Historical Biblical Archaeology and the Future

The New Pragmatism

Historical Biblical Archaeology and the Future

The New Pragmatism

edited by

Thomas E. Levy

Equinox Publishing Ltd

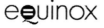

London   Oakville

Published by

UK: Equinox Publishing Ltd., 1 Chelsea Manor Studios, Flood Street, London SW3 5SR
USA: DBBC, 28 Main Street, Oakville, CT 06779

www.equinoxpub.com

First published 2010

Library of Congress Cataloguing-in-Publication Data
A catalogue record for this book is available from the Library of Congress

ISBN   9781845532574   (hardback)
        9781845532581   (paperback)

Typeset by Forthcoming Publications Ltd
www.forthcomingpublications.com

Printed and bound by Lightning Source

For Norma Kershaw

Visionary, patron of archaeology in the Levant, and dear friend

With affection

TEL

Contents

Abbreviations

AmAnt	*American Antiquity*
AASOR	Annual of the American Schools of Oriental Research
ABD	*Anchor Bible Dictionary*, edited by D. N. Freedman (6 vols.; New York, 1992)
ADAJ	Annual of the Department of Antiquities of Jordan
ARA	Annual Review of Anthropology
BA	*Biblical Archaeologist*
BAR	*Biblical Archaeology Review*
BASOR	*Bulletin of the American Schools of Oriental Research*
CA	*Current Anthropology*
CAARI	Cyprus American Archaeological Research Institute
IAA	Israel Antiquities Authority
IEJ	*Israel Exploration Journal*
JAA	*Journal of Anthropological Archaeology*
JAS	*Journal of Archaeological Science*
JBL	*Journal of Biblical Literature*
JEA	*Journal of Egyptian Archaeology*
JNES	*Journal of Near Eastern Studies*
JSOT	*Journal for the Study of the Old Testament*
JSOTSup	Journal for the Study of the Old Testament: Supplement Series
NEA	*Near Eastern Archaeology*
OBOSA	Orbis biblicus et orientalis: Series archaeologica
PEFQS	*Palestine Exploration Fund Quarterly Statement*
PEQ	*Palestine Exploration Quarterly*
SAA	State Archives of Assyria
SEL	*Studi Epigrafici e Linguistici sul Vicino Oriente antico*
SJOT	*Scandinavian Journal of the Old Testament*
VT	*Vetus Testamentum*
VTSup	Supplements to Vetus Testamentum
ZDPV	*Zeitschrift des deutschen Palästina-Vereins*

Preface

Thomas E. Levy

The archaeology of the southern Levant is synonymous with the 'Holy Land'—the region that includes modern Israel, Jordan, the Palestinian territories, Lebanon, Syria, and the Sinai Peninsula. This land bridge between Africa and southwest Asia and the two core areas of ancient Near Eastern civilization—Egypt and Mesopotamia—has played a central role in the evolution of human societies from the emergence of modern humans in the Middle Paleolithic over 200,000 years ago to the changing dynamics of global politics today. Relatively 'recently' in this long sequence of social change, some 6,000 years ago, scholars begin to trace the origins of Monotheism and the Abrahamic tradition that is so central to three of the great world religions—Judaism, Christianity, and Islam. To be fair, there are other Holy Lands around the world from India's fertile Tamil Nadu region to the peak of Mt. Shasta in northern California. However, statistics from the *Encyclopedia Britannica* indicate that over 50% of the world population belongs to one of the monotheistic religions whose roots are in the ancient Near East. The Hebrew Bible or Old Testament is central to these three great religions in different ways and levels of commitment. Written primarily in Biblical Hebrew and some Aramaic, the Hebrew Bible is the Jewish Bible. In Christianity, the Old Testament forms the first of the two-part Christian Biblical canon. For Islam, both the Hebrew Bible and New Testament are regarded as divinely revealed works and Muslims are especially familiar with biblical personages and events as presented in the Koran. This very short apologia is a simple testimony to the fact that there are an incredibly large number of people on the planet who have a direct or indirect relationship with the Hebrew Bible—as a sacred text that continues to play an unusually powerful role in Western and Middle Eastern culture from religion to the arts. For these reasons, there is a huge audience, religious and secular, interested in the historicity of the Hebrew Bible.

The books that make up the Jewish Scriptures include the *Pentateuch* or Five Books of Moses (Genesis, Exodus, Leviticus, Numbers, and Deuteronomy), *The Prophets* (Joshua, Judges, Samuel, Kings; Isaiah, Jeremiah, Ezekiel; Hosea, Joel, Amos, Obadiah, Jonah, Micah, Nahum, Habakkuk, Zephaniah, Malachi), and *The Writings* (Psalms, Proverbs, Job, Song of Songs, Ruth, Lamentations, Ecclesiastes, Ester, Daniel, Ezra–Nehemiah, Chronicles). When these texts are analyzed using the tools of modern Biblical scholarship and contextualized in relationship to extra-Biblical ancient texts from the Middle East and science-based approaches to the archaeological record, researchers are in a unique position to re-examine the Hebrew Bible in new and exciting ways to explore its historical dimensions. It is in this spirit that the essays in this book take a contemporary look at the relationship between sacred and ancient historical texts from the southern Levant and the archaeological record.

The occasion for producing this book was the establishment of the 'Norma Kershaw Endowed Chair in the Archaeology of Ancient Israel and Neighboring Lands' by Norma and Reuben Kershaw to the University of California, San Diego's Judaic Studies Program (JSP). This is the university's first endowed faculty chair in the Department of Anthropology and is one of six endowed chairs in

Judaic Studies. At the University of California, endowed chairs are teaching/research positions occupied by distinguished scholars. The university provides the teaching/research position and pays the salary of the person appointed to the endowed chairs. The permanent endowed fund created by philanthropic gifts provides perpetual annual income in support of the teaching and research activities of the person holding the chair. University colleagues must nominate a potential chair holder and the appointment is then ratified by the academic senate. When asked why the Kershaws decided to endow this chair, Norma said 'Our goal is to strengthen the research and scholarship of already superb programs in Judaic Studies and the Department of Anthropology at UCSD... We reside in Southern California, and find it natural to help support a Southern California university and provide for UCSD's outstanding faculty and students'.

The holder of the Kershaw chair must have an expertise in the archaeology of ancient (Iron Age) Israel and one of its neighbours; and it is assumed that the university will insure that the next recipient of this endowed chair will hold these credentials. My own journey to this honor began in 1971 when I was a 17-year-old volunteer on the Hebrew Union College excavations at Tel Gezer directed by Professor William G. Dever in Israel's Shephela region. As one of the first interdisciplinary research expeditions in Israel the Gezer excavation was an extremely exciting place to be for a young student. Bill's lectures were riveting and I soon worked my way into the orbit of the Gezer staff by becoming the unpaid photographer's assistant. With a state-of-the-art air-conditioned darkroom on-site, this was a wonderful place to hang out. In my enthusiasm for this job, I would leap from balk to balk (there were many at the Gezer excavations) to help set up each photograph. One day, to my horror, I accidently kicked one of the project's very expensive Hasselblad cameras off a balk overlooking a Middle Bronze Age cyclopean gate. The photographer was very sympathetic and the secret of my deed was kept until a few years ago when I finally made my confession to Bill. In 1975, when I was an undergraduate studying at the Department of Anthropology at the University of Arizona, Bill arrived as a new faculty member from Jerusalem where he had directed both the Nelson Glueck School of Biblical Archaeology and the W.F. Albright Institute of Archaeological Research. There were wonderful professors at the U of A who I was able to study with, including Michael B. Schiffer, Norman Yoffee, Arthur Jelinek, and Dever and each of these scholars had a very positive influence on me. Several years after the Gezer experience, I was back in the Mediterranean working at a Neolithic village site in Greece's Thessaly district on a joint UCLA –University of Thessaloniki project directed by Professors Maria Gimbutas and Demetrious Theocharis. Infatuated by Greece, its culture both past and present, and the prospect of excavating a tiny Neolithic island site in the northern Sporades with Dr. Theocharis, by 1976, I was on my way to study economic prehistory at the University of Sheffield with a focus on Aegean prehistory. After a year of learning Greek and creating a 3D computer model on the university's 'Main Frame' computer (large sets of punch cards were used to program the computer in those days)—Professor Theocharis died suddenly and my chances of doing field work in Greece evaporated overnight. I was devastated and at a loss with what to do with my floundering graduate student career. Fortunately, I had just met a wonderful (and stunningly beautiful) young woman named Alina, who was rapidly becoming my 'girl friend'. Just when I thought of throwing the towel in and returning to my home in the LA wasteland known as the San Fernando Valley, she said I would be crazy to leave my studies in the UK after having invested so much energy (and money). That was the beginning of my reliance on Alina's clear-eyed assessment of the world. I'm grateful to say we have just celebrated our 30th wedding anniversary and she continues to be beautiful and erudite. Pulling myself up by the boot-straps after much angst, I went to see one of the young lecturers in the Sheffield archaeology department, Graeme Barker, who served as an unofficial advisor for me. It was Graeme who said, 'You worked in Israel before, why don't you try doing a field project there for your PhD?' Thanks to Graeme's advice, it was then that I embarked on my professional career in Levantine archaeology and haven't looked back since. This led to living in Israel for 13 years, the growth of our family with Ben and Gil, and work at the Negev Museum where I established a museum for Bedouin culture and served as assistant director of two excellent American research centers in Jerusalem—the W.F. Albright Institute of Archaeological Research under Sy Gitin and the Nelson Glueck School of Biblical Archaeology at the Hebrew Union College under Avraham Biran.

The professorial positions in Levantine archaeology and Biblical Hebrew and Related Languages at UC San Diego are due to the late Professor David Noel Freedman—one of the 20th century's most distinguished Hebrew Bible scholars. As part of the Judaic Studies Program, when Noel was hired at UCSD, he insisted that these two positions be created. William (Bill) Propp received the latter position and I the former. During the peak of our program, with its focus on Hebrew Bible and archaeology, our faculty included Noel (Hebrew Bible), Richard Elliott Friedman (Hebrew Bible), William Propp (Hebrew Bible), David Goodblatt (ancient Jewish history), and myself. By having a focused group of research professors, our small program gained national and international recognition. However, since Friedman's retirement and Noel Freedman's recent death, our program is in a state of flux. At the time of writing this Preface, due to the financial crisis the University of California and our program have had a set-back because the administration has frozen all new job hires—including endowed chair positions. That said, the archaeology program at UCSD remains strong. When I joined the faculty in 1992, Guillermo Algaze, a Mesopotamian specialist, was the only one other archaeologist in the Department of Anthropology. Together we established an undergraduate degree program in anthropological archaeology. Over the years, we have been joined by Paul Goldstein, a South Americanist, and Geoff Braswell, a Mesoamerican specialist. Over much of this period, we have been fortunate to have Robert McC. Adams, the distinguished Near Eastern archaeologist, as an adjunct professor deeply involved in our program so that today we have over 20 graduate students doing PhD research with us. With the establishment of the Kershaw chair, teaching and research in the field of the archaeology of ancient Israel and its neighboring lands is assured in perpetuity.

Since joining the faculty at UCSD, in addition to being a part of the Department of Anthropology, I have been blessed with being a member of the Judaic Studies Program which provides the stimulating focus on Israel, Jordan, the Palestinian territories, and adjacent areas. Beginning in 1993, we carried out the first UCSD archaeology field school at the site of Shiqmim that focused on social evolution during the formative Chalcolithic period in Israel's northern Negev desert. This was an outgrowth of work that began as part of my doctoral dissertation. From 1994 to 1996, to better understand the processes that led to the rise of urbanism during the Early Bronze Age, we began to investigate the Halif Terrace site and its surroundings near Kibbutz Lahav. Toward the end of the 1996 season, while eating lunch in the kibbutz dining room, my friend Dodik Shohani came to our table and said that Pierre Bikai, the director of the American Center of Oriental Research (ACOR) in Amman was visiting the area and would I like to meet him. After showing Pierre around the site, he abruptly said 'Tom, you should work in Jordan; come and visit me after your excavation and I will show you around. If you rent a 4-wheel drive vehicle, I'll drive'. I will always be grateful to Pierre for introducing me to so many wonderful people in Jordan, including the then Director General of the Department of Antiquities of Jordan (DOA), Ghazi Bisheh, who warmly welcomed me to begin work there. By March of 1997, in anticipation of working in the ancient Faynan copper ore zone of southern Jordan, I invited two long-term researchers there to join me on a National Geographic Society sponsored expedition to reconstruct an unknown late prehistoric copper trade route from Faynan to Shiqmim in the Beersheva valley. Mohammad Najjar, then the Director of Excavations and Surveys for DOA, and Andreas Hauptmann of the German Mining Museum, joined Pierre, several Israeli colleagues including David Alon and Dodik, me, and a large group of donkeys and their Bedouin owners to begin a 150 km trek across the deserts of southern Jordan and Israel in search of the ancient trade route. Since then, Mohammad has been co-director in all our field work in Faynan and Andreas and serves as our project archaeometallurgist. The friendship and collegiality with these individuals is one of the pleasures of field work. As our research in Faynan is a deep-time study of the role of mining and metallurgy on social evolution from the Neolithic through Islamic times, we have been fortunate over the years to have the support of the Director General of DOA in Jordan, Fawwaz al-Khrayshah, in all our research endeavors. Since 2002, our research has focused on the Iron Age sequence of copper production in Faynan. Consequently, it is only since 2002 that my primary archaeological research has focused on the period that is most closely linked to the Hebrew Bible and other ancient texts from that period. Over the years, working in Jordanian, I have been fortunate to work and develop important friendships with Mohammad Defala, Juma Ali, Ibrahim Ibn Juma Ali, Howeid Sayadin, and many other members of the Quraiqira village. In addition, the help and support of Yehya Khaled, director of the Royal Society for the Conservation of Nature in Jordan, and Chris Johnson, Director, Wild Jordan, in the field is greatly appreciated.

In late 2005, the California Institute of Telecommunications and Information Technology (Calit2) was opened on the campus of UC San Diego. According to the Calit2 mission statement, it represents an experiment in inventing the university research environment of the future that can continue to fuel innovation in the global economy. It:

- builds horizontal links among departments to foster multidisciplinary studies.
- creates research teams consisting of members who can be located anywhere because of the Internet.
- supports involvement by faculty, students, industry, government, and community partners.
- enables prototyping in Calit2 'living laboratories'.
- provides technical professionals as the bridge between academia and industry.

On the opening day of Calit2, Alina and I went to see the incredible series of demonstrations and 'open-houses' where guests were treated to visits in laboratories ranging from Virtual Reality to Nano fabrication to robotics and an introduction to an array of the latest IT tools needed to create cyberinfrastructure for the sciences and humanities of the future. In his welcoming remarks, Calit2 director Ramesh Rao invited all UCSD faculty members to contact him if they had a project they wished to present to Calit2 for support. My interests in Digital Archaeology seemed a natural for Calit2 collaboration so I scheduled an appointment with Ramesh. A week later I arrived at his office with my Powerpoint presentation ready to go. Instead of plugging in, he asked me to sit at a small table and tell him 'my dreams'. This was the beginning of an academic and research adventure that I'm deeply involved in. With the establishment of the Center of Interdisciplinary Science for Art, Architecture and Archaeology (CISA3), I was asked to become an Associate Director and we now have a variety of 'Cyber-archaeology' projects, including the MedArchNet (Mediterranean Archaeology Network) and Digital Archaeology Atlas of the Holy Land (DAAHL) with Stephen Savage, Pottery Informatics with Neil Smith and Avshalom Karasik, On-site GIS-based Digital Archaeology, Virtual Reality (VR) with Kyle Knabb, and more. As Dominique Rissolo, archaeologist and Executive Director of the Waitt Institute for Discovery said after his first visit to the UCSD institute, 'Calit2/CISA3 is the Dreamworks of archaeology'. The future of world cultural heritage research is closely linked to new developments in Information Technology. Thus, it is both extremely stimulating and an honor to be associated with Calit2/CISA3.

One of the most satisfying things about being a faculty member at a great research university like UCSD is the opportunity to interact with and teach talented students—both undergraduates and graduates. My philosophy has been to try to carry out cutting-edge archaeological research in terms of new developments in both theory and method. By having a strong field component to Levantine archaeology it is possible to reach this goal, and at the same time incorporate students into the research endeavor. Most of my graduate students started their archaeological studies with me by being a part of one of our archaeological field school expeditions in Israel or Jordan. I'm very proud of these former and current students and protégés who have worked and published with me over the past 30 years based on our work in the deserts of Israel and Jordan. In addition, through the years, hundreds of talented undergraduates from UCSD and other institutions have played a key role in both the field and laboratory aspects of my research and for this I'm grateful. I am especially grateful to Alina for all her love, support, and collaboration in all my work. Finally, I sincerely appreciate the friends and colleagues who have contributed to this book, which is a celebration of how in the 21st century archaeologists and Biblical scholars can reawaken interest in issues concerning the anthropology and historicity of the Hebrew Bible and other ancient Near Eastern texts that are central to more than half the world's population.

Thomas Levy
March 21, 2010
San Diego, California

Kershaw chair inauguration at UCSD, April 30, 2006.
Top row, from left to right: William G. Dever, William H.C. Propp, Thomas E. Levy, David Goodblatt, Jodi Magness; bottom row, left to right: Rueben Kershaw, Norma Kershaw.

Celebrating the inauguration of the UCSD Norma Kershaw Endowed Chair
in the Archaeology of Ancient Israel and Neighboring Lands, April 30th, 2006 (photograph by
Gene Lally)

1.
INTO THE FUTURE—
NEW TRENDS IN HISTORICAL
BIBLICAL ARCHAEOLOGY

1 The New Pragmatism

Integrating Anthropological, Digital, and Historical Biblical Archaeologies

Thomas E. Levy

Abstract

Over the past three decades or so, Biblical Archaeology, or the archaeology of the Old Testament, has suffered as a paradigm of scientific archaeological investigation. In this chapter I would like to suggest a new pragmatic approach to what should be referred to as 'historical Biblical Archaeology'. The approach advocated here is a type of historical archaeology where researchers strive to understand the relationship between sacred and other ancient texts and the archaeological record in the same way that historical archaeologies around the world should attempt to confront ancient texts and the archaeological record. Following a discussion of the history of Biblical archaeological research in the Southern Levant, the historical Biblical Archaeology paradigm suggested here is discussed, followed by an example based on recent research in the Iron Age of southern Jordan.

This study advocates treating the archaeology of the Southern Levant that intersects with the Hebrew Bible like all other historical archaeologies where sacred and ancient texts interface with the archaeological record. The Southern Levant includes Israel, Jordan, the Palestinian territories, southern Lebanon and Syria, and the Sinai Peninsula, and is often referred to as the 'Holy Land'. Examples of archaeologies that deal with sacred text and the material record around the world include: the Icelandic Sagas and Scandinavia (Friðriksson 1994; Saga 1970), the Mahabharata, ancient Vedic literatures and India (Insoll 2001; Veer 2001), the New Testament and the Southern Levant (Ascough 2006; Saldarini *et al.* 2004), Gnostic literatures in Egypt (Kasser, Meyer, and Wurst 2006; Walsh 2006), Islamic texts and the Middle East (Horton 2005; Insoll 1999), Ancient Greek texts and the Aegean (Fisher, Wees, and Boedeker 1998; Yamauchi 2004) and more. All of these historical archaeologies share an underlying drive to examine the underlying confluences between the archaeological record and aspects of the sacred text that may have an historical foundation. In Western Europe and North America, from as early as the 19th century CE, interest in the Biblical Archaeology and the Middle (Near) East was primarily fueled by a desire to investigate their Judeo-Christian roots of the Bible lands. In fact, the growth of specialized disciplines such as Egyptology and Assyriology were sparked early on by a desire to understand the ancient civilizations of Egypt and Mesopotamia mostly because of the nature of their role in the history of the peoples and places mentioned in the Old Testament. Today, however, interest in the intersection between the Hebrew Bible, Egyptology, Assyriology, and Mesopotamian archaeology are minor at best with only a handful of interested scholars focused on these confluences (Hallo and Lambert 1998; Hoffmeier 1996; Hoffmeier, Millard, and Millar 2004; Kitchen 2003). Perhaps the main reason interest has waned over recent decades is the growth of the Biblical minimalist paradigm that has sought to lessen historical underpinnings of the Hebrew Bible (cf. Davies 1992; Levy 2000; Thompson 1999). To set the stage for a more pragmatic historical Biblical Archaeology, it is important to present a snapshot of the intellectual history of Biblical Archaeology since the 20th century CE.

The Golden Age of Biblical Archaeology

The period between the First and Second World Wars represent what the British archaeologist Roger Moorey (Moorey 1991) refers to as the 'Golden Age of Biblical Archaeology'; it was a time when the field flourished and had an unprecedented scholarly authority in the academies of North America and Western Europe. This 'fluorescence' was based mostly on the intellectual leadership of the great American Orientalist, William Foxwell Albright, who was a polymath and commanded expertise in disciplines ranging from field archaeology, to Biblical Studies, Northwest Semitic languages, Assyriology, and more (Levy and Freedman 2008). Albright worked passionately to establish Biblical Archaeology as an independent discipline that intellectually encompassed all of ancient Near Eastern studies related to the Bible and geographically extended from Gibraltar to the Indus Valley (Albright 1932a, 1971). During his tenure as the director of the newly built American School of Oriental Research (ASOR) in what is today East Jerusalem, between the years 1920 to 1935, Albright took advantage of permanent and semi-annual residence in Palestine to carry out some of the first scientific excavations in the country that were rapidly synthesized and published. At this time, it was his archaeological excavations and rapid publication of the little-known site of Tell Beit Mirsim in the Shephela foothills south of Jerusalem that gave Albright immediate respect among both the early 20th-century archaeological and biblical scholarly communities working in the 'Holy Land'. This pioneer work established the first sound archaeological chronology of Palestine for much of biblical history (spanning the Middle Bronze to Iron Ages, ca. 2000–500 BCE) (Albright 1926, 1938, 1943) and provided a series of tangible cultural material anchors for situating the Hebrew Bible in the land of the Bible. When Albright left the directorship at ASOR to focus permanently on graduate teaching and research at Johns Hopkins University, he passed the mantle of directing ASOR to one of his most talented and energetic protégés, Nelson Glueck.

Glueck, an important leader in Biblical Archaeology during its zenith, became director of Jerusalem's ASOR (now called the W.F. Albright Institute of Archaeological Research—AIAR). Like his mentor, Glueck, as director of ASOR took the opportunity of carrying out the first large-scale systematic archaeological field surveys in Transjordan, thereby establishing the foundation for all subsequent archaeological investigations of this important region (Glueck 1934, 1935, 1939, 1940, 1944). Following Israel's Independence War in 1948, the American School of Oriental Research fell under Jordanian administration and Glueck was unable to access it for political reasons. This resulted in Glueck beginning a program of extensive surveys in the southern Negev desert of the newly founded state of Israel (Glueck 1960). By 1957, Glueck was the long-standing president of the Hebrew Union College-Jewish Institute of Religion (HUC-JIR), the major wing of Reform Judaism in the United States. The presidency of HUC-JIR provided Glueck with the clout to begin a major building campaign in Israel to create a new American archaeological center in Jerusalem (on the west side of the then divided city) devoted to post-graduate research in Biblical and archaeological and related research. Initially called the Hebrew Union College-Biblical Archaeological School, following Glueck's death, it was renamed the 'Nelson Glueck School of Biblical

Archaeology' (NGSBA). During the last decade of his life, Glueck became so popular a 'public intellectual' in the 1960s that he appeared on the cover of *Time Magazine* and spoke at the inauguration of President John F. Kennedy in 1960 (Brown and Kutler 2005; Dever 2000; Stern 1980; Wright 1959).

The third scholar to help consolidate the intellectual prominence of Biblical Archaeology in North America during its 'Golden Age' was the Harvard University professor, G. Ernst Wright. Wright was a leading Hebrew Bible scholar and Levantine archaeologist who studied under W.F. Albright and was instrumental in formulating university-sponsored archaeological field schools in Palestine (Drew-McCormick Archaeological Expedition to Shechem, 1956–74), Israel (Hebrew Union College Biblical and Archaeological School Expedition at Tell Gezer, 1964–65), and Cyprus (the Joint American Expedition to Idalion 1971–74) as a formal means of training future generations of Biblical archaeologists. He published widely and founded the popular periodical *The Biblical Archaeologist* (now known as *Near Eastern Archaeology*) as a means of engaging the English-reading public with new research and issues concerning Biblical Archaeology.

Biblical and Syro-Palestinian Archaeology in North America

Although cracks appeared in Albright's Biblical Archaeology paradigm as early as the 1950s (J.J. Finkelstein 1958), it was only after the death of Albright, Glueck, and Wright in the early 1970s that William G. Dever, a student of Wright's, initiated a systematic onslaught to change Biblical Archaeology into a more 'secular' field known as 'Syro-Palestinian' archaeology (Dever 1980, 1981, 1982, 1992, 1993a). By 1975, Dever had moved to the University of Arizona following his long-term residence in Jerusalem during which time he served as director of both the NGSBA and AIAR. While residing in Israel, Dever worked closely with Glueck and Wright in establishing the new interdisciplinary American excavations at Tel Gezer that followed the field school model established by Wright at Shechem. Dever's arrival in Tucson coincided with the peak of the 'processual' archaeology paradigm in the American academy (Binford 1962; Binford and Binford 1968; Watson, LeBlanc, and Redman 1971). Some of the dominant thinkers during the zenith of processual and theoretical archaeology, such as Michael B. Schiffer (Schiffer 1975, 1976, 1983), William Rathje (Rathje 1971, 2001), and Norman Yoffee (Yoffee and Cowgill 1988), taught at the University of Arizona at this time. As an enthusiastic undergraduate in the Department of Anthropology, I had the good fortune of studying with these young professors, including William Dever, who became one of my most influential mentors during his first year at the university.

Following on the heels of many social and intellectual changes in the 1960s, the rise of processual archaeology paradigm was characterized by an array of rigorous theoretical and methodological approaches rooted in model testing, the application of the scientific method, and the displacement of the previous very descriptive 'culture historical' paradigm of archaeological research. In many respects, the 'New Archaeology' revolution took on the excitement of the rebellious social movements that were characteristic of the multitude of social changes that were occurring throughout the US and many European societies in the 1960s and early 1970s (Gitlin 1987; Wells 1994). I believe the intellectual paradigm shift among archaeologists working in the major US research universities, such as the University of Arizona, profoundly influenced Dever's project to rebel against the traditional descriptive 'Biblical Archaeology' that he was trained in and had been a superb practitioner of at Shechem and Tel Gezer (Davis 2004; Dever 1974; Dever and Lance 1978; Dever, Lance, and Wright 1970), and forge what he viewed at the time as a secular Syro-Palestinian archaeology. Dever's (cf. 1982: 103-4) critique was well founded for a number of reasons. For example, he argued: (a) that 'Biblical Archaeology' had no independent rationale, methodology, objectives, status or support; (b) that when Biblical Archaeology is defined as 'bridge builder', intersecting

Syro-Palestinian archaeology, epigraphy, Assyriology, and Egyptology, and encompassing Albright's broad geographic definition, it simply represents the entirety of ancient Near Eastern studies and loses meaning as a separate field; (c) that the idea that 'Biblical Archaeology' should dominate the field of Syro-Palestinian archaeology, which spans remote prehistory to the Ottoman period, made it passé; and finally (d) that 'Biblical Archaeology' as a 'peculiarly American' phenomenon that grew out of biblical theology movements that crystallized in the 1950s under Albright, Glueck, and Wright, had little resonance with mainstream archaeology practiced in the United States following the advent of the 'New Archaeology'. Dever's effort to disembowel Biblical Archaeology from professional North American archaeology in the 'Holy Land' was more successful than he may have anticipated. There were extensive debates at professional meetings, symposia, and congresses, about the future of Biblical Archaeology in North America, Europe and especially Israel (Biran 1993).

British, European, and Australian archaeologists played a critical role in the development of Iron Age archaeology in the Southern Levant and this is touched on below. However, following the Second World War, researchers from the United States played an increasingly prominent role through large-scale field and publication projects. With the development of the newly established countries of Israel, Jordan, and the changing political fortunes of the Palestinian territories, local universities and research organizations developed their own approach to the Iron Age archaeology of their respective lands, and it is important to distinguish this from what happened in North America.

Archaeology as a Discipline in Israel, Palestine, and Jordan

While scholars such as Albright and Glueck helped influence the theoretical foundations of archaeology in the newly established state of Israel, the major departments of archaeology at Israeli universities developed administrative structures that were inclusive and included the full range of archaeological activities in the country from prehistory to Islamic times. At the Hebrew University of Jerusalem, the first local university 'Department of Archaeology' was founded in 1934, and in 1967 it became the 'Institute of Archaeology' devoted to both teaching and research (http://archaeology.huji.ac.il/about/about.asp) spanning prehistoric to historic periods. Similarly, Tel Aviv University developed both the 'Institute of Archaeology' in 1969 (initiated by the late Professor Y. Aharoni) as a research facility and a 'Department of Archaeology and Ancient Near Eastern Cultures' to teach the archaeology, cultures, history, and languages of the 'Land of Israel and of the ancient Near East from the prehistoric to the end of the Classical periods' (http://www.tau.ac.il/humanities/archaeology/about_us_department.html). The University of Haifa also founded its archaeology with a 'Department of Land of Israel Studies' that later morphed into a 'Department of Archaeology' and an 'Institute of Archaeology' to facilitate research activities. Later, the Haifa Department of Maritime Civilizations, and the Leon Recanati Institute for Maritime studies (http://maritime.haifa.ac.il/) were established. At Bar Ilan University, archaeology was first established as part of the 'Department of Land of Israel Studies' but, more recently, an 'Institute of Archaeology' was founded to coordinate both teaching and research goals. And at Ben-Gurion University of the Negev, archaeology has been taught since its inception as part of the 'Department of Bible, Archaeology and Ancient Near Eastern Studies'. Most recently, in 1996, the Kimmel Center for Archaeological Science was established at the Weizmann Institute, aimed at educating a new generation of researchers who would be familiar with both the natural sciences and archaeology (http://www.weizmann.ac.il/kimmel-arch). The mission of the Kimmel Center focuses on establishing a cohesive group of archaeological scientists who both teach and carry out state-of-the-art research of significance to world archaeology and cultural studies. What is of interest for our discussion of 'Biblical Archaeology' here is the early commitment (certainly by 1934 at the Hebrew

University) of Jewish archaeologists in Palestine to build their university archaeology departments in a 'secular' format. This is the type of organization envisioned in the 'Syro-Palestinian archaeology' model that Dever was trying to establish in the United States. Granted the establishment of departments in 'Land of Israel Studies' may have nationalistic overtones at Bar Ilan and Haifa universities, however, both made conscious decisions to be more inclusive by establishing 'Institutes of Archaeology' to embrace the scientific and professional communities both inside and outside Israel. While prehistory, 'Biblical Archaeology', and classical archaeology remain areas of specialization at Israeli universities, they do not offer specific degrees in these fields. Degrees are awarded in 'archaeology'.

In the Palestinian National Authority and territories, Al-Quds University established the 'Institute of Islamic Archaeology' in 1992, offering M.A. degrees in Islamic Archaeology. An-Najah National University in Hebron has a 'Department of Archaeology' offering a B.A. degree in archaeology with a focus on Islamic archaeology and conservation. Bethlehem University has no formal degree program but teaches a number of archaeology courses in their diploma in tour guiding curriculum. The Islamic University of Gaza, established in 1978, has a Department of History and Archaeology. While the emphasis is on Classical and Islamic archaeology, 'Biblical Archaeology' is covered in a course entitled 'Ancient Arab History and The Prophet Age'. At Birzeit University, the Department of History and Archaeology offers two academic programs leading to a B.A. degree in history with a minor in either political science or Palestinian archaeology. Previously, Birzeit University had a 'Palestinian Institute of Archaeology' that was established in 1988 by the American archaeologist and former director of the AIAR, Albert Glock (Fox 2001; Glock 1994). Early on, the institute of archaeology at Birzeit published works on Biblical Archaeology, most probably due to Glock's involvement in the excavations at the biblical site of Taannek in the northern West Bank (Nashef *et al.* 1998). For many years, Birzeit University has carried out a major 'fieldwork documentation and archaeological excavation project at Khirbet Birzeit' that has focused on the Ottoman history of this village site—a subject more closely linked to the Palestinian population living in the region today. In Glock's last article published in the *Journal of Palestine Studies*, he observed that, 'For the Palestinians, the missing element (in the archaeology of Palestine) was the intellectual connection with Islamic tradition' (1994: 77). Glock's essay was written in the midst of the first Intifada. In considering the then state of affairs, he wrote:

> In the absence of a Palestinian government, the resources required to tell the Arab story have not been properly collected or preserved. Nor has evidence of the material culture been adequately protected or, where possible, restored... What is required is a documentation center. And equally necessary is access to the deep and rich archaeological record, the still-buried resource required to document and illustrate the Arab past in Palestine. (1994: 79)

As Adel Yahya (2005: 72) points out, 'it is most regrettable that the first Palestinian Institute of Archaeology at Birzeit never recovered from the tragic assassination of Prof. Glock in 1992, and it was closed down in 2003 because of financial problems'. It is under these difficult conditions that burgeoning Palestinian archaeological institutions have touched on biblical historical and other archaeologies, but have emphasized the Classical and Islamic periods for their primary research activities.

In contrast, Jordan has over twenty public and private universities. However, in order to understand the pedagogy of historical Biblical Archaeology in Jordan, we will highlight only those universities that have large degree programs and field projects in archaeology. Jordan's oldest academic institution for teaching archaeology is the Department of Archaeology established in 1962 at the University of Jordan in Amman (http://www.ju.edu.jo/faculties/FacultyofHumanities/ Archaeology/ Pages/overview.aspx). It offers B.A. and M.A. degrees in Near Eastern Archaeology and has both an archaeological and heritage museum aimed at training. As one of Jordan's largest research universities, the department carries out teaching, field work, and research on all archaeological periods, from prehistory to the Islamic periods. The department is in the process of establishing a Ph.D. program and an institute of archaeology to enhance research, excavation, and restoration, as well as to enhance public appreciation of cultural heritage in Jordan. Yarmouk University in the north of the country established the Faculty of Archaeology and Anthropology in 1984 and comprises four academic departments—Archaeology, Anthropology, Repertoires, and Conservation and Management. In the south of the country, Mu'tah University, located near Kerak, has a Department of Archaeology and Tourism with research projects and teaching spanning prehistory to Islamic times (http://www.mutah.edu.jo/index.php?option =com_content&task=view&id=122&Itemid= 246). In general, the major universities in Jordan have followed an inclusive model of teaching and research in all the archaeological periods represented in the country with an emphasis on how archaeology can contribute to national tourism and conservation needs.

The call to establish a separate *independent discipline* of Syro-Palestinian archaeology in the United States was a reaction to the failure of Biblical Archaeology, after having achieved such prominence in American society due primarily to the genius of Albright and the tenacity and energy of his protégés Glueck and Wright, in promoting this paradigm. Even after the Biblical Archaeology paradigm had begun to develop cracks, it remained a hard act to follow. Dever's solution was to replace Albright's 'Biblical Archaeology' paradigm with a less text-driven one, an archaeology based on interdisciplinary research and model testing along the lines promoted by the 'New Archaeology'; and by one that had a more narrowly focused geographic locale situated the land of Palestine and Syria. But why 'Syro-Palestine' and not simply the Palestine highlighted in one of Albright's own iconic volumes summarizes the region, such as *The Archaeology of Palestine* (Albright 1971)? I believe that the idea for a 'Syro-Palestinian' archaeology was influenced in the 1970s and 1980s because many scholars assumed that greater Syria was the primarily center of cultural influence on the history of Palestine throughout the ages—especially with regard to the influences of religion and social order for the formation of Canaanite society from the Early Bronze to Iron Ages (Aharoni 1979; de Vaux 1971; Dever 1987; Kenyon 1979; Kenyon and Moorey 1987). Secondly, scholarly movement between Israel and neighboring countries was not easy prior to the signing of peace treaties between Israel and Egypt in 1979 and Jordan in 1994. With the opening up of travel and social interaction in the region, especially after 1994, it is possible to see an increase in the use of the less geographically specific and more political neutral words 'Levant' or 'Levantine' in scholarly citations to refer to the region known as the 'Holy Land'. Emblematic of this change was the amalgamation of the 'British School of Archaeology in Jerusalem' (BSAJ) and the 'British Institute in Amman for Archaeology and History' (BIAAH) into the 'Council of British Research in the Levant' CBRL in 1998. It is important to highlight the pedigree of the term 'Syro-Palestinian' and its gradual replacement by the term 'Levant' or 'Levantine' because the latter is a more culturally and politically neutral term that more accurately reflects the tapestry of countries and peoples of the region, without assuming directionality of cultural influence. If a primary goal of historical archaeology in the Levant, regardless of chronological period, is to be as objective as possible, it is important to embrace the term 'Levantine archaeology' today. While historical Biblical Archaeology focuses mostly on the Southern Levant, Levantine archaeology extends north along the eastern Mediterranean littoral and includes modern Turkey, Cyprus and all of Syria and Lebanon. This may seem like a semantic argument; however, when scholarly and public dialogue is a primary goal for advancing knowledge and cultural understandings, this term opens rather than closes doors. In hindsight, the idea that there should be an independent discipline capable of replacing the 'Biblical Archaeology' paradigm may have been a natural reaction to the crisis of conscience at the time. However, from the perspective of the 21st century, it is more appropriate to speak of a 'specialization' in historical Biblical Archaeology—one of the facets of Levantine archaeology that span prehistory to Islamic specializations.

Toward a New Pragmatism for Historical Biblical Archaeology

When Levantine archaeologists work on those periods that intersect most closely with the Hebrew Bible, traditionally the Bronze and Iron Ages (ca. 3600–500 BCE), emotions and passions often overtake the ultimate goal of investigating the relationship between sacred and other ancient texts and the archaeological record. Recently, Daniel Yankelovich (2008), the noted social thinker and pioneer of the *New York Times*/Yankelovich poll, presented his ideas for helping the United States cope with the overwhelming problems it is currently facing. To help solve these problems, Yankelovich has argued for a 'New Pragmatism'—a distinctively American philosophy that can help solve these problems by transcending partisanship to foster cooperation and strengthen our universities. As Yankelovich (2008) points out, the New Pragmatism is based on 'Pragmatism' (a distinctly American philosophy that has a history of strengthening the country's problem-solving capabilities), a method that will transcend partisanship and encourage cooperation, and a means to update our universities. Similarly, a pragmatic approach to historical Biblical Archaeology will help develop new and innovative ways of objectively tackling the problem of investigating sacred and other historical texts and the archaeological record. The result will be more cooperation between the different scholarly communities involved in this research domain and a re-integration of the public in the work of the academy. The primary American philosophers behind Pragmatism include Charles Pierce (Moore and Charles 1993), William James (James and Olin 1992), John Dewey (Hickman 1990), and George Herbert Mead (Baldwin 1986). The term 'Pragmatism' was originated by Pierce, who viewed it more as a technique to find answers rather than a philosophy. As a philosophy, pragmatism views the truth of a proposition or idea in its observable consequences—a far cry from metaphysics and post-modern thought. According to Yankelovich (2008), the popular understanding of Pragmatism is correct but needs to be embellished in the 21st-century world. Accordingly, to be 'pragmatic' is to be practical and action-oriented rather than theoretical; experimental ('try it out and see if it works'); one should be open to compromise, incremental solutions, and adhere to the 'art of the possible' and be more concerned with solving concrete problems than with grand visions. To push the 'New Pragmatism' agenda forward, Yankelovich argues for a value driven paradigm based on freedom of thought and action; opportunities to develop one's gifts and capabilities, trust in public judgment; faith in optimism/hope/trust/ cooperation; opposition to authoritarianism/dogma/ideology/fundamentalism; and the development of a strong utopian/reformist tradition.

There are many lessons to be learned here for bridging the gap that has plagued 'Biblical Archaeology' over the past 30 years between the minimalist and maximalist/historical scholars' interest in biblical studies and archaeology. Now that we are in the 21st century, it is necessary to take up Dever's (1993b) call for a secular 'Biblical Archaeology', taking it a step forward and making it more inclusive and less laden by ideology. By taking a more pragmatic approach to the type of historical archaeology advocated here, we can draw together a wide range of resources that will propel the discipline to higher levels of research. To make this work, we need to find ways collectively to harness the scholarly communities interested in historical Biblical Archaeology (archaeology, anthropology, biblical studies, scientific analytical fields, telecommunications and information technology); funding resources; the possibility of re-establishing historical Biblical Archaeology as a important intellectual resource for societies especially interested in the Abrahamic tradition; and the tradition of archeology as a consumer, user, and innovator interested in testing new theories and methods for research.

Some Problems with 'Biblical Archaeology' Today

The debates between the minimalist and maximalist 'schools' have reached an end in terms of promoting significant research gains and new understandings concerning the relationship between sacred text and archaeology (Coote 1990; Garbini 1988, 2003; Masalha 2006; Thompson 1999; Whitelam 1996). As scholars continue to promote these steadfast positions, they are in a state of denial as to the 'health' of the field. In many cases, ideology has become so embedded in the research projects of both schools that they have lost sight of the practicality of using mutually agreed-upon tools and methodologies. This has led some of our most prominent scholars to pander to an ideologically divided public in North America, Europe, and the Middle East (Dever 2001; Finkelstein and Silberman 2001, 2006; Thompson 1999) to the point that the scientific underpinnings of historical Biblical Archaeology are ignored by the public. In giving up a public platform for the topic of 'Biblical Archaeology' by changing the title of their public outreach magazine to *Near Eastern Archaeology*, our main North American scholarly research organization—ASOR—handed the public 'bully pulpit' to a private, non-academic organization—the Biblical Archaeology Society (BAS), which publishes the very popular *Biblical Archaeology Review* (*BAR*) magazine. As BAS has developed an extensive public following, they compete with ASOR and the Society for Biblical Literature (SBL) each year in setting the agenda for discourse on issues related to the Bible and archaeology at their annual seminar meetings held at the same time as the ASOR/SBL meetings. Perhaps this is a good thing, but historical biblical archaeologists should be leading these kinds of public initiatives. By setting the agenda, BAS has indeed raised important issues such as the need to publish the Dead Sea Scrolls in a faster and more egalitarian manner, and, more recently, questioning the analytical studies of important artifacts linked to people or institutions mentioned in the Old and New Testaments. By not spearheading public outreach in North America, Levantine archaeologists may have lost the ability to communicate outside the academy. This may have created some irreverence for practitioners of 'Biblical Archaeology' on the part of the secular public, the reason being that the archaeologists themselves are not taking charge of this aspect of archaeological discourse.[1] Thus, there are a number of cultural reasons for the erosion of the status of 'Biblical Archaeology' in the North American and European public sphere. First, there is a growing gap between the experts (mostly archaeologists and biblical scholars) and the public for reasons outlined above; second, there is a polarization within the field by the *démodé* debate between the biblical 'minimalists' and 'maximalist' scholars; and finally, there are the 'culture wars' between the left and right in Western society where many members on the left are intolerant of faith-based communities and those on the right are prejudiced against supporters of evolutionary theory and other positions that trickle down to the complete erosion of interest in the Bible and its centrality in the history, philosophy, law, and other dimensions of Western culture to the point that it is not taught in the majority of K-12 public schools in the United States today.

By disengaging the public from 'Biblical Archaeology', professional organizations in North America and Western Europe have become self-isolating communities. It takes hard work to engage the public, professional organizations, university departments, or individual scholars. Consequently, although many researchers acknowledge that the divisiveness that characterized the divide between biblical minimalists and maximalists and Levantine archaeologists and biblical scholars has narrowed, they are unwilling to overcome the cultural obstacles that continue to hamper bringing the

---

1. Concern about public outreach by North American archaeologists working in the Levant was recently evidenced by a major session on 'Archaeology and the Media' held at the 2008 annual meetings of the American Schools of Oriental Research (ASOR) in Boston.

archaeology of sacred text (in this case the Hebrew Bible) and archaeology into the forefront of social discourse. It is not enough to throw money at the problem by paying for conferences and the construction of curricula and websites that work to erase the centrality of the Hebrew Bible in Western culture history. Instead, for those of us working and researching in the United States (and perhaps it will influence other countries as well), we need to begin by restoring some of the traditional American philosophical frames of reference for our field that will allow us to innovate and rise above the scholarly bickering that has made biblical studies and, for us, 'Biblical Archaeology', almost irrelevant in our society compared to what it was just over 30 years ago. Part of the answer can be borrowed from Yankelovich's call for the 'New Pragmatism' aimed at solving many of the overwhelming problems facing American society today. As there is a 'trickle-down' effect in which many of the problems facing American society in general have also shaped scholarly discourse across the academy, we can learn much from Yankelovich's model for our field.

For historical Biblical Archaeology, aspects of the 'New Pragmatism' can help drive the field forward in a very positive direction. However, the popular understanding that a pragmatic approach to our field means disengagement with theory is incorrect. Leaving aside the minimalist/maximalist debate, for over a decade researchers have made great strides in testing social and historical models against the Iron Age archaeological record of the Southern Levant (Bienkowski and van der Steen 2001; Faust 2006; Finkelstein 1995; Halpern 1999; Joffe 2002; LaBianca 1999; Levy 2003; Levy and Holl 2002; Masters 2001; Porter 2004; Routledge 2004; Schloen 2001). Thus, for historical Biblical Archaeology in the 21st century, theory and model-testing based on the acquisition of robust datasets, as promoted by the best work of both processual and post-processual archaeology, should be a primary aim of the field.

The best way to insure this positive growth pattern is to emphasize advancements in methods and theory that will enable researchers to achieve a pragmatic approach to historical Biblical Archaeology. There are multiple ways to achieve methodological advancement in our field. First, we need to follow the scientific method of research by asking problem-oriented questions, conducting background research, building hypotheses, testing hypotheses through experimentation, analysis of the data collection, and the publication or communication of the results (Binford 2001; Hodder 2006; Schiffer 2000). As new advances in science and technology appear on the world scene at a remarkable pace, we need to be committed to experimentation with these new methodologies with constant feedback through peer review and other communication tools. Our methodologies need to evolve in tandem with the understanding that we live in evolving cultures both as groups and individuals. In this way, methodologies can also help drive new theoretical approaches and the investigation of new models related to historical Biblical Archaeology. As methodology underlies a more pragmatic approach to our field, there needs to be an emphasis on understanding the specific historical context and circumstances in which observations, experiments, and data collection take place. By developing the most rigorous of methodologies, the results can be examined for different theoretical points of view until the most parsimonious explanation is achieved.

To advance the spread of the New Pragmatism beyond the walls of the academy, Yankelovich (2008: 15) argues that entrepreneurship and innovative thinking are needed at all levels of society. Applying this paradigm to resurrecting public interest in historical Biblical Archaeology in societies on the world scene, a concerted effort needs to be made to integrate teaching, research, government, institutional, private foundations, nonprofits, and commercial organization around themes that intersect the interests of these disparate groups. Some examples of new pragmatic initiatives in archaeology that seek this kind of integrative pragmatic approach include the US National Science Foundation funded Brown University project entitled 'Computer Vision Research: Promoting Paradigm Shifts in Archaeology' (funded at ca. $2.6 million); the Norwegian Research Council sponsored 'Global Moments in the Levant Project' at the University of Bergen (supported at ca. $2.4 million);

the Digital Archaeological Record (tDAR) cyberinfrastructure/digital information infrastructure for archaeology that is being developed with support from a major NSF grant (http://www.tdar.org/confluence/display/TDAR/Home); the multi-million Euro project 'Reconstructing Ancient (Biblical) Israel: The Exact and Life Sciences Perspective' European Union award to Israel Finkelstein of Tel Aviv University and Steve Weiner, Weizmann Institute of Science; and the 'MedArchNet—Mediterranean Archaeology Network' and 'DAAHL–Digital Archaeological Atlas of the Holy Land' project initiative at the Center of Interdisciplinary Science for Art, Architecture and Archaeology (CISA3), a part of the California Institute of Telecommunication and Information Technology (Calit2) at UC San Diego and supported by the Worldwide Universities Network (WUN—http://www.wun.ac.uk) discussed below (see http://daahl.ucsd.edu/DAAHL and http://cisa3.calit2.net/arch/news/ medarchnet). Although I was not trained as a Biblical archaeologist, when the UC San Diego's Jabal Hamrat Fidan (now Edom Lowlands Regional Archaeology Project—ELRAP) deep-time study of ancient mining and metallurgy began its focus on the Iron Age in southern Jordan's Edom region, I felt compelled to take a very pragmatic approach to the field work (Levy and Najjar 2007). Most important was the need to insure that archaeological data collected in the field could be brought home in digital form in the most streamlined and efficient way. These efforts in on-site digital archaeology (Levy *et al.* 2001c) helped evolve a number of integrated pragmatic approaches to working with robust cultural heritage datasets that are described below and have important implications for research and public outreach not only for archaeology and anthropology, but all aspects of world cultural heritage.

When methodological advances are used in conjunction with new theories, as well as those borrowed from anthropology, other fields of social sciences, and the humanities, it is possible to produce innovative interpretations in historical Biblical Archaeology that go beyond description and move beyond identifying important confluences between the Hebrew Bible (and other ancient texts) and the archaeological record. The importance of identifying these confluences has been discussed by W.G. Dever (2001, 2003, 2005); however, these linkages are only the first step in the search for historical and anthropological explanation. Armed with confluences between text and archaeology, researchers have already begun to investigate a number of exciting anthropological directions that can be applied to the 2nd- and 1st-millennium BCE Levantine archaeological record. Some of these topics include the following:

1. *Ethnogenesis in biblical societies*: Israelites, Philistines, Edomites, Moabites, and others (Bunimovitz and Faust 2001; Faust 2006; Killebrew 2005; Levy and Holl 2002)
2. *The Role of technological innovation* in structuring Iron Age societies (Ben-Yosef *et al.* 2008a, 2008b; Berna *et al.* 2007; Eliyahu-Behar *et al.* 2008; Friedman *et al.* 2008; Frumkin and Shimron 2006; Grattan, Gilbertson, and Hunt 2007; Hauptmann 2007; Karasik 2008; Klein and Hauptmann 1999; Levy *et al.* 2008a; Mazar *et al.* 2008, Shahack-Gross and Finkelstein 2008; Weinberger, Sneh, and Shalev 2008)
3. *Ancient world systems, trade and evolution of Iron Age polities*: Israel, Judah, Edom, etc. (Ben-Shlomo, Maeir, and Mommsen 2008; Bienkowski and van der Steen 2001; Hunt, Gilbertson, and El-Rishi 2007; Marriner, Morhange, and Doumet-Serhal 2006; Marriner, Morhange, and Saghieh-Beydoun 2008; Shahack-Gross *et al.* 2005)
4. *Secondary state formation in the Iron Age* (Albert *et al.* 2008; Finkelstein 1998, 1999; Halpern 1996, 1999; Joffe 2002; Knauf 1992; LaBianca 1999; LaBianca and Younker 1995; Levy *et al.* 2005b; Masters 2001; Routledge 2000a)
5. *Ethnoarchaeology and ethnography*: models for Iron Age technology, settlement, social organization (Bilu 2006; Levy *et al.* 2008b; Marx 2006; Tuzin 2006)
6. *Action/experimental archaeology*: reconstructing Trade Routes, Technology, etc. (Abbo *et al.* 2008; Charles *et al.* 2003; Levy 2007)

As historical Biblical Archaeology focuses more and more on problems of broad anthropological interest, there seems to be a concerted effort by researchers to employ science-based methods and analytical techniques to be able to test hypotheses with as objective methods as possible.

The Pragmatic Approach for Historical Biblical Archaeology in Action: Toward Finer Control of Time, Space, and Datasets

On-Site Digital Archaeology—Controlling for Context in Historical Biblical Archaeology

For archaeologists around the world, their two most precious commodities are the control of 'time' and 'space' to measure and assess the cultural and historical processes that drive their research interests. Historical biblical archaeologists are especially interested in measuring socio-historical change at the sub-century level of temporal resolution and recent advances in on-site digital archaeology will allow them to document the location of artifacts, ecofacts, architecture, and all aspects of the archaeological record with the highest degree of precision—one of the most important variables to control when conducting historical archaeological fieldwork and subsequent analyses. As the collection of dating samples, whether they are organic remains (fruit and other seeds, charcoal, etc.) for radiocarbon dating or artifacts that provide evidence for dating such as scarabs, seal impressions, unique imported pottery, etc., it is essential to record the location of these dating samples with the highest degree of precision in three dimension (X, Y, and Z coordinates). Locked into absolute 3D space in their cultural context, these artifacts can then be analyzed with a battery of dating techniques from seriation to high precision radiocarbon dating and consequently modeled using statistical and conventional archaeological methods to achieve sub-century dating. On-site digital archaeology methods surpass traditional non-digital methods that are still widely used on archaeological sites in the Southern Levant such as 'Dumpy' or Builder's levels, measure tapes, and line levels because the latter rely on 'skilled use', which consequently introduce multiple situations where error in data recording can occur. Digital recording tools such as the 'Total Station' that combines an electronic theodolite (tansit), an electronic distance measurer and software that is run on a data collector or external computer, or a GPS (Global Positioning System) have revolutionized the surveying industry by providing the surveyor accurate and timely positioning data (Fosburgh and Paiva 2001). When these developments in digital surveying are coupled with the power of Geographic Information Systems (GIS) that have become such an essential tool for archaeological data management and analysis (Westcott and Brandon 2000; Wheatley and Gillings 2002), it is possible for historical Biblical archaeologists to harness the most precise suite of data recording tools to locate precious artifacts and ecofacts in space. It is the seamless integration of these digital surveying tools and GIS that have made the on-site digital archaeology system developed at UCSD's Edom Lowland Project a model for historical Biblical Archaeology field work (Levy and Smith 2007). All archaeologists agree that because archaeological excavation is destructive, we must develop, and I would add continue to refine, our recording methods to insure we do our best to document the archaeological record that we actively destroy (Archer and Bartoy 2006; Barker 1977; Hester, Shafer, and Feder 1997; Maschner and Chippindale 2005; Renfrew and Bahn 2008; Roskams 2001; Zimmerman et al. 2002). The history of archaeological excavation around the world and in particular the Southern Levant is one linked to increasingly improved methodologies that accompany new interpretive paradigms of the historical archaeology record. A brief review of this co-evolutionary linkage in the Southern Levant is presented next.

Background to Excavation Methodology in the Holy Land

A wag once said that archaeological excavation is the science of destruction. While some impressive buildings and other architectural features may be revealed through excavation and subsequently preserved by those interested in cultural heritage, the layers above the structure will have been destroyed. If researchers want to explore layers beneath the exposed structure, they will have to destroy it in order to reveal the lower deposits. This unfortunate reality was recognized long ago by Sir Flinders Petrie (d. 1942) who conducted the first scientific excavations in Palestine at Tel Hesi in 1890 and who, in 1904, published his highly regarded book *Methods and Aims of Archaeology*. For archaeology in the Holy Land, it seems that major paradigm shifts are accompanied by important advances in excavation methodologies. Thus, the beginning of scientific archaeology in Palestine was ushered in by Petrie in the late 19th century CE. This was followed by methodological improvements at the 1909–10 Samaria excavations by George A. Reisner and Clarence Fisher, who developed a meticulous recording and classification system coupled with the debris-layer technique of excavation (King 1983), and W.F. Albright's 1926 to 1932 excavations at Tell Beit Mirsim, where he used the site to establish a ceramic dating framework for the Biblical periods by correlating typological changes with the stratigraphy and special imported finds spanning the 2nd and 1st millennia BCE (Levy and Freedman 2008). During this inter-war period, often referred to as the 'Golden Age of Biblical Archaeology' (Moorey 1991), the 1927 to 1935 University of Chicago excavations at Megiddo became a model for massive-scale excavation of biblical sites accompanied by P.L.O. Guy's pioneering use of aerial photography based on an electrically controlled plywood camera suspended from a hydrogen balloon (King 1983: 78). Some of the other large-scale excavations at biblical sites at this time took place at Beth Shan from 1921–33 (Rowe and FitzGerald 1930), Tell en Nasbeh (Badè 1934; McCown, Wampler, and Badè 1947), Beth Shemesh from 1928 to 1933 (Grant 1929), Lachish (Tell ed Duweir) from 1932–38 (Torczyner *et al.* 1938; Tufnell, Inge, and Harding 1940), and Ai (et Tell) from 1933 to 1935 (Marquet-Krause 1949). As Philip King (1983: 78) has pointed out, the problem with these enormous excavation projects using the Megiddo project as a model is that it was simply too large to be efficient—furthermore, it was too destructive.

Following the Second World War and the establishment of the State of Israel, the growth of Israeli universities and their own Department of Antiquities led to a distinctive excavation methodology that focused on large-scale broad horizontal exposures at sites such as Tel Beersheva, Arad, Lachish, Masada, and Hazor (Dever 1980). During this period, Kathleen Kenyon worked at the site of Jericho on the West Bank of what was then the Hashemite Kingdom of Jordan. There she developed one of the most important stratigraphic excavation techniques used in the Holy Land. This technique, referred to as the Wheeler–Kenyon method, is summarized in her 1952 book, *Beginning in Archaeology* (and later in Kenyon 1961) published the same year she began working at Jericho. Like her predecessors, Kenyon used a deep trench to sample the mound at Jericho. However, rather than crudely chop through the site, she utilized tight stratigraphic control and careful recoding based on the use of 5 × 5 meter squares where stratified layers and features were carefully excavated and sections preserved for drawing. Trained area supervisors were put in charge of parts of the trench so that they could control the excavation in a responsible manner. By the mid-1960s and early 1970s, a number of important North American excavations were carried out in Jordan's West Bank at sites such as Tell Taanach under Paul Lapp, and in Transjordan most notably at Tell Hesban, where Siegfried Horn established the Madaba Plains Project that continues to this day (Clark *et al.* 2010; Herr, Clark, and Trenchard 2001; LaBianca *et al.* 1990). During this period North American researchers in Israel re-investigated a number of important tel sites dating to the Biblical periods, including Tell el Hesi, Tell Jemmeh, and Tel Gezer. In terms of excavation methodology, the excavations at Gezer became the model for an American-style approach that utilized the Wheeler–Kenyon method, but outside of the trench (Dever and Lance 1978). Consequently, an excavation 'field' could include 20 or more 5 × 5 meter squares forming a kind of 'ice-cube tray' configuration where 1 meter balks were left between each excavation unit. An experienced supervisor was placed inside each excavation square who was responsible for recording all aspects of the excavation in this small area and an overall field supervisor was in charge summarizing the overall excavations for the field. The result of this approach was an over bureaucratization of the recording process with too many different hands involved in recording process. The result was a profusion of locus, wall, feature, and other summary documents that were extremely difficult to summarize. This led to a very time-consuming synthesis process that delayed the publication of data. The Israeli approach at this time put less stress on leaving baulks (for stratigraphic profile study) every 4 meters, and focused more on making larger scale exposures to reveal the complete plans of ancient architecture at a site. Rather than involve a multitude of excavation square supervisors, the Israeli approach was to have one field or area supervisor and an assistant supervisor responsible for all recording that may be called the 'open air' exposure method. The result was a more streamlined approach that was more conducive to synthesis than that used by many North American projects. An unintended consequence of the open-air approach was the desire to carry out the almost complete excavation of a site, leaving little for subsequent excavations to excavate on a scale similar to the large-scale excavations carried out during the inter-war years. Examples of these massive removals of archaeological layers include Tel Beersheva (Aharoni 1973), Tel Arad (Aharoni 1967; Aharoni, Naveh, and Rainey 1981), Hazevah (Cohen and Yisrael 1995a, 1995b), Kadesh Barnea (Cohen and Bernick-Greenberg 2007), and many Iron Age sites in the Negev desert (Cohen and Cohen-Amin 2004). While excellent interdisciplinary excavations have taken place in the Southern Levant over the past decade at historical biblical archaeology sites, none have utilized a completely integrated on-site GIS digital archaeology system as utilized in the Edom Lowlands Regional Archaeology Project described below. Some of the major interdisciplinary excavations projects recently working include: Tel es-Safi (Maeir *et al.* 2008), Tel Hazor (Ben-Tor 2002), Megiddo (Finkelstein, Ussishkin, and Halpern 2006; Piasetzky and Finkelstein 2005), Tel Rehov (Bruins, van der Plicht, and Mazar 2003a; Mazar *et al.* 2008), Tel Beth Shean (Mazar 2001, 2006), Tel Miqne (Gitin 2005), Tel Dor (Eliyahu-Behar *et al.* 2008; Gilboa and Sharon 2008), Khirbat al-Mudayna (Daviau and Chadwick 2007; Daviau and Dion 2002), Khirbat al-Mudayna al-'Aliya (Routledge 2000b, 2004; Routledge and Porter 2007), Dhiban (Porter *et al.* 2007), the Madaba Plains Project (Geraty 2007; Herr 2002; Herr and Clark 2007; Clark *et al.* 2010; LaBianca and Walker 2007; Younker 2007), among others. While many of these projects have employed a variety of digital tools for surveying, geophysical prospecting, and data analyses, among other tasks, none have applied an integrated on-site digital archaeology system rooted in GIS to insure the most accurate recording of archaeological data in the course of excavation. To tackle the sub-century dating issues that lay at the core of historical Biblical Archaeology, the next paradigm shift in this field will be accompanied by the adoption of totally integrated on-site digital archaeology systems. The following discussion outlines how such a system evolved with my own work in Israel and Jordan (Levy *et al.* 2001c).

A Personal View of On-Site Digital Archaeology and its Beginnings in the Southern Levant

When I joined the faculty at the UC San Diego in 1992, after living in the Middle East for over 13 years, I lost the opportunity to jump into my pick-up truck and drive for a few hours to my various research sites in the northern Negev desert. Also lost was the chance to check, on a daily basis, the artifact collections from our various expeditions that were housed in the beautiful laboratories and storage facilities of the Nelson Glueck School of Biblical Archaeology in Jerusalem. During my last expedition in Israel at the Early Bronze I Age (ca. 3600–3000 BCE) Nahal Tillah project near Kibbutz Lahav in 1994–96 (Levy et al. 2001b; Levy and van den Brink 2002), being based at UCSD, I realized how important it was to record as much data as possible using newly available digital cameras so that all special artifact finds collected during the excavation could be 'taken home' digitally for further study. However, since total stations were still quite expensive at that time and data collector technology and GIS was not advanced to the stage that it could be used easily in the field, we continued to rely on the traditional paper-based recording techniques rather than those based on digital assets. Similarly, during the first years (1997–98) that I worked in Jordan, we continued to use an analogue-recording system with hand-drawn day plans, locus, and other data forms filled by hand—we lacked any digital tools other than the same digital video camera that we used in Israel that had the capability of shooting individual photos at 3 MP resolution. By 1999, hand-held data recorders were powerful and rugged enough to allow us to couple them with Leica total stations that had dropped markedly in price by the end of the decade. My decision to 'go digital' that year during our major excavations at the Early Bronze III–IV (ca. 2700–2000 BCE) copper manufactory at Khirbat Hamra Ifdan (KHI) (Levy et al. 2002) and the Pre-Pottery Neolithic village of Tel Tifdan (Levy 2007; Twiss 2007) caused a great deal of angst among our staff who were compelled to stay up working until midnight for untold weeks before we finally began to iron out the flaws in the on-site digital archaeology system. An additional season of excavation at KHI in 2000 enabled us to perfect the on-site digital archaeology system to the point that we published one of the first papers on the subject with the Society of American Archaeology (Levy et al. 2001c). By 2002, our research concerning the social dimensions of ancient mining and metallurgy began to explore the nature of Iron Age copper production in Jordan's Faynan district. As this period is closely tied to the Hebrew Bible, it became clear that if the digital archaeology system was coupled with high precision radiocarbon dating, it would be possible to achieve sub-century dating. Consequently, this would put our research in a strong position to test questions related to the 12th–6th-century BCE history of Biblical Edom. The following section briefly describes the UCSD digital archaeology system.

GIS-based Excavation Recording at ELRAP, Faynan District, Jordan

A brief summary of the on-site GIS digital archaeology system (Levy and Smith 2007) used by our team, co-directed by Mohammad Najjar and me in Jordan's Faynan region, is presented below, along with some suggestions of where we need to go from here. While GIS has been around a long time, beginning in the 1950s, with its application in archaeology growing over the years with archaeological settlement pattern studies (Rua 2009; Westcott and Brandon 2000; Wheatley and Gillings 2002; Zimmerman et al. 2002), it has been slow in becoming the standard 'tool of choice' for fully integrating on-site archaeological data recording. It is hoped that exposure to the ELRAP on-site GIS digital archaeology system will help this application become a standard for historical Biblical archaeologists. The nexus of the ELRAP on-site digital archaeology is the GIS Data Center (served with an ArcGIS platform); as archaeologists, we need to visualize, question, examine, and understand the archaeological record and the human behavior reflected therein (Fig. 1). As indicated above, all of the recording systems used by archaeologists since the early days of Sir Flinders Petrie use maps to portray excavation data, the belief being that the map is superior over tables and spreadsheets for understanding the social and historical context of the material record, as well as patterns in the spatial data. The development of daily graphic diaries to record the progress of excavations makes archaeological recording a natural forum for GIS. This is because long ago archaeologists recognized that maps and spatial analysis are the most important tools for understanding patterns in excavation data–the key to understanding ancient human behavior. According to the National Science Foundation, GIS is a computer-based system for capture, storage, retrieval, analysis, and display of spatial data. Thus, archaeological excavation and archaeological datasets are particularly suitable to GIS because they are rooted in space, defined by their x, y, and z coordinates, which can be defined by a variety of coordinate systems (latitude/ longitude, Universal Transverse Mercator [UTM], etc.). The GIS combines layers of data about an artifact, ancient site, or any point where x, y, and z (elevation) coordinates are recorded to give the archaeologist a better understanding of its context. The ELRAP project recognized this back in 1999 (Levy *et al.* 2001c) when it was realized that understanding the meaning of artifact and settlement pattern data could be embellished through the integration of a wide range of data in different formats, such as maps (topographic, soil, geology, artifact, etc.), digital photographs and video, artifact analysis data sets, and more. This integrative approach to on-site digital archaeology is outlined in the flow-chart below (Fig. 1).

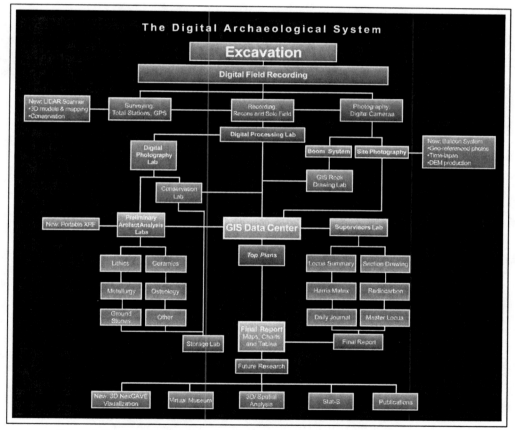

Figure 1. On-Site GIS Digital Archaeology system (3.0) as used by ELRAP in Jordan

Archaeological excavation produces a plethora of data, ranging from contextual excavation loci such as floors, pits, hearths, architectural features, etc., to artifacts such as pottery, lithics, metals, groundstone, archaeometallurgical finds, and more. To record the x, y, and z coordinate of each artifact or archaeological feature with the highest degree of precision, a Total Station or GPS unit is used for each measurement, which is then automatically given a unique sequential ID reference referred to as its EDM (or Electronic Distance Measurer) number in the data recorder. While many electronic survey instruments come with built-in data collectors, the ELRAP project uses TDS Rcon data collectors using SoloField TDS software that collects user-entered data on a specific point (a special find artifact, architectural feature, etc.) or a set of points (a polygon shape representing a locus) and triggers the Total Station or GPS unit to record the coordinates for the point or polygon data. Currently, the ELRAP project uses a list of 180 different identifiable special finds and features on a 'Descriptor Code' list stored in the Recon data collector so that each point that is shot with the Total Station or GPS unit can be assigned a meaningful cultural variable. At the end of each excavation day, these data are exported as an ArcGIS shapefile on a powerful GIS designated PC Laptop computer in the expedition 'Clean Lab' located in a rented house in the Bedouin village of Qurayqira—the largest modern settlement in our research area which has continuous electricity.

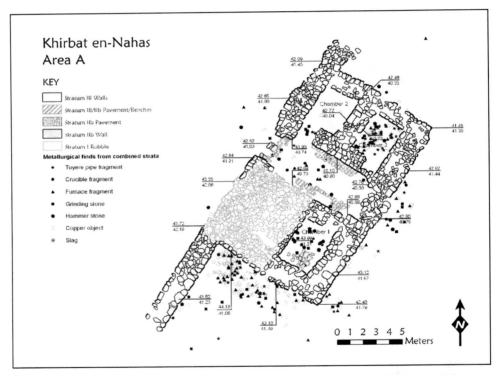

Figure 2. Map of the fortress gate house (Area A) at the Iron Age site of Khirbat en-Nahas (Jordan) produced in the field using ArcGIS in 2006. Note the range of metallurgical artifacts plotted in relation to the gatehouse map.

The shapefile contains both the spatial information for each point and polygon recorded on site that day as well as a spreadsheet database with the data entered for each recorded artifact or locus. Thus, both map and tabular data are produced instantaneously. The organization of the GIS Data Center and its team, the procedures used to insure mistakes made in the field during the data collection process are caught before those data are entered into the GIS, and the production of daily top plans and rapid production of publication-quality maps can be found in Levy and Smith (2007). An example of a GIS-produced final publication map can be seen in Figure 2, which illustrates the 10th–9th century BCE gatehouse in Area A at Khirbat en-Nahas (KEN) with distribution of metallurgical artifacts. As seen here, it is easy to select any assemblage of material culture (in this case, general categories of artifacts related to metallurgy) and plot them. Using GIS, Figure 2 combines broad categories of slag, ground stone, and other artifacts and has plotted them where they were found in the Gatehouse excavations regardless of strata. When viewed on a computer, each artifact data point has a 'hot link' to photographs of that artifact making it easy for the researcher to access virtually each artifact recorded at the site.

Thus, On-Site GIS Digital Archaeology is crucial for the excavation of historical biblical sites (and those from any period) because of its ability to record archaeological data with the highest degree of precision and integrate so many formats and sources of data collected in the field. These include digital photography from the field and lab, 3D artifact scan data, conservation data, storage data, field supervisor records (locus summaries, section drawings, Harris matrix, radiocarbon data, daily journal, master loci list, final report), specialist data and analyses (stone tool/lithics, ceramics, metallurgy, osteology, ground stone, zooarchaeology, geomorphology, etc.), along with the full range of data collected with imaging tools from satellite remote sensing data (Gallo *et al.* 2009; Siart, Eitel, and Panagiotopoulos 2008; Wiseman and El-Baz 2007), multispectral image data, geophysical data (Witten 2006), archaeological survey data collected with GPS units and Total Stations. In addition to integrating a whole range of datasets into one coherent database, the GIS has many strong tools for further analyses and manipulations of the data (such as statistical calculations of spatial relations of artifacts and sites, cross-cutting analyses of different types of finds, etc.), previously impossible to make 'by hand'.

In short, On-Site GIS Digital Archaeology provides a 'one stop shop' for recording, storing, integrating and analyzing all archaeological data collected in the field and laboratory in a way that streamlines studies and provides a basis for interdisciplinary collaborative research. In the era of computers, the GIS becomes essential for archaeological data management, if only for the simple fact that any archaeological excavation produces thousands or tens of thousands of data points, which can never be fully assessed using 'traditional' methods of research. With the rapid growth of digital file size resulting from the use of more and more digital recording tools on excavations (i.e. LIDAR scanning, 3D artifact scanning, digital SLR photography, and more), faster field computers with larger data-storage capability will be needed. Interest in viewing data in 3D means that the future field computer(s) will also need to be able to process and display 3D data.

Digital Artifact Informatics—Beginning with Pottery

Since the early systematic studies of 3rd to 1st millennia BCE sites in the Holy Land by W.F. Albright at Tell Beit Mirism (Albright 1932b, 1938, 1943), pottery has been at the center of historical Biblical archaeological investigation for dating (Amiran, Beck, and Zevulun 1970), identifying ethnic identity (Faust 2004, 2006), and ancient trade patterns (Bienkowski and van der Steen 2001). Advances in computer computation and digital 3D scanning have opened up new possibilities for more rigorous investigations of historical Biblical Archaeology questions (http://cisa3.calit2.net/arch/research/digitalpotery.php). Pottery is the dominant artifact found on sites dating to the Biblical periods, but these are usually found in the form of pottery sherd fragments that provide only a partial view of the artifact. The Digital Pottery Informatics Project aims to systematize the collection and input of pottery into a ceramic database that would make these finds visible to researchers worldwide over the Internet. The system integrates new methods for reconstructing 3D digital versions of the pottery, either through direct 3D scanning of the object, or through the application of algorithms for reconstructing 3D images based on scans of one or more sherds that appear to come from the same source object. CISA3 is also developing methods for extrapolating the 3D construction of pottery artifacts based on 2D photos of the pottery—a capability that could quickly make available 3D versions of thousands of objects in the archaeology record for which only 2D images are available.

In its initial format, the Digital Pottery Informatics Project is converting the Iron Age ceramic database composed of published archaeological excavations reports of the Southern Levant into 3D format, which will allow the pottery data to be queried via the Digitial Archaeological Atlas of the Holy Land (DAAHL, another CISA3 project—http://daahl.ucsd.edu). The majority of ceramic publications in the Iron Age Southern Levant are published as two-dimensional drawings in books and articles. Consequently, they lose key three-dimensional information on these vessels. By vectorizing published reports in ceramic databases, we are able to recover the 3D data. Once the vessels are vectorized, a unique mathematical algorithm can be extracted from the vessel so that it can be stored and classified by its 3D shape and curvature. This information can then be exported to any 3D rendering program. This project is being spearheaded by N.G. Smith and me of CISA3 (http://cisa3.calit2.net/arch/research/digitalpotery.php) in collaboration with Avshalom Karasik and Uzy Smilansky of the Weizmann Institute of Science (Israel), who, with A. Gilboa, I. Sharon, and others who have been at the forefront of applying quantitative methods to ceramic analyses in the Southern Levant (Gilboa *et al.* 2004; Karasik 2008; Karasik *et al.* 2004). The digital archaeology project is continuously evolving as new developments in portable digital technologies come on the market or are developed by my research lab, graduate students, and colleagues at CISA3.

CISA3's early work on this project also includes direct 3D scanning of pot sherds uncovered at various sites in Jordan and Israel, using a high-precision, 3D structured light FlexScan scanner. The scanner allows each nuance of the object to be recovered. Once the 3D scan of the object is retrieved, a mathematical computation can be run to determine the exact shape and stance of the vessel. The final result—either from 2D ceramic illustrations or 3D scans—is a digital 3D model that can be visually manipulated in three dimensions (including in 3D immersive environments) and also analyzed and compared with other vessels according to its mathematical curvature function. However, these kinds of multivariate datasets can be created for any realm of material culture from stone tools to metal artifacts to zooarchaeological remains. These exciting data will be accessible through Google Earth and other tools that permit them to be geo-located at the precise point where the pottery or sherds were recovered by the archaeologist.

Controlling for Sub-Century Time—High Precision Radiocarbon Dating and Historical Biblical Archaeology

For archaeologists, the control of time is essential for measuring culture evolution, modeling environmental change over different time-scales, and identifying historical events and personages in the archaeological record. It will be suggested here that only through the integration of multiple dating methods and sources can a degree of objectivity and accuracy be gained for addressing sub-century dating problems in historical Biblical Archaeology. As noted above, early archaeologists working in the Holy Land, such as Sir Flinders Petrie (1972), were instrumental in developing innovative methods not only for field excavation, but also relative dating methods to measure various archaeological phenomena such as the temporal placement of human burials, archaeological sites, and cultural strata. Petrie's development of contextual seriation analysis of Egyptian pottery from the site of Diospolis Parva was the first example of an objective relative dating method to determine the chronological sequence of artifacts without being able to refer to a fixed time scale. This was based on the ordering of artifacts in a typological sequence and known generically as seriation, where similar objects can be ordered together in a succession or series (Marquardt 1978; Renfrew and Bahn 2008). One of the problems with these types of seriation studies is knowing which end of the artifact seriation is the oldest. However, when the artifacts in the seriation can be placed in a stratigraphic order based on contextual observations in an archaeological site(s), it is possible to know which end of the artifact seriation is oldest. By the 1950s, frequency seriation was developed where the proportional abundance, or frequency, of a ceramic or stone tool style was studied, producing distinctive graphs known as 'battleship curves' (Barros 1982; Brainerd 1951; Meighan 1977; Robinson 1951). The rise and fall of the popularity of artifact styles is detected through seriation. Some of the best examples of frequency seriation are the work on changes in New England tombstone motifs over a ca. 150 year period by James Deetz (Dethlefsen and Deetz 1966) and Frank Hole's frequency seriation of bowl types in the Deh Luran Plain of Iran corroborated by stratigraphic excavations (Hole 1984). However, as Robert Drennan (Drennan 1979) points out, in trying to use seriation analyses (or any other analytical method), its efficacy is a limitation on the conclusions that can be drawn. For Drennan, some data sets will produce positive results with seriation and others will not. Other dating tools, such as the use of epigraphic data including Egyptian scarabs and amulets (Eggler and Keel 2006; Keel 1997; Levy et al. 2005a; Munger 2003, 2005; Rowe 1936) can also give extremely informative dates for archaeological deposits, however the role of site formation processes, the problem of amulets being re-cycled as heirlooms, and other factors means these objects can not be the single source of dating archaeological phenomena on historical Biblical archaeological sites. Even though historical Biblical archaeologists encounter 'type fossils' of certain artifact types, such as six-chambered gates, ashlar palaces, Greek Proto-geometric pottery, Red burnished pottery, and other material remains are generally ascribed to the 10th century BCE, the precise dating of these objects in the Iron Age II sub-century dating sequence are still debated (Finkelstein 2005b; Mazar 2005). Similarly, changes in epigraphic styles on certain artifacts must be used with caution when trying to ascertain the date of an object with writing found in the archaeological record (Schniedewind 2005). New approaches to sub-century dating are being developed as a result of recent archaeo-intensity research carried out by geo-scientists in the ELRAP project (Ben-Yosef et al. 2009). The most pragmatic approach to help solve sub-century dating problems in historical Biblical Archaeology is to combine all these dating methods with objective high precision radiocarbon dating.

To borrow some insights from Thomas Kuhn's monumental work *The Structure of Scientific Revolutions* (1962), it is fair to say that at the beginning of the 21st century a major paradigm shift toward more science-based research in historical Biblical Archaeology occurred. This came to fruition in 2001 with a concerted effort to publish considerable suites of radiocarbon dates from Iron Age sites, such as Tel Dor (Gilboa and Sharon 2001), Tel Beth Shean, Tel Safi (Maeir 2008), and Tel Rehov (Mazar and Carmi 2001). In addition, conferences have been held that specifically addressed the need for applying ^{14}C dating to Iron Age sites (Bruins 2001), and in 2003, with the publication of high precision radiocarbon dates from Tel Rehov applicable to historical Biblical Archaeology questions such as the Egyptian Pharoah Shishak's military campaign in Palestine that represents an important confluence of extra-Biblical historical and archaeological data and the Hebrew Bible.

Radiocarbon dating has been around since Willard Libby discovered the method as a result of his research during World War II concerning cosmic radiation—the sub-atomic particles that constantly bombard the earth, producing high-energy neutrons that react with nitrogen atoms in the atmosphere and produce atoms of carbon-14 called radiocarbon (^{14}C; Renfrew and Bahn 2008: 142) (Libby 1955). ^{14}C is unstable because it has eight neutrons in the nucleus rather than the usual six found in regular carbon (^{12}C). The instability of ^{14}C promotes its radioactive decay at a regular rate, and Libby calculated that it takes 5568 years for half of the ^{14}C in any organic sample to decay. This is known as half-life, and while modern radiocarbon dating labs have shown that a more accurate half-life figure is 5730 years, for consistency labs continue to use 5568 years. ^{14}C is produced in the atmosphere and continuously absorbed by living plants through carbon dioxide and by animals that eat plants or other animals. As soon as a plant or animal dies, the uptake of ^{14}C stops and decay begins. Libby was awarded a Nobel Prize for inventing a method of measuring the rate of radiocarbon decay. When first developed, Libby assumed that radiocarbon decayed at a constant rate through time. However, in the 1960s researchers discovered that the rate varies due primarily to changes in the strength of the earth's magnetic field and other variables. This inaccuracy was demonstrated by tree-ring dating, a method that enables scientists to correct or calibrate radiocarbon dates in relation to calendar dates. As Renfrew and Bahn (2008:143) point out, radiocarbon dates obtained from tree-rings show that before ca. 1000 BCE, dates expressed in radiocarbon years are increasingly too young in relation to true calendar years. In other words, before 1000 BCE trees (and all other living things) were exposed to greater concentrations of atmospheric ^{14}C than they are today. By obtaining radiocarbon dates systematically from the long tree-ring master sequences of bristlecone pine (from North America) and oak (from northern Europe), scientists have been able to plot radiocarbon ages against tree-ring ages (in calendar years) to produce calibration curves back to around 8500 BCE.

Thomas Higham (2009) of the Oxford Radiocarbon Accelerator Unit (ORAU) provides a very handy overview of the radiocarbon dating method, measurement, applications, age calibration, pretreatment of samples, and other related issues. Radioactive-based clocks in geosciences in general (of which radiocarbon is part) are extremely reliable, accurate, and rooted in modern science. To doubt these methods today is like doubting the fact that the earth is moving around the sun; the fact that we do not easily understand the physics behind the method ('we' as 'us archaeologists') does not make the method less reliable.[2]

Before the paradigm shift noted above, archaeologists working on Iron Age sites were averse to using radiocarbon dating as a regular part of their analytical 'tool box' because it was assumed that pottery typologies and small finds such as scarabs and other material culture 'type fossils' were sufficient for dating archaeological phenomena from the Biblical periods. What is new for historical Biblical Archaeology is the realization that it is now possible to achieve improved resolution of radiocarbon dating using the high precision AMS (accelerator mass spectrometry) method that requires much smaller organic sample sizes (ca. 5–10 mg compared with + 100 mg for the traditional Liquid Scintillation [LS] counting method) and the application of statistical analysis (Bronk Ramsey 2005) to achieve reliable sub-century dating that is so important for answering historical questions.

Reproducibility between laboratories is a key plank in establishing methodological confidence. Inter-laboratory comparisons are, therefore, a regular activity among the radiocarbon community—to test comparability of laboratory measurements and improve routine dating. Measurements are made for a variety of sample types (charcoal, wood, bone, etc.) to insure comparability between radiocarbon labs. Various laboratories sometimes publish their 'known age test data' and the results of the intercomparison exercises are published in the journal *Radiocarbon* for both AMS and conventional counting labs.

There are at least seven different radiocarbon calibration curves, but for archaeologists working in the Southern Levant, IntCal04 (Reimer *et al.* 2004) is the most commonly used for calibrating terrestrial material from the Northern Hemisphere. This is the most recent curve produced by the international radiocarbon community and it extends from 26,000 to 0 cal BP by combining radiocarbon determinations from tree-rings, uranium-thorium dated corals, and varve-counted marine sediments. Through our period of interest, however, the curve comprises only decadal tree-rings measured using high precision conventional decay counting. There are sections of the calibration curve that are flat, meaning that two samples of the same age in radiocarbon years can be 400 years apart in calendar years. For historical Biblical Archaeology this is a significant problem because for the period ca. 800 to 400 BCE in calendar years the calibration curve is flat, meaning it is impossible

---

2. I am indebted to Erez Ben-Yosef for pointing this out.

to test sub-century questions during this particular period. If we take one of the radiocarbon dates from the Iron Age excavations of a copper smelting mound in Jordan as an example (Levy *et al.* 2008a) calibrated to the 10th century BCE, the accuracy of radiocarbon dates means working not only with the center of a radiocarbon date (i.e. 2764 BP) but also its error estimate indicated by + (i.e. 2764 $\pm$ 25 BP), which produces an age range in calendar years for the radiocarbon determination. Depending on where the radiocarbon date falls on the calibration curve, some age ranges will be narrower and hence, more precise than others. Once a calibration curve has been established, it is by no means a static achievement. For example, for the past two decades, every 4 or 5 years, further extensions and additional measurements are added and the curve and its length and precision improve further. Currently, much work is being expended extending the curve back to the limit of the radiocarbon method at around 55,000 BP.

To facilitate the calibration of radiocarbon dates from archaeological sites, there are a variety of computer-based calibration programs available with OxCal (hosted by ORAU) and CALIB (hosted by the University of Washington and University of Belfast) being the most commonly used by Levantine archaeologists. Prior to the use of computers, calibration was undertaken by hand using the intercept method (Renfrew and Bahn 2008: 146). Today, computer calibration programs are widely available on the Radiocarbon website (www.radiocarbon.org) or at a variety of laboratory web sites (e.g. ORAU https://c14.arch.ox.ac.uk/oxcal for the OxCal calibration program). To find the best fit of a ^{14}C date sample and calibration curve, the computer provides age ranges based on probability distributions. The best fit is simply the correspondence of the ^{14}C date with the calibration curve that is based on 10-year blocks of tree ring wood dated by three or four laboratories. A Bayesian method has recently been used to find the best fit for the calibration curve because the order of the dates taken from the 10-year ring blocks is known. As each ^{14}C date has an error of 4 or 5 years, Bayesian modeling has tended to smooth the curve to a limited degree. In a recent paper dealing with the debate over the dating of the Santorini eruption ca. 1630 BCE, Malcolm Wiener (Wiener 2009a, 2009b) raises a number of important questions regarding the use of high precision radiocarbon dating for sub-century dating problems, including what happens if researchers in the Mediterranean zone use different calibration curves, such as the older IntCal98 (Stuiver *et al.* 1998) instead of the currently recommended IntCal04 (Reimer *et al.* 2004). He suggests there might be slight differences in the 'wiggly' parts of the curve where IntCal04 might result in greater smoothing (as seen at Tel Rehov, for instance); however, the differences are only of the order of 4 or 5 years (Mazar *et al.* 2005). At this juncture, one should use IntCal04 when running calibrations for historical Biblical Archaeology samples.

As Christopher Bronk Ramsey (2005: 63) points out, Bayesian statistical analysis:

> becomes essential when trying to resolve high resolution chronological issues with radiocarbon dating. The complex nature of the calibration curve means that intuitive fitting is extremely difficult to achieve. The strength of such mathematical analysis lies not only in the conclusions that it allows us to draw from complex data but also in the demonstration of what we cannot resolve given the available information.

Bayesian modeling, an ingenious coupling of relative stratigraphic information, high precision radiocarbon dates, and large sample sizes, is capable of improving the resolution of difficult sub-century dating issues in historical Biblical Archaeology. While there continue to be debates about the application of high precision radiocarbon dating in this branch of historical archaeology (Bruins, van der Plicht, and Mazar 2003a, 2003b; Finkelstein 2005a, 2005b; Finkelstein and Piasetzky 2003; Higham *et al.* 2005; Levy *et al.* 2005b, 2008a; Levy, Higham, and Najjar 2006; Levy, Najjar, and Higham 2007; Mazar 2005; Piasetzky and Finkelstein 2005; Sharon *et al.* 2005; Van der Plicht and Bruins 2005; van der Steen and Bienkowski 2005b; van der Steen and Bienkowski 2006), there can be little doubt that the paradigm shift alluded to above has happened and that radiometric dating should be a required method in every historical Biblical archaeologist's tool box.

A Case Study in Historical Biblical Archaeology from Khirbat en-Nahas, Jordan

Since 2002, the UCSD–DOAJ ELRAP project in Jordan's Faynan district has focused its research on tackling the problem of the role of mining and metallurgy on the formation, maintenance, and ultimate collapse of Iron Age polities in the region known as Edom in the Hebrew Bible (Levy and Najjar 2007). As ELRAP is an anthropological archaeology project which aims as using the best dating tools available, when research began it was assumed that the Iron Age chronology established by Crystal Bennett (Bennett 1966, 1982) and Piotr Bienkowski (Bennett 1977; Bennett and Bienkowski 1995; Bienkowski 2001a, 2001b, 2001c; Bienkowski and Bennett 2003; Bienkowski and Sedman 2001; Bienkowski and van der Steen 2001) was correct. These researchers, who carried out Iron Age excavations on the highland plateau of Edom at sites such as Umm el-Biyara, Tawilan, Busayra and other locales argued that the Iron Age in Edom was a relatively short period that began in the 7th century BCE and extended into the 6th century BCE. The low chronology established by Bennett and Bienkowski for Edom is a relative chronology based on the dating of one 7th-century BCE seal impression an Edomite king that is restored as 'Qos-Gabr, King of Edom' found at Umm el-Biyara and whose name is also recorded on Prism B of Esarhaddon dated to 673–72 BCE and in a description of Ashurbanipal's first campaign of 667 BCE (Bienkowski 1992: 99) and a series of small finds. The result of Bennett's important work (the first large-scale systematic Iron Age excavations in Edom's plateau) was the relative dating of the small finds and especially Iron Age ceramics of the region to the end of the Iron Age. This effectively removed discussion of the earlier centuries of the Iron Age (especially the 9th–12th centuries BCE) from historical modeling. Subsequently, the late Iron Age ceramic typologies established for Edom based on these excavations dated all Iron Age sites in the region to the very end of the Iron Age sequence (Hart 1987, 1988, 1989; Hart and Knauf 1986; Oakshott 1978, 1983). Using this relative chronology, researchers such as Gary Pratico (Pratico 1985, 1993) totally discounted the pioneer survey and excavation work of the pioneer archaeologist Nelson Glueck who carried out the first systematic work in Edom and identified a significant 10th-century BCE Iron Age occupation there (Glueck 1940). Today, however, stratified excavations in the lowlands of Edom using the on-site GIS digital archaeology methods described above coupled with a significant high precision radiocarbon dating project have pushed the Iron Age of this part of Jordan back to the 12th century BCE. This pragmatic approach has opened up new research opportunities for investigating the rise and collapse of complex societies in Edom and their relationship to the Hebrew Bible and other ancient Near Eastern texts.

Since 2002, our team has carried out a wide range of Iron Age excavations including two major seasons at the KEN copper production center (Levy *et al.* 2004, 2005b, 2008a), the watch tower site of Rujm Hamra Ifdan [RHI] (Levy *et al.* 2008a), the mortuary complex at Wadi Fidan 40 (Levy, Adams, and Muniz 2004; Levy *et al.* 2005a), a small sounding at the secondary copper production center of Khirbat al-Jariyeh [KAJ], and a number of full coverage intensive surveys of the main wadis in the Faynan district (Levy *et al.* 2001a, 2003; Witten *et al.* 2000). A considerable suite of Iron Age radiocarbon dates have been produced from the ELRAP–DOAJ excavations. To date, a total of 81 high precision radiocarbon dates have been processed for KEN. Of these, 37 have been published (Higham *et al.* 2005; Levy *et al.* 2004, 2005b) from the stratified excavations at KEN and nine additional samples come from the earlier probes at KEN made by the German Mining Museum (Hauptmann 2007). An additional 35 dates have recently become available from the ORAU and will be published in the near future. However, for the purposes of this chapter, a small sequence of those dates from the recent excavations at one of the public/administrative building at KEN will be presented. Nine dates have been processed for KAJ and will soon be published. Five dates have been published for RHI (Levy *et al.* 2008a) and seven from Wadi Fidan 40 (Levy, Adams, and Shafiq 1999; Levy *et al.* 2005a). Taken together, there is no question that a number of socio-economic phenomena related to complex societies and large-scale populations were at work in the Edom lowlands during the earlier centuries of the Iron Age (especially the 10th and 9th centuries BCE) were not accounted for in earlier Iron Age research or in the old chronology used in this region. As seen in Figure 3, over 400 years of history are now added to the Iron Age chronology of Edom when high precision radiocarbon dates from well-controlled stratigraphic excavations are combined. This approach not only provides an additional 400 years to the chronology, but also the ability to subdivide these years into fine sequences of layers and phases using the on-site GIS digital archaeology. By taking a pragmatic approach to the Iron Age archaeology of Edom rooted in an anthropological approach to historical Biblical Archaeology, one not wedded to historical assumptions based on or against the Hebrew Bible, the data now speaks for itself, allowing researchers to explore a wide range of socio-cultural topics discussed at the beginning of this chapter.

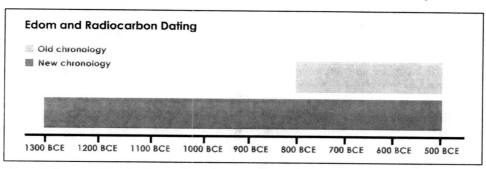

Figure 3. A new radiocarbon based chronology for Iron Age Edom in light of dates obtained from sites in the lowland region of Edom (Faynan district, Jordan).

To facilitate this discussion of a pragmatic approach to historical Biblical Archaeology, eight previously unpublished radiocarbon dates from the most recent excavations at KEN are examined in what follows. The 2006 excavations in Area T at KEN provide a good example of the importance of high precision radiocarbon dating and Bayesian modeling of archaeological phenomenon related to historical Biblical Archaeology. More than 70 years ago, Nelson Glueck (Glueck 1934, 1940) suggested that many of the buildings visible on the site surface at KEN dated to the 10th century BCE and that some of the larger structures were linked to administrative activities at this ancient copper production site. As our 2002 excavations focused on sampling the fortress gatehouse, the upper levels of a slag mound and a small building in proximity to the German Mining Museum's soundings (Fritz 1996), one of the goals of the 2006 season was to sample some of the large structures at the site. With this in mind, a large mound (labeled Area T) consisting of collapsed stone blocks representing an ancient building situated on the eastern side of KEN was selected for excavation (Fig. 4). This was the first of four large stone mounds to be sampled at the site.

After approximately three weeks of careful excavation, a fairly well preserved building was revealed with four rooms and one stairwell surrounding a courtyard. The stairs, located in the southwest corner of the building, seem to lead to a tower that was associated with the Area T building that measures ca. 10.78 m × 11.93 m in area (Figs. 5, 6). The map illustrated in Figure 7 was produced using the on-site GIS digital archaeology system briefly outlined above and described in detail elsewhere (Levy and Smith 2007).

Figure 4. Area T, Khirbat en-Nahas during initial stage of excavation, 2006
(photo by T.E. Levy, UCSD Levantine Archaeology Laboratory).

Figure 5. Overview of Iron Age public building excavated at Khirbat en-Nahas, Area T, with room
and structures labeled (photo by T.E. Levy, UCSD Levantine Archaeology Laboratory).

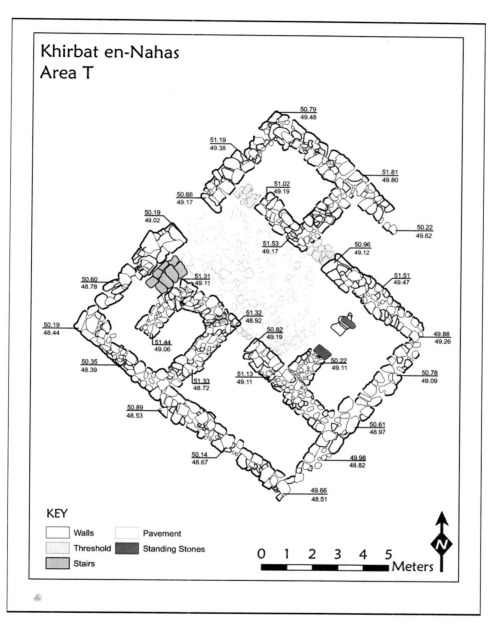

Figure 6. Map of Area T, Khirbat en-Nahas 2006 produced using the ELRAP on-site GIS digital archaeology system.

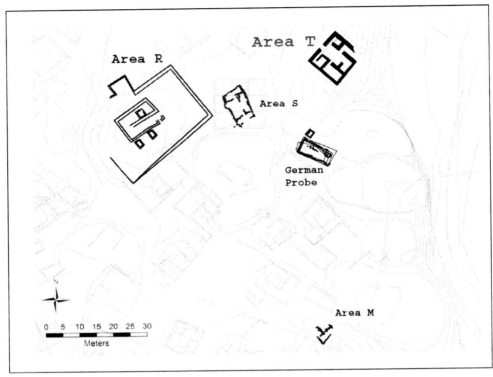

Figure 7. Location of Area T in relation to other excavations
carried out in the eastern quarter of Khirbat en Nahas, Jordan

The 2006 excavations in Area T were supervised by Adolpho Muniz in consultation with
Mohammad Najjar and me. A total of six strata were identified in Area T and labeled from the
surface down as T1a, T1b, T2a, T2ab, T2b, and T3. In general, T1a represents the mass of collapsed wall stones without any sediment matrix. Below this, Stratum T1b consists of wall collapse
with sediment fill. This fill was found both inside and outside the structure and extended to above
the floor levels. Stratum T2a represents the final occupation phase of the Area T building consisting
of various ash deposits and activity areas. Below this, Stratum T2ab represents loci and features
associate with both occupation phases, such as thresholds to all rooms and the stairs leading to the
tower. Stratum 2b embodies the main occupation phase. Finally, below the building foundations is
Stratum T3, which is characterized by thick layers of crushed slag and metallurgical debris (Fig. 5).
Like many other quarters of KEN, such as Areas S, R, and M (Levy *et al.* 2008a), the building in
Area T was built on top of an existing industrial slag mound. The 2006 excavations only penetrated
approximately 1 meter into these industrial deposits situated beneath the building. When the
excavations began, we assumed the Area T building would date to the 9th century BCE like the
nearby structure exposed in Area S and another by the German mining museum [Fig. 7] (Fritz
1996; Levy *et al.* 2005b). While some pottery and other finds were found in the Area T building
that place it in the Iron Age, the assemblage is too small to produce definitive dates for
the various strata. Preliminary analyses of the ceramics at the site carried out by Neil Smith and me
have demonstrated that many Iron Age ceramic types characteristic of 7th century BCE sites on the

Oxford Sample #	Oxford Series	Locus	Locus Description	Area		
Sample Description		d13C	Uncalibrated Date	Stratum	1 Sigma	2 Sigma
OxA-18947	EDOM2006_T_10KEN_06_T_EDM4114	1566	Ash Layer		T3	1021 – 928 BC	1111 – 909 BC
charcoal, Acacia sp.		d13=-23.69	2833 ± 30			
OxA-18948	EDOM2006_T_10KEN_06_T_EDM4107	1580	Fill: Dark Brown-reddish mixed with Ash-Room 5		T3	1007 – 928 BC	1052 – 901 BC
charcoal, Phoenix dactylifera		d13=-21.05	2819 ± 29			
OxA-18949	EDOM2006_T_10KEN_06_T_EDM40290	1517	Fill and Wall Collapse		T1b	895 – 814 BC	902 – 808 BC
charcoal, Indeterminate		d13=-21.89	2701 ± 26			
OxA-18950	EDOM2006_T_10KEN_06_T_EDM40686	1526	Fill Beneath Wall Collapse		T1b	996 – 911 BC	1015 – 849 BC
charcoal, Tamarix sp.		d13=-26.20	2797 ± 27			
OxA-18951	EDOM2006_T_10KEN_06_T_EDM40488	1541	Ash Layer		T2a	922 – 844 BC	975 – 829 BC
charcoal, Tamarix sp.		d13=-23.50	2755 ± 26			
OxA-18952	EDOM2006_T_10KEN_06_T_EDM40989	1578	Compact Mud (Floor) Mixed with Ash and Slag		T2a	997 – 921 BC	1043 – 896 BC
charcoal, Phoenix dactylifera		d13=-23.73	2805 ± 28			
OxA-18953	EDOM2006_T_10KEN_06_T_EDM40908	1561	Floor-Ash Layer		T2b	1043 – 941 BC	1112 – 922 BC
charcoal, Tamarix sp.		d13=-25.08	2844 ± 25			
OxA-18954	EDOM2006_T_10KEN_06_T_EDM41107	1599	Fill		T3	1041 – 937 BC	1111-918 BC
charcoal, Retama raetam		d13=-21.76	2840 ± 26			

Table 1. Radiocarbon determinations and calibrations for Area T, Khirbat en-Nahas, Jordan.

highland plateau of Edom have their origin as early as the 9th and 10th centuries BCE in the lowlands (Smith and Levy 2008). In spite of this, the best objective means for dating Iron Age deposits in this region is high precision radiocarbon dating coupled with Bayesian modeling.

As seen in Table 1, there are eight radiocarbon determinations now available for the building in Area T. Of these, two come from Stratum T1b (OxA-18980, OxA-18981), one from Stratum T2a (OxA-18982), two from Stratum T2b (OxA-18983, OxA-18984), and three from the lowest exposure beneath the foundations of the building in Stratum T3 (OxA-18947, OxA-18948, OxA-18985). Similar to all the previously published dates from KEN (Levy *et al.* 2004; Levy *et al.* 2005b, 2008a), the new dates from Area T all pre-date the 8th century BCE and span the late 9th to early 12th century BCE at two standard deviations. Taken together, the entire suite of ^{14}C dates for KEN now lay to rest critiques of the radiocarbon dates which have suggested that significant metal production took place at the site in the 7th and 8th century BCE (Finkelstein 2005a; Finkelstein and Piasetzky 2008; Finkelstein and Silberman 2006; van der Steen and Bienkowski 2005a, 2006). Even more informative, when the Area T radiocarbon dates are modeled using OxCal's Bayesian analysis, some important insights are gleaned concerning the occupational history of the building and this area of KEN.

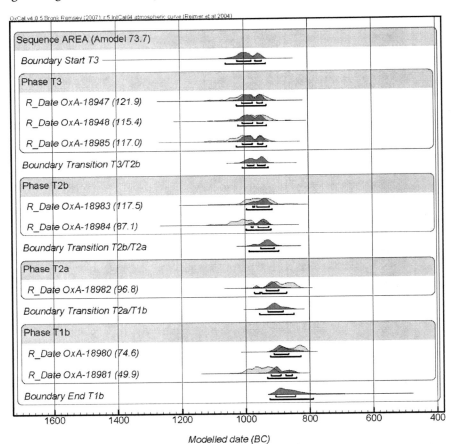

Figure 8. Model for Area T, Khirbat en-Nahas,
with original ORAU determinations from all strata.

Figure 8 shows there are no outliers, so all the radiocarbon dates can be used in the model. Keeping in mind that the Area T building was established on top of a deeply stratified industrial slag mound, and that our excavations penetrated approximately 1 meter into the slag below the building foundations, the last smelting operations to take place in Area T the end of the Stratum T3 sequence that ends 1021–944 BCE according the model. However, given the fact that this represents the top of the slag mound that pre-dates the construction of the building, this represents as near the end of the period when smelting took place in Area T as is currently possible to determine. Of great significance for the construction of the Area T building is the start of the Stratum T2b sequence which is after 1007–926 BCE. One problem with the dates from Stratum T3 is the fact that they are bimodal. However, when compared with the dates from the later strata in this area (see Fig. 8), the difference in calendrical years is minor.

When the probability distributions for the span of time in years for the three main strata are plotted (Fig. 9), it is possible to estimate the length of time over which the various layers accumulated. This means that the upper meter of industrial material in Stratum T3 accumulated over a ca. 45 year period, that the main Stratum T2b occupation lasted for ca. 40 years, that Stratum T2a was a very brief interlude lasting ca. 5 years and that Stratum T1b, representing the collapse and abandonment of the building, lasted ca. 60 years until the site was totally abandoned (Fig. 4, 9).

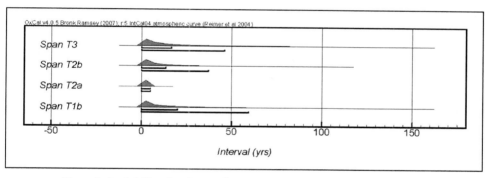

Figure 9. Probability distribution for the span of time in years in each of the four main strata in Area T, Khirbat en-Nahas, Jordon

In several recent papers, my colleagues and I suggested some of the possible confluences between the Hebrew Bible, ancient Egyptian texts and the Iron Age archaeological record at KEN intersect (Levy 2005b, 2008a, 2008b; Levy *et al.* 2005b, 2008a). In this brief discussion, it is sufficient to say that the new excavations and radiocarbon dates from Area T demonstrate major industrial scale copper production from the beginning to mid-10th century BCE. Like other areas at KEN, such as Area M (Levy *et al.* 2008a), there was a major reorganization at the site that may relate to the military campaign of the Egyptian king Shoshenq I at the end of the 10th century BCE (Finkelstein 2002; Kitchen 1992, 2003, 2004; Shortland 2005).

Conclusion

This paper has discussed a number of issues where pragmatic approaches to historical Biblical Archaeology are crucial today. Rather than being wedded to an ideology, whether it be religious, political, or academic, the on-site GIS digital archaeology methods described here coupled with the growing range of science-based approaches to archaeological materials, provide the most objective path to follow when investigating the interface between archaeology and historical biblical archaeological research.

Acknowledgments

I would like to thank Erez Ben-Yosef, Neil Smith, Adolfo Muniz, Kyle Knabb, Aren Meir, Ami Mazar, Malcolm Weiner, Mark Robinson, Aaron Gidding, and Ian Jones. A full study of the most recent ^{14}C dates from Khirbat en-Nahas is forthcoming. I am especially grateful to my friends and colleagues, Tom Higham for his help with the radiocarbon dating discussion and analyses presented here, and Mohammad Najjar for our many discussions and joint field work together in Jordan. I would also like to thank sincerely Dr. Fawwaz Al-Kharaysheh, and Dr. Ghazi Bisheh, former Director Generals of the Department of Antiquities of Jordan, for all their help and support through the years and Dr. Barbara Porter, Director, and Dr. Chris Tuttle, Associate Director, and Dr. Pierre Bikai, former Director, ACOR, Jordan for all their help and friendship. Special thanks to Erez Ben-Yosef for commenting on an earlier draft of this study, Kyle Knabb for producing the GIS map, and Cristian Horta for help with the graphics. I'm grateful to Alina Levy for input on this chapter, her love, and strong support. This chapter and edited book are dedicated with affection to Norma Kershaw.

References

Abbo, S., I. Zezak, E. Schwartz, S. Lev-Yadun, and A. Gopher (2008) Experimental Harvesting of Wild Peas in Israel: Implications for the Origins of Near East Farming. *JAS* 35: 922-29.

Aharoni, Y. (1967) *Excavations at Tel Arad: Preliminary Report on the Second Season, 1963* (Tel Aviv: University of Tel Aviv).

—(1973) *Beer-Sheba I: Excavations at Tel Beer-Sheba, 1969–1971 Seasons* (Tel-Aviv: Tel-Aviv University Institute of Archaeology).

—(1979) *The Land of the Bible: A Historical Geography* (Philadelphia: Westminster Press).

Aharoni, Y., J. Naveh, and A.F. Rainey (1981) *Arad Inscriptions: Judean Desert Studies* (Jerusalem: Israel Exploration Society).

Albert, R.M., R. Shahack-Gross, D. Cabanes, A. Gilboa, S. Lev-Yadun, M. Portillo, I. Sharon, E. Boaretto, and S. Weiner (2008) Phytolith-rich Layers from the Late Bronze and Iron Ages at Tel Dor (Israel): Mode of Formation and Archaeological Significance. *JAS* 35: 57-75.

Albright, W.F. (1926) The Excavations at Tell Beit Mirsim I. *BASOR* 23: 2-14.

—(1932a) *The Archaeology of Palestine and the Bible* (New York: Fleming H. Ravell).

—(1932b) *The Excavation of Tell Beit Mirsim*. I. *The Pottery of the First Three Campaigns* (AASOR 12; New Haven: American Schools of Oriental Research).

—(1938) *The Excavation of Tell Beit Mirsim*. II. *The Bronze Age* (AASOR 17; New Haven: American Schools of Oriental Research).

—(1943) *The Excavation of Tell Beit Mirsim*. III. *The Iron Age* (AASOR 21-22; New Haven: American Schools of Oriental Research).

—(1971) *The Archaeology of Palestine* (Glouchester, MA: Peter Smith; originally published by Penguin Books).

Amiran, R., P. Beck, and V. Zevulun (1970) *Ancient Pottery of the Holy Land* (New Jersey: Rutgers University Press).

Archer, S.N., and K.M. Bartoy (2006) *Between Dirt and discussion: Methods, Methodology, and Interpretation in Historical Archaeology. Society for Historical Archaeology Conference on Historical Underwater Archaeology* (New York: Springer).

Ascough, R.S. (2006) Cities of Paul: Images and Interpretations from the Harvard New Testament Archaeology Project—Edited by Helmut Koester. *Religious Studies Review* 32: 124-25.

Badè, W.F. (1934) *A Manual of Excavation in the Near East: Methods of Digging and Recording of the Tell en-Nasbeh Expedition in Palestine* (Berkeley: University of California Press).

Baldwin, J.D. (1986) *George Herbert Mead: A Unifying Theory for Sociology* (Masters of Social Theory 6; Newbury Park, CA: Sage Publications).

Barker, P. (1977) *Techniques of Archaeological Excavation* (New York: Universe Books).

Barros, P.L.F. d. (1982) The Effects of Variable Site Occupation Span on the Results of Frequency Seriation. *AmAnt* 47: 291-315.

Ben-Shlomo, D., A.M. Maeir, and H. Mommsen (2008) Neutron Activation and Petrographic Analysis of Selected Late Bronze and Iron Age Pottery from Tell es-Safi/Gath, Israel. *JAS* 35: 956-64.

Ben-Tor, A. (2002) Hazor—A City State between the Major Powers: A Rejoinder. *Scandinavian Journal of the Old Testament* 16: 303-8.

Ben-Yosef, E., T.L. Levy, R. Shaar, H. Ron, and M. Najjar (In prep) Archaeomagnetic Intensity Spike Recorded in High Resolution Slag Deposit from Historical Biblical Archaeology Site in Southern Jordan. In *UC San Diego ELRAP Research*, San Diego.

Ben-Yosef, E., H. Ron, L. Tauxe, A. Agnon, U. Avner, M. Najjar, T.E. Levy, and A. Genevey (2008a) Application of Copper Slag in Geomagnetic Archaeointensity Research. *Journal of Geophysical Research* 113: 1-26.

Ben-Yosef, E., L. Tauxe, H. Ron, A. Agnon, U. Avner, M. Najjar, and T.E. Levy (2008b) A New Approach for Geomagnetic Archaeointensity Research: Insights on Ancient Metallurgy in the Southern Levant. *JAS* 35: 2863-79.

Ben-Yosef, E., L. Tauxe, T.E. Levy, R. Shaar, H. Ron, and M. Najjar (2009) Archaeomagnetic Intensity Spike Recorded in High Resolution Slag Deposit from Historical Biblical Archaeology Site in Southern Jordan. *Earth and Planetary Science Letters* 287: 529-39.

Bennett, C.M. (1966) Umm el-Biyara. *Revue Biblique* 73: 400-401, pl. XXIIb.

—(1977) Excavations at Buseirah, Southern Jordan, 1974: Fourth Preliminary Report. *Levant* 9: 1-10.

—(1982) Neo-Assyrian Influence in Transjordan. *Studies in the History and Archaeology of Jordan* 1: 181-87.

Bennett, C.M., and P. Bienkowski (1995) *Excavations at Tawilan in Southern Jordan* (Oxford: The British Institute at Amman for Archaeology and History/Oxford University Press).

Berna, F., A. Behar, R. Shahack-Gross, J. Berg, E. Boaretto, A. Gilboa, I. Sharon, S. Shalev, S. Shilstein, N. Yahalom-Mack, J.R. Zorn, and S. Weiner (2007) Sediments Exposed to High Temperatures: Reconstructing Pyrotechnological Processes in Late Bronze and Iron Age Strata at Tel Dor (Israel). *JAS* 34: 358-73.

Bienkowski, P. (1992) The Date of Sedentary Occupation in Edom: Evidence from Umm el-Biyara, Tawilan and Buseirah. In Bienkowski 1992: 99-112.

—(2001a) Busayra and Judah: Stylistic Parallels in the Material Culture. In Mazar 2001a: 310-25.

—(2001b) The Iron Age and Persian Periods in Jordan. In *Studies in the History and Archaeology of Jordan VII* (Amman: Department of Antiquities): 265-74.

—(2001c) Iron Age Settlement in Edom: A Revised Framework. In *The World of the Aramaeans II: Studies in History and Archaeology in Honour o Paul-Eugen Dion*, edited by P.M.M. Daviau, J.W. Wevers, and M. Weigl (JSOTSup 325; Sheffield: Sheffield Academic Press): 257-69.

Bienkowski, P. (ed.) (1992) *Early Edom and Moab: The Beginning of the Iron Age in Southern Jordan* (Sheffield: J.R. Collis Publications).

Bienkowski, P., and C.M. Bennett (2003) *Excavations at Busayrah* (Oxford: Oxford University Press).

Bienkowski, P., and L. Sedman (2001) Busayra and Judah: Stylistic Parallels in the Material Culture. In Mazar 2001a: 310-25.

Bienkowski, P., and E. van der Steen (2001) Tribes, Trade, and Towns: A New Framework for the Late Iron Age in Southern Jordan and the Negev. *BASOR* 323: 21-47.

Bilu, Y. (2006) The Rise of a New Negev Cult Center Today: Baba Sali's Sanctuary in Netivot, Israel. In Levy 2006: 75-92.

Binford, L.R. (1962) Archaeology as Anthropology. *AmAnt* 28: 217-25.

—(2001) *Constructing Frames of Reference: An Analytical Method for Archaeological Theory Building Using Hunter–Gatherer and Environmental Data Sets* (Berkeley: University of California Press).

Binford, S.R., and L.R. Binford (eds.) (1968) *New Perspectives in Archaeology* (Chicago: Aldine Publishing).

Biran, A. (ed.) (1993) *Biblical Archaeology Today, 1990: Proceedings of the Second International Congress on Biblical Archaeology* (Jerusalem: Israel Exploration Society/The Israel Academy of Sciences and Humanities).

Brainerd, G.W. (1951) The Place of Chronological Ordering in Archaeological Analysis. *AmAnt* 16: 301-13.

Bronk Ramsey, C. (2005) Improving the Resolution of Radiocarbon Dating by Statistical Analysis. In Levy and Higham 2005: 57-64.

Brown, J.M., and L. Kutler (2005) *Nelson Glueck: Biblical Archaeologist and President of Hebrew Union College—Jewish Institute of Religion* (Cincinnati: Alumni Series of the Hebrew Union College Press).

Bruins, H.J. (2001) Near East Chronology: Towards an Integrated C-14 Time Foundation. *Radiocarbon* 43: 1147-54.

Bruins, H.J., J. van der Plicht, and A. Mazar (2003a) C-14 dates from Tel Rehov: Iron-age Chronology, Pharaohs, and Hebrew Kings. *Science* 300: 315-18.

—(2003b) Response to Comment on '14C Dates from Tel Rehov: Iron-Age Chronology, Pharaohs, and Hebrew Kings'. *Science* 302: 568c-568d.

Bunimovitz, S., and A. Faust (2001) Chronological Separation, Geographical Segregation, or Ethnic Demarcation? Ethnography and the Iron Age Low Chronology. *BASOR* 322: 1-10.

Charles, M., C. Hoppé, G. Jones, A. Bogaard, and J.G. Hodgson (2003) Using Weed Functional Attributes for the Identification of Irrigation Regimes in Jordan. *JAS* 30: 1429-41.

Clark, D.R., L.G. Herr, O. LaBianca, and R. Younker (eds.) (2010) *The Madaba Plains Project: Forty Years of Archaeological Research into Jordan's Past* (London: Equinox).

Cohen, R., and H. Bernick-Greenberg (2007) *Excavations at Kadesh Barnea (Tell el-Qudeirat) 1976–1982* (Israel Antiquities Authority Reports 34; Jerusalem: Israel Antiquities Authority).

Cohen, R., and R. Cohen-Amin (2004) *Ancient settlement of the Negev Highlands*, vol. II (Jerusalem: Israel Antiquity Authority).

Cohen, R., and Y. Yisrael (1995a) The Iron Age Fortresses at En Haseva. *Biblical Archaeologist* 58: 223-35.

—(1995b) *On the Road to Edom—Discoveries from 'En Hazeva* (Jerusalem: Israel Museum).

Coote, R.B. (1990) *Early Israel—A New Horizon* (Minneapolis: Fortress Press).

Daviau, P.M.M., and R. Chadwick (2007) Shepherds and Weavers in a 'Global Economy': Moab in Late Iron Age II—Wadi ath-Thamad Project (Khirbat al-Mudayna). In Levy *et al.*, eds., 2007: 309-14.

Daviau, P.M.M., and P.E. Dion (2002) Economy-Related Finds from Khirbat al-Mudayna (Wadi ath-Thamad, Jordan). *BASOR* 328: 31-48.

Davies, P.R. (1992) *In Search of 'Ancient Israel'* (JSOTSup 148; Sheffield: JSOT Press).

Davis, T.W. (2004) *Shifting Sands: The Rise and Fall of Biblical Archaeology* (Oxford: Oxford University Press).

Dethlefsen, E., and J. Deetz (1966) Death's Heads, Cherubs, and Willow Trees: Experimental Archaeology in Colonial Cemeteries. *AmAnt* 31: 502-10.

Dever, W.G. (1974) *Gezer II: Report of the 1967–70 Seasons in Fields I and II* (Jerusalem: Hebrew Union College).

—(1980) Archeological Method in Israel: A Continuing Revolution. *BA* 43: 41-48.

—(1981) The Impact of the 'New Archaeology' on Syro-Palestinian Archaeology. *BASOR* 242: 15-29.

—(1982) Retrospects and Prospects in Biblical and Syro-Palestinian Archeology. *BA* 45: 103-7.

—(1987) The Contribution of Archaeology to the Study of Canaanite and Early Israelite Religion. In *Ancient Israelite Religion: Essays in Honor of Frank Moore Cross*, edited by P. Miller, P. Hanson, and S. McBride (Philadelphia: Fortress Press): 209-47.

—(1992) Syro-Palestinian and Biblical Archaeology. In *The Anchor Bible Dictionary*, vol. 1, edited by D.N. Freedman (New York: Doubleday): 354-67.

—(1993a) Review: Syro-Palestinian Archaeology 'Comes of Age': The Inaugural Volume of the Hesban Series: A Review Article. *BASOR* 290-91: 127-30.

—(1993b) What Remains of the House that Albright Built? *BA* 56: 25-35.

—(2000) Nelson Glueck and the Other Half of the Holy Land. In *The Archaeology of Jordan and Beyond: Essays in Honor of James A. Sauer*, edited by L.E. Stager, J.A. Greene, and M.D. Coogan (Winona Lake, IN: Eisenbrauns): 114-21.

—(2001) *What Did the Biblical Writers Know and When Did They Know It?* (Grand Rapids: Eerdmans).

—(2003) *Who were the Israelites, and Where Did They Come From?* (Grand Rapids: Eerdmans).

—(2005) Some Methodological Reflections on Chronology and History-Writing. In Levy and Higham 2005: 413-21.

Dever, W.G., and H.D. Lance (eds.) (1978) *A Manual of Field Excavation: Handbook for Field Archaeologists* (Jerusalem: Hebrew Union College).

Dever, W.G., H.D. Lance, and G.E. Wright (1970) *Gezer I: Preliminary Report of the 1964–66 Seasons* (Jerusalem: Hebrew Union College).

Drennan, R.D. (1979) How to Succeed in Seriation without Really Trying. *AmAnt* 44: 171-72.

Eggler, J., and O. Keel (2006) *Corpus der Siegel-Amulette aus Jordanien—Vom Neolithikum bis zur Perserzeit* (Fribourg: Academic Press Fribourg).

Eliyahu-Behar, A., S. Shilstein, N. Raban-Gerstel, Y. Goren, A. Gilboa, I. Sharon, and S. Weiner (2008) An Integrated Approach to Reconstructing Primary Activities from Pit Deposits: Iron Smithing and other Activities at Tel Dor under Neo-Assyrian Domination. *JAS* 35: 2895-2908.

Faust, A. (2004) Mortuary Practices, Society and Ideology: The Lack of Iron I Burials in the Highlands in Context. *IEJ* 54: 174-90.

—(2006) *Israel's Ethnogenesis: Settlement, Interaction, Expansion and Resistance. Approaches to Anthropological Archaeology* (London: Equinox).

Finkelstein, I. (1995) *Living on the Fringe—The Archaeology and History of the Negev, Sinai and Neighbouring Regions in the Bronze and Iron Ages* (Sheffield: Sheffield Academic Press).

—(1998) The Great Transformation: The 'Conquest' of the Highlands Frontiers and the Rise of the Territorial States. In Levy 1995: 349-65.

—(1999) State Formation in Israel and Judah—A Contrast in Context, a Contrast in Trajectory (Middle-Eastern Biblical Archaeology). *Near Eastern Archaeology* 62: 35-52.

—(2002) The Campaign of Shoshenq I to Palestine—A Guide to the 10th-century-BCE Polity (Examining the Territorial-Political Systems of Iron-Age-II Canaan). *ZDPV* 118: 109-35.

—(2005a) Khirbet en-Nahas, Edom and Biblical History. *Tel Aviv* 32: 119-25.

—(2005b) A Low Chronology Update—Archaeology, History and Bible. In Levy and Higham 2005: 31-42.

Finkelstein, I., and E. Piasetzky (2003) Comment on '14C Dates from Tel Rehov: Iron Age Chronology, Pharoahs, and Hebrew Kings'. *Science* 302: 568b.

—(2008) Radiocarbon and the History of Copper Production at Khirbet en-Nahas. *Tel Aviv* 35: 82-95.

Finkelstein, I., and N.A. Silberman (2001) *The Bible Unearthed—Archaeology's New Vision of Ancient Israel and the Origin of its Sacred Texts* (New York: Free Press).

—(2006) *David and Solomon—In Search of the Bible's Sacred Kings and the Roots of Western Tradition* (New York: Free Press).

Finkelstein, I., D. Ussishkin, and B. Halpern (2006) *Megiddo IV: The 1998–2002 Seasons* (Tel Aviv: Emery and Claire Yass Publications in Archaeology).

Finkelstein, J.J. (1958) The Bible, Archaeology, and History: Have the Excavations Corroborated Scripture? *Commentary* 27: 341-49.

Fisher, N.R.E., H.v. Wees, and D.D. Boedeker (1998) *Archaic Greece: New Approaches and New Evidence* (London: Duckworth; Swansea: Classical Press of Wales; Oakville, CT: D. Brown Book Co.).

Fosburgh, B., and J.V.R. Paiva (2001) Surveying with GPS. *American Congress on Surveying and Mapping, March.*

Fox, E.L. (2001) *Sacred Geography: A Tale of Murder and Archaeology in the Holy Land* (New York: Henry Holt/Metropolitan Books).

Friðriksson, A. (1994) *Sagas and Popular Antiquarianism in Icelandic Archaeology* (Avebury: Ashgate Publishing).

Friedman, E.S., A.J. Brody, M.L. Young, J.D. Almer, C.U. Segre, and S.M. Mini (2008) Synchrotron Radiation-based X-ray Analysis of Bronze Artifacts from an Iron Age Site in the Judean Hills. *JAS* 35: 1951-60.

Fritz, V. (1996) Ergebnisse einer Sondage in Hirbet en-Nahas, Wadi el-'Araba (Jordanien). *ZDPV* 112: 1-9.

Frumkin, A., and A. Shimron (2006) Tunnel Engineering in the Iron Age: Geoarchaeology of the Siloam Tunnel, Jerusalem. *JAS* 33: 227-37.

Gallo, D., M. Ciminale, H. Becker, and N. Masini (2009) Remote Sensing Techniques for Reconstructing a vast Neolithic Settlement in Southern Italy. *JAS* 36: 43-50.

Garbini, G. (1988) *History and Ideology in Ancient Israel* (London: SCM Press).

—(2003) *Myth and History in the Bible* (Sheffield: Sheffield Academic Press).

Geraty, L.T. (2007) How Crossing Jordan made the Difference: The Case of the Madaba Plains Project, 1967–2007. In Levy *et al.*, eds., 2007: 107-10.

Gilboa, A., A. Karasik, I. Sharon, and U. Smilansky (2004) Towards Computerized Typology and Classification of Ceramics. *JAS* 31: 681-94.

Gilboa, A., and I. Sharon (2001) Early Iron Age Radiometric Dates from Tel Dor: Preliminary Implications for Phoenicia and Beyond. *Radiocarbon* 43: 1343-51.

—(2008) Between the Carmel and the Sea: Tel Dor's Iron Age Reconsidered. *Near Eastern Archaeology* 71: 146.

Gitin, S. (2005) Excavating Ekron: Major Philistine City Survived by Absorbing Other Cultures. *Biblical Archaeology Review* 31: 40-56.

Gitlin, T. (1987) *The Sixties: Years of Hope, Days of Rage* (New York: Bantam Books).

Glock, A. (1994) Archaeology as Cultural Survival: The Future of the Palestinian Past. *Journal of Palestine Studies* 23: 70-84.

Glueck, N. (1934) *Explorations in Eastern Palestine*, I (AASOR 14; New Haven: American Schools of Oriental Research).

—(1935) *Explorations in Eastern Palestine*, II (AASOR 15; New Haven: American Schools of Oriental Research).

—(1939) *Explorations in Eastern Palestine*, III (AASOR 18-19; New Haven: American Schools of Oriental Research).

—(1940) *The Other Side of the Jordan* (New Haven: American Schools of Oriental Research).

—(1944) On the Trail of King Solomon's Mines. *National Geographic* 85: 233-56.

—(1960) *Rivers in the Desert—A History of the Negev* (New York: Grove Press).

Grant, E. (1929) *Beth Shemesh (Palestine): Progress of the Haverford Archaeological Expedition* (Haverford, PA: Biblical and Kindred Studies).

Grattan, J.P., D.D. Gilbertson, and C.O. Hunt (2007) The Local and Global Dimensions of Metalliferous Pollution Derived from a Reconstruction of an Eight Thousand Year Record of Copper Smelting and Mining at a Desert-Mountain Frontier in Southern Jordan. *JAS* 34: 83-110.

Hallo, W.W., and W.G. Lambert (1998) The Context of Scripture. I. Canonical Compositions from the Biblical World. *Journal of Theological Studies* 49: 210.

Halpern, B. (1996) The Construction of the Davidic State: An Exercise in Historiography. In *The Origins of the Ancient Israelite States*, edited by V. Fritz and P.R. Davies (Sheffield: Sheffield Academic Press): 44-75.

—(1999) Power, Kingdom and State: Socio-cultural Sketches on the Origins and Development of Israelite Monarchy. *Journal of the American Oriental Society* 119: 149-51.

Hart, S. (1987) The Edom Survey Project 1984–85: The Iron Age. In *Studies in the History and Archaeology of Jordan 3*, edited by A. Hadidi (Amman: Department of Antiquities): 287-90.

—(1988) Excavations at Ghrareh, 1986: Preliminary Report. *Levant* 20: 89-99.

—(1989) The Archaeology of the Land of Edom (Ph.D. diss., Macquarie University).

Hart, S., and E.A. Knauf (1986) Wadi Feinan Iron Age Pottery. *Newsletter of the Institute of Archaeology and Anthropology, Yarmouk University* 1: 9-10.

Hauptmann, A. (2007) *The Archaeo-metallurgy of Copper—Evidence from Faynan, Jordan* (New York: Springer).

Herr, L.G. (2002) *Madaba Plains Project: The 1994 Season at Tall al-'Umayri and Subsequent Studies* (Madaba Plains Project Series 5; Berrien Springs, MI: Andrews University Press in cooperation with the Institute of Archaeology).

Herr, L.G., and D.R. Clark (2007) Tall al-'Umayri through the Ages. In Levy *et al.*, eds., 2007: 121-28.

Herr, L.G., D.R. Clark, and W.C. Trenchard (2001) Madaba Plains Project: Excavations at Tall Al-'Umayri, 2000. *Annual of the Department of Antiquities of Jordan* 45: 237-52.

Hester, T.R., H.J. Shafer, and K.L. Feder (1997) *Field Methods in Archaeology*. Mountain View, CA: Mayfield.

Hickman, L.A. (1990) *John Dewey's Pragmatic Technology* (The Indiana Series in the Philosophy of Technology; Bloomington: Indiana University Press).

Higham, T. (2009) Radiocarbon Dating: Method, Measurement, Applications, Age Calibration, and Pretreatment. *Radiocarbon Web-Info*, http://www.c14dating.com/agecalc.html.

Higham, T., J. van der Plicht, C. Bronk Ramsey, H.J. Bruins, M. Robinson, and T.E. Levy (2005) Radiocarbon Dating of the Khirbat-en Nahas Site (Jordan) and Bayesian Modeling of the Results. In Levy and Higham 2005: 164-78.

Hodder, I., ed. (2006) *Archaeological Theory Today* (Malden, MA: Polity Press).

Hoffmeier, J.K. (1996) *Israel in Egypt—The Evidence for the Authenticity of the Exodus Tradition* (New York: Oxford University Press).

Hoffmeier, J.K., A. Millard, and A.R. Millar (eds.) (2004) *The Future of Biblical Archaeology: Reassessing Methodologies and Assumptions: The Proceedings of a Symposium August 12–14, 2001 at Trinity International University* (Grand Rapids: Eerdmans).

Hole, F. (1984) Analysis of Stucture and Design in Prehistoric Ceramics. *Wolrd Archaeology* 15: 326-47.

Horton, M. (2005) Islam and Historical Archaeology. *The Journal of African History* 46: 147-48.

Hunt, C.O., D.D. Gilbertson, and H.A. El-Rishi (2007) An 8000-year History of Landscape, Climate, and Copper Exploitation in the Middle East: The Wadi Faynan and the Wadi Dana National Reserve in Southern Jordan. *JAS* 34: 1306-38.

Insoll, T. (1999) *The Archaeology of Islam* (Social Archaeology; Oxford/Malden, MA: Blackwell Publishers).

—(2001) *Archaeology and World Religion* (London/New York: Routledge).

James, W., and D. Olin (1992) *William James: Pragmatism, in Focus* (Routledge Philosophers in Focus Series; London/New York: Routledge).

Joffe, A.H. (2002) The Rise of Secondary States in the Iron Age Levant. *Journal of the Economic and Social History of the Orient* 45: 425-67.

Karasik, A. (2008) Applications of 3D Technology as a Research Tool in Archaeological Ceramic Analysis. In *Beyond Illustration: 2D and 3D Digital Technology as Tools for Discovery in Archaeology*, edited by B. Frischer and A. Dakouri-Hild (Oxford: British Archaeological Reports International Series 1805; Oxford: Archaeopress): 113-16.

Karasik, A., I. Sharon, U. Smilansky, and A. Gilboa (2004) Typology and Classification of Ceramics Based on Curvature Analysis. *Computers Applications and Quantitative Methods in Archaeology—CAA 2003*: 472-75.

Karasik, A., and U. Smilansky (2008) 3D Scanning Technology as a Standard Archaeological Tool for Pottery Analysis: Practice and Theory. *JAS* 35: 1148-68.

Kasser, R., M.W. Meyer, and G. Wurst (2006) *The Gospel of Judas: From Codex Tchacos* (Washington, DC: National Geographic).

Keel, O. (1997) *Corpus der Stempelsiegel-Amulette aus Palästina/Israel. Von den Anfängen bis zur Perserzeit. Katalog Band I: Von Tell Abu Farag bis 'Atlit. With Three Contributions by Baruch Brandl* (OBOSA 13; Freiburg: Schweiz-Göttingen).

Kenyon, K.M. (1961) *Beginning in Archaeology* (New York: Praeger).

—(1979) *Archaeology in the Holy Land* (4th edn; London: Benn).

Kenyon, K.M., and P.R.S. Moorey (1987) *The Bible and Recent Archaeology* (rev. edn; London: British Museum Publications).

Killebrew, A.E. (2005) *Biblical Peoples and Ethnicity—An Archaeological Study of Egyptians, Canaanites, Philistines, and Early Israel, 1300–1100 B.C.E.* (Atlanta: Society of Biblical Literature).

King, P.J. (1983) *American Archaeology in the Middle East* (Philadelphia: The American Schools of Oriental Research).

Kitchen, K.A. (1992) The Egyptian Evidence on Ancient Jordan. In Bienkowski 1991: 21-34.

—(2003) *On the Reliability of the Old Testament* (Grand Rapids: Eerdmans).

—(2004) *The Third Intermediate Period in Egypt (1100–650 BC)* (Oxford: Oxbow Books).

Klein, S., and A. Hauptmann (1999) Iron Age Leaded Tin Bronzes from Khirbet Edh-Dharih, Jordan. *JAS* 26: 1075-82.

Knauf, E.A. (1992) The Cultural Impact of Secondary State Formation: The Cases of the Edomites and the Moabites. In Bienkowski 1992: 47-54.

Kuhn, T.S. (1962) *The Structure of Scientific Revolutions* (Chicago: University of Chicago Press).

LaBianca, O.S. (1999) Salient Features of Iron Age Tribal Kingdoms. In *Ancient Ammon*, edited by B. MacDonald and R.W. Younker (Studies in the History and Culture of the Ancient Near East 17; Boston: Brill): 19-23.

LaBianca, O.S., L.A. Haynes, L.E. Hubbard, and L.G. Running (1990) *Sedentarization and Nomadization: Food System Cycles at Hesban and Vicinity in Transjordan. Hesban, 1* (Berrien Springs, MI: Institute of Archaeology: Andrews University Press).

LaBianca, O., and B. Walker (2007) Tall Hisban: Palimpsest of Great and Little Traditons of Transjordan and the Ancient Near East. In Levy *et al.*, eds., 2007: 111-20.

LaBianca, O.S., and R.W. Younker. (1995) The Kingdoms of Ammon, Moab and Edom: The Archaeology of Society in Late Bronze/Iron Age Transjordan (ca. 1400–500 BCE). In Levy 1995: 399-415.

Levy, T.E. (2000) The Mythic Past Biblical Archaeology and the Myth of Israel. *Science* 289: 1145.

— (2007) *Journey to the Copper Age—Archaeology in the Holy Land* (San Diego: San Diego Museum of Man).

—(2008a) Ethnic Identity in Biblical Edom, Israel and Midian: Some Insights from Mortuary Contexts in the Lowlands of Edom. In *Exploring the Longue Durée: Essays in Honor of Lawrence E. Stager*, edited by D. Schloen (Winona Lake, IN: Eisenbrauns): 251-61.

—(2008b) 'You shall make for yourself no molten gods'—Some Thoughts on Archaeology and Edomite Ethnic Identity. In *Sacred History, Sacred Literature: Essays on Ancient Israel, the Bible, and Religion in Honor of R.E. Friedman on His 60th Birthday*, edited by S. Dolansky (Winona Lake, IN: Eisenbrauns): 239-55.

Levy, T.E., R.B. Adams, J.D. Anderson, N. Najjar, N. Smith, Y. Arbel, L. Soderbaum, and M. Muniz (2003) An Iron Age Landscape in the Edomite Lowlands: Archaeological Surveys along the Wadi al-Guwayb and Wadi al-Jariyeh, Jabal Hamrat Fidan, Jordan, 2002. *Annual of the Department of Antiquities Jordan* 47: 247-77.

Levy, T.E., R.B. Adams, A. Hauptmann, M. Prange, S. Schmitt-Strecker, and M. Najjar (2002) Early Bronze Age Metallurgy: A Newly Discovered Copper Manufactory in Southern Jordan. *Antiquity* 76: 425-37.

Levy, T.E., R.B. Adams, and A. Muniz (2004) Archaeology and the Shasu Nomads-Recent Excavations in the Jabal Hamrat Fidan, Jordan. In *Le-David Maskil: A Birthday Tribute for David Noel Freedman*, edited by W.H.C. Propp and R.E. Friedman (Winona Lake, IN: Eisenbrauns): 63-89.

Levy, T.E., R.B. Adams, M. Najjar, A. Hauptmann, J.A. Anderson, B. Brandl, M. Robinson, and T. Higham (2004) Reassessing the Chronology of Biblical Edom: New Excavations and 14C Dates from Khirbat en-Nahas (Jordan). *Antiquity* 78: 863-76.

Levy, T.E., R.B. Adams, and R. Shafiq (1999) The Jabal Hamrat Fidan Project: Excavations at the Wadi Fidan 40 Cemetery, Jordan (1997). *Levant* 31: 293-308.

Levy, T.E., R.B. Adams, A.J. Witten, J. Anderson, Y. Arbel, S. Kuah, J. Moreno, A. Lo, and M. Waggoner (2001a) Early Metallurgy, Interaction, and Social Change: The Jabal Hamrat Fidan (Jordan) Research Design and 1998 Archaeological Survey: Preliminary Report. *Annual of the Department of Antiquities of Jordan* 45: 159-87.

Levy, T.E., D. Alon, E.C.M. Van Den Brink, E. Kansa, and Y. Yekutieli (2001b) The Protodynastic/Dynasty 1 Egyptian Presence in Southern Canaan: A Preliminary Report on the 1994 Excavations at Nahal Tillah, Israel. In *Studies in the Archaeology of Israel and Neighboring Lands in Memory of Douglas L. Esse*, edited by S.R. Wolff (Chicago: The Oriental Instiute of the University of Chicago): 407-38.

Levy, T.E., J.D. Anderson, M. Waggoner, N. Smith, A. Muniz, and R.B. Adams (2001c) Interface: Archaeology and Technology—Digital Archaeology 2001: GIS-Based Excavation Recording in Jordan. *The SAA Archaeological Record* 1: 23-29.

Levy, T.E., and D.N. Freedman (2008) William Foxwell Albright: A Biographical Essay. *Proceedings of the National Academy of Science*: 1-29.

Levy, T.E., T. Higham, C. Bronk Ramsey, N.G. Smith, E. Ben-Yosef, M. Robinson, S. Munnger, K. Knabb, J. Schulze, P., M. Najjar, and L. Tauxe (2008a) High-precision Radiocarbon Dating and Historical Biblical Archaeology in Southern Jordan. *Proceedings of the National Academy of Sciences* 105: 16460-465.

Levy, T.E., T. Higham, and M. Najjar (2006) Response to van der Steen & Bienkowski. *Antiquity* 80: 3-5.

Levy, T.E., and A.F.C. Holl (2002) Migrations, Ethnogenesis, and Settlement Dynamics: Israelites in Iron Age Canaan and Shuwa-Arabs in the Chad Basin. *JAA* V21: 83-118.

Levy, T.E., A. Levy, R. Sthapathy, S. Sthapathy, and S. Sthapathy (2008b) *Masters of Fire—Hereditary Bronze Casters of South India* (Bochum: German Mining Museum).

Levy, T.E., and M. Najjar (2007) Ancient Metal Production and Social Change in Southern Jordan: The Edom Lowlands Regional Archaeology Project and Hope for a UNESCO World Heritage Site in Faynan. In Levy *et al.*, eds., 2007: 97-105.

Levy, T.E., M. Najjar, and T. Higham (2007) Iron Age Complex Societies, Radiocarbon Dates and Edom: Working with the Data and Debates. *Antiguo Oriente 5*: 13-34.

Levy, T.E., M. Najjar, A. Muniz, S. Malena, E. Monroe, M. Beherec, N.G. Smith, T. Higham, S. Munger, and K. Maes (2005a) Iron Age Burial in the Lowlands of Edom: The 2004 Excavations at Wadi Fidan 40, Jordan. *Annual of the Department of Antiquities Jordan* 49: 443-87.

Levy, T.E., M. Najjar, J. van der Plicht, N.G. Smith, H.J. Bruins, and T. Higham (2005b) Lowland Edom and the High and Low Chronologies: Edomite State Formation, the Bible and Recent Archaeological Research in Southern Jordan. In Levy and Higham 2005: 129-63.

Levy, T.E., and N.G. Smith (2007) On-Site Digital Archaeology: GIS-Based Excavation Recording in Southern Jordan. In Levy *et al.*, eds., 2007: 47-58.

Levy, T.E., and E.C.M. van den Brink (2002) Interaction Models, Egypt and the Levantine Periphery. In *Egypt and the Levant—Interrelations from the 4th Through the Early 3rd Millennium BCE, New Approaches to Anthropological Archaeology*, edited by E.C.M. van den Brink and T.E. Levy (London and New York: Continuum): 3-38.

Levy, T.E. (ed.) (1995) *The Archaeology of Society in the Holy Land* (London: Leicester University Press).

—(2003) *The Archaeology of Society in the Holy Land* (3rd edn; New Approaches to Anthropological Archaeology; London: Leicester University Press/Continuum).

—(2006) *Archaeology, Anthropology and Cult* (London: Equinox).

Levy, T.E., P.M.M. Daviau, R. Younker, and M. Shaer (eds.) (2007) *Crossing Jordan: North American Contributions to the Archaeology of Jordan* (London: Equinox).

Levy, T.E., and T. Higham (eds.) (2005) *The Bible and Radiocarbon Dating: Archaeology, Text and Science* (London: Equinox).

Libby, W.F. (1955) *Radiocarbon Dating* (Chicago: University of Chicago Press).

Maeir, A.M. (2008) Zafit, Tel. In *The New Encyclopedia of Archaeological Excavations in the Holy Land 5: Supplementary volume*, edited by E. Stern (Jerusalem: Israel Exploration Society): 2079-81.

Maeir, A.M., A. Zukerman, S.J. Wimmer, and A. Demsky (2008) A Late Iron Age I/Early Iron Age II Old Canaanite Inscription from Tell es=Safi /Gath, Israel: Palaeography, Dating, and Historical-Cultural Significance. *BASOR*: 39-71.

Manning, S.W., and M.J. Bruce (eds.) (2009) *Tree-Rings, Kings, and Old World Archaeology and Environment: Cornell Dendrochronology-Archaeology Conference in Honor of Peter Ian Kuniholm* (Oxford: Oxbow Books).

Marquardt, W.H. (1978) Advances in Archaeological Seriation. In *Advances in Archaeological Method and Theory*, edited by M.B. Sciffer (New York/San Francisco/London: Academic Press): 257-314.

Marquet-Krause, J. (1949) *Les Fouilles de 'Ay (et-Tell) 1933–1935* (Paris: P. Guethner).

Marriner, N., C. Morhange, and C. Doumet-Serhal (2006) Geoarchaeology of Sidon's Ancient Harbours, Phoenicia. *JAS* 33: 1514-35.

Marriner, N., C. Morhange, and M. Saghieh-Beydoun (2008) Geoarchaeology of Beirut's Ancient Harbour, Phoenicia. *JAS* 35: 2495-2516.

Marx, E. (2006) Tribal Pilgrimages to Saints' Tombs in South Sinai. In Levy 2006: 54-74.

Masalha, N. (2006) *The Bible and Zionism: Invented Traditions, Archaeology and Post-colonialism in Palestine-Israel* (New York: Zed Books).

Maschner, H.D.G., and C. Chippindale (2005) *Handbook of Archaeological Methods* (Lanham, MD: AltaMira Press).

Masters, D. (2001) State Formation Theory and the Kingdom of Ancient Israel. *JNES* 60: 117-31.

Mazar, A. (2001) Radiocarbon Dates from Iron Age Strata at Tel Beth Shean and Tel Rehov. *Radiocarbon* 43: 1333-42.

—(2005) The Debate over the Chronology of the Iron Age in the Southern Levant: Its History, the Current Situation, and a Suggested Resolution. In Levy and Higham 2005: 15-30.

—(2006) *Excavations at Tel Beth-Shean, 1989–1996* (Jerusalem: Israel Exploration Society: Institute of Archaeology, the Hebrew University of Jerusalem).

Mazar, A. (ed.) (2001a) *Studies in the Archaeology of the Iron Age in Israel and Jordan* (Sheffield: Sheffield Academic Press).

Mazar, A., H.J. Bruins, N. Panitz-Cohen, and J. van der Plicht (2005) Ladder of Time at Tel Rehov—Stratigraphy, Archaeological Context, Pottery and Radiocarbon Dates. In Levy and Higham 2005: 193-255.

Mazar, A., and I. Carmi (2001) Radiocarbon Dates from Iron Age Strata at Tel Beth Shean and Tel Rehov. *Radiocarbon* 43: 1333-42.

Mazar, A., D. Namdar, N. Panitz-Cohen, R. Neumann, and S. Weiner (2008) Iron Age Beehives at Tel Rehov in the Jordan Valley. *Antiquity* 82: 629-39.

McCown, C.C., J. Wampler, and W.F. Badè (1947) *Tell en-Nasbeh Excavated under the Direction of the Late William Frederic Badè* (Berkeley, CA: Palestine Institute of Pacific School of Religion and the American Schools of Oriental Research).

Meighan, C.W. (1977) Recognition of Short Time Periods through Seriation. *AmAnt* 42: 628-29.

Moore, E.C., and S.P.S.I.C. Charles (1993) *Charles S. Peirce and the Philosophy of Science: Papers from the Harvard Sesquicentennial Congress* (Tuscaloosa: University of Alabama Press).

Moorey, P.R.S. (1991) *A Century of Biblical Archaeology* (Louisville, KY: Westminster/John Knox Press).

Munger, S. (2003) Egyptian Stamp-Seal Amulets and their Implications for the Chronology of the Early Iron Age. *Tel Aviv* 30: 66-82.

—(2005) Stamp-seal Amulets and Early Iron Age Chronology—An Update. In Levy and Higham 2005: 381-404.

Nashef, K., G. Friend, F.S. Frick, W.E. Rast, a.-F. Ma'had al-Athar (1998) *Tell Taannek, 1963–1968* (Publications of the Palestinian Institute of Archaeology; Birzeit: Palestinian Institute of Archaeology, Birzeit University).

Oakshott, M.F. (1978) A Study of the Iron Age II Pottery of East Jordan with Special Reference to Unpublished Material from Edom (Ph.D. diss., University of London).

—(1983) The Edomite Pottery. In *Midian, Moab and Edom: The History and Archaeology of Late Bronze and Iron Age Jordan and North-West Arabia*, edited by J.F.A. Sawyer and D.J.A. Clines (Sheffield: JSOT Press): 53-63.

Petrie, W.M.F. (1972) *Methods & Aims in Archaeology* (New York: B. Blom; originally published 1904).

Piasetzky, E., and I. Finkelstein (2005) 14C Results from Megiddo, Tel Dor, Tel Rehov and Tel Hadar: Where Do They Lead Us?. In Levy and Higham 2005: 294-301.

Porter, B.W. (2004) Authority, Polity, and Tenuous Elites in Iron Age Edom (Jordan). *Oxford Journal of Archaeology* 23: 373-95.

Porter, B., B. Routledge, D. Steen, and F. al-Kawamlha (2007) The Power of Place: The Dhiban Community through the Ages. In Levy *et al.*, eds., 2007: 315-22.

Pratico, G.D. (1985) Nelson Glueck's 1938–1940 Excavations at Tell el-Kheleifeh: A Reappraisal. *BASOR* 259: 1-32.

—(1993) *Nelson Glueck's 1938–1940 Excavations at Tell el-Kheleifeh—A Reappraisal* (AASOR 3; Atlanta: Scholars Press).

Rathje, W.L. (1971) The Origin and Development of Lowland Classic Maya Civilization. *AmAnt* 36: 275-85.

—(2001) *Rubbish! The Archaeology of Garbage* (Tucson: University of Arizona Press).

Reimer, P.J., M.G.L. Baillie, E. Bard, A. Bayliss, J.W. Beck, C.J.H. Bertrand, P.G. Blackwell, C.E. Buck, G. Burr, K.B. Cutler, P.E. Damon, R.L. Edwards, R.G. Fairbanks, M. Friedrich, T.P. Guilderson, A.G. Hogg, K.A. Hughen, B. Kromer, F.G. McCormac, S. Manning, C. Bronk Ramsey, R.W. Reimer, S. Remmele, J.R. Southon, M. Stuiver, S. Talamo, F.W. Taylor, J. van der Plicht, and C.E. Weyhenmeyer (2004) INTCAL04 Terrestrial Radiocarbon Age Calibration, 0–26 kyr BP. *Radiocarbon* 46/3: 46: 1029-58.

Renfrew, C., and P. Bahn (2008) *Archaeology—Theories, Methods, and Practice* (5th edn; New York: Thames & Hudson).

Robinson, W.S. (1951) A Method for Chronologically Ordering Archaeological Deposits. *AmAnt* 16: 293-301.

Roskams, S. (2001) *Excavation* (Cambridge Manuals in Archaeology; Cambridge/New York: Cambridge University Press).

Routledge, B. (2000a) The Politics of Mesha: Segmented Identities and State Formation in Iron Age Moab. *Journal of the Economic and Social History of the Orient* 43: 221-56.

—(2000b) Seeing through Walls: Interpreting Iron Age I Architecture at Khirbat al-Mudayna al-'Aliya. *BASOR*: 37.

—(2004) *Moab in the Iron Age: Hegemony, Polity, Archaeology* (Philadelphia: University of Pennsylvania Press).

Routledge, B., and B. Porter (2007) A Place in-between: Khirbat al-Mudayna al-'Aliya in the Early Iron Age. In Levy *et al.*, eds., 2007: 323-29.

Rowe, A. (1936) *A Catalogue of Egyptian Scrabs, Scaraboids and Amulets in the Palestine Archaeology Museum* (Cairo: Imprimerie de Institut Francais).

Rowe, A., and G.M. FitzGerald (1930) *The Four Canaanite Temples of Beth-shan* (Philadelphia: published for the University Museum by the University of Pennsylvania Press).

Rua, H. (2009) Geographic Information Systems in Archaeological Analysis: A Predictive Model in the Detection of Rural Roman Villae. *JAS* 36: 224-35.

Saga, S. (1970) *The Saga of the Icelanders*, translated by J. McGrew (New York: Twayne Publishers).

Saldarini, A.J., A.J. Avery-Peck, D.J. Harrington, and J. Neusner (2004) *When Judaism and Christianity Began: Essays in Memory of Anthony J. Saldarini* (Supplements to the Journal for the Study of Judaism 85; Leiden/Boston: Brill).

Schiffer, M.B. (1975) Behavioral Chain Analysis: Activities, Organization, and the Use of Space. *Fieldiana: Anthropology* 65: 103-19.

—(1976) *Behavioral Archeology* (New York: Academic Press).

—(1983) Toward the Identification of Formation Processes. *AmAnt* 48: 675-706.

—(2000) *Social Theory in Archaeology: Foundations of Archaeological Inquiry* (Salt Lake City: University of Utah Press).

Schloen, D. (2001) *The House of the Father as Fact and Symbol: Patrimonialism in Ugarit and the Ancient Near East* (Winona Lake, IN: Eisenbrauns).

Schniedewind, W.M. (2005) Problems in the Paleographic Dating of Inscriptions. In Levy and Higham 2005: 405-12.

Shahack-Gross, R., R.-M. Albert, A. Gilboa, O. Nagar-Hilman, I. Sharon, and S. Weiner (2005) Geoarchaeology in an Urban Context: The Uses of Space in a Phoenician Monumental Building at Tel Dor (Israel). *JAS* 32: 1417-31.

Shahack-Gross, R., and I. Finkelstein (2008) Subsistence Practices in an Arid Environment: A Geoarchaeological Investigation in an Iron Age Site, the Negev Highlands, Israel. *JAS* 35: 965-82.

Sharon, I., A. Gilboa, E. Boaretto, and A.J.T. Jull (2005) The Early Iron Age Dating Project—Introduction, Methodology, Progress Report and an Update on the Tel Dor Radiometric Dates. In Levy and Higham 2005: 65-92.

Shortland, A.J. (2005) Shishak, King of Egypt: The Challenges of Egyptian Calendrical Chronology. In Levy and Higham 2005: 43-54.

Siart, C., B. Eitel, and D. Panagiotopoulos (2008) Investigation of Past Archaeological Landscapes using Remote Sensing and GIS: A Multi-method Case Study from Mount Ida, Crete. *JAS* 35: 2918-26.

Smith, N.G., and T.E. Levy (2008) The Iron Age Pottery from Khirbat en-Nahas, Jordan: A Preliminary Study. *BASOR* 352: 1-51.

Stern, E.N. (1980) *Dreamer in the Desert—A Profile of Nelson Glueck* (New York: KTAV).

Stuiver, M., P.J. Reimer, E. Bard, J.W. Beck, G.S. Burr, K.A. Hughen, B. Kromer, G. McCormac, J. van der Plicht, and M. Spurk (1998) INTCAL98 Radiocarbon Age Calibration, 24,000-0 cal BP. *Radiocarbon* 40: 1041-83.

Thompson, T.L. (1999) *The Mythic Past: Biblical Archaeology and the Myth of Israel* (New York: Basic Books).

Torczyner, H., *et al.* (1938) *Lachish 1 (Tell ed Duweir). I. The Lachish Letters* (Wellcome Archaeological Research Expedition to the Near East publications 1; London: published for the trustees of the late Sir Henry Wellcome by the Oxford University Press).

Tufnell, O., C.H. Inge, and G.L. Harding (1940) *Lachish II (Tell ed Duweir) the Fosse Temple*. London/New York/Toronto: Oxford University Press).

Tuzin, D. (2006) Cults, Shrines, and the Emergence of Regional Ritual Centers: The View from New Guinea. In Levy 2006: 34-53.

Twiss, K.C. (2007) The Zooarchaeology of Tel Tif'dan (Wadi Fidan 001), Southern Jordan. *Paleoorient* 33: 127-45.

Van der Plicht, J., and H.J. Bruins (2005) Quality Control of Groningen 14C Results from Tel Rehov—Repeatability and Intercomparison of Proportional Gas Counting and AMS. In Levy and Higham 2005: 256-70.

van der Steen, E., and P. Bienkowski (2005a) 'Our Response to: How many fortresses do you need to write a preliminary report?. Wadi Arabah Web Site: http://www.wadiarabahproject.man.ac.uk/opening.

—(2005b) 'Review of Levy *et al.* 2004 Antiquity Article. Wadi Araba Project Web Site—www.wadiarabahproject.man.ac.uk.

—(2006) Radiocarbon Dates from Khirbat en-Nahas: A Methodological Critique. *Antiquity* 80: 1-3.

Vaux, R. de (1971) Palestine in the Early Bronze Age. In *The Cambridge Ancient History*, vol. 1, Part 2 (Cambridge: Cambridge University Press): 208-37.

Veer, P. van der (2001) *Imperial Encounters: Religion and Modernity in India and Britain* (Princeton, NJ: Princeton University Press).

Walsh, R. (2006) The Gospel According to Judas: Myth and Parable. *Biblical Interpretation: A Journal of Contemporary Approaches* 14: 37-53.

Watson, P.J., S.A. LeBlanc, and C.L. Redman (1971) *Explanation in Archeology—An Explicitly Scientific Approach* (New York: Columbia).

Weinberger, R., A. Sneh, and E. Shalev (2008) Hydrogeological Insights in Antiquity as Indicated by Canaanite and Israelite Water Systems. *JAS* 35: 3035-42.

Wells, T. (1994) *The War Within: America's Battle Over Vietnam* (Berkeley: University of California Press).

Westcott, K.L., and R.J. Brandon (eds.) (2000) *Practical Applications of GIS for Archaeologists* (London/Philadelphia: Taylor & Francis).

Wheatley, D., and M. Gillings (2002) *Spatial Technology and Archaeology—The Archaeological Applications of GIS* (London/New York: Taylor & Francis).

Whitelam, K.W. (1996) *The Invention of Ancient Israel: The Silencing of Palestinian History* (New York: Routledge).

Wiener, M. (2009a) Cold Fusion: The Uneasy Alliance of History and Science. In Manning 2009: 277-92.

—(2009b) Reply to the papers by Manning *et al.* and Friedrich *et al.* In Manning and Bruce 2009: 317-32.

Wiseman, J., and F. El-Baz (2007) *Remote Sensing in Archaeology* (Interdisciplinary Contributions to Archaeology; New York: Springer).

Witten, A. (2006) *Handbook of Geophysics and Archaeology* (London: Equinox).

Witten, A.J., T.E. Levy, R.B. Adams, and I.J. Won (2000) Geophysical Surveys in the Jebel Hamrat Fidan, Jordan. *Geoarchaeology* 15: 135-50.

Wright, G.E. (1959) Is Glueck's Aim to Prove That the Bible is True? *The BA* 22: 101-8.

Yahya, A.H. (2005) Archaeology and Nationalism in the Holy Land. In *Archaeologies of the Middle East—Critical Perspectives*, edited by S. Pollock and R. Bernbeck (Malden, MA: Blackwell Publishing): 66-77.

Yamauchi, E. (2004) Homer and Archaeology: Minimalists and Maximalists. In *The Future of Biblical Archaeology—Reassessing Methodologies and Assumptions*, edited by J.K. Hoffmeier and A. Millard (Grand Rapids: Eerdmans): 69-90.

Yankelovich, D. (2008) The New Pragmatism—Coping with America's Overwhelming Problems. In *Viewpoint Learning Inc.* (La Jolla: Viewpoint Learning): 32.

Yoffee, N., and G.L. Cowgill (eds.) (1988) *The Collapse of Ancient States and Civilizations* (Tucson: The University of Arizona Press).

Younker, R. (2007) Highlights from the Heights of Jalul. In Levy *et al.*, eds., 2007: 129-36.

Zimmerman, L.J., W. Green, S.L. Black, K. Jolly, J.M. Collins, B. Molyneaux, D.L. Carmichael, R.H. Laffery, C.R. Ewen, K.D. Sobolik, L.P. Sullivan, and S.T. Childs (2002) *Archaeologist's Toolkit* (Walnut Creek, CA: Altamira Press).

2 Re-Constructing Biblical Archaeology

Toward an Integration of Archaeology

and the Bible

Shlomo Bunimovitz and Avraham Faust

Abstract

For over a century, the archaeology of the Land of Israel went hand in hand with the Bible. Biblical Archaeology, the outcome of this interaction, has been normally conceived as the handmaiden of the biblical texts, authenticating and illustrating them. Whether motivated by theological or secular agenda, the main tenet of Biblical Archaeology was political history. In spite of recent claims for the emancipation of archaeology from the tyranny of the biblical texts, the archaeological agenda is still biblical, pursuing questions related to biblical historiography. Paradoxically, however, due to its problematic nature, the use of the Bible in archaeological discourse is considered today almost illegitimate.

We envision a different integration between archaeology and the Bible. On the one hand, an archaeological agenda, independent of the biblical text, will open a much wider range of social and cultural questions. On the other, using the Bible as a cultural document to answer these questions will restore its central place in the archaeological discourse of the biblical period. Conceiving of both biblical texts and ancient material artifacts as cultural documents, we believe that their inspection will be fruitful and enlightening. Words and artifacts can give us access to the mindset of the people of the biblical period. Encapsulated in both are the worldviews, cosmology, perceptions of landscape, ideology, symbolism, etc. of the people who produced them. The insights gained by this approach will eventually result in a better understanding of biblical political history.

Introduction

Biblical Archaeology is currently under crisis. On the one hand, some of its practitioners are seeking to emancipate the archaeology of the Land of Israel from the tyranny of the biblical text that has dictated the discipline's agenda for many years. In their opinion, archaeology must take the leading role in the historical and historiographical study of the biblical period (especially Finkelstein 1996a, 1998; Finkelstein and Silberman 2001, 2006; Herzog 1999, 2001; see also Ussishkin 2003). On the other hand, in spite of the new vistas of research opened to archaeology by its great theoretical progress, the issues considered worth pursuing by these scholars are hardly different from those that interested Biblical Archaeology since its early days, namely, the deeds of kings, military campaigns, major destructions, etc. Furthermore, though the Bible is all but eliminated from most of the current archaeological discourse due to the dark shadow cast over its historicity (below), the agenda of current Biblical Archaeology is paradoxically still driven by biblical historiography (cf. Finkelstein and Silberman 2001, 2006).

In this essay, we suggest to renew the dialogue between archaeology and the Bible but in a completely different manner. First and foremost, we argue for a new archaeological agenda not dictated by the biblical texts—an agenda that will focus on the wide array of social and cultural questions stemming from the plethora of material finds of the biblical period (mainly from the Iron Age, 12th–6th centuries BCE). Yet, the agenda must integrate the Bible in addressing these questions, since it is a cultural document encapsulating invaluable information about the social and ideological world of the society that has produced this material culture. The new integration will infuse fresh air into Biblical Archaeology's sails, and will restore the Bible to its central position in the archaeological discourse of the biblical period.

Archaeology and Bible: Ambivalent Relations

Since its inception in the 19th century, the archaeology of the Land of Israel has gone hand in hand with the Bible (for comprehensive summaries, see, e.g., Moorey 1991; Bunimovitz 1995, 2000; Silberman 1982, 1995; Davis 2004; see also Levy, this volume). 'Biblical Archaeology'—the fruit of this unique combination—was initially conceived as the handmaiden of biblical studies whose task was to illustrate the biblical world and shed light on its historical and cultural background (e.g. Davis 2004: 3-20). Later, it was used to prove the authenticity of the biblical text. The curriculum of Biblical Archaeology and its attitude to the Bible were shaped especially during its 'Golden Age' between the two world wars, and reflected the intellectual and ideological background of the 'Founding Fathers' of the discipline (Dever 1985; Moorey 1991: 25-78). The spiritual world of William F. Albright and his students, most notably G. Ernest Wright, was anchored in the religious life of the United States in the late 19th and early 20th century (For Albright see: Running and Freedman 1975; Van Beek 1989; Long 1997; Levy and Freedman 2008; and the critical articles by Jack M. Sasson, Neil A. Silberman, William G. Dever and Burke O. Long in *Biblical Archaeologist* 56 [1993]; also *NEA* 65 [2002]. For Wright see: Dever 1980; King 1987; and the articles in *Biblical Archaeologist* 50 [1987]: 5-21.) They attempted to establish the historicity of the biblical narratives in face of the 'threat' posed by German biblical criticism. Biblical Archaeology developed, therefore, as a sub-discipline of biblical studies, a vehicle for supplying external and objective evidence that would refute the theoretical assumptions of 'high criticism'. Its goals were to identify the 'period of the Patriarchs', to prove the historicity of the Israelite conquest of Canaan, and to place Israelite monotheism in its appropriate position within the ideological history of the ancient Near East. Improvements in archaeological methodology, the establishment of ancient Near Eastern chronology and construction of the region's cultural history—all important achievements of Albright school—were not intentional goals of themselves. Apparently they were but tools helping to create an historical interpretative framework through integration of archaeological finds, biblical text, and external textual sources (see, e.g., Dessel 2002).

Paradoxically, though the 'Israeli school' of Biblical Archaeology that developed mainly after the establishment of the State of Israel in 1948 was secular, its scope and interest paralleled those of the Albright school. For the first generation of Israeli archaeologists, the Bible served as a founding document of the nation's history. Archaeology played an important role in affirming the links of the newly founded state with its ancient past and its ancestral land (Bar-Yosef and Mazar 1982; Yadin 1985; Stern 1987; Dever 1989a; Silberman 1989; Geva 1992). No wonder, then, that the lion's share of the archaeological enterprise was related to the Bible—a tendency dubbed by W.G. Dever (1989b: 49*; 1993: 710) 'secular fundamentalism'. Although the interpretative framework of the

Israeli school reflected ethnic and national sentiments more than religious interests, it focused on the same historical aspects that were at the core of the Albright school, namely the Israelite conquest of Canaan, the monumental building activities of the kings of Israel and Judah, military campaigns, mass destructions, etc. The two branches of Biblical Archaeology—the American and the Israeli—were busy, therefore, in a search for evidence for 'big' historical and political events and for royal enterprises, thus viewing the Bible as a primary historical source, both relying on it and affirming it. In this 'monumental' archaeology, no place was found for the study of social and cultural process, nor for close acquaintance with the daily life of the 'silent majority'.

Several important developments, however, shook Biblical Archaeology during the 1970s and 1980s. On the American side, the influence of the 'new archaeology', although not always direct and explicit, was felt (Dever 1981, 1992; see also Levy, this volume). New archaeology's a-historical, and even anti-historical attitude was probably partially responsible for the growing will to sever the connection between archaeology and the Bible and to 'liberate' the former from the 'yoke' of the latter. Dever (1985) even called for secularization of the discipline, under the banner of 'Syro-Palestinian Archaeology' (replacing now the old fashioned 'Biblical Archaeology'). This movement was accompanied by the adoption of scientific and technological advances and their incorporation in archaeological excavations—also resulting from the influence of the 'new archaeology' of the time (Dever 1981; see, however, Dever 1993: 707). In the Israeli side, too, major shifts took place as a consequence of the large archaeological surveys in the highlands following the Six-Day War of June 1967 (see mainly: Kochavi 1972; Zertal 1992–2005; Finkelstein, Lederman and Bunimovitz 1997; Finkelstein and Magen 1993; Ofer 1994, 1998; see also Frankel *et al.* 2001; Gal 1992). These surveys brought with them fresh conceptual innovations to Biblical Archaeology, but at the same time, ironically, eroded its connection with the Bible.

First and foremost, the surveys brought into the forefront the 'people without history'—the rural population that was the backbone of past societies but had been ignored by both ancient elite's historical writing and by the modern 'urban biased' and 'tell minded' archaeologists (Ahlström 1982: 25; London 1989; a conspicuous outcome of this change, along with the indirect influence of the 'new archaeology', is the plethora of settlement patterns and demographic studies that followed the surveys, e.g. Broshi and Gophna 1984, 1986; Finkelstein 1988: 324-35; Broshi and Finkelstein 1992; Finkelstein and Gophna 1993, and many others).

Second, the reconstruction of settlement and demographic history of the Land of Israel introduced a long-term perspective (*longue durée*) in which ancient Israel was brought into normal, 'secular' cultural evolution, in contrast to its unique, almost 'super-historical' position in the eyes of some biblical archaeologists of previous generations (Finkelstein 1988, 1994, 1995, 1996b; Bunimovitz 1994). Third, environmental and ecological factors, previously ignored, became the basis for explaining not only the structure of daily life and sociopolitical organization in ancient Canaan and Israel, but also culture change (Finkelstein 1989, 1993; Stager 1985, 1988). As an outcome of the above new directions, short episodic historical events lost their popularity as adequate explanation for culture change and were substituted by slow, long-term changes that are deep-structured within the geographical-ecological setting of the historical scene.

The distancing of settlement archaeology from the history of 'events' signaled the growing chasm between cultural interpretation of the archaeological record and the biblical text. If the Israelite settlement in Canaan can be explained by ethnographic analogies for the settling of pastoral nomads groups, the ecology of the highlands, and long-term cyclical settlement processes (Finkelstein 1988, 1992, 1994), then the biblical text becomes redundant.[1]

---

1.   In perspective, the broadening of the research program in the archaeology of the Land of Israel, which took place in the 1980s and early 1990s (see its culmination in Levy 1995), reflected a break with the biblical agenda, though not necessarily with the Bible. However, as we shall see below, this widening of

A similar process of disengagement from the text can be seen also in the traditional archaeological study of the central *tells,* which has always relied on historical events documented in the Bible. Even here, there has been a growing discontent with the 'secular fundamentalism' that simplistically viewed the biblical narratives as history, and a call to 'liberate' the archaeology of the Iron Age from the 'tyranny' of the Bible was loudly voiced. The historicity of large parts of the biblical text has been questioned vis-à-vis the archaeological reality; the well-known narratives were deprived of any historicity and were attributed to the ideological and theological world of late monarchic Judah (reflecting the new disciplinary discourse influenced by the 'minimalist' school, see below; Herzog 1999, 2001; Finkelstein and Silberman 2001). An apt expression of this process is the drastic revision of the Iron Age chronology, which empties the biblical description of the glorious United Monarchy, and delays the formation of the state in Israel and Judah (Finkelstein 1996a, 1999).

In tandem with the above changes, an even more dramatic process of completely undermining the credibility of the biblical text took place during the 1990s. A group of biblical scholars had totally negated the validity of the Bible as an historical source for early Israel and even the monarchic period. These scholars, sometimes dubbed 'minimalists' or 'nihilists', claimed that the Bible was composed only in the Persian, the Hellenistic, or even the Roman period, and therefore had no relevance for the study of the Iron Age (e.g. Davies 1992; Thompson 1992, 1999, 2000; Lemche 1994, 1998; Whitelam 1996). Though this small group of scholars have not convinced mainstream biblical and historical scholarship (see, e.g., various works in Day 2004) and was severely criticized (e.g. Rainey 1994; Halpern 1995; Dever 1998, 2001; Pasto 1998; Rendsburg 1999; Barr 2000), it had an immense impact on the scholarly discourse, including archaeology. Thus, many scholars, including those that are not necessarily inscribed to the 'minimalist' school, completely refrain nowadays from referring and relying on the biblical text. Using the Bible (in whatever capacity) is seen today as problematic and in many instances is simply avoided.

Despite the above, and notwithstanding the vociferous plea to 'liberate' archaeology from the burden of the biblical text, the agenda of Iron Age archaeology in the Land of Israel is currently still dictated by the Bible (most notably, Finkelstein and Silberman 2001, 2006; even the great scientific progress achieved in the utilization of ^{14}C in the archaeology of the Iron Age in Israel [e.g. Levy and Higham 2005a] is, to a large extent, an outcome of the debate over the historicity of David and Solomon). The anthropologically oriented research program that developed in the 1980s was abandoned, and once again the central themes include the United Monarchy, the emergence of the kingdoms of Israel and Judah, the status of Jerusalem as a capital, etc.—all issues stemming from biblical historiography. Surprisingly, even radical critics of the historicity of the biblical narratives did not turn to alternative research themes abundant in modern archaeology (e.g. economic structures, core-periphery relations, social organization, socioeconomic stratification, power relations, symbolism, gender, and more). Rather, they remained within the domain of biblical historiography, and devoted lengthy studies to prove their arguments regarding, for example, the non-existence of the United Monarchy (e.g. Wightman 1990; Finkelstein 1996a, 1999, 2003; Niemann 2000; note that opposing views were also 'dragged' into extensive discussion of those issues, e.g., Stager 2003; Mazar 2004, and many others; see also the vast literature on the United Monarchy and Iron Age chronology). Even though archaeology is the vehicle for their arguments, at the end of the day the discussion revolves around biblically driven issues. Apparently, the questions asked at the forefront of current archaeological research of the biblical period are similar to the ones dealt with by Albright and his students generations ago, even if the answers to these questions are diametrically different (cf. Finkelstein and Silberman 2001).

---

research horizons was short lived, and from the mid-1990s one can identify an unfortunate retreat to the more limited research agenda of previous generations of Biblical Archaeology.

We thus face today a paradoxical situation that leads Biblical Archaeology into a cul-de-sac: while its scientific agenda is still dictated predominantly by biblical historiography, the Bible itself, due to its problematic nature as an historical source, has been cast out of the archaeological discourse and its use has become almost illegitimate.

'New Biblical Archaeology': The Archaeological Record and the Biblical Text as Cultural Products

The developments in the 1970s and 1980s and the indirect influence of the new archaeology, as discussed above, led to a growing chasm between the Bible and archaeology. This divide, however, led to some dissatisfaction. W.G. Dever, probably the most vocal advocate for a 'secular' Syro-Palestinian archaeology during in the 1980s, called in the early 1990s for a 'New Biblical Archaeology' (1993). Dever realized that the total split between the two fields was more than he bargained for. The texts, problematic as they might be, are still important in the attempt to study the Iron Age. He therefore called for a new cooperation between archaeologists and biblical scholars and envisioned an ideal, synthetic history of ancient Israel comprised both of 'sacred history' (based largely upon biblical texts) and of 'secular history' (based on Iron Age archaeology in Israel and the ancient Near East). In the meantime, however, he was ready to compromise for the two histories running parallel to each other (1993: 711). Disappointingly, Dever's plea to rebuild Biblical Archaeology along new lines of construction was, generally speaking, unheeded.[2]

Embracing the idea of a 'New Biblical Archaeology', we suggest a re-construction of Biblical Archaeology founded on a different integration between archaeology and the Bible. On the one hand, we call for an archaeological agenda not dictated by the biblical text, which will place cultural and social issues at the center of the discussion, hence expanding our research questions. On the other hand, integrating the Bible as a cultural document in the quest for the answers to these questions will restore the biblical text to its central place within the archaeological discourse.

The archaeology of the Land of Israel in general, and that of the biblical period in particular, has produced a rich and detailed database, originating from a wealth of institutionalized and salvage excavations, as well as from extensive surveys conducted all over the country. This wealth of information, unparalleled in other countries, has not been fully used yet, especially in regard to social and cultural questions. As emphasized above, archaeological studies of the Iron Age period concentrated mainly on questions of political history, chronology, typology, etc. Progress in world archaeology in the last decades has enriched the discipline with a plethora of theoretical and practical approaches and immensely enlarged the range of issues dealt with by archaeologists as well as advancing the ways to tackle them. These issues include, for example, social organization, political

---

2.   Recently, Levy and Higham (2005b: 5-6) defined 'New Biblical Archaeology' as Biblical Archaeology embracing 'science-based methodologies to control time (chronometric methods) and space (e.g. Geographic Information Systems [GIS] and other digital processing technologies)' (see also Levy, this volume). While applauding this suggestion, which calls for a better-controlled Biblical Archaeology, we find it too narrow as a platform for a 'New Biblical Archaeology'. It does not directly address the need for a more sophisticated integration between the biblical texts and the archaeological finds, nor do new methodologies necessarily transform an old agenda (cf. Clarke 1973: 11). For example, the extensive and sophisticated use of ^{14}C in the debate over the chronology of the 10th century (see the various papers in Levy and Higham 2005a; see also Bruins, Van der Plicht, and Mazar 2003; Finkelstein and Piasetzky 2006; and Sharon *et al.* 2007, and many others) does not change the fact that the debate is still over Great Kings and Great Deeds. Numerous additional scientific methods and procedures, currently applied in the field, also fall short of solving the problems we are facing. While producing new data, it still requires explanation and interpretation. In our view, these should be created within an anthropological framework.

structures, spatial analysis, gender, social stratification, ideology, etc. (see, e.g., Renfrew and Bahn 1996; Johnson 1999; Hodder 2001). A thorough restudy of the rich Iron Age archaeological database at our hands, in light of the new disciplinary insights, will undoubtedly bring into relief various behavioral patterns of the period's society that demand explanation. It should be emphasized that no such patterns could have been discerned in the past, since the research perceptions and questions were different (for the linkage between the two, see, e.g., Trigger 1980; 1989: 1-26; Hodder 1986: 14-17; Shanks and Hodder 1995; Bunimovitz and Greenberg 2006).

The method to explain the newly revealed patterns includes comprehensive reference to the cultural context in which they were embedded. Despite the problems involved in using the Bible as an historical source, there is no doubt that it is a cultural document that incorporates contemporary, Iron Age 'layers' and can provide valuable information about Iron Age society. The incidental information contained in the Bible, just like the language of the people, provides insights into the social and spiritual world in which they created their material culture. As Murray (1998: xxxi) wrote: 'It does not matter whether the stories…are true… And even a forgery is an important piece of evidence for the period that perpetrated it… This principle of unconscious revelation through representation…is one of the most powerful tools in the modern historian's study of mentalities'. And in King and Stager's (2001: 7) words: '[F]or our purposes, then, it matters little whether the biblical accounts are "true" in the positivistic sense of some historians and biblical scholars… The stories must have passed some test of verisimilitude, that is, having the appearance of being true or real. In this sense, the biblical accounts and many other ancient accounts, however self-serving and tendentious, become grist for the cultural historian's mill'.

Both the biblical text and the period's material culture are cultural products of the very same society. Both words and artifacts open a door into the cognitive world of the people who created them: they represent worldviews, cosmology, spatial perception, ideology, symbolism, etc. The present approach 'places texts and maps in the same role as anthropological descriptions or natural scientific laws… Unlike these sources, as products of the society under study, they enable us to give *interpretation from within* that society. That is, they may enable us to give the same interpretation to archaeological material as people from within that society would have given' (Dark 1995: 57, emphasis in the original).

A few studies conducted by us recently demonstrate the new approach presented here, and its potential (see also Faust 2005).

1) The phenomenon of directing Iron Age buildings and settlements in ancient Israel to the east, and avoiding the west, went unnoticed by previous scholarship (Faust 2001). Because this tendency is not explicitly mentioned in the text it was not looked for in the past, and was revealed only by a scrutiny of the archaeological data.

The tendency to direct doorways of structures to the east and avoid the west influenced not only dwellings but also city gates. Moreover, it appears that it even had an impact on Iron Age urban planning (Faust 2001, 2002). An examination of various climatic and functional considerations does not explain the phenomenon. Many ethnographic studies, however, have demonstrated the strong influence that cosmological principles can have on the planning of buildings and settlements (e.g. Wheatley 1971; Oliver 1987; Waterson 1997), and that in many cases the east is preferred (e.g. Parker Pearson and Richards 1994: 15; Har-El 1984; Frazer 1968: 47). In the case of the ancient Israelites, however, we have additional information. The common Biblical Hebrew word for east is *qedma* (forward), while the west is *ahora* (backward) (e.g. Drinkard 1992a, 1992b). As Malamat (1989: 67) phrased it: 'The early Israelite ego faced east'. Moreover, additional words for those directions indicate that the east had a good connotation while the west had a bad one. The common word for west in Biblical Hebrew is *yam*, literary 'Sea', which is the most conspicuous element in this direction. But the word *yam*, beside designating a large body of water and westerly orientation, had some other meanings as well, and in many cases it represents the forces of chaos, sometimes personified in the *Leviathan* or other legendary creatures (Lewis 1993: 335; see also Ahlström 1986: 49; Stoltz 1995: 1397-98; Keel 1978: 23, 35, 49, 50, 55, 73-75).

The matching of the archaeological pattern, human tendency to prefer the east, and the evidence that the Israelites not only oriented themselves to the east but had even attributed positive and negative meaning to the various directions, seem to be sufficient to conclude that the Israelites viewed the east as a hospitable place (and the west as an inhospitable one), and this is the reason for the eastward orientation of structures and settlements. Still, it appears that the available evidence allow us to go one step further. Ezekiel 40–48 describes the temple in Jerusalem. It is clear that the description is not historical, and, at best, contains some historical elements, but this is irrelevant for the present discussion. According to this description, the Temple courts had three gates each, the main one in the east, and two others in the south and north. It is striking that no entrance is described in the west. Perhaps more important is the description of the eastern gates. This is the main gate through which Ezekiel enters the temple (40:4ff.). Later, however, the eastern gate is described as being closed, since this is the gate through which God is entering the Temple (44:2; see also 43:1-4 and ch. 46). The matching of the description with the archaeological data—where east is preferred and west is avoided—is therefore complete.

Thus, an archaeological pattern, along with language and texts (which are used as a substitute for human informants), seem to give an important insight into some of the cosmological principles of the ancient Israelites. This is because both the texts and the archaeological finds are cultural products reflecting the perception and beliefs of the society that produced them. Notably, the entire discussion, including the biblical one, stemmed from an archaeological agenda.

2) Another example is the well-known four-room house. This house is the dominant type of domestic building in Ancient Israel from the beginning of the Iron Age until the Babylonian Exile. As such, numerous studies were devoted to its origins and the ethnic identity of its inhabitants (e.g., Shiloh 1970, 1973; Netzer 1992; Holladay 1992, 1997; Ji 1997). The popularity of the four-room house was explained as either expressing its close relation with the Israelites (without elaborating the reasons for this relation) and/or its functional suitability to the needs of the Iron Age peasants, regardless of their ethnicity. Neither of these explanations, however, seem to account for the synchronic and diachronic dominance of the four-room house as a preferable architectural type in all levels of Iron Age settlement (from cities to hamlets and farmsteads), all over the country (both in highlands and lowlands), for almost 600 years(!). Moreover, the plan served as a template not only for dwelling, but also for public buildings, and even for the late Iron Age Judahite tombs (e.g. Barkay 1999). The fact that the house disappeared in the 6th century seems also to refute any 'functional' explanation, as no changes in peasant life and no architectural or agricultural inventions took place at the time. We have therefore suggested that an adequate explanation for the unique phenomenon of the four-room house must relate to the ideological/cognitive realm (Bunimovitz and Faust 2002, 2003; Faust and Bunimovitz 2003). Formed in the Iron Age I to fulfil the functional needs of the hill-zone settlers, the four-room house took shape during the process of ethnic negotiation and boundary construction that accompanied the Israelite ethnogenesis. Some of its architectural characteristics (few of them revealed by Access Analysis) reflect Israelite values and ethnic behavior: e.g. egalitarian ethos, purity, privacy, and cosmology. These are reflected in the spatial syntax of the house, as well as in the biblical text. Moreover, because the Israelites were preoccupied with Order (Douglas 1966), once this kind of house became typical, it eventually became the appropriate and 'right' one. It is thus the dialectic between function, process, and mind that created the 'Israelite House' which once crystallized long-lived for hundreds of years and disappeared following the destruction of the kingdoms of Israel and Judah, when its creators and maintainers lost coherence and were dispersed.

Whether all the explanations raised by us for the specific plan of the four-room house and its popularity will prove to be correct is irrelevant at the moment. We should stress that the entire discussion and all lines of reasoning stemmed from an archaeological agenda. Even the discussion of purity laws and their relevance to the Israelite household had been developed in an attempt to explain an archaeological pattern.

Summary

The archaeology of the Land of Israel has been shadowed from its inception by texts. Over the years it has become apparent that the biblical text is a problematic source for comprehensive historical reconstructions. This understanding, among other developments and influences, led to its marginalization within the archaeological discourse. Still occupied today by 'big questions' about biblical history, Iron Age archaeology has pushed aside the Bible itself, placing Biblical Archaeology at a dead-end.

We propose to *reverse* the usual scientific procedure in Biblical Archaeology. The research agenda should be archaeological/anthropological, relying on patterns identified in the archaeological record. Explanation of these patterns, however, should include *all* lines of evidence, with an important place reserved for the biblical texts. From a cultural perspective, the Bible as an 'unconscious revelation' is invaluable.

The new procedure will not only expand our research questions and restore the importance of the texts in the archaeological discourse, but may also be of importance for historical-political reconstructions—the main substance of 'traditional' Biblical Archaeology. Political aspects are, after all, part of a larger cultural environment (cf. Bunimovitz and Faust 2001). Thus, a better understanding of the political facets of a society demands acquaintance with its cultural facets—an aspect usually overlooked by the archaeology of Iron Age Israel.

While 'liberating' the research agenda from the 'shackles' of the Bible, it is rather the new approach to Biblical Archaeology suggested here that reinstates the Bible at the heart of the archaeological discourse of the Iron Age.

References

Ahlström, G.W. (1982) *Royal Administration and National Religion in Ancient Palestine* (Leiden: Brill).

—(1986) *Who Were the Israelites* (Winona Lake, IN: Eisenbrauns).

Barr, J. (2000) *History and Ideology in the Old Testament: Biblical Studies at End of a Millennium* (New York: Oxford University Press).

Barkay, G. (1999) Burial Caves and Dwellings in Judah during Iron Age II: Sociological Aspects. In *Material Culture, Society and Ideology: New Directions in the Archaeology of the Land of Israel*, edited by A. Faust and A. Maeir (Ramat Gan: Bar-Ilan University): 96–102 (Hebrew).

Bar-Yosef, O., and A. Mazar (1982) Israeli Archaeology. *World Archaeology* 13: 310-25.

Biran, A., and J. Aviram (eds.) (1993) *Biblical Archaeology Today, 1990. Proceedings of the Second International Congress on Biblical Archaeology. Pre-Congress Symposium: Population, Production and Power. Supplement* (Jerusalem: Israel Exploration Society).

Broshi, M., and I. Finkelstein (1992) The Population of Palestine in the Iron Age II. *BASOR* 287: 47-60.

Broshi, M., and R. Gophna (1984) The Settlement and Population of Palestine during the Early Bronze Age II-III. *BASOR* 253: 41-53.

—(1986) Middle Bronze Age II Palestine: Its Settlements and Population. *BASOR* 261: 73-90.

Bruins, H.J., J. van der Plicht, and A. Mazar (2003) ^{14}C Dates from Tel Rehov: Iron-Age Chronology, Pharaohs and Hebrew Kings. *Science* 300 (5617): 315-18.

Bunimovitz, S. (1994) Socio-Political Transformations in the Central Hill Country in the Late Bronze–Iron I Transition. In Finkelstein and Na'aman 1994: 179-202.

—(1995) How Mute Stones Speak: Interpreting What We Dig Up. *BAR* 21: 58-67, 96-100.

—(2000) Cultural Interpretation and the Bible: Biblical Archaeology in the Postmodern Era. *Cathedra* 100: 27–46 (Hebrew).

Bunimovitz, S., and A. Faust (2001) Chronological Separation, Geographical Segregation or Ethnic Demarcation? Ethnography and the Iron Age Low Chronology. *BASOR* 322: 1–10.

—(2002) Ideology in Stone: Understanding the Four Room House. *BAR* 28: 32–41, 59–60.

—(2003) Building Identity: The Four Room House and the Israelite Mind. In Dever and Gitin 2003: 411–23.

Bunimovitz, S., and R. Greenberg (2006) Of Pots and Paradigms: Interpreting the Intermediate Bronze Age in Israel/Palestine. In *Confronting the Past: Archaeological and Historical Essays on Ancient Israel in Honor of William G. Dever*, edited by S.J. Gitin, J.E. Wright, and J.P. Dessel (Winona Lake, IN: Eisenbrauns): 23-31.

Clarke, D. (1973) Archaeology: The Loss of Innocence. *Antiquity* 47: 6-18.

Dark, K.R. (1995) *Theoretical Archaeology* (London: Duckworth).

Davies, P.R. (1992) *In Search of Ancient Israel* (Sheffield: Sheffield Academic Press).

Davis, T.W. (2004) *Shifting Sands: The Rise and Fall of Biblical Archaeology* (New York: Oxford University Press).

Day, J. (2004) *In Search of Pre-Exilic Israel* (London: T&T Clark).

Dessel, J.P. (2002) Reading Between the Lines: W.F. Albright 'in' the Field and 'on' the Field. *NEA* 65: 43-50.

Dever, W.G. (1980) Biblical Theology and Biblical Archaeology: An Appreciation of G. Ernest Wright. *Harvard Theological Review* 73: 1-15.

—(1981) The Impact of the 'New Archaeology' on Syro-Palestinian Archaeology. *BASOR* 242: 15-29.

—(1985) Syro-Palestinian and Biblical Archaeology. In *The Hebrew Bible and Its Modern Interpreters*, edited by D.A. Knight and G.M. Tucker (Chico, CA: Scholars Press): 31-74.

—(1989a) Archaeology in Israel Today: A Summation and Critique. *AASOR* 49: 143-52.

—(1989b) Yigael Yadin: Prototypical Biblical Archaeologist. *Eretz-Israel* 20: 44*-51*.

—(1992) Archaeology, Syro-Palestinian and Biblical. In *ABD* 1:354-67.

—(1993) Biblical Archaeology: Death and Rebirth. In Biran and Aviram 1993: 706-22.

—(1998) Archaeology, Ideology, and the Quest for an 'Ancient,' or 'Biblical' Israel. *NEA* 61: 39–52.

—(2001) *What Did the Biblical Writers Know and When Did They Know it?* (Grand Rapids: Eerdmans).

Dever, W.G., and S. Gitin (eds.) (2003) *Symbiosis, Symbolism and the Power of the Past: Canaan, Ancient Israel and Their Neighbors from the Late Bronze Age through Roman Palestine* (Winona Lake, IN: Eisenbrauns).

Drinkard, J.F. (1992a) Direction and Orientation. In *ABD* 2:204.

—(1992b) East. In *ABD* 2:248.

Douglas, M. (1966) *Purity and Danger: An Analysis of Concepts of Pollution and Taboo* (London: Routledge & Kegan Paul).

Faust, A. (2001) Doorway Orientation, Settlement Planning and Cosmology in Ancient Israel during Iron Age II. *Oxford Journal of Archaeology* 20: 129–55.

—(2002) Accessibility, Defense, and Town Planning in Iron Age Israel. *Tel Aviv* 29: 297-317.

—(2005) Israelite Society in the Period of the Monarchy: An Archaeological Perspective (Jerusalem: Yad Ben Zvi [Hebrew]).

Faust, A., and S. Bunimovitz (2003) The Four Room House: Embodying Iron Age Israelite Society. *NEA* 66: 22–33.

Finkelstein, I. (1988) *The Archaeology of the Period of Settlement and Judges* (Jerusalem: Israel Exploration Society).

—(1989) The Emergence of the Monarchy in Israel the Environmental and Socio-Economic Aspects. *JSOT* 44: 43-74.

—(1992) Pastoralism in the Highlands of Canaan in the Third and Second Millennia B.C.E. In *Pastoralism in the Levant: Archaeological Materials in Anthropological Perspective*, edited by O. Bar-Yosef and A. Khazanov (Madison: Prehistory Press): 133-42.

—(1993) The Sociopolitical Organization of the Central Hill Country in the Second Millennium B.C.E. In Biran and Aviram 1993: 119-31.

—(1994) The Emergence of Israel: A Phase in the Cyclic History of Canaan in the Third and Second Millennia BCE. In Finkelstein and Na'aman 1994: 159-78.

—(1995) The Great Transformation: The 'Conquest' of the Highlands Frontiers and the Rise of the Territorial States. In Levy 1995: 349-65.

—(1996a) The Archaeology of the United Monarchy: An Alternative View. *Levant* 28: 177-87.

—(1996b) Ethnicity and Origin of the Iron I Settlers in the Hughlands of Canaan: Can the Real Israel Stand Up? *BA* 59: 198-212.

—(1998) Bible Archaeology or Archaeology of Palestine in the Iron Age? A Rejoinder. *Levant* 30: 167-73.

—(1999) State Formation in Israel and Judah. *NEA* 62: 35-52.

—(2003) City-States to States: Polity Dynamics in the 10th–9th Centuries B.C.E. In Dever and Gitin 2003: 75-83.

Finkelstein, I., and R. Gophna (1993) Settlement, Demography, and Economic Patterns in the Highlands of Palestine in the Chalcolithic and Early Bronze Periods and the Beginning of Urbanism. *BASOR* 289: 1-22.

Finkelstein, I., Z. Lederman, and S. Bunimovitz (1997) *Highlands of Many Cultures: The Southern Samaria Survey I. The Sites*, vols. 1 and 2 (Tel Aviv: Institute of Archaeology Tel Aviv University).

Finkelstein, I., and Y. Magen (eds.) (1993) *Archaeological Survey of the Hill Country of Benjamin* (Jerusalem: Israel Antiquities Authority).

Finkelstein, I., and E. Piasetzky (2006) The Iron I–IIA in the Highlands and Beyond: [14]C Anchors, Pottery Phases and the Shshenq I Campaign. *Levant* 38: 45-61.

Finkelstein, I., and N.A. Silberman (2001) *The Bible Unearthed: Archaeology's New Vision of Ancient Israel and Its Sacred Texts* (New York: Touchstone).

—(2006) *David and Solomon: In Search of the Bible's Sacred Kings and the Roots of the Western Tradition* (New York: Free Press).

Finkelstein, I., and N. Na'aman (eds.) (1994) *From Nomadism to Monarchy: Archaeological and Historical Aspects of Early Israel* (Jerusalem: Yad Izhak Ben-Zvi and Israel Exploration Society).

Frankel, R., N. Getzov, M. Aviam, and A. Degani (2001) *Settlement Dynamics and Regional Diversity in Ancient Upper Galilee: Archaeological Survey of Upper Galilee* (Jerusalem: Israel Antiquities Authority).

Frazer, D. (1968) *Village Planning in the Primitive World* (London: Studia Vista).

Gal, Z. (1992) *Lower Galilee During the Iron Age* (ASOR Dissertation Series 8; Winona Lake, IN: Eisenbrauns).

Geva, S. (1992) Israeli Biblical Archaeology in its Beginning. *Zemanim* 42: 93-102 (Hebrew).

Halpern, B. (1995) Erasing History: The Minimalist Assault on Ancient Israel. *Bible Review* 11: 26-35, 47.

Har-El, M. (1984) Orientation and Mapping in Biblical Lands. *Israel—People and Land* 1: 157-68 (Hebrew).

Herzog, Z. (1999) The Canaanite City between Ideology and Archaeological Reality. In *Material Culture, Society and Ideology: New Directions in the Archaeology of the Land of Israel*, edited by A. Faust and A. Maeir (Ramat Gan: Bar-Ilan University): 42-50 (Hebrew).

—(2001) Deconstructing the Walls of Jericho. *Prometheus* 4: 72-93.

Hodder, I. (1986) *Reading the Past* (Cambridge: Cambridge University Press).

—(2001) *Archaeological Theory Today* (Oxford: Polity Press).

Holladay, J.S. (1992). House, Israelite. In *ABD* 3:308-18.

—(1997) Four Room House. In *The Oxford Encyclopedia of Archaeology in the Near East*, vol. 2, edited by E.M. Meyers (New York: Oxford University Press): 337–41.

Ji, C.H.C. (1997) A Note on the Iron Age Four-Room House in Palestine. *Orientalia* 66: 387-413.

Johnson, M. (1999) *Archaeological Theory: An Introduction* (Oxford: Blackwell).

Keel, O. (1978) *Symbols of the Biblical World: Ancient Near-Eastern Iconography and the Book of Psalms* (New York: The Seabury Press).

King, P.J. (1987) The Influence of G. Ernest Wright on the Archaeology of Palestine. In Perdue, Toombs, and Johnson 1987: 15-29.

King, P.J., and L.E. Stager (2001) *Daily Life in Ancient Israel* (Louisville: Westminster/John Knox).

Kochavi, M. (ed.) (1972) *Judaea, Samaria, and the Golan: Archaeological Survey 1967–1968* (Jerusalem: Archaeological Survey of Israel).

Lemche, N.P. (1994) Is it Still Possible to Write a History of Ancient Israel? *SJOT* 8: 165-90.

—(1998) *The Israelites in History and Tradition* (Louisville: Westminster/John Knox)

Levy, T.E. (ed.) (1995) *The Archaeology of Society in the Holy Land* (Leicester: Leicester University Press).

Levy, T.E., and D.N. Freedman (2008) William Foxwell Albright: A Biographical Essay. *Proceedings of the National Academy of Science*: 1-29.

Levy, T.E., and T. Higham (2005b) Introduction: Radiocarbon Dating and the Iron Age of the Southern Levant. In Levy and Higham 2005a: 3-14.

Levy, T.E., and T. Higham (eds.) (2005a) *The Bible and Radiocaron Dating: Archaeology, Text and Science* (London: Equinox).

Lewis, T.J. (1993) Israel, Religion of. In *The Oxford Companion to the Bible*, edited by B.M. Metzger and M.D. Coogan (Oxford: Oxford University Press): 332-36.

London, G. (1989) A Comparison of Two Contemporaneous Lifestyles of the Late Second Millennium B.C. *BASOR* 273: 37–55.

Long, B.O. (1997) *Planting and Reaping Albright* (University Park: Pennsylvania State University Press).

Malamat, A. (1989) *Mari and the Early Israelite Experience* (The Schweich Lectures 1984; Oxford: Oxford University Press).

Mazar, A. (2004) Jerusalem in the 10th Century BCE—the 'Half-Full' Glass. In *New Studies on Jerusalem: The 10th Volume*, edited by E. Baruch and A. Faust (Ramat Gan: Bar-Ilan University): 11-22.

Murray, O. (1998) Introduction. In J. Burckhardt, *The Greeks and Greek Civilization* (New York: St. Martin's Press): xi–xliv.

Moorey, P.R.S. (1991) *A Century of Biblical Archaeology* (Louisville: Westminster/John Knox).

Netzer, E. (1992) Domestic Architecture in the Iron Age. In *The Architecture of Ancient Israel from the Prehistoric to the Persian Period*, edited by A. Kempinski and R. Reich (Jerusalem: Israel Exploration Society): 193-201.

Niemann, H.M. (2000) Megiddo and Solomon: A Biblical Investigation in Relation to Archaeology. *Tel Aviv* 27: 61-74.

Ofer, A. (1994) 'All the Hill Country of Judah': From a Settlement Fringe to a Prosperous Monarchy. In Finkelstein and Na'aman 1994: 92-121.

—(1998) The Judean Hills in the Biblical Period. *Qadmoniot* 115: 40-52 (Hebrew).

Oliver, P. (1987) *Dwellings, the House Across the World* (Oxford: Phaidon Press).

Parker Pearson, M., and C. Richards (1994) Ordering the World: Perceptions of Architecture, Space and Time. In *Architecture and Order, Approaches to Social Space*, edited by M. Parker Pearson and C. Richards (London: Routledge): 1-37.

Pasto, J. (1998) When the End is the Beginning? Or When the Biblical Past is the Political Present: Some Thought on Ancient Israel, 'Post Exilic Judaism', and the Politics of Biblical Scholarship. *SJOT* 12: 157-202.

Perdue, L.G., L.E. Toombs, and G.L. Johnson (eds.) (1987) *Archaeology and Biblical Interpretation: Essays in Memory of D. Glenn Rose* (Atlanta: John Knox).

Rainey, A.F. (1994) The 'House of David' and the House of the Deconstructionists. *BAR* 20: 47.

Rendsburg, G.A. (1999) Down with History, Up with Reading: The Current State of Biblical Studies. *A Lecture at the McGill University Department of Jewish Studies Thirtieth Anniversary Conference, The Academy Reports to the Community, May 9–10, 1999* (an expanded text of this lecture with notes can be found online: http://www.arts.mcgill.ca/programs/jewish/30yrs/rendsburgh/index.html).

Renfrew, C., and P. Bahn (1996) *Archaeology: Theories, Methods and Practice* (London: Thames & Hudson).

Running, L.G., and D.N. Freedman (1975) *William Foxwell Albright: A Twentieth Century Genius* (New York: Two Continents).

Shanks, M., and I. Hodder (1995) Processual, Postprocessual and Interpretive Archaeologies. In *Interpreting Archaeology*, edited by I. Hodder *et al.* (London: Routledge): 3-29.

Sharon, I., A. Gilboa, A.J.T. Jull, and E. Boaretto (2007) Report on the First Stage of the Iron Age Dating Project in Israel: Supporting a Low Chronology. *Radiocarbon* 49: 1-46.

Shiloh, Y. (1970) The Four Room House—Its Situation and Function in the Israelite City. *IEJ* 20: 180-90.

—(1973) The Four Room House—The Israelite Type-House? *Eretz-Israel* 11: 277-85 (Hebrew).

Silberman, N.A. (1982) *Digging for God and Country* (New York: Doubleday).

—(1989) *Between Past and Present: Archaeology, Ideology, and Nationalism in the Modern Near East* (New York: Henry Holt).

—(1995) Power, Politics and the Past: The Social Construction of Antiquity in the Holy Land. In Levy 1995: 7-23.

Stager, L.E. (1985) The Archaeology of the Family in Early Israel. *BASOR* 260: 1-35.

—(1988) Archaeology, Ecology, and Social History: Background Themes to the Song of Deborah. In *Congress Volume: Jerusalem 1986*, edited by J.A. Emerton (VTSup 40; Leiden: Brill): 221-34.

—(2003) The Patrimonial Kingdom of Solomon. In Dever and Gitin 2003: 63-74.

Stern, E. (1987) The Bible and Israeli Archaeology. In Perdue, Toombs, and Johnson 1987: 31-40.

Stoltz, F. (1995) Sea. In *Dictionary of Deities and Demons in the Bible* (DDD), edited by. K. Van der Toorn, B. Becking, and P.W. Van der Horst (Leiden: Brill): 1390-1402.

Thompson, T.L. (1992) *Early History of the Israelite People from the Written and Archaeological Sources* (Leiden: Brill).

—(1999) *The Bible in History: How Writers Create a Past* (London: Jonathan Cape).

—(2000) Lester Grabbe and Historiography: An Apologia. *SJOT* 14: 140-61.

Trigger, B. (1980) Archaeology and the Image of the American Indian. *AmAnt* 45: 662-76.

— (1989) *A History of Archaeological Thought* (Cambridge: Cambridge University Press).

Ussishkin, D. (2003) Jerusalem as a Royal and Cultic Center in the 10th–8th Centuries B.C.E. In Dever and Gitin 2003: 529-38.

Van Beek, G.W. (ed.) (1989) *The Scholarship of William Foxwell Albright: An Appraisal* (Atlanta: Scholars Press).

Waterson, R. (1997) *The Living House: An Anthropology of Architecture in South-East Asia* (Singapore: Thames & Hudson).

Wheatley, P. (1971) *The Pivot of the Four Quarters: A Preliminary Inquiry into the Origins and Character of the Ancient Chinese City* (Edinburgh: Edinburgh University Press).

Whitelam, K.W. (1996) *The Invention of Ancient Israel: The Silencing of Palestinian History* (London: Routledge).

Wightman, G.J. (1990) The Myth of Solomon. *BASOR* 277-78: 5-22.

Yadin, Y. (1985) Biblical Archaeology Today: The Archaeological Aspect. In *Biblical Archaeology Today: Proceedings of the International Congress on Biblical Archaeology, Jerusalem*, edited by J. Amitai (Jerusalem: Israel Exploration Society): 21-27.

Zertal, A. (1992–2005) *The Manasseh Hill Country Survey* (2 vols.; Tel Aviv: Haifa University and the Ministry of Defense [Hebrew]).

3 Future Directions in the Study of Ethnicity in Ancient Israel

Avraham Faust

Abstract

Ethnicity has always been a central issue in Biblical Archaeology. Still, detecting ethnic groups in the archaeological record of ancient Israel in general, and identifying the Israelites in particular, have become less fashionable recently, with many scholars avoiding this altogether. The present article will analyze the reasons for this attitude, and, in light of anthropological approaches to ethnicity, will suggest a new method for the study of ethnic groups in the archaeological record of ancient Israel.

Ethnicity has always been a major theme in Biblical Archaeology. Recently, it became a focus of a heated debate, with several schools contesting the issue of Israelite ethnicity. Some aspects of the debate have even reached the mass-media, and are of great public interest.

Until not long ago, in the spirit of the culture-history school, 'archaeological cultures' were simply identified with 'peoples'. A notable example of this view is the Iron I culture of the highlands, which was identified as Israelite. Gradually, however, and mainly in the 1980s and 1990s, this view fell into disfavor. This development was due to both (1) the failure of this explanation to account for the expected archaeological patterns in the highlands, i.e., lack of Gibeonites, Jebusites, and other ethnic groups, in the archaeological record (e.g. Skjeggestand 1992), and (2) the indirect impact of the new (processual) archaeology, which viewed the study of ethnicity as a 'virtual pariah' (see below). These factors, combined with the more skeptical approaches to the biblical texts that became more prevalent as time progressed, all led almost to the abandonment of labels such as 'Israelites' from the archaeological discourse. Today, while a few scholars still speak of Israelites in discussing the Iron Age I, terms like 'proto-Israelites' have become more prevalent (e.g. Dever 1991: 87; 1992b; 1995a: 206-7; Williamson 1998: 147), and many prefer to avoid 'Israelites' altogether (e.g. Skjeggestand 1992; Lemche 1998; Thompson 1999; see also Finkelstein 1996).

The identification of ethnic groups in the archaeological record of ancient Israel in general, and the question whether we can speak of Israelites in the Iron I in particular, therefore became a highly contested issue. Today, it appears that we have almost reached a dead-end.

Biblical Archaeology and Anthropological Archaeology: An Introductory Note

As is widely known, there is a large theoretical gap between Biblical Archaeology and 'regular' (anthropological) archaeology (e.g. Bunimovitz and Faust, this volume; Levy, this volume;

Bunimovitz 2001; Dever 1981, 1992a; Geva 1992; see also Moorey 1991: 139-43). The archaeology of the Land of Israel along with that of neighboring regions was developed in the shadow of the texts (e.g. Moorey 1991). While no doubt an important source, the scientific agenda and research question of the emerging Biblical Archaeology were to a large extent dictated by preconceived knowledge and interest. Whether this was appropriate or not is a different question, but it definitely limited the discipline's agenda. While many early studies simply aimed at illustrating the texts, and later ones to prove or disprove them, it is clear that even today, regardless of one's position on the historicity of the Bible, the *agenda* of many is still dictated by the texts (see even Finkelstein and Silberman 2001). Among the main questions are those relating to wars, kings and prophets and to the events, or at least the background of the events, depicted in the Bible, and their historicity.

Many other 'archaeologies', however, were developed as a study of prehistory or a sub-discipline of anthropology, dealing with anthropological questions concerning households, family size, community organization, socio-economic stratification, economic systems, political organization, etc. (e.g. Trigger 1989; Renfrew and Bahn 1996; Johnson 1999). While there is a growing contact between Biblical Archaeology and anthropology, it is still not a major theme, and even the impact of the new (processual) archaeology, let alone post-processual approaches, on Biblical Archaeology was limited (Bunimovitz and Faust, this volume; Bunimovitz 2001; Dever 1981, 1997; Geva 1992; Davis 2004: 150-51; the unimportance of those strands of thought can also be seen in their almost complete absence from Davis's book).

Biblical Archaeology concentrates on issues that appear to be directly connected with biblical history or related debates, whether accepting their historicity or rejecting it (see most recently Finkelstein and Silberman 2001, 2006), and is usually not immersed in approaches and advances made in anthropology/anthropological archaeology (there are exceptions to this generalization, of course). And even when the research questions seemed to converge, scholars from the various sub-disciplines would engage them in a totally different way. Indeed, as we will see below, this can be best exemplified in the study of the Israelite ethnicity.

Cautiously, I would like to claim that this is not only a somewhat narrow approach which limits the research questions of our sub-discipline, but also a major hindrance in the attempts to answer the very questions biblical archaeologists have traditionally been interested in, in general, and to decipher issues relating to ethnicity in Biblical Archaeology, in particular.

On the positive side, the archaeology of ancient Israel (and Biblical Archaeology at large) has a much richer archaeological database than the archaeology of any other region in the world. In Israel alone, hundreds of planned excavations and thousands of salvage excavations were carried out, along with detailed surveys. This makes Israel an excellent archaeological field laboratory (e.g. Faust and Safrai 2005). But due to the above mentioned theoretical gap, this huge database is not used to advance anthropological-archaeological studies. Many excellent studies, conducted in other regions, are built on a very limited datasets, while ours, which is many times larger, is hardly 'used' for anthropological purposes at all. The 'gap', therefore, has a negative impact not only on Biblical Archaeology, but also, though on a different scale, on the general, anthropological archaeology.

With respect to ethnicity I would like to claim that part of the current 'dead-end' we are facing in the study of ethnicity in ancient Israel results from this partial interaction with anthropological archaeology and that the latter has much to contribute to the study of ancient ethnicities. On the other hand, I believe that 'our' rich database can contribute to general studies of ethnicity, including to the understudied issue of ethnogenesis, i.e., how ethnic groups are created.[1]

---

1.   Due to the nature of ethnicity, such an identity (i.e. ethnic identity) was already established when Europeans documented other societies. The study of what brought it about, and how it was formed, were

Ethnicity in Archaeology

The Culture History School

Archaeologists have always attempted to identify ethnic groups in the archaeological record. This endeavor was more or less the main agenda of the Culture History school, the dominant archaeological paradigm during most of the 20th century. Archaeologists working in this tradition equated 'archaeological cultures', identified by their material culture, with ethnic groups (e.g. Trigger 1989; Jones 1997; McNairn 1980). Childe succinctly explains the rationale for this approach: 'We find certain types of remains—pots, implements, ornaments, burial rites and house forms—constantly recurring together. Such a complex of associated traits we shall term "cultural group" or just a "culture". We assume that such a complex is the material expression of what today would be called a "people"' (1929: v-vi; but see also Childe 1951: 40). This approach was based on a normative understanding of culture, i.e., that norms or rules of behavior prescribe the practices and behaviors of members of any given group, as a result of shared ideas, worldviews, and beliefs (e.g. Jones 1997: 24; Johnson 1999: 16-17).

The New (Processual) Archaeology

The New Archaeology, which evolved in the 1960s and later came to be known as Processual Archaeology, generally failed to direct much attention to the identification of ethnic groups (e.g. Jones 1997: 5, 26-27, 111; De Boer 1990: 102). This school grew out of the dissatisfaction with the 'unscientific' nature of the Culture History school, specifically its inductive approach, its lack of rigorous scientific procedures, its descriptive nature, and, most important for our purposes, its normative approach to culture (Binford 1962, 1965). Much discussion was devoted to adaptation. The new school believed that archaeological remains were the product of a range of complex processes and not 'simply a reflection of ideational norms' (Jones 1997: 26).

Moreover, adherents of the New Archaeology school were interested in generalizations and laws, and disregarded the specific and the unique. Studies of differences and uniqueness, e.g., studies of specific ethnic identities, were consequently inconsistent with their scientific agenda (Trigger 1989: 312-19). It is further likely that the disinterest in discussions of ethnicity also resulted from the horrifying outcome of the racial archaeology, which was so prevalent in Europe (e.g. Hall 1997: 1-2). This so-called 'archaeology' collaborated with the justification of the Nazi claims of racial superiority and, as a consequence, contributed to the extermination of millions. Ethnicity was relegated to a minor role as a part of discussions on style, which were in themselves not of great concern (e.g. De Boer 1990: 102).

With the advent of New (Processual) Archaeology, therefore, the methodological foundations of the Culture History school and its normative approach to culture were heavily criticized and fell into disfavor (Binford 1962, 1965; see also Jones 1997; Trigger 1989; Ryman, O'Brien, and Dunnell 1997).

Changes in Anthropological Approaches to Ethnicity

At about the same time, however, revolutionary changes were occurring in the anthropological approach to ethnicity.

---

therefore usually beyond the realm of anthropological studies (but see Comaroff and Comaroff 1992; Faust 2006).

The most important development in the study of ethnicity in general came with the publication of *Ethnic Groups and Boundaries* (1969). In his introduction to the book, Barth (1969: 10-13) criticizes the conventional view of ethnic groups as 'culture-bearing units', by which he means groups sharing core values that find representation in cultural forms (1969: 10-11). Barth defines ethnic groups as, in essence, a form of social organization; its critical criterion is an ability to be identified and distinguished among others, or in his words, allowing 'self-ascription and ascription by others' (1969: 11, 13). Ethnic identity here is not determined by biological or genetic factors but is subject to perception and is adaptable. Barth's views had an immense impact in the social sciences, and probably even more so in archaeology, so much so that in Emberling's overview of the study of ethnicity in archaeology, works on the subject are referred to as B.B. (before Barth) or A.B. (after Barth) (1997: 295; see also Jones 1997: 60). With his work, emphasis shifted from the shared elements or characteristics of a group to the features that distinguish it from others. It was the contact between groups that was seen as essential for the formation of the self-identity of a group (see also Cohen 1985), which is thus clearly manifested in its material culture.

Following these developments in anthropology and sociology, archaeologists have also come to understand that ethnicity is too complex to be merely identified with a material or an archaeological culture (see, e.g., Hodder 1982a); it is fluid, it is merely one of several attributes of an individual's complete identity, and it is subjective (e.g. Shenan 1989, 1991; Emberling 1997; Schortman, Urban, and Ausec 2001; Jones 1997, and bibliography there). This new understanding of ethnicity also seemed appropriate for several Post-Processual approaches to archaeology that were beginning to develop (e.g. Hall 1997: 142; Jones 1997: 5-6).

Archaeology and Ethnicity: The Response

As observed in existing groups, the subjective nature of ethnicity has led some scholars to question the ability of archaeologists to identify ethnic groups in the material record of extinct societies (see Jones 1997: 109-10, 124; with regard to the Levant, see Herzog 1997).[2] Yet in most cases, clear relationships between material culture and ethnicity can be identified, however complicated they may be (McGuire 1982; Kamp and Yoffee 1980; Emberling 1997, and others; see also Howard 1996: 239-40), and the potential of archaeological inquiry to deal with such issues should not be underestimated.

The new anthropological approaches to ethnicity were propagated at a time of change in archaeological thinking. New/Processual Archaeology, at least in its original orthodox version, was the target of increasing criticism, primarily by what came to be known as Post-Processual archaeologists (e.g. on various grounds, Trigger 1989; Hodder 1991, 1992, and others; see even Flannery 1973). The Post-Processual approaches (some of them at least) reinstated a different, yet normative approach to culture, which did not seek to desert older approaches entirely (Hodder 1991: 1; Bunimovitz 1999: 147-48). Today archaeology is much more responsive to the study of ethnicity, acknowledging its subjective nature. Today's approaches, including both Post-Processual approaches and the new Cognitive/Processual Archaeology (Renfrew 1994), tackle problems concerning ideology and worldviews and in dealing with symbols. We shall expand on this issue below. In the meantime, however, we should turn to the study of Israelite ethnicity.

---

2. Note that some claim that ethnicity is modern, and that there were no ethnicities in the past (based on works such as Anderson 1983; Gellner 1983). This view, which is based on studies of modern nationalism, seems unfounded (e.g. Hall 1997; Smith 1986, 1994; Banks 1996; Atkinson 1994; Comaroff and Comaroff 1992, and many others; see also Grosby 2002), and need not be discussed here.

History of Research of Israelite Ethnicity

Identifying the Israelites in the Iron Age Archaeological Record

The Iron Age I settlement in the highlands is a well-known phenomenon which drew much scholarly interest and was discussed in detail by many scholars (e.g. Finkelstein 1988; Gottwald 1979; Callaway 1983; Stager 1998; Mazar 1992; Dever 2003). The following quote from Dever (1994: 215) summarizes the phenomenon:

> In the late 13th–12th cents. B.C. there occurred a major influx of new settlers into the hill country, especially from Jerusalem northward to Shechem. Hundreds of small villages were now established, not on the remains of destroyed or abandoned Late Bronze Age Urban Canaanite sites, but de novo. These villages are characterized chiefly by their hilltop location and lack of defensive walls...

Indeed, the locations and material remains of the Iron I agricultural villages indicate a rather different lifestyle from that of the Late Bronze Age, the settlements of which were concentrated mainly in the valleys and plains and were highly stratified. The Iron Age settlements were rural and concentrated in an area that was relatively uninhabited in the preceding centuries (e.g. Finkelstein 1988; Dever 1994; 1995a: 204). Their inhabitants lived in a new type of building called the three- or four-room house (or its proto-type). The finds from the Iron Age hill country villages were poor and rudimentary. While pottery forms had Late Bronze Age antecedents, the assemblages typically included a limited pottery repertoire, consisting of cooking pots, bowls, and storage jars, which were mainly of the collared rim type.

Until the 1990s, scholarly consensus held that these settlers constituted 'early Israel,' corresponding to the period of the Judges in the Bible (e.g. Albright 1961; Aharoni 1979: 193-94; Finkelstein 1988). This concept was based on the assumption that the settlement of the Israelite tribes as mentioned in the Bible was synonymous with the material remains uncovered by archaeologists, a seemingly secure identification in light of the mentioning of Israel as an ethnic group in the Merenptah stele, dating to the end of the 13th century BCE (Stager 1985a; Na'aman 1994: 247-49; Bloch-Smith and Alpert Nakhai 1999: 77).

The material culture of these sites was therefore seen, in the tradition of the dominant cultural history school, as representing the Israelites (e.g. Mazar 1992: 287-95). This approach can be exemplified by the various attempts made to deduce the Israelite character of Megiddo Stratum VI from the presence of several characteristics, mainly the collared rim jar (Albright 1937; Aharoni 1970; Esse 1991, 1992, and references).

Questioning the Identification

Gradually, however, serious doubts arose on the direct equation of these material remains with the Israelites. Criticism focused on the discrepancy between the territories supposedly inhabited by Israelites, and the distribution of their assumed material markers. According to Ibrahim, for example, the presence of both four-room houses and collared rim jars in Transjordan outside of the area of the Israelite settlement is clearly problematic evidence (Ibrahim 1975, 1978, and others). He concludes: 'The presence of the collared-rim jar during the late 13th–12th centuries cannot be attributed to one single ethnic group. The origin and the long use of the type under discussion, whenever and wherever, ought to be considered in connection with a social-economic tradition' (1978: 124). And similar discrepancies were observed in the distribution of the four-room house (e.g. Ibrahim 1975; Mazar 1980: 74-75; Finkelstein 1996: 204-5), leading many scholars to conclude that the unique connection between this building type and the Israelites is incorrect, and that the four-room house, as well as collared rim jars, should be explained by their functionality and suitability for life in highland farming communities (many of those discrepancies do not stand scrutiny, but this is beyond the scope of the present article; see Faust 2006). Notably, these explanations were in implicit accordance with the adaptation spirit of the New Archaeology.

Furthermore, various scholars have pointed to the heterogeneity of Early Iron Age society in the region, and to the fact that there is no evidence that the highland's 'material culture' was distinctively Israelite, as opposed to being Jebusite, Hivite, Moabite, etc. (Miller and Hayes 1986: 85), or of any other group which, according to the Bible, inhabited the region at the time. The texts indicated that, although the area was inhabited by Israelites during the Iron Age II, there were also other groups in the region during the Iron Age I (e.g. the Gibeonites, Josh. 9; the Jebusites, Judg. 19:10-11; 2 Sam. 5:5-7; and others). Since the attempts to identify more than one 'archaeological culture' in the highlands failed, many scholars concluded that we should not identify the highland's archaeological culture with the Israelites.

Indeed, the problems with Iron I ethnic labels initially concentrated on the question of how to distinguish an Israelite from a member of any other group inhabiting the region at the time, as mentioned in the Bible (B. Mazar 1981; Ahlstrom 1984; A. Mazar 1994: 90-91; Finkelstein 1988: 28, 65; see also Skjeggestand 1992: 165, 176, 177, 185; Stager 1998: 1367; Kempinski 1995: 60). However, not only were the basic concepts of the Culture History school never questioned, but they were directly responsible for the dissatisfaction with the identification of the Israelites with the highland material culture. The inapplicability of the term Israelites was based on our inability to differentiate between Israelite 'culture' and other 'cultures' in the archaeological record, and was therefore still in the spirit of the Culture History school.

The observation of these issues was also accompanied by a more cautious approach to the issue of identifying ethnic groups in the archaeological record—what has been called 'pots and peoples' (e.g. Parr 1978; but see already Engberg 1940). While a cautious and even negative approach was typical of the New Archaeology (e.g. Renfrew 1993; Jones 1997: 5, 26-27; see above), it had only an indirect influence on Syro-Palestinian archaeology. However, although these two lines of criticism—the problematic distribution of traits on the one hand and the indirect impact of the skepticism of the New Archaeology toward the study of ethnicity on the other—occurred together, it should be stressed that they are not complementary, if not contradictory (Faust 2006). Both, however (along with, as we shall see below, the strong influence of skeptic approaches of the minimalist school) have gradually raised doubts over the once popular identification of the Israelites with these Iron I material traits.

Ironically, although those dealing with the archaeology of ancient Israel still work to a large extent in the tradition of the Cultural History school, it seems that the evaluation of ethnicity—the center of this approach—has changed.

Thus, what might be seen as a failure of the old-fashioned culture history school to identify the Israelites, was taken as a proof that the Israelites cannot be identified archaeologically in the Iron Age, and hence (according to some) that there was no such group.

Solutions and Problems

With these challenges, putting the Israelite label on the settlers in the highlands became increasingly problematic. At the time, Finkelstein suggested that we should treat all groups living in the Iron I highlands as Israelites (1988: 27-28) on the rationale that regardless of their ethnic affiliation during the Iron I, they became Israelite from the 10th century BCE onward after the formation of the monarchy (see also Mazar 1990b: 95-96).

Finkelstein's solution was a subject of criticism, particularly by Skjeggestand (1992). The critics based much of their argumentations on Finkelstein's misleading conclusion that the Iron Age I pottery forms of the highlands were very different from their Late Bronze Age predecessors

(Skjeggestand 1992: 170 n. 24; Dever 1995a; 2000: 69 n. 21). The assumption of the critics was that the similarity in pottery forms (and perhaps in other traits as well) between the Late Bronze Age and the Iron Age I indicates continuity in population and culture, therefore invalidating the applicability of the term Israelite for these (Canaanite) Iron I settlers.[3] The question of how can we differentiate Israelites from Canaanites or identify the Iron I settlers came to the forefront.

In order to avoid the problem, W.G. Dever suggested calling the highland's Iron I population 'Proto-Israelite' (1991: 87; 1992b; 1995a: 206-7; see also Williamson 1998: 147). Dever's rationale seems to have been based on his awareness that this population had indeed constituted an ethnic group, and that this, together with the mentioning of Israel in the Merenptah stela and the continuity of material culture from Iron I to Iron II in the hill country (when there is no doubt about the identity of the population), is a sufficient justification to use the term. Like Finkelstein, he partially used the consensus on the Iron Age II reality as a basis for conclusions on a previous period.

At the same time, however, the minimalist school was 'established'. This school, which is also referred to as the nihilistic, deconstructionist, and Copenhagen school, and is led by figures such as Lemche, Thompson, Whitelam, and Davies (although they differ on some matters, their views are similar enough to label them a school), has attempted to undermine the relevancy of the term Israel to Iron Age society, beginning with the Iron I, but continuing well into the Iron II (see, e.g., Whitelam 1996; Thompson 2000).[4] Thompson's approach is representative; he claims that his study leaves no room for ethnic unity within the highland regions (2000: 156; see also Davies 1992: 69). The very existence of ancient Israel has been questioned (despite denials; for example, by Lemche 1998: 63), thus dragging the debate to other grounds. This is not the place for a detailed discussion of this school and its political-ideological views (as has been detailed by many, e.g., Dever 1998: 50; Pasto 1998; Rendsburg 1999; see also Rainey 1994 and various papers in Levine and Mazar 2001), but it should be emphasized that these scholars have usually offered no new evidence or even new insights into the discussion. Generally, their writings show inaptitude in both archaeological theory and even archaeological data (e.g. Dever 1998: 46; Faust 2006). They have, however, greatly influenced academic discourse, even if indirectly, especially in their denial of Israelite ethnicity (e.g. Thompson 2000: 165).

Within this new intellectual environment, Finkelstein re-examined the archaeological evidence for Israel's existence in the highlands during the Iron Age I and took a more critical stance. Referencing earlier papers by Dever (1995b, 1995c), whose title included the phrase, 'will the real Israel please stand up?,' he wrote a paper whose title included the question 'Can the Real Israel Stand Up?' There, he claimed that since the pottery forms continue Late Bronze Age antecedents and the characteristic architectural forms of the highlands are found in the lowlands and Transjordan, these cannot be seen as Israelite (Finkelstein 1996). He concluded that the only criterion that can be used to infer the presence of Israelites at the time is the absence of pig bones (Finkelstein 1996: 206). Yet, despite this he concluded that the Israelites cannot be recognized in the Iron Age I archaeological record, but only in that of the Iron II (Finkelstein 1996: 209).

---

3.   Notably, the confusion between the issues of ethnic identity and 'origins', exemplified here, had enhanced the feeling of a 'dead-end'. The two issues are related, of course, but are not the same, and should be dealt with separately (see the detailed discussion in Faust 2006). Notably, the present paper deals mainly with the question of identity and does not cover the question of origins. In the past, debate over the latter relied to a large extent simply on the presence or absence of foreign items or traits. The question of Israel's origins in relation to ethnogenesis has been discussed in detail recently by Levy and Holl (2002), as part of a larger study which also considered other examples. This work can serve as an example for the great potential of anthropological approaches also to the study of the origins of ancient Israel.

4.   And even later (Thompson 1999; 2000: 155-57).

The Current State of Research into Israelite Ethnicity: A Dead End

Today, the prevalent attitude toward the study of ethnicity is one of skepticism (see also Edelman 2002; although this might be changing now, see recently Levy and Holl 2002; Dever 2003; Bloch-Smith 2003; Miller 2004; Killebrew 2005; Faust 2006). Due to the above, many have abandoned the term 'Israelite', with some scholars preferring the term 'proto-Israelites' while others avoiding 'Israelites' altogether (although it is not always clear what term they do prefer). Each side seems to entrench itself in its position, and the issue of Israelite ethnicity, which turned into one of the major issues in the study of ancient Israel, seems unresolved.

Identifying Ethnicity in the Archaeological Record

While the problem of identifying the Israelites in the archaeological record appears almost impossible to solve, there are many instances, in other parts of the world, in which ethnic groups are identified archaeologically (despite the much smaller archaeological database, see e.g., McGuire 1982; Clark 2001; Hodder 1982; Hall 1997, and many others; for a general overview and many references, see also Emberling 1997; Faust 2006: 15-19, and references).

So what went wrong here? Clearly, the present skeptical approach regarding the ability of archaeology to tackle the question of ethnicity is unwarranted, when examined on a world-scale. It appears that the skeptical stance prevalent in the archaeology of ancient Israel is to a large extent a result of the failure of biblical archaeologists (most of whom are still working in the spirit of the culture history school) to identify the 'archaeological cultures' of the Israelites, Gibeonites, Jebusites, etc., and to distinguish between them. As we have seen above, it is the failure to distinguish between those archaeological cultures, along with the skeptical approaches in biblical studies and the indirect negative influence of the (long ago dead) new archaeology which have led to the currently held pessimistic assessment. Clearly, the skeptical stance is based on very shaky methodological foundations.

Identifying Ethnicity in the Archaeological Record: Some Preliminary Observations

It is accepted today that social groups define themselves in relation to, and in contrast with, other groups (Barth 1969; see also R. Cohen 1978a: 389; A.P. Cohen 1985: 558). The ethnic boundaries of a group are not defined by the sum of cultural traits contained by it but by the idiosyncratic use of specific material and behavioral symbols as compared with other groups (McGuire 1982: 160; see also Kamp and Yoffe 1980: 96; Emberling 1997: 299; Barth 1969: 14, 15; Hall 1997: 135). McGuire (1982: 163) points out that overt material symbols of ethnic identity (ethnic markers, e.g., yarmulke) are the clearest evidence of the maintenance of an ethnic boundary. However, such markers are scarce in the archaeological record. Furthermore, grasping the symbolic significance of artifacts can be extremely difficult. While all groups may communicate messages of identity through material culture, the vehicles used differ by group, message, and context. Which artifact can express a boundary of a group depends on the ideas people in that society have about what 'an appropriate artifact for group marking' is (Hodder 1991: 3), but the selection may seem arbitrary to outside observers. One group might choose elements of clothing, while another might choose ceramics. Pinpointing those elements of material culture that were meaningful to any particular group, and determining when to attribute significance to an observed variation in the distribution of certain artifacts is, therefore, a complicated endeavor.

Notably, in addition to ethnic markers, ethnicity can also be identified by 'ethnically specific behavior', or more accurately, by the material correlates of such behavior. Such behavioral differences might include, in McGuire's (1982: 163) words, 'variations in rubbish disposal patterns...or differences in floor plans of dwellings, which reflect differing behavioral requirements for space'.

This ethnic behavior is much easier to identify than ethnic markers, as archaeology is to a large extent a 'behavioral science'. As an instructive example, one can consider the 'Parting Ways' site in Plymouth, Massachusetts, which was inhabited by freed African slaves following the American Revolution (Deetz 1996: 187-211). Excavations at the site revealed a material culture generally similar to that of contemporary sites, but as observed by Deetz (1996: 210), there existed real differences in house construction, trash disposal, and community arrangement as compared to these sites—differences that could have been overlooked based on a 'traditional' analysis of the artifacts themselves. So it is not the artifacts themselves that necessarily carry any ethnic importance, but the use made of these artifacts that is potentially important. Another, better known, example, is the lack of pig bones in Israelite sites. This is not the place to discuss the relation between pig consumption and ethnicity (Hesse 1986, 1990; Hesse and Wapnish 1997; Faust 2006: 35-40), but it is clear that if they bear any connection, the absence of pigs is not an ethnic marker but a result of an ethnic behavior.

It should also be noted that in many cases there are elements (artifacts, decoration, etc.), that are used to convey messages to other members of the group, and are connected to intra-group communication. In many cases, however, those elements are not spread evenly across the human landscape, and are used by members of a specific group only—the group which uses it for its inter-group communication—hence, as a by-product, they 'are likely to offer not only good but the best evidence of "ethnicity" generally preserved in the archaeological record' (David *et al.* 1988: 378; see also Hodder 1982).

Notably, social dimensions such as economic status, prestige, religion, occupation, urban or rural setting, and other factors may all affect the symbolic content of artifacts (McGuire 1982: 164; see also Kamp and Yoffee 1980: 97; London 1989; Skjeggestand 1992: 179-80; Orser and Fagan 1995: 215-16; Emberling 1997: 305-6, 310-11; see also Finkelstein 1996: 204). Contradictions between different kinds of symbols may confound interpretations even further, such as when a member of an ethnic group characterized by a low economic status attains a higher status, or in elite dwellings, when the finds might include both symbols of solidarity with the local group along with symbols of solidarity with its peers. The latter message might at times contradict the former.

In order to differentiate between the various 'combinations of effects,' a full examination of the society should be undertaken to identify all the social dimensions relevant to material culture production and symbolization (see Kamp and Yoffee 1980). Only after the other elements have been identified can we attribute ethnic labels to some traits of material culture. The second step, of course, should be to find the tangible connection between those material traits and the ethnic group under discussion. The difficulties inherent in any attempt to identify symbolic traits in the archaeological record require the use of a very large database, but also that attention be given to written sources. Although sometimes quite problematic, a careful examination of these sources is needed in order to extract maximum information and gain insights into the society in question (see also Hall 1997: 142).

The Way Forward

As we have seen, the archaeology of ancient Israel is still, to a large extent, divorced from anthropology. That poses a clear problem to any attempt to study ethnicity, which is, after all, an anthropological question.

It is insufficient, however, simply to conduct better, more anthropologically oriented studies of 'ethnicity' in the Iron Age. Ethnicity is but one aspect of social life, and probably the most illusive of them (Renfrew 1993: 20), and it cannot be studied in isolation from other aspects of society. Likewise, it should only be tackled after such issues as economic structure, inequality, class, gender, social organization, cosmology, and worldviews have been adequately dealt with. Unfortunately, much of the study of Israelite ethnicity has been conducted only as a by-product of studies by scholars more focused on the reconstruction (or deconstruction) of political, or biblical, history. Whereas they correctly understood that the general history of ancient Israel is inseparable from the issue of ethnicity, most of these scholars did not pay attention to other aspects of Israelite society and this is a major obstacle in any attempt to gain a real insight into Israelite ethnicity. Only when combined with detailed studies of all aspects of Israelite society is there a good chance of identifying ethnicity in the period's archaeological record.

Archaeology of the Israelites

Space is insufficient for a serious discussion of archaeology and Israelite ethnicity, but in the following few paragraphs I would like to hint at several promising directions (for a detailed discussion see Faust 2006).

The possible importance of food habits, and mainly the avoidance of pigs, is a well-known example of a trait that seems to have been ethnically meaningful during the Iron Age. While not without problems (e.g. Hesse and Wapnish 1997), it is commonly accepted today that the Israelites avoided the consumption of pork, and that this variable is ethnically sensitive (see even Finkelstein 1996: 206).

To this, one can now add additional variables. Following a detailed discussion of various aspects of Israelite society (e.g. Faust 2005, 2006, in press), several patterns, which are not connected with class, wealth, occupation, gender, or similar factors, can be identified and, moreover, be directly connected with ethnic behavior. Among those, one can list the tendency of the Israelites not to decorate their pottery, to avoid imported pottery, to bury their dead in simple inhumations (during most of the Iron Age), and several other traits, many of which seems to share a common denominator, and appear to result from a shared ethos: an ethos of simplicity and egalitarianism which was created as part of a boundary maintenance during Israel's ethnogenesis (Faust 2006; see also Faust 2004). Some of these traits partake in Israelite society's *internal* communications and negotiations, but as a by-product can serve as clear indications for Israel's external boundaries (for a detailed discussion, see Faust 2006, and references). Most traits, however, were chosen directly as part of negotiations (and boundary maintenance) with other groups, and are therefore in explicit contrast with traits and behaviors of those groups (Faust 2006; see also Levy and Holl 2002: 112-13).

Summary and Conclusions

The widespread skeptical approaches toward the ability of archaeology to identify ethnic groups in the archaeological record of ancient Israel are unwarranted. It is based on the failure of the culture-history approach to identify archaeological cultures which correspond with the groups mentioned in the Bible on the one hand, and on outdated views on the nature of the archaeology of ethnicity on the other.

The existing gap between the archaeology of ancient Israel and anthropological archaeology is damaging, and is partially responsible for the dead-end we are facing when studying ethnicity in ancient Israel. Indeed, a number of more anthropological or anthropologically oriented studies conducted recently (Levy and Holl 2002; Dever 2003; Bloch-Smith 2003; Miller 2004; Killebrew 2005; Faust 2006) identify ancient Israel archaeologically, and will, in my opinion, change what seems currently like a 'skeptic' discourse.

While better-informed studies of ethnicity will overcome what appears like a dead-end, it should be stressed that this is not sufficient. Biblical Archaeology should not only open up to more 'theoretical' or 'anthropological' studies of ethnicity, but widen its research agenda, in order to embrace the study of society in all its aspects. One cannot study ethnicity in isolation, even if it is a 'hot' and 'sexy' issue, as it is but one, very complex aspect of society.

A detailed study of the societies involved will enable us to learn about family structure, community organization, wealth, economic structures, gender relations, etc., which in turn will allow us to identify ethnic behaviors, and even ethnic symbols. Only detailed knowledge will allow us insights into the society's cognitive world, including its identity.

The relations between Biblical Archaeology and anthropological archaeology, however, need not be one-sided, i.e., the former borrowing from the latter. Due to our extremely large database, the archaeology of ancient Israel has much to contribute to general anthropology. Due to the hundreds of planned excavations, thousands of salvage excavations, and extensive surveys, we currently posses enough data against which the conclusions of various studies can be examined and checked. In this respect, Israel is an archaeological laboratory, which was practically not used by general archaeology. The availability of many texts, as problematic as they are, is also a great advantage for the study of ethnic markers and behaviors. Texts are, after all, cultural documents of the society that produces them, regardless of their historicity (Murray 1998: xxxi; King and Stager 2001: 7). This is, therefore, another potential strength of our sub-discipline (see also Bunimovitz and Faust, this volume), and it supplements the advantages of our vast material database even further.

And this is the great promise that lies in Biblical Archaeology: Not only would a better interaction between Biblical Archaeology and anthropological archaeology help and greatly improve Biblical Archaeology in general and the study of ethnicity in ancient Israel in particular, but Biblical Archaeology has a great potential to contribute to anthropology. We should use this potential.

References

Aharoni, Y. (1970) New Aspects of Israelite Occupation in the North. In *Near Eastern Archaeology in the Twentieth Century: Essays in Honor of Nelson Glueck*, edited by J. Sanders (New York: Garden City): 254-67.

—(1979) *The Land of the Bible: A Historical Geography* (Philadelphia: Westminster Press).

Ahlstrom, G.W. (1984) Giloh: A Judahite or Canaanite Settlement? *IEJ* 34: 170-72.

Albright, W.F. (1937) Further Light on the History of Israel from Lachish and Megiddo. *BASOR* 68: 22-26.

—(1961) *The Archaeology of Palestine* (Harmondsworth: Penguin).

Anderson, B. (1983) *Imagined Communities: Reflections on the Origins and Spread and Nationalism* (London: Verso).

Atkinson, R.R. (1994) *The Origins of the Acholi of Uganda before 1800* (Philadelphia: University of Pennsylvania Press).

Banks, M. (1996) *Ethnicity: Anthropological Constructions* (London and New York: Routledge).

Barth, F. (1969) Introduction. In *Ethnic Groups and Boundaries*, edited by F. Barth (Boston: Little, Brown & Co.): 9-38.

Binford, L.R. (1962) Archaeology as Anthropology. *AmAnt* 28: 217-25.

—(1965) Archaeological Systematics and the Study of Culture Process. *AmAnt* 31: 203-10.

Bloch-Smith, E. (2003) Israelite Ethnicity in Iron I: Archaeology Preserves what is Remembered and What is Forgotten in Israel's History. *JBL* 122: 401-25.

Bloch-Smith, E., and B. Alpert Nakhai (1999) A Landscape Comes to Life: The Iron I Period. *NEA* 62/2: 62-127.

Bunimovitz, S. (1999) Lifestyle and Material Culture: Behavioral Aspects of 12th Century B.C.E. Aegean Immigrants in Israel and Cyprus. In *Material Culture: Society and Ideology: New Directions in the Archaeology of the Land of Israel*, edited by A. Faust and A. Maeir (Ramat Gan: Bar-Ilan University): 146-60 (Hebrew).

—(2001) Cultural Interpretation and the Bible: Biblical Archaeology in the Postmodern Era. *Cathedra* 100: 27-46 (Hebrew).

Callaway, J.A. (1983) A Visit With Ahilud. *BAR* 9/5: 42-53.

Childe, G.V. (1929) *The Danube in Prehistory* (Oxford: Oxford University Press).

—(1951) *Social Evolution* (New York: Henry Schuman).

Clark, J.J. (2001) *Tracking Prehistoric Migrations. Pueblo Settlers among the Tonto Basin Hohokam* (Tucson: University of Arizona Press).

Cohen, A.P. (1985) *The Symbolic Construction of Community* (Chichester/London: Ellis Horwood & Tabistock).

Cohen, R. (1978a) Ethnicity: Problem and Focus in Anthropology. *ARA* 7: 379-403.

Comaroff, J., and J. Comaroff (1992) *Ethnography and Historical Imagination* (Boulder: Westview Press).

David, N., J. Sterner, and K. Gavua (1988) Why Pots are Decorated. *CA* 29: 365-89.

Davies, P. (1992) *In Search of 'Ancient Israel'* (Sheffield: Sheffield Academic Press).

Davis, T.W. (2004) *Shifting Sands: The Rise and Fall of Biblical Archaeology* (New York: Oxford University Press).

De Boer, W.R. (1990) Interaction, Imitation, and Communication as Expressed in Style: The Ucayali Experience. In *The Uses of Style in Archaeology*, edited by M.W. Conkey and C.A. Hastorf (Cambridge: Cambridge University Press): 82-104.

Deetz, J. (1996) *In Small Things Forgotten: An Archaeology of Early American Life* (New York: Anchor).

Dever, W.G. (1981) The Impact of the 'New Archaeology' on Syro-Palestinian Archaeology. *BASOR* 242: 15-29.

—(1991) Archaeological Data on the Israelite Settlement: A Review of Two Recent Works. *BASOR* 284: 77-90.

—(1992a) Archaeology: Syro-Palestinian and Biblical. In *ABD* 1:354-67.

—(1992b) How To Tell A Canaanite from an Israelite? In *The Rise of Ancient Israel*, edited by H. Shanks (Washington: Biblical Archaeology Society): 26-56.

—(1994) From Tribe to Nation: State Formation Processes in Ancient Israel. In *Nouve Fondenzioni Nel Vicino Oriente Antico. Realta' E Ideologia*, edited by S. Mazzoni (Pisa: Giardini Editori e Stampatori in Pisa): 213-29.

—(1995a) Ceramics, Ethnicity, and the Questions of Israel's Origins. *BA* 58/4: 200-213.

—(1995b) Will the Real Israel Please Stand Up? Archaeology and Israelite Historiography. *BASOR* 297: 61-80.

—(1995c) Will the Real Israel Please Stand Up? Part II: Archaeology and the Religions of Ancient Israel. *BASOR* 298: 37-58.

—(1997) Biblical Archaeology. In *Oxford Encyclopedia of Archaeology in the Near East* (New York: Oxford University Press): 315-19.

—(1998) Archaeology, Ideology, and the Quest for an 'Ancient' or 'Biblical' Israel. *NEA* 61/1: 39-52.

—(2003) *Who Were the Israelites and Where Did They Come From?* (Grand Rapids: Eerdmans).

Edelman, D. (2002) Ethnicity and Early Israel. In *Ethnicity and the Bible*, edited by M.G. Brett (Leiden: Brill): 25-55.

Emberling, G. (1997) Ethnicity in Complex Societies: Archaeological Perspectives. *Journal of Archaeological Research* 5/4: 295-344.

Engberg, R. (1940) Historical Analysis of Archaeological Evidence: Megiddo and the Song of Deborah. *BASOR* 78: 4-9.

Esse, D.L. (1991) The Collared Store Jar: Scholarly Ideology and Ceramic Typology. *SJOT* 2: 99-116.

—(1992) The Collared Pithos at Megiddo: Ceramic Distribution and Ethnicity. *JNES* 51: 81-103.

Faust, A. (2004) Mortuary Practices, Society and Ideology: The Lack of Highlands Iron Age I Burials in Context. *IEJ* 54: 174-90.

—(2005) *The Israelite Society in the Period of the Monarchy: An Archaeological Perspective* (Jerusalem: Yad Ben Zvi [Hebrew]).

—(2006) *Israel's Ethnogenesis: Settlement, Interaction, Expansion and Resistance* (London: Equinox).

—(in press) *The Archaeology of Israelite Society in Iron Age II* (Winona Lake: Eisenbrauns).

Faust, A., and Z. Safrai (2005) Salvage Excavations as a Source for Reconstructing Settlement History in Ancient Israel. *PEQ* 137: 139-58.

Finkelstein, I. (1988) *The Archaeology of the Period of Settlement and Judges* (Jerusalem: Israel Exploration Society).

—(1996) Ethnicity and the Origin of the Iron I Settlers in the Highlands of Canaan: Can the Real Israel Stand Up? *BA* 59/4: 198-212.

Finkelstein, I., and N. Na'aman (eds.) (1994) *From Nomadism to Monarchy* (Jerusalem: Yad Ben-Zvi).

Finkelstein, I., and N.A. Silberman (2001) *The Bible Unearthed: Archaeology's New Vision of Ancient Israel and the Origin of its Sacred Texts* (New York: Touchstone).

—(2006) *David and Solomon: In Search of the Bible's Sacred Kings and the Roots of the Western Tradition* (New York: Free Press).

Flannery, K.V. (1973) Archaeology with a Capital S. In *Research and Theory in Current Archaeology*, edited by C.L. Redman (New York: Wiley): 47-53.

Gellner, E. (1983) *Nations and Nationalism* (Oxford: Blackwell).

Geva, S. (1992) Israeli Biblical Archaeology—The First Years. *Zmanim* 42: 92-102 (Hebrew).

Gottwald, N.K. (1979) *The Tribes of Yahweh* (New York: Orbis Books).

Grosby, S. (2002) *Biblical Ideas of Nationality: Ancient and Modern* (Winona Lake, IN: Eisenbrauns).

Hall, J.M. (1997) *Ethnic Identity in Greek Antiquity* (Cambridge: Cambridge University Press).

Herzog, Z. (1997) Phoenician Occupation at Tel Michal: The Problem of Identifying Ethnic-National Groups from Archaeological Assemblages. *Michmanim* 11: 31-44 (Hebrew).

Hesse, B. (1986) Animal Use at Tel Miqne-Ekron in the Bronze Age and Iron Age. *BASOR* 264: 17-28.

—(1990) Pig Lovers and Pig Haters: Patterns of Palestinian Pork Production. *Journal of Ethnobiology* 10: 195-225.

Hesse, B., and P. Wapnish (1997) Can Pig Remains be Used for Ethnic Diagnosis in the Ancient Near East? In *The Archaeology of Israel: Constructing the Past, Interpreting the Present*, edited by N.A. Silberman and D. Small (JSOTSup 237; Sheffield: Sheffield Academic Press): 238-70.

Hodder, I. (1982) *Symbols in Action: Ethnoarchaeological Studies of Material Culture* (Cambridge: Cambridge University Press).

—(1991) *Reading the Past* (Cambridge: Cambridge University Press).

—(1992) *Theory and Practice in Archaeology* (London: Routledge).

Howard, M.C. (1996) *Contemporary Cultural Anthropology* (New York: HarperCollins).

Ibrahim, M.M. (1975) Third Season of Excavation at Sahab, 1975 (Preliminary Report). *ADAJ* 20: 69-82.

—(1978) The Collared-Rim Jar of the Early Iron Age. In Moorey and Parr 1978: 116-26.

Johnson, M. (1999) *Archaeological Theory: An Introduction* (Oxford: Blackwell).

Jones, S. (1997) *The Archaeology of Ethnicity: Constructing Identities in the Past and Present* (London: Routledge).

Kamp, K., and N. Yoffee (1980) Ethnicity in Western Asia during the Early Second Millennium B.C.: Archaeological Assemblages and Ethnoarchaeological Perspectives. *BASOR* 237: 85-104.

Kempinski, A. (1995) To What Extent were the Israelites Canaanites? *Archeologya: Bulletin of the Israel Association of Archaeologists* 4: 58-64 (Hebrew).

Killebrew, A.E. (2005) *Biblical Peoples and Ethnicity: An Archaeological Study of Egyptians, Canaanites, Philistines, and Early Israel 1300–1100 B.C.E.* (Atlanta: SBL).

King, P.J., and L.E. Stager (2001) *Life in Biblical Israel* (Louisville: Westminster/John Knox Press).

Lemche, N.P. (1998) The Origin of the Israelite State—A Copenhagen Perspective on the Emergence of Critical Historical Studies of Ancient Israel in Recent Times. *SJOT* 12: 44-63.

Levine, L.I., and A. Mazar (2001) *The Controversy Over the Historicity of the Bible* (Jerusalem: Yad Ben-Zvi [Hebrew]).

Levy, T.E., and A.F.C. Holl (2002) Migrations, Ethnogenesis, and Settlement Dynamics: Israelites in Iron Age Canaan and Shuwa-Arabs in the Chad Basin. *JAA* 21: 83-118.

London, G. (1989) A Comparison of Two Contemporaneous Lifestyles of the Late Second Millennium B.C.'. *BASOR* 273: 37-55.

Mazar, A. (1980) *Excavations at Tell Qasile*. Part 1. *The Philistine Sanctuary: Architecture and Cult Objects* (Qedem 12; Jerusalem: Hebrew University).

—(1990) Iron Age I and II Towers at Giloh. *IEJ* 40: 77-101.

—(1992) The Iron Age I. In *The Archaeology of Israel*, edited by A. Ben-Tor (New Haven: Yale University Press): 258-301.

—(1994) Jerusalem and its Vicinity in Iron Age I. In Finkelstein and Na'aman 1994: 70-91.

Mazar, B. (1981) The Early Israelite Settlement in the Hill Country. *BASOR* 241: 75-85.

McGuire, R.H. (1982) The Study of Ethnicity in Historical Archaeology. *JAA* 1: 159-78.

McNairn, B. (1980) *The Method and Theory of V. Gordon Childe* (Edinburgh: Edinburgh University Press).

Miller, J.M., and J.H. Hayes (1986) *A History of Ancient Israel and Judah* (Philadelphia: Westminster Press).

Miller, R.D. (2004) Identifying Earliest Israel. *BASOR* 333: 55-68.

Moorey, P.R.S. (1991) *A Century of Biblical Archaeology* (Louisville: Westminster/John Knox Press).

Moorey, R., and P. Parr (eds.) (1978) *Archaeology in the Levant: Essays for Kathleen Kenyon* (Warminster: Aris & Phillips).

Murray, O. (1998) Introduction. In J. Burckhardt, *The Greeks and Greek Civilization* (New York: St. Martin's Press): xi-xliv.

Na'aman, N. (1994) The 'Conquest of Canaan' in the Book of Joshua and in History. In Finkelstein and Na'aman 1994: 218-81.

Orser, C.E., and B.M. Fagan (1995) *Historical Archaeology* (New York: HarperCollins).

Parr, P.R. (1978) Pottery, People and Politics. In Moorey and Parr 1978: 202-9.

Pasto, J. (1998) When the End is the Beginning? Or When the Biblical Past is the Political Present: Some Thought on Ancient Israel, 'Post Exilic Judaism', and the Politics of Biblical Scholarship. *SJOT* 12: 157-202.

Rainey, A.F. (1994) The 'House of David' and the House of the Deconstructionists. *BAR* 20/6: 47.

Rendsburg, G.A. (1999) Down with History, Up with Reading: The Current State of Biblical Studies. *A Lecture at the McGill University Department of Jewish Studies Thirtieth Anniversary Conference: The Academy Reports to the Community*, May 9–10, 1999 (an expanded text of this lecture with notes can be found online: http://www.arts.mcgill.ca/programs/jewish/30yrs/rendsburgh/index.html).

Renfrew, C. (1993) *The Roots of Ethnicity, Archaeology, Genetics and the Origins of Europe* (Rome: Unione Internazionale degli Instituti de archaeologia, storia e storia dell arte in Roma).

—(1994) Toward a Cognitive Archaeology. In *The Ancient Mind: Elements of Cognitive Archaeology*, edited by C. Renfrew and E.B.W. Zubrow (Cambridge: Cambridge University Press): 3-12.

Renfrew, C., and P. Bahn (1996) *Archaeology: Theories, Methods and Practice* (London: Thames & Hudson).

Ryman, R.L., M.J. O'Brien, and R.C. Dunnell (1997) *The Rise and Fall of Culture History* (New York: Plenum Press).

Schortman, E.M., P.A. Urban, and M. Ausec (2001) Politics with Style: Identity Formation in Prehispanic Southern Mesoamerica. *American Anthropologist* 103/2: 312-30.

Shenan, S. (1991) Some Current Issues in the Archaeological Identification of Past Peoples. *Archaeologia Polona* 29: 29-37.

Shennan, J.S. (1989) Introduction: Archaeological Approaches to Cultural Identity. In *Archaeological Approaches to Cultural Identity*, edited by J.S. Shennan (London: Unwin Hyman): 1-32.

Skjeggestand, M. (1992) Ethnic Groups in Early Iron Age Palestine: Some Remarks on the Use of the Term 'Israelite' in Recent Literature. *SJOT* 6: 159-86.

Smith, A. (1986) *The Ethnic Origins of Nation* (Oxford: Blackwell).

—(1994) The Politics of Culture: Ethnicity and Nationalism. In *Companion Encyclopedia of Anthropology*, edited by T. Ingold (London: Routledge): 706-33.

Stager, L.E. (1985) Mernephtah. Israel and the Sea Peoples: New Light on an Old Relief. *Eretz Israel* 18: 56*-64*.

—(1998) Forging an Identity: The Emergence of Ancient Israel. In *The Oxford History of the Biblical World*, edited by M.D. Coogan (New York: Oxford University Press): 123-75.

Thompson, T.L. (1999) *The Bible in History: How Writers Create A Past* (London: Jonathan Cape).

—(2000) Lester Grabbe and Historiography: An Apologia. *SJOT* 14/1: 140-61.

Trigger, B. (1989) *A History of Archaeological Thought* (Cambridge: Cambridge University Press).

Whitelam, K.W. (1996) *The Invention of Ancient Israel: The Silencing of Palestinian History* (London: Routledge).

Williamson, H.G.M. (1998) The Origins of Israel: Can We Safely Ignore the Bible? In *The Origins of Early Israel—Current Debate: Biblical, Historical and Archaeological Perspectives*, edited by S. Ahituv and E.D. Oren (Beer-Sheva: Ben-Gurion University of the Negev): 141-51.

4 Biblical Archaeology as Social Action

Two Case Studies

David Ilan

Abstract

In many ways archaeology is a unique discipline. Though grounded in scholarship it has great appeal to the lay public and great potential as a participatory enterprise. Though grounded in the past, archaeology is embedded in the present and bears ramifications for the future. This is where politics come into play. This chapter describes two projects that seek to take advantage of these facets, projects which unabashedly adopt social and political agendas. One of these is an attempt to create a mutually invested relationship between an archaeological site (Givat Sher) and a community (Modi'in) and the other addresses questions of collective memory, narrative construction and political (dis)enfranchisement.

Biblical Archaeology was initially a European/American pursuit that served to illuminate and concretize the biblical world. In no small measure this was a reaction to Enlightenment rationalism, a paradigm which threatened the old certainties of biblical truth and even threatened the anchor of Judeo-Christian faith (e.g. Levy and Freedman 2008; Moorey 1991: 1-24; Silberman 1991; Trigger 1989: 102-3). At the same time, however, the earliest Biblical Archaeology adopted tools borne of rationalist thought and science: historical-geographical survey, systematic, stratigraphic excavation and material culture typology. But whatever form it took, whatever methods it employed, it was essentially an academic, elitist pursuit whose results only sometimes trickled down to the public, and even then in the form of filtered, already-interpreted knowledge.

In Israel the public was first engaged in the late 1920s, when the Zionist movement, almost as an afterthought, comprehended the potential of Biblical Archaeology as one means of legitimizing the Zionist enterprise (e.g. Elon 1994; Moorey 1991: 87-88; Shavit 1987). With the creation of the State of Israel in 1948, archaeology was integrated officially into the national *modus operandi*; the state began issuing stamps and currency with archaeological motifs (Zahavy 2009) and the army and Israeli volunteers participated in archaeological field work. The excavations at Tel Qasile, Hazor and Arad, for example, coincided with the arrival and settlement, in temporary tent camps and development towns, of immigrants, mainly from Arabic-speaking countries. Large-scale archaeological excavations were seen as an avenue of stopgap employment, cheap labor and as an educational opportunity—an opportunity to inculcate a biblical but secular historical narrative. As has been shown elsewhere, however (Shavit 1987), this last purpose was never truly realized and the larger

Israeli public pretty much ignored the program of Biblical Archaeology. The net result has been erosion in the public concern for cultural resources of antiquity, which seems be reflected in the reduction in state-sponsored archaeological work and concurrently, a gradual privatization of cultural resource management (Killebrew 1997).

All the contributors to this volume believe that archaeology still has redeeming social and cultural value, whatever the current that flows in the public mind. This being so, the question then becomes: What can we do to enhance the position of antiquity as a cultural resource? From another perspective I also ask: Can archaeology add to the public's quality of life? These are universal questions, but in the present paper I examine two case studies based on projects initiated by the Nelson Glueck School of Biblical Archaeology of the Hebrew Union College—Jewish Institute of Religion in Israel.

These two projects involve two different communities (the new Jewish town of Modi'in and the mixed Arab–Jewish population of the Galilee) and address two different sets of concerns. At the same time the two projects rest upon a common underlying conceptual and ideological foundation. Below, I outline the two projects, their goals, methodologies and interim results. The conclusions offered at the end concern the future of archaeology as social and political action.

The Givat Sher, Modi'in Community Archaeology Project[1]

Problem: The Mutual Alienation of Archaeological Research and the Public

While archaeology was an important part of Israeli national discourse in the nation-building phase, this is no longer the case (Killebrew forthcoming). With a few exceptions, archaeological sites are not frequently visited and tend to fall into disrepair; this is even true for some sites administered by the National Parks Authority. For most Israelis, archaeology is, at best, a curiosity. More often, it is just not on the radar. This lack of public concern for archaeology as a cultural resource contributes to the destruction of archaeological sites by plunder, development, vandalism and by simple neglect. Assuming the non-salubrious nature of this status quo, the question is: How to we rectify the situation? Previous research suggests that local community involvement is one key element (e.g. Edwards 1998; Marshall 2002) and our own experience in the field bears this out. What follows below is a series of statements regarding the relationship between the public and archaeology. Each statement is accompanied by a hypothesis concerning the possible solution to, or amelioration of, the social and archaeological problematic.

1. *Archaeology is an elitist pursuit.* For the most part, archaeology is an introverted, exclusive affair. It is administered by specialists acting either to answer research questions or to salvage cultural heritage threatened by development. In Israel the physical expediters of this work are usually paid laborers and, less often, volunteers or students who often pay a lot of money to dig. *Hypothesis: If the actual act of discovery becomes more accessible to a wider public, that public will become more invested in its archaeological heritage and more positively inclined toward professional archaeologists.*

2. *Archaeological sites are part of the existing natural and human environment.* Archaeological sites can be a nuisance (for developers, for example) or a boon (for plunderers, but also for the general public that sees cultural resources as a quality-of-life issue). *Hypothesis: If archaeologists actively pursue a program of education about, and appreciation of, archaeological resources the public will respond by actively resisting destruction of archaeological heritage.*

---

1. The primary investigators for the Givat Sher project are the author, Yuval Gadot, Yoav Farhi and Ron Lavi. The latter three are all residents of Modi'in or neighboring Maccabim.

3. *The community living closest to an archaeological site is the most likely to feel a sense of identification and appreciation for that site.* This may be especially so for newer towns where open spaces are at a premium. *Hypothesis: a program targeting and actively involving the local community most proximate to an archaeological site has the best chance of achieving long-term voluntary curatorship of that site, whether by organized or ad hoc means.*

Givat Sher: A Brief Description[2]

Horvat Sher (Umm es-Sur in Arabic)[3] was first mentioned in the publication of the British Survey of Western Palestine, conducted at the close of the 19th century (Conder and Kitchener 1882: 161). Since then it has been visited by several archaeological surveyors who reported various features—stone columns, walls and strange stone edifices of unknown function (Shavit n.d.).

Well-dressed stones can be seen in some of the terrace walls, indicating residential use. Sherds collected from the surface of the site teach us that the place was first settled during the Hellenistic period, during which time there existed a thriving village with a synagogue at nearby Umm el Umdan. Umm el Umdan was excavated several years ago by the Israel Antiquities Authority and tentatively identified by the excavators as ancient Modi'in of the Maccabees (Weksler-Bdolach, Onn, and Rapuano 2003).

The second period of occupation is the end of the Byzantine period (this is also the period during which the Talmud coalesced). A stone lintel with two crosses carved into it must have belonged to a church, so there was clearly a Christian community here. One question is, were there other groups here too?

The last period the site was settled is the medieval period, when it must have been a small farmstead, probably occupied by Moslem peasants. Today the area is a semi-wild olive grove, perhaps planted just prior to the 1948 war by peasants from the neighbouring village of Salbit, who fled with the onset of war (Khalidi 1992: 410; the site of Salbit is now occupied by a religious kibbutz, Sha'alabim).

Our research is still in its infancy. We now have our eye on the hill to the east where all the ruins reported by the explorers of old are found (this is part of our concession). Here we can make out stone-fenced enclosures and a great many agricultural installations—wine and oil presses, cisterns, terrace walls and threshing floors. The many stone huts and caves may have been dwellings. The date of these features is unknown, but our work in the coming years should provide answers.

Project Goals

Our primary goal in the Givat Sher project is to provide the people of Modi'in and its surrounding settlements with a fun, outdoor, educational activity. Academic research is truly secondary here. Honest.

Nevertheless, we have other motivations as well, as might be deduced from the assumptions and hypotheses listed above. For one thing, we fear for the future of the Modi'in region's archaeological heritage. Our feeling is that a community project that highlights the wealth and wonder of this heritage, one that involves hands-on exploration, will give the participants a desire to protect that heritage in an active way—to keep an eye on the bulldozers and a lookout for telltale signs of plunder. More generally, we feel that if archaeology is enjoyed by large numbers of individuals, and if these kinds of projects are set up in other parts of the country, we can build an archaeological 'lobby' that will help further protection of heritage throughout the country, in the long term.

---

2. A detailed preliminary report for the Givat Sher project appears in Farhi *et al.* 2009.
3. Horvat Sher is the name of the archaeological site; Givat Sher refers to the entire hill.

Our research goals are intended to be influenced by the community. To put it more academically, our research question is: Can social science and humanities research be conducted by professionals when non-professionals are posing the research questions? Clearly, this is partly a matter of establishing dialogue and presenting non-professionals with preliminary information that will enable them to formulate questions. At this point the questions we are addressing are: Who lived here before us, Jews, Christians, Moslems? Did they live together or do successive occupations represent homogeneous communities? If I find something, can I take it home with me?

Project Execution

In the Summer of 2003 Yuval Gadot, a graduate student at Tel Aviv University at the time and a resident of the new town of Modi'in, approached me with concern, and a proposal. Modi'in was developing at a rapid pace and open green spaces, archaeological sites included, were the bone of contention between developers and the municipality on the one hand and the citizens of Modi'in on the other. His proposal: to turn Givat Sher—a pristine Mediterranean maquis-covered hill and archaeological site of unknown qualities—into an active 'archaeological park', with the Hebrew Union College as the sponsoring institution. This was to be done in cooperation with the Society for the Preservation of Nature in Israel (SPNI), which already had a foothold in the town's education system and amongst the town's 'green' element.[4]

Starting September 1, 2003 the park was adopted by the nearby 'Nitzanim' elementary school, which uses Givat Sher for all kinds of outdoor activities. The formal act of adoption was intended to encourage local communities to take responsibility for the natural and cultural heritage within their purview. It is also a statement of 'stakeholdership', emphasizing community goals rather than research objectives that are purely academic. The school's adoption program includes a two-week excavation in the spring where students, parents and teachers all dig together. This event is followed by three more weeks of excavation, one more week in spring and two in the summer. During this time other citizens from the Modi'in area and beyond can join in—though again, young children must be accompanied by an adult. Altogether, approximately 600 people work at the site during the five-weeks we are in the field each year. We have estimated that about 20% of the excavators return for more than one day of digging. This rate generally increases toward the end of the season. In total, we reckon that around 2200 people have excavated at Horvat Sher in four seasons of work. Only 'Archaeological Seminars' excavations can claim larger numbers of participants, and these are mostly visitors from abroad. (Archaeological Seminars is a successful, for-profit, educational enterprise that has been working in recent years at Tel Maresha [Gertzberg 2006].)

Concurrently, the entire site and its surroundings have been subject to intensive survey, carried out mainly by high-school-age students and archaeologists (mainly Y. Gadot). The survey emphasizes landscape archaeology, i.e. the registry and mapping of landforms, vegetation cover, soils and agricultural and industrial installations (Farhi et al., in press). Geomagnetic survey has also been conducted in and near the excavation areas in order to better comprehend architectural layout and subterranean features, such as caves and cisterns, and to facilitate decision making as far as where to continue working in the future.

---

4.   I would like to take this opportunity to thank Sharona Houri and Tal Kimche of the SPNI for their part as equal partners in this project. Their experience with primary school education was crucial to the success of the Givat Sher initiative. Most instructive for all of us were the discussions that resulted from conflicts between preservation of nature and archaeological excavation.

Figure 1. Jewish pupils and parents of a 5th grade class from the Nitzanim Elementary School in Modi'in. Digging at Givat Sher over several seasons has generated a sense of identification and invested interest amongst many of the townspeople.

Figure 2. Sieving at Givat Sher: the staff were surprised at how well younger children could carry out even the more demanding rituals of a full-fledged archaeological excavation.

One of the great unknowns concerned the quality and standard of excavation that could be expected from inexperienced and often very young workers. Raw recruits are placed in topsoil and fill contexts, where they find a great deal of cultural material without doing any damage. In this way, initiates learn the tools and techniques of excavation—to discern pottery, glass, tesserae, bone and metal—before they graduate to more sensitive archaeological contexts. Many of the returnees are becoming highly proficient. Admittedly, some never graduate from topsoil and fills.

Classroom study is generally part of the program; several preparatory lessons are taught either by the HUC staff, SPNI educators or the school teachers themselves. Follow-up is also essential—a vitrine was set up at Nitzanim Elementary displaying some of the finds from previous seasons and the city of Modi'in is planning to build a regional museum. Finally, a yearly symposium, dealing with the history, archaeology and geography of the Modi'in region, has been established by the vice mayor of Modi'in, Mr. Alex Weinraub. The proceedings are published in Hebrew. This is the place to note that the Modi'in Municipality is also a full partner in the Givat Sher community archaeology project, providing logistical support, publicity and lots of positive feedback.

Preliminary Conclusions

There is a palpable sense that the community has responded positively. Most citizens of Modi'in and its surrounding villages know about the community excavation and view it as something special that their city offers its residents. Unfortunately, most of them don't know that the primary instigator is Hebrew Union College, but this is secondary at the moment. Givat Sher is now a popular picnic site and vandalism is not a significant problem so far. I can also offer up several more specific conclusions:

1.   Given well-thought-out parameters, inexperienced excavators, even very young children, can dig and even dig well. With enough encouragement and perseverance these volunteers might become an important sector in the archaeological 'work force' of the future.

2.   Community archaeology programs involve, by definition, multiple partners, or 'stakeholders' in modern cultural resource management (CRM) jargon. Networking with multiple partners requires a significant amount of energy and time. And it requires negotiating what are sometimes conflicting agendas.

3.   If we archaeologists are willing to invest of ourselves we can be public servants in the most direct and concrete of ways. By being so we can also help to strengthen local identity and enhance quality of life. In terms of long-term self-interest, community archaeology leads to increased protection of archaeology patrimony and creates a long-term positive image for the discipline.

4.   With all the energy expended on dealing with multiple stakeholders, we have found that it is still possible to carry out a rigorous scientific research project that includes research questions, methodological discussion, hypothesis testing and the presentation of conclusions (Farhi *et al.*, in press)

5.   Excavating a multi-period site occupied in turn by Jews, Christians, Muslims and then again, Jews, creates the opportunity to explore the subject of multiple and conflicting narratives. This can be an inroad for political sophistication and the avoidance of black-and-white perceptions of a complex political reality. Moreover, a community that excavates a multi-period site gains an appreciation of long-term historical and ecological processes, in a way that increases environmental awareness.

The Tel Dan 'Digging for Coexistence' Project[5]

Problem: Archaeology in Israel has been an integral part of constructing the Zionist narrative. Palestinians are excluded from this narrative by Jews and non-local Christians, reject it from their own perspective and, as a byproduct, are alienated from archaeology.

Brief Description

The Tel Dan excavation project was conceived in 1966 by Avraham Biran, first as a salvage dig and then as a standard research excavation (for a chronicle of excavations, see Biran 1996, 2002). It is one of the northernmost sites in modern Israel and is part of one of Israel's most visited national parks. As such it is a major conceptual reference point for establishing Israel's territorial integrity—not a foregone conclusion in the present state of affairs.

The culture history of Tel Dan consists mainly of Bronze Age and Iron Age levels, including much that is monumental in scale—fortifications, public buildings and a national cult place mentioned in the Bible (e.g. 1 Kgs 12:29). The Israeli government Tourism Corporation and the Nature Reserves and Parks Authority have also made a large investment in restoration and reconstruction work. In no small measure this is because Tel Dan exhibits some of the most visible and impressive ancient Israelite remains in the country, though some of these are probably Aramean (Arie 2008). More detailed accounts of the findings at Tel Dan can be found in Biran (1993, 1994) and Ilan (1997).

Assumptions

1. As a 'biblical' site, Tel Dan is part of the biblical narrative cherished by Christians and Jewish Israelis (more specifically, Zionist Israelis). In and of itself, this is natural and positive.

2. Tel Dan, like other biblical sites, is not considered part of Palestinian cultural heritage, not by most Palestinians (whether Muslim or Christian) and certainly not by most Jewish Israelis.

3. Jewish collective memory, as informed by the biblical narrative and later rabbinic sources, asserts a territorial claim on the Land of Israel. At the same time, Palestinian collective memory, as informed by generations of Palestinians who have lived in Palestine long before, during and after the influx of modern Zionist immigrants, asserts a territorial claim on Palestine, which essentially corresponds to the Land of Israel.

4. Neither Israeli Jews nor Palestinians show any large-scale inclination to leave their homeland or to abandon their territorial claim.

5. While peace negotiations may result in a two-state solution (and even if they don't) the 'Jewish State' (Israel) will continue to contain a large Arab population (not to mention Druze and others). If this country's inhabitants wish to achieve the quality of life fostered by peace, we should find a way to live together.

6. A discussion of the distant past, where the roots of our conflict lie, can be a starting point for peaceful coexistence. Archaeological excavation at a biblical site is a good platform for this discussion. This is especially true when working with youth, whose minds are less conditioned, when digging is fun and when the program takes place in a neutral setting.

---

5. The Tel Dan 'coexistence project' is directed by the author, Mr. Ali Ayoub (scoutmaster of the town of Shfar'am) and Mr. Omar Asfour (Geography and Heritage teacher at the Kabul Village High School).

Project Goals

At its foundation, this project emphasizes co-existence. This greater goal may be furthered by creating a forum for dialogue and communication between Palestinians and Jews, mainly Jewish Israelis. Non-Jewish and non-Palestinian students and volunteers have a role to play as facilitators and commentators. More specific goals include:

1. Imparting an understanding of the chronological and cultural framework of ancient history. This framework serves as the foundation for the more philosophical debates concerning interpretation of the remains of the past that come later.

2. Imparting an understanding of how archaeological, historical and literary data can be interpreted in different ways, depending on the background of the interpreter and the questions she or he is asking.

3. Imparting an understanding of how Palestinians, Christians, Muslims, Jews, Israelis, Americans, Arabs, etc. have arrived at their own interpretive syntheses (meta-narratives), how these narratives differ, and why.

4. Providing the students and volunteers with an enjoyable experience that will result in a more intimate and personal understanding of people who are portrayed as the 'enemy', demonized by ingrained prejudice, political demagoguery and media complicity. These young people, who are the future, should learn that there is someone to talk to on the other side.

5. Move dirt and discover the past.

Project Execution

The Hebrew Union College Tel Dan Expedition has hosted a group of 20 Jewish and Arab junior high school students over three excavation seasons between 2003 and 2007. These students come from the western Galilee villages of Shfar'am, Kabul, Hanita, Harduf and the eastern Galilee village of Jish (Gush Halav). They are a pre-selected group, mostly being comprised of good students who *want* to participate and view participation as a sort of prize—an all-expenses-paid archaeology jamboree. They also show up with curiosity about, and a willingness to deal with, 'the other'.

Until now the students have come for one week only. This is due to financial limitations; we would like to be able to host at least two groups of 20 each for two further weeks in the season. We find that it is best for the students to comprise a minority within the larger group of older students and volunteers from around the world. The latter provide a framework and atmosphere of intellectual seriousness and emotional maturity that establishes healthy limits and expectations for the younger students.

Ideally, the Galilee students get together in six meetings before the dig commences, to learn the basics of archaeology—stratigraphy, typology and digging technique. One of the meetings is a field trip to a local archaeological site. These meetings are the first opportunity for the students to get to know each other. In fact, this has not always worked out, given the reality of busy parents, busy kids and driving distances. Experience has taught us, however, that such preliminary meetings make for a better dig experience.

Thus far the Galilee students have arrived for the second or third week of excavation. This ensures that the older students and volunteers, who have absorbed excavation technique, can guide the younger ones. It also ensures, once again, that the younger kids enter a clear framework of operation with clear expectations. The younger students do everything the older students do: digging, sieving, pottery washing, pottery sorting and the like. They do not attend the same lectures however. Rather, we conduct parallel before-dinner lectures and discussions about archaeology and after-dinner sessions that deal with politics, competing narratives and interpretation of data and interpersonal relations. It is here that the most difficult discussions and confrontations take place.

Figure 3. Jewish and Arab kids working together with American and European volunteers at Tel Dan in 2005. The act of discovery and the nature of hard work were highly effective bonding mechanisms.

Figure 4. Jewish and Arab kids washing pottery at Tel Dan under the supervision of Hebrew Union College student Greg Snyder. This was an opportunity to explore the implications of Bronze and Iron Age artifacts for the Arab-Israeli conflict.

Every session so far has ended on a good note—many kids continue to be in contact with each other and with the older students and volunteers. Many want to come back the next season (only two are chosen to do so).

Preliminary Conclusions

The Tel Dan project is more overtly political than the Givat Sher/ Modi'in project. It addresses directly the source of the conflict in the Middle East between Israel and the Arabs. As a result the atmosphere can be tenser at times and the outcome is less predictable. Since its inception in 2005 the Tel Dan 'Digging for Coexistence' project has led us to the following conclusions:

- When people work together in close contact, within a defined framework with a monitoring presence, doing something they enjoy, social and psychological barriers fall and mutual trust is gradually instilled. This is also true for groups with a history of enmity. We know this works at least for young people. Fear of the demonized 'other', lack of mutual respect and besmirched honor are key factors in the Middle East conflict. If we can alleviate these factors, we will have done half our work.
- When different groups of people with different cultural and political perspectives gather together to explicitly examine differing historical narratives sparks may fly, but critical appraisal voiced openly introduces empowering possibilities. Working in real-time archaeology makes the deconstruction of historical narrative less threatening, since a powerful tool of narrative construction is immediately at hand. The examination of competing narratives by conflicted parties can lead to new understandings and openings for accommodation. There is room in Palestine/Israel for everyone and for both sides' narratives; it is not a zero-sum equation.
- It seems that the presence of a third group actor—the students and volunteers from abroad—creates a neutral atmosphere. The young Jewish and Palestinian students become part of an ongoing intellectual enterprise that is not an artificial construct designed solely as political action. We believe this reduces the stakes and therefore the potential for anxiety. The foreign volunteers also serve as observers and facilitators.
- Some of these youngsters may go on to study archaeology and to do research that is reflexive and politically aware. In any event, we hope that their experience at Tel Dan will be a course in the foundation of coexistence and part of an ongoing, open discourse about the meaning of the past for the present and the future.

Conclusions

In the preceding sections I have presented two different archaeological projects that have a social action component. These projects differ in some ways and in other ways they are similar. The Givat Sher/Modi'in project is oriented toward the local community and its stakeholders. The Tel Dan project is more international in scope and more overtly political in the strategic sense.

Certainly, there are limitations to working with inexperienced volunteers; these are mainly logistical. Working with neophytes requires a careful selection of venue, where limited dig experience and motor capabilities can be mediated by less sensitive archaeological contexts and readily available staff.

What do these two projects have in common? For one thing it is clear that archaeology can be used as a tool of social and political action; it is highly effective as such. Contrary to our initial expectations, according to which we anticipated young people as being the target group, this is true for youth and for adults of all ages. Archaeology can give people a more nuanced, long-term perspective of their place in the land and in history. The conflict in the Middle East is comprised of a thousand nuances. If we can instill a sense of complexity and demonstrate the possibility of multiple perspectives, our public may become more amenable to seeing the viewpoint of the other side.

Archaeology constructs stories out of material remains of the past (Shanks 1992: 186-88). Those who take part in creating the story, and those who consume the story, share an experience of emotional exposure and intimacy. This shared experience is the stuff of group solidarity. Perhaps, in our own small way, this newly fabricated group solidarity counters, or at least balances, the more negative forms of group solidarity—chauvinism, racism and nationalism. Archaeology *can* make a positive difference.

References

Arie, E. (2008) Reconsidering the Iron Age II Strata at Tel Dan: Archaeological and Historical Implications. *Tel Aviv* 35: 6-64.

Biran, A. (1993) Dan. In E. Stern (ed.), *The New Encyclopedia of Archaeological Excavations in the Holy Land* (Jerusalem: Carta): 323-32.

—(1994) *Biblical Dan* (Jerusalem: Hebrew Union College-Jewish Institute of Religion, Israel Exploration Society).

—(1996) A Chronicle of Excavations. In *Dan I, A Chronicle of the Excavations, the Pottery Neolithic, the Early Bronze Age and the Middle Bronze Age Tombs*, edited by A. Biran, D. Ilan and R. Greenberg (Annual of the Nelson Glueck School of Biblical Archaeology; Jerusalem: Hebrew Union College-Jewish Institute of Religion): 7-64.

—(2002) A Chronicle of Excavations. In *Dan II, A Chronicle of the Excavations and the Late Bronze Age 'Mycenaean' Tomb*, edited by A. Biran and R. Ben Dov (Annual of the Nelson Glueck School of Biblical Archaeology; Jerusalem: Hebrew Union College—Jewish Institute of Religion): 3-32.

Conder, C.R., and R.R. Kitchener (1882) *The Survey of Western Palestine*. III. *Samaria* (London: Committee of the Palestien Exploration Fund).

Edwards, J. (1998) The Need for a 'A Bit of History', Place and Past in English Identity. In *Locality and Belonging*, edited by N. Lovell (London/New York: Routledge): 147-67.

Elon, A. (1994) Politics and Archaeology. *New York Review of Books* 41 (September): 14-20.

Farhi, Y., Y. Gadot, D. Ilan, J. Pincus-Ben Avraham, I. Taxel, L. Tsfania and S. Bechar (2009) The Givat Sher-Modi'in Community-Based Excavation: Preliminary Report on the 2004–6 Seasons. *Strata: Bulletin of the Anglo-Israel Archaeological Society* 27: 89-150.

Gertzberg, C.O. (2006) Amateur Archaeologists Get the Dirt on the Past. *New York Times*. July 16, 2006. Travel Section (http://travel2.nytimes.com/2006/07/16/travel/16family.html).

Ilan, D. (1997) Tel Dan. In E. Meyers (ed.),*The Encyclopedia of Near Eastern Archaeology* (Oxford: Oxford University Press): 107-12.

Khalidi, W. (1992) *All That Remains: The Palestinian Villages Occupied and Depopulated by Israel in 1948* (Beirut: Institute for Palestine Studies).

Killebrew, A.E. (1997) Development and Archaeology. In *The Oxford Encyclopedia of Archaeology in the Near East*, vol. 2, edited by E.M. Meyers (New York: Oxford University Press): 151-56.

—(forthcoming) Who Owns the Past? Archaeological, Ideological, and Economic Considerations on Interpreting and Presenting the Past in Israel. In *Filtering the Past, Building the Future*, edited by L. Swartz-Dodd and R. Boytner (Tucson, AZ: University of Arizona Press).

Levy, T.E., and D.N. Freedman (2008) William Foxwell Albright: A Biographical Essay. *Proceedings of the National Academy of Science*: 1-29.

Marshall, Y. (2002) What is Community Archaeology? *World Archaeology* 34: 211-19.

Moorey, P.R.S. (1991) *A Century of Biblical Archaeology* (Louisville, KY: Westminster/John Knox).

Shanks, M. (1992) *Experiencing the Past: On the Character of Archaeology* (London: Routledge).

Shavit, A. (n.d.) *The Gezer Map* (unpublished manuscript in the Israel Antiquities Authority archives).

Shavit, Y. (1987) 'Truth will rise from the earth': Points in the Development of the Public Jewish Interest in Archaeology (until the 1930s). *Cathedra* 44: 27-54 (Hebrew).

Silberman, N.A. (1991) Desolation and Restoration: The Impact of a Biblical Concept on Near Eastern Archaeology. *BA* 54: 76-86.

Trigger, B.G. (1989) *A History of Archaeological Thought* (Cambridge: Cambridge University Press).

Weksler-Bdolach, S., A. Onn, and Y. Rapuano (2003) Identifying the Hasmonean Village of Modi'in. *Kathedra* 109: 69-86 (Hebrew with English summary).

Zahavy, Y. (2009) *Archaeology, Stamps and Coins of the State of Israel* (Lulu.com).

5 The Archaeology of the Levant in North America

The Transformation of Biblical and Syro-Palestinian Archaeology

Aaron A. Burke

Abstract

This chapter addresses a fundamental shift in the definition of archaeological research in the Levant since the so-called demise of 'Biblical Archaeology' in the early 1990s. It asserts that a consensus has emerged regarding the identity of this discipline throughout North America, which is now known as the archaeology of the Levant. The adoption of this term by archaeologists working in the Levant appears to reflect a fundamental shift that has occurred in the research agendas and strategies of North American scholars working within the region. In addition to an overview of programs in Levantine archaeology, suggestions are provided for the sustainability and growth of the discipline among North American institutions.

A little more than a decade ago after years of warning, William G. Dever (1995) proclaimed the death of 'Syro-Palestinian and Biblical Archaeology' in North America. He cited the rising costs of fieldwork, cutbacks in awards from funding agencies, reduced support for humanities, loss of church-related funding, the emergence of 'national schools' of archaeology, and Middle Eastern politics as the causes of this crisis. In the mid-1990s many college students who, like myself, were passionately interested in Syro-Palestinian archaeology felt faced with a dilemma after reading Dever's essay. The choice was either to give up before setting out to pursue an elusive career in archaeology and thereby avoid being unemployed with a 'useless' Ph.D. in the humanities, or pursue such a career knowing full well that we might remain unemployed after ten years of schooling. Over the past decade I have met numerous individuals who have made one or the other of these choices, and have viewed that choice in these terms. Nevertheless, had I not personally witnessed all too similar insecurities in corporate America I might also have pursued an entirely different career as a result of Dever's proclamation.

Although it is widely recognized today that Dever was correct regarding the disappearance of traditional 'Biblical Archaeology' (see Levy, this volume), the changes that have occurred within the discipline during the past two decades must not be viewed, however, as the death of a discipline but rather as a necessary, if painful, transformation of the study of what is appropriately identified today as the archaeology of the Levant. Thus, in what follows I will attempt to reflect upon the factors that have led to the emergence of Levantine archaeology in North America as an independent discipline, albeit born from 'Biblical' and 'Syro-Palestinian' archaeology. I will follow this with a broad survey of the research of a number of North American scholars who are engaged in archaeological research throughout the Levant. This review will serve to demonstrate that Levantine archaeology in North America has retained the advances of 'Biblical Archaeology', but has also recognized the need for redefining its objectives as an independent, diverse, and more vibrant discipline. Finally, I will conclude by considering the future of Levantine archaeology and suggest some practical strategies for assuring not only its survival but its growth within the university setting. I hope, therefore, that this contribution may be received as a positive vision of what the future of the archaeology of the Levant can still offer.

The Emergence of Levantine Archaeology in North America

A number of factors account for the gradual emergence during the past two decades of what is now widely identified as Levantine archaeology in North America. This approach has grown out of advances within 'Syro-Palestinian' archaeology, and before that from developments within 'Biblical' archaeology. This emergence is the result not only of the obstacles archaeology in this region has faced, some of which Dever has already articulated, but also out of a growing consensus regarding the appropriate terminology for the region and its family of cultures. Added to these factors are changes that have taken place among the priorities and strategies of individuals conducting archaeological field research in the Levant, as noted in the following section.

Although many of Dever's concerns regarding the demise of 'Biblical Archaeology' were perhaps shocking revelations during the mid-1990s (e.g. 1995, 1997, 1998, 2001), today it is evident that his concerns were pertinent not only to Levantine archaeology but also more generally to a funding crisis within the humanities. In Levantine archaeology this crisis has appeared all the more acute as a result of the fact that funding from other sources, such as church groups, has not only been lost but is for the most part no longer pursued except by a minority of institutions. While it is true that a great deal of funding previously came from confessional organizations, that funding from this source has been reduced—if not often entirely lost—does not condemn Levantine archaeology to failure. Rather, the keen awareness of this major change must drive us to seek funds from new sources, whether other organizations, individuals, or granting agencies—what we might call a 'broad-spectrum' approach to the solicitation of funds. It is important to recognize, however, that these trends that have been detrimental to higher education as a whole are, nevertheless, part of fundamental economic and demographic cycles, which for the most part remain beyond our abilities to change.[1] While these trends have certainly been detrimental to the humanities, as Dever has noted, other fields such as the sciences have not been protected from their effects and, thus they too have been forced to develop new strategies to cope with such uncertainties. Only months before starting a graduate degree program at the University of Chicago at the height of these uncertain times I recall taking a strange comfort in a *Chicago Tribune* article. It proclaimed that as in all other market sectors the hiring of university faculty remained cyclical (Worthington 1996). While the author painted a bleak picture for those 'on the market' at that time, the article provided a necessary reality

---

1. Note, however, that these are two predominantly unrelated trends, which when they are simultaneously at their worst, the effects are extremely acute. In the mid-1990s these trends included the lagging effects of a recession compounded by the lack of predicted demographic growth for colleges and universities. What long-term effects the recent economic downturn or crisis will have upon the discipline remain to be seen.

check at the start of a long and unpredictable road. That said, who could have anticipated the incredible economic developments between the mid-1990s and 2007, which was only been tapped in a most limited way for the funding and growth of Levantine archaeology?[2] From these observations it is safe to conclude that the funding of our discipline will by and large remain uncertain for the foreseeable future in the absence of concerted efforts to establish stable sources of funding for Levantine archaeology as a whole. Despite the fact that at present the state of humanities funding at North American institutions remains unfavorable, such funding structures alone cannot be relied upon to keep Levantine archaeology alive as a discipline.

What truly defines Levantine archaeology and will assure its survival will not alone be well-structured funding strategies, or unique, sound, and well-articulated research objectives for the Levant. The identification of the objectives of this discipline must begin, therefore, with a clear articulation of the appropriate terminology for our regionally focused discipline. Dever began this process when he revived the term 'Syro-Palestinian' archaeology in the late 1970s (2001). He suggested that the coverage of 'Syro-Palestinian' archaeology included 'southern-central Syria and Palestine…or more properly "Greater Canaan"' (2001: 62). One could argue, however, that after more than twenty years of advocacy, despite adoption of the term by some scholars, many, if not most, have demonstrated a predilection to identify this region as the *Levant*, a term which has been employed more frequently by European scholars.

The advantage of the term Levant is that, as defined by the scholars who have adopted it, its purview is not restricted to the areas identified, as, for example, by Dever. Rather, in common usage the Levant has also included western Syria, as well as the 'Amuq Valley and its tributaries in southern Turkey (e.g. the Hatay). Much work continues to be done in these regions, and not surprisingly this work is now of great interest to those studying the southern Levant (i.e. the region formerly identified as Syria-Palestine and including Canaan). Nevertheless, during the past thirty years most of the northern Levant has not been a part of the core curriculum and training of students of Syro-Palestinian archaeology at North American institutions. This fact is amply demonstrated by a survey of dissertations completed under North American scholars throughout this period. The overwhelming emphasis and scope of these works has been the southern Levant or, as the terms adopted in most of these Ph.D. dissertations suggest, 'Israel' and 'Canaan'. It is, however, only by considering the northern Levant alongside the south that it is possible to address broader historical and archaeological questions. These issues include, for example, the origins of the Amorites, the impact of the Sea Peoples along the Levantine coast, the origins of the Arameans, and Iron Age imperial policies in the Levant, to name but a few. To address these questions requires, therefore, a larger dataset than that which is offered by the archaeological record of the southern Levant alone.

Although the term *Levant* has been increasingly employed to describe this region over the past twenty years, it is worthwhile to articulate why this has occurred. Two primary bases present themselves: geography and material culture. The term came into wide currency in English during the sixteenth century to refer to the eastern Mediterranean, which encompassed all eastern Mediterranean countries from Turkey to Egypt (see Braudel 1972). In Near Eastern archaeology, however, use of the term has been restricted to the region that is essentially bounded by the mountains of southern Turkey to the north, the Euphrates and the Arabian Desert to the east, the Red Sea to the south, and the Mediterranean Sea and Pelusiac branch of the Nile to the west. This region shares a number of features that provide a degree of geographic continuity from north to south that warrant the application of a single geographic term. The greatest of these features, and the one responsible

---

2.   The author wishes to note that the original draft of this article was completed in May 2006, before the unforeseeable downturn in the global economy that, at least for the short term, appears to be the single greatest hurdle to the anticipated growth of academic positions, including those in Levantine archaeology.

for the formation of all of the others, is the Great Rift Valley, which bisects the region from north to south. Like the rivers of Egypt and Mesopotamia, this valley has served as an 'access corridor' for the movement of man and beast alike, and trade and communication. In a similar manner, the coastal plain (though extremely narrow in Lebanon) and the inland desert provided secondary axes of interconnectivity from north to south. From west to east most of the Levant also consisted of (1) a humid coastal plain (though of varying widths), (2) an inner mountain ridge, (3) the Great Rift valley, (4) a second mountain or highland ridge, as well as (5) an arid inland plateau.

The cultural continuity evident throughout the Levant during most historical periods, which supports treatment of the region under a single term, also stemmed largely from these geographical features. While it would be incorrect to suggest that the geography of this region in some way *determined* the development of its cultures, it did—for concerns related primarily to subsistence—encourage a degree of inter-dependence throughout most periods between the different regions within this zone. This interdependence usually outweighed the dependence of these regions upon and interaction with neighboring regions such as Egypt, Anatolia, or Mesopotamia. Therefore, aspects of the material culture of the Levant that reflect these interconnections bear the strongest categorical and stylistic similarities to regions *within* this zone during almost every archaeological period from the Neolithic to the Ottoman period. Thus, it is evident that the Levant constitutes a contiguous (though not homogenous) cultural zone akin to Mesopotamia and Egypt, the continuity of which were largely shaped by their principal geographic features. Nevertheless, despite such a well-reasoned basis for the identification of Levantine archaeology, the adoption of this term by many scholars has been, for the most part, simply the result of individual attempts to consider a wider, yet relevant, cultural corpus than that which is suggested by the use of terms like Canaan, Israel, or even Syria-Palestine.

Regardless of the manner in which the term has come into common use, for a couple of additional reasons it seems clear that the *Levant* will remain the term of choice. In the first place scholars have shown a penchant for the term Levant, despite the fact that the term 'Syria-Palestine' has been advocated since the late 1970s. This is evident from the fact that no journal or series today has adopted a title that includes 'Syria-Palestine'. However, the journal *Levant* has been published since 1969 and since 1990 *Ägypten und Levante* has also attracted a plethora of papers relating to the archaeology of this region. Furthermore, a search through any electronic database of titles reveals an overwhelming adoption of the term 'Levant' when compared to 'Syria-Palestine' for archaeological studies. Undoubtedly, this is mostly due to the fact that 'Syria-Palestine' is, correctly speaking, the title for a Roman administrative division of the Levant created by Hadrian (Millar 1993). The term 'Syria-Palestine' also carries political overtones that inadvertently evoke current efforts to establish a full-fledged Palestinian state. Scholars have recognized, therefore, that—for at least the time being—they can spare themselves further headaches by adopting the term *Levant* to identify this region. In light of these widely recognized trends it is, therefore, the responsibility of those of us working within the discipline to advance this terminology and educate the public regarding its significance and geographical scope.

North American Archaeologists in the Levant

The locations of excavations by North American scholars and their research agendas constitute the strongest evidence that Levantine archaeology has emerged as an independent discipline within Near Eastern archaeology. Since 1992, for example, all of the archaeology positions that have been filled, which are discussed here, have been filled by scholars who may be identified first and foremost as Levantine archaeologists according to the terms outlined above. While most of the positions held by these individuals could formerly have been identified with 'Biblical' or 'Syro-Palestinian' archaeology, few of these scholars are at present working within the boundaries of ancient Israel. Whereas for many decades scholars in 'Biblical' or 'Syro-Palestinian' archaeology did not especially concern themselves with the results of northern excavations (i.e. in Lebanon, western Syria, and the 'Amuq—the exception being Ugarit), today these regions feature prominently within the research agendas of North American archaeologists working in the Levant. Thus, the research interests of Levantine archaeologists, as illustrated below, appear to be increasingly concerned with topics of greater interest to Near Eastern archaeologists and anthropologists than they are to biblical scholars.

Let us begin with research institutions that offer Ph.D. programs in Near Eastern archaeology with a track in Levantine archaeology. Seven institutions in North America host such programs, which are supported by the presence of not only a Levantine archaeologist, but also other Near Eastern archaeologists. These include Harvard University, the University of Chicago, the University of Toronto, Pennsylvania State University, and now the University of California at San Diego (UCSD), Los Angeles (UCLA), and most recently at Berkeley (UCB). While the official titles of many of these positions often continue to include explicit reference to Israel, the research of scholars at these institutions confirms that the scope of archaeological research in the Levant continues to broaden beyond the boundaries defined by 'Biblical' and 'Syro-Palestinian' archaeology.

Since 1985, Lawrence E. Stager (Harvard '75) has held the Dorot chair in the Archaeology of Israel at Harvard University. Stager's contributions to questions related to the archaeology of the family and daily life in ancient Israel (King and Stager 2001; Stager 1985), like the results of his excavations at Ashkelon (Stager 1993, 2002; Johnson 2008, Stager, Schloen, and Master 2008), are very well known. Prior to assuming his post at Harvard, Stager held the professorship in Syro-Palestinian archaeology at the University of Chicago's Oriental Institute from 1974 to 1986. During that time he carried out excavations at Idalion in Cyprus from 1971 to 1980 (Stager and Walker 1974) and at Carthage in Tunisia from 1975 to 1979 (Stager 1980). Stager's biblical interests also nearly led him along with Douglas Esse to excavate Harran on the border of Turkey and Syria. Although this project was thwarted by political roadblocks, this ultimately resulted in the excavation of the site of Ashkelon in Israel beginning in 1985. There can be little doubt that Stager's archaeological insights are the product of his diverse archaeological experience, including work outside of Israel (e.g. 1992), thus illustrating the value of a research agenda defined by the far reach of Levantine cultures. Furthermore, his experiences serve as an excellent reminder that many unexpected circumstances have led Levantine archaeologists to choose the sites they have excavated, and yet to continue to conduct research related to Levantine cultures. Over the more than twenty years since he has held his position at Harvard, Stager has trained a cadre of students in the archaeology of ancient Israel. A number of these students have taken up influential positions ensuring that Stager's work will influence our understanding of the archaeology of the southern Levant for decades to come.

The North American institution with perhaps the longest established tradition of exploration in the Levant is the Oriental Institute at the University of Chicago. Throughout the many decades since its work at Megiddo (1925–39) and Tel Ta'yinat (1935–38) the Oriental Institute's role in the archaeology of the Levant has been limited. Since 1994, J. David Schloen has held the appointment in Syro-Palestinian archaeology at Chicago resulting in Oriental Institute excavations at Yaqush and Alala, and Schloen's serving as co-director of the Leon Levy Expedition to Ashkelon. Thus, in more than a decade of work the Oriental Institute has been involved in excavations throughout the breadth of the Levant including sites from the Early Bronze Age through the classical periods. Schloen's study of social structure in the Levant and the Near East during the Bronze Age, now referred to as the 'house of the father' model, provides unique insights into social theory, kinship, and demography for the Levant (1993a, 1993b, 2001). His forthcoming work on social structure in the Levant during the Iron Age promises to be equally thought provoking. While Schloen's research interests in social theory address fundamental questions of significance to 'Biblical Archaeology', namely as they concern a greater understanding of the social dynamics of ancient Israel and its Levantine neighbors, his approach underscores the importance of the Levantine context of such questions, rather than an exclusively Israel-centered approach. In addition to this research, the recent rolling out of the Oriental Institute sponsored *Online Cultural Heritage Research Environment* (OCHRE),[3] developed by David and Sandra Schloen, also represents a major contribution to the management of cultural heritage data from the ancient Near East. This initiative supports the observation that scholars in Levantine archaeology also continue to pioneer theoretical, methodological, and technological developments of importance to Near Eastern archaeology that will fundamentally affect the availability and accessibility of archaeological information.

In 1997 Timothy Harrison assumed his position at the University of Toronto in the archaeology of Syria-Palestine. Harrison's research interests, excavation experience, and approaches epitomize the nature of Levantine archaeology today. Since his graduate work at the University of Chicago, Harrison has been extensively involved in the Madaba Plains Project in Jordan. His dissertation research was an outgrowth of his research on the Early Bronze Age in Jordan and the influence of his advisor, the late Douglas Esse (Harrison 1995). He has co-directed excavations at Tel Yaqush in Israel, and served as the director of excavations of the Tell Madaba Archaeological Project, although shortly after undertaking this project he began to pursue an archaeological project in the 'Amuq Valley. This latest development is not entirely surprising given his relationship to the Oriental Institute, which was responsible for surveying the 'Amuq (Braidwood 1937; Braidwood, Braidwood, and Haines 1960). His efforts led to the renewal of excavations at Tell Ta'yinat, which had not been excavated since 1938 (Haines 1971; McEwan 1937). Following several seasons of survey and geophysical analysis (Batiuk, Harrison, and Pavlish 2005), the early excavation seasons have revealed impressive finds related to the Late Bronze Age–Iron I transition in the 'Amuq. Harrison's recent publication of *Megiddo 3* (2005), which featured Stratum VIA materials first discovered by Douglas Esse (1991, 1992), has also placed him squarely in the midst of the debate raging over the Iron Age chronology of the southern Levant. In short, Harrison's diverse research in Israel, Jordan, and the 'Amuq in Turkey at sites ranging from the Early Bronze Age through the Iron Age demonstrates the regional and temporal breadth that is becoming increasingly characteristic of archaeological research in the Levant.

In 2001 Ann Killebrew filled one of the most recently established positions in the archaeology of Israel within the Classics and Ancient Mediterranean Studies Department at Pennsylvania State University. As a result of her graduate research at the Hebrew University of Jerusalem and her participation in excavations at Ekron, she has undertaken extensive research on the Philistines with a special focus on the Philistine ceramic assemblage (e.g. Killebrew 1998). Her publication of final reports from the Tel Miqne-Ekron excavation project promises to shed still further light on the Philistine material culture in the coming years. Killebrew's research has also culminated in a recent monograph on ethnicity in the southern Levant from ca. 1300 to 1100 BCE (2005). As with the scholars mentioned above, her regionally diverse excavation experience, throughout Israel and recently in Cilicia in Turkey, as well as her interest in addressing broad questions such as ethnicity in the Levant, underscore the need for a wider regional perspective that has become a requisite of Levantine archaeology.

Since 1992 the greatest gains in positions within the field of Levantine archaeology have taken place within the University of California system. These include the notable endowment of a chair at UC San Diego (the pretext for this volume) and the creation of a new position in the archaeology of Israel at UCLA, and the recent hiring of a Levantine archaeologist at UC Berkeley. The first of these

---

3. See http://ochre.lib.uchicago.edu/.

positions resulted from the appointment of Thomas E. Levy as Professor of Anthropology and Judaic Studies in the Anthropology Department at UC San Diego in 1992 (see Levy, this volume). Although it is not identified by title as a position in the archaeology of the Levant, the endowment of the Kershaw chair in the Archaeology of Ancient Israel and Neighboring Lands assures the survival of this position as part of the anthropology and Judaic studies programs at San Diego for the foreseeable future. Levy's work on Chalcolithic sites in the Negev like Shiqmim (Levy 1987), Gilat (Levy 2006), on Chalcolithic and Early Bronze Age relations between Egypt and the southern Levant (Levy and van den Brink 2002), and his more recent excavations in the Faynan district of southern Jordan are among his many contributions, which demonstrate the broad scope of his work. Within a field usually dominated by textually focused inquiry, the highlight of Levy's contribution to Levantine archaeology today is his sophisticated incorporation of innovative anthropological approaches to traditional problems in Levantine archaeology (e.g. Levy 1995; Levy and Higham 2005), from experimental archaeology to regional and material analyses. As his most recent excavations at Khirbet en-Nahas already indicate (Levy *et al.* 2004; for additional bibliography, see Levy, this volume), his continuing work will assuredly provide still greater insights into the earlier than expected emergence of the state of Edom in Iron Age Transjordan. Given the limitations of the textual corpus for this region, Levy's anthropologically driven approach and use of varied analytical tools is particularly well suited to the problems that still remain to be addressed. Levy has recognized the importance of a fully Levantine perspective to problems in the archaeology of the region and he is therefore collaborating with the Global Moments in the Levant (GML) project to produce the Digital Archaeological Atlas of the Holy Land (DAAHL).[4] The anthropological and spatial-temporal approaches that Levy has pursued highlight the direction that Levantine archaeology has taken in the years since the demise of 'Biblical Archaeology'.

A second position within the University of California system was opened in 2005 at the University of California, Los Angeles. The position, which I hold, originally conceived of as one in the archaeology of the Levant, was cast as a traditional appointment in 'The Archaeology of Ancient Israel and Early Judaism'. However, for the reasons cited in this article, I have sought to identify the position as one in the archaeology of the Levant with a field research focus in the southern Levant, specifically Israel, where since 2007 UCLA has conducted joint excavations in Jaffa as part of The Jaffa Cultural Heritage Project. Established in 2007, the Jaffa Cultural Heritage Project is a multidisciplinary and multi-faceted archaeological research project with the aim of researching, publishing, conserving, and presenting Jaffa's archaeological heritage (Burke and Burke 2008). My research interests in warfare and state formation as well as in comparative analysis of Bronze and Iron Age Levantine cultures employ a broad historical and regional perspective (e.g. Burke 2004, 2007, 2008, and in press), which is aided by the use of GIS in archaeological analysis (e.g. Batiuk and Burke 2005).

A third and what seems to be an unexpected position in Levantine archaeology that may further improve the prospects for the discipline in the years ahead has emerged at the University of California at Berkeley (UCB). This outcome results from the hiring of Benjamin Porter, a graduate of the University of Pennsylvania (Porter 2007), who assumed the post in 2008 in Near Eastern Archaeology, a position that was widely expected to be filled by a Mesopotamian archaeologist. Porter's archaeological fieldwork at Dhiban in Jordan serves as yet another example of the regional diversity among the research interests of North American Levantine archaeologists. That he is a graduate of the Department of Anthropology at the University of Pennsylvania is also a fitting development for a discipline that William Dever had sought for nearly three decades to infuse with greater anthropological rigor.

---

4.   See http://daahl.ucsd.edu/daahl.

Other research institutions have also recognized the importance of the archaeology of ancient Israel for a long time in one form or another in their graduate programs, though these institutions have not sought to establish a position in the archaeology of the Levant within their Near Eastern civilizations programs. Among such institutions—to single out but a few—are the University of Pennsylvania, Johns Hopkins (once the home of William F. Albright), Brown, Yale, Cornell, UC Berkeley, University of Michigan at Ann Arbor, and the University of Arizona. All of these universities, and still others, routinely offer courses in the archaeology of Israel, and yet none of these well-funded institutions have sought to create a post for a full-time Levantine archaeologist. How positions, such as the one once filled by Albright, fade away is amply demonstrated by the recent example at the University of Pennsylvania. Between 1997 and 2004 the endowed James B. Pritchard Chair in Biblical Archaeology and Related Fields resided in the Department of Anthropology at the University of Pennsylvania where it was held by Bruce Routledge and before him by James Sauer (1981–88). Unfortunately, what has been appropriately characterized as a 'folding chair', because it was not securely attached to a specific department, has, in fact, been removed from the Anthropology Department since Routledge's departure. Thus, the future of the archaeology of the Levant at the University of Pennsylvania is now in serious doubt. Although this is not yet a reason for complete despair, a concerted effort would be necessary if this position is ever to be revived, strengthened, and secured.

In addition to the seven positions supported by research institutions with graduate programs in Levantine archaeology, a closer look reveals a number of other faculty positions within Levantine archaeology throughout North America, which support the identification of a vibrant discipline with a broad mandate. These positions, like those above, illustrate the diversity of research within Levantine archaeology and demonstrate the persistence of interest in the archaeology of ancient Israel, despite the changes that have occurred across the discipline. As for some of the positions in the archaeology of Israel which were, for example, feared lost by Dever in 1995, two prominent ones have been retained and continue with a focus on the archaeology of ancient Israel. The Pacific School of Religion filled its position with Aaron J. Brody (Harvard University, '97), while the position at Pittsburgh Theological Seminary (PTS) was filled by Ron E. Tappy (Harvard University, '92) in 1997. Tappy now leads an expedition to the previously unexplored site of Tel Zeitah near the border of ancient Philistia in Israel and serves as the director of the James L. Kelso Bible Lands Museum at PTS.

Other students of Lawrence Stager have also added to the number of university positions held by Levantine archaeologists, with a continued focus predominantly on ancient Israel. Wheaton College has emerged as a potential contributor in the archaeology of ancient Israel under the direction of Daniel Master (Harvard University, '01). A number of students have already completed a Masters degree through this program and have gone on to enroll in Ph.D. programs in Levantine archaeology as well as in biblical studies. Susan Cohen (Harvard University, '00), too, has recently assumed a position at Montana State University. In 2006 she began excavations at a new site in northern Israel following her excavations of a Middle Bronze Age cemetery at Gesher (Garfinkel and Cohen 2007). In 2008 John Monson, a student of Larry Stager (Harvard University, '97), joined the faculty at Trinity Evangelical Divinity School.

Since the early 1990s William G. Dever's students from the University of Arizona have filled a number of positions while maintaining research concentrations in the archaeology of ancient Israel (for the most recent list of students, see Nakhai 2003). As a result, Dever's students occupy positions in History, Anthropology, and Judaic Studies programs throughout North America—the types of programs that typify the job prospects for graduates in Levantine archaeology. While it has been argued that IAA (Israel Antiquities Authority) requirements, among other things, have made fieldwork for many of his students difficult, notably due to a lack of affiliation with archaeological institutes, two of Dever's students are presently leading active field projects in Israel and Jordan. Steven Ortiz, Associate Professor of Archaeology and Biblical Backgrounds at Southwestern Baptist Theological Seminary (University of Arizona, '00), has, for example, recently partnered with Samuel Wolff (University of Chicago, '86) of the IAA and has renewed excavations at Gezer. Randall Younker, Professor of Old Testament and Biblical Archaeology and director of the Institute of Archaeology at Andrews University (University of Arizona, '97), continues the ongoing work of the Madaba Plains Project with a consortium of institutions. The work of these scholars demonstrates the potential that still remains for fieldwork in the southern Levant through collaborations with local archaeologists, despite concerns to the contrary. Thus, the now defunct University of Arizona program continues to contribute to the diversity of field research by North American archaeologists in the Levant by assuring the continued presence of North American institutions in archaeological research in Israel, in particular, but also Jordan during a period when many Levantine archaeologists have begun to pursue exploration of sites outside of Israel.

Another position that must be mentioned is at Emory University in 'Hebrew and Biblical Archaeology' in the Department of Middle Eastern and South Asian Studies. It has been held since 1980 by Oded Borowski (University of Michigan, '79), whose work on agriculture and daily life in ancient Israel is well known (1987, 2003). Borowski currently serves along with Paul F. Jacobs (Mississippi State University) as co-director of Phase III of the Tell Halif excavations in Israel as part of the Lahav Research Project. Despite the resources of Emory University and its involvement in field excavations, the position has not generated graduate students in the archaeology of the Levant, presumably due to a lack of supporting faculty in Near Eastern archaeology. Nevertheless, since sufficient Jewish and Biblical studies faculty are already present at Emory, the position should be viewed as one which could potentially support a graduate program in Levantine archaeology, if one or two other Near Eastern archaeologists were to be hired.

The diversity of research interests that characterize Levantine archaeology today over and against the former approach of 'Biblical Archaeology' are apparent in Canada as much as they are in the United States. Several scholars in Canada, for example, are best identified as Levantine archaeologists based on their field projects and research interests. P.M. Michèle Daviau of Wilfred Laurier University, for example, who is also a member of the graduate faculty in the Department of Near and Middle Eastern Civilizations at the University of Toronto, has worked extensively in the southern Levant. She is currently the director of the Wadi ath-Thamad Project and is conducting excavations at Khirbat al-Mudayna in central Jordan. Daviau is especially interested in Iron Age towns, and ceramic technology and classification. Many will, of course, be familiar with her work on Bronze Age houses and their furnishings in the southern Levant (1993). Edward Banning at the University of Toronto, who has conducted excavations for a number of years in the prehistoric occupation of the Wadi Ziqlab in Jordan, must also be mentioned here. Like Thomas Levy, Banning's anthropological approaches have been widely celebrated as innovative contributions within an often old-fashioned field. Since 1998, Michel Fortin of Laval University in Quebec has conducted excavations at the 70 ha site of Tell 'Acharne (possibly to be identified as ancient Tunip) in the Orontes Valley in Syria. There he is also conducting a survey of the surrounding valley (Fortin 2006). Since the start of the project, Fortin has, for example, worked extensively with members of the Geomatics (GIS) department at Laval to develop database software for analysis and dissemination of data from this project. His diverse research experience, which includes a dissertation that was focused on fortresses in Middle Bronze Age Cyprus (Fortin 1981), and excavations in eastern Syria at Tell 'Atij and Tell Gudeda from 1986 to 1993, typify the diversity of experience among Levantine archaeologists today that so dramatically distinguishes their research agendas from those that characterized traditional 'Biblical Archaeology'.

The Future of Levantine Archaeology in North America

Despite substantive changes that have resulted in the emergence of Levantine archaeology, significant obstacles remain to be addressed before Levantine archaeology will be on a solid footing within the humanities. In what follows, I identify three major obstacles and potential strategies for addressing each of them in order to attempt to assure the sustainability and growth of Levantine archaeology. I conclude by observing that the role of the North American scholar in Levantine archaeology is more important than ever and that fundamentally our role is a unique and necessary one.

While there is probably no need to defend the purpose of Levantine archaeology to those within the discipline, our foremost concern must be, however, with the immediate obstacle posed by university administrations that view our discipline as either unnecessary or irrelevant. (The same concern applies for any number of smaller disciplines in Near Eastern studies, such as Assyriology.) While it is one thing to identify generic obstacles to Levantine archaeology, it is quite another to identify individuals within our own institutions who play a role in the future of research and work to secure their support. For it is not a lack of interest among the public, college, or graduate students, or even among the highest echelon of the academy in North America where substantive opposition lies. Rather, opposition is most common among short-sighted deans and pencil-pushing university bureaucrats who are almost exclusively concerned with numerical justifications for the university's bottom line.

Several strategies can be implemented by Levantine archaeologists to assure the satisfaction and support of university administration. First, since Levantine archaeology by and large falls within the humanities, it is possible to exploit this classification to considerable effect, since Levantine archaeology offers one of the most appealing subjects to undergraduates in the humanities. An emphasis, for example, on using Levantine archaeology courses (such as in the archaeology of Israel, the history of Jerusalem, or the religion of ancient Israel) to meet writing or other core university requirements can guarantee Levantine archaeology not only visibility, but also substantial institutional support. At UCLA an upper divisional writing requirement can be met by taking 'Jerusalem the Holy City'. Because the course is extremely popular, offered throughout the year to approximately four hundred students, it generates numerous Teaching Assistantships that thereby support graduate students. Other comparable ideas might include exploiting the cultural heritage of the Levant by means of art and archaeology courses addressing its roles as the birthplace of the world's three major monotheistic religions, the alphabet, and cultures such as the Phoenicians. Second, the incorporation of undergraduates in faculty research, as has been modeled at the University of San Diego by Thomas Levy and the University of Southern California by Bruce Zuckerman, also possesses potential to garner substantial institutional support (i.e. funding for research) and publicity. Third, summer travel programs offered for college credit, by reducing the university's overall costs per credit hour, can also be negotiated to provide fiscal returns for funding faculty research projects. While some countries may be 'off-limits' for taking students for fieldwork, others, as noted above, are not, and creative solutions can be found to overcome institutional bureaucracy that on the surface may appear to hinder the prospects for such projects. Finally, those holding positions in Levantine archaeology must also be prepared to identify potential donors who will not only support our research projects (which is already quite often done), but might also consider endowing a university position in Levantine archaeology (a far less frequent request) in order to assure its perpetuity. To the best of my knowledge such specific endeavors have only been undertaken twice in North America for Levantine archaeology, which have resulted in endowed chairs at Harvard University and the University of California, San Diego.

Despite the most proactive efforts of individual scholars and the support of university administrators, Levantine archaeology will always be faced with certain obstacles. The greatest of these, which has always plagued Near Eastern archaeology, is that it is and has always been a fundamentally unpredictable endeavor. Threats may come from within our own institutions (e.g., insurance concerns) or without (e.g. political circumstances may emerge at any moment that prevent the conduct of field research). Levantine archaeology—not unlike its sister disciplines in Egypt, Anatolia, and Mesopotamia—must, therefore, be prepared for such circumstances. The terms we employ, therefore, to define the *raison d'etre* of Levantine archaeology must be sufficiently flexible to accommodate a wide range of research interests and strategies for their implementation. This I took into account when I recast my own research focus as 'The Archaeology of the Levant'. While much of my research and what I teach will certainly focus on ancient Israel, defining my position as one in Levantine archaeology allows me to justify teaching a range of subjects both to graduates and undergraduates with greater topical, regional, and temporal breadth. Fundamentally, however, the change in terminology also reflects how I perceive the field to have changed, which has occurred even since I began my graduate studies in the mid-1990s.

To cope with the uncertainties of the region in which we work we must also consider a strategy of *regional diversification* in our fieldwork, which might involve exploration of sites and regions that have formerly been given less consideration within the framework of 'Biblical Archaeology'. As the above survey indicates, perhaps for the first time in the history of Levantine archaeology the largest, active, foreign-led projects excavating Bronze and Iron Age sites and conducting surveys seem to be in the northern Levant, rather than in the south. These include Alala, Tell Tayinat, the Aleppo citadel excavations, Ugarit, Tell 'Acharne, Tell Afis, Ebla, Tell Qarqur, Sidon, and the survey around Homs, among others. While this may be the result of a temporary set of circumstances (prior to the start of fieldwork in Israel by several American institutions, including UCLA), explicit efforts must be made not only to keep abreast of the developments coming out of western Syria, Lebanon, and the 'Amuq, but also to encourage the incorporation of these results in our graduate students' research. Syria, for example, offers extraordinary untapped potential for the exploration of Iron Age Aramean states and, despite political concerns over the past few years, several American projects have continued their fieldwork in Syria. Levantine archaeology, however, is fortunate enough to be able to justify a strategy of continued fieldwork, despite geopolitical concerns, by means of the exploration of, for example, Phoenician sites throughout the Mediterranean or sites of interest to the study of the Sea Peoples whether in Cyprus, on the coast of Anatolia, or in the Aegean.

A similar and related strategy for assuring the stability of archaeological research in Levant, despite geopolitical concerns, is involvement in a variety of research activities (i.e. other than excavation). While archaeological fieldwork may be prohibitive for scholars at many institutions (at least in the leading and funding of projects), there is ample room for cooperation and collaboration on many other projects that seek to synthesize data from more than one hundred years of archaeological research in the Levant. The spate of White-Levy Publication grants providing for the publication of archaeological remains are the clearest indication of the quantities of material that remain unpublished and, therefore, remain essentially outside of existing archaeological syntheses. Furthermore, more effort must be made to tap geospatial data from relevant sources as has been done for Mesopotamia (e.g. satellite data, aerial photography, etc.). A number of tools in addition to the Internet, such as Geographic Information Systems and sophisticated database programs like OCHRE, provide ample opportunity to facilitate this type of synthesis (e.g. the DAAHL project).

Insofar as it may be possible to identify a variety of obstacles to Levantine archaeology, it is necessary to note that if not given proper consideration, the greatest obstacle to the success of Levantine archaeology may actually be insufficient attention to pedagogy. Examples of the effects of pedagogical failure include insufficient or over specialization, inadequate training in related disciplines, and the inability to communicate with both specialists and non-specialists. These and other failures will give Levantine archaeology the reputation of a navel-gazing enterprise. With so few research institutions offering positions in Levantine archaeology it is necessary for graduate students who wish to improve their chances of finding employment today to achieve the greatest breadth possible while acquiring basic proficiencies in Near Eastern languages, history, biblical studies, and, I would advocate, at least one technical specialty (such as ceramic analysis, GIS, remote sensing, materials analysis, etc.). It would be a tragedy if the greatest strength of 'Biblical Archaeology', namely the emergence of a rigorous effort to integrate text and archaeology, was completely lost as a result of the emergence of an anthropologically focused Levantine archaeology. However, if Levantine archaeology is to continue to distinguish itself in the realm of text and archaeology we must continue to expect extensive language training by graduate students, which includes no less than Hebrew and the first-millennium cognate languages of its neighbors. Therefore, students should likewise seek proficiency in Akkadian and other Northwest Semitic Languages such as Ugaritic. Language proficiencies cannot be sacrificed in light of the need for technical specialties such as training in GIS or ceramic analysis during eleventh-hour negotiations between graduate students and their advisors. The two skills offer completely different insights, and thus it may be concluded that technologically driven studies that do not take into account relevant textual data will remain at best marginally relevant to scholarship in Levantine archaeology. Furthermore, as the debate regarding biblical minimalism demonstrates, students must also continue to receive a modicum of training in biblical studies if they are to interact responsibly with scholarship in the archaeology of ancient Israel, which still constitutes something in the order of ninety percent of the archaeological data available for the Levant.

Inasmuch as the success of Levantine archaeology depends upon the efforts of established scholars, graduate students are truly those who will shape the future of the discipline. However, to succeed in this capacity they must each identify—at the outset of their studies—the target market to which they hope to position themselves and thus improve their chances for employment. At the start of my graduate work I was encouraged to choose from one of two main emphases that would improve my chances for employment: biblical studies or anthropology. Students making such a decision should not, however, conclude that they are engaging exclusively in only one of these activities in their research simply because of the choice they must make to become marketable, even if they accept one type of position or another. Nevertheless, when it comes down to courses taken and research experience, the student must ultimately be able to win over a search committee; few committees will be convinced that a prospective applicant is equally competent in both fields. In short, jobs have been and will continue to remain few and far between for those who identify themselves solely as 'Biblical' or 'Syro-Palestinian' archaeologists. This trend can be discerned, for example, in the fact that over the past decade our discipline has seen a decrease in the receptivity of biblical studies to Levantine archaeology, while there has been a general increase in positions available in anthropology to Near Eastern archaeologists at large. By positioning ourselves as Near Eastern archaeologists with a specialty in the Levant and with the ability to teach in areas of broad interest with respect to historical, biblical, and Near Eastern studies we will broaden the prospects for the placement of graduate students and ultimately the expansion of Levantine archaeology.

Setting aside for the moment all strategies for the sustenance and growth of Levantine archaeology, the most important role that North American (if not also European) scholars working in the Levant can play within Levantine archaeology as a whole may be one of cultural academic mediation. This is readily evident when one considers that seven nations fall within the boundaries of the cultural zone identified as the Levant and that political, let alone academic, relationships between many of these nations remain virtually non-existent. Such a mediatory role is already borne by some foreign scholars, in a capacity as academic bridges between segregated communities of scholars whose research foci are defined by the geographical limits of the nations in which they work, either as northern Levantine (scholars in Syria and Lebanon) or southern Levantine (Israel, Jordan, and Palestine). Collaborative analytical research projects, such as those mentioned above, offer the greatest potential to bridge this gap.

Conclusions

Despite the emergence of Levantine archaeology, 'Biblical Archaeology' as a discipline will no doubt persist in its older manifestation at many bible colleges and seminaries. However, this sanctuary may soon also be threatened, as many such schools appear to favor increasingly an exclusive focus on literary approaches to the bible. As is evident, narrowly defined positions such as in 'Biblical Archaeology' are much more difficult for many institutions to justify, particularly as these institutions desire faculty to provide broader interdisciplinary course offerings. The survival of Levantine archaeology, like its siblings Egyptian, Mesopotamian, Anatolian, and Iranian archaeology, will require, therefore, that its value be recognized as more than simply the preservation of 'Biblical Archaeology' under another name. To survive and grow as a discipline Levantine archaeology must ultimately be accorded a place within institutions that acknowledges the major contributions of Levantine civilization, such as, for example, the origin of the alphabet, as well as the fact that out of the Levant the three major monotheistic religions emerged. Still it is obvious that institutional recognition and financial support alone constitute but a few of the steps necessary for the success of Levantine archaeology. Nevertheless, only through the endowment of positions can we offer any fundamental security for the future of our discipline—our students.

Acknowledgments

I would like to thank Tom Levy for inviting me to contribute to this volume in celebration of the endowment of and his subsequent conferral of the Kershaw Chair in the Archaeology of Israel and Neighboring Lands at the University of California, San Diego. I also wish to express my sincerest appreciation to Norma Kershaw whose efforts are proving fundamental to the future of Levantine archaeology, especially within the University of California. As one who has only just joined the University of California (at Los Angeles) in the Archaeology of Ancient Israel, it is most encouraging to witness such a substantive improvement in the prospects for our discipline. I cannot but also express the hope that this is just the beginning of a new era in Levantine archaeology that will see additional growth at other universities throughout North America.

I would also like to thank Carol Wald, Katherine Burke, William Schniedewind, and George Pierce all of whom read drafts of this article.

References

Batiuk, S., and A.A. Burke (2005) The Tell Atchana Mapping and GIS Project. In Yener 2005: 145-52.
Batiuk, S., T.P. Harrison and L. Pavlish (2005) The Ta'yinat Survey, 1999–2002. In Yener 2005: 171-92.
Borowski, O. (1987) *Agriculture in Iron Age Israel* (Winona Lake, IN: Eisenbrauns).
—(2003) *Daily Life in Biblical Times* (Society of Biblical Literature: Archaeology and Biblical Studies 5; Atlanta: Society of Biblical Literature).
Braidwood, R.J. (1937) *Mounds in the Plain of Antioch: An Archeological Survey* (Oriental Institute Publications 48; Chicago: University of Chicago Press).
Braidwood, R.J., L.S. Braidwood, and R.C. Haines (1960) *Excavations in the Plain of Antioch: The Earlier Assemblages, Phases A–J* (Oriental Institute Publications 61; Chicago: University of Chicago Press).

Braudel, F. (1972) *The Mediterranean and the Mediterranean World in the Age of Philip II* (translated by S. Reynolds; New York: Harper & Row).

Burke, A.A. (2004) The Architecture of Defense: Fortified Settlements of the Levant during the Middle Bronze Age (Ph.D. diss., University of Chicago).

—(2007) Magdalūma, Migdālîm, Magdoloi, and Majādīl: The Historical Geography and Archaeology of the Magdalu (Migdāl). *BASOR* 346: 29-57.

—(2008) *'Walled Up to Heaven': The Evolution of Middle Bronze Age Fortification Strategies in the Levant* (Studies in the Archaeology and History of the Levant 4; Winona Lake, IN: Eisenbrauns).

—(In press) 'More Light on Old Reliefs: New Kingdom Egyptian Siege Tactics and Asiatic Resistance'. In *Exploring the Longue Durée: Essays in Honor of Lawrence E. Stager*, edited by J.D. Schloen (Winona Lake, IN: Eisenbrauns): 57–68.

Burke, A.A., and K.S. Burke (2008) Investigating a Forgotten Port: The Jaffa Cultural Heritage Project. *Backdirt* 2008: 70-75.

Daviau, P.M.M. (1993) *Houses and Their Furnishings in Bronze Age Palestine: Domestic Activity Areas and Artefact Distribution in the Middle and Late Bronze Ages* (JSOT/ASOR Monograph 8; Sheffield: JSOT Press).

Dever, W.G. (1995) Death of a Discipline. *BAR* 21/5: 50–55, 70.

—(1997) Biblical Archaeology. In *The Oxford Encyclopedia of Archaeology in the Near East*, edited by E.M. Meyers (5 vols.; New York: Oxford University Press): I:315-19.

—(1998) Archaeology, Ideology, and the Quest for an 'Ancient' or 'Biblical' Israel. *NEA* 61/1: 39-52.

—(2001) *What Did the Biblical Writers Know and When Did They Know It? What Archaeology Can Tell Us about the Reality of Ancient Israel* (Grand Rapids: Eerdmans).

Esse, D.L. (1991) Megiddo Revisited. *The Oriental Institute Annual Report* 1990–91: 32–35.

—(1992) The Collared Pithos at Megiddo: Ceramic Distribution and Ethnicity. *JNES* 51/2: 81-103.

Fortin, M. (1981) Military Architecture in Cyprus during the Second Millennium B.C. (Ph.D. diss., University of London).

—(2006) À la recherche de l'ancienne Tunip à Tell Acharneh dans l'Oronte. In *Les espaces syro-mésopotamiens. Dimensions de l'expérience humaine au Proche-Orient ancien*, edited by P. Butterlin, M. Lebeau and B. Pierre (Subartu 17; Turnhout: Brepols).

Garfinkel, Y., and C. Cohen (eds.) (2007) *The Middle Bronze Age IIA Cemetery at Gesher: Final Report* (Boston: American Schools of Oriental Research).

Haines, R.C. (1971) *Excavations in the Plain of Antioch II* (Oriental Institute Publications 95; Chicago: University of Chicago Press).

Harrison, T.P. (1995) Life on the Edge: Human Adaptation and Resilience in the Semi-Arid Highlands of Central Jordan during the Early Bronze Age (Ph.D. diss., University of Chicago).

—(2005) *Megiddo 3: Final Report on the Stratum VI Excavations* (Chicago: Oriental Institute of the University of Chicago).

Johnson, B.L. (2008) *Ashkelon 2: Imported Pottery of the Roman and Late Roman Periods* (Final Reports of the Leon Levy Expedition to Ashkelon 2; Winona Lake, IN: Eisenbrauns).

Killebrew, A.E. (1998) Ceramic Craft and Technology during the Late Bronze and Iron I Ages: The Relationship between Pottery Technology and Cultural Diversity (Ph.D. diss., Hebrew University).

—(2005) *Biblical Peoples and Ethnicity: An Archaeological Study of Egyptians, Canaanites, Philistines, and Early Israel 1300–1100 B.C.E.* (Archaeology and Biblical Studies 9; Atlanta: Society of Biblical Literature).

King, P.J., and L.E. Stager (2001) *Life in Biblical Israel* (Library of Ancient Israel; Louisville: Westminster John Knox).

Levy, T.E. (ed.) (1987) *Shiqmim I: Studies Concerning Chalcolithic Societies in the Northern Negev Desert, Israel (1982–1984)* (Oxford: British Archaeological Reports).

—(1995) The *Archaeology of Society in the Holy Land* (New York: Facts on File).

—(2006) *Archaeology, Anthropology and Cult: The Sanctuary at Gilat, Israel* (London: Equinox).

Levy, T.E., R.B. Adams, M. Najjar, A. Hauptmann, J.D. Anderson, B. Brandl, M.A. Robinson, and T. Higham (2004) Reassessing the Chronology of Biblical Edom: New Excavations and [14]C Dates from Khirbat en-Nahas (Jordan). *Antiquity* 4: 863-76.

Levy, T.E., and E.C.M. van den Brink (eds.) (2002) *Egypt and the Levant* (Edinburgh: T. & T. Clark).

Levy, T.E., and T. Higham (eds.) (2005) *The Bible and Radiocarbon Dating: Archaeology, Text and Science* (London: Equinox).

McEwan, C.W. (1937) The Syrian Expedition of the Oriental Institute of the University of Chicago. *American Journal of Archaeology* 41: 8-16.

Millar, F. (1993) *The Roman Near East, 31 BC–AD 337* (Cambridge, MA: Harvard University Press).

Nakhai, B.A. (ed.) (2003) *The Near East in the Southwest: Essays in Honor of William G. Dever* (Boston: American Schools of Oriental Research).

Porter, B. (2007) The Archaeology of Community in Iron I Central Jordan (Ph.D. diss., University of Pennsylvania).

Schloen, J.D. (1993a) Caravans, Kenites, and *casus belli*: Enmity and Alliance in the Song of Deborah. *Catholic Biblical Quarterly* 55(3): 18–38.

—(1993b) The Exile of Disinherited Kin in KTU 1.12 and KTU 1.23. *JNES* 52/3: 209-20.

—(2001) *The House of the Father as Fact and Symbol: Patrimonialism in Ugarit and the Ancient Near East* (Studies in the Archaeology and History of the Levant 2; Winona Lake, IN: Eisenbrauns).

Stager, L.E. (1980) The Rite of Child Sacrifice at Carthage. In *New Light on Ancient Carthage*, edited by J.G. Pedley (Ann Arbor: University of Michigan Press): 1-11.

—(1985) The Archaeology of the Family in Ancient Israel. *BASOR* 260: 1-35.

—(1992) The Periodization of Palestine from Neolithic through Early Bronze Times. In *Chronologies in Old World Archaeology*, edited by R.W. Ehrich (Chicago: University of Chicago Press): 1:22-41; 2:46-60.

—(1993) Ashkelon. In *The New Encyclopedia of Archaeological Excavations in the Holy Land*, edited by E. Stern (2nd English edn; 4 vols.; Jerusalem: Israel Exploration Society): 1:103-12.

—(2002) The MB IIA Ceramic Sequence at Tel Ashkelon and Its Implications for the 'Port Power' Model of Trade. In *The Middle Bronze Age in the Levant: Proceedings of an International Conference on MB IIA Ceramic Material, Vienna, 24th–26th of January 2001*, edited by M. Bietak (Contributions to the Chronology of the Eastern Mediterranean 3; Wien: Österreichischen Akademie der Wissenschaften): 353-62.

Stager, L.E., J.D. Schloen, and D.M. Master (eds.) (2008) *Ashkelon 1: Introduction and Overview (1985–2006)* (Winona Lake, IN: Eisenbrauns).

Stager, L.E., and A.M. Walker (1974) *American Expedition to Idalion, Cyprus: First Preliminary Report, Seasons of 1971 and 1972* (Supplement to the Bulletin of the American Schools of Oriental Research 18; Cambridge, MA: American Schools of Oriental Research).

Worthington, R. (1996) Struggling Ph.D.s Learning about Supply, Demand. *Chicago Tribune*: 1.

Yener, K.A. (ed.) (2005) *The Amuq Valley Regional Projects*. Vol. 1, *Surveys in the Plain of Antioch and Orontes Delta, Turkey, 1995–2002* (Chicago: Oriental Institute of the University of Chicago).

II.
SOME APPLICATIONS

6 'Biblical Archaeology' and Egyptology

Old and Middle Kingdom Perspective*

Miroslav Bárta

Abstract

Egyptology and Biblical Archaeology meet only rarely. The roots of this evolution are difficult to ignore, yet over the past decades the situation has improved significantly, especially due to the latest field projects in the Eastern Delta in Egypt and the Sinai peninsula. This contribution seeks to provide a basic overview of relevant data and latest research in the field of the Biblical and Egyptian archaeology during the Old and Middle Kingdom/Early Bronze Age III and IV and Middle Bronze Age II. The Old Kingdom evidence seems to indicate relatively strong Egyptian interests in the Eastern border and the countries beyond it (wooden statues of prisoners, titles of high officials of the state, imported vessels). The same holds true for the Middle Kingdom (Sinuhe, the Annals of Amenemhat II, Execration texts). Even more surprising may be the evidence emerging from the First Intermediate Period, indicating that mutual contacts continued even after 4.2 kya BP event. Thus the current evidence may challenge the still-popular notion that Egypt of the third and early second millennia BCE has very little to offer to the current biblical discourse.

The 21st century offers many exciting possibilities for exploring the relationship between the Egyptian archaeological record, archaeological data from the southern Levant and the Hebrew Bible. By employing rigorous methodologies of both ancient historical research (Halpern 1988) and archaeology (Levy and Higham 2005) over the past few decades, it is possible to explore these relationships anew. It is a common belief that following the unification of Egypt around 3000 BCE the high level of intensive contacts between Egypt and the Levant was significantly lessened. These contacts were intensive for most of the fourth millennium BCE, and their peak may be found in the opulent equipment of the tombs of Pre-dynastic rulers of Upper Egypt of the Naqada III period, such as that of Uj and several others (van den Brink 1992; van den Brink and Levy 2002; Hartung *et al.* 2001; Hartung 2002). The traditional overland Way of Horus lost its previous importance for the sake of the maritime route connecting Egypt with Byblos (Marcus 1998)—what Lawrence Stager

* I am indebted to Professor T.E. Levy, University of California, San Diego, for many valuable comments, suggestions and improvements over earlier versions of this article. All mistakes are, of course, mine.

refers to as the 'Byblos Run' (Stager 1992). Following the First Dynasty and the disappearance of the Egyptian presence from the Gaza strip and northern Negev, Egypt turned its attention to the exploration of Sinai, the Western Desert and military pacification of Nubian territories. It was only during the Sixth Dynasty that the contacts seem to be revived to a certain degree. Yet, is this traditional paradigm still correct? How does the new evidence fit our traditional views? Do new projects with different research strategies in the field in Egypt and with a more contextual approach to previously known evidence contribute to current discourse? And how?

It is interesting to note that the beginnings of the modern archaeological research in Egypt were connected not only with the challenge posed by the pyramids of Giza but also a clear intention to identify and excavate biblical sites. The founding of the Egypt Exploration Society in 1883 (later reorganized into the Egypt Exploration Fund) followed the example of the Palestinian Exploration Fund. One of its priorities was to 'organize excavations in Egypt with a view to the elucidation of the History and Arts of Ancient Egypt and the illustration of the Old Testament narrative, so that it has to do with Egypt and the Egyptians; also to explore sites connected with Greek history or with the antiquities of the Coptic Church' (Davis 2004: 28-29). One notable difference in comparison with the Biblical Archaeology of the time (persisting well into the first half of the 20th century) was that Egyptian archaeology also paid reasonable attention to New Testament sites. This was how E. Naville and W.F. Petrie made their way into Egypt. Later on, however, the attention of Egyptian Archaeology was consumed by the discovery of the tomb of Tutankhamun, which left its everlasting imprint on the discipline. At the same time, however, Egyptian archaeology has always been confronted with finds covering a much wider area of interest than say Biblical Archaeology or even Syro-Palestinian archaeology (e.g. Amarna tablets, Moran 1992). Despite what has been said, Egyptology as a discipline remained, with a few exceptions, to some extent isolated. Only recently one can observe a clear trend in Egyptology, which may be defined as a reconciliation of the evidence from Egypt with ever-increasing data provided by Syro-Palestinian archaeology (in Dever's sense [Dever 1985a]; Hoffmeier and Millard 2004).

In this contribution concerning the future of Biblical Archaeology, as an Egyptologist, I would like to re-evaluate some characteristics of two different historical periods. The first one represents the final stage of the Old Kingdom period (2686–2160 BCE) in Egypt, the Sixth Dynasty (2345–2160 BCE). The second period represents the beginning of the Twelfth Dynasty (1985–1773 BCE)—the early re-formation of the second stage of the Egyptian state traditionally known as the Middle Kingdom and the period immediately preceding it (the First Intermediate Period [FIP]) (Shaw 2000). This is the timeframe that roughly corresponds to the Early Bronze Age III Period (2700–2200 BCE), Middle Bronze Age I/EB IV (2200–2000 BCE) and MB IIa (2000–1750 BCE) (Mazar 1990; Stern 1992). I will attempt to demonstrate that there is substantial, sometimes also new evidence, indicating a higher degree and broader scope of contacts then previously assumed. What should also emerge is that despite the formally different terms used by both disciplines, their chronological trajectories and socio-cultural traits are very similar.

I. General Kaaper and the King Raneferef

Some authors, such as E. Marcus and R. Gophna (Marcus 1998; Gophna 2002), suppose that trade contacts between Egypt and Canaan continued during the Old Kingdom. This trade was mediated by Palestinian coastal cities that have not been adequately excavated yet (Marcus 2002). The main objection to this assumption is obvious: there is simply no proof of this as yet.

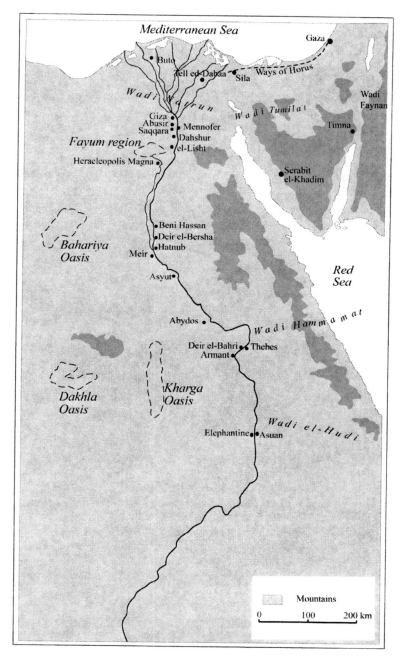

Figure 1. Map of Egypt

The current generally accepted scholarly opinion maintains the idea that for the most part of the Old Kingdom there were minimal contacts between both regions and that the Egyptians themselves limited their activity to the protection of the Eastern border and the strategically important 'Ways of Horus' that provided access to Sinai (Redford 1993; Hoffmeier 2006). However, this hypothesis was taken for granted because of the missing evidence (Oren 1973; Yekutieli 2002 with references). That said, if there was only minimal contact, we should be able to prove it. In support of this line of argument, one can bring some epigraphic evidence from tombs at Giza and Abu Sir dated to the 25th and 24th century BCE, showing that there was at least one 'Overseer of the Way of Horus' (the 'way' written in singular), a Fifth-Dynasty official, Hekenkhenenu (Hassan 1953: 49-52). He was, among various other offices, also *'adj-mer* administrator of the desert, overseer of the deserts, overseer of the army and great of the tens of Upper Egypt'. These data indicate that he was not only of a high social standing but that he was also largely involved in the administration of the border zones of the country, such as deserts, and that this office may have required his engagement with the army administration as well.

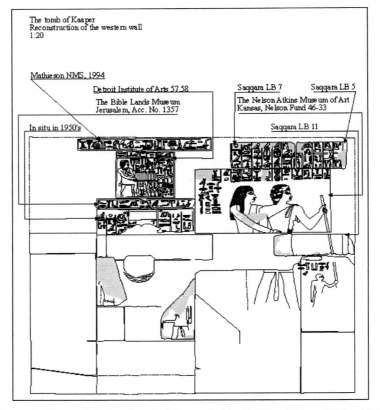

Figure 2. West wall in the chapel of Kaaper in Abusir (Bárta 2001: 176 fig. 4.24)

Another official, Kaaper, came to light relatively recently. His tomb was excavated in 1991 by the Czech Institute of Egyptology and his early Fifth Dynasty L-shaped chapel contained some important titles providing new evidence for our debate (Bárta *et al.* 2001 and Fig. 2 here). Kaaper served at several garrisons as a military scribe and it is very probable that these garrisons were stationed along the Ways of Horus. This is in accordance with parallel development in southwestern Canaan which came under the sphere of dominance of local city states (Miroschedji 2006). This was likely the reason why the Egyptians considered it necessary to fortify their Eastern border so as to demarcate their own spheres of interest. At the same time, it was a way for the Egyptians to secure the entrance route leading to the resources of the southern Sinai exploited from the Third Dynasty onwards. In addition, Kaaper was not only 'Scribe of the Army of the king in Wenet, Serer, Tepa, Ida', but also scribe in the 'Terraces of Turquoise and the Western and Eastern foreign lands' (Fischer 1959; Helck 1962).

The evidence for the sites Wenet, Serer, Tepa and Ida (?) is extremely sparse during the given period and it is probably of some importance that with only one exception they are not attested in later periods (Ahituv 1982). This corroborates, together with determinatives for fortified enclosures in their toponyms, their supposed character: relatively short-lasting fortified military camp-sites with Egyptians troops situated behind the north-eastern Egyptian border. It is equally possible that these sites were surrounded by camps of semi-nomadic local populations who provided some economic support for the Egyptian mining caravans to Sinai, as was the case with the New Kingdom forts on the Ways of Horus (Oren 1987). The fact is that after the EB I period, there are no more Egyptian settlements or any other proof of Egyptian presence in southern Canaan (Brandl 1992; Marcus 1998). The only likely option is to seek the location of Wenet, Serer, Tepa and Ida (?) along the north Sinai coastal line connecting the Egyptian eastern Delta with western Asia. The fact that the Wadi Maghara quarries are referred to by Kaaper in this connection (as Terraces of Turquoise) makes this reconstruction even more intelligible. This part of Sinai with the site of Wadi Maghara was one of the most important spheres of interest to the Old Kingdom pharaohs outside Egyptian territory (Mumford 1999).

Finally, one is tempted to conclude that, given Kaaper's two more unusual titles—'herdsman of dappled cattle' and 'scribe of the pasture land(s) of the dappled cattle', he was also involved with the administration of the traditional grazing areas, probably located in the Eastern Delta.

Kaaper may have lived during the time of the King Sahura. Zahi Hawas and Tarek el-Awadi began to excavate the causeway of his mortuary Abu Sir complex in the 1990s. The results of their expedition brought to light what is now considered to be the most complete record of the architecture and decoration of such a monument for the entire Third millennium BCE (El-Awadi 2006). Among many unique scenes there is an inscription describing an expedition of King Sahura to the unknown country of Bat. According to El-Awadi, it seems that its location was somewhere beyond Sinai and thus it may be located in today's southern Israel/ Palestine or even in Jordan.[1]

In connection with the royal mortuary complexes of the Fifth Dynasty in Abu Sir, located south of Cairo, it is worth having a closer look at the wooden statues of the so-called 'bound prisoners' representing enemies of Egypt. They were found in the mortuary temple of the king Raneferef discovered by the Czech mission in Abu Sir (Verner *et al.* 2006). These statues include the Asiatics, the Libyans and Nubians. It is interesting to observe that several well-preserved statues of the Asiatics are not stylized in order to make a generally understandable reference to the 'Asiatic enemies'. On the contrary, the statues are reasonably different in terms of their wigs and facial features.[2] This may be a good indication of the fact that the Egyptians had reliable knowledge of what lay beyond their border to the east and were able to make a distinction between various Levantine populations (Fig. 3).

---

1. T. El-Awadi (personal communication, 24 July 2007).
2. Benešovská 2006: 409, fig. 2.7.47; 412, 2.7.51; 414, 2.7.52 and 2.7.53.

Figure 3. Wooden statues of Asiatic prisoners discovered in Abu Sir, JE 981812, Excav. No. 773g/I/84 and JE 981812, Excav. No. 773k/I/84 (Archive of the Czech Institute of Egyptology)

Some time later we find evidence for 'preventive' military strikes against south Canaan. One of the most famous reports may be found with Abydos' Weni (Strudwick 2005: 352-57). Weni's extensive report may be complemented by two scenes from tombs at Saqqara and Deshasheh that show Asiatic walled settlements under siege (Kanawati and McFarlane 1993: pls. 26–27; McFarlane 2000, pl. 48). It is important to note that most of the reports of military campaigns and the scenes of destruction of towns are dated to the late Fifth and early Sixth Dynasties. It is generally held that already during this period Egypt was losing some of her power and dominance (Mumford and Parcak 2004; Mumford 2006). These military campaigns may therefore paradoxically indicate growing instability within the state and its increasing weakness, which was disguised in these pre-emptive strikes.

Beside this sporadic evidence, we have no other indication of direct trade contacts between Egypt and south Canaan during the Old Kingdom period. The major trade contact was undoubtedly played out by the maritime trade with Byblos. If we therefore automatically posit that the *raison d'être* of the city states of southern Canaan was the demand by the Egyptian market, we have to suppose a mediator capable of realizing the transactions. This is probable mainly because of the fact there is no indication whatsoever of direct trade of any sort or communication between Egypt and Canaan. It seems that this mediator could have been Byblos. This would also explain satisfactorily the occurrence of Canaanite EB III metallic ware in Egyptian tombs. However, more recent discoveries made in Abu Sir may argue for a complementary or alternative hypothesis.

II. 'Master of Imports', Qar Junior

Surprising new evidence has been brought to light quite recently, during the course of the Czech excavations in South Abu Sir. The family tomb complex of the vizier Qar and his sons in Abu Sir contained several burial chambers with a wealth of different classes of burial goods (Bárta and Vodera 2002; Bárta 2006; Bárta *et al.* 2007). There are two classes of artifacts that deserve our attention in this context: the large storage amphoras and assemblages of copper implements. They were discovered in several archaeological contexts. Probably the richest was the burial chamber of Qar Junior (Fig. 4).

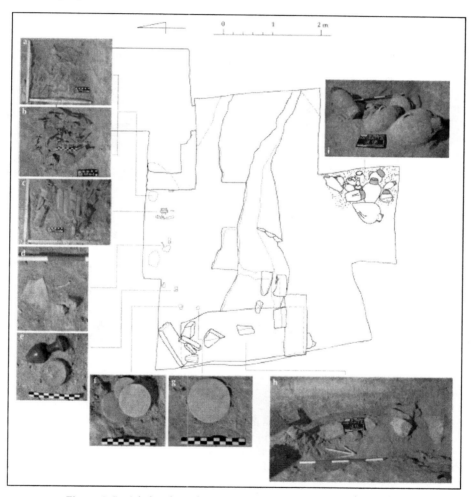

Figure 4. Burial chamber of Qar Junior in Abusir, distribution of finds
(Bárta *et al.* 2009: 170 fig. 6.2.23)

Qar Junior's burial chamber consisted of two parts: a western niche which contained the burial installation proper (a rectangular cavity cut in the limestone floor of the room measuring 2.50 × 1.00 m and 1.00 m deep), measuring 4.30 × 2.00 m, and the eastern, longer part of 5.20 × 2.20 m in ground plan, reserved for the burial equipment. On its floor were found rich remains of the original burial equipment. In the northeast corner of the chamber there was a huge copper hoard consisting of hundreds of implements. It is estimated that its weight was not less than 3.0 kg. Further to the west, still along the north wall of the chamber, there were birds and cattle bones and ribs, residue from the original meat offerings. In front of the sarcophagus pit, lying on the floor, were found several miniature plates of limestone and some other miniature stone vessels. The copper tools may be divided into several groups: razors, flat chisels, cross-cut chisels, knife blades, hooks and sticks (Reisner 1942; Kanawati and Hassan 1996 and Fig. 5 here).[3]

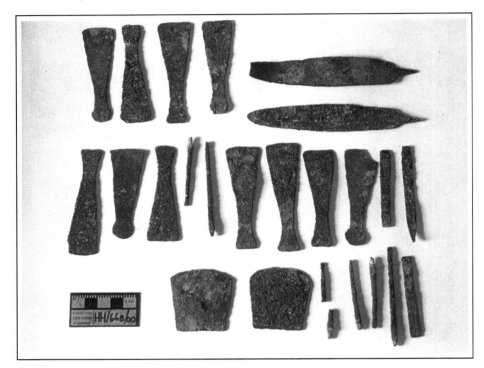

Figure 5. Copper implements from the tomb of Qar Junior (Bárta *et al.* 2009: pl. 28.2)

The copper implements were of essential importance in ancient Egyptian stone-working industry and building (beside many other crafts) and temples and tombs decoration. Copper tools used in combination with hard stone and wooden tools and abrasives (such as dolerite hammers and wooden mallets) were fairly suitable even for most laborious tasks (Arnold 1991: 257–67). It is a well-known fact that copper was considered to be a very important ore and one of its major known Old Kingdom sources, the site of Wadi Maghara in Sinai, was protected by many apotropaic

---

3.   Cf. Reisner 1942, pls. 43c (G 2150), 64f (G 4631 B), 69e (G 4520 A) or more recent Saqqara finds in Kanawati and Hassan 1996: pl. 13, TNE94:69, tomb of Kaaper.

compositions showing Egyptian pharaoh smiting his enemies. The access route to it started on the western shore of the Red Sea and was protected by a fortress built by the Egyptians (El-Markha Plain Site 345; cf. Mumford and Parcak 2004).

The fortress was discovered only recently by G. Mumford's expedition to South Sinai (Mumford 2006) and represents a unique piece of evidence for a more permanent presence of the Egyptians beyond the Eastern frontier. It has also been shown that the demand for copper was enormous. Dennis Stocks was able to demonstrate the copper tools needed to procure the granite sarcophagus chest of King Khufu situated in his pyramid at Giza necessitated more than 434 kg of copper and large quantities of many other materials (Stocks 2003). Based on the above evidence, it seems likely that currently known sources of copper in the Sinai Peninsula may not have been sufficient to sustain the 'pharaonic appetite' for copper. In this light, recent discoveries made by T.E. Levy *et al.* (2002) and his expedition at the Early Bronze III–IV site of Khirbet Hamra Ifdan in Jordan may provide a new perspective on this issue. The finds at Khirbat Hamra Ifdan represent the largest copper production site and possibly the largest source of copper ore known from the third millennium BCE in the whole southeastern Mediterranean basin (Levy *et al.* 2002; Hauptmann 2000, 2007 and Fig. 6 here). Moreover, formal comparison of the tools discovered in Abu Sir and at this site show very close similarities (Fig. 7). Was there a direct link between Jordan and Egypt during the Old Kingdom? Could this be the region of Bat? The definite solution will be provided by the comparative analysis of the copper implements and ultimately through archaeometallurgical provenance studies. The affirmative result would not come as a surprise given the FIP (EB IV) data collected by M. Haiman (1996).

Figure 6. Site of Khirbet Hamra Ifdan
(photographed with permission of T.E. Levy)

Figure 7. Comparison of copper implements from Abusir (above) and Khirbat Hamra Ifdan (Photos: Top—Czech Institute of Egyptology; Bottom—UCSD Levantine Archaeology Laboratory).

Of great interest is a group of fifteen vessels deposited and found *in situ* in the southeast corner of the burial chamber of Qar Junior (Excav. Nos. 86, 1-15/HH/2001, Fig. 8a here). The vessels were almost completely preserved and most of them were still sealed with Nile mud lids. Given the context, originally all of them must have been sealed. The vessels may be divided into two groups. The first of them consisted of six imitations of Syro-Palestinian amphoras—large, flat-bottomed jars, with or without two handles (nos. 2, 3, 4, 5, 6 and 12) made of Nile silt matrix (Sowada 2001). In the literature, this specimen of pottery is traditionally known as 'Combed Ware' (Greenberg and Porat 1996). Finely polished mud lids were about 8 cm high and flat on the top (diam. about 11 cm)(compare contemporary and almost identical finds from Giza tomb shaft G 2381 A [Impy]: Reisner and Smith 1955: 54, fig. 54, pl. 52g). The seals of these six exemplars were almost intact and still bore readable imprints of one cylinder seal with finely carved hieroglyphic signs. According to the inscriptions, it is clear that the jars were sealed in Egypt, at the estate of Qar Junior. It is interesting to put these jars into historical contexts as the praxis of their inclusion in the burial equipment of high officials during the Old Kingdom is not singular. During the Fourth Dynasty they occur in elite tombs of high officials buried in Giza (Helck 1962: ware 'Q', and 'R'). During this period, the vessels were associated only with elite members of the society, mostly of royal origin, and exclusively with men (with but one exception).

Figure 8a. Pottery from the burial chamber of Qar Junior (Photo—Jo. Malátková)

Figure 8b. Drawing of ceramic storage jar from Qar Junior's burial chamber (Courtesy of Czech Institute of Egyptology).

One question is inescapable: Are the Fifth- and Sixth-Dynasty jars associated with the Levant genuine imports or not? According to Karin Sowada (2001), who studied Abu Sir pieces as well as those from Fourth-Dynasty Giza, they represent real imports. T. Rzeuska (pers. comm.) in her treatment of the Saqqara specimens from the Polish excavations arrived at a contrary conclusion.

It must be said, however, that there is a qualitative difference between the Saqqara and Abu Sir exemplars—the matrix they are made of, which is Nile silt. Moreover, in one case, Excav. No. 86-1/HH/2000, it is more than evident that the vessels were produced in Egypt and designed to imitate the luxurious imports containing highly valued wine (Fig. 8b). It is a two-handled amphora with a flat bottom and out-turned neck with a roll rim. At the place where the neck joins the body of the amphora is a plastic collar with an imitation rope decoration. The surface of the vessel is a red–orange colour with a partly preserved white wash, and shows clear traces of the 'combing' technique typical of imported amphoras known from Old Kingdom Egypt. Given the poor firing, the softness of the sherd and its appearance upon fracture (Nile Silt A), it must be concluded that it is a copy of a genuine vessel of the type produced in Egypt.

This type of vessel has been classified as 'collared rim pithoi' with a narrow neck. Re-evaluation of this type of pottery has shown that it occurs from the Chalcolithic period onwards and its geographic distribution includes Cyprus, northern Syria, Anatolia, the middle and upper Eufrates and Israel. Close contemporary and typological parallels to this item have been found at several sites in Israel (Yannai 2006). What makes the Abu Sir piece so unusual is the combination of the collar with two handles, which is so far unattested in the original material and therefore most likely an invention of the Egyptian craftsman who conflated characteristic features of two different pottery types (for details, see Bárta *et al.* 2007).

Figure 9. Scene with imported pottery from the mastaba of Ptahshepses (Photo—M. Bárta)

New light on this issue may be thrown by the latest discovery in the famous mastaba of Ptahshepses in Abu Sir. During the fall season 2005 a new relief fragment came to light.[4] Despite its weathered state, it provides fresh evidence for imported vessels. It shows an offering bearer of higher social standing (as indicated by his pointed kilt) carrying on his left shoulder a vessel typologically identical with those found in Abu Sir South (Fig. 9). It is the only evidence of this kind known from the Old Kingdom residential area. The mastaba of Ptahshepses is well known both for its historically important owner and its architecture and decoration. Ptahshepses was among the highest members of the state, one of the first who was given the privilege of marrying a royal daughter. The architecture of his mastaba may be labeled as 'daunting' and its decoration program as 'unrivaled' in his time (Bárta 2006). This may be why he chose to include such an unparalleled scene in his decoration. In this light it is highly unlikely that a man of such status would make use of a 'faked' or an imitation piece of pottery in order to emulate highly prestigious commodity and thus his status, since he was a real vizier (e.g. almighty deputy) of the ruler. The importance ascribed to this 'vehicle' of high status during the Fourth and Fifth Dynasties highlights the Sixth-Dynasty milieu, when officials of lower standing were using the 'faked' pottery as a means of social-status identification in the afterlife.

III. Copper Traders of the EB IV?

Following the collapse of the Old Kingdom during the 22nd century BCE we are faced with corresponding significant changes on the Egyptian periphery—in the settlement area of southern Canaan. During this period we observe the virtually complete disappearance of cities and large settled areas in northern and Central Palestine and the appearance of small settlements in Transjordan, the Jordan valley and in Negev and the Sinai with a preference for herding, dry-farming and stock breeding. There are exceptions to this general trend, such as the urban center at Khirbet Iskander in Jordan (Richard 1987). This general picture of the subsistence economy is also confirmed by the animal offerings in EB IV tombs, consisting mainly of goat and sheep (Greenhut 1995). This shift in the economy was probably the result of a combination of factors, such as the warming and drying of the climate (Dalfes, Kukla and Weiss 1997; Issar and Zohar 2004), and the disappearance of their perhaps 'too-tight relationship' with the vanishing Old Kingdom period in Egypt demonstrated above all by the loss of a large 'international' market (Esse 1989).

There is no indication whatsoever that a change in the subsistence pattern would have been a response to some sudden natural calamity such as an epidemic. It has been estimated that the EB III population consisted of about 100,000–150,000 inhabitants and the density of EB IV sites throughout the region seems to correspond with this number. In other words, the major change occurring at the transition between EB III and EB IV, most likely a complex process including a major climate change, collapse of the Egyptian market and shift in the subsistence strategies in most parts of the Levant, had no significant impact on the population size (Dever 2003). Comparable data emerge from the FIP in Egypt. The collapse of central administration and almost complete disappearance of central institutions did not mean that there was no administration at all, nor that there would have been a major decline in population size. Instead, the territory of the Egyptian state disintegrated into smaller provincial chiefdoms run and administered by local elites.

There are numerous settlements that attest to the nature of the period—some of which have been excavated (Cohen and Cohen-Amin 2004). One of the principal ones is the site of Beer Resisim in the Central Negev highlands (Dever 1985b). This was a single period occupation site consisting of several dozen circular sleeping huts made of stone, measuring 2–4 m in diameter, roofed with

---

4.   The block has never been published. Its publication is in preparation by my colleague B. Vachala.

timber and chalk slabs and plaster construction usually resting on a central pillar. The finds attest to some dry farming of wheat or barley whereas copper ingots may indicate long-distance trade, as was the case with the EB I and II sites. Each cluster of circular huts for both sleeping and other activities was grouped around an open court. It seems that each cluster may be assigned to a single family unit consisting of one male, 1–3 females and 2–6 children. The whole population residing in Beer Resisim may be estimated as being about 40–80 persons (Dever 1985b). This evidence indicates that local pastoral populations could had been involved in long-distance copper trade.

The sites of Jebel Qa'aqir in the southern Hebron Hills and several sites in Transjordan such as Khirbat Iskander and Bab ed-Dhra show clearly that there was no marked break or major discontinuity during the transition of EB III and EB IV (Richard 2003: 294–300). This is indicated primarily by the undisturbed pottery sequence. Another indication for a continuum in terms of the population and its cultural traits is represented by the EB IV cemeteries. The manifold typology of individual tomb types also shows some Syrian influence during this period (Greenhut 1995). Based on the 1999–2000 excavations at Khirbat Hamra Ifdan (KHI) in the Faynan district, a similar picture is emerging from this part of southern Jordan (Levy *et al*. 2002; Adams 2000). Last but not least, there is a clearly discernible tumuli tradition in Sinai and Negev continuing, as mentioned earlier, in the EB IV that is most likely a continuation of EB I–II tumuli mortuary traditions (Greenhut 1995).

Based on these data, it is important to ask if there were any contacts between Egypt and Canaan at all during the EB IV and, if so, what was their nature. M. Haiman's (1996) study has indicated that there might have been a relatively intensive copper trade between Egypt and south Canaan undertaken by the Asiatic population precisely during this period. His conclusions were based on permanent and temporary sites discovered mostly in the Central Negev highlands. The distribution pattern of these sites shows that most of the temporary sites were connected with the permanent ones. Moreover, they were situated in a belt 30 km wide to the south of them and covered the area extending from the southwest of the Dead Sea westwards to the Nile Delta along the line of the northern Sinai sea shore. More importantly, the whole area is characterized by the same uniform culture traits of the pottery S group.

One of the most instructive sites was Har Yaroham. On this site, almost 30% of Stratum C was occupied by industrial activity. There were found about 30 installations and magazines with a significantly large number of hammer stones, mortars and grinding stones. Along with these features, the site contained many stone installations with ashes and other traces of intensive burning and a large number of copper chips and fragments of copper ingots everywhere on the site. Altogether 19 ingots were found in area C. Much similar evidence was discovered at sites such as En Ziq, Har Zayyad and Mashabbe Sade (Cohen and Cohen-Amin 2004). This means that a significant number of sites in Negev had these traces of copper hammering and transportation activities. Since the temporary sites consisted mainly of single huts suitable only for sleeping, it is certainly possible that they were used by the caravan members on their way to or from Egypt.

According to Haiman (1996), it is possible that the EB IV fortified city of Khirbat Iskander (where remains of copper working were also found), Iktanu, Bab ed Dhra, Aroer, Tell el-Hayat, Ader, Tell Um Hammad and other cities may have organized the whole copper caravan trade with copper that may have originated from the Faynan district to the south (Richard 1987). In this light, it is probably correct to speak of the EB IV period in terms of urban regression, rather than of a nomadic interlude. It seems that the centre of development during the EB IV period was lying to the east of the Jordan river. The red slipped and burnished pottery of the EB III period (platters, bowls, jars, jugs and so on) also demonstrates the same continuity.

However, up to the present time, there is no EB IV/FIP site in the Eastern Delta that would confirm the supposed copper trade. It seems quite plausible that the site of Wadi Faynan could be a major source of copper ore for EB IV Egypt. The imports to Egypt during this period can be summarized as follows: copper, bronze, cedar wood, perhaps some Levantine pottery and lapis lazuli. The Egyptian could pay the prices in gold, luxurious items such as stone vessels, jewellery, carnelian beads, turquoise or even the cattle. Most of these commodities belong, however, to the so-called invisible items that are impossible to be tracked down by archaeology as they leave almost no remains along the trade routes. Only recently it was also confirmed that Timna copper mines were in operation during this time and thus this area may be also included in the above considerations (Yekutieli, Shalev and Shilstein 2005). But archaeological evidence is not the only source of information that we can successfully expose to modern scholarship.

IV. Deconstructing Sinuhe

Moving on, 20th-century BCE Egypt presents us with a completely different record. Following the re-unification, Egypt resumes its stately shape and organization. Its rulers organized military campaigns against Canaan and undoubtedly knew very well what was going on to the east of Egypt. One of the best testimonies of the period of the forthcoming Twelfth Dynasty may be the literary composition of Sinuhe (Bárta 2003). It was used for several centuries as one of the most fundamental sources for learning Middle Egyptian grammar in ancient Egypt as witnessed by frequent finds on New Kingdom ostracas. As such it has been frequently analysed by modern Egyptologists primarily for its language, grammatical features and general historical significance, being considered to be a politically stimulated work of art serving its specific pedagogic purpose (Parkinson 2002: 149ff.). Proper historical evaluation of the story and interpretation of individual passages has become a matter of dispute far less frequently. To simplify the matter a bit, one could say that the story has usually been taken as a masterpiece of literature yet entirely fictional. In 1996, K.A. Kitchen added his voice in support of the historicity of Sinuhe. He based his argument on comparison with historically relatively accurate biographies of ancient Egyptian high officials.

Studies of this subject matter by A. Rainey, however, resulted in his complete dismissal of Sinuhe's story as a possible source of information for the situation in the Levant at the beginning of the 20th century BCE (Rainey 1972, 2006). Looking at the text from an archaeological perspective, it may be said at the beginning that despite the completely fictional story, many points of the narrative use facts that fit particularly well with our knowledge of the period based on other, entirely independent perspectives (Bárta 2003). This holds true for Egypt as well as for the Levant.

Sinuhe's fictitious account—we still possess no evidence that he was an actual individual—is dated to the beginning of the second millennium BCE. Its author is unknown, which is typical of ancient Egyptian literature, in which authorship was not considered an important issue (Loprieno 1996, *passim*; Redford 2000). Sinuhe's story may be summarized as follows: the first king of the Middle Kingdom, Amenemhat I, is assassinated while his son Senusret I is off leading a military campaign against the Bedouin in the Western Desert. After the king's death, messengers are dispatched to his son in order to inform him about the circumstances of his father's demise. Senusret leaves the army, which is on its way back to Egypt, and speeds to Egypt to suppress the potential revolt in the capital. The high courtier Sinuhe overhears the message of the royal envoys and, out of fear of being considered among those responsible for the assassination, sets flight. He eventually leaves Egypt and joins the south Levantine Bedouin to the northeast of the Egyptian frontier. The Bedouin chieftain develops an affection for Sinuhe, marries his daughter to him, gives him part of his tribe, and assigns territory to him. Sinuhe spends most of his life here, surrounded by his new family. However, he is also compelled to defend his position at the head of his tribe. Thus, one day a giant arrives, the hero of the land of Retjenu, to challenge Sinuhe to battle in order to take possession of his property. The following day Sinuhe fights an almost hopeless duel; in the end, however, he is victorious. This story was, according to some scholars, the inspiration of the account of the duel of David and Goliath, dating to almost a millennium later (Lanczkowski 1958; Bárta 2003). In the end Sinuhe, encouraged by the king, returns to Egypt in his old age, where he is welcomed as a close friend of the king, who takes care of him and has a tomb built for him in the necropolis. Thus Sinuhe's existence in the afterlife is guaranteed.

Despite the fact that the story is considered to be fictitious, many descriptions and events included in it correspond to the conditions and environment that we know from the contemporary archaeological and written evidence from Syria-Palestine. Sinuhe's story takes place in the context of the political, economic and human events of ancient Egypt and Syria-Palestine during the twentieth and nineteenth centuries BCE (Bárta 2003). A similar conclusion was reached simultaneously by Kitchen who considers this period to be the real cultural background of Genesis 14 (Kitchen 2003: 313ff.).

Sinuhe's story was conceived by its author(s) above all as a political composition, on the basis of which Amenemhat's son and successor was to be cleared of all charges concerning his possible participation in the assassination of his father or its organization. This is also attested by the passages celebrating King Senusret I (once in a hymn, the second time in a letter from Sinuhe to the king). At the same time, however, Sinuhe's account is also a description of the life of a loyal Egyptian official, who, despite his flight from Egypt (as a consequence of the 'intention of God', as he himself makes clear), remains true to the principles characterizing the Egyptian official, i.e. loyalty to the Egyptian king, religiosity—Sinuhe never conceived of worshipping foreign gods despite his lengthy stay abroad—and the desire to be buried in the Egyptian homeland in the vicinity of his lord. To an extent, Sinuhe's text gives an impression of an ethical treatise. It is thus even now extremely difficult to determine its genre; it is a fairy tale and at the same time a political manifesto with typical biographical elements (for details, see Bárta 2003; Blumenthal 2005).

Sinuhe's account, one of the most interesting works of ancient Egyptian literature, remains one of the most frequently discussed literary sources from the Middle Kingdom. From this era, two partially damaged papyri with the composition are preserved, namely Papyrus Berlin 3022 (abbreviated in egyptological literature as B), which has a damaged beginning and contains altogether 311 lines, and Papyrus Berlin 10499 (abbreviated as R), which contains 203 lines and a preserved beginning. The popularity of Sinuhe's account is attested by the fact that it continued to be copied for several subsequent centuries.

Sinuhe's account describes southern Levant as tribal and makes no reference to permanent or fortified settlements (Bárta 2003: 36ff.; Tallet 2005). Moreover, the area is the arena of extra-tribal conflicts—he even becomes involved in one of them. As a head of 'his' adopted tribe, he has to fight a duel against a 'Strong of Retjenu'—a hopeless duel that he eventually wins. The structure of the story may well be the precursor of the much later famous duel of David and Goliath as described in the Hebrew Bible (Bárta 2003: 49ff.; comp. Blumenthal 2005).

V. The Middle Kingdom Influx from the East

Given the wealth of published material found in clear stratigraphic contexts from Egypt, and the lack of other evidence, it is sites from Egypt such as Tell el-Dab'a, the pyramid necropolis at Lisht and the Kom el-Rabia settlement of Memphis that can shed some more light on the chronology of this period and support the 'Middle' chronological variant of A. Mazar, W.G. Dever and others, placing the beginning of the MB IIa to the first decades of the 20th millennium BCE (Mazar 1986). This has important implications for ultimately examining the relationship of the archaeological and historical records of Egypt and the southern Levant with the periods often associated with the Patriarchs mentioned in the Hebrew Bible.

The magisterial work of D. Arnold on the Middle Kingdom pottery from the pyramid necropolis at Lisht has shown clearly that imports of Canaanite pottery in Egypt first occur only during the second half of the Middle Kingdom, starting with the reigns of Senusret III and Amenemhat III. The same result was reached by the Egypt Exploration Society excavation at Kom el-Rabia at Memphis (Arnold, Arnold and Allen 1995; Bourriau 1990).

It is above all the stratigraphy of Tell el-Dab'a that provides the cornerstone for any attempt to classify the available evidence. The recent study by E. Czerny *et al.* (1999) shows that the early Middle Kingdom 'Asiatic' artifacts are limited to a layer labeled by the excavators as F/1, Str. e. In this layer, together with Egyptian pottery, coarsely fired hand-made cooking pots of Palestinian EB IV period were discovered, also attesting to a behavioral interface with a probable trade-like pattern between the Canaanite and Sinai nomads during this time. The petrographic composition of several sherds has shown that some of the clays are non-Egyptian and supposedly originate from south Sinai or the area of Arad. Is it possible that these sherds were left behind by south Levantine nomads grazing their herds in the Delta during the early Middle Kingdom, a possibility alluded to also in the story of Sinuhe.

Moreover, it has convincingly been shown by Czerny, Boessneck and Driesch that during the Middle Kingdom it was probably the Pelusiac branch of the Nile that represented the eastern border of Egypt (Czerny, Boessneck and Driesch 1999: 14–15; Butzer 2002). Tell el-Dab'a at this time played a vital role as one of the important site on the Ways of Horus from Egypt to Palestine and Sinai (thus its ancient Egyptian name 'Opening of Tow Ways'), and it may even be interpreted as one of the border sites. Generally speaking, we can observe that most of the MBII sites in Delta are concentrated along the eastern bank of the Pelusiac branch of the Nile or along the two principal communication routes: Wadi Tumilat and the Ways of Horus.

The initial settlement (Stratum F/1) of the Canaanites in Tell el-Dab'a goes back to the late Twelfth Dynasty, to the reign of Senusret III who seems to be the first ruler to pay some attention to this settlement. The settlement exemplifies architecture that is foreign in Egypt—the so-called 'Mittelsaal- and Breitraumhäuser'. This settlement also included cemeteries attached to the houses. The tombs are constructed in a purely Egyptian manner. It is interesting that about 50% of the male burials contained weapons, a clear indication that these settlers were soldiers in the military service of the Egyptian king. Clearly, they were also engaged in other activities, such as participation in expeditions to Sinai, organized presumably from Tell el-Dab'a. The inscriptions from Wadi Maghara attest to this fact and most of them are dated to the reign of Amenemhat III. They clearly show that Asiatic soldiers were accompanying these expeditions. Some of the expeditions were even headed by an Asiatic, as in the case of Imeni. Moreover, it seems that their camps in the Sinai were supplied by Asiatic tribes, for example by that of Khebded, who was the brother of the prince of Retjenu.

This seems to be supported by the pottery of Canaanite origin in well-dated contexts in Egypt. Disregarding a single find of a sherd with a rope imprint decoration of a questionable early Twelfth-Dynasty date, the first more precisely dated exemplars come from the tomb complex LNP Tomb 756 from Lisht North. These were two juglets of Levantine painted ware and the tomb was dated to the reigns of Amenemhat II, Senusret II and Senusret III (Arnold, Arnold and Allen 1995).

From the reign of Sesostris III (1878–43 BCE), one can observe features connected to increasing urbanism in Palestine that may fall into MB IIb 'urban phase' (Dever 1997). The evidence compiled by S. Cohen shows that there were 131 sites in Canaan with attested MB II levels. Only 19 settlements were fortified. It must be noted, however, that most of these sites were not fortified prior to the middle phase of MB IIa (Cohen 2002). The evidence known so far seems to indicate that during the MB IIa, the number of fortified sites was relatively low, and that cemeteries and tombs dominated. Broschi and Gophna (1986) estimate that the MB IIa population was about 106,500 (calculating 250 individuals per hectare).

No effective model has yet been proposed that would explain the mechanism of the process leading to the return of urbanism in the area. Currently we assume that this process consisted of the interplay of several contributing factors, such as the cooling of the climate, increasing humidity and temperature at the beginning of this period (Issar 1998), more sophisticated and elaborate water management providing cities with cisterns and rock-cut wells (Miller 1980), and the re-ensuing need for long-distance trade and its coordination by local elites of the city states (Dever 1993). Recently, a model for urbanization during 3rd-millenium BCE Syria has been developed by A. Potter (2002) emphasizing the ritual aspects of communal cemeteries and the ancestral cult mechanisms. It is very likely that these factors could also have been in operation during later historical periods in the area.

Many of these settlements and cemeteries in Canaan provided numerous Egyptian finds. These finds have always attracted the interest of archaeologists, since objects bearing royal names could often be used as chronological indicators. There has been much discussion of Egyptian finds in Canaan during this period. Older views included those claiming that there was intensive trade with Egypt and that Egypt attempted to establish new colonies in the region. More recent studies show unequivocally that this theory does not fit the evidence. It is more likely that the Middle Kingdom resumed the standing Old Kingdom policy of fortresses and occasional preventive strikes and that these finds owe much to late Twelfth-Dynasty development and later (Ben Tor 2003).

What does the Egyptian Twelfth Dynasty tells us? Not much, but still we can glean some information from the limited sources for the period under discussion. Above all, it is interesting to note that during the Middle Kingdom there is not a single depiction of the Egyptian king smiting his enemies as used to be standard during the Old Kingdom, although Amenemhat I had already firmly re-established the Egyptian presence in Sinai at Serabit el-Khadim (Mumford 1999).

If we look at the Annals of Amenemhat II from Mitrahina, we see that the number of Asiatic captives from two settlements was about 1500 people (Altenmüller and Moussa 1991 and Fig. 10). This gives us a picture of Asiatic settlements at the end MB IIa 'pre-urban' period, when small fortified sites were already emerging:

> S16—Return of the army and the military unit that were sent to destroy the fortress Iwai and subvert the fortress Iasy. Number of captives that were brought from these two foreign lands:
> Asiatics: 1,554,
> Bronze and wood: axes—10, sickles—33, blades—12, saws—4 a 1/4, knives—79,
> S 17—...fragments of copper: 646 deben (8,5 kg), New copper: 125 deben (1,6 kg).

If we compare these with the commodities that were brought from a single expedition to Byblos, we see clearly where the Egyptian sphere of interest was and the difference in amount of the procured items:

> S18—Return of expedition that was sent forth to Byblos in two ships. It brings:
> Silver: 1,676 a 1/2 deben (22 kg),
> S19—bronze: 48,882 deben (635 kg), copper: 15,961 deben (207 kg), white lead: 1410 deben (18 kg), marble: 13 stones, abrasive sand: 16,588 deben (215 kg), polishing sand: 39,556 deben (514 kg)...
> S21—...Asiatics—men and women: 65...

From the evidence above it is clear that southern Canaan was considered as a potential enemy that had to be subdued with military might and fortresses. Egypt's number one economic connection remained Byblos. It is interesting to note that whereas during the reign of Senusret I Canaan is described as a land of Bedouin, Amenemhat II considers it important in his Annals to mention that he subjugated two fortresses in Canaan (given the booty listed, quite small ones) and that the last military campaign dates to the reign of Senusret III, probably against Sekhem yet with a very dubious outcome (Tallet 2005: 172-77). As urbanism developed during the latter half of MB IIA, and reached its peak in the 17th century BCE in southern Canaan in a power formation centering on Sharuhen (Oren 1997), one gets the impression that as soon as there were numerous city states, the Egyptians were no longer willing to take their chances venturing into Canaan. They preferred, at least it seems, to renew and re-establish borders in Nubia as Senusret III did or to intensify trade with Byblos and focus on expeditions to Sinai—from the reign of Amenemhat III, at least 49 inscriptions are known from Serabit el-Khadim. Indeed, it is striking that from the reigns of the wealthiest pharaohs, no true military campaigns against the Asiatics are known. Thus from the diachronic perusal of the Middle Kingdom written sources a picture emerges with different priorities during different periods.

Figure 10. Annals of Amenemhat I in Mit Rahineh (Photo—courtesy of J. Malek)

Another vital source of our information about Canaan during the Middle Kingdom are several groups of Egyptian Execration texts dated from 1,850—1,750 BCE designed to defeat on a magical level the forces hostile to the pharaoh and Egypt. These come from the Nubian site of Mirgissa (dated as 1900–1850 BCE), Berlin group (Sesostris III or early Amenemhet III) and Saqqara/Brussels group (about 20–40 years later than the Berlin group) (see Redford 1993: 87–93 for a detailed treatment of the issue). Even though these texts were purely magical, and their structure and composition was to a high degree a matter of formalism, we can discern vital differences and shifts in their factual information. In the earlier texts, the Mirgissa and Berlin groups, several chiefs are connected with one toponym, in six cases no fewer than three. In the Brussels group, each place is connected just with one ruler. In the Mirgissa texts four toponyms refer to coastal sites—Byblos, Ulazza, and probably Anaki and Mugar—of which one is in Transjordan and none in central Palestine. The Berlin group refers to coastal toponyms—Arkata, Ashkelon, Ulazza and Byblos—and in three cases to maritime sites—Anaki, Mugar and Sapa. The picture that emerges is that of a rural country with several city states along the coast.

The Brussels group, on the other hand, being about two generations later, seems to be much more logically structured and, in principle, the listing of sites follows the main communication roads. This group quotes about four times as many sites as the Berlin group, is well organized and seems to reflect a change in the geopolitical situation in the region, with much settlement inland. How are we to explain this phenomenon? Is it just a chance that the texts look as they do? Despite their much-disputed historical significance or irrelevance, given the progress in chronology, we may claim that they reflect the actual development in Canaan. And what were the sources of the Egyptians? The answer is given already in Sinuhe's story when he mentions that all Egyptian messengers going northwards and returning southwards stopped and stayed with him. It seems feasible that it was these Egyptian messengers that kept the Egyptian administration well informed about current development to the northeast of the Egyptian eastern border. As shown here, the power of the 'Tale of Sinuhe' for re-examining the relationship between Egyptology, the archaeology of the southern Levant and the Hebrew Bible can not be minimized.

VI. Summary and Outlook

It is not an easy matter to foresee the further development of the relationship between Egyptology and Biblical Archaeology. Looking at the interconnections between Egyptology and Biblical Archaeology it becomes evident that a crucial role was played, as has been always claimed, by the Eastern Delta in Egypt and the Sinai peninsula, in the changing relationship between the two regions from late Pre-Dynastic to the Old Kingdom period times. It seems that both archaeological and epigraphic evidence from Egypt and Canaan support the conclusion that MB IIA started at the beginning of the 20th century BCE and was contemporary with formation of the Middle Kingdom state in Egypt. In view of the recent policy of the Supreme Council of Antiquities in Egypt to boost archaeological excavation of the Delta, it may be expected that some newly discovered Eastern Delta sites will shed some further light on the subject, especially for the EB IV period.

In my opinion, the current intensive research in the field of Historical Biblical Archeology should evaluate and make detailed reference to what is going on in Egyptology in general and in Egyptian archaeology specifically. What may be worthy of reconsideration is more intensive collaboration of the specialists from both respective fields. The Tell el-Borg project (Hoffmeier 2004) may serve as a stimulating example. It may be also expected that the EB IV period may change in the near future basically because more and more cemeteries dating to the late Sixth Dynasty and the First Intermediate period are being excavated. The Old Kingdom evidence seems to indicate relatively strong Egyptian interests in the Eastern border and the countries beyond it (as evidenced by wooden statues of prisoners, titles of high officials of the state, imported vessels). The same holds true for the Middle Kingdom (the Annals of Amenemhat II, Execration texts). Thus the current evidence may challenge the still-popular notion that the Egypt of the 3rd and early 2nd millennia BCE has very little to offer to the current Biblical discourse.[5] It is difficult to expect some new results without a prior expenditure of effort and specific research, in particular the Old Kingdom contacts and interactions with the Levant and Middle Kingdom as a real Egyptian backdrop of Genesis 14 and the patriarchal period certainly deserve close attention in the future. It may be expected that the new evidence and old 'facts' dressed in new, more fitting suit may provide some clues for future research.

---

5.   Cf. Hoffmeier and Millard 2004, which neglects the discussed period entirely.

References

Adams, R.B. (2000) The Early Bronze Age III–IV Transition in Southern Jordan: Evidence from Khirbet Hamra Ifdan. In *Ceramics and Change in the Early Bronze Age of the Southern Levant*, edited by G. Philip and D. Baird (Sheffield: Sheffield Academic Press): 379–401.

Ahituv, S. (1984) *Canaanite Toponyms in Ancient Egyptians Documents* (Jerusalem: Magnes Press, Hebrew University).

Altenmüller, H., and A. Moussa (1991) Die Inschrift Amenemhets II. aus dem Ptah-Tempel von Memphis. Ein Vorberricht. *Studien zur altägyptichen Kultur* 18: 1–48.

Arnold, D. (1991) *Building in Egypt: Pharaonic Stone Masonry* (Oxford: Oxford University Press).

Arnold, D., F. Arnold and S. Allen (1995) Canaanite Imports at Lisht, the Middle Kingdom Capital of Egypt. *Ägypten und Levante* 5: 3–32.

El-Awadi, T. (2006) Pyramid Causeway in the Old Kingdom; Evolution of the Architecture and Definition of the Relief decoration Program (Ph.D. diss., Charles University, Prague).

Bárta, M. (2001) Abusir V: The Cemeteries at Abusir South I (Prague: SETOUT).

—(2003) *Sinuhe, the Bible, and the Patriarchs—with a Foreword by Thomas E. Levy* (Prague: SETOUT).

—(2005) Architectural Innovations in the Development of the Non-royal Tomb during the Reign of Nyuserra. In *Structure and Significance: Thoughts on Ancient Egyptian Architecture*, edited by P. Jánosi (Vienna: Verlag der Österreichischen Akademie der Wissenschaften): 105-30.

—(2006) The Sixth Dynasty Tombs in Abusir: Tomb Complex of the Vizier Qar and his Family. In *Old Kingdom Art and Archaeology Proceedings*, edited by M. Bárta (Praha: Academia): 45–62.

Bárta, M., and K. Vodera (2002) *Memories of 4500 Years Ago* (Foto–Grafika: Brandýs n. Labem).

Bárta, M. *et al.* (2009) *Abusir XIII: Tomb Complex of the Vizier Qar, his Sons Qar Junior and Senedjemib, and Iykai. Abusir South 2* (Prague: Czech Institute of Egyptology).

Benešovská, H. (2006) Statues from the Pyramid Complex of the King Raneferef. In Verner *et al.* 2006: 360-467.

Ben Tor, D. (2003) Egyptian-Levantine Relations and Chronology in the Middle Bronze Age: Scarab Research. in *The Synchronisation of Civilisations in the Eastern Mediterranean in the Second Millenium B.C. II*, edited by M. Bietak (Vienna: Verlag der Österreichischen Akademie der Wissenschaften): 239-48.

Blumenthal, E. (2005) Sinuhes Feindbilder. In *Feinde und Aufrührer: Konzepte von Gegnerschaft in ägyptischen Texten besonders des Mittleren Reiches*, edited by H. Felber (Leipzig: Verlag der Sächsischen Akademie der Wissenschaften zu Leipzig): 32–61.

Bourriau, J. (1990) Canaanite Jars from New Kingdom Deposits at Memphis, Kom el-Rabia. *Eretz-Israel* 21: 18-26.

Brandl, B. (1992) Evidence for Egyptian Colonization of the Southern Coastal Plain and Lowlands of Canaan during the Early Bronze I Period. In van den Brink 1992: 441-76.

van den Brink, E.C.M. (ed.) (1992) *The Nile Delta in Transition: 4th–3rd Millenium B.C.* (Tel Aviv: The Israel Exploration Society).

Brink, E.C.M. van den, and T.E. Levy (eds.) (2002) *Egypt and the Levant: Interrelations from the 4th through the Early 3rd* Millennium BCE (London/New York: Leicester University Press).

Butzer, K.W. (2002) Geoarchaeological Implications of Recent Research in the Nile Delta. In van den Brink and Levy 2002: 83–97.

Cohen, R., and R. Cohen-Amin (2004) *Ancient Settlement of the Negev Highlands*, II (Jerusalem: The Israel Antiquity Authority).

Cohen, S. (2002) *Canaanites, Chronology, and Connections: The Relationship of Middle Bronze Age IIA Canaan to Middle Kingdom Egypt* (Studies in the Archaeology and History of the Levant 3; Winona Lake, IN: Eisenbrauns).

Czerny, E., J. Boessneck and A.v.d. Driesch (1999) *Tell el-Dab'a IX: eine Plansiedlung des frühen Mittleren Reiches* (Wien: Österreichische Akademie der Wissenschaften).

Dalfes, H.N., G. Kukla and H. Weiss (eds.) (1997) *Third Millennium BC Climate Change and Old World Collapse* (Berlin/New York: Springer).

Davis, T.W. (2004) *Shifting Sands: The Rise and Fall of Biblical Archaeology* (Oxford: Oxford University Press).

Dever, W.G. (1985a) Syro-Palestinian and Biblical Archaeology. In *The Hebrew Bible and its Modern Interpreters*, edited by D. Knight and G.M. Tucker (Philadelphia: Fortress Press): 31-74.

—(1985b) Village Planning at Be'er Resisim and Socio-economic Structure in Early Bronze Age IV Palestine. *Eretz Israel* 18: 18–28.

—(1993) The Rise of Complexity in Palestine in the Early Second Millenium BCE. In *Biblical Archaeology Today, 1990: Proceedings of the Second International Congress on Biblical Archaeology, Jerusalem, June 1990* (Jerusalem: Israel Exploration Society): 98-109.

—(1997) Settlement Patterns and Chronology of Palestine in the Middle Bronze Age. In Oren 1997: 285-301.

—(2003) Social Structure in the Early Bronze IV Period in Palestine. In *The Archaeology of Society in the Holy Land*, edited by T.E. Levy (London/New York: Continuum): 282-96.

Esse, D.L. (1989) Secondary State Formation and Collapse in Early Bronze Age Palestine. In *L'urbanisation de la Palestine à l'âge du Bronze ancien. Bilan et perspectives des recherches actuelles*, edited by P. de Miroschedji (*BAR* IS 527; Oxford: Oxbow Books): 81–107.

Fischer, H.G. (1959) A Scribe of the Army in a Saqqara Mastaba of the Early Fifth Dynasty. *JNES* 18/4: 260-65.

Gophna, R. (2002) Elusive Anchorage Points along the Israel Littoral and the Egyptian–Canaanite Maritime Route during the Early Bronze Age I. In van den Brink and Levy 2002: 418-21.

Greenberg, R., and N. Porat (1996) A Third Millennium Levantine Pottery Production Center: Typology, Petrography, and Provenance of the Metallic Ware of Northern Israel and Adjacent Regions. *BASOR* 301: 5–24.

Greenhut, Z. (1995) EB IV Tomb and Burial in Palestine. *Tel Aviv* 22/1: 3–46.

Haiman, M. (1996) Early Bronze Age IV Settlement Pattern of the Negev and Sinai Deserts: View from Small Marginal Temporary Sites. *BASOR* 303: 1–32.

Halpern, B. (1988) *The First Historians: The Hebrew Bible and History* (San Francisco: Harper & Row).

Hartung, U. (2002) Imported Jars from Cemetery U at Abydos and the Relations between Egypt and Canaan in Predynastic Times. In van den Brink and Levy 2002: 437-49,

Hartung, U., L.J. Exner, N. Porat, and Y. Goren (2001) *Umm el-Qaab II: Importkeramik aus dem Friedhof U in Abydos (Umm el-Qaab) und die Beziehungen ägyptens zu Vorderasien im 4. Jahrtausend v. Chr* (Mainz am Rhein: P. von Zabern).

Hassan, S. (1953) *Excavations at Giza, 1935–1936. VII. The Mastaba of the Seventh Season and their Description* (Cairo: Government Press).

Hauptmann, A. (2000) *Zur frühen Metallurgie des Kupfers in Fenan* (Der Anschnitt Beiheft 11; Bochum: Deutsches Bergbau-Museum).

—(2007) *The Archaeo-metallurgy of Copper—Evidence from Faynan, Jordan* (New York: Springer).

Helck, W. (1962) *Die Beziehungen Ägyptens zu Vorderasien im 3. und 2. Jahrtausend v. Chr.* (Ägyptologische Abhandlungen 5; Wiesbaden: Harrassowitz).

Hoffmeier, J.K. (2004) The North Sinai Archaeological Project's Excavations at Tell el-Borg (Sinai): An Example of the 'New' Biblical Archaeology? In Hoffmeier and Millard 2004.

—(2006) 'The Walls of the Ruler' in Egyptian Literature and the Archaeological Record: Investigating Egypt's Eastern Frontier in the Bronze Age. *BASOR* 343: 1–20.

Hoffmeier, J.K., and A. Millard (eds.) (2004) *The Future of Biblical Archaeology: Reassessing Methodologies and Assumptions* (Grand Rapids: Eerdmans).

Issar, A.S. (1998) Climate Change and History during the Holocene in the Eastern Mediterranean Region. In *Water, Environment and Society in Times of Climatic Change*, edited by A.S. Issar and N. Brown (Dordrecht/Boston/London: Kluwer Academic Publishers): 113-28.

Issar, A.S., and M. Zohar (2004) *Climate Change: Environment and Civilization in the Middle East* (Berlin: Springer).

Kanawati, N., and A. Hassan (1996) *The Teti Cemetery at Saqqara. Vol. 1, The Tombs of Nedjem-em-pet, Ka-aper and Others* (Sydney).

Kanawati, N., and A. McFarlane (1993) *Deshasha: The Tombs of Inti, Shedu and Others* (Sydney: Australian Centre for Egyptology).

Kitchen, K.A. (1996) Sinuhe: Scholarly Method versus Trendy Fashion. *Bulletin of the Australian Centre for Egyptology* 6: 55–63.

—(2003) *On the Reliability of the Old Testament* (Grand Rapids: Eerdmans).

Lanczkowski, G. (1958) Die Geschichte vom Riesen Goliath und der Kampf Sinuhes mit dem Starken von Retenu. *Mitteilungen des Deutschen Archäologischen Instituts Abteilung Kairo* 16: 214-18.

Levy, T.E., R.B. Adams, A. Hauptmann, M. Prange, S. Schmitt-Strecker and M. Najjar (2002) Early Bronze Age Metallurgy: A Newly Discovered Copper Manufactory in Southern Jordan. *Antiquity* 76(292): 425-37.

Levy, T.E., and T. Higham (eds.) (2005) *The Bible and Radiocarbon Dating: Archaeology, Text and Science* (London: Equinox).

Loprieno, A. (ed.) (1996) *Ancient Egyptian Literature: History and Forms* (Leiden/New York/Cologne: Brill).

Maeir, A.M., and P. de Miroschedji (eds.) (2006) *'I will Speak the Riddle of Ancient Times': Archaeological and Historical Studies in Honor of Amihai Mazar on the Occasion of his Sixtieth Birthday* (Winona lake, IN: Eisenbrauns).

Marcus, E.S. (1998) Maritime Trade in the Southern Levant from Earliest Times through the Middle Bronze IIA Period (Ph.D. diss., Oxford University).

—(2002) Early Seafaring and Maritime Activity in the Southern Levant from Prehistory through the Third Millenium BCE. In van den Brink and Levy 2002: 403-21.

Mazar, A. (1990) *Archaeology of the Land of the Bible* (New York: Doubleday).

Mazar, B. (1986) The Middle Bronze Age in Canaan. In *Benjamin Mazar: The Early Biblical Period. Historical Studies*, edited by S. Ahituv and B.A. Levine (Jerusalem: The Israel Exploration Society): 1-33.

McFarlane, A. (2000) *Mastabas at Saqqara: Kaiemheset, Kaipunesut, Kaiemsenu, Sehetepu and Others* (The Australian Centre for Egyptology: Reports 20; Oxford: Aris & Phillips).

Miller, R. (1980) Water use in Syria and Palestine from the Neolithic to the Bronze Age. *World Archaeology* 11/3: 331-41.

Miroschedji, P. (2006) At the Dawn of History: Sociopolitical Developments in Southwestern Canaan in Early Bronze Age III. In Maeir and de Miroschedji 2006: 55–78.

Moran, W.L. (1992) *The Amarna Letters* (Baltimore: Johns Hopkins University Press).

Mumford, G. (2006) Tell Ras Budran (Site 345): Defining Egypt's Eastern Frontier and Mining Operations in South Sinai during the Late Old Kingdom (Early EB IV/MB I). *BASOR* 342: 3–67.

Mumford, G.D. (1999) Wadi Maghara. In *Encyclopedia of the Archaeology of Ancient Egypt*, edited by K.A. Bard (London/New York: Routledge): 876-78.

Mumford, G.D., and S. Parcak (2004) Pharaonic Ventures into South Sinai: El-Markha Plain Site 346. *JEA* 89: 83-116.

Oren, E.D. (1973) The Overland Route between Egypt and Canaan in the Early Bronze Age: Preliminary Report. *IEJ* 23: 198-205.

—(1987) The 'Ways of Horus' in North Sinai. In *Egypt, Israel, Sinai: Archaeological and Historical Relationships in the Biblical Period*, edited by A.F. Rainey (Tel Aviv): 69–119.

—(1997) The 'Kingdom of Sharuhen' and the Hyksos Kingdom. In Oren 1997: 253-83.

Oren, E.D. (ed.) (1997) *The Hyksos: New Historical and Archaeological Perspectives* (Philadelphia: The University Museum, University of Philadelphia).

Parkinson, R.B. (2002) *Poetry and Culture in Middle Kingdom Egypt* (London/New York: Continuum).

Potter, A. (2002) The Dynamism of Death: Ancestors, Pastoralism, and the Origins of a Third-Millennium City in Syria. *BASOR* 325: 1–36.

Rainey, A.F. (1972) The World of Sinuhe. *Israel Oriental Studies* 2: 369-408.

—(2006) Sinuhe's World. In Maeir and de Miroschedji 2006: 277-99.

Redford, D.B. (1993) *Egypt, Canaan and Israel in Ancient Times* (Cairo: The American University in Cairo Press).

—(2000) Writings and Speech in Israelite and Ancient Near Eastern Prophecy. In *Writings and Speech in Israelite and Ancient Near Eastern Prophecy*, edited by E. Ben-Zvi and M.H. Floyd (Atlanta: Society of Biblical Literature): 145-218.

Reisner, G.A. (1942) *A History of the Giza Necropolis*, vol. 1 (London: Harvard University Press).

Reisner, G.A., and W.S. Smith (1955) *A History of the Giza Necropolis*. Vol. 2, *The Tomb of Hetep-heres the Mother of Kheops* (Cambridge, MA: Harvard University Press).

Richard, S. (1987) Questions of Nomadic Incursions at the End of the 3rd Millennium B.C. In *Studies in the History and Archaeology of Jordan III*, edited by A. Hadidi (Amman/London/New York: Routledge & Kegan Paul): 241-46.

—(2003) The Early Bronze Age in the Southern Levant. In *Near Eastern Archaeology: A Reader*, edited by S. Richard (Winona Lake, IN: Eisenbrauns): 286–303.

Shaw, I. (ed.) (2000) *The Oxford History of Ancient Egypt* (Oxford: Oxford University Press).

Sowada, K. (2001) Egypt in the Eastern Mediterranean during the Old Kingdom: A Re-Appraisal of the Archaeological Evidence (Faculty of Arts diss., University of Sydney).

Stager, L.E. (1992) The Periodization of Palestine from Neolithic through Early Bronze times. In *Chronologies in Old World Archaeology*, edited by R. Ehrich (3rd edn; Chicago: University of Chicago Press): 22-41.

Stern, E. (ed.) (1992) *The New Encyclopedia of Archaeological Excavations in the Holy Land*, vol. 4 (New York: Simon & Schuster).

Stocks, D.A. (2003) *Experiments in Egyptian Archaeology: Stoneworking Technology in Ancient Egypt* (London/New York: Routledge).

Strudwick, N. (2005) *Texts from the Pyramid Age* (Leiden/Boston: Brill).

Tallet, P. (2005) *Sésostris III et la fin de la XIIe dynastie* (Paris: Pygmalion).

Verner, M. *et al.* (2006) *Abusir IX : The Pyramid Complex of Raneferef. The Archaeology* (Prague: Academia).

Yannai, E. (2006) The Origin and Distribution of the Collared-rim Pithos and Krater: A Case of Conservative Pottery Production in the Ancient Near East from the Fourth to the First Millenium BCE. In Maeir and de Miroschedji 2006: 89–112.

Yekutieli, Y. (2002) Settlement and Subsistence Patterns in North Sinai during the Fifth to Third Millennia BC. In van den Brink and Levy 2002: 422-33.

Yekutieli, Y., S. Shalev and S. Shilstein (2005) 'En Yahav—A Copper Smelting Site in the 'Arava'. *BASOR* 340: 1–21.

7 New Perspectives on Levantine Mortuary Ritual

A Cognitive Interpretive Approach to the Archaeology of Death

Aaron J. Brody

Abstract

Two intramural burials from Late Bronze I Ashkelon are presented and analyzed using a cognitive interpretive approach. Further components of the mortuary rituals associated with each internment, beyond the burial itself, are determined through stratigraphic analysis aided by interpretive insights from ethnohistoric and ethnographic sources. It is argued that using complementary classes of archaeological, textual, pictorial, and ethnographic data expands B. Bartel's schema of burial archaeology and allows for a fuller understanding of the cultural practices and beliefs that accompanied death and burial in the southern Levant.

Introduction

Death, the treatment of the dead, and the responses of the living elicited by death, are occurrences charged with sacred significance that entail prescribed ritual behavior (Hertz 1960; Van Gennep 1960: 146-65; Huntington and Medcalf 1979; Thomas 1987; Chesson 2001). Processual studies of the archaeology of death, however, have moved away from interpreting the religious or ritual aspects of burials, which were emphasized in pre-processual archaeological studies (Chapman and Randsborg 1981: 2-6). Instead, Processual research has developed a set of societal hypotheses tested through mortuary evidence (Saxe 1970; Binford 1971; Tainter 1978; O'Shea 1984; see collected studies in Brown 1971; Chapman, Kinnes, and Randsborg 1981). Post-processual works on the theory of mortuary archaeology have critiqued these Processual social interpretations, concluding that burials are an imperfect measure of society since they are the product of ritual activity and not of normative cultural behavior (Pader 1982; Parker Pearson 1982: 100-101, 2000). Recent studies have sought to combine aspects of both Processual and Post-processual theory to produce a more integrative approach to interpreting the archaeology of death and burial (Keswani 2004; Rakita et al. 2005).

The significance of mortuary data as aspects in the study of the religion and ritual of extinct cultures has been recognized in works on the archaeology of cult or religion, as well (Sears 1961: 227-29; Alexander 1979: 217-19; Renfrew 1985: 17; 1994: 52-53; Johansen 1986: 72-73; Renfrew and Bahn 1991: 363; Insoll 1999: 166-200; 2004). Certain Near Eastern and Classical archaeological studies have also derived ritual interpretations from burial data with the aid of textual and/or depictive sources pertaining to death, the treatment of, and beliefs regarding the dead (Al-Khalesi 1977; Spencer 1982; Cooley 1983; Salles 1987, 1995; Pollock 1991; Bloch-Smith 1992; Antonaccio 1995; Ilan 1995, 1996; Toynbee 1996; Keswani 2004: 9, 50-51, 101-4; Laneri 2007). These classes of data are generally not available to archaeological theorists researching prehistoric or proto-historic societies.

Two Late Bronze (LB) I, Canaanite graves excavated by the Leon Levy Expedition at Ashkelon provide a case study in the archaeological interpretation of mortuary ritual. What follows is an analysis of the stratigraphy and contents of these tombs, and interpretations based on analogous mortuary concepts and practices known ethnohistorically from the texts from Ugarit and the Hebrew Bible and ethnographically from studies of death and burial in traditional societies (Ucko 1969; Watson 1980; Trinkaus 1984; Marcus and Flannery 1994: 55-57; Simpson 1995). This cognitive-interpretive approach (Renfrew and Zubrow 1994) allows for a reconstruction of aspects of the funeral ceremonies and beliefs about the dead in LB I Ashkelon that goes beyond just the presentation of the archaeology of the burials. This expands on the schema of Bartel who views burial archaeology as reflecting only one component of mortuary practice, the interment (1982: 52-55). At Ashkelon further components of burial ritual described by Bartel can be determined archaeologically through stratigraphic analysis in conjunction with interpretive insights from ethnohistoric and ethnographic sources.

The Stratigraphic Location and Comparative Material

Tel Ashkelon, located on the southern Mediterranean coast of modern Israel, was an important stopping point along the maritime and overland routes that linked the Egyptian Delta to the Levant, and beyond to Mesopotamia (Stager 1991; 1993: 103; Stager *et al.* 2008). The site was a gateway city, connecting localized commerce and goods, which flowed in from a regional hinterland, with a larger, international exchange network. These local and international networks were in use during the LB I, the period of our burials, but also help explain Ashkelon's almost continual habitation from the Chalcolithic through Medieval periods (Stager 1993: 103; Stager *et al.* 2008).

Two tombs were uncovered in the courtyard of a LB I (ca. 1550–1400 BCE) household (F169 and L165/F116, fig. 1).[1] Our area of excavation was limited as it was exposed at the bottom of a step trench, which has left an incomplete picture of the architectural context for the graves. Despite this, the southern edges of two LB I rooms remain, each with beaten earth floors. Outside of these rooms was a large courtyard area, which included several features such as hearths and pits that attest to the domestic nature of the context. The two burials were cut into this domestic courtyard.

---

1. For a map of the site and the location of the excavation area that contained the burials, Grid 38 Lower, see Stager *et al.* eds. 2008. I would like to thank Professor Lawrence Stager, Director of the Leon Levy Expedition to Ashkelon, for permission to research and publish these two burials. The phasing of this area was taken from the end of season report for the 1990 excavations in Grid 38 Lower by Dr. Elizabeth Bloch-Smith, grid supervisor and stratigrapher for the area. I would like to thank Liz for making sense of a very complicated area, and for her patience and support in working with me as a young square supervisor. For MB–LB cave tombs from Ashkelon's Grid 50 see Baker 2003.

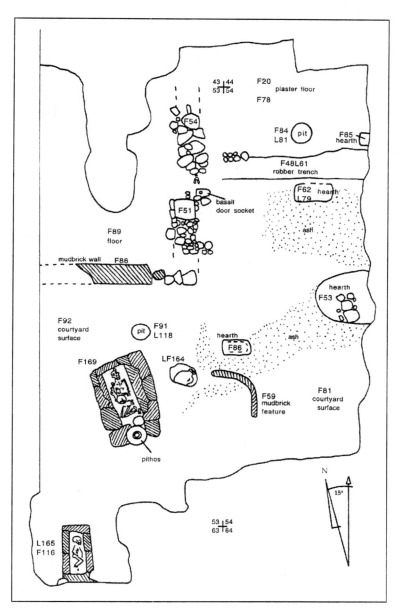

Figure 1. Tombs and associated architectural remains, Tel Ashkelon, Grid 38 Lower, Squares 44/53/54/63, Localized Phase II, Late Bronze Age I. Drawing: Elizabeth Bloch-Smith and Aaron Brody.

Intramural burials in structural tombs are rare in LB Palestine. Parallels exist only at the neighboring site of Tell el-'Ajjul and to the north at Megiddo and Ta'anach (Lapp 1969: 27-28; Gonen 1992a: 98-120). The tradition of intramural burial in structural tombs is known further afield at the coastal sites of Tyre and Ugarit, both of which were involved in maritime trade with the southern Levant (Bikai 1978: 6, 65; Margueron 1983; Salles 1987, 1995).[2] However, the vast majority of burials in LB Palestine, both along the coast and in the hill country, are found in cemeteries outside of city walls (Gonen 1992a).

Intramural burials in the southern Levant reflect a Canaanite urban tradition that began in the Middle Bronze (MB) IIA and continued through the LB I (Gonen 1992a: 21; Hallote 1995: 103-5). The practice stops in the LB II, for reasons that are not well understood. Sites with earlier MB intramural burials include 'Ajjul, Megiddo, Ta'anach, and Tel Dan, and a group of Hyksos, or southern Canaanite, built tombs from sites in the Egyptian Delta (Petrie 1931, 1932, 1933, 1934; Loud 1948; Tufnell 1962; Lapp 1969: 27-28; Van den Brink 1982; Ilan 1995, 1996; Holladay 1997: 196, 223-26).

Given the overwhelming tendency in Canaan to place the dead outside of city walls, why were some individuals buried intramurally? Explanations range from economic to spiritual or social motivations: an ancestral tomb provides a very literal claim to a piece of property, allowing the living to demonstrate ownership of land dating back to at least the time of the oldest interred relative (Brichto 1973; Bloch-Smith 1992: 110-21); the burying of a venerated family member near one's home allows this ancestor to be remembered, respected, and possibly invoked by relatives, since the deceased's spirit could have beneficial or detrimental influence over the living (Fustel de Coulanges 1873: 36; Hallote 1995: 105-7); and a specialized area for the interment of an exclusive group's dead (intramural minority vs. extramural majority)[3] is likely representative of the practices of a 'corporate group that has rights over the use and/or control of crucial but restricted resources...likely attained and/or legitimized by means of lineal decent from the dead' (Goldstein 1981: 61; see also Morris 1991).

It is probable that intramural burials served all three of these functions. They bolstered claims of an elite group to ancestral rites over urban land, while providing kinship links to powerful spirits. These ties to dead ancestors, in turn, reinforced religious status and economic standing of related individuals or families.[4]

A Description of the Burials

The two intramural burials at Ashkelon were of a young child and a young adult woman, both placed in structural tombs (Brody 2008; Dawson 2008). The child was buried in a simple, rectangular tomb of mudbrick (Fig. 2.3). The child's age was around three years at the time of death; because of the immature nature of the skeletal remains its sex is indeterminate (Dawson 2008). The walls of the tomb were made of mudbrick two courses high, and the structure was sealed over with a mudbrick covering.

---

2.   For fuller references to the scattered reports of tombs from Ugarit and its port Minet el-Beida, see Spronk (1986: 142 n.1). For the tomb from Tyre, this study assumes the contemporaneity of the burials in Tyre Stratum XVIII and the features in Stratum XVII, a possibility already suggested by the excavator. See Bikai (1978: 15 n. 8).

3.   In Hallote's quantification of Middle Bronze Age burials, intramural interments make up 17 percent of the sample, leaving 83 percent of burials outside of city walls (1995: 105, fig. 4).

4.   Later elite burials of Israelite kings, royal families, and some court functionaries are intramural (Bloch-Smith 1992: 116-19). Royal, Phoenician burials from Byblos are also intramural (Montet 1928).

The structure contained the skeleton of the child placed in a semiflexed position on its left side, head pointing northeast and facing the east-southeast. The legs were flexed to the east-southeast, with the right foot resting on top of the left. The right upper arm ran straight along the torso, with the lower arm bent across the ribs and the hand resting on the pelvic area. The left upper arm extended out from the body, slightly, with the lower arm bending down towards the legs. The skeleton's left hand was not preserved. The arms of the child have likely moved slightly from their original burial position due to decomposition (Dawson 2008). The orientation of the tomb itself follows that of the contemporary architecture used by the living, like other examples of intramural structural tombs (Fig. 1) (Van den Brink 1982: 39-44; Gonen 1992a: 118-20; Ilan 1996).

Interred with the child were two vessels imported from Cyprus, a Base-Ring I jug and juglet, and a small, rectangular piece of ostrich eggshell, approximately 3 × 3 cm. The juglet was placed upright near the head of the child, tucked in the space between the back of its skull and the western wall of the tomb (Figs. 2.4, 3.11). The jug was placed on the east side of the tomb, and the vessel's body may have been cradled in the deceased's left arm (Figs. 2.4, 3.12). The spout of the jug was positioned towards the dead child's face, with its opening near the child's mouth. The fragment of ostrich eggshell was found below the feet of the skeleton. Though it was the sole fragment in the tomb, it may have originally belonged to an ostrich eggshell drinking vessel, which are commonly found among offerings in MB intramural structural tombs from Tell el-Dab'a and other contemporary burials in Canaan (Van den Brink 1982: 51-52, 83-89).

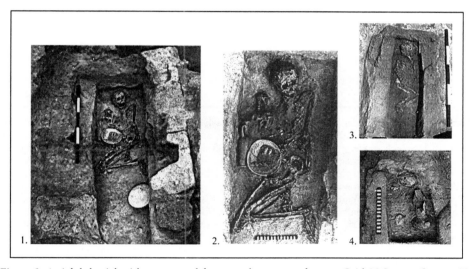

Figure 2. 1. Adult burial, pithos removed from southern part of grave. Grid 38 Lower, Square 53, Feature 169. 2. Adult burial, detail with grave goods. 3. Child burial with grave goods removed. Grid 38 Lower, Square 63, Feature 116, Layer 165. 4. Detail of Cypriot vessels near the child's head. All Photos: Leon Levy Expedition to Ashkelon/Carl Andrews.

The second tomb, an interment of a young adult, was rectangular and built out of three courses of mudbrick (Fig. 2.1). Based on skeletal analysis, the age is determined to be in the early twenties, and the sex is female (Dawson 2008). Typologically, the tomb architecture has close parallels in LB

I and II structural tombs from Tell el-'Ajjul (Gonen 1992a: 80-82).[5] Notches were cut into the Ashkelon tomb's uppermost course of bricks in order to hold wooden boughs used to close over the burial. These boughs were covered with a white, lime plaster, and fused to the mudbrick with a grey silt mortar.

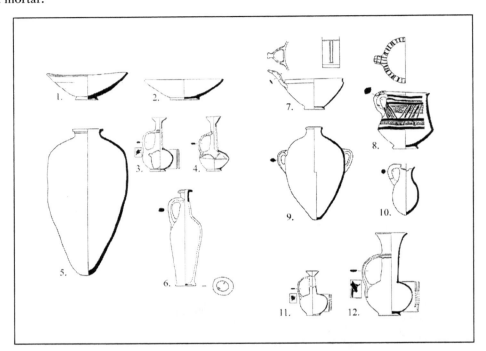

Figure 3. *Vessels interred with the adult burial*: 1. Bowl; rounded, direct rim; ring base; core: pink-buff; surface: pink-buff. 2. Bowl; rounded, direct rim; ring base; core: pink-buff, few small sand and white inclusions; surface: pink-buff. 3. Cypriot Base-Ring I juglet; direct rim; ring base; core: pink; surface: pink, red-brown slip, burnished; raised designs. 4. Cypriot Base-Ring I juglet; direct rim; ring base; core: pink; surface: pink, red-brown slip, burnished; raised designs. 5. Pithos; everted rim; core: pink to dark grey, many very small to small dark grey inclusions; surface: pink, white plaster. 6. Cypriot Red Lustrous Ware flask; everted rim; ring base; core: pink; surface: pink, red slip, burnished; potter's marks on bottom of base. *Vessels from fill above sealed adult tomb*: 7. Cypriot Base-Ring I bowl; direct rim; ring base; wishbone handle; core: grey-brown; surface: pink to pinkish red; brown slip; burnished; raised designs. 8. Bichonical jug; flared rim; ring base; core: pink, sand inclusions; surface: pink; buff slip, red and dark brown decoration. 9. Storage jar; upright rim; core: pink, many very small to small white inclusions; surface: pink. 10. Juglet; no rim; core: buff, few small white and small organic inclusions; surface: buff. *Vessels interred with the child*: 11. Cypriot Base-Ring I juglet; direct rim; ring base; core: pink; surface: pink, red-brown slip, burnished; raised designs. 12. Cypriot Base-Ring I jug; direct rim; ring base; core: pink, grey interior; surface: pink, brown to red slip, burnished; raised designs.

---

5.   Several major differences between the Ashkelon tomb and the structural tombs from 'Ajjul should also be noted: unlike the Ashkelon tomb, the 'Ajjul tombs were extramural; they were equipped with stepped entryways, which allowed for easy access in and out of the tomb; and they frequently contained multiple burials.

The young woman was interred in a semiflexed position on her back, her head pointing up, facing slightly to the east (Figs. 2.1, 2.2). Both legs were tightly flexed towards the west, just fitting into the width of the tomb, with the right knee against the western side and her left foot pressed against the eastern side. Her left arm extended straight down at her side, with a slight bend in the lower arm, and her left hand placed to the side and underneath her pelvis. Her right upper arm extended straight down her side, with the lower arm flexed across her body, the right hand falling over the left arm. Her body and the tomb were oriented due north, not along the line of the contemporary architecture (Fig. 1).

Grave goods included a food offering of sheep/goat chops and a small bird placed in a bowl of local manufacture, located by the woman's right side (Figs. 2.2, 3.2). This meal is evident from the faunal remains of sheep/goat ribs, and the bones of a pigeon or dove, found in situ in the bowl. Meal offerings were common in other intramural burials in structural tombs, and included birds, sheep, goats, and other species like pig, cow, and fish, mimicking the varied diet of elite Canaanites (Tufnell 1962: 8; Lapp 1969: 28; Boessneck 1976; Van den Brink 1982: 50-51, 56, 58-59; Horwitz 1996). Next to this bowl of food was a Red Lustrous Ware flask, most likely imported from Cyprus (Figs. 2.2, 3.6) (Eriksson 1991). This flask may have held some liquid, like wine or water, to help wash down the meal. A second bowl was located south of the interred's left foot, propped against the east wall of the tomb (Figs. 2.1, 3.1). No visible remains were discerned in this bowl. This vessel may have held organics, although none were discovered in a flotation sample processed from the bowl. Just south of this second bowl was a large pithos, which was built into the mudbrick of the closing end of the tomb construction (Figs. 1, 3.5). This pithos may have stored a liquid meant for the deceased. The pithos is close in typology to MB pithoi, Bonfil's Type 5 (1992: 29, fig. 5.3). It is possible that the MB pithos type continues into the LB I at Ashkelon, or that the pithos is an heirloom vessel.

Other offerings in the large grave at Ashkelon were of a more personal nature. A small, rounded limestone cobble was placed on the dead woman's head. This stone was clearly worked, as is demonstrated by its flake scars, and shows wear marks at one end, which indicate its possible use in grinding (Fig. 4.1). Two Cypriot Base-Ring I juglets were placed in the crook of her right arm (Figs. 2.2, 3.3-4). These closed vessels, with tall necks and small mouths, may have held favored perfumed oils or perhaps an opiate (Merrillees 1989).

Clothing and adornment is also evident from material remains in the tomb. Two small, bronze straight pins were found on the skeleton: one was just below the acromial end of the left clavicle, the other was symmetrically placed on the right side; however, the right clavicle was not preserved (Fig. 4.4-5). Underneath the skeleton's right shoulder was a grey, metal object with a cross section resembling a squared bracket. This may have been some sort of pin or fastener. A positive identification is difficult because the object was poorly preserved and virtually disintegrated when excavated. This object angled from beneath the right shoulder to below the right side of the jaw, and appeared to continue under the skull. Perhaps it represents a fastener for a cloak, or similar clothing, though this is speculative. A carved, ivory roundel was discovered in her pelvic area (Fig. 4.6). This appears to have been used for holding a belt or sash, given its shape and location at the woman's waist. Parallels exist in a contemporary burial from the neighboring site of 'Ajjul, where Petrie refers to the object as a 'belt toggle' (1933: pl. 49, burial 305), and in an LB I cave burial from Megiddo (Guy 1938: pl. 152.8, 9, 10, burial 1145B). The hole carved in the center of the ivory has sharp edges on both sides of the object, showing no evidence of use wear where a rope or sash would have rubbed.[6] This suggests that the ivory roundel was new at the time of interment.

---

6. I would like to thank Glenda Friend for sharing this observation with me while examining the artifact.

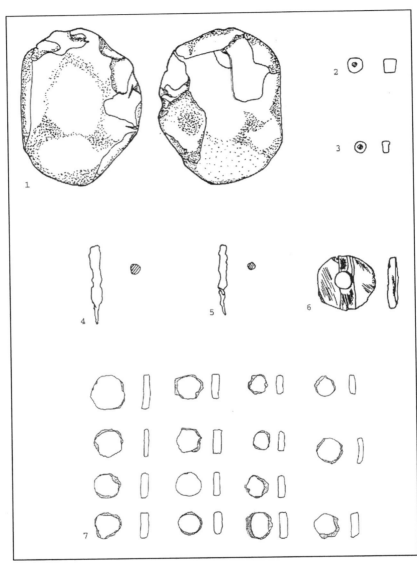

Figure 4. Non-ceramic finds interred with the adult burial: 1. Dorsal and ventral views of worked stone; spherical cobble; white limestone. 2. Cylindrical bead; frit; dull, matt white with olive green accents. 3. Cylindrical bead; frit; dull, matt red-umber. 4. Straight pin from skeleton's left side; copper alloy; highly patinated. 5. Straight pin from skeleton's right side; copper alloy; highly patinated. 6. Worked ivory disk. 7. Ceramic jar stoppers; thirteen from fill above tomb, upper two in fourth column from fill inside of tomb.

Jewelry in the burial consisted of five beads remaining from a necklace, which were found clustered together in the area of the sternum. Three of the beads were heirloom scarabs, identified and studied by O. Keel, and two were small, cylindrical beads made from frit (Fig. 4.2-3). The scarabs range in date from the 13th–15th Dynasties, all of which predate the LB I (Ashkelon scarab numbers 71, 72, and 113, Keel 1997: 716, 730). These heirloom scarabs were of various colors—green jasper, light brown, and white—while the frit beads were red-umber and white with olive green inclusions. Strung together, these scarabs and frit beads would have made a colorful necklace.

After the young woman was laid to rest, her tomb was covered with wooden boughs, held in place with a mud mortar, and plastered shut. This covering is unique among structural tombs. The comparable tombs from 'Ajjul and the Egyptian Delta were sealed over with mudbrick superstructures of varying designs or slabs of kurkar sandstone (Van den Brink 1982: 19-39; Gonen 1992a: 80-82; 1992b: 152). Those from sites further north were both built and covered with fieldstones (Loud 1948: 89-134; Lapp 1969: 27-29; Ilan 1996). This reflects the varying availabilities of building materials for sites in different regions of Canaan. Small fieldstones and cobbles were placed on top of and next to these plastered wooden boughs sealing over the Ashkelon tomb. It is not clear that these stones were simply part of the covering of the tomb, as some on top of the mudbrick walls appear to be arranged in rows and not just thrown in as fill.

On top of the sealed tomb and below the courtyard surface, from which the cist was cut for the burial, a space .85-.77 m deep remained. In the southeastern part of this space above the sealed tomb, a Cypriot Base-Ring I bowl, local biconical drinking mug, local storage jar, and a third of an entire skeleton of a sheep were discovered clustered together (Fig. 3.7-9). The storage jar was placed upright with two ceramic body sherds covering the mouth of the vessel. Next to this concentration of vessels was the large ceramic pithos, mentioned above as built into the mudbrick courses of the southern closing wall of the tomb architecture (Fig. 3.5). This pithos also was utilized after the tomb was sealed, since a dipper juglet (Fig. 3.10) was placed next to the pithos, stratigraphically above the timbers and small stones that closed the deceased in her grave. This juglet aided, either symbolically or literally, in removing liquid from the large jar. The pithos may have been originally built into the tomb to provide additional liquid refreshment for the deceased, but the positioning of the juglet next to the pithos suggests that it was also in use after the burial was sealed.

Other items of note from the fill above the tomb and below the courtyard surface include thirteen ceramic jar stoppers (Fig. 4.7). These may indicate the opening of vessels by the graveside that were not deposited on top of the tomb. Three other ceramic jar stoppers were discovered in the fill inside the tomb. Over twenty pieces of chert debitage, four chert blade fragments, two chert-cobble hammer/grinding stones, a basalt quern fragment, and twelve charred olive pits were unearthed in the same fill matrix above the sealed burial in which the concentration of whole vessels and jar stoppers were discovered. A scarab was found in this same fill, just below the courtyard surface, which has been dated by O. Keel from the second half of the 15th to the beginning of the 18th Egyptian Dynasty, 1600–1500 BCE (Ashkelon scarab number 36, Keel 1997: 702). This provides a *post quem* for the covering of the burial that agrees with the LB I date of the tomb, which is based on pottery typology and stratigraphy of the associated habitation remains, as well as the LB IIA date of the subsequent phase verified by local ceramics and imported Late Helladic IIIA wares.

A further offering of a storage jar was uncovered just adjacent to the young adult's tomb at Ashkelon, cut into the courtyard surface (LF164 fig. 1). Inside of this storage jar were a bowl, a juglet, and a fragment of a sheep's skull. Because of the position of this offering, it cannot be determined whether it was stratigraphically later or earlier than those found clustered on top of the sealed tomb. The storage jars from both offering groups are typologically similar, and both were found with rectangular body sherds placed over their mouths to 'seal' the jars.

Parallels for offerings discovered on top of, and next to burials come from MB intramural structural tombs at Tel Dan, Tell el-Dab'a, and Tell el-Maskhuta (Van den Brink 1982: 33, 35, 38, 50-51; Bietak 1989: 35*; 1990: 11*-14*; 1991; Ilan 1996: 183-87, 204-11; Holladay 1997: 196).[7] The practice of leaving offerings external to burials continues on in the later Iron Age at Achziv, and is evident from Phoenician sites in the western Mediterranean, such as Carthage, Trayamar, and Toscanos (Gras, Rouillard, and Teixidor 1991: 138-40). Similar deposits are also known from the Bronze and Iron Age Aegean and Cyprus, and from Roman evidence (Renfrew 1972: 432-33; Antonaccio 1995: 199-243; Toynbee 1996: 50-54, 61-64; Herscher 1997: 31).

Ritual Interpretations

The Child Burial

The orientation of a grave or the placement of the body within a tomb can encode societal beliefs regarding the dead or the realm of the dead (Thomas 1987: 456). The child burial at Ashkelon was oriented along the line of the contemporary architecture, however, which relates more to the practicality of the living. The child was laid out on its side, in a semi-flexed position, perhaps mimicking an attitude of sleep. In the Ugaritic epic of Aqhat, the slain hero, already interred in his grave [Ugaritic *qbr*], is disturbed and roused from 'his sleep' [Ugaritic *shnth*] (*KTU* 1.19:III:44-45). Several MB tombs from Baghouz, in eastern Syria, and Jericho contained the remains of wooden beds or rush mats on which the deceased were laid, quite literally, to rest, presumably mimicking an attitude of sleep (Du Mesnil Du Buisson 1948: 36; Kenyon 1993: 680). In the Hebrew Bible, death is likened to making a bed in Sheol, the Israelite netherworld (Ezek. 32:25; Job 17:13; McCullough 1962: 373).

The Cypriot jug interred with the child seems to have been nestled in its left arm, with the vessel's spout resting above the child's mouth, as if the child were meant to drink the contents. The second vessel, a Cypriot juglet, rested behind the child's head. A similar clustering of vessels near children's mouths or heads is evident in earlier, MB intramural burials in structural tombs from Tell el-Dab'a and Tel Dan (Bietak 1991: 134, 202, 210, 229, 252, 274; Ilan 1996: 179, 183). It is possible that this suggests the intent of the surviving relatives to provide nourishment for their children's spirits. Food offerings left with interred adults, like that in the neighboring tomb at Ashkelon, seem to be in positions where the adult spirit would feed itself.

The fragment of ostrich eggshell, placed in the child's grave, may have held symbolic protective or regenerating qualities as the egg is associated with the concepts of life and birth. This interpretation is based on studies of ostrich eggshells, eggshell containers, and decorated eggshells that come from later Phoenician tombs in the western Mediterranean. In the context of these seventh- to second-century BCE tombs, ostrich eggs are viewed as having apotropaic qualities, and are linked to magical ideas of regeneration as a symbol of life placed in a context related to death (Moscati 1988: 456; Gras, Rouillard, and Teixidor 1991: 138-40). As the cultural descendants of the Canaanites, it is not surprising that the Phoenicians carry on the practice of placing ostrich eggs in burials, a custom that is already prevalent in MB interments in Canaan.

---

7.   The most detailed evidence for this practice is found in Bietak's report on the burials from Dab'a, which illustrates at least sixteen adult burials with post-funeral offerings and ten separate offering deposits related to tombs (1991). It is likely that similar external offerings were made at the Middle Bronze and Late Bronze structural tombs from 'Ajjul, Megiddo, and Ta'anach; however, the excavation reports do not detail these sorts of data. I would like to thank David Ilan for discussing the Tel Dan material with me, and possible parallels to the burials at Ashkelon.

The placement of imported, Cypriot pottery and a prestige item like the fragment of an ostrich eggshell (vessel?) with a dead child suggests the high social status of the child's family. It is unlikely that the Cypriot vessels or the eggshell were actually personal possessions of the deceased, since they are somewhat 'adult' in nature. Rather, these grave goods were likely items from the child's household or extended family.

The Young Adult Burial

The placement of the young adult burial along a cardinal direction shows planning and intent on the part of those who built the tomb structure. Whether this direction encodes any ritual significance is difficult to interpret. North [Ugaritic *Zpn* = Hebrew *Zapon*], the orientation of her burial, was important in Canaanite belief systems as the location of the deified mountain, Mt. Zapon, and the home of the storm god (Clifford 1972: 57-79; Astour 1975: 318-24). In Ugaritic myth, this storm god is brought down to the netherworld by its ruler, the god of death, but is rescued and brought back to rule the realm of the living (*KTU* 1.5–1.6).

Cross-cultural comparisons suggest that burials oriented to the cardinal directions often reflect a connection between the interred and the sunrise or sunset (Binford 1971: 12-13; Rahtz 1978: 3-6). In Ugaritic eschatology, the sun-goddess, Shapshu, ruled over the underworld, for it was she who traveled between the world of the living and that of the dead in her daily cycle of rising and setting (Lewis 1989: 35-46). Through this cycle, it was also the sun-goddess who accompanied the spirits of the dead on the journey from their earthly abode to their new home in the netherworld. Canaanite burials from the Middle and Late Bronze Ages, however, do not show any strict consistency in their orientation, which could point to standard intent or beliefs on the part of the living who constructed the graves (Van den Brink 1982: 39-44; Gonen 1992a: 18; Hallote 1995: 102-3). It should be noted that although the burial was directed to the cardinal points, the head was faced upwards and only turned slightly towards the east and the rising sun.

The meal offering, consisting of sheep or goat chops, a small bird, and a possible beverage held in the Red Lustrous Ware flask, is representative of a belief in a spirit of the deceased that needed sustenance. Further foods and liquids may have been held in the bowl and pithos at the southern end of the tomb. M. Bietak has interpreted similar meals, present in MB intramural structural tombs from Tell el-Dab'a, as 'sufficient for the daily needs of the dead' (1990: 13*). I contend that this interpretation is based on ancient Egyptian concepts of the afterworld, as tombs for Egyptians were typically provisioned with grave goods, including foodstuffs, which were meant to serve the everyday needs of the dead soul in a paradisiacal afterlife (Spencer 1982: 45-73, 139-64). However, those buried in the MB tombs at Dab'a are not Egyptians but rather southern Canaanites (Van den Brink 1982: 67), who held different cultural concepts from Egyptians regarding death and the afterlife.

The Canaanite netherworld was not a paradise like its Egyptian counterpart, but rather a dark, dreary place, a realm for the spirits of the dead (Gaster 1962; Astour 1980; Xella 1995). In Ugaritic eschatology the underworld is referred to simply as *'arz*, 'the earth'. This realm of the dead is a dank place where the spirits dwell, comparable in concept to Sheol and Hades, the netherworlds of biblical Israel and classical Greece; it is located below the firmament, the realm of the living. Dead ancestors, known from Ugarit as *rp'm* and in biblical Israel as *repa'îm*, were respected by living relatives in ceremonies alluded to textually (Caquot 1960; L'Heureux 1974, 1979; Pope 1977, 1981; Pitard 1978; Horwitz 1979; Bordreuil and Pardee 1982; Levine and Tarragon 1984; Spronk 1986: 161-96; Lewis 1989: 14-16; Rouillard 1999; but see Schmidt 1994: 71-93, 267-73 for a contradictory opinion). It is possible that intramural tombs from Ashkelon, elsewhere in Canaan, and the Egyptian Delta were placed in household courtyards of the wealthy to keep these spirits of the deceased ancestors, the *rp'm*, close by the family, for reasons that I have discussed above.

Some studies of modern burials and mortuary rituals have stressed that nourishment is placed in tombs not to feed the dead throughout eternity, but rather to provide sustenance during the transitory journey of the deceased into the world of the dead (Van Gennep 1960: 153-54; Thomas 1987: 455). This seems a more likely analogy for Canaanite rituals, rather than viewing the food offering as representing a meal for eternity, as does Bietak. The West Semitic underworld is not a realm for the soul to feast and enjoy a continuation of its earthly life but rather a grim resting place for the shades.

The material culture discovered in the fill above the tomb of the young adult woman is indicative of rites carried on after she was sealed in her grave. The collection of open and closed vessels, a bowl, tankard, storage jar, pithos, and dipper juglet, is a pottery repertoire suitable for the storage and serving of liquids and foods. The jar stoppers, olive pits, stone tools, and bones of a third of a sheep are additional material evidence, which suggests that there was a feast enjoyed by mourners for the deceased, the remains of which were then placed on top of the grave in further tribute to the dead. It is known from certain modern, traditional cultures that objects used in mortuary rituals are considered to be tainted and not suitable for further use in the world of the living, and are thus left at the grave (Hartland 1928: 430-31).

Such mourning feasts are known as the *mrzh* or *mrz'* in Ugaritic and Phoenician texts, and *marzeah* in later Hebrew Bible writings (Eissfeldt 1966, 1969; Porten 1968; Miller 1971; Pope 1972, 1979–80, 1981; Greenfield 1974; Fenton 1977; Friedman 1979–80; Spronk 1986: 196-202; King 1988, 1989; Lewis 1989: 80-94; McLaughlin 2001; see Schmidt 1994: 62-66 for a contradictory view).[8] These feasts were part of funeral ceremonies performed by the living involving the rite of passage of the dead spirit from the community into the netherworld (Van Gennep 1960: 153-54). A possible *mrzh* is depicted on the sarcophagus of the Phoenician king Ahiram, which shows the dead king enthroned with a meal set on a table before him. A procession of mourners approaches the funerary meal, some bring further offerings in storage jars and bowls, and one mourner leads a ram, presumably as a sacrifice to the dead ruler (Montet 1928; Aimé-Giron 1943; Haran 1958; Chéhab 1970; Porada 1973). These offerings are reminiscent of the material goods left on top of the woman's tomb at Ashkelon.[9]

Funeral feasts are also attested among the modern, traditional communities of the Levant, and take place at several specific times after the burial of the dead (Granqvist 1965: 85-90, 97-100; in general see Hartland 1928: 434-37; Thomas 1987: 455). In certain cultures these meals for the dead stop once the journey of the deceased's spirit to the netherworld is believed to be complete, although further offerings may be given on the anniversary of a death or a specific day of atonement. The Phoenicians, later cultural descendants of the Canaanites, celebrated a memorial day for the dead and left offerings at tombs (Appian, *Roman History* XII.84, 89; Cicero, *Pro Scauro* VI.11; Justin, XVIII.6.6, Lucian, *De Dea Syria* 6; Gsell 1920: 466-68; Gras, Rouillard, and Teixidor 1991: 138-39); and there are a variety of post-funerary ceremonies celebrated for the dead in modern traditional societies in the Middle East (Simpson 1995: 248-49). It is possible that the

---

8.   There is no scholarly consensus regarding the translation of the terms *mrzh/mrz'* in Ugaritic. Some take the meaning to be a funeral meal or feast, others view it as a socio-religious association, while others see the mourning meal as an aspect of a broader *marzeah* institution. Unfortunately the Ugaritic texts are ambiguous, and thus open to broad interpretation. Given the relative clarity of the passage in the book of Jeremiah (16:5-8) describing a house of *marzeah* as a place of mourning and feasting, and the similarities in cultural practices between Israelites and the people of Ugarit, it seems that the occasional reading of *mrzh/mrz'* in Ugaritic as a funeral feast is appropriate. This goes against the extreme views of Schmidt (1994: 66). See the pertinent comments of Lewis (1989: 94).

9.   For other studies linking archaeological remains with the *mrzh/marzeah*, see Cooley and Pratico 1994: 90; Cockerham 1995; Salles 1995: 183-84; Herscher 1997: 31-32; Holladay 1997: 196.

offering located near the young adult tomb, consisting of a storage jar with a bowl, dipper juglet, and fragment of a sheep's skull, was made after the initial burial rites had ended. This must remain as a hypothesis as it cannot be demonstrated stratigraphically, or by the typology of the vessels. This material, representative of a container for liquids, a juglet for serving portions, a bowl to drink or eat out of, and a skull fragment from a meal or sacrifice, could be the remains of another feast held in honor of the deceased.

Mortuary Rituals with Little or No Archaeological Correlates

There are other aspects of Canaanite mortuary ritual known from Ugaritic texts that would leave little or no archaeological traces. These include special preparation of the body before burial and the mourning rituals of the living. These practices are not unique to Canaan, as they are paralleled in Israelite society and numerous modern, traditional cultures.

In traditional Levantine villages, for instance, the dead are ritually cleansed, clothed in special garb, and shrouded before interment (Wensinck 1917: 56-77; Granqvist 1965: 58-67; Simpson 1995: 241).[10] Evidence of clothing and adornment from the young adult burial at Ashkelon include two straight pins, a possible metal pin or fastener behind her right shoulder, an ivory roundel to hold a sash-like belt, and scarabs and other beads from a necklace. None of these material remains, however, demonstrate that the woman was dressed in special clothing for burial. Nor is her jewelry distinctly apotropaic; it shows no discernable stylistic or color properties meant to protect the wearer (Simpson 1995: 246). As noted earlier, the ivory roundel has no marks from use wear. This suggests that the belt hoop was not used by the woman during her life but rather was new at her time of burial.

Canaanite mourning rituals that accompany death and burial, such as wailing, rending garments or the wearing of sackcloth, cutting hair, lacerating flesh, throwing dust or straw on one's head, and the voicing of lamentations are known textually from Ugarit and the Hebrew Bible (*KTU* 1.5:VI:11-25; 1.5:VI:26-1.6:I:29; 1.15:V:12-14; 1.19:IV:10-26; 1.61:13-34; Lev. 19:26; Deut. 14:1; Ezek. 27:28-36). Some of these practices are shown on the sarcophagus of the Phoenician king Ahiram, which depicts female mourners whose tops have been removed, or torn, so that they hang over their skirts. Some of these women beat their chests while others tear at their hair.[11] It is likely that similar ceremonial demonstrations of grief and mourning accompanied the burials at Ashkelon but they cannot be demonstrated archaeologically.[12]

---

10.   Some early translations of the Ugaritic Aqhat epic, line *KTU* 1.19:III:41, have the dead hero buried 'in a shroud', based on a faulty cognate link of Ugaritic *knrt* with Arabic *kanara* (Pitard 1994: 32-33, 36). This is not a correct reading, and should not influence our interpretation of burial practices at Ugarit (see Pitard 1994). Recently a Chalcolithic burial has been discovered in a cave near Jericho that was covered in a linen shroud (see Schick 1998), and several of the LB IIB burials at Tell es-Sa'idiyeh had remnants of cloth preserved in bitumen or fused to metal objects, which the excavator suggests may have been from shrouds (see Pritchard 1980: 15, 21-23). Otherwise evidence of cloth in excavations, let alone burials, is extremely rare.

11.   The Ugaritic epic of Aqhat details the weeping of women mourners in the king's palace (*KTU* 1.19:IV:10-26). Wailing female mourners are known from Israelite sources (Jer 9:17-20, for further citations see de Vaux 1961; Olyan 2004: 49-51), and is a practice detailed in Middle Eastern ethnographic examples which may include the hiring of professional women who are paid to wail for the dead (Wensinck 1917: 78-95; Granqvist 1965: 92-96).

12.   It is possible that the pieces of chert debitage or the chert blade fragments, discovered in the fill above the sealed tomb, were used in ceremonial hair cutting or laceration; however, they may have been used for cutting food, or may have been brushed in the fill after having been originally deposited on the courtyard surface. Closer study of these flaked-stone artifacts and their residue analysis is required to approach these questions. In later Phoenician and Punic burials, bronze razors are found on occasion that may have been used for ritual hair cutting or shaving.

Conclusions

Through an analysis of the stratigraphy and contents of the intramural, structural tombs from LB I Ashkelon, I have demonstrated that several components of mortuary ritual, besides the interment, may be discerned in the archaeology of burials. Ritual interpretations from the tombs are aided by ethnohistorical evidence for concepts related to death, burial, and mortuary ceremonies that lead toward a more balanced historical Biblical Archaeology. Further comparisons may be drawn between the LB I burials at Ashkelon and ethnographic studies of death and burial in Middle Eastern, and other modern, traditional cultures. Utilizing complementary classes of archaeological, textual, pictorial, and ethnographic data, one can go beyond the mere description of burials, as outlined in Bartel's schema, and present a fuller understanding of the cultural practices and beliefs that accompanied death and burial in the southern Levant.[13]

References

Äimé-Giron, N. (1943) Essai sur l'âge et la succession des rois de Byblos d'après leurs inscriptions. *Annales du service des antiquités de l'Égypte* 42: 283-338.

Albright, W.F. (1968) *Yahweh and the Gods of Canaan* (New York: Doubleday).

Alexander, J.A. (1979) The Archaeological Recognition of Religion: The Examples of Islam in Africa and 'Urnfields' in Europe. In *Space, Hierarchy and Society: Interdisciplinary Studies in Social Area Analysis*, edited by B.C. Burnham and J. Kingsbury (BAR International Series 59; Oxford: British Archaeological Reports): 215-28.

Al-Khalesi, Y. (1977) The Beit Kispim in Mesopotamian Architecture: Studies of Form and Function. *Mesopotamia* 12: 53-81.

Alster, B. (ed.) (1980) *Death in Mesopotamia* (Mesopotamia 8; Copenhagen: Akademish Forlag).

Antonaccio, C.M. (1995) *An Archaeology of Ancestors: Tomb Cult and Hero Cult in Early Greece* (Lanham, MD: Rowman & Littlefield).

Astour, M.C. (1975) Place Names. In *Ras Shamra Parallels*, II, edited by L.R. Fisher (Rome: Pontificum Istitutum Biblicum): 249-369.

—(1980) The Nether World and its Denizens at Ugarit. In Alster 1980: 227-38.

Avigad, N., and J.C. Greenfield (1982) A Bronze Phiale with a Phoenician Dedicatory Inscription. *IEJ* 32: 118-28.

Baker, J. (2003) The Middle and Late Bronze Age Tomb Complex at Ashkelon, Israel: The Architecture and Funeral Kit (Ph.D. diss., Brown University, RI).

Bartel, B. (1982) A Historical Review of Ethnological and Archaeological Analyses of Mortuary Practice. *JAA* 1: 32-58.

Bayliss, M. (1973) The Cult of Dead Kin in Assyria and Babylonia. *Iraq* 35: 115-25.

Bietak, M. (1989) Servant Burials in the Middle Bronze Age Culture of the Eastern Nile Delta. *Eretz-Israel* 20: 30*-43*.

—(1990) The Concept of Eternity in Ancient Egypt and the Bronze Age World: An Archaeological Approach. *Eretz-Israel* 21: 10*-17*.

—(1991) *Tell el-Dab'a V* (Österreichische Akademie der Wissenschaften Denkschriften der Gesamtakademie 9; Vienna: Österreichischen Akademie der Wissenschaften).

Bikai, P.M. (1978) *The Pottery of Tyre* (Warminster: Aris & Phillips).

Binford, L.R. (1971) Mortuary Practices: Their Study and their Potential. In Brown 1971: 6-29.

---

13.   For a similar use of archaeological, textual, and ethnographic data to interpret burials from a social/ethnic perspective, see Levy *et al.* 2004. I would like to thank Tom Levy for sharing this article with me and for inviting me to contribute to this symposium volume.

Biran, A., D. Ilan, and R. Greenberg (eds.) (1996) *Dan I: A Chronicle of the Excavations, the Pottery Neolithic, the Early Bronze Age & the Middle Bronze Age Tombs* (Israel: Nelson Glueck School of Biblical Archaeology).

Bloch-Smith, E. (1992) *Judahite Burial Practices and Beliefs about the Dead* (JSOTSup 123; JSOT/ASOR Monograph Series 7; Sheffield: Sheffield Academic Press).

Boessneck, J. (1976) Verteilung der Tierknochenfunde über die Flächen und Gräber. In *Tell el-Dab'a III* (Österreichische Akademie der Wissenschaften Denkschriften der Gesamtakademie 5; Wien: Österreichischen Akademie der Wissenschaften): 9-18.

Bonfil, R. (1992) MB II Pithoi in Palestine. *Eretz-Israel* 23: 26-37 (Hebrew).

Bordreuil, P., and D. Pardee (1982) Le rituel funéraire ougaritique RS. 34.126. *Syria* 59: 121-28.

Brichto, H.C. (1973) Kin, Cult, Land and Afterlife: A Biblical Complex. *Hebrew Union College Annual* 44: 1-54.

Brody, A.J. (2008) Late Bronze Age Canaanite Mortuary Practices. In Stager *et al.* 2008: 515-31.

Brown, J.A. (ed.) (1971) *Approaches to the Social Dimensions of Mortuary Practices* (Memoirs of the Society for American Archaeology 25; American Antiquity 36/3).

Buttrick, G.A., *et al.* (eds.) (1962) *The Interpreter's Dictionary of the Bible* (New York: Abingdon Press).

Campbell, S., and A. Green (eds.) (1995) *The Archaeology of Death in the Ancient Near East* (Oxbow Monograph 51; Oxford: Oxbow).

Caquot, A. (1960) Les rephaim ougaritiques. *Syria* 37: 75-93.

Chapman, R., and K. Randsborg (1981) Approaches to the Archaeology of Death. In Chapman, Kinnes, and Randsborg 1981: 1-24.

Chapman, R., I. Kinnes, and K. Randsborg (eds.) (1981) *The Archaeology of Death* (Cambridge: Cambridge University Press).

Chéhab, M. (1970) Observations au sujet du sarcophage d'Ahiram. *Mélanges de l'Université St. Joseph* 46: 107-17.

Chesson, M.S. (ed.) (2001) *Social Memory, Identity, and Death: Anthropological Perspectives on Mortuary Rituals*. Vol. 10, *Archaeological Papers of the American Anthropological Association* (Naperville: American Anthropological Association).

Clifford, R.J. (1972) *The Cosmic Mountain in Canaan and the Old Testament* (Cambridge, MA: Harvard University Press).

Cockerham, C.L. (1995) Burial Practice at Tell Dothan: Was Tomb 1 a *byt mrzh*? (M.A. diss., Gordon-Conwell Theological Seminary, MA).

Cooley, R.E. (1983) Gathered to his People: A Study of a Dothan Family Tomb. In *The Living and Active Word of God: Studies in Honor of Samuel J. Schultz*, edited by M. Inch and R. Youngblood (Winona Lake, IN: Eisenbrauns): 47-58.

Cooley, R.E., and G.D. Pratico (1994) Gathered to his People: An Archaeological Illustration from Tell Dothan's Western Cemetery. In *Scripture and Other Artifacts: Essays on the Bible and Archaeology in Honor or Philip J. King*, edited by M.D. Coogan, J.C. Exum, and L.E. Stager (Louisville, KY: Westminster John Knox Press): 70-92.

Cross, F.M. (1973) *Canaanite Myth and Hebrew Epic* (Cambridge, MA: Harvard University Press).

Dawson, L. (2008) Osteological Analysis of the Human Remains from the Late Bronze Age Tombs of Grid 38. In *Ashkelon I: Introduction and Overview 1985-2000*. Vol. 3, *Studies in the Archaeology and History of the Levant*, edited by L.E. Stager *et al.* (Winona Lake, IN: Eisenbrauns): 531-32.

Du Mesnil du Buisson, C. (1948) *Baghouz, l'ancienne Corsote* (Leiden: E.J. Brill).

Eissfeldt, O. (1966) Etymologische und archäologische erklärung alttestamentlicher Wörter. *Oriens Antiquus* 5/2: 165-76.

—(1969) Kultvereine in Ugarit. In *Ugaritica 6* (Paris: Librairie Orientalite Paul Geuthner): 187-95.

Ellis, A.G., and B. Westley (1965) Preliminary Report on the Animal Remains in the Jericho Tombs. In *Excavations at Jericho 2, the Tombs Excavated in 1955-8*, edited by K.M. Kenyon (London: British School of Archaeology in Jerusalem): 694-703.

Eriksson, K. (1991) Red Lustrous Wheelmade Ware: A Product of Late Bronze Age Cyprus. In *Cypriot Ceramics: Reading the Prehistoric Record*, edited by J.A. Barlow, D.L. Bolger, and B. Kling (University Museum

Monograph 74; Pennsylvania: The University Museum of Archaeology and Anthropology, University of Pennsylvania): 81-96.

Fenton, T.L. (1977) The Claremont 'MRZH' Tablet, its Text and Meaning. *Ugarit-Forschungen* 9: 71-75.

Friedman, R.E. (1979–80) The *MRZH* Tablet from Ugarit. *Maarav* 2: 187-206.

Fustel de Coulanges, N.D. (1873) *The Ancient City*, translated by Willard Small (Garden City, NY: Doubleday Anchor).

Gaster, T.H. (1962) Dead, Abode of the. In Buttrick *et al.* 1962: 787-88.

Goldstein, L. (1981) One-Dimensional Archaeology and Multi-Dimensional People: Spatial Organization and Mortuary Analysis. In Chapman, Kinnes, and Randsborg 1981: 53-69.

Gonen, R. (1992a) *Burial Patterns and Cultural Diversity in Late Bronze Age Canaan* (Winona Lake, IN: Eisenbrauns).

—(1992b) Structural Tombs in the Second Millennium B.C. In *The Architecture of Ancient Israel: From the Prehistoric to the Persian Periods*, edited by A. Kempinski and R. Reich (Jerusalem: Israel Exploration Society): 151-60.

Granqvist, H. (1965) *Muslim Death and Burial: Arab Customs and Traditions Studied in a Village in Jordan* (Societas Scientiarum Fennica Commentationes Humanarum Litterarum 34.1; Helsinki: Helsingfors).

Gras, M., P. Rouillard, and J. Teixidor (1991) The Phoenicians and Death. *Berytus* 39: 127-76.

Greenfield, J.C. (1973) Un rite religieux araméen et ses parallèles. *Revue Biblique* 80: 46-52.

—(1974) The Marzeaʾ as a Social Institution. *Acta Antiqua* 22: 451-55.

Gsell, S. (1920) Les pratiques funéraires. In *Histoire ancienne de l'Afrique du nord IV* (Paris: Librairie Hachette): 426-69.

Guy, P.L.O. (1938) *Megiddo Tombs* (The University of Chicago Oriental Institute Publications 33; Chicago: University of Chicago Press).

Hallote, R.S. (1995) Mortuary Archaeology and the Middle Bronze Age Southern Levant. *Journal of Mediterranean Archaeology* 8/1: 93-122.

Haran, M. (1958) The Bas-Reliefs on the Sarcophagus of Ahiram King of Byblos. *IEJ* 8: 15-25.

Hartland, E.S. (1928) Death and Disposal of the Dead. In *Encyclopaedia of Religion and Ethics IV*, edited by J. Hastings (New York: Scribner's): 411-44.

Hastings, J. (ed.) (1928) *Encyclopaedia of Religion and Ethics I* (New York: Scribner's).

Herscher, E. (1997) Representational Relief on Early and Middle Cypriot Pottery. In *Four Thousand Years of Images on Cypriote Pottery*, edited by V. Karageorghis, R. Laffineur, and F. Vandenabeele (Brussels: Vrije Universiteit): 25-35.

Hertz, R. (1960) A Contribution to the Study of the Collective Representation of Death. In *Death and the Right Hand*, translated by R. and C. Needham (Glencoe, IL: The Free Press): 27-86.

Holladay, J.S. (1997) The Eastern Nile Delta During the Hyksos and Pre-Hyksos Periods: Toward a Systemic/Socioeconomic Understanding. In *The Hyksos: New Historical and Archaeological Perspectives*, edited by E.D. Oren (University Museum Monograph 96; Philadelphia: The University Museum, University of Pennsylvania): 183-252.

Horwitz, L.K. (1996) Animal Bones from the Middle Bronze Age Tombs at Tel Dan. In Biran, Ilan, and Greenberg 1996: 268-77.

Horwitz, W.J. (1979) The Significance of the Rephaim. *Journal of Northwest Semitic Languages* 7: 37-43.

Huntington, R., and P. Metcalf (1979) *Celebrations of Death: The Anthropology of Mortuary Ritual* (Cambridge: Cambridge University Press).

Ilan, D. (1995) Mortuary Practices at Tel Dan in the Middle Bronze Age: A Reflection of Canaanite Society and Ideology. In Campbell and Green 1995: 117-39.

—(1996) The Middle Bronze Age Tombs. In Biran, Ilan, and Greenberg 1996: 161-329.

Insoll, T. (1999) *The Archaeology of Islam* (Oxford: Blackwell).

—(2004) *Archaeology, Ritual, Religion* (London: Routledge).

Johansen, Ø. (1986) Religion and Archaeology: Revelation or Empirical Research? In *Words and Objects: Towards a Dialogue between Archaeology and History of Religion*, edited by G. Steinsland (Oslo: Norwegian University Press): 67-77.

KAI = Donner, H., and W. Röllig (1962–64) *Kanaanäische und Aramäische Inschriften* (3 vols.; Wiesbaden: O. Harrassowitz).

Keel, O. (1997) *Corpus der Stempelsiegel-Amulette aus Palästina/Israel von den Anfängen bis zur Perserzeit. Katalog Band 1: Tel Abu Farag-Atlit* (Orbis Biblicus et Orientalis, Series archaeological 13; Fribourg, Switzerland: University of Fribourg Press).

Kenyon, K.M. (1993) Jericho. In *The New Encyclopedia of Archaeological Excavations in the Holy Land 2*, edited by E. Stern (New York: Simon & Schuster): 674-80.

Keswani, P. (2004) *Mortuary Ritual and Society in Bronze Age Cyprus* (London: Equinox).

King, P.J. (1988) The Marzeah Amos Denounces. *Biblical Archaeology Review* 14: 34-45.

—(1989) The Marzeah: Textual and Archaeological Evidence. *Eretz-Israel* 20: 98*-106*.

KTU = Dietrich, M., O. Loretz, and J. Sanmartin (eds.) (1976) *Die keilalphabetischen Texte aus Ugarit* (Alter Orient und Altes Testament 24; Neukirchen–Vluyn: Neukirchener Verlag).

Laneri, N. (ed.) (2007) *Performing Death: Social Analyses of Funerary Traditions in the Ancient Near East and Mediterranean* (Oriental Institute Seminars 3; Chicago: University of Chicago Press).

Lapp, P. (1969) The 1968 Excavations at Tell Ta'annek. *BASOR* 195: 2-49.

Levine, B.A., and J.-M. de Tarragon (1984) Dead Kings and Rephaim: The Patrons of the Ugaritic Dynasty. *Journal of the American Oriental Society* 104: 649-59.

Levy, T.E., *et al.* (2004) Archaeology and the Shasu Nomads: Recent Excavations in the Jabal Hamrat Fidan, Jordan. In *Le-David Maskil: A Birthday Tribute to David Noel Friedman*, edited by R.E. Friedman and W. H. Propp (Biblical and Judaic Studies 9; Winona Lake, IN: Eisenbrauns): 63-89.

Lewis, T. (1989) *Cults of the Dead in Ancient Israel and Ugarit* (Atlanta: Scholars Press).

L'Heureux, C. (1974) The Ugaritic and Biblical Rephaim. *Harvard Theological Review* 67: 265-74.

—(1979) *Rank Among the Canaanite Gods: 'El, Ba'al, and the Repha'im* (Atlanta: Scholars Press).

Loud, G. (1948) *Megiddo II* (The University of Chicago Oriental Institute Publications 42; Chicago: University of Chicago Press).

Marcus, J., and K.V. Flannery (1994) Ancient Zapotec Ritual and Religion: An Application of the Direct Historical Approach. In Renfrew and Zubrow 1994: 55-74.

Margueron, J. (1983) Quelques reflexions sur certaines pratiques funeraires d'Ugarit. *Akkadica* 32: 5-31.

McCullough, W.S. (1962) Bed. In Buttrick *et al.* 1962: 372-73.

McLaughlin, J.L. (2001) *The Marzeah in the Prophetic Literature: References and Allusions in Light of Extra-Biblical Evidence* (Supplements to Vetus Testamentum 86; Leiden: Brill).

Merrillees, R.S. (1989) Highs and Lows in the Holy Land: Opium in Biblical Times. *Eretz-Israel* 20: 148-54.

Miller, P.D. (1971) The MRZH Text. In *The Claremont Ras Shamra Tablets*, edited by L.R. Fisher (Rome: Pontifical Bible Institute): 37-48.

Montet, P. (1928) La tombe d'Ahiram. In *Byblos et l'Égypte* (Paris: Librairie orientaliste Paul Geuthner): 215-38.

Morris, I. (1991) The Archaeology of Ancestors: The Saxe/Goldstein Hypothesis Revisited. *Cambridge Archaeological Journal* 1/2: 147-69.

Moscati, S. (1988) Ostrich Eggs. In *The Phoenicians*, edited by S. Moscati (New York: Abbeville): 456-63.

Olyan, S. (2004) *Biblical Mourning: Ritual and Social Dimensions* (Oxford: Oxford University Press).

O'Shea, J.M. (1984) *Mortuary Variability: An Archaeological Investigation* (Orlando, FL: Academic Press).

Pader, E.-J. (1982) Death and Ritual: Anthropological and Archaeological Perspectives. In *Symbolism, Social Relations and the Interpretation of Mortuary Remains* (BAR International Series 130; Oxford: British Archaeological Reports): 36-68.

Parker Pearson, M. (1982) Mortuary Practices, Society, and Ideology: An Ethnoarchaeological Study. In *Symbolic and Structural Archaeology*, edited by I. Hodder (Cambridge: Cambridge University Press): 99-113.

—(2000) *The Archaeology of Death and Burial* (College Station: Texas A & M University Press).

Petrie, F. (1931) *Ancient Gaza I: Tell el Ajjul* (London: British School of Archaeology in Egypt).

—(1932) *Ancient Gaza II: Tell el Ajjul* (London: British School of Archaeology in Egypt).

—(1933) *Ancient Gaza III: Tell el Ajjul* (London: British School of Archaeology in Egypt).

—(1934) *Ancient Gaza IV: Tell el Ajjul* (London: British School of Archaeology in Egypt).

Pitard, W.T. (1978) The Ugaritic Funerary Text RS 34.126. *BASOR* 232: 65-75.

—(1994) The Reading of *KTU* 1.19:III:41: The Burial of Aqhat. *BASOR* 293: 31-38.

Pollock, S. (1991) Of Priestesses, Princes and Poor Relations: The Dead in the Royal Cemetery of Ur. *Cambridge Archaeological Journal* 1/2: 171-89.

Pope, M. (1972) A Divine Banquet at Ugarit. In *The Use of the Old Testament in the New and Other Essays: Studies in Honour of William F. Stinespring*, edited by J. Efird (Durham, NC: Duke University Press): 170-203.

—(1977) Notes on the Rephaim Texts from Ugarit. In *Essays on the Ancient Near East in Memory of Jacob Joel Finkelstein*, edited by M. de Jong Ellis (Memoirs of the Connecticut Academy of Arts and Sciences 19; Hamden, CT: Archon): 163-82.

—(1979–80) Le *mrzh* à Ougarit et ailleurs. *Les annales archéologique arabes syriennes* 29-30: 141-43.

—(1981) The Cult of the Dead at Ugarit. In *Ugarit in Retrospect*, edited by G.D. Young (Winona Lake, IN: Eisenbrauns): 159-79.

Porada, E. (1973) Notes on the Sarcophagus of Ahiram. *Journal of the Ancient Near Eastern Society of Columbia University* 5: 355-72.

Porten, B. (1968) The Marzeah Association. In *Archives from Elephantine* (Berkeley: University of California Press): 179-86.

Pritchard, J.B. (1980) *The Cemetery at Tell es-Sa'idiyeh, Jordan* (University Museum Monograph 41; Philadelphia: The University Museum, University of Pennsylvania).

Rahtz, P. (1978) Grave Orientation. *Archaeological Journal* 135: 1-14.

Rakita, G.F.M., *et al.* (eds.) (2005) *Interacting with the Dead: Perspectives on Mortuary Archaeology for the New Millennium* (Gainesville: University of Florida Press).

Renfrew, C. (1972) *The Emergence of Civilization: The Cyclades and the Aegean in the Third Millennium B.C.* (London: Methuen).

—(1985) *The Archaeology of Cult: The Sanctuary at Phylakopi* (London: The British School of Archaeology at Athens).

—(1994) The Archaeology of Religion. In Renfrew and Zubrow 1994: 47-54.

Renfrew, C., and P. Bahn (1991) Symbols for the Other World: The Archaeology of Religion. In *Archaeology: Theories, Methods, and Practice* (New York: Thames & Husdson): 358-63.

Renfrew, C., and E.B.W. Zubrow (eds.) (1994) *The Ancient Mind: Elements of Cognitive Archaeology* (Cambridge: Cambridge University Press).

Rouillard, H. (1999) Rephaim. In *Dictionary of Deities and Demons in the Bible*, edited by K. van der Toorn *et al.* (Leiden: Brill): 692-700.

Salles, J.-F. (1987) Deux nouvelles tombes de Ras Shamra. In *Ras Shamra-Ougarit III: Le centre de la ville*, edited by M. Yon (Editions Recherche sur les Civilisations 72; Paris: ADPF): 157-95.

—(1995) Rituel mortuaire et rituel social à Ras Shamra/Ougarit. In Campbell and Green 1995: 171-84.

Saxe, A.A. (1970) Social Dimensions of Mortuary Practices (Ph.D. diss., University of Michigan; Ann Arbor: University Microfilms).

Schick, T. (1998) *The Cave of the Warrior: A Fourth Millennium Burial in the Judean Desert* (IAA Reports 5; Jerusalem: The Israel Antiquities Authority).

Schmidt, B.B. (1994) *Israel's Beneficent Dead* (Forschungen zum Alten Testament 11; Tübingen: J.C.B. Mohr).

Sears, W.H. (1961) The Study of Social and Religious Systems in North American Archaeology. *CA* 2/3: 223-46.

Simpson, S. (1995) Death and Burial in the Late Islamic Near East: Some Insights from Archaeology and Ethnography. In Campbell and Green 1995: 240-51.

Spencer, A.J. (1982) *Death in Ancient Egypt* (London: Penguin Books).

Spronk, K. (1986) *Beatific Afterlife in Ancient Israel and in the Ancient Near East* (Alter Orient un Altes Testament 219; Neukirchen-Vluyn: Neukirchener).

Stager, L.E. (1991) *Ashkelon Discovered* (Washington, DC: Biblical Archaeological Society).

—(1993) Ashkelon. In *The New Encyclopedia of Archaeological Excavations in the Holy Land 1*, edited by E. Stern (New York: Simon & Schuster): 103-12.

Stager, L.E. *et al.* (eds.) (2008) *Ashkelon 1: Introduction and Overview, 1985–2000.* Vol. 3, *Studies in the Archaeology and History of the Levant* (Winona Lake, IN: Eisenbrauns).

Tainter, J.A. (1978) Mortuary Practices and the Study of Prehistoric Social Systems. In *Advances in Archaeological Method and Theory 1*, edited by M.B. Schiffer (New York: Academic): 105-41.

Thomas, L.-V. (1987) Funeral Rites, translated by K. Anderson. In *The Encyclopedia of Religion 5*, edited by M. Eliade (New York: Macmillan): 450-59.

Toynbee, J.M.C. (1996) *Death and Burial in the Roman World* (Baltimore: The Johns Hopkins University Press).

Trinkaus, K.M. (1984) Mortuary Ritual and Mortuary Remains. *CA* 25: 674-79.

Tufnell, O. (1962) The Courtyard Cemetery at Tell El-'Ajjul, Palestine. *University of London Bulletin of the Institute of Archaeology* 3: 1-37.

Ucko, P.J. (1969) Ethnography and Archaeological Interpretation of Funerary Remains. *World Archaeology* 1: 262-80.

Van den Brink, E.C.M. (1982) *Tombs and Burial Customs at Tell el-Dab'a* (Beiträge zur Ägyptologie 4; Cairo: Berichte des Österreichischen Archäologischen Institutes).

Van Gennep, A. (1960) *The Rites of Passage*, translated by M.B. Vizedom and G.L. Caffee (Chicago: University of Chicago Press).

Vaux, R. de (1961) Death and Funeral Rites. In *Ancient Israel, its Life and Institutions*, translated by J. McHugh (London: Darton, Longman & Todd): 56-61.

Watson, P.J. (1980) The Theory and Practice of Ethnoarcheology with Special Reference to the Near East. *Paléorient* 6: 55-64.

Wensinck, A.J. (1917) *Some Semitic Rites of Mourning and Religion* (Verhandelingen der Koninklijke Akademie van Wetenschappen te Amsterdam, Afdeeling Letterkunde 18/1; Amsterdam: Müller).

Xella, P. (1995) Death and the Afterlife in Canaanite and Hebrew Thought. In *Civilizations of the Ancient Near East*, vol. 3, edited by J.M. Sasson (New York: Scribner's): 2059-70.

8 Under the Shadow of the Four-Room House

Biblical Archaeology Meets Household Archaeology in Israel

Assaf Yasur-Landau

Abstract

This paper surveys the history of household archaeology in Israel using three main case studies: the Israelites, the Philistines, and the Canaanites. Much attention has been given to the study of Israelite four-room houses and their contents, mainly to answer questions of ethnogenesis and establishing ethnic demarcators in the material culture. At the same time, Philistine houses have been studied for more or less the same reasons—the search for the Philistine ethnicity and origin, which is in many ways a mirror image of the search for Israelite ethnicity by archaeological means. The study of Canaanite households was, however, until recently, curiously neglected, with little or no interest in reconstructing Canaanite social structure, gender relations, and manifestations of ethnicity.

> Furthermore, you are aware that I have entered an empty house... (Taanach Letter 2; trans. A. Rainey in Rainey and Notley 2006: 76).

Introduction

The domestic group, along with its archaeological manifestation in domestic assemblages, merits a focus of research in its own right not only because it is the social group best represented in the archaeological record, but also because its practices within the domestic sphere relate directly to economy, political organization, and social structure (Tringham 1991: 101). Household archaeology set out to investigate the multiple facets of culture embedded in household activities, among which are aspects of gender, religion, economy (such as storage and production), status, political structure, and ethnicity (Wilk and Rathje 1982; Hendon 1996). It is not only the archaeology of men, but also of women and children, often rendered invisible in the archaeological record (Scott 1997). The domestic arena, inseparable from family and kinship, is where socialization begins.

Here, by observing and imitating the behavior of others, one acquires some of the most important elements of one's identity, among them kinship (lineage) and language. It is within the home that *habitus*, the core of self-identity, resides (Bourdieu 1990: 53). It determines the individual's dispositions toward social constructs and practices, and establishes the sense of self at an early age (Jones 1997: 88). Household archaeology is also the method to detect minorities, such as migrants, servants, or slaves. The house acts as a replicator of culture, yet not necessarily of the dominant one; in this private sphere it is possible to manifest identities candidly, in a manner which would have been difficult in the public sphere. Such is the case in houses of migrants, preserving traditions from their countries of origin (Burmeister 2000: 542).

Despite the great benefits household archaeology can afford the study of ancient societies, Biblical Archaeology, or the archaeology of Syro-Palestine, it is only in recent years that the integrated study of household assemblages has begun to receive its due attention in field projects in Israel. According to Meyers, this neglect, as well as the focus on monumental architecture in research, results from the 'way Syro-Palestinian archaeology has been driven, since its nineteenth-century beginnings, by information in written sources'. He goes on to claim that 'the existence of such materials from the Bronze and Iron Ages has given researchers the impression…that they have access to more direct information about the past than the 'mute stones' themselves can provide' (2003a: 187). While I agree that published analyses of entire arrays of activities occurring within the domestic space are still rather rare occurrences in the archaeology of the second- and first-millennia BCE in Israel, I will try to portray in this short article the more complex relations existing between Biblical Archaeology and household archaeology. It will be argued that the agenda and the interest of Biblical Archaeology did not lead to a neglect of household archaeology, but rather to a use of domestic assemblages that was limited to answer narrow questions, mostly related to the ethnicity and group identities of the Israelites and the Philistines. However, the search for ethnicity in Iron I houses resulted, in many cases, in a plethora of studies addressing broader aspects of culture. Finally, I will point to a major lacuna in the study of households: the rather astounding disregard of Middle and Late Bronze Canaanite houses.

Building Houses for Ancient Israel

The treatment of Iron I and II household assemblages was determined, to a large extent, by a complex combination of concern for the ethnic identity of the ancient Israelites and close adherence to the biblical narrative as a source for household activities.

The close connections, and sometimes tension between reconstructed display and actual archaeological remains are clearly evident in one of the earliest attempts made in modern Israel to present ancient, biblical Israelite lifestyle: the reconstructed Israelite four-room house on display at the permanent exhibition in the Ceramics Pavilion at the Eretz Israel Museum, in Tel Aviv, which was opened to the public in June 1966.[1] The concept for the exhibition was devised by Ruth Amiran, who had been, at the time, working on her magnum opus on the ancient pottery of the Holy Land (1966, Hebrew edition). The aim was to present to the public finds from the time of the Israelite Monarchy in their context; the new exhibition piece was presented in the brochure as 'the private dwelling of the Israelite Monarchy period (10th–7th centuries B.C.E.)'. The carefully reconstructed

---

1.   I am very grateful to Dr. Uza Zevulun, former director of the Ceramics Pavilion, for the information on the early days of the reconstructed Israelite house (e-mail of Feb. 7, 2008). Dr. Irit Ziffer has very kindly provided me with photos and brochures of the reconstructed house.

house is approached through the main hall of the Ceramics Pavilion. The visitor goes through glass doors, straight into the central space of the four-room building (Fig. 1), reconstructed as an open space. The visitor can then look unhindered into the other rooms of the house, which include two closed spaces—a living room, in which a dinner set is placed on a colorful rug, and a sleeping area. Also displayed is a roofed work area in which there are a cooking *tabun*, a large footbath, and a loom. The strong connection with the biblical narrative is made in the accompanying brochure, which is laden with biblical quotes relating to the objects and activities exhibited. The use of natural materials for this reconstruction, such as wood, reeds, stone, basketry, and rugs dyed with natural colors, as well as the display of authentic, well-preserved artifacts, turns the visit to an aesthetic dive into the past and a potent educational tool.[2]

Figure 1. The reconstructed four-room house at the Eretz Israel museum. Photo: Leonid Padrul, Eretz Israel Museum, Tel Aviv, courtesy of Dr. Irit Ziffer.

In the reconstructed house, however, not a single complete domestic assemblage is represented, but, rather, there is an attempt to create a 'typical' house by combining finds from several sites, crossing regional, temporal, and perhaps even ethnic boundaries. The house contains Iron II finds from the excavations at Arad in the Negev, side by side with reconstructions inspired by finds from Judah, such as a loom reconstructed after finds from Lachish. The plan of the house, on the other hand, as well as the building materials used for its reconstruction, was inspired by an Iron I four-room building found by Benjamin Mazar in Area A at Tell Qasile, an Iron Age site located on the grounds of the Eretz Israel Museum, and easily visible from the Ceramics Pavilion. Choosing a plan

---

2.   I saw this exhibition for the first time in the late 1970s with my grandfather Michael Landau, during a visit to the museum that doubtlessly sparked in me a keen interest in archaeology. The house is still visited by many groups of schoolchildren every year, and it is, arguably, one of the most influential loci for forming public notions on life in ancient Israel.

of a nearby house seems highly logical, especially bearing in mind Tell Qasile's important place in the history of Israeli archaeology, having been, in 1949, the first site for which a digging permit was issued by the newly independent State of Israel. This notwithstanding, the excavator, Benjamin Mazar, had designated the site as a Philistine one and attributed the destruction of the site at the end of Stratum X to David (Mazar 1980: 9-10). Only the following, rather meager settlement of Stratum IX was dated to the days of the United Monarchy. The Philistine nature of the site, and its floruit in Iron Age I, were further strengthened by the excavations of a succession of Philistine temples by Amihai Mazar, beginning in the late 1970s and on (Mazar 1980, 1985). However, clear ethnic boundaries were kept in the museum for years to come: The finds from the tel, coming from both the Philistine temple and the residential area, were displayed in a separate pavilion located in a small structure on the tel, which was closed a few years ago. The reconstructed house includes no Philistine finds—not even those found in the house, the plan of which had been used for the reconstruction.

The shift in the heart of scholarly interest from discussions concerning Iron Age II and the kingdoms of Israel and Judah, to a fierce debate between competing theories on the origin and ethnogenesis of ancient Israel during the last two decades of the twentieth century (Killebrew 2006: 181-85; T.E. Levy, this volume) had a profound influence on the analysis of domestic assemblages.[3] By the early 1990s, doubts concerning the archaeological manifestations of the unified conquest of Canaan by the Israelites, as it appears in the book of Joshua (Albright's 'unified conquest theory'), had reached even mainstream textbooks (e.g. Mazar 1990: 330-31; 1992). The absence of any other literary source for the study of the settlement of the Israelites, as well as debates on the origin of the Israelites, be they new arrivals or descending from the Canaanite culture of the Late Bronze Age, has led to an urgent need for sharpened archaeological tools that will enable the 'Israelite ethnicity' to be identified. As most highland sites of the twelfth and eleventh centuries BCE were domestic sites (with the exception of the 'Bull Site' and perhaps Shiloh), the question of 'pots and people' was, by default, thrown into the domestic arena. The desire to see an archaeological materialization of the biblical narrative of the settlement of the nomadic Israelites in the central hill country had led to the envisioning of Iron I houses as fossilized tents—the manifestation in stone of nomadic dwellings. The plan of the four-room house, generally considered to be an Israelite innovation, was compared to nomads' tents (Fritz 1977; Herzog 1984: 75-77; Shiloh 1970). Similarly, the round outline of settlements such as Tel Masos and ʿIzbet Ṣartah were compared by Finkelstein to the outline of Bedouin encampments (1988: 237-50). While the tyranny of the text did not determine the results of the inquiry, it certainly dictated an extremely narrow research question. The study of household assemblages was unidimensional and selective in its scope, ignoring aspects of gender, household production, and status in the houses of the early Israelites. At the same time, the focus on questions of group identity led to the rapid development of an archaeological discourse of sophisticated theory. The retreat from straightforward equations of 'pots and people', such as the unqualified attribution of the 'collar-rim' jar and the 'four-room building' to the Israelites, started in the early 1990s (e.g. Mazar 1992: 287-92). By the mid-1990s, discussions of Israelite ethnicity stood in the forefront of archaeological research, combining archaeological and anthropological theories of ethnicity and group identity with an integrative use of a wide array of material culture remains—from survey data to house plans and from pottery to animal bones (e.g. Dever 1995;

---

3.   There are two exceptions dealing with household assemblages of the Iron Age II. Geva's study of the urban plan of Hazor in the eighth century BCE has used the different artifacts found in each room (1989: Appendix 1) in an effort to recognize the function of each space. Following a somewhat similar methodology, Singer-Avitz (1996) conducted a detailed, intra-site, functional analysis of the well-excavated site of Iron II households of Beer-Sheba.

Finkelstein 1996). Furthermore, it seems that the quest for group identity in the houses of the ancient Israelites became, at times, a catalyst for the study of ethnicity in other periods of history; for example, the December 1995 issue of *The Biblical Archaeologist* aimed, as stated by the editor (Magness 1995), to go beyond the study of Israelites and Philistines. Accordingly, this anthology includes five articles on periods spanning the time between the Middle Bronze Age ('Hyksos' in Egypt) and Iron Age II.

Despite the fact that the 1990s studies on Israelite ethnogenesis have used household assemblages of Iron Age I as mines from which only the ores of ethnicity were extracted, it seems that, almost unintentionally, the use of archaeological theory has opened slightly the floodgates of household activities analysis, including the archaeology of gender. The twenty-first century opened with the Centennial Symposium of the W.F. Albright Institute of Archaeological Research, which included a large section on the history of the family. In the published volume, five of the eight articles appearing in the 'history of the family' section deal with Iron Age I and II, showing the great potential in studying household assemblages, which is beyond questions of group identity. These new approaches to the archaeology of the family include ideological aspects of the four-room building (Bunimovitz and Faust 2003); gender and household production (Meyers 2003b); and household cult (Ackerman 2003). This section culminates in a rich narrative 'more in the nature of a dream report than in the style of a scholarly paper' (van der Toorn 2003: 393) on nine months of village life among the Iron I highland peasants.

At the same time, King and Stager's seminal book, *Life in Biblical Israel* (2001), had explored virtually every aspect of life in Iron Age Israel—from household through subsistence to political structure—combining the biblical text with archaeological finds and ethnographic evidence. The desire to educate biblical archaeologists in modern archaeological theory is seen in Meyers's (2003a) key article 'Engendering Syro-Palestinian Archaeology: Reasons and Recourses', which includes a broad review of key publications in the archaeology of gender and the archaeology of household. With Hendon, Rappaport, Conkey, and Spector becoming household names also in Near Eastern Archaeology, have the floodgates really opened for the study of household archaeology, or do we still practice archaeology under the shadow of the four-room building? The answer is given quite bluntly in Meyers's article, which, while criticizing the inability of Syro-Palestinian archaeology to shake off its Biblical Archaeology origins (2003a: 187), depicts two images of houses—both(!) reconstructions of the four-room house. Volume 66 of *Near Eastern Archaeology* (2003), dedicated to 'House and Home in the Southern Levant', contains articles corresponding to the periods in which household archaeology is of interest to the research: of five articles, two deal with Roman-Byzantine houses (from the period of the Mishnah and Talmud), one with the Neolithic house (the first houses ever built), and two with the four-room house (Faust and Bunimovitz 2003; Clark 2003), presenting innovative and intriguing insights to the psyche of the ancient Israelites. None of the articles in this volume, or in the Centennial Symposium of the W.F. Albright Institute of Archaeological Research volume, for that matter, deal with the houses of the Bronze Age. Have the Canaanites become the new homeless people of the biblical world?

A Mirror Image: The Philistine House

The study of Philistine households began as what may be seen at first as a parallel to the Israelite ethnogenesis project of the 1990s. The paradigm of Philistine ethnogenesis and settlement was formed by Albright (1932: 58) and Alt (1944), based on a rather limited number of Egyptian texts, and supported by an even more limited amount of archaeological data available back then. Taking at face value the words of Ramses III and his successors (recorded in Medinet Habu and in the

Great Papyrus Harris), they argue that the Sea Peoples were defeated by the Egyptians in Year 8 of Ramses III, then settled as vassals in Egyptian strongholds (interpreted by Albright and Alt as the Egyptian centers in southern Canaan). After a short period of time, they conclude, the Sea Peoples broke the Egyptian yoke and formed their own political system.

The exposure of relatively vast Iron I deposits at Tel Miqne/Ekron as well as at Ashkelon had sparked, in the 1990s, a renewed discussion on the characteristics of Philistine ethnicity and its distinctive, non-local, Aegean nature. The finds provided additional material culture traits for the 'Aegean checklist' (already including fineware and Aegean-style pottery), such as Aegean-type cooking jugs and coarseware kalathoi, Aegean-style loomweights, and unique pottery kilns (Dothan 1989; Stager 1995). As house plans from both sites have not been published until very recently (e.g. Dothan and Zukerman 2004; Master 2005) the discussion on matters of ethnicity has been limited mostly to pottery and other portable objects. However, it was made clear by the excavators that the house architecture was different from that of the Canaanite or Israelite houses, in the use of Aegean-style hearths (Stager 1995: 347). Furthermore, the Tel Miqne/Ekron excavations, as well as the excavation at Ashkelon, also opened the way for studies on behavioral aspects of Philistine migration, such as changes in animal husbandry and economy (Hesse 1986, 1990). The ostensibly 'parallel lives' of Philistine and Israelite houses during the 1990s may have been, in fact, not parallel, but rather two parts of the same narrative, ardent to determine distinct ethnic boundaries in the formative period of the biblical world. This tendency is explicitly put forward in Bunimovitz and Yasur-Landau's (1996) comparison between Israelite and Philistine manifestation of ethnicity through pottery. Furthermore, the emphasis on pigs in the Iron I Philistine economy was used by Finkelstein (1996: 206; 1997: 227-30), dealing with Israelite ethnicity as an antithesis to the lack of pig remains in 'proto-Israelite' sites and as a possible indication of an Iron I taboo on pig among the Israelites. This is despite Hesse and Wapnish's (1997) advice to limit the use of pig remains as ethnic demarcators. At the same time, the Aegean aspect of the Philistine material culture, and hence Philistine ethnicity, was defined as being different from the preceding Canaanite material culture of the thirteenth century (e.g. Killebrew 1998). However, defining Philistine ethnicity was not accompanied by a definition of Canaanite ethnicity through material culture.

The late 1990s saw the appearance of new methodological approaches in the study of the Philistines, putting more emphasis on aspects of human activity than on objects, and, thus, paving the road to an investigation of household assemblages that does not center entirely on demarcation of ethnic boundaries. A gradual shift is noticeable from the 'checklist' approach, which enumerates material culture traits that are indicative of an Aegean migration, to an approach concentrating on behavioral patterns that reflect a change in the way of life, ideology, and economy. New topics that have been investigated stress the importance of ancient foodways (Killebrew 1992; Yasur-Landau 1992) as well as details of pottery production (Killebrew 1996, 1998) to the study of ancient ethnicity. The study of aspects of gender in the Philistine migration (Yasur-Landau 1999; Bunimovitz and Yasur-Landau 2002) has also gone beyond the study of ethnicity; data from Ashdod of architecture and spatial distribution of accompanying finds have been used to reconstruct ancient social structures and to suggest the important role of intercultural marriages in Philistine society. The meticulous recording system of finds at Tel Miqne/Ekron has enabled Mazow (2005) to conduct the first full quantitative spatial analysis of multiple household assemblages in Philistia. There is no doubt that the similarly detailed record of excavations at Ashkelon (Master 2005; Cross and Stager 2006) will inspire similar studies. It seems that similar to the case of Iron I Israelites, the archaeology of the Philistines is moving steadily away from the limited questions of 'pots and people' and from historically oriented questions posed by textually biased agendas, and toward the theoretically complex realm of household archaeology.

No Ethnicity—No Home for the Canaanites

The prosperous present of household archaeology of the Israelites and Philistines is not shared by the Canaanites. Curiously, the keen archaeological interest in twelfth-century BCE ethnicity was not translated into a study of Canaanite ethnicity through an analysis of household assemblages; this is despite the fact that early twelfth-century Canaanite assemblages were available from well-excavated sites such as Lachish, Megiddo, Ashdod, and even Tel Miqne/Ekron. One possible reason for the exclusion of the Canaanites from the study of ethnicity was the similarity between Canaanite and Israelite material culture noted above, which also hindered the search for the Israelite ethnicity. Without the 'ethnicity phase' of the 1990s, the trajectory of Canaanite household archaeology of the Middle and Late Bronze Age, although admittedly within the range of the chronological and cultural interests of Biblical Archaeology, differs much from that of the Israelites or the Philistines.

Figure 2. A Canaanite Family from Jericho. After Kenyon 1977: fig. 63.

Kenyon's find of wooden furniture in the Jericho tombs, mainly in Tomb H 18, was likely a catalyst for the unusual representation of a reconstructed Middle Bronze room and a household scene in Jericho (Kenyon 1979: Fig. 63) (Fig. 2). The visible corner of the room is inhabited by no less then six people: two women, a man, and three children. The material culture objects in the room are based on finds from the Jericho tombs: large storage jars with a dipper juglet in the corner together with a wooden stool and a wicker basket; an oil lamp in a niche in a wall; a table laden with a wooden fruit bowl, an alabaster bowl, and an inlayed box. The setting of the figures reflects a patriarchal notion: the man sits on a stool, holding one of the children; one of the women is standing before him, holding a bowl; and the other woman is ladling some liquid from the storage jars. Another (male?) child is sitting behind the man, chewing on what may be a stylos(?), while a naked toddler is crawling on the floor, its hands on a wooden bed. Despite this extremely evocative depiction, nothing in Kenyon's narrative (1979: 175) relates to the family that is depicted, but rather it mentions only the objects!

Tubb, speaking of the need to create an 'Archaeology of Canaan', laments the fact that 'the development of highly refined sequences, based predominantly on minute changes in pottery styles, disguised the fundamental problem in Canaanite archaeology, that is, the difficulty in relating the archaeological findings, such as we have, in any meaningful way to the people'. 'Detailed pottery sequences... may all be well and good', he continues, 'but what do they say about the Canaanites and how they lived?' However, instead of looking for answers about Canaanite society in the multitude of Canaanite houses excavated and published, Tubb concludes that 'the material remains recovered from excavations are simply inadequate and insufficient to allow for a well-rounded historical and social reconstruction of life in ancient Canaan' (2003: 141). A similar sentiment, blaming the dearth of data, was sounded by Killebrew (2006: 109), who noted that 'numerous Late Bronze Age domestic structures have been excavated in Canaan, but due to their poor preservation or inadequate publication, the topic remains obscure'.

I suspect that lack of data was not the main reason for the neglect of Canaanite households. The early years of the 1990s have given two conspicuous examples of the great potential for the study of Canaanite domestic assemblages, even with the less-than-perfect record at hand. The potential of household assemblages, even those coming from old excavations with an incomplete archaeological database, for the understanding of behavioral patterns within them, is manifested in Daviau's (1993) groundbreaking work on Middle and Late Bronze Age houses. This work has also established, for the first time, an implicit methodology for the analysis of household assemblages, the 'functional paradigms' (1993: 47-51), defining criteria for the identification of food preparation, storage, pottery production, textile manufacture, personal adornment, economic affairs, and animal care.

Ziffer's (1990) catalogue for the exhibition *At That Time the Canaanites Were in the Land* offers a unique treatment of aspects of Canaanite daily life inside the Canaanite house: from drinking and eating practices to furniture, clothing, and jewelry. A description of Middle Bronze IIB houses found by Garstang in Jericho reveals that many domestic activities were conducted in the upper floors, such as weaving and storage, while the lower floors were used as shops (1990: *17). The exhibition itself included the reconstruction of a Middle Bronze house from Jericho (1990: *9-*10) made of mud bricks similar in size to those of the Jericho houses, and roofed using materials available in ancient Jericho. The house included a storeroom, as well as a living room, which was fashioned and furnished, with great attention to detail, in a manner very similar to Kenyon's reconstruction.

The renewed interest in household practices during the last decade has passed over the Canaanite houses of the Middle and Late Bronze Age. A notable exception is Panitz-Cohen's (2006) study of two phases of a patrician house at Tel Batash/Timnah, in which she uses spatial analysis of finds to reconstruct activity areas and to estimate the number of people residing within the house. Unfortunately, this is an isolated case. Canaanite practices are often referred to in the context of a dialectic relationship between Canaanites and Philistines or Israelites—the Canaanites never the focus of the argument. There has been therefore little attempt to explore Canaanite household practices in their own right. Thus, for example, Faust and Bunimovitz (2003), in an article dedicated to the study of the four-room house, use access analysis in order to characterize the 'typical Canaanite-Phoenician dwelling', but they do so without giving reference to the specific Canaanite houses used for the preparation of the diagram they present.

In sharp contrast to Iron Age I, there are multiple written sources relating to the Late Bronze Age. The Egyptian control over Canaan in the fifteenth–thirteenth centuries BCE left a massive volume of historical record ranging from inscriptions of Egyptian pharaohs to the El Amarna texts. These texts, portraying Canaan as the arena for intervention of foreign powers, have doubtlessly influenced the choice of research questions regarding the archaeological record, which are traditionally concerned with the international arena, e.g., questions on the nature of Egyptian presence in Canaan and interaction with the local rulers; on international trade with Cyprus and the Aegean; and on production of elite art (Bunimovitz 1995; Killebrew 2006: 21-49, 51-92). The Late Bronze Age seems to be the last period in the traditional span of Biblical Archaeology in which texts reign supreme. Bunimovitz duly noted (1995: 328) that the tyranny of the text and of historical context 'seems to be the main reason for the provinciality of Levantine archaeology—namely, its persistent reluctance to take advantage of its tremendously rich archaeological, historical and ethnographic data in order to produce, test and improve general, worldwide archaeological models and theories'. However, new cuneiform texts found at Hazor and elsewhere (Horowitz *et al.* 2006) continue to feed the hope that a large archive is destined to be found in a major Late Bronze site that will provide critical information on Canaanite society, lifestyle, and politics. Even problems in history and historical geography arising from the El Amarna texts were resourcefully answered by optical and chemical provenance studies of the tablets themselves (Goren, Finkelstein, and Na'aman 2004). Canaanite houses have been therefore overlooked in research not due to an agenda specifically opposing household archaeology, but more simply because research questions on the Middle and Late Bronze Age had been dictated, to a large extent, by available texts, and could be addressed mainly by using those same texts. On the other hand, questions that could be answered by analyses of household assemblages were never raised.

Precisely this type of question was put forward by Schloen in his book *The House of the Father as Fact and Symbol* (2001), arguing that over the entire ancient Near East, and especially in Canaan and Israel, in which the basic structures of society exhibited much uniformity throughout the Bronze and Iron Ages, society was based on the 'patrimonial house model' (2001: 50-53), and the entire social order was based on the 'root metaphor' of the 'house of the father'. The polity is seen as an extension of the household of the ruler, and relative status is referred to in kinship terms: 'brother' used between equals, 'father' used to address a superior, and 'son' to relate to an inferior. Of great relevance for the understanding of society in biblical times is Schloen's argument for continuity in the structure of society between the Late Bronze Age Canaanites and the Iron Age Israelites (2001: 135-36). In both, the basic household unit was the 'patriarchal joint household', and the extended family in which several generations cohabited the same structure. Such continuity could easily explain the rise of the Israelite Monarchy as a 'Patrimonial kingdom' (King and Stager 2001: 4-5) not as an antithesis to Canaanite society, but rather as its direct successor in terms of social structure. Schloen indeed uses household archaeology to support his arguments, investigating demography and domestic space in Iron Age Israel (Schloen 2001: 135-83) as well as in Late Bronze Age Ugarit (2001: 317-47). Conspicuously missing is a comparison of an analysis of houses and palaces of Late Bronze Canaan with the literary evidence for the 'patrimonial house model' (which does exist in the El Amarna letters; 2001: 257). A first step in this direction was taken by Panitz-Cohen that argues for the existence of a 'patriarchal joint household' in Late Bronze Tel Batash/Timnah (2006: 192-93). Other studies investigating the non-elite aspects of Canaanite society, such as Falconer's (1995) and Faust's (2005) studies on village life during the Middle Bronze Age, or Ebeling and Yorke's (2004) study on grinding as a daily maintenance activity, may eventually close the gap in our knowledge of daily life during the Middle and Late Bronze Age. An example for the potential of household archaeology in the study of ancient society, as well as in breaking the ethnically oriented tendencies in household archaeology, comes from the excavations and publication of Building 00/K/10 at Megiddo, unearthed during 1996 and 1998, in excavations directed by Israel Finkelstein, David Ussishkin, and Baruch Halpern. This courtyard house of Level K-4 (Chicago's Stratum VIA) was violently destroyed by the fire that consumed the entire stratum (Fig. 3).[4] Arie (2006: 249), studying the pottery from the building, has noted that the ceramic tradition that it belonged to is a direct continuation of the Late Bronze Canaanite tradition of Megiddo, and he thus argues that the inhabitants of this Iron I building were Canaanites, making this a rare example of a study devoted to an Iron I domestic assemblage that is not Israelite or Philistine.

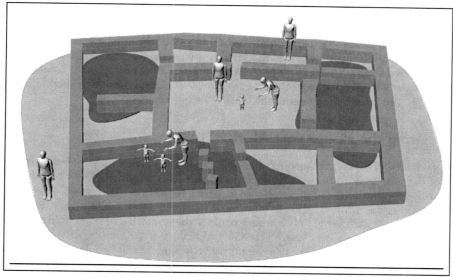

Figure 3. The burnt courtyard building 00/K/10 at Megiddo. Shaded area indicate intense burning. The presence of adults and children is reconstructed according to skeletal material (after Gadot and Yasur-Landau 2006: fig. 33.1).

In the final synthesis of activities that took place in the building (Gadot and Yasur-Landau 2006) data have been used from the numerous reports on various aspects of material culture and also other finds from the house, published in *Megiddo IV* (Finkelstein, Ussishkin, and Halpern 2006). The careful recording of the position of pottery, bones, flint, and human remains enabled a reconstruction of the various activities carried out within the house, answering questions of household production and the timing of household activities, and even relating to aspects of gender and to the size of the household group.

Building 00/K/10 was an ordinary house in Megiddo of Stratum VIA—inconspicuous in its size and wealth, and in the social status of its inhabitants. To judge from the remains of four or five adults and three children found in its ruins, it was most likely the residence of an extended or joined family unit; perhaps several generations lived together, or married and unmarried kin shared the

---

4.   Once it was established that the use of the house ended in sudden disaster, sealing not only the entire domestic assemblage, but also the human remains of the people trapped within it, meticulous data-collection techniques were implemented, aimed at the reconstruction of every aspect of life in the building (Gadot *et al.* 2006: 94).

house together with their children (Gadot and Yasur-Landau 2006: 591-92). The lack of signs for full-time craft specialization, as well as the evidence for the preparation of flint blades to be used in farming, indicates that the inhabitants were farmers who resided within the city boundaries. Their economy was supplemented by part-time crafts, such as weaving and the making of bone and antler implements. Maintenance activities, such as cooking and child care, and crafts, such as spinning and weaving, were practiced by women, active in the inner, more secluded parts of the house. Other crafts may have been practiced outside the house by either men or women (Gadot and Yasur-Landau 2006: 587-91).

The finds inside the house enable reconstruction of some of the events that occurred within it on its last day. The fact that storage jars found in the house were empty and that no storage of grain was found may suggest that the disaster struck after a period of shortage, or before the harvest. It seems that devastation was swift, and caught most if not all of the inhabitants of the house before they could flee. During this time, an adult, possibly a woman, was in the kitchen cooking while taking care of two children. Another woman was working in the nearby inner courtyard. Several other adults were also struck down by the destruction; one, found outside the building, may have died elsewhere and been buried next to the house by survivors.

Repopulating the House that Albright built

Biblical, or Syro-Palestinian, archaeology has only rarely been aimed fully to reconstruct 'biblical society' of the Bronze and Iron Ages through the potent tools of household archaeology. Thus, it missed precious opportunities to gain firsthand insights into the lives of the people mentioned in the Bible and in other ancient Near Eastern sources. It would be a mistake, however, to assume that Biblical Archaeology had played only a negative role in the formation of household archaeology in the Levant. Some works, such as Stager's (1985) *Archaeology of the Family*, Ziffer's (1990) reconstruction of Canaanite life, and Daviau's (1993) work on Middle and Late Bronze Age houses and their furnishing, preceded most canonical theoretical works on household archaeology, such as those of Blanton (1994) and Hendon (1996). The questions put forward by many scholars during the 1990s regarding ethnicity and ethnogenesis, despite being inspired in many cases by text-biased attitudes and resulting in a narrow scientific inquiry of domestic assemblages, have nonetheless opened the door to other studies dealing with the households of the Israelites and the Philistines. With the New Pragmatism, interdisciplinary approach (T.E. Levy, this volume), and additional attention given to the study of aspects of gender, household production, and the economic, social, and political structure of household groups, the empty houses of the Bronze and Iron Ages will once again be filled with the people of the past, 'and the streets of the city will be filled with boys and girls playing in its streets' (Zech. 8:5).

References

Ackerman, S. (2003) A Home with the Goddess. In Dever and Gitin 2003: 455-68.
Albright, W.F. (1932) *The Excavation at Tell Beit Mirsim I: The Pottery of the First Three Campaigns* (AASOR 12; New Haven: American Schools of Oriental Research).
Alt, A. (1944) Ägyptische Tempel in Palästina und die Landnahme der Philister. ZDPV 67: 1-20.
Arie, E. (2006) The Iron Age I Pottery: Levels K-5 and K-4 and an Intra-Site Spatial Analysis of the Pottery from Stratum VIA. In Finkelstein, Ussishkin, and Halpern 2006: 191-298.
Blanton, R.E. (1994) *Houses and Households: A Comparative Study* (New York/London: Plenum Press).
Bourdieu, P. (1990) *The Logic of Practice* (Stanford, CA: Stanford University Press).
Bunimovitz, S. (1995) On the Edge of Empires—Late Bronze Age (1500–1200 BCE). In Levy 1995: 320-31.

Bunimovitz, S., and A. Faust (2003) Building Identity: The Four-Room House and the Israelite Mind. In Dever and Gitin 2003: 411-23.

Bunimovitz, S., and A. Yasur-Landau (1996) Philistine and Israelite Pottery: A Comparative Approach to the Question of Pots and People. *Tel Aviv* 23: 88-101.

—(2002) Women and Aegean Immigration to Cyprus in the Twelfth Century BCE. In *Engendering Aphrodite: Women and Society in Ancient Cyprus*, edited by D. Bolger and N. Serwint (CAARI Monograph 3; Boston: American Schools of Oriental Research): 211-22.

Burmeister, S. (2000) Archaeology and Migration: Approaches to an Archaeological Proof of Migration. *CurrAnthr* 41.4: 539-67.

Clark, D.R. (2003) Bricks, Sweat and Tears: The Human Investment in Constructing a 'Four-Room' House. *NEA* 66/1–2: 34-43.

Cross, F.M., and L.E. Stager (2006) Cypro-Minoan Inscriptions Found in Ashkelon. *IEJ* 56: 129-59.

Daviau, P.M.M. (1993) *Houses and Their Furnishings in Bronze Age Palestine* (Sheffield: Sheffield Academic Press).

Dever, W.G. (1995) Ceramics, Ethnicity, and the Question of Israel's Origins. *BA* 58/4: 200-213.

Dever, W.G., and S. Gitin (eds.) (2003) *Symbiosis, Symbolism, and the Power of the Past* (Winona Lake, IN: Eisenbrauns).

Dothan, T. (1989) The Arrival of the Sea Peoples: Cultural Diversity in Early Iron Age Canaan. *AASOR* 49: 1-22.

Dothan, T., and A. Zukerman (2004) A Preliminary Study of the Mycenaean IIIC:1 Pottery Assemblages from Tel Miqne-Ekron and Ashdod. *BASOR* 333: 1-54.

Ebeling, J.R., and R.M. Yorke (2004) The Archaeology of the Daily Grind: Ground Stone Tools and Food Production in the Southern Levant. *NEA* 67/2: 108-17.

Falconer, S.E. (1995) Rural Responses to Early Urbanism: Bronze Age Household and Village Economy at Tell el-Hayyat, Jordan. *Journal of Field Archaeology* 22/4: 399-419.

Faust, A. (2005) The Canaanite Village: Social Structure of Middle Bronze Age Rural Communities. *Levant* 37: 105-25.

Faust, A., and S. Bunimovitz (2003) The Four Room House: Embodying Iron Age Israelite Society. *NEA* 66/1–2: 22-31.

Finkelstein, I. (1988) *The Archaeology of the Israelite Settlement* (Jerusalem: Israel Exploration Society).

—(1996) Ethnicity and Origin of the Iron I Settlers in the Highlands of Canaan: Can the Real Israel Stand Up? *BA* 59/4: 198-212.

—(1997) Pots and People Revisited: Ethnic Boundaries in the Iron Age. In Silberman and Small 1997: 216-37.

Finkelstein, I., D. Ussishkin, and B. Halpern (eds.) (2006) *Megiddo IV: The 1998–2002 Seasons* (Tel Aviv: Institute of Archaeology of Tel Aviv University).

Fritz, V. (1977) Bestimmung und Herkunft des Pfeilerhauses in Israel. *ZDPV* 93: 30-45.

Gadot, Y., and A. Yasur-Landau (2006) Beyond the Finds: Reconstructing Life in the Courtyard Building of Level K-4. In Finkelstein, Ussishkin, and Halpern 2006: 583-600.

Gadot, Y., M. Martin, N. Blockman, and E. Arie (2006) Area K (Levels K-5 and K-4: The 1998–2002 Seasons). In Finkelstein, Ussishkin, and Halpern 2006: 87-103.

Geva, S. (1989) *Hazor, Israel: An Urban Community of the Eighth Century B.C.E.* (Oxford: British Archaeological Reports).

Goren, Y., I. Finkelstein, and N. Na'aman (2004) *Inscribed in Clay: Provenance Study of the Amarna Tablets and Other Ancient Near Eastern Texts* (Tel Aviv: Tel Aviv University/Institute of Archaeology).

Hendon, J.A. (1996) Archeological Approaches to the Organization of Domestic Labor: Household Practice and Household Relation. *Annual Review of Anthropology* 25: 45-61.

Herzog, Z. (1984) *Beer Sheba II: The Early Iron Age Settlements* (Tel Aviv: Tel Aviv University/Institute of Archaeology).

Hesse, B. (1986) Animal Use at Tel Miqne-Ekron in the Bronze Age and Iron Age. *BASOR* 264: 17-27.

—(1990) Pig Lovers and Pig Haters: Patterns of Palestinian Pork Production. *Journal of Ethnobiology* 10/2: 195-225.

Hesse, B., and P. Wapnish (1997) Can Pig Remains Be Used for Ethnic Diagnosis in the Ancient Near East? In Silberman and Small 1997: 238-70.

Horowitz, W., T. Oshima, and S. Sanders (2006) *Cuneiform in Canaan: Cuneiform Sources from the Land of Israel in Ancient Times* (Jerusalem: Israel Exploration Society/Hebrew University of Jerusalem).

Jones, S. (1997) *The Archaeology of Ethnicity: Constructing Identities in the Past and Present* (London/New York: Routledge).

Kenyon, K.M. (1979) *Archaeology in the Holy Land* (4th edn; London and New York: Methuen).

Killebrew, A. (1992) *Functional Analysis of Thirteenth and Twelfth Century BCE Cooking Pots* (paper presented at the ASOR/SBL Annual Meeting, San Francisco).

—(1996) Pottery Kilns from Deir el-Balah and Tel Miqne-Ekron. In *Retrieving the Past: Essays on Archaeological Research and Methodology in Honor of Gus W. Van Beek*, edited by J.D. Seger (Winona Lake, IN: Eisenbrauns): 131-59.

—(1998) Ceramic Typology and Technology of Late Bronze II and Iron I Assemblages from Tel Miqne-Ekron: The Transition from Canaanite to Philistine Culture. In *Mediterranean Peoples in Transition: Thirteenth to Early Tenth Centuries BCE*, edited by S. Gitin, A. Mazar, and E. Stern (Jerusalem: Israel Exploration Society): 379-405.

—(2006) *Biblical People and Ethnicity: An Archaeological Study of Egyptians, Canaanites, Philistines, and Early Israel 1300-1100 B.C.E.* (Leiden: Brill).

King, P.J., and L.E. Stager (2001) *Life in Biblical Israel* (Louisville, KY: Westminster John Knox Press).

Levy, T.E. (ed.) (1995) *The Archaeology of Society in the Holy Land* (New York: Leicester University Press).

Magness, J. (1995) From the Guest Editor. *BA* 58/4.

Master, D.M. (2005) Iron I Chronology at Ashkelon: Preliminary Results of the Leon Levy Expedition. In *The Bible and Radiocarbon Dating*, edited by T.E. Levy and T. Higham (London: Equinox): 337-48.

Mazar, A. (1980) *Excavations at Tell Qasile: Part One—The Philistine Sanctuary* (Qedem 12; Jerusalem: Institute of Archaeology, Hebrew University of Jerusalem).

—(1985) *Excavations at Tell Qasile: Part Two—Various Objects, The Pottery, Conclusions* (Qedem 20; Jerusalem: Institute of Archaeology, Hebrew University of Jerusalem)

—(1990) *Archaeology of the Land of the Bible 10,000–586 B.C.E.* (New York/London: Doubleday).

—(1992) The Iron Age I. In *The Archaeology of Ancient Israel*, edited by A. Ben-Tor (New Haven/London): 258–301.

Mazow, L.B. (2005) Competing Material Culture: Philistine Settlement at Tel Miqne-Ekron in the Early Iron Age (Ph.D. diss., The University of Arizona).

Meyers, C. (2003a) Engendering Syro-Palestinian Archaeology: Reasons and Resources. *NEA* 66/4: 185-97.

—(2003b) Material Remains and Social Relations: Women's Culture in Agrarian Households of the Iron Age. In Dever and Gitin 2003: 425-44.

Panitz-Cohen, N. (2006) Distribution of Finds, Activity Areas and Population Estimates. In *Timnah (Tel Batash) III: The Finds from the Second Millennium BCE*, edited by N. Panitz-Cohen and A. Mazar (Qedem 45; Jerusalem: Institute of Archaeology, Hebrew University of Jerusalem): 173-94.

Rainey, A.F., and R.S. Notley (2006) *The Sacred Bridge: Carta's Atlas of the Biblical World* (Jerusalem: Carta).

Schloen, J.D. (2001) *The House of the Father as Fact and Symbol: Patrimonialism in Ugarit and the Ancient Near East* (Winona Lake, IN: Eisenbrauns).

Scott, E. (1997) Introduction: On the Incompleteness of Archaeological Narratives. In *Invisible People and Processes: Writing Gender and Childhood into European Archaeology*, edited by J. Moore and E. Scott (London: Leicester University Press): 1-12.

Shiloh, Y. (1970) The Four-Room House: Its Situation and Function in the Israelite City. *IEJ* 20: 180-90.

Singer-Avitz, L. (1996) Household Activities at Beersheba. *Eretz-Israel* 25: 166-74.

Stager, L.E. (1985) The Archaeology of the Family in Ancient Israel. *BASOR* 260: 1-35.

—(1995) The Impact of the Sea Peoples in Canaan (1185–1050 BCE). In Levy 1995: 332-48.

Toorn, K. van der (2003) Nine Months among the Peasants in the Palestinian Highlands: An Anthropological Perspective on Local Religion in the Early Iron Age. In Dever and Gitin 2003: 393-410.

Tringham, R. (1991) Households with Faces: The Challenge of Gender in Prehistoric Architectural Remains. In *Engendering Archaeology: Women and Prehistory*, edited by J.M. Gero and M.W. Conkey (Oxford: Blackwell): 93-131.

Tubb, J.N. (2003) Canaan as a Cultural Construct. In *One Hundred Years of American Archaeology in the Middle East: Proceedings of the American Schools of Oriental Research Centennial Celebration, Washington, DC, April 2000*, edited by D.R. Clark and V.H. Matthews (Boston, MA: ASOR): 137-43.

Wilk, R.R., and W.L. Rathje (1982) Household Archaeology. *American Behavioral Scientist* 25: 617-39.

Yasur-Landau, A. (1992) The Philistine Kitchen—Foodways as Ethnic Demarcators. In *Eighteenth Archaeological Conference in Israel, Abstracts* (Tel Aviv [Hebrew]): 10.

—(1999) The Daughters of Philistia: Towards a Methodology of Gender and Migration in Archaeology. In *Material Culture, Society and Ideology: New Directions in the Archaeology of the Land of Israel*, edited by A. Faust and A. Maeir (Ramat-Gan: Bar Ilan University): 67-75 (Hebrew with an English summary).

Ziffer, I. (1990) *At That Time the Canaanites Were in the Land* (Tel Aviv: Muze'on Erets-Yiśra'el).

9 The Philistines and their Material Culture in Context

Future Directions of Historical Biblical Archaeology for the Study of Cultural Transmission

Ann E. Killebrew

Abstract

This paper reviews different methodological and theoretical approaches to culture transmission in general and as applied to the Philistines in particular. Recent archaeological evidence is then summarized that challenges simplistic 20th-century Eurocentric hyper-diffusionist migration interpretations and linear narratives that portray the Philistines as a group of 'Mycenaean' refugees fleeing the Greek mainland and/or the western Aegean. New directions for future research regarding the transmission of Aegean-style material culture in the eastern Mediterranean are proposed and their implications for the biblical Philistines. In this way, this paper contributes to efforts to forge a more pragmatic historical Biblical Archaeology for the southern Levant.

The Philistines, well known in biblical lore as one of ancient Israel's most treacherous enemies, have fascinated biblical scholars, archaeologists and the general public for well over a century. During the 20th century, the search for the Philistines centered on mounds associated with the Philistines in the biblical account—Tel Miqne (Ekron), Tell es-Safi (Gath), Ashdod, Ashkelon and Gaza.[1] At these five sites, often dubbed the 'Pentapolis' cities, an especially elegant Aegean-style material culture was uncovered that scholars have unanimously attributed to the Philistines. This incongruity of the

---

1.   The identifications of Tel Miqne (Khirbet el-Muqanna) with biblical Ekron (Dothan and Gitin 2008), Tel Ashkelon (Tell el Khadra) with biblical Ashkelon (Avi-Yonah and Eph'al 1993; Stager 2008) and Tel Ashdod (Isdud) with biblical Ashdod (M. Dothan 1993) are accepted by most scholars and confirmed by excavations at these sites. Recent excavations at Tel es-Safi (Maeir 2008b) also seem to confirm its identification with Gath. Several sites have been suggested as the location of biblical Gaza, including Tell el-'Ajjul and Tell Harube, the latter situated under the modern city of Gaza. Most scholars today accept the largely unexcavated Tell Harube as the location of ancient Gaza (see, e.g., Albright 1938; Kempinski 1974; Ovadiah 1993).

biblical depiction of the Philistines as uncouth and uncivilized with the discovery of a very sophisticated culture has served to increase popular fascination and scholarly interest in these vilified people. The publication of T. Dothan's 1982 now classic book, *The Philistines and their Material Culture*, represented the first comprehensive study of the Philistines and remains the major reference work on the topic until today. As outlined by Dothan in her book and expanded upon in later publications, the Philistines emerged from the ruins of the Bronze Age and arrived in the southern coastal plain of Canaan, bringing with them a distinctive Aegean-style culture. The hallmark of Philistine material culture is its ceramic assemblage. In its earliest stratigraphic phase, these vessels are characterized by their fine ware and monochrome paint decoration, somewhat misleadingly designated as 'Mycenaean IIIC'.[2] Associated with these decorated vessels are Aegean-style plain wares, comprising mainly bowls, kraters and cooking pots and smaller numbers of jars and jugs. Other aspects of Philistine material culture, including cultic objects, architectural features, cuisine, and crafts and technology, also display Aegean-style features. Remarkably, this early phase of Philistine material culture representing their initial settlement in the 12th century BCE has been found only at the five Pentapolis cities mentioned in Josh. 13:2-3, lending credence to the historical relevance of the biblical account. Bichrome pottery, a later development of the decorated monochrome Mycenaean IIIC assemblage, is characterized by its painted black and red decoration that incorporates both Aegean-style and 'Levantine' features. This pottery has been found throughout the southern coastal plain and corresponds to a period of expansion of Philistine settlement and influence during the 11th century BCE, a development that is also reflected in the biblical text describing the Philistines initial victories against the Israelites.[3] Armed with this evidence and building on earlier research (see, e.g., Dothan and Dothan 1992: 3-11 for a history of research), Dothan (1982; see also Dothan and Dothan 1992) argued that the appearance of this new Aegean-style material culture excavated at the Pentapolis cities represented a migrating group of west Aegean peoples fleeing destruction and chaos on the Greek mainland during the final years of the 13th and early 12th centuries BCE. In spite of a plethora of recent archaeological discoveries in the eastern Mediterranean that indicates a far more complex scenario of cultural transmission leading up to the appearance of Aegean-style material culture in the east, the majority of scholars continue to endorse the model of a unidirectional mass-migrations of 'Greek' or western Aegean peoples to explain the appearance and diffusion of Aegean-style culture in the east in general and at Philistine sites in particular.[4] In nearly all

---

2.   The use of 'Mycenaean IIIC' is misleading when used in the Philistine context because the term refers to a very specific category of Mycenaean-style pottery that does not always accurately reflect the development of this Aegean-style in the east. As I have discussed elsewhere, the decorated Philistine repertoire most closely resembles the Aegean-style pottery produced on Cyprus, specifically Decorated Late Cypriot III and White Painted Wheelmade III wares that are wheel-made with a light fabric decorated with a dark matt paint (see Killebrew 1998b: 395 for a discussion of these terms).

3.   See, e.g., the biblical accounts of their encounters with Samson (especially Judg. 15–16) and Saul (especially 1 Sam. 31). According to the Bible, their influence began to decline during the reign of King David. (e.g. 2 Sam. 5–8). For overviews of the biblical evidence regarding the Philistines, see e.g. Dothan 1982: 13-21; Singer 1994; Ehrlich 1996; and Machinist 2000 who review the evidence sequentially as related in the biblical account. See Finkelstein (2002) who categorically states that the biblical narrative of Philistine–Israelite encounters represents a late monarchic 7th-century BCE reality with little relevance to historical reconstructions of earlier periods, a view that in my opinion does not adequately represent the complexity of the biblical account.

4.   See, e.g., Barako 2003; Dothan 1989, 1995, 1998, 2000, 2003; Dothan and Zukerman 2004; Mazar 1985, 1988; Stager 1995; Yasur-Landau 2003a, 2003b, 2005. In most of these works, 'Aegean' is synonymous with the Greek mainland, Crete or the west Aegean islands. Noteworthy is the continued neglect of archaeological evidence from the east Aegean and the western and southwestern coasts of modern-day Turkey, in spite of considerable new data from these regions. See Silberman (1998) regarding the Eurocentric focus of research into Philistine origins and also Chami (2007) for a discussion of how modern Western preconceptions of race

treatments of the early Philistines, the focus largely has been placed on origins, diffusion and acculturation, or inter-group and vertical (e.g. hierarchical or linear) transformation, with little consideration for processes that involve intra-group and horizontal transmission. Similarly, overly simplistic analyses of the literary transmission of the Philistines in the biblical text continue to characterize much of the recent scholarly investigations. In what follows, I review methodological and theoretical approaches to culture transmission in general and as applied to the Philistines in particular. The recent archaeological evidence is then summarized that challenges simplistic 20th-century Eurocentric hyper-diffusionist migration interpretations and linear narratives that portray the Philistines as a group of 'Mycenaean' refugees fleeing the Greek mainland and/or the western Aegean. I conclude with suggestions for new venues of future research regarding the transmission of Aegean-style material culture in the east and its implications for the biblical Philistines. In this way, this paper contributes to efforts to forge a more pragmatic historical Biblical Archaeology for the southern Levant (see Levy, this volume).

Approaches to Cultural Transmission and Change and Biblical Archaeology

During the first six decades of the 20th century, culture-historically oriented views of the nature of culture and its transmission dominated anthropological and archaeological thought (see, e.g., Lyman, O'Brien and Dunnell 1997 for an overview). These scholars, whose interests generally focused on tracing histories and origins of specific nations or ethnic groups, employed diffusion and migration, two often overlapping mechanisms to explain the transfer of culture traits and ideas from one society to another. Migration can be defined as a specific type of diffusion characterized by the arrival of a new group and material culture that replaces or overwhelms an indigenous people, usually via conquest and/or colonization. Diffusion, in its broadest sense, encompasses all external processes that spread cultural traits, including migration (see, e.g., stimulus, or trans-cultural, diffusion as developed by Kroeber 1940). But in some scholarly traditions, diffusion is differentiated from migration and refers specifically to less direct mechanisms of transmission such as trade, imitation, colonialism or imperialism. Several theoretical models dominated cultural diffusion literature during this period. Heliocentric diffusion, or hyper-diffusionism, advocates that similar cultures originated from one center and that technological innovation happened once. A second view proposes that cultures originate from several cultural 'hearths', hubs or culture circles (*kulturkreise*). An additional approach, often termed evolutionary diffusionism, posits that societies and cultures are influenced from the outside but share traits that create conditions where similar innovations develop independently, resulting in parallel evolution (see, e.g., Shennan 1996; Trigger 2006: 211-313 for an extensive bibliography and history of research regarding diffusionist and migration traditions in archaeological and anthropological research).

Beginning in the 1960s, these notions of cultural diffusion came under assault by anthropologists and archaeologists trained in the social sciences. With few exceptions, such as Biblical Archaeology that remained closely affiliated with classical or biblical academic traditions, culture-historical explanations of material culture change fell out of favor and largely disappeared from mainstream archaeological literature during the final decades of the 20th century. These increasingly assertive intellectual challenges to traditional humanities-based approaches to the past gave rise to a 'new' or 'processual' archaeology that placed a premium on the importance of environment, functionality and scientifically based measureable models, systems or universal paradigms for interpreting the

---

shaped diffusionist reconstructions in Africa. A similar Eurocentric bias in favor of the west Aegean evidence may be a result of historical events of the past centuries in the region.

past. A key tenet of processual archaeology was the rejection of diffusion and migration as means of cultural change. Rather, it attempted to address broader mechanisms of cultural transmission, such as learning frameworks and intergenerational transmission approaches to explain material culture patterns. Research questions that targeted mechanisms responsible for the transmission of cultural continuity were preferred over more traditional investigations of cultural origins and methods of diffusion (see, e.g., Trigger 2006: 314-85 for an overview).

Despite the fact that migration and diffusion had fallen out of favor as key factors of cultural transmission in most anthropological and archaeological circles, this conceptual approach remained a primary paradigm and concern in Biblical Archaeology. Especially in recent studies of the Philistines, these mechanisms of cultural change continue to play a key role. In particular, the view of a unidirectional diffusion via migration from the west Aegean and acculturation or assimilation studies dominates the majority of publications on the topic. Only recently have scholars begun to challenge this century-long paradigm of a direct unidirectional link between Mycenaean Greece/west Aegean and Philistine cultures (see, e.g., Killebrew 1998a, 1998b, 2000, 2003; 2005: 197-245; 2007, 2008; Killebrew and Lev-Tov 2008; see also, e.g., Maier 2008a). With the notable exception of E.S. Sherratt's insightful study of economic systems and its impact on cultural transmission at the end of the Late Bronze Age in the eastern Mediterranean, few studies have departed from the diffusionist frameworks regarding our understanding of the Philistines (see, e.g., Sherratt 1992, 1998, 2000, 2003; see also Bauer 1998).

During the past decade, there has been a renewed interest in the mechanisms of both intra- and inter-group transmission. This revival is in part inspired by the social sciences that traditionally have focussed on modes of transmission and processes rather than the more narrowly defined concerns of cultural change resulting from diffusion and migration. Cultural transmission, the preferred term in most literature, is a broader and more complex approach that considers innovation, evolution, environment, economy, diffusion, migration and learning modes. Culture is interpreted as 'transmittable' via a variety of directions—i.e. vertically, horizontally or obliquely. Thus cultural transmission by definition is conceived as being three-dimensional rather than linear, the latter a feature that characterizes many culture-historical approaches (see, e.g., Shennan 1996; Clarke 2005a, 2005b; Phillips 2005; Eerkens and Lipo 2007; O'Brien 2008; Stark, Browser and Horne 2008 for treatments of the topic). Considered in light of recent discoveries in the eastern Aegean and northern Levant, this expanded tool kit for investigating cultural transmission is an especially suitable framework for re-examining the Philistine phenomenon. Before discussing new directions for the study of Philistine material culture, I will briefly review the major salient features of their material culture within its broader eastern Mediterranean context (for general summaries see Killebrew 2005: 209-20 and Maeir 2008a).

Characteristics of Early Philistine Material Culture

During the past three decades, large-scale excavations at three sites—Tel Miqne-Ekron, Ashkelon and Tell es-Safi/Gath—have added tremendously to our understanding of the Philistines (see Dothan and Gitin 2008 [Ekron]; Maeir 2008b [Gath]; Master 2005; Stager 2008 [Ashkelon] for recent summaries and updated bibliographies). The material culture uncovered at these three sites, considered together with the findings from Ashdod and Gaza, displays similar non-indigenous, Aegean-style[5] features that characterize Philistine sites. These new traits are evident in several categories of

---

5.   I use the term 'Aegean-style' to characterize Philistine material culture, in contrast to 'Aegean' or 'Mycenaean', which was the dominant adjective used in scholarly literature. By adding the word 'style' to 'Aegean,' my intention is to emphasize the complexity of the development and transmission of this particular

material culture, including ceramic vessels, cultic practices, architectural features, cuisine and various industries and technologies (see Killebrew 2005: 197-246 for a detailed discussion and comprehensive bibliography; for an updated general survey, see Maeir 2008a).

Pottery

The locally produced Iron I Philistine pottery repertoire includes decorated fine and undecorated plain wares as well as cooking vessels that are distinguished from indigenous assemblages by their shape, decoration, fabric and formation techniques (for recent studies of aspects of this assemblage, see, e.g., Killebrew 1999, 2000; 2005: 219-30; Dothan and Zukerman 2004; Yasur-Landau 2005; Ben-Shlomo *et al.* 2008). Remarkably, while most research continues to highlight the connections between mainland Greece/west Aegean connections, features of the earliest monochrome and undecorated plain wares from Philistine sites find their closest parallels in shape, decoration and technology with Cypriot and Cilician assemblages (e.g. Killebrew 1998a, 1999, 2000; 2005: 230; 2007). Although several ceramic studies have begun to address issues of cultural transmission beyond diffusion (e.g. Yasur-Landau 2005; Uziel 2007) vis-à-vis specific features of the Philistine ceramic assemblage, still lacking is a more comprehensive diachronic and synchronic study of this Aegean-style repertoire that addresses both intra-regional and inter-regional developments.

Cult

Several features of Philistine material culture associated with cult represent a clear break from long-term indigenous traditions, including lion-headed cups, incised bovine scapulae and female figurines. Lion-headed cups make their first appearance in the southern Levant during the Iron I period, especially at sites associated with the Philistines. The stylistic inspiration of these vessels is usually traced to rhyta from Bronze Age contexts on mainland Greece and Crete (Dothan 1982: 231; Barako 2000: 523). However, as pointed out by Meiberg (in press), several morphological and functional features of these vessels distinguish them from west Aegean examples. The closest comparisons with the Philistine rhyta are those from Bronze Age Anatolia and North Syria where these vessels have a longstanding tradition.

Incised bovine scapulae are another class of artifacts associated with cultic practices. Numerous examples have been recovered from Iron I and early Iron IIA levels associated with the Philistine settlements (see, e.g., Dothan 1998: 155; Zukerman *et al.* 2007) and at other sites along the southern Levantine coast (see, e.g., Tel Dor: Stern 1994: 96, fig. 409; 2000: 199, fig. 10.6). Most examples of incised scapulae are known from Cyprus, where they have been found in cultic contexts at several Late Cypriot IIIA sites (Webb 1985). Although their function remains a mystery, two possibilities have been suggested: either they were used for divination (Webb 1985: 324-28) or as parts of musical instruments (Karageorghis 1990: 159).

Nicknamed 'Ashdoda' in honor of the site where she was first discovered, these distinctive female figures are one of the hallmarks of Philistine cult. They are usually compared to similar

---

material culture style that spread, either via trade, imitation, emulation, migration or other means of transmission, over a large area of the Aegean and later in several regions in the Levant during the Late Bronze Age and early Iron Ages. In using the word 'Aegean' in its geographical sense, I include all regions bordering on the Aegean Sea. Unfortunately, the term 'Aegean' as used by most scholars usually refers to cultures associated with the west Aegean mainland and islands, reflecting a Eurocentric view of the Aegean Sea. Greek and 'Greek-style' material culture is one of many cultural styles and ethnic groups inhabiting the Aegean Sea region from earliest times to the present. My use of the term 'Aegean-style' refers to the predominant material culture style in the Aegean that developed as a result of multi-directional influences and contacts between the various groups and cultures situated at many sites along the shores of the Aegean Sea during the final decades of the Late Bronze Age and continuing into the early Iron Age.

Mycenaean female figurines known from the west Aegean (see Dothan 1982: 234; Yasur-Landau 2001: Table 1). However, no less significant sources of inspiration are figurines found on Cyprus in Late Cypriot IIC–IIIA and earlier contexts, while I. Singer (1992: 432-50) suggests these figurines should be identified with the Anatolian mother goddess Kubaba/Kybele (also see Morris 2001 for a discussion of Late Bronze Aegean east–west interactions and Anatolian contributions to Greek religion). I contend that Ashdoda is best understood as a hybridization of Aegean, Anatolian and Cypriot styles and influences (see Killebrew 2005: 217-18 for a summary; see also Mazar 2000 for a general discussion of Philistine cult, including temple architecture).

Architectural Features

Over the past few decades extensive architectural remains have been uncovered at Philistine sites. Hearths are one of the most distinctive elements of Philistine architecture, a feature unknown in the southern Levant prior to the appearance of this Aegean-style culture. Hearths first appear in Asia Minor and on Crete. During the second millennium BCE, they are well documented in Asia Minor, in the east and west Aegean, on Cyprus and in Cilicia, and later at Philistine sites, hinting at the complex multi-directional nature of Late Bronze Age cultural interaction (see Karageorghis 1998; 2000: 266, for a general discussion; Barako 2001: 14-15 Table 2). Although most literature has emphasized the comparison of hearths on the Greek mainland (e.g. Dothan 2003: 196-201), the closest parallels to the more modest circular, rectangular or square domestic hearths typical in Philistia are found on Cyprus (Killebrew 2005: 210-16).

Crafts and Technology: Textile and Ceramic Production

Two Aegean-style classes of artifacts found at Philistine sites and associated with a professional textile industry include stone or terracotta bathtubs and spool-shaped ceramic weights. Stone and terracotta bathtubs are documented from second-millennium sites in the Aegean. In later contexts these tubs appear on Cyprus during the Late Cypriot IIC and IIIA periods. Typically these installations have been interpreted as bathtubs for bathing, or for use in purification rites (for a detailed discussion, see Karageorghis 2000: 266-74; Dothan 2003: 202). More recently, L. Mazow (2007) has presented convincing evidence that at least some of these tubs were used either for scouring or fulling wool. Further evidence for a significant textile industry is attested to by increasing numbers of Aegean-style non-perforated reel or spool-shaped loom weights found at Tel Miqne-Ekron and Ashkelon (see Yasur-Landau 2009). In addition to non-indigenous textile manufacturing techniques, pottery technology associated with the Aegean-style Philistine assemblage also represents a break from centuries-long local Bronze Age pottery production practices. These changes are evident in clay selection and preparation, vessel formation techniques and firing temperatures (see, e.g., Nissenbaum and Killebrew 1995; Killebrew 1996; 1998b: 397-401).

Cuisine

The dramatic leap in the quantities of pig bones is one of the most noteworthy changes that marks the transition from the Late Bronze to Iron I levels at Philistine sites. This rise in the role of pork in the Philistine diet is accompanied by a marked increase in the consumption of beef. In the earliest Iron I phases at Tel Miqne-Ekron, pig bones make up at least 13% of the assemblage, increasing in percentages through the 11th century. This phenomenon is matched at other Philistine sites and indicates the maintenance of clearly defined boundaries for at least two centuries. The appearance of Aegean-style table wares and cooking pots also signals significant changes in dietary practices. Most scholars have traced these dietary practices to the west Aegean. However, it should be noted that pork consumption was widespread in the Bronze Age Aegean, Anatolia and Europe. What can be concluded with certainty is that a well-defined cultural boundary existed between what can be called Indo-European vs. Semitic areas of influence, indicating the intrusive character of the Philistine Iron I diet (see Killebrew and Lev-Tov 2008 for a recent analysis and relevant bibliography; see also Hesse 1986; Hesse and Wapnish 1997).

Mention should also be made of an exceptional find of a dog burial from an early Iron Age level at Ekron. The placement of the dog's head between its hind legs and cut marks on its neck vertebrae suggest that the animal had been sacrificed. This discovery brings to mind Anatolian rites where a puppy, kid and piglet were sacrificed to cure epidemics. Dog consumption is also known from several sites in Bronze Age Greece but was not practiced during the Bronze Age southern Levant (see Killebrew and Lev-Tov 2008: 344-45 for a discussion and relevant bibliography; see also Stager 1991 regarding later dog burials). These new data concerning Philistine material culture, taken together with the older datasets, provide new avenues for interpreting the Philistine phenomenon.

Beyond Diffusion and Migration

As outlined above, Philistine material culture is one of the best documented and most distinctive Iron Age cultural assemblages in the eastern Mediterranean. Carefully excavated stratigraphic sequences and detailed typologies provide an excellent database from which to embark on new directions in Philistine research. However, still lacking is an adequate understanding of the complex mechanisms and processes involved in the transmission of Aegean-style culture during the final decades of the Late Bronze Age leading up to the Philistine phenomenon. Unfortunately much past and present research on the topic remains mired in hyper-diffusionist and unidirectional migration models to explain the transmission of Aegean-style material culture, both in the Late Bronze and early Iron Ages, as outlined above.

Following I. Rouse (1986: 11-14), I suggest two types of diffusion—stimulus and complex—as approaches that can be used to clarify diffusionist aspects of the cultural transmission of Aegean-style culture. During the closing decades of the Late Bronze, prior to the appearance of the Philistines, west Aegean-style material culture manufactured in production centers outside of the Greek mainland spread in popularity throughout the Aegean and eventually to Cyprus. Often ignored in many of the studies of the diffusion of Aegean-style material culture is the multi-directional sharing of cultural features and the impact of hybridization and cross fertilization between cultures located on the Aegean coasts (see Maran 2004 for one of the few studies of multi-directional cultural interchange in the Late Bronze Age Aegean; see also Mountjoy 1998 and 1999 regarding regional variations of Mycenaean pottery in the Aegean). This more gradual transmission of culture, an aspect of which can be termed stimulus diffusion, represents both external and internal transference and transmission of information, ideas or elements of material culture. Although small-scale migration doubtlessly played a role, additional factors were crucial in the cultural transmission and interactions between cultures of the Aegean. These mechanisms could include other forms of human contact (e.g. intermarriage), gift exchange and trade, imitation/emulation/learning, ideology and agency, or the impact of individual action. How and why this transmission occurred has yet to be adequately investigated, in part due to a priori notions and biases regarding spheres and direction flows of cultural transmission during the 14th through early 12th centuries BCE.

Complex diffusion, which best describes the transmission of the initial phase of Philistine material culture in the southern coastal plain, is not common and is difficult to prove in the archaeological record. Complex diffusion refers to transference of a complete set of traits and ideas to another culture or region during a relatively short period of time and is usually a result of large-scale population movements, migrations, conquests, colonization and the forced displacement or transfer of populations. As outlined above, the initial appearance of Philistine material culture includes the wholesale transfer of an entire complex of Aegean-style material culture to the southern Levant and can best be understood as a result of well-planned colonization and migration (see Dommelen 1997: 306 regarding colonization, and Killebrew 2005: 197-202; 2007). Although the early Philistine material culture appears suddenly and full-blown at the Pentapolis cities, recent excavations at Ashkelon, Tel es-Safi/Gath and Tel Miqne-Ekron illustrate the existence of inter-site variations, reflecting the complexity of scenarios and means of transmission of Aegean-style material culture at each of these sites. Although initially useful to conceptualize cultural processes at work, the concepts of assimilation, acculturation and creolization models today do not adequately address the mechanisms at work in the cultural transmission of later phases of Philistine material cultures (see, e.g., Stone 1995). In recent years, several publications have begun to explore internal mechanisms of cultural transmission and the exchange of information in Iron Age Philistia and in neighboring regions (e.g. Yasur-Landau 2005 and Uziel 2007). However, these studies are hampered by their limited scope and a priori presumptions of a unidirectional west Aegean transmission of Aegean-style material culture and of the Philistines in particular.

We are now well positioned to embark on new avenues of inquiry regarding the biblical Philistines. These include research questions relating to cultural and economic interaction between the urban Philistine centers, the surrounding countryside and neighboring regions. Thus far little is known regarding the workings of regional markets and exchange systems during much of the Iron Age in Philistia and elsewhere. Mechanisms of internal cultural transmission have largely been ignored in Philistine research. These could include human cognitive structures, learning modes involved with production or acquisition, experimentation, copying error and innovation, or the consideration of both external and internal transmission processes responsible for stylistic variations of material culture (see, e.g., Eerkens and Lipo 2007; Stark, Bowser and Horne 2008 for an overview and case studies). The impact of demography and population numbers on transmission and cultural diversity or the potential impact of individuals involved with production has also not been investigated (see, e.g., Henrich and Boyd 1998; Lipo 2001; Henrich 2004). An understanding of the mechanisms responsible for the transmission of general structures versus specific features of material culture could be especially effective in the analysis of Philistine and other Aegean-style pottery assemblages (see, e.g., Washburn 2001; Mesoudi and Whiten 2004). These suggestions represent just a small sampling of possible future research directions that incorporate both external and internal modes of cultural transmission in the study of the Philistines and their material culture that will lead to a more pragmatic historical Biblical Archaeology.

References

Albright, W.F. (1938) The Chronology of a South Palestinian City, Tell el-'Ajjul. *American Journal of Semitic Languages and Literature* 60: 337-59.

Avi-Yonah, M., and Y. Eph'al (1993) Ashkelon. In Stern 1993: 121-30.

Barako, T.J. (2000) The Philistine Settlement as Mercantile Phenomenon? *American Journal of Archaeology* 104/3: 513-30.

—(2001) The Seaborne Migration of the Philistines (Ph.D. diss., Harvard University).

—(2003) One if by Sea...Two if by Land: How did the Philistines Get to Canaan? One: By Sea. *BAR* 29/2: 26-33, 64, 66.

Bauer, A.A. (1998) Cities of the Sea: Maritime Trade and the Origin of Philistine Settlement in the Early Iron Age Southern Levant. *Oxford Journal of Archaeology* 17: 149-67.

Ben-Shlomo, D., I. Shai, A. Zukerman and A.M. Maeir (2008) Cooking Identities: Aegean-Style Cooking Jugs and Cultural Interaction in Iron Age Philistia and Neighboring Regions. *American Journal of Archaeology* 112: 225-46.

Chami, F.A. (2007) Diffusion in the Studies of the African Past: Reflections from New Archaeological Findings. *African Archaeological Review* 24: 1-14.

Clarke, J. (ed.) (2005a) *Archaeological Perspectives on the Transmission and Transformation of Culture in the Eastern Mediterranean* (Levant Supplementary Series 2; Oxford: Oxbow Books).

—(2005b) Cultural Transmissions and Transformations. In Clarke 2005a: 1-6.

Dever, W.G., and S. Gitin (eds.) (2003) *Symbiosis, Symbolism, and the Power of the Past: Canaan, Ancient Israel, and their Neighbors from the Late Bronze Age through Roman Palaestina. Proceedings of the Centennial Symposium W.F. Albright Institute of Archaeological Research and American Schools of Oriental Research Jerusalem, May 29–May 31, 2000* (Winona Lake, IN: Eisenbrauns).

Dommelen, P. van (1997) Colonial Constructs: Colonialism and Archaeology in the Mediterranean. *World Archaeology* 28: 305-23.

Dothan, M. (1993) Ashdod. In Stern 1993: 103-19.

Dothan, T. (1982) *The Philistines and their Material Culture* (Jerusalem: Israel Exploration Society).

—(1989) The Arrival of the Sea Peoples: Cultural Diversity in Early Iron Age Canaan. In *Recent Excavations in Israel: Studies in Iron Age Archaeology*, edited by S. Gitin and W.G. Dever (AASOR 49; Winona Lake, IN: Eisenbrauns): 1-14.

—(1995) Tel Miqne-Ekron: The Aegean Affinities of the Sea Peoples' (Philistines') Settlement in Canaan in Iron Age I. In Gitin 1995: 41-59.

—(1998) Initial Philistine Settlement: From Migration to Coexistence. In Gitin, Mazar and Stern 1998: 148-61.

—(2000) Reflections on the Initial Phase of Philistine Settlement. In Oren 2000: 145-58.

—(2003) The Aegean and the Orient: Cultic Interactions. In Dever and Gitin 2003: 189-213.

Dothan, T., and M. Dothan (1992) *People of the Sea and the Search for the Philistines* (New York: Schribner).

Dothan, T., and S. Gitin (2008) Miqne, Tel (Ekron). In Stern 2008: 1051-59.

Dothan, T., and A. Zukerman (2004) Preliminary Study of Mycenaean IIIC:1b Assemblages from Tel Miqne-Ekron and Ashdod. *BASOR* 333: 1-54.

Eerkens, J.W., and C.P. Lipo (2007) Cultural Transmission Theory and the Archaeological Record: Providing Context to Understanding Variation and Temporal Changes in Material Culture. *Journal of Archaeological Research* 15: 239-74.

Ehrlich, C.S. (1996) *Philistines in Transition: A History from 1000–730 B.C.E.* (Leiden: E.J. Brill).

Finkelstein, I. (2002) The Philistines in the Bible: A Late-Monarchic Perspective. *JSOT* 27: 131-67.

Gitin, S. (ed.) (1995) *Recent Excavations in Israel: A View to the West* (Dubuque, Iowa: Kendall/Hunt).

Gitin, S., A. Mazar and E. Stern (1998) *Mediterranean Peoples in Transition: Thirteenth to Early Tenth Centuries BCE* (Jerusalem: Israel Exploration Society).

Hesse, B. (1986) Animal Use at Tel Miqne-Ekron in the Bronze Age and Iron Age. *BASOR* 264: 17-28.

Hesse, B., and P. Wapnish (1997) Can Pig Remains be Used for Ethnic Diagnosis in the Ancient Near East? In *The Archaeology of Israel: Constructing the Past, Interpreting the Present*, edited by N.A. Silberman and D.B. Small (JSOTSup 239; Sheffield: Sheffield Academic Press): 238-70.

Henrich, J. (2004) Demography and Cultural Evolution: Why Adaptive Cultural Processes Produced Maladaptive Losses in Tasmania. *AmAnt* 69: 197-221.

Henrich, J., and K. Boyd (1998) The Evolution of Conformist Transmission and Between-Group Differences. *Evolution and Human Behavior* 19: 215-42.

Hitchcock, A., R. Laffineur and J. Crowley (eds.) (2008) *DAIS The Aegean Feast, Proceedings of the 12th International Aegean Conference, University of Melbourne, Centre for Classics and Archaeology, 25–29 March 2008* (AEGAEUM 29; Liège: Université de Liège).

Karageorghis, V. (1990) Miscellanea from Late Bronze Age Cyprus. *Levant* 22: 157-59.

—(1998) Hearths and Bathtub in Cyprus: A 'Sea Peoples' Innovation? In Gitin, Mazar and Stern 1998: 276-82.

—(2000) Cultural Innovations in Cyprus Relating to the Sea Peoples. In Oren 2000: 255-79.

Kempinski, A. (1974) Tell el-'Ajjul—Beth-Aglayim or Sharuhen? *IEJ* 24/3-4: 142-52.

Killebrew, A.E. (1996) Pottery Kilns from Deir el-Balah and Tel Miqne-Ekron. In *Retrieving the Past: Essays in Honor of Gus W. Van Beek*, edited by J.D. Seger (Winona Lake, IN: Eisenbrauns): 135-62.

—(1998a) Aegean and Aegean-Style Material Culture in Canaan during the 14th–12th Centuries BC: Trade, Colonization, Diffusion or Migration? In *The Aegean and the Orient in the Second Millennium: Proceedings of the 50ᵗʰ Anniversary Symposium Cincinnati, 18–20 April 1997*, edited by R.L. Laffineur and G.

Emanuele Greco (Aegaeum 18; Annales d'archéologie égéenne de l'Université de Liège et UT-PASP; Austin: University of Texas at Austin): 159-71.

—(1998b) Ceramic Typology and Technology of the Late Bronze II and Iron I Assemblages from Tel Miqne-Ekron: The Transition from Canaanite to Early Philistine Culture. In Gitin, Mazar and Stern 1998: 379-405.

—(1999) Late Bronze and Iron I Cooking Pots in Canaan: A Typological, Technological and Functional Study. In *Archaeology, History and Culture in Palestine and the Near East Essays in Memory of Albert E. Glock*, edited by T. Kapitan (ASOR Books 3; Atlanta: Scholars Press): 83-126.

—(2000) Aegean-Style Early Philistine Pottery in Canaan during the Iron I Age: A Stylistic Analysis of Mycenaean IIIC:1b Pottery and its Associated Wares. In Oren 2000: 233-53.

—(2003) The Southern Levant during the 13th–12th Centuries BCE: The Archaeology of Social Boundaries. In *Identifying Changes: The Transition from Bronze to Iron Ages in Anatolia and its Neighbouring Regions: Proceedings of the International Workshop Istanbul, November 8–9, 2002*, edited by B. Fischer, H. Genz, É. Jean and K. Köroğlu (Istanbul: Türk Eskiçağ Bilimleri Estitüsü): 117-24.

—(2005) *Biblical Peoples and Ethnicity: An Archaeological Study of Egyptians, Canaanites, Philistines, and Early Israel, 1300–1100 B.C.E.* (Society of Biblical Literature Archaeology and Biblical Studies 9; Atlanta: Society of Biblical Literature; Leiden: Brill).

—(2007) The Philistines in Context: The Transmission and Appropriation of Mycenaean-Style Culture in the East Aegean, Southeastern Coastal Anatolia and the Levant. In *Cyprus, the Sea Peoples and the Eastern Mediterranean: Regional Perspectives of Continuity and Change*, edited by T.P. Harrison. Special issue of *Scripta Mediterranea* XVII–XVIII: 81-103.

—(2008) Aegean-Style Pottery and Associated Assemblages in the Southern Levant: Chronological Implications Regarding the Transition from the Late Bronze II to Iron I and the Appearance of the Philistines. In *Israel in Transition: From Late Bronze II to Iron IIA (c. 1250–850 BCE): The Archaeology*, edited by L.L. Grabbe (European Seminar in Historical Methodology 7; London: T. & T. Clark): 54-71.

Killebrew, A.E., and J. Lev-Tov (2008) Early Iron Age Feasting and Cuisine: An Indicator of Philistine-Aegean Connectivity. In Hitchcock, Laffineur and Crowley 2008: 339-46.

Kroeber, A.L. (1940) Stimulus Diffusion. *American Anthropologist* 40/1: 1-20.

Laffineur, R., and R. Hägg (eds.) (2001) *Potnia: Deities and Religion in the Aegean Bronze Age: Proceedings of the 8th International Aegean Conference/8e Reconte égéenne internationale, Göteborg, Göteborg University, 12–15 April 2000* (Aegaeum 22; Liège: Université de Liège).

Lipo, C. (2001) *Science, Style and the Study of Community Structure: An Example from the Central Mississippi River Valley* (BAR International Series 918; Oxford: British Archaeological Reports).

Lyman, R.L., M.J. O'Brien and R.C. Dunnell (1997) *The Rise and Fall of Culture History* (New York: Plenum Press).

Machinist, P. (2000) Biblical Traditions: The Philistines and Israelite History. In Oren 2000: 53-83.

Maeir, A. (2008a) Aegean Feasting and other Indo-European Elements in the Philistine Household. In Hitchcock, Laffineur and Crowley 2008: 347-52.

—(2008b) Zafit, Tel. In Stern 2008: 2079-81.

Maran, J. (2004) The Spreading of Objects and Ideas in the Late Bronze Age Eastern Mediterranean: Two Case Examples from the Argolid of the 13th and 12th Centuries B.C. *BASOR* 336: 11-30.

Master, D. (2005) Iron I Chronology at Ashkelon: Preliminary Results of the Leon Levy Expedition. In *The Bible and Radiocarbon Dating: Archaeology, Text and Science*, edited by T.E. Levy and T.F.G. Higham (London: Equinox): 337-48.

Mazar, A. (1985) The Emergence of Philistine Culture. *IEJ* 35: 95-107.

—(1988) Some Aspects of the 'Sea Peoples' Settlement. In *Society and Economy in the Eastern Mediterranean (c. 1500–1000 B.C.): Proceedings of the International Symposium Held at the University of Haifa from the 28th of April to the 2nd of May 1985*, edited by M. Heltzer and E. Lipiński (Orientalia lovaniensia analecta 23; Leuven: Peeters): 251-60.

—(2000) The Temples and Cult of the Philistines. In Oren 2000: 213-32.

Mazow, L.B. (2007) The Industrious Sea Peoples: The Evidence of Aegean-Style Textile Production in Cyprus and the Southern Levant. In *Cyprus, the Sea Peoples and the Eastern Mediterranean: Regional Perspectives of Continuity and Change*, edited by T.P. Harrison. Special issue of *Scripta Mediterranea* XVII–XVIII: 291-322.

Meiberg, L. (In press) Philistine Lion-Headed Cups: Aegean or Anatolian? In *The Philistines and Other 'Sea Peoples'*, edited by A.E. Killebrew and G. Lehmann (Atlanta: Society of Biblical Literature).

Mesoudi, A., and A. Whiten (2004) The Hierachical Transforamtion of Event Knowledge in Human Cultural Transmission. *Journal of Cognition and Culture* 4: 1-24.

Morris, S.P. (2001) Potnia Aswiya: Anatolian Contributions to Greek Religion. In Laffineur and Hägg 2001: 423-34.

Mountjoy, P. (1998) The East Aegean–West Anatolian Interface in the Late Bronze Age: Mycenaeans and the Kingdom of Ahhiyawa. *Anatolian Studies* 48: 33-67.

—(1999) *Regional Mycenaean Decorated Pottery* (Rahden, Westf.: M. Leidorf).

Nissenbaum, A., and A.E. Killebrew (1995) Stable Isotopes of Carbon and Oxygen as a Possible New Tool for Estimating Firing Temperatures of Ancient Pottery. *Israel Journal of Chemistry* 35: 131-36.

O'Brien, M.J. (ed.) (2008) *Cultural Transmission and Archaeology: Issues and Case Studies* (Washington, DC: SAA Press).

Oren, E. (ed.) (2000) *The Sea Peoples and their World: A Reassessment* (University Museum Monograph 108; University Museum Symposium Series 11; Philadelphia: University Museum, University of Pennsylvania).

Ovadiah, O. (1993) Gaza. In *The New Encyclopedia of Archaeological Excavations in the Holy Land 2*, edited by E. Stern (Jerusalem: Israel Exploration Society): 408-17.

Phillips, J. (2005) A Question of Reception. In Clarke 2005: 39-74.

Rouse, I. (1986) *Migrations in Prehistory: Inferring Population Movement from Cultural Remains* (New Haven: Yale University Press).

Shennan, S. (1996) Cultural Transmission and Cultural Change. In *Contemporary Archaeology in Theory: A Reader*, edited by R.W. Preucel and I. Hodder (Social Archaeology Series; Oxford: Blackwell): 282-96.

Sherratt, E.S. (1992) Immigration and Archaeology: Some Indirect Reflections. In *Acta Cypria: Acts of an International Congress on Cypriote Archaeology Held in Göteborg on 22–24 August 1991*, Part 2, edited by P. Åström (Jonsered: Åströms): 315-45.

—(1998) 'Sea Peoples' and the Economic Structure of the Late Second Millennium in the Eastern Mediterranean. In Gitin, Mazar and Stern 1998: 292-313.

—(2000) Circulation of Metals and the End of the Bronze Age in the Eastern Mediterranean. In *Metals Make the World Go Round: Supply and Circulation of Metals in Bronze Age Europe*, edited by C. Pare (Oxford: Oxbow Books): 82-98.

—(2003) The Mediterranean Economy: 'Globalization' at the End of the Second Millennium B.C.E. In Dever and Gitin 2003: 37-62.

Silberman, N.A. (1998) The Sea Peoples, the Victorians, and Us: Modern Social Ideology and Changing Archaeological Interpretations of the Late Bronze Age Collapse. In Gitin, Mazar and Stern 1998: 268-75.

Singer, I. (1992) Towards the Image of Dagon, the God of the Philistines. *Syria* 69: 431-50.

—(1994) Egyptians, Canaanites and Philistines: The Period of the Emergence of Israel. In *From Nomadism to Monarchy: Archaeological and Historical Perspectives of Early Israel*, edited by I. Finkelstein and N. Na'aman (Jerusalem: Yad Izhak Ben-Zvi): 282-338.

Stager, L. (1991) Why Were Hundreds of Dogs Buried at Ashkelon? *BAR* 17: 26-42.

—(1995) The Impact of the Sea Peoples in Canaan (1185–1050 BCE). In *The Archaeology of Society in the Holy Land*, edited by T.E. Levy (New York: Facts on File): 332-48.

—(2008) Tel Ashkelon. In Stern 2008: 1578-86.

Stark, M.T., B.J. Browser and L. Horne (eds.) (2008) *Cultural Transmission and Material Culture: Breaking Down Boundaries* (Tucson: University of Arizona Press).

Stern, E. (1994) *Dor, Ruler of the Sea: Twelve Years of Excavations at the Israelite-Phoenician Harbor Town on the Carmel Coast* (Jerusalem: Israel Exploration Society).

Stern, E. (ed.) (1993) *The New Encyclopedia of Archaeological Excavations in the Holy Land 1*, edited by E. Stern (Jerusalem: Israel Exploration Society):

—(2008) *The New Encyclopedia of Archaeological Excavations in the Holy Land 5: Supplementary Volume* (Jerusalem: Israel Exploration Society).

Stone, B.J. (1995) The Philistines and Acculturation: Culture Change and Ethnic Continuity in the Iron Age. *BASOR* 298: 7-32.

Trigger, B.G. (2006) *A History of Archaeological Thought* (2nd edn; New York: Cambridge University Press).

Uziel, J. (2007) The Development Process of Philistine Material Culture: Assimilation, Acculturation and Everything in between. *Levant* 29: 165-73.

Washburn, D.K. (2001) Remembering Things Seen: Experimental Approaches to the Process of Information Transmittal. *Journal of Archaeological Method and Theory* 8: 67-99.

Webb, J.M. (1985) The Incised Scapulae. In *Excavations at Kition V: The Pre-Phoenician Levels, Part II*, edited by V. Karageorghis; Nicosia: Department of Antiquities, Cyprus): 317-28.

Yasur-Landau, A. (2001) The Mother(s) of all Philistines? Aegean Enthroned Deities of the 12th–11th Century Philistines. In Laffineur and Hägg 2001: 329-43.

—(2003a) One if by Sea…Two if by Land: How Did the Philistines Get to Canaan? Two: By Land. *BAR* 29/2: 34-39, 66-67.

—(2003b) The Many Faces of Colonization: Twelfth Century Aegean Settlements in Cyprus and the Levant. *Mediterranean Archaeology and Archaeometry* 3: 45-54.

—(2005) Old Wine in New Vessels: Intercultural Contact, Innovation and Aegean, Canaanite and Philistine Foodways. *Tel Aviv* 32: 168-91.

—(2009) Behavior Patterns in Transition: Eleventh-century B.C.E. Innovation in Domestic Textile Production. In *Exploring the Longue Durée: Essays in Honor of Lawrence E. Stager*, edited by J. David Schloen (Winona Lake, IN: Eisenbrauns): 507-16.

Zukerman, A., L. Kolska-Horwitz, J. Lev-Tov and A.M. Maier (2007) A Bone of Contention? Iron IIA Notched Scapulae from Tell es-Safi/Gath, Israel. *BASOR* 347: 57-81.

10 Judha, Masos and Hayil

The Importance of Ethnohistory and Oral Traditions

Eveline J. van der Steen

Abstract

In this paper I look at two 'applications' of ethnohistory, or historic anthropology, both rooted in the Arab world in subrecent periods. The first is the concept of tribal state formation, using the formation of the emirate of Ibn Rashid in the 19th century CE as a model to hypothesize on the history of Iron Age II Tel Masos (Khirbet Msas) in the Negev. The second study looks at the formation and transformation of oral traditions in a tribal society, and tries to trace the origins of the story cycle of David, and of the United Kingdom.

Introduction

As Tom Levy has stated in his introduction to this volume, there is a need for greater 'pragmatism' in how we go about trying to understand the past. Archaeology, history, studies of literature, religious studies, scientific techniques, all can and must be used interactively in our studies if we want to gain a greater insight into why, or even whether history developed as we believe it did. Whereas the role of anthropology in archaeology has always been significant in the understanding of material remains, as a field of study this has largely been limited to 'primitive' societies, prehistory rather than history. In what I hope counts as a pragmatic approach, I apply recent history to a more distant, historical past, the understanding of which has been shaped for centuries by the literary sources it created. I investigate these literary sources using other literary sources, Western travel accounts of subrecent socio-political constructs, and the precipitation of centuries of local oral traditions.

The concept of Early State formation in the southern Levant has stirred up a lot of dust in recent times. First there is the controversy about the United Monarchy, triggering a heated, and at times vicious debate among opposing parties (the 'low chronology' debate; see Kletter 2004 for an extensive overview of the literature; Herzog and Singer-Avitz 2004). Next there is the discussion about the nature of the Early States that materialized in the Iron Age II, and how we can use the limited evidence at our disposal to understand them (Routledge 2004; Bienkowski and van der Steen 2001; LaBianca and Younker 1998; articles by Stager, Finkelstein, and Mazar in Dever and Gitin 2003). The discussion about the United Monarchy is well known and will not be repeated here, since its main bone of contention is a 50-year dating discrepancy in a period that is notoriously difficult to date. This paper rather looks at anthropological parallels that may be used to clarify the developments in the Beersheba valley, particularly the rise of the Iron Age trading polity at Tel Masos (Khirbet Msas). The chronology established by Herzog and Singer-Avitz (2004) will be used in this application.

In the second part of the paper I look at oral traditions in Arabic Bedouin society; and I speculate about ways in which the process of story-telling may have influenced our perception of the history of early Israel, and created the great story cycle of the United Kingdom.

Tribal Societies in Anthropological Research

The anthropological and ethnoarchaeological study of tribes and tribal societies has seen a kaleidoscope of approaches and appraisals since Evans-Pritchard did his seminal study on the Nuer and Elman Service laid out his evolutionary model of bands—tribes—chiefdoms and states. Both the evolutionary model and the notion of tribe itself have been rejected (Fried 1975) at various stages as being too rigid and too theoretical (see Parkinson 2002 for an introduction into the various stages the concept of 'tribe' went through in anthropology). The concept of tribe, however, has proven resilient as a hypothesis that may throw light on social organization in many historical periods and regions (Parkinson 2002; Eickelman 1989; McNutt 1999; Khoury and Kostiner 1990 *passim* are a tiny selection from the available literature).

The contemporary written sources of most historical periods show that tribes, or kin-based social structures headed by a local leader, played an important part in the social organization of the region. Egyptian sources from the Middle Kingdom until well into the Iron Age mention the presence of tribal groups in the southern Levant: Shasu and Shutu (Giveon 1971; Koenig 1990; Levy *et al.* 2004a). The Assyrian and Babylonian sources from the Old Babylonian period onwards mention the presence of tribal groups on the edges of the 'civilized' world ('Amorites', see Fleming 2004 for the most recent and thorough treatment of the subject); the bible is full of references not only to the twelve tribes of Israel, but also to the tribes surrounding them, and the interaction between them. Before that, the Mesha inscription mentions groups that are generally seen as tribes: the 'men of Sharon' and the 'men of Maharith', and I have recently suggested that Daibon may have been Mesha's 'tribe' (van der Steen and Smelik 2007) rather than the name of his town.

Later Assyrian and Babylonian sources (Eph'al 1982) mention the presence of Arabs and Qedarites, nomadic tribes on the edges of the vassal kingdoms of the southern Levant.

The Nabataeans were a bedouin tribe that established itself on both sides of the Wadi Arabah, and the Romans interacted with the local tribes on the borders of their empire (Ball 2000: 31-36), as did the Byzantines (Mayerson 1994 *passim*; Graf 1978, 1997). From the Islamic conquest onwards the history of the region is one of continuous interaction between Arab tribes, with frequently changing power relations (the various historical introductions in Max Oppenheim's *Die Beduinen* (1939, 1943, 1952, 1967/68) still seem to give the most complete tribal history of the region (also the writings of various Arab scholars, particularly Ibn Khaldun; see also Rosenthal 1967).

This paper focuses on one particular period in the history of the Ottoman empire, and a specific group of written sources: the accounts of Western travellers, most of which were published in the 19th century. The 18th and especially the 19th century CE saw an increase in exploration and travel in the Near East by Westerners: British, American, German, French. They came for various reasons. Many were exploring the biblical lands with the aim of mapping the country and identifying biblical place-names (such as Robinson and Smith [1841–42]), some were perfecting their disguise as Arabs, in order to embark on completely different missions (John Lewis Burckhardt [1822, 1831] and Ulrich Jasper Seetzen [1854–59] being the most famous), some were based in the country as representatives of Western nations (for example James Finn [1878] who was consul in Jerusalem, or

Edward Rogers, vice consul first in Haifa and later in Damascus, whose sister, Mary Eliza, wrote a fascinating account of domestic life in Palestine [1862/1989]) or exploring the entrepreneurial possibilities of the region (Oliphant 1880), some were missionaries, such as William Lethaby (Durley ca. 1910) and Archibald Forder (1909/2002), both based in Kerak, and many others were simply looking for adventure and romance. Some, especially in later periods, were doing actual anthropological research (Musil 1907/8; 1928a being the most important of these).

All these travellers looked with a Western eye. They described, for a Western audience, a society that was basically alien, even though some of them became very familiar with it. Their outsider's observations recorded customs, politics, and social organization in a way a local observer would not bother to do. The period they described, the 19th century up to World War I, was one in which the tribes were virtually independent, particularly in Transjordan, the southern desert areas and the Arabian Peninsula, in spite of being formally subjected to the Ottoman empire. Modern ethnographic research, even though it is more strictly adhering to the rules of anthropological observation, is limited in that it cannot explore this society anymore, simply because it has ceased to exist, routed out by modern political powers and modern technology. The tribes may still exist—and research has shown that many tribal features are strong enough to have survived a century of modern Western intrusion (Shryock 1997: 150-51, 161, 237-42)—but the tribally oriented political landscape of the 19th century has disappeared.

Obviously, these 19th-century accounts were biased in many ways, towards either excessive romanticism, such as the accounts of Anne Blunt or Richard Burton, or the opposite, Western culturocentrism, such as the travels of Irby and Mangles or John Lloyd Stephens, biases which have to be taken into account in reading these sources. Some show a much more profound understanding of the society, often based on a good knowledge of the language, than others. Together they paint a relatively complete picture of the political and social landscape of the 19th century, of the tribal and territorial politics, power relations, and economy of the tribes that inhabited the region.

It is this political landscape, shaped by almost independent intertribal interaction, with a distant superpower that sometimes interfered with local politics, but remained mostly in the background, that is used here as an explanatory model, to understand and interpret the literary sources and the material culture of the early Iron Age.

Tribal State Formation in the 19th Century

The 18th and 19th centuries saw the development of various semi-independent policies in the southern realm of the Ottoman empire. In the north of the Levant the empire still constituted a tangible, albeit erratic, and generally hated presence. In the southern Levant, specifically south of Salt in Jordan, and south of Hebron in Palestine, the empire's authority was practically nil, with the possible exception of the port of Gaza. Any dealings the empire had with the population of these areas had to be negotiated on a basis of equality. The empire had an interest in the south because of the Hajj route, which went from several centres in the north to Mecca and Medina on a yearly basis. The various routes had to be kept safe and usable, which involved keeping Hajj stations at various points, providing water to the pilgrims, and, even more important, paying off the tribes on the routes, to keep them from robbing the pilgrims. That this was no absolute guarantee for the pilgrim's safety is shown by the numerous recorded reports of raiding and robbing of the pilgrims (Browne 1806: 464; Seetzen 1854: II, 341; Burckhardt 1822: 309, 413; 1831: 13, 221; Lynch 1849: 260; Palmer 1871: 429). The empire was also dependent on the tribes for their normal trade, in coffee that came from the Moccha region in the Yemen, textiles and silks from India or slaves from Egypt and Muscat. This trade was for all practical purposes controlled by the tribes, who formed and protected the trade caravans, provided the camels and did most of the buying and selling. The wealth of the Shammar, in the Nejd region of Arabia, was largely the result of their regular trade caravans (compare Ball 2000: 34), and control of the market in Hayil. Since the most common means of transport, for all purposes, was the camel, and the breeding of camels was the main occupation of many of the larger tribes, the Ottoman government was dependent on these tribes. Nevertheless, clashes between the government and tribal forces were common, and were exploited by the tribes to establish their independent position. Only during the short period of Muhammad Ali Pasha's rule (1830–41) were the most powerful tribes subjected, and Robinson and Smith (1841–42: 156) record that even the Howeitat and the Beni Sakhr paid their taxes to the government: one camel for every two tents.

In this political sphere, shortly after the defeat of Muhammed Ali and Ibrahim Pasha, a change in power took place within the leadership of one of the tribes of the Shammar confederation in central Arabia (the most detailed information about this period in the history of the region can be found in al-Rasheed 1991; Wallin 1854/1979; Palgrave 1866; Doughty 1921; Blunt 1881/2002; Euting 1896; Musil 1928b).

The Shammar were a confederation of four independent tribes: the Sinjara, the Abda, the Aslam and the Tuman. Among them lived another tribe, the Beni Tamim, descendents of an ancient tribe of agriculturalists, who had their own villages in the Shammar territories.

In 1836 Abdallah Ibn Rashid, cousin of the paramount sheikh of the Abda, rebelled against his cousin, and after a short exile in Riadh, deposed his cousin with the support of the Ibn Saud leaders. Abdallah was an ambitious man, and he immediately started to expand the power of the Abda.

The Egyptian army, which had come close to overthrowing the Ottoman empire ten years earlier, had been confined to the Arabian peninsula by the international powers, and the Wahhabi Ibn Saud emirate was beginning to recover from its earlier defeat. A renewed struggle between these two powers for supremacy broke out on the peninsula. In this unstable political climate the Shammar felt the need for a strong leader, in order not to be crushed between the two competing powers. This is probably the reason why the independent Shammar tribes, the Sinjara, the Aslam and the Tuman, rallied behind Abdallah and started to look to him as their overall leader. Never before had the confederation had a central leader or a leading tribe. They had always been independent, cooperating and supporting each other when called upon, on a basis of equality. So the structure of the confederation was fundamentally changed, with the take-over of Ibn Rashid. He maintained the oasis of Hayil as his home base, but most of his time was spent in raids and wars. Nevertheless he found time to expand his home town, and it began to transform from a small oasis into a central place.

Abdallah died in 1847. He was succeeded by his son Talal, supported by the Shammar. Under Talal's rule the structure of the Shammar confederation, and particularly of the leadership, reached a new stage, and became more state-like. He started to use the title of amir (al-Rasheed 1991: 53). This added a layer of power to the political structure of the confederation, effectively changing it into a three-tiered hierarchy. The amir was both ruler of the confederation, and leader of the Abda, equal to the sheikhs of Sinjara, the Aslam and the Tuman.

Talal ibn-Rashid focused on the consolidation of his power, further developing Hayil into a centre of both power and trade. He enlarged and finished Barzan, the palace started by the Ibn Ali and continued by his father. He encouraged foreign traders, including Jews and Christians, to settle in Hayil. International trade became one of his economic mainstays. He was known for his liberality (al-Rasheed 1991: 57-58; Palgrave 1866: 91-93; Musil 1928b: 239), which he pursued in the face of the religious intolerance of the Wahhabis, to whom he was still formally subjected. He also consolidated his power outside his capital, restoring old date gardens and settlements, and creating new date gardens with fortified houses in the centre (Musil 1928b). Under his rule the emirate expanded further, a process that reached its zenith during the long rule of Mohammed Ibn Rashid. Although the Ibn Rashid had been accepted as the leading family of the confederation, the succession after

Talal's death was a bloody affair. His brother Mitab, who succeeded him, was murdered within a year by Talal's eldest son, Bandar. Bandar, in his turn, was murdered by Talal's youngest brother, Muhammad, who was supported by the tribes. Muhammad murdered most of the male contestants to the throne. In spite of that, or perhaps because of it, his rule became not only the longest in the history of the Shammar emirate, lasting from 1869 to 1897, but also the most benevolent and prosperous. At the height of its power the domain of the emirate extended towards Jauf, while Palmyra paid tribute to the Rashidis (Musil 1928b: 243). Hayil became a major trade centre. Muhammad reversed the relationship with the Ibn Saud, and received tribute from them.

After Mohammad's death the decline set in. His successor and nephew, Abdel-Aziz, was killed in battle against the Ibn Saud, who were now supported by the British. After his death a struggle over the succession broke out. This was but one of the factors that contributed to the downfall of the emirate. With the support of the British, the Saudis regained their power, and international trade was declining because of the construction of the Hijaz and Baghdad railways, and the construction of the Suez canal. During World War I the Rashidis sided with the Ottoman empire, but some of the tribal sheikhs supported the British, which caused the emirate to fall apart. In 1921 the Rashidis were expelled from Hayil, and that was the end of their emirate.

The Concept of Tribal State or Kingdom
The concept of tribal state or kingdom was introduced in Khouri and Kostiner (1990) but its definition has remained rather loose. The first efforts at defining a 'tribal kingdom' in Near Eastern society was made by LaBianca (1999) with a tentative trait-list, to which several 'traits' have been added (van der Steen 2005).

1. A tribal alliance or confederation would evolve into a tribal kingdom usually under influence of outside pressure or threat.
2. The rise, at the right moment, of a strong man who is acceptable to all the tribes, either because he is an outsider, or because his personal qualities are enough to overcome tribal competition.
3. The pre-monarchical tribal social structure would not be extinguished by the rise of kings. A 'class-based' society, with an urban class controlling a 'rural class' would not evolve.
4. Basic features of tribal society would continue to exist, such as the association of tribes with their traditional territories; an economy that continues to take place on the scale of the individual tribes; and overlapping of territories among tribes for different economic purposes.
5. The intra- and intertribal social organization would be used and adapted in order to accommodate the bureaucracy that was the result of the kingdom structure.
6. Tribal hinterlands would be administered from a central place, but most people would still be living in the hinterlands, in their own traditional tribal territory.
7. Power structures within the kingdom were heterarchical rather than hierarchical: there could be several power bases on the same level, basing their power on different resources, such as economic, religious or political resources.
8. The maintenance of a central militia, to protect the interests of the kingdom as a whole.
9. Although the leaders did not control the economy, they did reap considerable benefits, which they used to consolidate their power by executing prestige projects, maintaining a standing army and 'buying' the cooperation of the tribal leaders.

Most of the traits mentioned here are evident in the history of the Rashidi emirate.

The Shammar were subjected to the recovering Wahhabi Ibn Saud regime, but traditionally they resisted them (Oppenheim 1939: 134). The Egyptian forces of Muhammad Ali had been thrown back on the peninsula, and tried to consolidate their power there. Fear of being crushed between the two competing powers drew the rather loose confederation of the Shammar closer together (al-Rasheed 1991: 48).

Nevertheless, without a uniting force within the confederation itself, they would not have been able to withstand the pressure and eventually shake off the superior forces of the Ibn Saud and the Egyptians. This uniting force was the charismatic person of Abdallah. His claims to leadership were both ascribed and achieved. As a minor member of the leading family of the Abda, they could easily be legalized in the eyes of the Abda tribe, while he also had the support of Faisal Ibn Saud, to whom the Shammar were still subjected.

It was, however, his success in battles and raids (with the material gain that was usually the strongest incentive for those raids) as well as his charismatic and strong personality, that won over the other tribes. Wallin describes 'His intrepidity and manliness, his strict justice, often inclining to severity, his unflinching adherence to his word and promise, of a breach of which he was never known to have rendered himself guilty; and, above all,...his unsurpassed hospitality and benevolence towards the poor, of whom, it was a well-known thing, none ever went unhelped from his door' (Wallin 1854/1979: 68).

Even though Abdallah Ibn Rashid was still very much a tribal sheikh, he consolidated his power by various strategies. One important change from the traditional tribal organization was the creation and maintenance of a standing militia. The basis for this militia was laid in Abdallah's guerrilla days, when he was fighting his cousin over the leadership of the Abda. Tribes had no professional militias. Every man capable of carrying a weapon would take part in battles and raids, and afterwards return to his flocks or fields. Abdallah's guerrilla band consisted of a combination of personal slaves, and kinsmen from his Jaafar clan of the Abda. The kinsmen based their loyalty to Abdallah on their kinship relation, but the slaves were attached to the man himself. In later periods the Jaafar section of the militia lost its central position (al-Rasheed 1991: 137), but the slaves, supplemented by deserters from the Egyptian army and others (Euting 1896: I, 201), continued to form the core of the militia-cum-police-force and contributed much to the security and peace of the region (Wallin 1854/1979: 183; Blunt 1881/2002: I.260). The tribesmen, however, would still take part in major wars and raids, largely on a voluntary basis (any coercion was largely psychological and honour-related: Euting 1896: 206-8), and stimulated by the prospect of booty. These raiding expeditions did much to cement the confederation.

Abdallah also continued the building of the palace started by his predecessor in Hayil, and which would eventually be finished by his son Talal. In Wallin's time (around 1845) the oasis contained some 210 houses, whereas in Euting's time, in 1885, it was a major town surrounded by walls, and with various quarters, also separated by walls, one of which accommodated the Persian traders (Euting and his companions were lodged in this quarter), while another housed the over 1000 slaves of the amir. Palgrave's estimation of 20,000 inhabitants is (as are most of his estimates) wildly exaggerated, but it must have been an impressive town. The Rashidi palace was the largest building. Next to it were the mosque and the main market. The Palace had a large courtyard, where the emir held court every morning. These sessions were open to everybody with a complaint, and were presided over by the emir himself, assisted by a Qadi, a judge. Several travellers have described these sessions (Euting 1896: 201-5; Palgrave 1866: 97-98; Doughty 1921: 606-9). The palace was surrounded by a wall, with high towers, meant both to impress and to set the leadership apart from its subjects, unlike a tribal sheikh, who would traditionally have camped among them.

International trade was also concentrated in the town, on its numerous markets. The position of the town, on some of the major trade routes, as well as on one of the main Hajj routes (the Darb Zobeida), made it a natural centre for economic activity, a circumstance that was recognized and fully exploited by the Rashidi rulers. Talal and his brother and successor Muhammad both encouraged foreign traders to settle in the town and the revenues they received in the form of taxes greatly increased their wealth.

Hayil was thus turned into a central place, the centre of both political power and economic activity.

The tribal structure of the confederation was not disrupted by the rise of the Rashidis or by the adding of an extra 'layer of power' over the existing structure. The sheikhs and the leading families of the separate asha'ir retained their independence. It was Ibn Rashid who had to negotiate the support of these tribal sheikhs, through gifts of food, money and weapons. The organization of the mainstays of the economy, date cultivation and cattle breeding, were the domain of the separate tribes, and the amirs could get access to these goods only through the tribal sheikhs. The individual tribes could participate in raids that were organized by the amirs, and they generally would, because of the gain, but there was no obligation. Tribal territories also remained intact. In order to control this system, the amirs needed wealth, which they gained by several means. Talal created new date gardens in order to increase his wealth and influence, without disrupting the existing social or economic structure. Other revenues came from taxes on trade, which was concentrated in Hayil, the tribute paid by subjected tribes outside the Shammar territory (the Shammar tribes did not pay tribute) and subsidies from the Ottoman government, which hoped to gain the support of the Shammar through the amirs. This became especially important in the 20th century, when the international powers were trying to gain influence among the Arabian tribes (al-Rasheed 1991: 74-84).

That the tribal structure of the Shammar remained intact became clear during and after WW I. Ibn Rashid continued to support the Ottoman empire in spite of strong pressure from the British. However, he could not control the loyalties of the tribes: after the war several tribes lost confidence in the Ibn Rashid leadership, and went over to the side of Ibn Saud and Emir Hussein (al-Rasheed 1991: 218, 224ff.).

Tribal Society in the Early Iron Age

Speculations about the social organization of early Israel are rife, and usually based on anthropological models taken from a variety of tribal societies (McNutt 1999; Eickelman 1989; de Geus 1976; Lemche 1985, to name a few). Studies about the political organization of the region are less frequent.

The general picture is that of an egalitarian coexistence of tribes or clans, all with more or less the same lifestyle: settled in various regions in unwalled villages, living off the land, exploiting a mixture of agricultural and animal resources. Conflict is generally directed outwards, against Amalekites, Midianites, Philistines and others. In light of the later editing of the early history of Israel in the Bible this is understandable, as the editors wanted to stress the organic unity of 'Israel', and would have glossed over any accounts of internal conflict among the chosen tribes. The reality must have been harsher, and less peaceful, if the subrecent history of the region is to be taken as a model. An overview of tribal politics in the 19th century (and other subrecent periods; see Oppenheim 1943) shows that these are much more complex than is often assumed when the early history of Israel is reviewed. Coalitions were temporary, usually made with the purpose of fighting other tribes, and changed frequently. Territorial conflicts were common, and raids would be carried out not only for gain but also to establish power relations (van der Steen 2004). Interaction between what later would become the tribes of Israel must have followed this pattern to a large extent. Rare remnants of these conflicts may have been preserved in the stories about the change of territory of Dan, and the conflict with Benjamin.

Around the turn of the millennium or somewhat later, depending on which chronology one prefers, a more complex social organization emerged that eventually led to the rise of the kingdoms of Israel and Judah (whether or not via the stage of a United Kingdom). This relatively straightforward development has also been assumed for the surrounding regions, Ammon, Moab and Edom. With the Bible being our only written source for the period, and archaeology being a relatively coarse tool for detecting short-term and temporary changes in the socio-political organization of a town, village or region, there seems little else we can look to. On the other hand, the fact that temporary and short-lived development cannot be detected, or pinpointed exactly, does not mean that it did not occur. Sources for the southern Levant in subrecent periods reveal a complex and changeable society, governed by intertribal relationships and conflicts.

In the south, in the desert, were nomadic tribes, but they have attracted little interest from scholars, although they are occasionally associated with Amalek (Finkelstein 1995: 104 with references), or with the later Edomites (Na'aman 1992).

One example is the community of Khirbet Msas, in the Beersheba valley. This site flourished in the 11th and 10th centuries, and formed part of a polity that was based on long-distance trade (Finkelstein 1995: 114-18, 120-23; Herzog and Singer-Avitz 2004: 227). It coincided with industrial activity in Khirbet en-Nahas, in the Faynan district in Southern Jordan, a site heavily involved in copper mining (Levy *et al.* 2005; Higham *et al.* 2005; but see the discussion on www.wadiarabahproject.man.ac.uk/ and van der Steen and Bienkowski 2006 for a critical assessment of the dates), as well as with a surge of small settlements in the Negev highlands to the south of it.

The Archaeological Record of a Trade Polity

The archaeological record shows an expansion in the south at the end of Iron Age I. The Beersheba valley saw the growth of a string of settlements, of which Tel Masos (Khirbet Msas) was the oldest and the most complex. Other major sites were Arad and Beersheba.

Arad. Orna Zimhoni (1985) has proposed a date for Arad str. XI in the 9th century on the basis of parallels with Lachish str. IV. Stratum XII, consequently, must have been the stratum that was destroyed by Sheshonq in ca. 925, since it is the earliest Iron Age stratum on the site. Zimhoni also states that Arad str. XII may have been much more substantial than the excavators suggested, with a surrounding wall (Zimhoni 1985: 86-87; Aharoni 1981: 181; *contra* Herzog 1994: 138). It was clearly a village, however, with houses built in a rather loose fashion, not displaying any strong central control. The pottery repertoire of str. XII closely resembles that of str. XI, which also suggests an occupation late in the 10th century. The pottery of Arad str. XII (Aharoni 1984: pl. 1–4) is comparable to that of Masos str. II and Beersheba str. VII (see below).

Masos. Tel Masos (Khirbet Msas) is located in the narrow pass between the plain of Arad and the plain of Beersheba, beside the main waterwells. The pottery of Masos str. II is comparable to that of Arad str. XII (Herzog 1994: 138), and should therefore be dated to the 10th century (Finkelstein 2002: 114; Herzog and Singer-Avitz 2004: 219).

The first evidence of occupation at Tel Masos appears in the 12th or 11th century, with a number of storage pits and some cooking areas. Soon, however, these were replaced with courtyard houses, in which Philistine and Canaanite pottery was found (Fritz and Kempinski 1983: 73, 81). Other finds include a number of copper objects and remains of ingots (1983: 10, 38) and a stamp seal. Masos str. II, which followed str. III immediately, was the largest and most important site of the region. It consisted of several enclosed compounds, with isolated houses in between. There were pillared storehouses, and Phoenician, Canaanite and Midianite pottery was found, particularly in the earlier stages. A metalsmith's workshop was found, and an ivory lion's head possibly originating in Phoenicia. Comparison of the repertoire of Masos str. II with that of Arad shows that the Masos str. II pottery is somewhat earlier, but there are many shapes that are comparable to the Arad str.

XII pottery, and the high amount of slipped and burnished pottery also suggests a date early in the 10th century, starting perhaps at the very end of the 11th century. The pottery from Masos str. III shows a large overlap in types with that of str. II, and thus must have preceded it immediately. Early shapes, such as the cyma-shaped bowls, and the storage jars with ridged neck (Fritz and Kempinski 1983: pl. 131) suggest a rather long timespan for this stratum, but the dates ascribed to it by the excavators are clearly too early (also Finkelstein 1995, 2005). The architecture of both str. III and II consisted of clusters or compounds of dwellings, not built in a clearly defined architectural style: str. II consisted of clusters of houses, some of which contained mostly four-room buildings (area A; Fritz and Kempinski 1983: plan 2), whereas other areas contained mainly courtyard buildings. This stratum was destroyed, according to Finkelstein (2002: 116), by Shoshenq I in the second half of the 10th century. It was followed immediately by str. I, in which a citadel was built close to the walls, although other buildings seem to have continued in use with no or only minor changes. This stratum was only occupied for a short time, after which the site gradually declined and was deserted.

Beersheba. Beersheba was occupied more or less in the same period as Tel Masos. Beersheba str. IX consisted mainly of pits (Herzog 1984: 8), some of which may have been dwelling pits (1994: 130), and cooking areas. Most of the finds, pottery and other, suggest a basically agrarian and possibly pastoral existence, but some Philistine pottery was found, and one fragment of a Cypro-Phoenician juglet. In str. VIII the pits remained in use, but an actual house or building was added to the settlement (1984: 11). An iron arrowhead was found in the remains, and a bead, possibly of Egyptian origin. The pottery from Beersheba str. VIII is closest to that of Masos str. III and can thus be dated to the 11th century. In spite of the limited repertoire that has been published, the pottery from Beersheba str. VIII is varied, and suggests contacts with the coastal area. Beersheba str. VIII was not destroyed, but simply replaced by str. VII, which saw a complete change in architecture, with a planned lay-out, consisting of a row of houses with shared walls, and possibly a central compound. Many of the houses were built according to the four-room layout.

The pottery from Beersheba str. VII seems contemporaneous with that of Arad str. XII (Herzog 1994: 138) and should therefore be dated to the 10th century.

Other sites, such as Tel Ira, Tel Esdar or Nahal Yattir, seem to have been occupied in the same period.

The Negev Highlands. In the Negev highlands, to the south of the Beersheba valley, about 350 small sites have been found, dated to the 11th and 10th century (Cohen 1979; Cohen and Cohen-Amin 2004; Finkelstein 2002: 114; Haiman 1994, 2003). About 60 of these sites have been labeled 'fortresses' and associated with either the United Kingdom (Haiman 2007) or an independent desert polity (Finkelstein 1995: 103-14 with references; Herzog and Singer-Avitz 2004). The sites are dispersed over a large region, without a clear order or overall pattern. The pottery consisted of local Negev ware, and wheel-made 11th–10th-century pottery, while other artifacts consisted of grinding stones, mortars, stone basins and sickle blades, indicating a mixed pastoral/agrarian lifestyle for the inhabitants. Herzog and Singer-Avitz date these sites, on the basis of the pottery repertoire, to the same period as Masos str. II (Herzog and Singer-Avitz 2004: 226).

Khirbet en-Nahas. The Beersheba valley has always been a passageway between the coast and the Wadi Arabah. Copper, mined at Timna and in the Wadi Feinan, was transported along this route, and it was part of the Arabian trade route since the 8th century BCE and probably earlier (Singer-Avitz 1999; Jasmin 2006). At the end of the Late Bronze Age, when copper mining in Timna was controlled by Egypt, the Egyptians must have been responsible for transport of the copper; in that light it is interesting that the most extensive occupation in the Beersheba valley dates from after the Egyptian period.

Recent finds in the Wadi Fidan by Levy and Adams prove that mining activity restarted there between the 12th and the 10th centuries, probably conducted by independent tribal groups (Levy *et al.* 1999, 2001). More recent excavations at Khirbat en-Nahas in 2006 and 2009 directed by Levy and M. Najjar confirm the initial 13th–11th-century BCE initial production phases at the site with peak industrial scale production in the 10th and 9th centuries BCE (Levy *et al.* 2008).

The earliest slag layers dated so far in Wadi Feinan (Khirbet en-Nahas) were dated to the 12th century (Hauptmann 2000). The production seems to have increased into the 11th and 10th centuries (Levy *et al.* 2004: Table 1). Survey and excavation of the region suggest that these industrial activities were conducted by a local, semi-nomadic population (Levy, Adams and Shafiq 1999; Levy *et al.* 2001). There is no indication of control by external powers. The role of the Arabian trade (the incense trade) is still not clear, although Jasmin (2006) suggests the possibility that it was already active in the 11th century.

The Tribal Polity of Masos

In the absence of an external political power in the area, it is to be assumed that both the copper industry and trade were controlled by the local population. Nineteenth-century sources show that trade was a major economic activity among bedouin tribes, who controlled the means of transport and had the tribal connections to control the trade routes. The Howeitat in southern Jordan controlled trade through the Negev, conducting a trade caravan of up to four thousand camels to and from Egypt each year. There was regular trade between the Arabian Desert and Mesopotamia, conducted and controlled by the Shammar tribe. The Sherarat, a camel-breeding tribe in Jordan, were full-time traders who did not even have a territory of their own anymore.

The archaeological record of the region supports the hypothesis of the development of a complex tribal polity—a tribal state, with Tel Masos as its centre (what Finkelstein, following Rowton, calls a 'dimorphic chiefdom'). During the 12th and 11th centuries Masos was transformed from a simple oasis into a village. The oasis may have been used as a way station by tribes or clans involved in the copper trade through the Beersheba valley. It must, therefore, have been, or have become, part of the territory of this tribe. Eventually it was turned into a more permanent base, in order to be able to control the trade better. It had residential buildings, a possible administrative building, and already an abundance of foreign objects ranging from Phoenicia and Philistia to Midian, attesting to its role in the trade. The large amounts of copper found in the site testify to the importance of copper in this trade.

The heyday of Masos came with str. II, with the establishment of an administration and public buildings, storage facilities, various residential quarters and evidence of local industry. Traders and craftsmen were stimulated to settle in Masos, and it was turned into a central place, from which trade could effectively be controlled.

The transformation of Masos suggests a transformation of the tribal confederation that controlled trade, and possibly the copper industry, into a more structured polity, the beginnings of a tribal state, under the control of a strong leader, comparable to the rule of Talal Ibn Rashid and his brother Muhammad Ibn Rashid in Hayil in the 19th century. Other sites, that were probably already part of the trade route, were incorporated in the system, particularly Beersheba, with perhaps a supporting role for Arad.

This is also the period in which the Negev highlands, to the south of the Beersheba valley, became densely settled. Several explanations have been offered for this phenomenon. Haiman's suggestion that they were probably part of a larger polity makes sense (Haiman 2003, 2007). However, the polity that controlled these sites was not the United Monarchy, but the Masos tribal state—in the same way that Talal Ibn Rashid stimulated horticulture in his emirate by creating new date gardens (with fortified farms) in the Nejd, the Masos polity may have stimulated and controlled settlement in the Negev highlands, in order to increase the production of various commodities such as grain, and perhaps wine. Finkelstein's (1995: 104-9) rejection of their function as fortresses consequently also makes sense. They were fortified farmsteads with an agrarian function, subjected to and protected by the Masos polity.

Finkelstein suggests that Masos was destroyed by Shoshenq in an effort to control the trade route. This seems a plausible explanation that fits the concept of Masos as a tribal state controlling trade. The emirate of Ibn Rashid declined as a result of a combination of internal and external factors: lack of strong leadership, the withdrawal of support from a number of tribal leaders and pressure from the side of the great Ottoman and British powers. The polity at Masos seems to have made a last effort to regain its former hegemony, as suggested by the fortress in str. I, but it is clear that the economic centre of the trade moved to other sites, particularly Lachish (Herzog and Singer-Avitz 2004: 233) supported by Beersheba and Arad. This may well reflect the internal crumbling of the tribal state: the threat of the Egyptian forces may have induced tribes and tribal leaders of the Masos confederacy (or 'tribal state') to change loyalties, and to side with the Egyptians, and this could well have resulted in their taking over of the trade route. The architecture of these sites testifies to the presence of a developed polity, but also to a local one. We have no evidence of any other local polity than that of Masos. It is therefore most likely that rival segments within the Masos polity took over the trade route and further developed the state. The building of a fortress at Khirbet en-Nahas around this time may confirm this change in the organization of the system (Levy *et al.* 2005: 138-39; *contra* Finkelstein 2005: 122-23).

The Story of David, Tribal Hero

The story cycle of David, Solomon and the United Monarchy as related in the Bible has strong echoes of the history of the Ibn Rashid emirate. The existing leader, Saul, was deposed by a member of his own household, who then set out to unite the tribes of the coalition, and consolidate the kingdom, by defeating Israel's enemies, creating a capital for himself, and expanding the kingdom. His son, Solomon, focused on trade and international relationships, increasing the wealth of the realm and turning the relatively simple polity created by his father into a full-blown state. At the same time, the continuing tribal structure of the kingdom becomes clear, when after two generations of rulers it falls apart because separate tribes withdraw their loyalty.

Unfortunately for those who want to see these stories as reflections of a historical reality, archaeology has come up with practically no evidence for early statehood in the 10th century, focusing on Jerusalem. Those archeologists who favour the low chronology (Herzog and Singer-Avitz 2004; Finkelstein 2005, with literature) dismiss the existence of a United Kingdom altogether, and date every form of statehood in Judah to after the northern Omride dynasty. But even those who favour a high chronology (Mazar 2003; Stager 2003[1]) have a hard time of it, since particularly Jerusalem, the capital of the Kingdom, has revealed no evidence of being a central place in any form of polity (Steiner 1998, 2003). In the 10th century Jerusalem was a village, nothing more, and so the heart of the Kingdom did not really exist.

So what about the United Kingdom of David and Solomon, and the great architecture and wealth of Jerusalem? Where did these stories come from? For the earlier periods of Israel's history, the periods of the patriarchs and the judges, the general consensus among scholars is that they are a precipitation of oral traditions that have been transmitted over time. The literature on oral traditions for this period is vast (see Thompson 1992: 7-9, 100, with literature; Lemche 1999), but for

---

1. The most complete overview of the discussion until 2004, regardless of his position in it, is by Kletter (2004). See also recent work at Khirbet Qeiyafa in Garfinkel and Ganor 2008.

the period of the United Monarchy there is much less support for an oral prehistory, even though it is likely that literacy was not widespread, and information transmission must have been largely oral in the period of the United Kingdom (Jamieson-Drake 1991). Nor does any of the research look into what is 'closest to home' for the early Iron Age of Israel: the oral traditions of more recent tribal societies of the Near East.

Oral Traditions in Early Arab Society

Subrecent Arab society possessed a well-developed oral tradition, rooted in pre- and early Islamic tribal traditions (Heath 1996; Connelly 1986; Bailey 1991: 406-29). It incorporated both storytelling and poetry, narrative forms that were never clearly distinguished from each other. In pre-Islamic times popular narrative consisted of anecdotes, called *akhbar*, centred around important events and personalities, narrated in prose interspersed with poetry. One of the most important bodies of early popular narrative was the *Ayyam al-'Arab*, the 'battle days of the Arabs', dealing with tribal skirmishes, battles and feuds and the deeds of warriors and heroes from before the time of Islam.

A second important body of popular narrative was love stories, which developed mostly in the early days of Islam.

The third important tradition was poetry. Poets were highly regarded in pre-Islamic Arab culture, and many famous heroes and lovers were also famous poets (Heath 1996: 54-55; Bailey 1991).

Out of these early traditions developed a corpus of Arab heroic epic, generally featuring one Tribal Hero. Unlike the Arabian nights, which have their origins in the courtly traditions of the city, they originate in tribal, bedouin society, featuring the daily life of the tribe, in its religious and metaphysical beliefs, and in their need for group identification, often in response to external strife and pressure from other tribes. These themes determined the subject matter of the stories, which ranged from droughts and territorial issues, or the honour of women, to the actions of jinns and magical creatures, to tribal feuds, raiding and wars. According to Antony Smith (2000: 65), one of the most important traits of an ethnic community, or a tribe, is 'myths of common ancestry, and shared historical memories'.

The original narrative material for the epics consisted of rather loose collections of stories, featuring various heroes and heroines, which were often 'interchangeable' in the sense that the same story could be told featuring different heroes.[2] It was the nature of oral tradition itself that would eventually transform these groups of stories into heroic epics, the most famous of which are the Sirat Antar, the Sirat Beni Hilal and the Sirat ez-Zahir (Heath 1996; Connelly 1986; Lane 1871: 359-91). All of these are extensive epic stories, in prose or rhymed prose, interspersed with poetry, focusing on the life of one specific hero and his adventures. In the Sirat Beni Hilal the hero, Abu Zayd, undertakes to lead his tribe, the Beni Hilal, out of the Arabian desert and into their promised land in north Africa, stories rooted in the historical 10th- and 11th-century exodus of the Beni Hilal from the Arabian peninsula first into Egypt, and later into Tunisia. The Sirat Antar tells about the adventures of the pre-Islamic hero Antara ibn Shaddad of the tribe of Abs. The Sirat ez-Zahir is the romanticized story of the Mamluk Sultan Baybars.

Storytelling and the Creation of Oral Traditions

Storytellers, *hakawati*, existed until well into 20th-century Arab society, both in the town and the countryside. Travellers mention their existence, and the fact that everybody they met knew and could cite parts of the famous *siyar* (Burckhardt 1831: 47; 175; Wallin 1854/1979: 52; Doughty

---

2.   According to Crone (1987: 203, 213), the hadiths have the same background, originating in pre-Islamic folk traditions which were used to explain the text of the Qur'an.

1928: 263; Schumacher 1888: 131; Jennings-Bramley 1906: 25). By that time, all these stories had undergone a long formation process.

The 'mechanics' of story-telling and the way in which the interaction between the storyteller and his/her audience shapes the development of the oral traditions has received increasing attention in recent years, following the seminal study of Lord and Parry (1960). The influence of the audience in the composition and development of the story cannot be overestimated (Connelly 1986: 147; Heath 1996: 41-42 and n. 21).

Every time a story is performed by a storyteller, he 'recomposes' the story (Lord and Parry 1960: 13). The performer, the storyteller, is himself the composer, building the story around the narrative framework provided by his hero. The narrative material he draws from consists of a large corpus of traditional short stories, as well as material more directly relevant to the audience, drawn from their own surroundings and daily lives. He can, and does, use simple thematic units time and again with slight variations, in a way that may be compared to the use of formulas as described by Lord and Parry (1960: 30-67).[3]

Lane (1871: 380) comments on this interaction, and the need for the narrator to keep his audience interested by using inventions of his own, often using cliff-hangers in order to captivate his audience over long periods (also Heath 1996: 39-41, and n. 18). Connelly takes the issue furthest, and demonstrates how the epic (the Sirat Beni Hilal, in her case) can become part of an ongoing dialogue between the story-teller and his audience (1986: 149); how it can be used to create or confirm an ethnic identity (1986: 162); or to become the 'voice of the unspeakable', crossing both conventional and political boundaries (1986: 167), and voicing political views and veiled criticisms. The incorporation of themes taken from the daily life of the audience plays an all-important role in this. Heath recognizes yet another aspect of this incorporation of themes from daily life: he argues that the Sirat Antar must have gotten its final form in the Mamluk period, as some of the stories feature Crusaders, but nothing that can be related to later periods.

Until well into the 19th century, and again in the 20th century, these epic traditions were seen by the Arab elite as rural 'folk' traditions, not recognized as art or real poetry (they were largely in prose, interwoven with fragments of poetry). The traditions belonged to the lower, illiterate classes, generally the bedouin, in spite of the fact that they were read in the town coffee houses, and that the Sirat Antar was written down in the 15th century at the latest, at the request of sultan Mehmet II (Heath 1996: 43). The only exception to this general attitude seems to have been Ibn Khaldun who praised bedouin poetry (Rosenthal 1967: 457). In various periods the citation of the *siyar* was seen as subversive (Connelly 1986: 17).

However, with the recognition or recent rediscovery of the importance of Arab identity, they changed status (see also Heath 1996: 45ff.) and became an important representation of the Arab identity (Connelly 1986: 167). In Cairo in 1986 the Sirat Beni Hilal was cited every evening on national radio. Sirat Antar became a popular subject for movies in both Egypt and Syria until recently, almost turning Antar into a national hero (http://www.peplums.info/pep04.htm).[4]

The Sirat Antar

Heath (1996: 22-24) argues that the epic must have had a historical core, which can be dated to the 6th and 7th centuries. Historic Antara ibn Shaddad was the son of a black slave woman and a

---

3. In using the term 'formula' we have to keep in mind that Lord and Parry were looking at epic poems, whereas the Bedouin epics are largely prose. The 'formula' as defined by them is structural: a phrase or group of phrases that is varied according to the need of the narrator. The repetition of storylines in different contexts is thematic rather than structural. See also Heath 1996: 105-6.

4. Last accessed February 9, 2009

member of the clan of Qurad, of the northern Arabian tribe of the Beni Abs. Born as a slave, he won his freedom through skill in battle, gained a reputation for martial prowess and as a poet and lived to a ripe old age. He died early in the 7th century, possibly in a sand storm.

Legendary Antar must have started to replace historical Antara almost immediately after his death. The legendary Antar was unusually strong, even as a child. When he grew older, he fell in love with his cousin Abla. She was to be his great love, even though he had many other love affairs. Antar collected his own band of followers around him, with which he roamed the Arab world and had numerous adventures.

The short stories that must have made up the original collection of Antar stories started shortly after Antar's death, probably already in the pre-Islamic era. From their original versions they underwent a long formative process, in which the audience must have played an active part: they expressed their emotions and discussed the story with the narrator, who adapted it to please and move his audience. In many ways, discussed above, the stories are a reflection of the world in which the audience lived.

The fact that the Crusaders, or Franks, as they were called in the Arab world, play a role in many of the stories (even though Antar himself lived some 600 years earlier) demonstrates that this formative process must have lasted well into the Crusader period. No later political or historical events have been incorporated in the epic, so Heath concludes that shortly after the Crusader period the narrative must have crystallized into the Sira (Heath 1996: 29)

By this time the Sirat Antar had developed into a monumental epic, in which a number of themes recur in different contexts, creating a 'network of patterns' on which the storyteller relied to create the episodes of the epic, using the framework of the 'original' stories to build a narrative that could be endlessly expanded into a full-scale epic cycle.

In this 'network of patterns' Heath has discerned four central themes, a general sequence that classifies the Sirat Antar, in common with comparable epics from the same region, as a heroic epic (Heath 1996: 68):

1. *The rise of the hero*. Usually the hero is born under circumstances that already put him in a special position at birth. Often these circumstances are unfavourable, an extra barrier to overcome on his way to heroism: low descent (Antar was both black and a slave); or of high descent but without anybody knowing it, because of some mishap at his birth. At the same time, there are signs both surrounding his birth and/or his early youth, foretelling a great future. Often the heroes in bedouin heroic epic are exceedingly strong and intelligent as youths—both Antar and Abu Zayd, the hero of the Sirat Beni Hilal, were depicted as ferocious, strong and extremely intelligent. The skills he displays and the deeds he performs in his youth also set the future hero apart from his playfellows. There may be conflicts in which the hero becomes estranged from his tribe and has to go into hiding, often with an enemy of the tribe. This estrangement, and the ensuing need to become accepted by and reconciled with his own people, is a frequent theme in the epic literature. And finally, this is also the period in which the future hero acquires magic objects, collects followers and creates friendships that will help him in his future tasks. All these themes are found in the Sirat Antar and in various other Arab epic stories.

2. *The love story*. Arab heroic epic abounds with love stories. Antar's great love was his cousin Abla, whom he won by performing various heroic deeds. Besides that, he had many love affairs and erotic adventures. The love stories often repeat themselves, with different heroines, suggesting that these were favourite themes with audiences. A common theme is that of the wicked father-in-law, who demands an outrageous or impossible dowry as a way to get rid of the hero (Heath 1996: 77). The women themselves were

often strong personalities. Abla was famous for her jealousy, and Antar kept many of his marriages and love affairs secret from her. El-Gundubah's (Sirat Delhemmeh) great love was a heroine herself, who had beaten every man that came her way, and eventually had fled her father because she feared he would force her to marry an unworthy (Lane 1871: 141-42). She only married el-Gundubah because he beat her in battle.

3.   *Heroic service.* Once the hero has reached his destiny, and is recognized as a hero, his main purpose in life becomes to protect and serve the society that has proclaimed him their champion. In practice the activities of the hero change little: he fights, rescues, saves, attacks and defends. But the main goal has changed. While in the first stage of his life the purpose of these activities is to prove himself as a hero, in this stage the purpose becomes detached from the hero's personal motives: he serves. The larger-than-life aspect of his service becomes clear not only in the numbers of enemies the hero slays, but also in what Heath calls his 'personal code of honour', which transcends the accepted laws of society. This may again cause conflicts with his tribe and his followers as the hero will follow his own code: he will protect strangers, even against his own tribe if necessary, and he will give up the duty of revenge out of mercy. Very often the hero has also won renown as a poet. Antar would not rest until one of his poems was accepted among the Mu'allaqat, the poets' 'hall of fame': the seven poems that were suspended in the Ka'ba as being the ultimate poems of the pre-Islamic period.

4.   *The death of the hero.* The death of the hero is usually composed of three parts: the death scene, burial and mourning and revenge, which then provides the storyteller with opportunities for more stories and adventures.

The similarities of the story cycle of David with this analysis of the Sirat Antar are immediately obvious: David's disadvantage at being a younger son, 'of no consequence', the prediction of Samuel of his kingship, his battles as a youngster, his friendship with Jonathan, even the acquisition of a 'magic sword' (the sword of Goliath), his estrangement from Saul, which made him flee to the traditional enemies of Israel, the Philistines, with his own band of followers, until he could be recognized as the hero he is.

The love stories are no less telling: the bride price for Michal, which is the classic theme of the wicked father-in-law, the encounter with Abigail and the erotic adventure of Bathseba bathing on the roof.

As a hero, or king, David also behaved according to the heroic tradition: serving his people by beating Israel's enemies and enlarging the kingdom, and bringing peace and prosperity. His personal code of honour brought him into occasional conflict with his followers, especially in showing mercy to enemies. His qualities as a poet are well-known.

Many of these themes can be considered universal, not only in Near Eastern narrative tradition, but also in Western European traditions—Western fairytales and sagas provide ready examples. Other themes are more closely interwoven with the tribal societies that prevailed in the region around the 10th century BCE.

The comparison suggests a similar development for the David stories as has been described for the Sirat Antar.

David may have been a historical figure (although that does not follow from the stories) about whom a collection of hero stories circulated. These stories were taken up by storytellers and expanded upon, complemented with hero tales borrowed from other traditions (e.g. the slaying of Goliath, which originally seems to have featured a hero named Elhanan). Other themes may have included veiled criticisms of the government. This process may have continued for several centuries, ever expanding the corpus of stories connected to David and gradually transforming it into an epic.

Because of this it has become impossible to discern which, if any, of the themes may have formed part of the original framework. However, the nature of the stories, and their thematic closeness to the Sirat Antar, suggest strongly that they originated in a tribal society, rather than in a state-like one.

The final recording and editing of the story cycle may also have a parallel with the most recent fate of the Arabic *siyar*. They became part of the pan-Arabic ethnic revival, and after centuries of being seen as base folk culture, they were rehabilitated and used to promote ethnic and national awareness. The heroic cycle of David, such as it was, may have seemed, to the editors of the bible, eminently suitable to create and consolidate ethnic awareness and ethnic pride, in a time when that was most called for. David was the prototypical, ideal national hero.

It is even possible (but this is even more speculative) that tales about the legendary leader/ruler of the tribal state of Masos may have survived as a separate story cycle about a legendary trader-king, famous for his fabulous wealth and wisdom, and may eventually have become incorporated in the larger story cycle of the United Kingdom.[5]

References

Aharoni, M. (1984) The Pottery from Strata 12–11 of the Iron Age Citadel at Arad. *Eretz-Israel* 15: 181-204 (Hebrew).

Aharoni, Y. (1981) *Arad Inscriptions* (Jerusalem: Israel Exploration Society).

Bailey, C. (1991) *Bedouin Poetry from Sinai and the Negev: Mirror of a Culture* (Oxford: Clarendon Press).

Ball, W. (2000) *Rome in the East* (London/New York: Routledge).

Bienkowski, P., and E.J. van der Steen (2001) Tribes, Trade and Towns: A New Framework for the Late Iron Age in Southern Jordan and the Negev. *BASOR* 323: 21-47.

Blunt, A. (1881) *A Pilgrimage to Nejd, the Cradle of the Arab Race* (London: Murray).

Browne, W.G. (1806) *Travels in Africa, Egypt and Syria from the Year 1792 to 1798* (London: Cadell & Davies/Longman, Hurst, Rees & Orme).

Burckhardt, J.L. (1822) *Travels in Syria and the Holy Land* (London: Murray).

—(1831) *Notes on the Bedouins and Wahhabis, Collected during his Travels in the East* (London: Murray).

Cohen, R. (1979) The Iron Age Fortresses in the Central Negev. *BASOR* 236: 63-75.

Cohen, R., and R. Cohen-Amin (2004) *Ancient Settlement in the Negev Highlands. II. Iron Age and Persian Period* (IAA Reports 20; Jerusalem: Israel Exploration Society).

Connelly, B. (1986) *Arab Folk Epic and Identity* (Berkeley/Los Angeles/London: University of California Press).

Crone, P. (1987) *Meccan Trade and the Rise of Islam* (Oxford: Blackwell).

Dever, W.G., and S. Gitin (eds.) (2003) *Symbiosis, Symbolism and the Power of the Past* (Winona Lake, IN: Eisenbrauns).

Doughty, C.M. (1928) *Travels in Arabia Deserta* (2nd edn; New York: Boni & Liveright).

Durley, T. (ca. 1910) *Lethaby of Moab* (London: Marshall Brothers).

Eickelman, D.F. (1989) *The Middle East: An Anthropological Approach* (Englewood Cliffs, NJ: Prentice-Hall).

Eph'al, I. (1982) *The Ancient Arabs: Nomads on the Border of the Fertile Crescent 9th–5th centuries B.C.* (Jerusalem: Magness Press).

Euting, J. (1896–1914) *Tagbuch einer Reise in Inner-Arabien, vol. I and II* (Leiden: Brill).

Finkelstein, I. (1995) *Living on the Fringe: The Archaeology and History of the Negev, Sinai and Neighbouring Regions in the Bronze and Iron Ages* (Sheffield: Sheffield Academic Press).

—(2002) The Campaign of Shoshenq I to Palestine: A Guide to the 10th Century BCE Policy. *ZDPV* 118/2: 109-35.

---

5.   Even though I admit this is highly speculative, it may not be as far-fetched as it seems. Palgrave, who visited Hayil in the time of Talal, the son of Abdallah Ibn Rashid, relates that legends about Abdallah were already circulating among the population (Palgrave 1873: 85).

—(2003) City-states to States: Polity Dynamics in the 10th–9th Centuries B.C.E. In Dever and Gitin 2003: 75-83.

—(2005) Khirbet en-Nahas, Edom and Biblical History. *Tel Aviv* 32: 119-25.

Finn, J. (1878) *Stirring Times, or Records from Jerusalem Consular Chronicles of 1853 to 1856* (London: C. Kegan Paul).

Fleming, D.E. (2004) *Democracy's Ancient Ancestors: Mari and Early Collective Governance* (Cambridge: Cambridge University Press).

Forder, A. (1909/2002) *Ventures among the Arabs in Desert, Tent and Town* (Piscataway, NJ: Gorgias Press).

Fried, M.H. (1975) *The Notion of Tribe* (Menlo Park, CA: Cummings).

Fritz, V., and A. Kempinski (1983) *Ausgrabungen auf der Khirbet el-Msas (Tell Masos)* (Wiesbaden: Harrassowitz).

Garfinkel, Y., and S. Ganor (2008) Khirbet Qeiyafa: Sha'arayim. *Journal of Hebrew Scriptures* 8:2-10.

Geus, C.H.J. de (1976) *The Tribes of Israel: An Investigation into some of the Presuppositions of Martin Noth's Amphictyony Hypothesis* (Assen: van Gorcum).

Giveon, R. (1971) *Les Bédouins Shasu des documents égyptiens* (Leiden: Brill).

Graf, D. (1978) The Saracens and the Defense of the Arabian Frontier. *BASOR* 229: 1-26.

—(1997) *Rome and the Arabian Frontier: From the Nabataeans to the Saracens* (Aldershot, Hants.: Ashgate Variorum Collected Studies Series).

Haiman, M. (1994) The IA II Sites of the W. Negev Highlands. *IEJ* 44/1–2: 33-61.

—(2003) The 10th Century B.C. Settlement of the Negev Highlands and Iron Age Rural Palestine. In *The Rural Landscape of Ancient Israel*, edited by A. Maeir, S. Dar and Z. Safrai (BAR International Series 1121; Oxford: British Archaeological Reports): 71-90.

—(2007) Pastoralism and Agriculture in the Negev in the Iron Age II. In *On the Fringe of Society*, edited by B. Saidel and E.J. van der Steen (BAR International Series 1657; Oxford: British Archaeological Reports): 57-62.

Hauptmann, A. (2000) *Zur frühen Metallurgie des Kupfers in Fenan/Jordanien* (Der Anschnitt 11; Bochum: Deutsches Bergbau Museum).

Heath, P. (1996) *The Thirsty Sword: Sirat Antar and the Arabic Popular Epic* (Salt Lake City: University of Utah Press).

Herzog, Z. (1984) *Beer-Sheba II. The Early Iron Age Settlements* (Tel Aviv: Institute of Archaeology and Ramot Publishing).

—(1994) The Beer-Sheba Valley: From Nomadism to Monarchy. In *From Nomadism to Monarchy: Archaeological and Historical Aspects of Early Israel*, edited by I. Finkelstein and N. Na'aman (Jerusalem: Israel Exploration Society): 122-49.

Herzog, Z., and L. Singer-Avitz (2004) Redefining the Centre: The Emergence of State in Judah. *Tel Aviv* 31/2: 209-44.

Higham, T., J. van der Plicht, C. Bronk Ramsey, H.J. Bruins, M. Robinson and T.E. Levy (2005) Radiocarbon Dating of the Khirbat en-Nahas Site (Jordan) and Bayesian Modeling of the Results. In Levy and Higham 2005: 164-78.

Ibn Khaldun/F. Rosenthal (1967) *The Muqaddimah: An Introduction to History. Translated from the Arabic by Franz Rosenthal* (London: Routledge & Kegan Paul).

Jamieson-Drake, D.W. (1991) *Scribes and Schools in Monarchic Judah: A Socio-archeological Approach* (Sheffield: Almond Press).

Jasmin, M. (2006) The Emergence and First Development of the Arabian Trade Across the Wadi Arabah. In *Crossing the Rift: Resources, Routes, Settlement Patterns and Interaction in the Wadi Arabah*, edited by P. Bienkowski and K. Galor (London: Council for British Research in the Levant): 143-50.

Jennings-Bramley, W.E. (1906) The Bedouin of the Sinaitic Peninsula. *PEFQS* 23-33, 103-9, 197-205, 250-58.

Khoury, P.S., and J. Kostiner (eds.) (1990) *Tribes and State Formation in the Middle East* (Berkeley: University of California Press).

Kletter, R. (2004) Low Chronology and United Monarchy: A Methodological Review. *ZDPV* 120: 13-54.

Koenig, Y. (1990) Les textes d'envoûtement de Mirgissa. *Revue d'Egyptologie* 41: 101-25.

LaBianca, O.S. (1999) Salient Features of Iron Age Tribal Kingdoms. In *Ancient Ammon*, edited by B. MacDonald and R.W. Younker (Leiden: Brill): 19-23.

LaBianca, O.S., and R.W. Younker (1998) The Kingdoms of Ammon, Moab and Edom: The Archaeology of Society in Late Bronze/Iron Age Transjordan (ca. 1400–500 BC). In *The Archaeology of Society in the Holy Land*, edited by T.E. Levy (London/New York: Continuum): 399-415.

Lane, E.W. (1871) *An Account of the Manners and Customs of the Modern Egyptians, Written in Egypt during the Years 1833, –34 and 35* (London: Murray).

Lemche, N.P. (1985) Early Israel, Anthropological and Historical Studies on the Israelite Society before the Monarchy. *VT* 37: 357-85.

Levy, T.E., R.B. Adams, and A. Muniz (2004a) Archaeology and the Shasu Nomads-Recent Excavations in the Jabal Hamrat Fidan, Jordan. In *Le-David Maskil: A Birthday Tribute for David Noel Freedman*, edited by W.H.C. Propp and R.E. Friedman (Winona Lake, IN: Eisenbrauns): 63-89.

Levy, T.E., R.B. Adams, M. Najjar, A. Hauptmann, J.D. Anderson, B. Brandl, M.A. Robinson and T. Higham (2004b) Reassessing the Chronology of Biblical Edom: New Excavations and 14C Dates from Khirbat en-Nahas (Jordan). *Antiquity* 302, online: http://www.anthro.ucsd.edu/~tlevy/Archaeology_in_the_Levant/Publications_files/Early%20Bronze%20Age%20Metallurgy.pdf.

Levy, T.E., R.B. Adams and R. Shafiq (1999) The Jabal Hamrat Ifdan Project: Excavations at the Wadi Fidan 40 Cemetery, Jordan (1997). *Levant* 31: 293-308.

Levy, T.E., R.B. Adams, A.J. Witten, J. Anderson, Y. Arbel, S. Kuah, J. Moreno, A. Lo and M. Wagonner (2001) Early Metallurgy, Interaction, and Social Change: The Jabal Hamrat Fidan (Jordan) Research Design and 1998 Archaeological Survey: Preliminary Report. *ADAJ* 45: 159-87.

Levy, T.E., T. Higham, C. Bronk Ramsey, N.G. Smith, E. Ben-Yosef, M. Robinson, S. Münger, K. Knabb, J. Schulze, P., M. Najjar, and L. Tauxe (2008) High-precision Radiocarbon Dating and Historical Biblical Archaeology in Southern Jordan. *Proceedings of the National Academy of Sciences* 105: 16460-65.

Levy, T.E., and T. Higham (eds.) (2005) *The Bible and Radiocarbon Dating: Archaeology, Text and Science* (London: Equinox).

Levy, T.E., M. Najjar, J. van der Plicht, N. Smith, H.J. Bruins and T. Higham (2005) Lowland Edom and the High and Low Chronologies. In Levy and Higham 2005: 129-63.

Lord, A.B., and M. Parry (1960) *The Singer of Tales* (Cambridge, MA: Harvard University Press).

Lynch, W.F. (1849) *Narrative of the US Expedition to the River Jordan and the Dead Sea* (Philadelphia: Lea & Blanchard).

Mayerson, P. (1994) *Monks, Martyrs, Soldiers and Saracens: Papers on the Near East in Late Antiquity* (Jerusalem: Israel Exploration Society).

Mazar, A. (2003) Remarks on Biblical Traditions and Archaeological Evidence Concerning Early Israel. In Dever and Gitin 2003: 85-98.

McNutt, P. (1999) *Reconstructing the Society of Ancient Israel* (London: Westminster John Knox Press).

Musil, A. (1907–8) *Arabia Petraea* (Vienna: Alfred Holder).

—(1928a) *The Manners and Customs of the Rwala Bedouin* (New York: The American Geographical Society).

—(1928b) *Northern Nejd: A Topographical Itinerary* (New York: The American Geographical Society).

Na'aman, N. (1992) Israel, Edom and Egypt in the 10th Century B.C.E. *Tel Aviv* 19: 71-93.

Oliphant, L. (1880) *The Land of Gilead, with Excursions in the Lebanon* (Edinburgh: William Blackwood & Sons).

Oppenheim, M. (1939) *Die Beduinen, band I* (Leipzig: Harrassowitz).

—(1943) *Die Beduinen, band II* (Leipzig: Harrassowitz).

—(1952) *Die Beduinen, band III* (Leipzig: Harrassowitz).

—(1967/68) *Die Beduinen, band IV* (Leipzig: Harrassowitz).

Palgrave, W.G. (1866) *Narrative of a Year's Journey through Central and Eastern Arabia (1862–63)* (London: MacMillan & Co.).

Palmer, E.H. (1871) *The Desert of the Exodus* (Cambridge: Deighton, Bell & Co.).

Parkinson, W.A. (2002) Introduction: Archaeology and Tribal Societies. In *The Archaeology of Tribal Societies*, edited by W.A. Parkinson (Ann Arbor, MI: International Monographs in Prehistory): 1-12.

al-Rasheed, M. (1991) *Politics in an Arabian Oasis: The Rashidis of Saudi Arabia* (London: Tauris).

Robinson, E., and E. Smith (1841–42) *Palästina und die südlich angrenzenden Länder : Tagebuch einer Reise im Jahre 1838 in Bezug auf die biblische Geographie unternommen von E. Robinson und E. Smith: nach den Original-Papieren mit historischen Erläuterungen* (Halle: Verlag der Buchhandlung des Waisenhauses).

Rogers, M.E. (1862/1989) *Domestic Life in Palestine* (London: Kegan Paul).

Routledge, B. (2004) *Moab in the Iron Age: Hegemony, Polity, Archaeology* (Philadelphia: University of Pennsylvania Press).

Schumacher, G. (1888) *The Jaulan* (London: Richard Bentley & Son).

Seetzen, U.J. (1854–59) *Reisen durch Syrien, Palaestina, Phoenizien, die Trans-Jordan länder, Arabia-Petraea und Unter Ägypten* (Berlin: G. Reimer).

Shryock, A. (1997) *Nationalism and the Genealogical Imagination: Oral History and Textual Authority in Tribal Jordan* (Berkeley: University of California Press).

Singer-Avitz, L. (1999) Beersheba—A Gateway Community in Southern Arabian Long-distance Trade in the Eighth Century B.C.E. *Tel Aviv* 26: 3-75.

Smith, A.D. (2000) *The Nation in History: Historiographical Debates about Ethnicity and Nationalism* (Cambridge: Polity Press).

Stager, L.E. (2003) The Patrimonial Kingdom of Solomon. In Dever and Gitin 2003: 63-74.

Steen, E.J. van der (2004) *Tribes and Territories in Transition* (Leuven: Peeters).

—(2005) Tribal State Foramtion. Paper presented at the seminar on Ottoman Archaeology, Jerusalem, June (Jerusalem: Albright Institute).

Steen, E.J. van der, and P. Bienkowski (2006) How Old is the Kingdom of Edom? A Review of New Evidence and Recent Discussion. *Antiguo Oriente* 4: 11-20.

Steen, E.J. van der, and K. Smelik (2007) King Mesha and the Tribe of Daibon. *Journal for the Study of the Old Testament* 32/2: 139-62.

Steiner, M.L. (1998) It's Not There: Archaeology Proves a Negative. *BAR* 24/4: 26-33, 62-63.

—(2003) The Evidence from Kenyon's Excavations in Jerusalem: A Response Essay. In *Jerusalem in Bible and Archaeology: The First Temple Period*, edited by A. Vaughn and A. Killebrew (Atlanta: Society of Biblical Literature): 347-63.

Thompson, T. (1992) *Early History of the Israelite People: From the Written and Archaeological Sources* (Leiden: Brill).

Wallin, G.A. (1854/1979) *Travels in Arabia (1845 and 1848)* (Cambridge: Oleander Press).

Zimhoni, O. (1985) The Iron Age Pottery of Tel Eton and its Relation to the Lachish, Tell Beit Mirsim and Arad Assemblages. *Tel Aviv* 12: 63-90.

11 The Four Pillars of the Iron Age Low Chronology

Daniel A. Frese and Thomas E. Levy

Abstract

The precise chronology of the Iron Age I–II in the southern Levant has been a matter of heated debate for over a decade. Over the course of the dispute, four major chronological anchors have been advanced in support of I. Finkelstein's low chronology: the date of Philistine monochrome pottery, the 9th-century pottery of Tel Jezreel, the construction style of Samaria Building Period I, and high-precision radiocarbon dating. We will review and assess all four of these arguments, and conclude that none of them add substantial support to the low chronology.

Introduction

The problem with Iron Age archaeology in the Levant is the lack of secure chronological anchors. For a period of about 400 years—between 12th-century Egyptian connections and 8th-century Assyrian conquests in the north—absolute dates have been assigned primarily based on relative chronology and historical considerations (Mazar 1997: 157). The flexibility provided by this window has made the exact chronology of the Iron I–II periods a matter of some debate. Since 1996, Israel Finkelstein has advanced his alternative, lower chronology—which initially differed from the traditional chronology by approximately one century (Finkelstein 1996). Many other scholars, however, have continued to defend the traditional chronology, or a slight variation of it: Amihai Mazar's 'modified conventional chronology'.[1]

In the past 13 years, through numerous articles, the difference of opinion between the two camps has been reduced to 60 years at most.[2] Dozens of sites and many different lines of evidence

---

1.   For the original suggestion of the modified conventional chronology, see Bruins, van der Plicht, and Mazar 2003a: 318; cf. also 2003b. For reference to further scholars who have adopted Mazar's chronology, see Mazar 2005: 21.

2.   Mazar's modified conventional chronology places the Iron I–II transition at ca. 980 BCE, whereas Finkelstein's low chronology originally placed it around 920 BCE. There are signs, however, that Finkelstein may have softened his position considerably. Finkelstein recently changed his views on some Iron Age strata at Megiddo based on newer ^{14}C dates (Finkelstein 2006). The implications of his paper are that, at Megiddo at least, the beginning of the Iron II has moved to ca. 965 BCE (+/- 40 years, based on radiocarbon dates)—a scant 15 years later than Mazar's suggestion. Finkelstein, however, has made no explicit concession to Mazar's chronology, has not spelled out a programmatic change in his own understanding of the chronology, and has not repeated this point about Megiddo since 2006. Indeed, Finkelstein still contends that the debated

are involved in the increasingly complex argumentation. In this paper we will review and assess the four major chronological anchors that Finkelstein has advanced in support of his low chronology: the date of Philistine monochrome pottery, the 9th-century pottery of Tel Jezreel, the construction of Samaria building period I, and high-precision radiocarbon dating.[3]

The Philistines' Arrival in Canaan

Finkelstein's point of departure for his low chronology was the entry of the Philistines into Canaan. He proposed that the commonly accepted view of the Philistines' arrival ca. 1175 BCE—along with their unique monochrome pottery—is almost a century too early.[4] His argument, put briefly, is this: in every stratum with finds from the 20th Dynasty in Egypt (1186–1069), there are no Philistine monochrome sherds. The converse is also true: if there is Philistine monochrome, there are no 20th-Dynasty remains. Since there is no way, reasons Finkelstein, that Philistines and Egyptians could have lived next-door to one another and not shared pottery, the separation of the material culture must be explained by positing a chronological separation: the Philistines came after the Egyptians had left. This conclusion pushed the absolute date of the easily identifiable Philistine monochrome pottery (as well as the subsequent bichrome pottery) to nearly a century later than it had been (Finkelstein 1995; 1998a: 167; 2005: 33). This armed Finkelstein with an absolute date (of sorts), which he could apply to every settlement that yielded stratified Philistine pottery—which is exactly what he did (Finkelstein 1996: 180-85).

The change in Iron I dating naturally affected Iron II strata as well: those previously associated with the 10th century BCE were now from the 9th century. Or to put it in biblical terms (which is unavoidable), what we thought was Solomon's town is actually Ahab's. In particular, Stratum VA–IVB at Megiddo has been singled out as a main point of contention, since its two monumental palaces and monumental 4-entry gatehouse have long been attributed to Solomon (cf. 1 Kgs 9:15).[5]

Responses

The response to Finkelstein's thesis was sharp. Most detractors disagreed with his primary assumption that a particular pottery type should be represented at all contemporary sites. A. Mazar provided three examples from ancient Canaan of distinct pottery confined to a specific region, presumably because of cultural or ethnic differences between these and neighboring communities (Mazar 1997: 158). Mazar's examples showed that it was entirely plausible to find a lot of distinct pottery in one town and not find any of the same in the contemporary town down the road

---

'Solomonic' Megiddo VA–IVB should be dated to the 9th century (2006: 182). Thus, we will limit our interpretation of Finkelstein's concession to this: at least concerning Megiddo, the chronology debate is less about the date of Iron I/Iron II transition than it is about defining specific strata as either 9th or 10th century. For Mazar's response to Finkelstein's paper, see Mazar 2008a: 330 n. 13 and Mazar 2008b: 101 n. 16.

3. For a list of secondary arguments raised by Finkelstein, see Appendix A. Mazar's chronology also has four main candidates for chronological anchors—see Appendix B for a brief summary of each with references to the literature.

4. The conventional date for the Philistines' appearance is dependent on Pharaoh Ramses III's descriptions of his battles against various immigrating Sea Peoples around this time—including one group named 'Pareshet' (= Philistines)—as well as the biblical references to Israel's wars with the Philistines in the period of the 'judges' and United Monarchy.

5. For the classic articulation of the Solomonic gatehouses at Megiddo, Hazor, and Gezer, see Y. Yadin 1960. The view advocated by D. Ussishkin (1980) that the gate is actually from the later Stratum VI does not seem to have been widely accepted.

—especially in the case of recently immigrated people groups. Many more examples of the same phenomenon, also from Bronze and Iron Age Canaan, were subsequently added by other excavators.[6] The lack of mixed Philistine monochrome and Egyptian material culture does not represent chronological separation, these scholars argued; it represents an ethnic or cultural separation. Further, they pointed out that Finkelstein's thesis is essentially an argument from silence, and that it would be reckless to shift so much chronology on such a basis: 'Arguments based on considerations such as the presence or absence of ceramic families...are unconvincing, especially when so much is at stake' (Ben-Tor and Ben-Ami 1998: 33). Finkelstein's response was to suggest that where a contemporary pottery type is missing in a particular stratum, we might view it as an occupational gap at that site (1998a: 167-68). In addition, he said that if scholars are going to make assumptions about human behavior (viz. not sharing pottery), we need a legitimate ethnographic model upon which to base this (1999b: 37).

S. Bunimovitz and A. Faust responded with important ethnographic parallels from sub-Saharan African tribes. They showed that people willingly and consciously eschewed using their neighboring tribe's material culture precisely because it represents the 'other' (2001: 3-5). They also pointed out the example of Tel Qasile, in which a great deal of Philistine pottery was found in one residential/cultic quarter, while none whatsoever was recovered from another sector of the same stratum, showing that the pottery must have been viewed as a cultural or ethnic marker (2001: 3-5). Finkelstein, however, was not convinced by these analogies either, saying that it is possible to prove anything one wants with ethnographic parallels (2002a: 118; 2005: 33). Bunimovitz and Faust's comparisons 'have nothing to do with the twelfth-century B.C.E. Levant', Finkelstein said, and 'their article has no relevance for the debate' (2002a: 119).

Finkelstein decided early that his arguments for the low chronology are separate from the issue of the Philistine's arrival (1998a: 167; cf. 2002a: 118).[7] Indeed, in a recent summary of the low chronology, Finkelstein gives primary support to his position by invoking Samaria's buildings, Jezreel's pottery, and radiocarbon dates (2005: 36-37). The late-Philistines argument has convinced few—and is no longer being touted as a direct support for the low chronology.

Jezreel Pottery

Another datum that Finkelstein uses to anchor his chronology is the pottery from Jezreel. Since the huge compound unearthed there is undoubtedly the second residence of the Omride kings as described in the Bible (1 Kgs 18:45; 2 Kgs 9:16), scholars on both sides agree that it was built in the 9th century (e.g. Coldstream and Mazar 2003: 40-43). Finkelstein has pointed out numerous times that pottery from this compound is identical with that of the debated Megiddo VA–IVB, and argues that therefore the stratum at Megiddo should also be dated to the 9th century (1996: 183; 1998a: 170; 2000a: 244; 2000b: 129; Finkelstein and Piasetzky 2003b: 773).

Two basic objections have been made to this argument. First, the site of Jezreel has been subject to extreme amounts of stratigraphic disturbance from antiquity through the past century. Due to these disturbances, strong objections have been voiced about the security of the loci from which the relevant pottery was taken (Mazar 1997: 161; 2005: 19; Ben-Tor and Ben-Ami 1998: 31; Ben-Tor 2000: 9-16). For example, A. Ben-Tor says:

---

6.   A. Ben-Tor and D. Ben-Ami added an example from Jericho (1998: 31), W. Dever added one from Gezer (1998: 47-49; 2005: 72), and S. Bunimovitz and A. Faust added two more from Philistia (2001: 2).
7.   See, however, one recent article in which Finkelstein has invoked ^{14}C dating to support his late Philistine presence argument (Finkelstein and Piasetzky 2007).

> A close study of the preliminary reports on all seasons of excavations at Jezreel shows that in all, 48 Iron Age loci were listed at Jezreel, and of these none meets these two minimal requirements [of being a secure locus]!... It is therefore incomprehensible to me why Finkelstein would choose such a site as Jezreel as his key site for the discussion of Iron Age chronology. (2000: 13)

Finkelstein and David Ussishkin, for their part, have both insisted that the loci are uncontaminated and the pottery should be used for comparison (Ussishkin 2000; Finkelstein 2000a: 243).

A more serious objection, made by many researchers, is that the pottery of the Iron IIA is basically the same for much of the 10th and 9th centuries (Ben-Tor and Ben-Ami 1998: 30; Halpern 2000: 102; Mazar and Carmi 2001: 1340; Mazar 2005: 19; Dever 2005: 75-76; Mazar 2007: 147-48).[8] Thus, the Jezreel compound and Megiddo VA–IVB might have the same pottery, but that does not necessarily mean they both represent the 9th century. We should point out that this argument is not a response to Finkelstein's chronology. Long-lived Iron IIA pottery was suggested half a century ago by Aharoni and Amiram (1958), and has since found support among other researchers (Ben-Tor 1992; Barkay 1992). Mazar has only recently been convinced on this point, publishing his own 'modified conventional chronology', by which Iron IIA pottery spans about 150 years and covers much of the 10th and 9th centuries.[9] The long duration of this pottery is shown most clearly at sites with numerous Iron IIA strata, like Hazor and Rehov, and can also be seen at Jezreel itself: the pottery from underneath the Omride compound at Jezreel is the same as that of the compound itself (Mazar 2005: 19). The long-lived Iron IIA pottery is also seemingly supported by a series of ^{14}C dates from Tel Rehov (Bruins, van der Plicht, and Mazar 2003a: 318). 'This, in my view', says Mazar, 'is the key to the resolution of our debate' (Mazar 2005: 19).

Finkelstein seems to realize that the pottery in question spans a long period. He says that the pottery in strata VI–IV at Rehov (all Iron IIA by Mazar's reckoning) is all 'very similar', such that it would be very difficult to detect contaminated loci (Finkelstein and Piasetzky 2003c: 284). And he admits that 'the significant time span of [the Iron IIA pottery] assemblage was already indicated by the excavations of the University of Chicago in the 1920s' (2003c: 291-92). But again, Finkelstein has not explicitly conceded the relevance of this point to the debate—instead he maintains that both the Jezreel pottery and the Megiddo VA–IVB pottery are from the 9th century. If it is true, however, that Iron IIA pottery remained unchanged during much of the 10th and 9th centuries—and this seems to be the case—then Finkelstein must prove a 9th-century date for Megiddo VA–IVB on other grounds.

Samaria Parallel

A third main argument for Finkelstein's low chronology is based on a comparison of Megiddo VA–VIB and Samaria building period I. The monumental palace unearthed in Samaria, like the palace at Jezreel, was built during the reign of Omri in the 9th century according to the biblical evidence (1 Kgs 16:23-24). Also like the case of Jezreel, all parties agree that the stratum in question represents the 9th century. Norma Franklin—a doctoral student of Finkelstein's—claims that there is a close parallel between stratum VA–IVB at Megiddo and the Building Period I of Samaria, which supports

---

8. One exception is A. Zarzeki-Peleg, who argues that there are a few pottery forms in the Jezreel enclosure that are not in the pre-building settlement or the under-building fills. She also says that this same pottery also shows up, among other places, in Megiddo IVA (and *not* VA–IVB), and thus Megiddo VA–IVB should be dated to the 9th century (1997: 284-87). See Finkelstein's objections to Zarzeki-Peleg's analysis in Finkelstein 1999a: 56.

9. Mazar previously held that the Iron IIA only covered 1000 to 925 BCE (Mazar 1990: 368); in his Modified Conventional Chronology it covers 980 to 840/830—about twice as long (Coldstream and Mazar 2003: 40-44). Mazar points out that a number of scholars have recently adopted his chronology (2005: 21).

a 9th-century date for the Megiddo stratum. The comparison in this case, however, is not based on pottery typology—it is based on parallels in the construction style of the two strata. Franklin compares three specific elements of Palace 1723 of Megiddo with Samaria I:

> To summarize, at Megiddo and Samaria, both palaces attest to the use of the short cubit of 0.45 meters, both palaces are built using roughly hewn ashlars devoid of drafted margins or intervening fieldstone courses, and significantly both palaces have unique masons' marks inscribed on the ashlars contained in their foundation courses. These three similarities testify to a clear technical, and therefore also a chronological, correlation between Samaria Building Period I and Megiddo Stratum V. (Franklin 2005a: 319; cf. 2005b: 143)

Finkelstein has repeatedly endorsed this argument as a point in favor of his chronology (Finkelstein 2000a: 244; 2000b: 129; 2002a: 125; 2004: 185; Finkelstein and Piasetzky 2003b: 773; 2006a: 384). Since one of us has critiqued this argument in detail elsewhere, we will give only a brief summary of the problems with the three points of Franklin's comparison: cubit length, ashlar style, and masons' marks.[10]

Short Cubits

Measurements of ancient Israelite structures are not the clean data one might imagine. This is mainly because, based on excavated buildings we can measure, the Israelites did not seem to care much for precision. It is almost impossible to divide any structure's dimensions into consistent units of length. Thus, for Franklin to prove that the two buildings in Megiddo and Samaria were based on the same cubit measure, she must round the measurements up or down to suit her conclusions—sometimes by relatively large amounts.[11] It is not at all clear, based on Franklin's measurements, that it is possible to determine which cubit was used for these buildings.

Additionally, it is just as important to determine when the cubit in question was used.[12] Why should we connect the 45 cm cubit with the 9th century but not the 10th? Franklin says that the short cubit in question—which most agree was borrowed from Egypt's 6-palm cubit—dates to the 22nd 'Libyan' Dynasty (935–730) of the Third Intermediate Period, which overlaps with Omri's 9th-century reign in Samaria (Franklin 2004: 90–91; 2005a: 321). This is true, but it is only part of the picture. The short cubit is also attested on two Egyptian cubit rods from the 18th Dynasty (1550–1295) of the New Kingdom,[13] and is in use as late as the 26th Dynasty (664–525) (Wilkinson 2005: 260).[14] Given such a large span of time in which the short cubit was used (over 600 years

---

10. For a more detailed discussion, see Frese and Freedman (2009) and cf. Ussishkin 2007. Both of these studies (conducted independently) come to similar conclusions, but there is very little overlap in the lines of argumentation. Franklin (2007) responds briefly to Ussishkin in the same volume.

11. For example, Franklin says that the podium attached to Megiddo's palace 1723 measures 16 short cubits on the north side. Sixteen short cubits equals 7.2 m, but the unit actually measured 'ca. 7.7 m' (Franklin 2004: 89). This is a difference of 'ca.' half a meter—out of only about 7 m total. For further examples and analysis, see Frese and Freedman 2009: 37*-38*.

12. Cubit measures may remain in use for very long periods of time. The Egyptian/Israelite royal cubit of 52.5 cm, for example, is attested in Canaan in the Early Bronze Age (Franklin 2004: 84), and it is still in use over a millennium later in 8th-century Israel (Barkay and Kloner 1986).

13. A cubit rod from the 18th Dynasty (1550–1295), now located in the Louvre Museum, includes 'markings for other kinds of internal cubit divisions, such as that for the short cubit (six palms)' (Clagett 1999: 9, cf. Fig. IV.25). The same is true of a cubit rod from Deir el Medina, now in the Museum of Turin (Scott 1942: 70–71). On the short cubit's attestation in the New Kingdom (1550–1069), cf. also Grandet 2001: 494. (Dates of Egyptian periods cited in the present discussion are from Kitchen 1991.)

14. Franklin concedes, in response to Ussishkin (2007), that the short cubit 'has a long history of use', but she says that 'it was used only for artistic works (e.g., sculptures) [in earlier periods]. Its use on architectural

minimally), finding a building set out according to this unit does not assure us that the building is from the 9th century (cf. Ussishkin 2007: 61).

Ashlar Masonry

Ashlar masonry, like cubit length, is not very precise in its chronological significance. It is attested at scores of sites spanning centuries—both before and after the Iron II period.[15] It is found as early as the Early Dynastic Period in Egypt (early third millennium BCE), and in the Late Bronze Age is found in Anatolia, Cyprus, and many sites in the Levant: Ugarit, Hazor, Megiddo, Taanach, Gezer, and Jerusalem (Wright 1985: 342; Sharon 1987: 31, 36; Silberman 1989).

Franklin specifically points out that the ashlars from Megiddo and Samaria are 'plain, roughly hewn blocks', with 'no interspersed fieldstones or marginal drafting' (2005a: 319). However, since such smooth-faced ashlars were used, e.g., in LB Ugarit and in the LB city gate of Megiddo, we should not insist that their appearance in Palace 1723 places this building in the 9th century.[16]

Moreover, as Y. Shiloh observes, different styles and grades of ashlar masonry are commonly attested within a single stratum—or even within a single building (1979: 66). It follows from this fact that masonry style and quality are not reliable chronological indicators.

Masons' Marks

Here is how Finkelstein describes the significance of the mysterious masons' marks found at Megiddo and Samaria:

> These [the marks at Megiddo] are found in one other site, in fact mainly—possibly only—in one other building in Israel—the palace of the Omride Dynasty at Samaria. These masons' marks are so distinctive that they must have been executed by the same group of masons. (Finkelstein 2005: 36)[17]

The first problem with this argument is that the marks at Megiddo and Samaria are not identical: out of the seventeen known shapes, only eight have been found at both sites (Franklin 2005b: 92). This is indeed significant—a 47% overlap in the characters could not be coincidental. But on the other hand, there is also significant divergence. The marks probably indicate a connection of some sort, but it is hasty to posit that the same masons must have been responsible for them, or that they must come from the same century.

Elsewhere, Franklin shows that the masons' marks in question have significant correspondences with, and are thus probably related to, the Carian alphabet (Franklin 2001: 107-11). She also points out that the Carian people are referred to in historical documents as stone masons, and she documents Carian letters that have been found inscribed on ashlars from Persia, Anatolia, and Egypt (2001: 112–13). Her suggestion, then, is that the masons responsible for the marks at Megiddo and Samaria were Carians—perhaps one of the 'Sea Peoples', who were hired or forced by Omri to build his palaces for him (2001: 114). Franklin concludes:

elements can only be dated back to the Third Intermediate Period in Egypt' (2007: 72). It is curious that—similar to her previous claims about the earliest attestation of the short cubit—Franklin does not refer to any authority to support these assertions. Moreover, even if the short cubit is only attested on art in earlier periods, this does not preclude its use for architecture.

15.   For a helpful (though not comprehensive) survey of sites where ashlar masonry is attested in the Levant and in which periods, see Sharon 1987: 30-31. Sharon's discussion is confined to ashlar masonry laid in headers and stretchers.

16.   On the Ugaritic ashlars, see Shiloh 1979: 73. The Late Bronze Age gate of Megiddo is still extant on-site. For a photograph, see Shiloh 1979: plate 35.

17.   Incidentally, Finkelstein is wrong about the uniqueness of these marks. See published examples in Macalister 1911: 179 fig. 106; 222; 281 fig. 149. See also Dever 1984: 209 and 1986: 17. Shiloh points out that the marks are also attested at Hazor (Shiloh 1979: 63).

Some of the masons' marks reappear over a long period and can be seen on Israelite, Southwest Anatolian, Egyptian and Persian stone and quarry work. Therefore the use of 'Carian-related alphabetic marks' as masons' marks throughout time may point to an enduring vocational rather than an ethnic link. (2001: 113)

If this is the case, then there is little room to insist that the characters inscribed at Megiddo and Samaria must be 'simultaneous'. It is at least equally plausible that the marks (and the similar ashlars) could come from one century apart, and that both Solomon (at Megiddo) and Omri (at Samaria) used foreign workers to build their palaces (cf. Mazar 2005: 21-22).

To sum up our above critique: the three points of comparison used by Franklin—the cubit length used, the style of ashlar masonry, and the use of masons' marks—do not individually or cumulatively have the chronological precision necessary to place the strata in question in the same century.

Radiocarbon Dating

Radiocarbon dating has been championed as something of a silver bullet for the chronology debate. Its appeal is obvious: we may potentially obtain absolute dates for any stratum from which we can retrieve a few bits of organic matter. There are, however, a number of difficulties involved with the method. Here our discussion will not focus on assessing all of the previously published RC dates to determine if they support the low chronology or not. Instead, we will address a couple of broader problems with the science of RC dates and their statistical analysis. Our remarks are thus applicable to parties on both sides of the chronology debate.

First, a bit of history. A major problem surfaced in 2003 when both Finkelstein and Mazar triumphantly asserted that RC dates had vindicated their chronologies (Bruins, van der Plicht, and Mazar 2003a; Finkelstein and Piasetzky 2003b: 777; 2003c: 291). The trouble, it turned out, was conflicting data. Some carbon samples measured in a lab in Rehovot, Israel, supported an ultra-low chronology (even lower than Finkelstein's) for the Iron I–II sequence at Dor.[18] Finkelstein and Piasetzky compared the published RC dates for Rehov, Megiddo, Tel Hadar, and Dor (including the very low dates), and concluded that 'the data unambiguously support the Low Chronology and disagree with the High Chronology' (2003b: 777). Mazar, however, suspected that the dates from the Rehovot lab were 'systematically too low by about a century', based on his own dates from both Rehovot and control measurements from another lab (Mazar 2004: 31-35). Mazar thus (rightly) questioned Finkelstein's conclusions because of the problematic Rehovot dates. Meanwhile, Mazar published a new set of RC dates that had been measured in multiple labs, and claimed that these dates supported his chronology (Bruins, van der Plicht, and Mazar 2003a). He did not, however, include his first (and low) Rehovot dates in his calculations, and Finkelstein (rightly) pointed out that Mazar could not simply ignore the inconvenient data (Finkelstein and Piasetzky 2003a; 2003c: 287). It was clear at this point that some work needed to be done in order to clarify which dates and which labs were to be trusted.

To do this, Boaretto et al. conducted a large, controlled intercomparison study involving the Rehovot lab and multiple other labs (Boaretto et al. 2005; Sharon et al. 2005). Scores of carbon samples were split up, prepared and measured in multiple laboratories, and the results compared. Boaretto et al. concluded that there is no observable laboratory bias: all dates between labs fall within 2 standard deviations of the mean (i.e. a 95% confidence interval). 'The null assumption of no difference between the labs cannot be negated at a reasonable statistical confidence level' (Boaretto et al. 2005: 54).

---

18. See Gilboa and Sharon 2001: 1343-51. The dates from Dor supported a chronology with an Iron I to Iron IIA transition at around 880–850 BCE (compared to Finkelstein's at ca. 920, and Mazar's at ca. 980).

But this conclusion is not very encouraging if one takes a look at their numbers. The 2-sigma (95% confidence) range that supposedly disproved any lab bias is a staggering 232 years.[19] That is to say, it is statistically acceptable if two different labs' measurements *of the same carbon sample* diverge by over two centuries. Such a difference might be acceptable in statistical terms, but if we are applying these dates to a sub-century chronology dispute, this is not a useful level of precision.

How are such large discrepancies possible? Some comments in Boaretto *et al.*'s article reveal fundamental problems with ^{14}C dating in general:

> The Fourth International Radiocarbon Intercomparison…demonstrates that while little or no bias can usually be detected between laboratories, ^{14}C measurements generally do not conform to the 'ideal' standard distribution. *The actual distribution under extensive replication is wider than the quoted errors*… Even after the exclusion of the more-obvious outliers and the recalculation of the central moments, *the observed distributions are wider than the theoretical expectation*. (2005: 43, emphasis added)

In other words, multiple measurements of the same carbon sample do not yield consistent results. The dates tend to be more scattered than we would expect.

This raises an important (perhaps the most important) issue: What type of precision may we expect from RC dates? The error estimate (standard deviation) of one measurement of a carbon sample might be anywhere from (ca.) 10 to 50 years, depending on the method of measurement.[20] If we add some statistical analysis, it is generally assumed, we can reduce our error estimates—and thus the range of plausible dates for a given sample—even further. Boaretto *et al.* optimistically stated that with large enough data sets, we will be able to solve the chronology debate. The solution 'will have to be based on numerous, replicated dates, taken from different sites and measured by different procedures. A large, replicated data set is the only way to overcome the inevitable noise in the model' (Boaretto *et al.* 2005: 54). In other words, given enough samples and measurements, we can average our way to the required precision.[21]

The same researchers published a new study in 2007 (Sharon *et al.*) with an enormous number of new RC data: 380 measurements of 105 carbon samples from 21 different sites in Israel. On their analysis, the new data contradict the conventional chronology and support the low chronology (Sharon *et al.* 2007: 1, 22-23).[22]

With so much replication and so many samples, we may evaluate whether their hopes for more precise measurements were realized. Each of their carbon samples was measured anywhere from 2–9 times, in many cases at multiple laboratories.[23] Each measurement—with its BP (before present) date and standard deviation—was combined with all other measurements of the same sample to give

---

19. The mean difference between the Tucson and Rehovot labs was only 9.96 years, but the standard deviation was 57.56 years (Boaretto *et al.* 2005: 46; cf. 47 Fig. 2).

20. PGC (proportional gas counting) and LSC (liquid scintillation counting), called 'conventional' forms of radiocarbon dating, can yield BP (before present) ages with very low standard deviations—around 15–18 years. AMS (accelerator mass spectrometry) readings, which allow very small (milligram) sample sizes, give error estimates of 30–45 years. Though the conventional methods are more precise, it is harder to find high-quality, short-life carbon samples (such as grains or olive pits) with enough material for these techniques.

21. Other scholars have been more cautious. Cf., for example, Bronk Ramsey's remarks: '…from the point of view of radiocarbon dating, where a single calibrated date rarely gives a range (95% probability) of less than 100–200 years, [a span of approximately 100 years] is too short a time interval to resolve easily' (Ramsey 2005: 57).

22. They say that 'The "conventional"/"High" chronology (i.e. the "real" transition being at 980 BCE or earlier) is completely excluded by all models' (2007: 22).

23. Additionally, two samples were only measured one time each.

a weighted average plus or minus a weighted standard deviation. How well the group of BP dates for each sample clustered together is reported by an alpha agreement index. The higher the alpha score, the more tightly the dates are clustered—with 100% being perfect agreement (as in the case of two samples that were only measured one time each).

Below (Fig. 1) we have grouped the samples according to the number of times they were measured, and the average alpha score for each group is reported.[24]

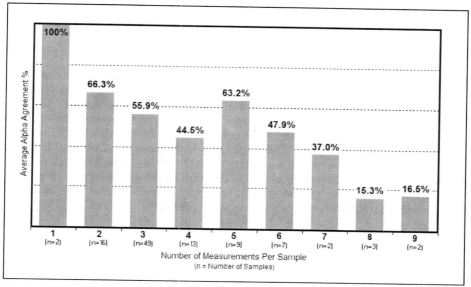

Figure 1: Average alpha score (how tightly the measurements of one sample cluster together) vs. the number of measurements per sample

As Figure 1 shows, the theoretical inconsistency discussed above is real. Generally speaking, the more times a sample was measured, the more scattered the measurements (and the lower the alpha score) became. In other words, the net result of multiplying RC measurements is *im*precision. Importantly, this also shows that the precision of the smaller date ranges provided by only one or two RC measurements may be illusory.

Despite this fact, Sharon *et al.* confidently report their data with very small weighted-average error estimates. To illustrate, we will look at one sample, which they measured 8 times (alpha = 38%). The sample was measured in 3 different laboratories, and the results as reported in Sharon *et al.* (2007: 29) are shown below in Figure 2.

---

24.   These numbers are derived from the primary data in Sharon *et al.* Sharon *et al.* have already removed 4 outlier dates from this data set: two measurements from among the samples measured 2-3 times each, and one each from the groups of 4–6 and 7–9 measurements per sample (2007: 24-40).

Site & context	Type	Sample	Analysis	^{14}C age (BP)	σ	W. AVG.	C. σ	Residual	χ^2	df	α
Qasile X L168	lathyrus	3931.1	Rehovot LSC	2853	20	2864	13	–0.559	7.51	7	38%
		3931.3	Rehovot AMS	2820	55			–0.8033			
		3931.4	Rehovot AMS	2930	56			1.17535			
		3931.5	Rehovot AMS	2936	41			1.7517			
		3931-1	Tucson AMS	2852	45			–0.2707			
		GrA25535	Groningen AMS	2864	40			–0.0045			
		GrA25710	Groningen AMS	2818	38			–1.2153			
		GrA25768	Groningen AMS	2897	44			0.7459			

Figure 2: Example of one carbon sample measured eight times by Sharon *et al.*

The 8 mean BP dates from this sample have a spread of 118 years. The weighted average of all measurements places the (hypothetical) true age of the sample at 2864 BP ('W. AVG.' in Fig. 2). The weighted standard deviation (C-sigma in Fig. 2) makes the 1-sigma range of BP dates from 2851–2877. Theoretically, if the BP age and standard deviation are correct, 68% of all mean BP ages should fall in this range. The wider 2-sigma range is 2838–2890, into which 95% of all mean BP ages should fall. However, 5 of the 8 mean BP ages actually measured (2820, 2930, 2936, 2818, 2897) fall outside of the 1 sigma range, and 4 of the 8 (2930, 2936, 2818, 2897) fall outside of the 2 sigma range. That is to say, half of the measured dates fall outside of the range where they should hypothetically fall—even though the hypothetical range was calculated from these same measured dates. The weighted average does not seem to represent the actual data (see Fig. 3).

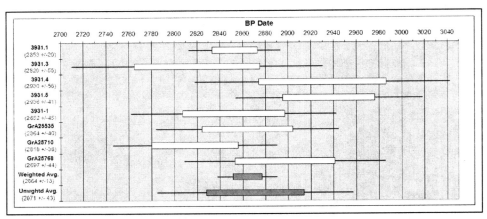

Figure 3. Sharon *et al'.*s sample #3931 from Qasile X. The 8 measurements of the sample are listed on the vertical axis, with mean BP age and standard deviation in parenthesis. The measured BP ages are represented by the top eight bars. The white portion of the bar represents the range of the 1-sigma (68%) confidence interval; the protruding black lines represent the 2-sigma (95%) range. The shaded bar second from the bottom represents Sharon *et al.*'s weighted average of the above 8 measurements, while the shaded bottom bar represents their unweighted 'cautious estimate' (on which, see below).

Sharon *et al.*'s method of calculating the error estimate of such a group of measurements is somewhat surprising: '…combining measurements always reduces the error estimate (regardless of how similar or dissimilar the actual measurements are!)' (2007: 9). In fact, using their calculation technique, 'given enough measurements of an event, one can asymptotically reduce the error-estimate to zero, no matter how noisy the replicated set is' (Sharon *et al.* 2005: 72). In other words, the more measurements we take of a sample, the more certain we may be that we have found its exact age—down to a single year—regardless of how much scatter there is among the repeated measurements. However, Sharon *et al.* seem to realize that their small error estimates may not adequately correspond to the data: 'There is some indication that conventional error-estimation techniques may tend to underestimate the actual deviation that would be obtained under extended replication' (2007: 9). Because of this, they also report alternative, unweighted BP date averages and errors (or whichever has the larger error estimate between the weighted and unweighted methods), which they call a 'cautious estimate' (2007: 9, 41-44). This method of calculation, they say, 'almost certainly overestimates' the standard deviation (2007: 9).

Returning to our example above, the 'cautious estimate' reported for this sample is 2871 BP +/- 43 (Sharon *et al.* 2007: 42). The considerably increased standard deviation of this average (43 years instead of 13) puts all 8 mean BP dates within the 2-sigma range, and 4 of the 8 within the 1-sigma range. This is a better description of the data (see 'Unweighted Average' in Fig. 3, above). The date range for the unweighted average, however, is fairly broad: the 2-sigma range is 172 years wide—a consequence of the date-scatter effected by measuring the sample eight times.

This example reveals a problem with using a weighted standard deviation for multiple measurements of the same sample. Such a procedure seems to be based on the assumption that the measurements are grouping more tightly than they actually are, and that we are zeroing in on the actual age with each additional measurement. The erratic nature of the data—apparent in wide range of dates in Fig. 3, above—should preclude the use of weighted standard deviations. It is unclear to us—especially in light of the candid admissions we saw above—why Sharon *et al.* report all of their primary data with such small weighted error estimates.[25]

Returning to the broader topic of applying RC dating to the chronology dispute, we will mention one further difficulty. The issues of date precision discussed above do not include conversion of the BP date into an absolute date, which requires the use of a troublesome calibration curve. The curve itself has a built-in error range (since it was made from RC dates), and its shape at any given BP date might produce multiple dates ranges in the case of a wiggle, or a huge (and therefore unhelpful) date range in the case of a plateau. In short, the data seldom yield clear, precise answers.

Conclusion

We are not, of course, advocating an abandonment of RC dating. On the contrary—it is an extremely useful tool, and we applaud Sharon *et al.*'s substantial efforts to clarify problems and utilize RC data to the extent possible. Our objection is to pushing the precision of our measurements beyond what the science is capable of supporting. We should admit the limits of RC dating: the (false) precision of weighted averages and error estimates should be sacrificed to achieve greater accuracy, even though the broader date ranges will be less helpful than we may have hoped. To sum up: radiocarbon dating does not (presently) seem capable of offering a definitive solution for our dispute over such a short period; it should instead be considered one of many lines of evidence that informs our chronological picture of the Iron Age.

---

25. Sharon *et al.* 2007: 24-40. It also seems that their final conclusion in favor of the low chronology makes exclusive use of such weighted averages, since their dates are reported with very low standard deviations—commonly as low as 10–15 years (Sharon *et al.* 2007: 19-21).

Conclusion

We have looked at four candidates advanced as chronological pegs in support of the low chronology, and have found that all of them are beset with problems: the Philistine pottery argument has not withstood scrutiny; long-life Iron IIA pottery undermines the potential absolute date from Jezreel; Franklin's arguments for the simultaneity of Megiddo Palace 1723 and Samaria Building Period I are not compelling; and radiocarbon dating does not (presently) seem capable of the sub-century precision we require. Without these four supports, there remains little to commend the low chronology.

Is it possible definitively to resolve this debate? There is room to hope so. The science of ^{14}C dating may become more and more precise—perhaps to the point that it will be even more accurate than pottery seriation. And there is always the possibility of a historically based chronological anchor. We may all hope for the day when, from a well-stratified destruction layer, we retrieve the elusive victory stele of Pharaoh Shishak.

Appendix A

Secondary Arguments for Finkelstein's Low Chronology

Among the many articles Finkelstein has published related to his low chronology are scattered references to other arguments, which we consider to be of a secondary nature. These range from issues he has raised repeatedly (#1) to offhanded suggestions, perhaps made tongue-in-cheek (#7). These deserve due consideration, but in contrast to his four major arguments discussed in the present paper, they are mostly historical considerations that are derived from the low chronology, rather than data that actually support it. They are:

1. *Hazael's destructions.* The low chronology provides missing destruction layers for the campaign of Hazael in the second half of the 9th century, which are documented both by the Bible and the Tel Dan stele (Finkelstein 1999a: 61; 1999b: 39; 2000a: 244; 2002a: 125; 2005: 36).

2. *The 9th-century 'Black Hole' in Judah.* Finkelstein says that the conventional chronology leaves an awkward occupational gap in the 9th century in Judah, but his low chronology closes this gap. Finkelstein calls this the 'prime advantage' of his chronology (Finkelstein 1996: 181-82; 1999b: 39).

3. *The missing 10th-century Jordan.* Our present data do not support the presence we expect in Transjordan. But the low chronology pushes the Iron I finds later, filling in the 10th-century gap (Finkelstein 1999b: 39).

4. *The chronology of proto-geometric pottery.* The low chronology closes the century-long gap between the dating of Late Proto-Geometric pottery in Greece (10th century) and the same pottery's appearance in the Levant (11th century) (Finkelstein 1999b: 39; 2005: 36).

5. Bit-Hilani *palaces.* Megiddo's *bit-hilani* style palace(s), by the conventional chronology, are dated to at least a century earlier than their supposed prototypes in north Syria. They should be placed in the same (i.e. the 9th) century (Finkelstein 1996: 185 n. 3; 1999b: 39).

6. *Inscriptional evidence.* Seals, bullae, ostraca, and monumental inscriptions are all attested in the 9th and especially the 8th century BCE—but not before this. The appearance of all of these items should match that of monumental construction with ashlar masonry and proto-aeolic capitals, which also attest a central government. Therefore,

the low chronology's dating of the monumental buildings in Megiddo to the 9th century is more consistent with the inscriptional data that indicate statehood (Finkelstein 1996: 185; 1999b: 39).

7. *The low chronology saves 10th-century Jerusalem*. 'Most important', his low chronology ' "saves" 10th century Jerusalem'—in that it relieves it of the gap in the 10th century by pushing the Iron I material down into the 10th century (Finkelstein 1999b: 39).

8. *State formation in the Levant*. The rise of states in the Levant began in the 9th century as an outcome of pressure from the Assyrians. All major states in the region—Aram Damascus, Moab, and Ammon—developed in the 9th century BCE. Israel should follow suit (Finkelstein 2000a: 244; 2005: 35).

Appendix B

Suggested Chronological Anchors in Support of A. Mazar's 'Modified Conventional Chronology'

1. *Arad*. The destruction of Arad XII should be associated with Pharaoh Shishak's late 10th-century campaign, since Shishak names Arad in his description of the campaign and this stratum is the best candidate for the destruction (Mazar 1997: 160-61; 2005: 19-20; 2007: 148). Thus Arad XII pottery—a typical Iron IIA assemblage—is from the 10th century and should be compared to similar assemblages from other southern sites. Finkelstein originally conceded this point (Finkelstein 1998a: 171; 2002b: 113-14; Finkelstein and Piasetzky 2006b: 57), but has recently changed his mind, saying that the identification of the destruction level with Shishak's campaign is weak for various reasons (Fantalkin and Finkelstein 2006: 19).

2. *The Negev Highland sites*. Similarly, Shishak names a number of desert sites among the towns he destroyed in the 10th century. These should be identified with the short-lived sites in the Negev Highlands, a number of which yielded simultaneous destruction layers dated by the excavators to the 10th century. Thus the pottery from these strata, which is also typical Iron IIA pottery, should be considered 10th century (Mazar 2005: 20; 2007: 151). Finkelstein also conceded this point (Finkelstein 2002b: 114; Finkelstein and Piasetzky 2006b: 57), but now has changed his view. The ashes found in the remains of these houses, says Finkelstein, are actually from domestic fireplaces, and the 'ashes' in the courtyard are actually only the remains of animal dung (Fantalkin and Finkelstein 2006: 20; Shahack-Gross and Finkelstein 2008). The sites, says Finkelstein, were abandoned and not destroyed by Shishak.

3. *Ta'anach*. This town is also mentioned by Shishak as a victim of his 10th century campaign, and there is only one possible stratum we may identify with this destruction. This stratum's (IIB) pottery should be used as a 10th-century anchor everywhere else it is found in the north, including the hotly debated stratum VA–IVB at Megiddo. Finkelstein disagrees with this point (originally raised by Stager 2003) on the basis of his different understanding of Ta'anach's stratigraphy (Finkelstein 1998a: 171; 1998b: 210-11; 2005: 38).

4. *14C dating*. A high quality series of RC dates of the Iron I–II strata of Tel Rehov seemingly supports the modified conventional chronology (Coldstream and Mazar 2003; Mazar *et al.* 2005: 250-54; Bruins *et al.* 2005; van der Plicht and Bruins 2005). Finkelstein points out that the data do not unambiguously support Mazar's chronology; they might also support his low chronology (Finkelstein and Piasetzky 2003a: 568b; 2003c: 287). A high quality series of RC dates of the Iron I–II strata of Tel Rehov

seemingly supports the modified conventional chronology (Coldstream and Mazar 2003; Mazar *et al.* 2005: 250-54; Bruins *et al.* 2005; van der Plicht and Bruins 2005). Finkelstein points out that the data do not unambiguously support Mazar's chronology; they might also support his low chronology (Finkelstein and Piasetzky 2003a: 568b; 2003c: 287). Published dates from Megiddo's debated Stratum VA-IVB also seem to place this stratum squarely in the 10th century (Mazar 2005: 27).

References

Aharoni, Y., and R. Amiram (1958) A New Scheme for the Subdivision of the Iron Age in Palestine. *IEJ* 8: 171-84.

Barkay, G. (1992) The Iron Age II–III. In Ben-Tor 1992: 302-73.

Barkay, G., and A. Kloner (1986) Jerusalem Tombs from the Days of the First Temple. *BAR* 12/2 (CD-ROM), edited by H. Shanks (Biblical Archaeology Society).

Ben-Tor, A. (ed.) (1992) *The Archaeology of Ancient Israel* (New Haven: Yale University Press).

—(2000) Hazor and the Chronology of Northern Israel: A Reply to Israel Finkelstein. *BASOR* 317: 9-16.

Ben-Tor, A., and D. Ben-Ami (1998) Hazor and the Archaeology of the Tenth Century. *IEJ* 48: 1-37.

Boaretto, E., A.J. Jull, A. Gilboa, and I. Sharon (2005) Dating the Iron Age I/II Transition in Israel: First Intercomparison Results. *Radiocarbon* 47/1: 39-55.

Bruins, H.J., J. van der Plicht, and A. Mazar (2003a) [14]C Dates from Tel Rehov: Iron-Age Chronology, Pharaohs, and Hebrew Kings. *Science* 300 (April 11): 315-18.

—(2003b) Technical Comment: Response to Comment on [14]C Dates from Tel Rehov: Iron-Age Chronology, Pharaohs, and Hebrew Kings. *Science* 302 (October 24): 568c.

Bruins, H.J., J. van der Plicht, A. Mazar, C.B. Ramsey, and S.W. Manning (2005) The Groningen Radiocarbon Series from Tel Rehov: OxCal Bayesian Computations for the Iron IB–IIA Boundary and Iron IIA Destruction Events. In Levy and Higham 2005: 272-93.

Bunimovitz, S., and A. Faust (2001) Chronological Separation, Geographical Segregation, or Ethnic Demarcation? Ethnography and the Iron Age Low Chronology. *BASOR* 322: 1-10.

Clagett, M. (1999) *Ancient Egyptian Science*. Vol. 3, *Ancient Egyptian Mathematics* (Philadelphia: American Philosophical Society).

Coldstream, N., and A. Mazar (2003) Greek Pottery from Tel Rehov and Iron Age Chronology. *IEJ* 53: 29-48.

Dever, W.G. (1984) Gezer Revisited: New Excavations of the Solomonic and Assyrian Period Defenses. *BA* 47/4: 206-18.

—(1986) Late Bronze Age and Solomonic Defenses at Gezer: New Evidence. *BASOR* 262: 9-34.

—(1998) Archaeology, Ideology, and the Quest for an 'Ancient' or 'Biblical' Israel. *NEA* 61/2: 39-52.

—(2005) Histories and Non-histories of Ancient Israel: The Question of the United Monarchy. In *In Search of Pre-Exilic Israel*, edited by J. Day (Proceedings of the Oxford Old Testament Seminar, JSOTSup 406; London: T&T Clark): 65-94.

Fantalkin, A., and I. Finkelstein (2006) The Sheshonq I Campaign and the 8th Century BCE Earthquake—More on the Archaeology and History of the South in the Iron I–IIA. *Tel Aviv* 33: 18-42.

Finkelstein, I. (1995) The Date of the Philistine Settlement in Canaan. *Tel Aviv* 22: 213-39.

—(1996) The Archaeology of the United Monarchy: An Alternative View. *Levant* 28: 177-87.

—(1998a) Biblical Archaeology or Archaeology of Palestine in the Iron Age? A Rejoinder. *Levant* 30: 167-73.

—(1998b) Notes on the Stratigraphy and Chronology of Iron Age Ta'anach. *Tel Aviv* 25: 208-18.

—(1999a) Hazor and the North in the Iron Age: A Low Chronology Perspective. *BASOR* 314: 55-70.

—(1999b) State Formation in Israel and Judah: A Contrast in Context, a Contrast in Trajectory. *NEA* 62/1: 35-52.

—(2000a) Hazor XII–XI with an Addendum on Ben-Tor's Dating of Hazor X–VII. *Tel Aviv* 27: 231-47.

—(2000b) Omride Architecture. *ZDPV* 116: 114-38.

—(2002a) Chronology Rejoinders. *PEQ* 134: 118-29.

—(2002b) The Campaign of Shoshenq I to Palestine: A Guide to the 10th Century BCE Polity. *ZDPV* 118: 109-35.

—(2004) Tel Rehov and Iron Age Chronology. *Levant* 36: 181-88.

—(2005) A Low Chronology Update: Archaeology, History, and Bible. In Levy and Higham 2005: 31-42.

—(2006) The Last Labayu: King Saul and the Expansion of the First North Israelite Territorial Entity. In *Essays on Ancient Israel in its Near Eastern Context: A Tribute to Nadav Na'aman*, edited by Y. Amit *et al.* (Winona Lake, IN: Eisenbrauns): 171-88.

Finkelstein, I., and E. Piasetzky (2003a) Comment on ^{14}C Dates from Tel Rehov: Iron Age Chronology, Pharaohs, and Hebrew Kings. *Science* 302 (October 24): 568b.

—(2003b) Recent Radiocarbon Results and King Solomon. *Antiquity* 77/298: 771-79.

—(2003c) Wrong and Right; High and Low: ^{14}C Dates for Tel Rehov and Iron Age Chronology. *Tel Aviv* 30: 283-95.

—(2006a) ^{14}C and the Iron Age Chronology Debate: Rehov, Khirbet en-Nahas, Dan and Megiddo. *Radiocarbon* 48: 373-86.

—(2006b) The Iron I–IIA in the Highlands and Beyond: ^{14}C Anchors Pottery Phases and the Shoshenq I Campaign. *Levant* 38: 45-61.

—(2007) Radiocarbon Dating and Philistine Chronology with an Addendum on el-Ahwat. *Egypt and the Levant* 17: 73-82.

Franklin, N. (2001) Masons' Marks from the 9th century BCE Northern Kingdom of Israel: Evidence of the Nascent Carian Alphabet? *Kadmos* 40: 107-16.

—(2004) Metrological Investigations at 9th and 8th c. Samaria and Megiddo. *Journal of Mediterranean Archaeology and Archaeometry* 4/2: 82-92.

—(2005a) Correlation and Chronology: Samaria and Megiddo Redux. In Levy and Higham 2005: 310-22.

—(2005b) State Formation in the Northern Kingdom of Israel: Some Tangible Symbols of Statehood (Ph.D. diss., Tel Aviv University).

—(2007) Response to David Ussishkin. *BASOR* 348: 71-73.

Frese, D.A., and D.N. Freedman (2009) Samaria I as a Chronological Anchor of Finkelstein's Low Chronology: An Appraisal. In *Eretz Israel* 29 (Ephraim Stern volume; Jerusalem: Israel Exploration Society): 36*-44*.

Gilboa, A., and I. Sharon (2001) Early Iron Age Radiometric Dates from Tel Dor: Preliminary Implications for Phoenicia and Beyond. *Radiocarbon* 43: 1343-51.

Grandet, P. (2001) Weights and Measures. In *Oxford Encyclopedia of Ancient Egypt*, vol. 3, edited by D. Redford (Oxford: Oxford University Press): 493-95.

Halpern, B. (2000) The Gate of Megiddo and the Debate on the Tenth Century. In *Congress Volume: Oslo 1998*, edited by A. Lemaire, and M. Saebo (VTSup 80; Leiden: E.J. Brill): 79-122.

Kitchen, K.A. (1991) The Chronology of Ancient Egypt. *World Archaeology* 23/2: 201-8.

Levy, T., and T. Higham (2005) *The Bible and Radiocarbon Dating: Archaeology, Text and Science* (London: Equinox).

Macalister, R.A.S. (1911) *The Excavation of Gezer 1902–1905 and 1907–1909*, vol. 1 (London: Palestine Exploration Fund).

Mazar, A. (1990) *Archaeology of the Land of the Bible 10,000–586 B.C.E.* (New York: Doubleday).

—(1997) Iron Age Chronology: A Reply to Israel Finkelstein. *Levant* 29: 157-67.

—(2004) Greek and Levantine Iron Age Chronology: A Rejoinder. *IEJ* 54: 24-36.

—(2005) The Debate over the Chronology of the Iron Age in the Southern Levant: Its History, the Current Situation, and a Suggested Resolution. In Levy and Higham 2005: 15-30.

—(2007) The Spade and the Text: The Interaction between Archaeology and Israelite History Relating to the Tenth–Ninth Centuries BCE. In *Understanding Ancient Israel*, edited by H.G.M. Williamson (Proceedings of the British Academy 143; Oxford: Oxford University Press): 143-71.

—(2008a) The Iron Age Dwellings at Tel Qasile. In *Exploring the Longue Durée: Essays in Honor of Lawrence E. Stager*, edited by D. Schloen (Winona Lake, IN: Eisenbrauns): 319-36.

—(2008b) From 1200 to 850 B.C.E.: Remarks on some Selected Archaeological Issues. In *Israel in Transition: From Late Bronze II to Iron IIa (c. 1250–850 BCE)*. Vol. 1, *The Archaeology*, edited by L.L. Grabbe (London: T&T Clark): 86-120.

Mazar, A., and I. Carmi (2001) Radiocarbon Dates from Iron Age Strata at Tel Beth Shean and Tel Rehov. *Radiocarbon* 43/3: 1333-42.

Mazar, A., H.J. Bruins, N. Panitz-Cohen, and J. van der Plicht (2005) Ladder of Time at Tel Rehov: Stratigraphy, Archaeological Context, Pottery and Radiocarbon Dates. In Levy and Higham 2005: 193-255.

Ramsey, C.B. (2005) Improving the Resolution of Radiocarbon Dating by Statistical Analysis. In Levy and Higham 2005: 57-64.

Scott, N. (1942) Egyptian Cubit Rods. *The Metropolitan Museum of Art Bulletin* 1/1: 70-75.

Shahack-Gross, R., and I. Finkelstein (2008) Subsistence Practices in an Arid Environment: A Geoarchaeological Investigation in an Iron Age Site, the Negev Highlands, Israel. *JAS* 35: 965-82.

Sharon, I. (1987) Phoenician and Greek Ashlar Construction Techniques at Tel Dor, Israel. *BASOR* 267: 21-42.

Sharon, I., A. Gilboa, E. Boaretto, and A.J. Jull (2005) The Early Iron Age Dating Project: Introduction, Methodology, Progress Report and an Update on the Tel Dor Radiometric Dates. In Levy and Higham 2005: 65-92.

Sharon, I., A. Gilboa, A.J. Jull, and E. Boaretto (2007) Report on the First Stage of the Iron Age Dating Project in Israel: Supporting a Low Chronology. *Radiocarbon* 49/1: 1-46.

Shiloh, Y. (1979) *The Proto-Aeolic Capital and Israelite Ashlar Masonry* (Qedem 11; Jerusalem: Institute of Archaeology, Hebrew University of Jerusalem).

Silberman, N.A. (1989) Glossary: Stones in Many Shapes and Sizes. *BAR* 15/4 (CD-ROM), edited by H. Shanks (Biblical Archaeology Society).

Stager, L. (2003) The Patrimonial Kingdom of Solomon. In *Symbiosis, Symbolism, and the Power of the Past: Canaan, Ancient Israel, and their Neighbors from the Late Bronze Age through Roman Palestine*, edited by W. Dever and S. Gitin (Winona Lake, IN: Eisenbrauns): 63-74.

Ussishkin, D. (1980) Was the Solomonic City Gate at Megiddo Built by King Solomon? *BASOR* 239: 1-18.

—(2000) The Credibility of the Tel Jezreel Excavations: A Rejoinder to Amnon Ben-Tor. *Tel Aviv* 27: 248-56.

—(2007) Megiddo and Samaria: A Rejoinder to Norma Franklin. *BASOR* 348: 49-70.

van der Plicht, J., and H.J. Bruins (2005) Quality Control of Groningen ^{14}C Results from Tel Rehov: Repeatability and Intercomparison of Proportional Gas Counting and AMS. In Levy and Higham 2005: 256-70.

Wilkinson, T. (2005) *The Thames & Hudson Dictionary of Ancient Egypt* (London: Thames & Hudson).

Wright, G.R.H. (1985) *Ancient Building in South Syria and Palestine* (Leiden: E.J. Brill).

Yadin, Y. (1960) New Light on Solomon's Megiddo. *BA* 23/2: 62-68.

Zarzeki-Peleg, A. (1997) Hazor, Jokneam and Megiddo in the Tenth Century B.C.E. *Tel Aviv* 24: 258-88.

III.
FROM TEXT TO TURF

12 Texts in Exile

Towards an Anthropological Methodology for Incorporating Texts and Archaeology

Tara Carter and Thomas E. Levy

Abstract

This paper explores the relationship between history, anthropology, and archaeology and offers a methodology for using ancient textual data in archaeological research. It examines the changing role of history in anthropological archaeology from archaeology's perceived role as the 'handmaiden' of history to its current status as an intellectual and methodological partner based on mutualism. When ancient historical texts are charged with emotion based on religious belief or nationalism, archaeology can provide an objective data source for examining the ancient textual historical record. The examples presented here are based on the Hebrew Bible and the Icelandic Sagas.

Archaeology and history have had a kind of love–hate relationship based on the perceived reliability of one being able to glean more 'truth' about the past than the other. Historians can boast that while they work with texts that convey *messages* revealing past *events*, archaeologists are left to manage *mute artifacts* that illustrate less specific *situations* (Vansina 1995: 370). Archaeologists, on the other hand, are quick to rejoin that while historians can only hope to examine the elite, an *indiscriminating* material record has granted them with admission into the daily life of all members of society (Brumfield 2000: 208-9). Representing one of the most negative views of archaeology is Philip Grierson (1959: 129) who wrote that:

> the archaeological evidence…in its very nature substitutes inference for explanation. It has been said that the spade cannot lie, but it owes this merit to the fact that it cannot even speak.

On the more positive side is John Moreland (2001), who argues that archaeologists and historians have now gone beyond a 'servant and master' relationship where the word always took precedence over artifacts. Middle-range theories and more rigorous hypothesis-testing models have served as a kind of methodological revolution within the discipline of archaeology in the last fifty years, effectively edging the profession above the rank as a 'handmaiden' to historical projects, where texts provided the social framework and artifacts simply the matter to illustrate or defend the word. While this partnership can be seen by a frequent use of radiocarbon dates obtained from excavations in historical projects, 'most historians are simply not interested in the results of archaeology'

(Vansina 1995: 369). This in part stems from a lack of understanding about archaeological methodology, but also from the dominant view that the reconstructions of the past generated by history and those by archaeology produce profound dissonances that are impossible to reconcile. This mutual incompatibility prohibits the two from neatly dovetailing into a coherent whole, and as such, has created a terse divide between what should be partnered enterprises.

The further one goes back in time, the more fractured these camps become (Ankersmit 1989; Robertshaw 2000). Early histories often read more like myth and general storytelling to the discerning modern eye, which has rattled the battle cry of some scholars to consign these categories of text to the realm of fiction and, therefore, squarely out of the range of viable data for both the historian and archaeologist alike. To complicate the matter even further, many early texts, such as *Beowulf*, the *Iliad*, and the Hebrew Bible (Old Testament), originated from an oral tradition, creating alarm over the *accuracy* and *faithfulness* of these texts. Should we think of the writers of these texts as recorders who did little more than set down on vellum or parchment the histories preserved through an oral storytelling tradition, or were these writers innovators, who used the names, places, and even themes from traditional stories as a mechanism of creating a kind of symbiosis between the word and the reader? This subject has been the flagship of literary critics who have phrased the debate between issues of *historicity*, where scholars agree that oral narratives can be preserved over multiple generations and later transferred to text, but that these texts must be evaluated for accuracy, and issues of *intertextuality*, where texts are seen as original creations that may resonate some elements of an older oral tradition, and must therefore be evaluated as a literary production rather than an historical one (Hanks 1989). Both of these positions have a seemingly unsolvable pitfall: without digital recorders, how can we ever know the historical content of oral narratives several centuries after the last storyteller had fallen silent?

At the root of all these debates is a methodological seed: how can text and the material record, dissimilar in nature and context, ever be integrated, and even more puzzling, how can texts that seem devoid of proper historical reporting be used as a viable pool of information for those aiming to reconstruct the past?[1] These concerns can be addressed by renegotiating the relationship between history and archaeology, re-centering our focus on how both artifacts and ancient texts play active roles in the production, negotiation, and transformation of social relations in past and present societies (Alcock 2002; Brumfield 2003: 207-8; Moreland 2001: 31; Van Dyke and Alcock 2003). Thus, we will argue that structurally similar critical methodologies can be applied to both archaeological and textual data to understand objectively the social context of ancient societies.

This paper proposes a methodology for incorporating ancient textual data based on examples from two disparate regions: the southern Levant or 'Holy Land' (modern Israel, Jordan, the Palestinian territories, southern Lebanon–Syria, and the Sinai Peninsula) and Iceland. What unite these two regions from a processual perspective are emotionally charged ancient texts that continue to play an important role in the lives of the peoples that live in these areas or in some way feel linked to these texts (Pálsson 1995).

The Bible, Sagas, and Archaeology Debate

For nearly 2000 years the Hebrew Bible has been viewed as a reliable source of history, accurately depicting the lifeways of Iron Age (ca. 1200–500 BCE) peoples in the Southern Levant (Barstad 1997). In recent years, however, the Hebrew Bible (hereafter, Bible) has been examined from two distinct perspectives or 'schools of thought'—a traditionalist perspective based on a close examination of the ancient languages, cultures and archaeological record of the Iron Age Middle East, and a

---

1. See also Paynter 2000.

'minimalist' position which sees the Bible as a form of textualism, a kind of fetishization of text emulating the beliefs and values of modern-day readers rather than a factual depiction of an Iron Age mentality. The contestation surrounding the historicity of the Bible is suitably characterized through the polarized 'maximalist–minimalist debate' found between Biblical scholars today (Dever 2001: 9; Long *et al.* 2002: 1-8). In its most extreme form, proponents of a maximalist school argue that the Bible must be viewed as *the Truth*, and therefore, one need not question the reliability or legitimacy of the Bible to relate a history of the Iron Age (Laughlin 2000: 10-16). Extreme minimalists or revisionists, however, posit that because the Bible contains numerous anachronisms and was edited and compiled well after the events it describes, it must be viewed as a form of a literary fiction, a 'thinly veiled fabrication that is a product of wish fulfillment' achieved through the invention of a social world that never existed (Thompson 1999: xii). Both sides of the debate routinely rely not only on the exegesis of biblical and extra-biblical texts, but also increasingly on archaeological data to demonstrate the authority of their theoretical positions (Ahlström 1991; Davies 1992, 1995, 1997; Dever 1991, 1995a, 1995b, 1997; Halpern 1996; Kitchen 2002). The maximalist–minimalist dialogue, driven by the quest for proving their intellectual paradigms to be the penultimate view of the Bible, has resulted in a cacophony of personal and disparaging name-calling and mud slinging, rather than a discussion on how lines of archaeological and textual data may bring to the fore the Bible's capacity to understand Iron Age social configurations (Finkelstein 1996; Finkelstein and Silberman 2001, 2002, 2006). Thompson, a representative of the minimalist position, charges that so-called maximalist scholars like Dever, an archaeologist, have 'invented a very strange, but not archaeologically coherent' view of the Iron Age, that reflects a 'history by committee' rather than a critical interpretation of available data (Thompson 1996: 27-28, 32). To retort, Dever has charged that Thompson, an Old Testament scholar, is not qualified to interpret sufficiently the complexities of archaeological data, and that Thompson's use of archaeology (see especially Thompson 1991) is at best prosaic, and at worst a means to furthering his own 'anti-establishment' agenda, that 'if carried through resolutely, opens the way to first to intellectual and social anarchy, then to Fascism' (Dever 2001: 259, 266). This form of intellectual squabbling does little to address our ability to understand the past, and can only stymie future research. Rather than addressing the concerns over the historicity of the Bible through a lens of proving or disproving the events depicted in the text, this paper will suggest that by framing the debate as a methodological issue, one can begin to propose an anthropological context for using the Bible and other ancient ethnohistorical documents from around the globe as an instructive tool, rather than a hindrance towards understanding past lifeways.

The new reassessment of the Bible is in part embedded within the larger debate spurred by postmodernism and the 'new literary critique' paradigms, which question the ability of text to reflect accurately reality (Clines and Exum 1993; Edelman 1991, 1993; Grabbe 1997; Hess 2002; Knauf 1991). These theoretical paradigms suggest that reality is contextual and multivocal, made up of an infinite arrangement of individual interpretations of experience, making it impossible to pin down a precise and single interpretation of the past. However, advocates of the postmodern paradigm were not the first to call into question the ability of ancient texts to reflect accurately history. During the first half of the 20th century, a form of literary criticism, known as 'book-prose', at the University of Copenhagen, concluded that the Icelandic Sagas, once unquestionably viewed as historical texts, were entirely a work of literary fiction (Byock 1992: 52). Book-prosists insisted that the Sagas should be analyzed for their masterful style, and unless archaeology could prove otherwise, they were not to be used as a representation of history, an insistence echoed in the current 'Copenhagen School's' approach towards analyzing the Bible (Kofoed 2002: 35-39). Texts, such as *The Iliad*, not least the Icelandic Sagas, once resoundingly applauded for their historicity, began to be scrutinized, resulting in the formation of two literary camps defined by German Norse literary historian Andreas Heusler (1908, 1914): the *Freiprosa* ('free-prose') who emphasized traditional oral narratives as likely sources for the origin of the stories captured in the Sagas; and the *Buchprosa* ('book-prose') who stressed the role of the individual writer (see also G. Sigurðsson 2004: 285). Scholars of the free-prose school suggested that while the Sagas contained elements of the fantastical, they were grounded in the social memory of societies preserved through a rich storytelling tradition, and as such, can be used by modern historians to help recreate the lifeways of medieval Icelanders. This approach was strongly contrasted by the book-prose school, which suggested that the Sagas were the work of individual authors, and relied only marginally on an older oral tradition. Therefore, the Sagas, and the Family Sagas in particular, were works of literary grandeur that invented a past through the genius of the author, and cannot be seen as containing any useful historical significance for understanding the settlement period of Iceland. At best, they reflect how authors in the 12th and 13th centuries would have liked their own contemporary society to behave, and were thus a kind of wish fulfillment rather than an accurate depiction of the past. While the 13th century was plagued with violence and corruption, audiences could take refuge in the world of heroism and honor depicted in Sagas about the settlement of Iceland. The intention of the author(s) was to create a world contrasted from his or her own troubling times, perhaps to inspire change, or perhaps merely to entertain. At worst, however, these texts were deliberate lies, used as a kind of propagandistic social capital by rivaling families, each using these texts to validate the claims of their families' superiority and right to rule. Through writing, a few specific families employed the efficacy of history, albeit a fictionalized invention, as a kind of state-building tool:

> [T]his representation of the past, initiated by Ari and elaborated to baroque proportions by the subsequent two centuries of scholarship, had little to do with any 'genuine' traditions about the *landnám* that may have existed at that time. Instead, it was probably generated by the social and cultural needs of the Icelandic intelligentsia in the High Middle Ages (Friðriksson and Vésteinsson 2003).

Writing, according to book-prose theory, was ultimately controlled by elites who possessed the finance and skill to commission the production of texts, and was by and large a reflection of elite interests and had little concern for maintaining a sense of historical accuracy. Further, scholars in the book-prose camp have raised the issue of the timing of when we first see texts being written: were the Sagas composed during the time of independent chiefs, or from a period when Icelanders saw themselves as marginalized citizens under the Norwegian Crown (Hastrup 1990: 280-95; 1992, 2004)? The first texts date to the 12th century (Ólason 1998, 2005; Quinn 2000) with a subsequent flourish of Saga writing in the 13th century. Why then and not before? The Family Sagas depict what has been referred to as a 'golden age', perhaps in an attempt to create a sense of Icelandic independence at a time when they in actuality had very little. *Landnámabók*, for example, combats the assertion that writing about the settlement is a waste of time, by suggesting that 'we can better meet the criticism of foreigners when they accuse us of being descended from slaves or scoundrels, if we know for certain the truth about our ancestry' (Pálsson and Edwards 1972: 6). Hastrup (1992) goes so far as suggesting the 'golden age' depicted in the Family Sagas reflects a society that never was, but was perhaps an invented society used as a model of what could be, if the Icelanders could only throw off the shackles of foreign domination:

> What we are witnessing is a paradoxical development of a dual history—one that was native and exclusively Icelandic, and another that was foreign and inclusive. The symbolic stress on distinction as traditionally conceived in both the literary and the oral tradition, gave rise to a particular view of Icelandicness that we term Uchronic. If Utopia is place out of the world, Uchronic is a time out of history. In many ways, I would argue, the Icelanders entertained a Uchronic vision of their history, symbolically reproducing the myth of distinction and autonomy, and of a society of free farmers (2004: 279).

If we are to take up the challenge of free-prosists and book-prosists alike, one must be able to examine methodologically each of these claims. These two theories share an inherent flaw: they have not put forth a means to evaluate critically their central tenets. Free-prose relies on the assumption that the thematically older Family Sagas are based on oral narratives, with book-prosists quick to retort that we have no recordings, no direct evidence of any oral narratives, making it impossible ever to know with any certainty that such a tradition in fact actually existed. Book-prose theories, on the other hand, advocate that the Sagas reflect an imaginary world, and are the creation of their authors, but these theories likewise offer no means of methodically 'proving' that the Saga writers wrote independently of a prescribed social memory of a past that actually existed. Nor have book-prosists aptly demonstrated that the Sagas were used as a kind of propaganda employed at the behest of a calculating chief. This kind of circular reasoning has forced the free-prose–book-prose debate to a standstill, and has unfortunately produced a fair amount of mud slinging along the way. These sorts of arguments are not useful, and do little to help us understand the lifeways of medieval Icelanders. Further, neither literary school has adequately grappled with the issue of defining what it meant by history and historicity. It is easy for modern researchers to fall into the trap of assuming that what we define as history today can be amendable to ancient and medieval texts. However, throughout the Middle Ages, historical treatises or *historia* were 'chronologically oriented narrative... History was [therefore] the literary product of scholarly activity and was placed within the field of grammar and rhetoric' (Würth 2005: 155). Medieval writers did not make the kinds of distinctions between the corporal and mystical in the same way that a modern historian might. The division between an experienced reality and a legendary world where men could come face to face with supernatural beings in the form of gods, beasts, and ghosts, was not firmly implanted in the medieval psyche. For example, it is unlikely that a man could live among the trolls, or battle a revenant as we are told in *Grettir's saga*, but it is likely that some individuals were legally declared outlaws and sentenced to live for a period of time in exile as is also described in this text. Likewise, some events may seem fantastical, such as Leifr Eiríksson sailing to Vínland, but have since been shown to based on fact, confirmed through archaeological investigations at L'Anse aux Meadows (Ingstad 1985; G. Sigurðsson 2004: 272; Wallace 2000).

All things considered, there is still a strong reticence among some historians to treat the Family and Contemporary Sagas as the distinct representations of historical periods that they describe, often concluding that both sets of text must either be grounded entirely in fiction, or if there are hints of historical themes embedded between the words depicting the battles between men and ferocious trolls, then these histories solely reflect the psyche of 13th- and 14th-century Saga writers and not the earlier periods of history these texts claim to depict (Whaley 2000). Proof of this is in the existence of two extreme portraits of Icelandic medieval society contained in the Sagas. These differences can be resolved by concluding that some accounts in these documents must be true, others are at best misinterpretations of the past, and at worst pure and deliberate fiction. However, we argue that by using an anthropological methodology we can begin to move our debates past the impossible task of proving or disproving the historicity of the sagas. Examining the historicity of texts like the Sagas and the Bible, therefore, requires an interdisciplinary methodology that incorporates both text and material culture in order to produce a social backdrop of not only the time in which these texts were written, but also of the period these texts wish to reflect. We are fortunate that there are several instances where the texts themselves explicitly address these issues. For example, in the introduction of *Heimskringla*, Snorri Sturlusson remarks on the value of accuracy in skaldic poetry written to commemorate the deeds of foreign princes and kings: 'We regard all that to be true which is found in those poems about their expeditions and battles. It is to be sure the habit of poets to give the highest praise to those princes in whose presence they are: but no one would have dared to tell them to their faces about deeds which all who listened, as well as the prince himself, knew were only falsehoods and fabrications. That would have been mockery, not praise' (Sturlusson [Aðalbjarnarson] 1979; cf. Karlsson 2000: 68). In a similar vein, Ari declares in his introduction of *Íslendingabók*: 'And whatever is missaid in this history, one is duty-bound to prefer what proves to be most true'. These statements directly reflect the author's concern for faithfully retelling the past, as well as the acknowledgment that the intended audience would not tolerate a deliberate distortion of the past.

These examples illustrate two crucial avenues for future Biblical and Saga research: first, scholars need to define explicitly the term history; and secondly, textual research can benefit from interdisciplinary studies. Acknowledging that the very definition of history is culturally and temporally specific brings to the fore the need to examine critically the historical standard modern researchers have placed upon ancient texts.

Although at first glance the Bible and the Icelandic Sagas may appear to have few similarities, they in fact share much in common. First, both are texts that have been looked upon as sacred and are a continued source of an ethnic and ideological identity. Second, both the Bible and the Sagas were unquestionably edited and compiled well after the events they describe and stem from both written and oral traditions (Dever 2001; Niditch 1996: 134; Sørensen 1992: 173), leading some to question the ability of these texts to paint an accurate depiction of the past. Third, both texts combine elements of prose, narratives, poems, and songs to depict the factual, the fictive, and the fabulous events of their ancestors. Fourth, in both the southern Levant and Iceland, the field of archaeology was initially shaped by their respective sacred texts. Through a summary analysis of the historicity of the Bible and the Icelandic Sagas, we suggest one can develop an anthropological methodology that incorporates both text and material culture, if that methodology can address three primary challenges: first, the methodology must be able to assess the ability of ancient texts to project an accurate image of not only its contemporary period, but those of its past as well; second, the methodology must address the limitations of memory and the methods by which oral traditions seek to maintain a consistent depiction of the past; and lastly, the methodology must be able to show that through an anthropological approach, one can broaden our definition of history as a record of past lifeways, rather than be confined to the traditional meaning of history as solely the chronological events and deeds of 'great men' and 'great battles'. Thus, we will address each of these challenges by examining how the historicity of the Bible and the Sagas have been disputed, and how a methodology grounded in anthropology can ably combine text and archaeological remains, imparting a panoramic vision rather than a synoptic view of the past.

The Social Context of the Bible and the Icelandic Sagas: Sources of Evidence

Before we can address the challenges raised against the historicity of the Bible and the Icelandic Sagas, a brief overview of the available sources of data is needed. These sources include not only the primary texts of the Bible and the Sagas, but other forms of written documentation as well as a rich archaeological dataset.

The Hebrew Bible

Both the Bible and the Sagas are made up of many books and can be thought of as a library, rather than a single body of work. The Dead Sea Scrolls represent the earliest evidence for the biblical text in the world and include some two hundred copies of biblical manuscripts. Most are written in Hebrew and date from the 3rd century BCE to the 1st century CE (Davies *et al.* 2002; Cross 1995).

The Hebrew Bible is comprised of the books of the Old Testament, which can be broadly divided into the Law Books or Pentateuch, History Books, Poetry and Wisdom Books and the Book of Prophets. In total, there are thirty-nine books written in ancient Hebrew almost entirely by anonymous authors (Drane 2000: 10, 22-25). The temporal setting of these books spans the creation, but focuses on a period of over one thousand years, centering prominently on the Iron Age (the end of the Late Bronze Age ca. 1200 BCE through the destruction of the first temple in Jerusalem in 586 BCE by the Babylonians), while the geographic setting extends from the southern Levant to parts of southern and western Syria (Mazar 1990: 295, 33). These thirty-nine books were 'woven into a composite, highly complex literary fabric sometime in the Hellenistic era, ca. 2nd century BCE' (Dever 2001: 2). Given the late date of the compilation of the Bible, some scholars have argued that the text was entirely composed in the Hellenistic era, while others argue that the majority of the texts were written and edited in the preceding Persian period, while still others posit that the final edited version of the Hebrew Bible is based on texts written during the Iron Age through the Persian Period (J.M. Miller 1993: 11-16). The concern over when these texts were written reflects the issue of the intentionality of the authors, grounded within their own historical time. Either the texts that make up the Hebrew Bible were composed during a period of independence of Israelite states, or it was arranged during a period of exile and marginalization of the Israelites, or it was written after the period of exile, as the Israelites were allowed to return to Syro-Palestine. These discrete historical episodes no doubt played a role in the shaping of these texts, leaving some to question the ability of these ancient writers to produce an unbiased account of an Iron Age society.

Extra-biblical Sources

In addition to the Bible, there are numerous extra-biblical texts relating to the southern Levant during the Iron Age. These include locally found scripts, such as victory stele (cf. Biran and Naveh 1993; Hasel 2003; J.M. Miller 1974), administrative lists, impressed inscriptions such as those found on stamped bullae (Avigad and Sass 1997), written economic transactions in ink found on ostraca (broken pieces of pottery with writing—Blenkinsopp 2000) inscribed objects such as pottery vessels that contain the name of the owner and occasionally the contents of the vessel, such as a Judean decanter that read 'belonging to Yehazyāhū' and 'dark wine' (Avigad 1972: 1-9), and tomb inscriptions such as those found at Khirbet el-Qôm in the West Bank (Dever 1999b). In addition to these local examples of writing, there are also numerous documents from Egypt and Mesopotamia that make references to persons and events depicted in the Bible. For example, the Merneptah Stela, a 7.5-meter-high monolith from the funerary temple in Thebes of Pharaoh Merneptah that documents the triumphs of his reign (1213–1203 BCE), including his military campaigns in Canaan relating that 'Israel is laid waste, his seed is not' (Hasel 2003; and in Halpern 1995: 29), and the Black Obelisk of the Assyrian king Shalmaneser III (reigned ca. 858–824 BCE) that relates 'in the 18th year of my rule...I received the tribute of the inhabitants of Tyre, Sidon, and Jehu, son of Omri' (Halpern 1995: 30). These non-Israelite inscriptions not only mention names and events found in the biblical texts, but they also skillfully reflect the fluidity and contact between these cultures during the late 13th–9th centuries BCE Iron Age.

The Archaeology of the Southern Levant

Along with textual data, we have a rich archaeological corpus of material culture from the southern Levant (Laughlin 2000; Levy 1995; Mazar 1990). The first systematic survey of Syro-Palestine began in the mid-19th century with the work of Edward Robinson, who was not an archaeologist, but correctly identified more than one hundred Iron Age sites (Robinson 1867). The actual birth of

Syro-Palestinian archaeology is accredited to Sir Flinders Petrie, the discoverer of the Merneptah stele in Egypt, who introduced two crucial archaeological concepts to the area: pottery typology and stratification (Mazar 1990: 11). The 'Golden Age' of Syro-Palestinian archaeology (ca. 1925 to 1945) was largely shaped by the excavations directed by William Foxwell Albright, Nelson Glueck, and G. Ernst Wright, who to varying degrees relied extensively on the Bible, especially for selecting sites and interpreting the meaning of Iron Age archaeological data (Moorey 1991; Silberman 1995: 14-19). Nearly all sites excavated during this 'Golden Age' of archaeology had a direct correlation with the Bible and it was widely viewed, especially by Wright, that archaeology could to some degree *prove* that the events and peoples mentioned in the Bible was an accurate historical account (Currid 1999; Silberman 1995: 15). Since 1945, however, archaeology in the southern Levant has moved away from a strict adherence to biblical texts, and more towards an interdisciplinary approach, with the goal of uncovering a social history of the Iron Age (Mazar 1990: 14-20). Archaeological data, including material remains, architectural features, burials, anthropogenic modifications to the landscape, floral and faunal remains, and the like are all independent, but not mutually exclusive, lines of evidence that can be used to uncover the activities of Iron Age peoples in this region (Levy 1995).

The Icelandic Sagas

The lines of data available for understanding the earliest lifeways of peoples in Iceland are no less numerous. Iceland is perhaps unique in that there is no indigenous population. The island was uninhabited until the 8th century CE, when a group of Irish monks established a small ephemeral colony. The Norwegian Vikings established the first permanent settlement of Iceland in the late 9th century. According to Norwegian texts, such as the *Book of Kings* (*Heimskringla*), the first settlers consisted of chiefs that had lost their clout in Norway; their kinfolk and supporters; and their slaves (Bagge 1992: 70-75). The textual evidence from Medieval Iceland includes the Sagas, an all-encompassing term used to include at least thirty-nine individual books that are often broadly organized into six types: sagas that take place outside of Iceland, most notably in Greenland and Vínland; the biographical sagas of kings, bishops, poets, and warriors; the biographical sagas of outlaws; heroic or epic sagas; the *Íslendingasögur* or the Family Sagas; and the *Samtíðarsögur* or the Contemporary Sagas (Kellogg 2001: liii-lxvi). The Family Sagas were edited and compiled from over one hundred Family Sagas, poems, songs, and short stories in the late thirteenth to early 14th century CE and describe Icelandic society during the initial colonial period (the so-called Viking Age of Iceland, ca. 870–1050 CE). Medieval Icelanders are depicted in the Family Sagas as fiercely independent people, who somehow managed to overcome the rough ocean currents of the Atlantic in open ships rather than remain embedded in the social turbulence of Norway; who staked their claim in an empty and arduous landscape; who created the first democratic assembly (*Althing*); and who peaceful coexisted with one another without the interference of a king. In contrast, the Contemporary Sagas were written as eyewitness accounts to the 12th- and 13th-century CE events they describe. These sagas, notably the *Sturlunga saga*, focus extensively on the turmoil of the early 12th century CE, when the chiefly system of social order in Iceland was polarized between two powerful chiefs, and the resulting civil war that paved the way for Norwegian intervention (Clover 1982, 1985). By 1262 CE, Iceland had become a colony of the Norwegian Crown, marking what is considered the 'dark ages of foreign rule' that lasted for the next 682 years (Hjálmarsson 1993: 58). As with the Bible, there are sharp divisions between saga scholars as to the historicity of these texts. Although there is no question as to when the Sagas were compiled there is, however, no agreement on how or when the stories contained in the Sagas were first documented. Some scholars, notably Sigurður Nordal (1940, 1953), have challenged the historicity of the Sagas, especially the Family Sagas, charging that the anonymous saga writers of the 13th century were not historians, but were rather writers who composed, not compiled, the so-called 'historical elements' of the Sagas, making these works an exemplary *fictitious* genre of literature (Byock 1992: 52; Friðriksson 1994: 10; Nordal 1940, 1953). Other saga researchers have suggested that the Family Sagas were transmitted and reshaped from pre-existing texts (Clover 1985: 279; Pálsson 1992: 1); while still others have suggested the Sagas were written from the histories told through an oral tradition (Niditch 1996: 20; Ong 1982: 31-39; Sørensen 1993: 173-79), noting that the literary style of these texts reflects an oral recitation and pointing out numerous references to orators within the Sagas (Sørensen 1992: 179). As with the Bible, a concern over how and when these texts originated reflects a deeper concern over the purpose or intentionality of the authors: were the Sagas composed during the time of independent chiefs, or from a period when Icelanders saw themselves as marginalized citizens under the Norwegian Crown?

'Extra-Saga' Sources

In addition to the Sagas, there are economic and legal documents from the Medieval Period, most notably the *Landnámabók* (*The Book of Settlements*; the literal translation is 'book of land taking'), a land registry, and the *Grágás* ('grey goose') or law books. There are several extant versions of the Book of Settlements that were more than likely penned by several different authors, but the original manuscript was probably written in the early half of the 12th century CE by a priest, Ari Þorgilsson or Ari the Learned. The Book of Settlements is a registry of the original land claims in Iceland, starting with the initial 9th-century CE colonization, as well as of the transfer of lands through inheritance and purchase dating from the tenth through the 12th century CE. The registry not only provides documentation of land ownership, it also provides a detailed genealogy of the first settlers of Iceland, providing us with some insights into who these settlers were as well as what their economic status and social reputation was (Pálsson and Edwards 1972: 8-13). For example, *Landnámabók* reports that at least twenty-three chieftains were part of the original 874 CE settlement and that these chiefs (*goðar*) brought with them their kinfolk, their slaves, and several hundred sheep and cattle (Pálsson and Edwards 1972: 2). The entries in the *Landnámabók* are organized by the names of the settlers. For each settler, a descriptive narrative is given on whom the settler was, where they had emigrated from, where they settled in Iceland, and any other interesting stories or events that occurred in the settler's lifetime. Often, a list of descendants is given for each settler as well. The Book of Settlements, therefore, provides us with direct evidence of who was able to acquire land in the initial colonization, as well as how land was later transferred through inheritance and sometimes purchase. In addition to the land and genealogical registry we also have the Grágás, a multi-volume collection of books containing the law codes of Medieval Iceland compiled in 11th and 12th centuries CE by an unknown author(s) (Dennis *et al*. 1980: 5-6). The Grágás contain resolutions and rulings of legal cases that emphasize a fixation on property rights in Medieval Iceland. The sections on the legality of ownership, when lands were alienable, and rules and regulations governing inheritance occupy the greater part of the Grágás. Immersed in these seemingly dry regulations over property rights are the social and economic transactions of Medieval Iceland, providing us with evidence of production, exchange, consumption, social inequality, economic specialization, and subsistence strategies, providing us with a second line of evidence for corroborating the political economy described in the Sagas.

The Archaeology of Iceland

As with the southern Levant, there is a history of archaeological projects that dates to the 19th century in Iceland (Friðriksson1994: 5-16). The earliest archaeological projects were conducted principally by Danish archaeologists, most notably Daniel Bruun in the late nineteenth and early

20th century, who were interested in discovering sites mentioned in the Sagas (Hansen 2001; Friðriksson 1994: 10). Little attention was paid to archaeological methodology and often fragmentary evidence was used to make very specific proclamations concerning the ability of the archaeological record to demonstrate the validity of the Sagas. The Sagas were viewed as unquestionably correct; if the archaeological record did not jibe with the Sagas, the burden of proof fell to the archaeological material to somehow find a way to corroborate with the text. By the 1950s, however, the historicity of the Sagas was in heavy dispute, and archaeology began to move away from relying on the Sagas. From the 1960s to the present, archaeological research in Iceland has been increasingly conducted by British scholars, and has tended to focus on environmental and agricultural issues, leaving the Sagas firmly out of view (Friðriksson 1994: 14-16).

With a firm understanding of lines of data used in the academic battlefield surrounding the historicity of the Bible and the Sagas in place, we can now begin to tease apart the three primary challenges leveled at attempts to use text and archaeology to paint a reliable image of the past:

- The ability of ancient texts to document a historical reality and our ability to comprehend that reality in the modern era.
- The ability of oral traditions to preserve a social memory of the past.
- The ability of archaeology to use 'things' to tap into the frequency of ancient voices.

The Ability of Text to Reflect Reality

Supporters and denouncers of the historical merit of the Sagas equally acknowledge the call for critically evaluating these texts. If we are to use ancient texts to get at a sense of a past reality, one must grapple with the distinction Halldór Laxness (1968) observes in his novel *Christianity at Glacier*: 'the difference between a novelist and a historian is this, that the former tells lies deliberately and for the fun of it; the historian tells lies in his simplicity and imagines he is telling the truth'. As Laxness suggests, when examining any text, sacred, medieval or otherwise, one must devise a strategy for establishing the *intention* of the document, as either a reflection of an invented or lived event. In doing so, we bring to the fore concern for the intentionality of the author; that is, the purpose for committing the telling of these events and ideas to a written format, and lastly, in making these ideas more permanent, who may have been the intended audience. Laxness also keenly observes that no text can ever reflect an entire universe of ideas and experiences of a society, and must choose to record only a glimpse of that universe, only a narrow portion of a historical reality.

However, psychology and cognitive psychology has demonstrated that this is not simply a question of honesty or objectivity, but is an issue of our mental mechanics, that in fact the structuring of our brains makes it pointless, if not inane, to have discussions over truth and subjectivity. Despite the once common belief among anthropologists and sociologists that identity and reality are the constructs of the collective community with whom we interact, the development of cognitive psychology has revealed a startling revelation: in neurological terms, each individual mind processes and creates a distinct and unique reality, confirmed physiologically by distinct neurological thumbprints or signatures, leading many scholars to suggest that there can in fact be no single or collective version of a 'true' reality (Halbwachs 1992; Roediger and Goff 1998; Schacter 1996). To complicate the matter even further, not only can there be in a sense multiple realities, but even at an individual level, reality is not static. Under different stimuli or contexts, the brain can process information differently, creating thousands of realities for every individual. Swiss linguist Ferdinand de Saussure had already noted this phenomenon in the mid-19th century when he observed that language events behaved like an open electrical circuit, arguing that all communication required at least two nodes to complete the circuit and successfully convey a message. Saussure (1959: 9) concluded that words, both verbal and written, are not defined by what they referred to, but by their relation to each other, since all successful communicative transmissions can only make sense in relation to the nodes or speakers. This means that even speakers of a shared language independently make words meaningful. While speakers of a shared language use a similar structure or hardware—grammar, syntax and the like—the web of associated significance and comprehension are in fact unique to the individual. Derrida (1973), building on Saussure's model, argued that speech events were not only determined by the relationships between nodes or participants, but that these relationships were also not fixed, and therefore changed depending on all the different contexts in which they were used (see also Hymes 1972). Individual comprehension is not fixed, but instead each individual has a multi-vocal repertoire of knowledge of their world which is in turn dependent on context. Building on all of these ideas are the fields of postmodernism and literary critique, which posit that the meaning of texts is likewise dependent on an individual's reading or interpretation of the relationship of the words, which is in turn dependant on how their mind builds relationships of understanding, which is in turn shaped by both context and past experience. This presents a particular problem for truly understanding ancient texts, whose authors are long gone and are in many instances anonymous, leaving behind no clues of the experiences that shaped the words they wrote. We as a modern audience run the risk of not understanding the intended goal of the author, which is, at best, always elusive, since any text, modern or ancient alike, can be interpreted in multiple ways depending on who the reader is. Embedded within the maximalist–minimalist debate, however, is a broader methodical concern raised by literary and postmodern critiques: can individuals, imbued by their own cultural and temporal epistemology, goals and ambitions, ever reveal past lifeways through the limitations of text? Postmodern critiques posit that not only must one be wary of not only the biases of the authors of these ancient texts, but we must also make a reflective turn and acknowledge that we, the academics, are ourselves not free of bias. Can historians and anthropologists, then, ever become literate readers of the clues left behind by ancient societies? *Intersubjectivity, discourse, epistemology, textualism, multivocality, multiplicity of readings*, and *relative truths* have become the watchwords of the vanguard of the new literary critics who urge historians to put aside problematic texts like the Sagas and the Bible, texts that were clearly redacted, stem from an older oral tradition, and still to this day evoke a wave of powerful emotions, rendering the modern reader incapable of reading objectively.

The advances in cognitive psychology do little to alleviate older social history assumptions, most notably those of French sociologist Michel Foucault. At the heart of all of Foucault's writing is the explicit notion that there are no absolute truths that one can actively seek. Truths are relative and contextual. Truth is, therefore, always defined and created by people; it does not exist on its own in nature. It is human beings that give meaning to their world and give meaning to what is fact and what is fiction. Foucault illustrates this by taking a historical look at how truth, value, and meaning have changed throughout time. However, Foucault's notion of history and truth is perhaps not all that different from Marx, who asserted that that 'men make their own history, but they do not make it just as they please' (1981: 15); or distinctly different from Vico's declaration that we can come to understand the past because men make their own history, that what they can know is what they have made, nor is it entirely different from Geertz's idea of culture whereby 'man is an animal suspended in webs of significance he himself has spun' (1973: 5). By its very nature, truth is shaped and defined by individuals and thus truth can be known if one is familiar with the cultural and historical context in which these truths were defined.

If truth is only relative to a particular historical context, how and why do people come to believe some things are true and some are false, a clear distinction we must make if we are to understand how and why the Bible or the Sagas should be seen as true or false representations. Foucault addresses this concern through his concept of 'discourse' as developed in *Discipline and Punish* (1977) and *The History of Sexuality* (1978), where he discusses how a discourse is ultimately a modality of power and the knowledge created by that power. A discourse defined by Foucault is somewhat different from what it means in linguistic terminology. Foucault defines discourse as a set of written texts on an area of technical or specialized knowledge. These areas produce specialists or experts who create a particular body of knowledge as well as a specialized vocabulary. These specialists always work together through a shared set of knowledge and vocabulary and are in communication with one another through writing and publishing, constantly reaffirming their notions of a 'regular constellation of ideas' by creating a consistency through the reenactment of citing one another (Foucault 1978: 5). This is what is often meant by textualism, a sort of fetishization of texts as not only the receptacles of knowledge, but also of power. Through texts, a discourse becomes productive: it produces specialists or experts, and vocabularies, but at the same time, it also produces power, which in turn produces subjects. A discourse, through text, then becomes the definer of what is acceptable and what is not in a particular society through the creation of categories, such as sane and insane, normal and abnormal, citizen and delinquent. Practices get labeled through these categories and then by extension, so, too, do individuals through their practice.

One means out of this morass is to acknowledge that while most modern historians would argue that *accuracy* is the single most important factor when evaluating any text claiming to be historical, accuracy is by far not the only goal in mind when transforming actions and events into words; *usability* of that past is also firmly considered when histories are written (Wertsch 2002: 35). This distinction made between accuracy and usability in fact reflects a basic distinction the human mind makes in order to store and recall different kinds of memories: individual or personal memories tend to focus on the accuracy of the detail, while collective or shared memories (i.e. public or cultural) operate on the usability of that memory (2002: 40-51). Usable histories are not static, but change given the demands of the society that use them. The past is remembered and re-remembered because that remembrance can serve the present needs or concerns of a society. Recently, a number of archaeological and historical examinations[2] have keenly demonstrated that ancient states, likewise, used writing technologies to shape and govern their polities: Egyptian pharaohs more than once attempted to erase unpopular predecessors from monuments and king's lists (Meskell 2003); Virgil's *Aeneid* utilized Homer's meta-history of the Trojan War at the expense of their Latin and Etruscan roots to create a new political and social identity that justified the Augustian program of a single ruler for the Roman world (Ando 2000); and the Vijayanagara Empire created an ancestral connection to the previous and once powerful Chola Empire to demonstrate its imperial status in India (Sinopoli 2003), to name just a few.

The Bible and the Sagas, likewise, contain a mixture of individual memories, shown by an emphasis on precise detail, as well as elements of a shared history that were malleable to the demands of society, simultaneously reflecting both the views of a past society depicted within the pages of these text, as well as the society that consigned these events through words onto the page. While some societies erect monuments to remember the past and create a sense of social solidarity, the ancient Israelites and the medieval Icelanders had their texts. The telling of these texts is the telling of the history of these people, and as such, served as a malleable form of social memory, 'the construction of the collective notion about the way things were in the past' (Van Dyke and Alcock 2003: 2). More was at play here than just remembering the deeds of individuals; the oral, and later written, narratives of the Bible and the Sagas were a transformative force, turning a blank landscape into one filled with meaning. The Bible and the Sagas are a material representation of the processes used to convert space to place, the backdrop for the actions of individuals throughout time.

---

2. See Van Dyke and Alcock's *Archaeologies of Memory* (2003) for a survey of archaeological and historical examinations of how ancient societies utilized the past for political, ideological, and economic endeavors.

If we acknowledge that social memory is itself malleable, are we left with the conclusion that because there can be no tangible truths outside of human motivation and manipulation, the entire enterprise of scientific learning and critical examinations of historical and social texts has in a sense been a farce (Kuznar 1997: 110-15)? Biblical minimalist scholars, such as Clines, seem to suggest the answer is yes, citing for example that when gauging the validity of various readings of Psalm 24 'there are no *right* interpretations, and no validity in interpretation beyond the assent of various interest groups' so that 'what counts as a valid interpretation in Cambridge does not necessarily do so in Guatemala City or in Jakarta, or Seoul... biblical interpreters have to give up the goal of determinate and universally acceptable interpretations, and devote themselves to producing inter-pretations they can sell—in whatever mode is called for by the communities they choose to serve' (Clines 1993: 87). Taken to this extraordinary length, the Bible can mean whatever we want it to; it can and has been reinvented many times over. To a certain degree studies on social memory suggest this argument is not without logic. There are numerous examples, beyond the use of the Sagas and the Bible, of invented traditions based on a politics of re-remembering the past in order to suit a society's current goals and agenda (Hobsbawn and Ranger 1983). One prime example is Trevor-Roper's (1983: 15) study of how the Scottish kilt woven in a tartan to represent clan affiliation is largely a modern invention, despite the popular assertion of its ancient origins. However, does this mean that one cannot evaluate how the politics of memory can play a role in shaping how we view the past? Trevor-Roper's analysis of the Scottish Highlands in fact clearly demonstrates that one can examine modern-day assessments of historical traditions and practices, mapping out a kind of practice history of the text. The fact that texts are not static, but are ripe with action and change should not invoke despondency in the academic community, but should evoke a joyous revelation of the possible new and tangible directions of investigation. This observation also implies that with careful scholarship, one can make strides in uncovering the history of a text, examining how it has changed over time and what influences might account for these changes (see, e.g., Friedman 1987).

Foucault himself echoes this observation when he states that individuals, as subjects, are 'consti-tuted in real practices—historically *analyzable* practices' (Rabinow 1984: 369, emphasis added). Therefore, one can come to understand the past through human action, recorded within the mark-ings of script and the material remains of the archaeological record. As Moreland suggests, 'it is, of course, true that the incompleteness of the record, our situatedness in the present, and our meth-odological naivety prevent us from producing a single reading of the past...but this does not mean that *any* reading of the past is as good as any other' (Moreland 2001: 116-17). The key to evaluat-ing texts is through an understanding of the cultural configurations of a society reflected in the text. To uncover these configurations, one must use all available sources of data: texts, archaeological remains, and ethnographic comparisons. It is crucial to emphasize that while unraveling the complexities of cultural configurations of societies (especially extinct societies visible solely through indirect observation) is never straightforward, it can be done if one employs a holistic and flexible methodology that allows us to make inferences and comparisons. If we assume otherwise, than one can never know anything, past or present, a brand of pessimism that seems not only unproductive, but also unwarranted. The same sort of criteria must also be applied to the ability of those individuals who compiled the Bible and the Sagas.

The Power of the Oral Tradition

The previous discussion has illustrated the potential for modern researchers to evaluate how histories are shaped and documented. However, we must also contend with the fact that the writers and compilers of the Bible and of the Sagas had their own sources to draw upon to evaluate the past. One such contested method was the ability of oral traditions to act as social memories of the past. Most scholars would agree that compilers of both the Bible and the Sagas had a number of other written sources to draw upon. As discussed in the beginning of this essay, for the southern Levant, there a numerous forms of extrabiblical texts, including a significant number of non-Israelite sources from Egypt and Mesopotamia (Halpern 1988). It is a possibility that these sorts of texts were available to those authors who compiled and edited the Bible. Halpern and many other scholars also suggest that were earlier written versions of events depicted in the Bible, with portions of stories finding their way into the final edited Hebrew Bible (1988: 16-18, 60-68; Freedman 1980; Propp 1999). While the compilers of the Sagas could look to a far more limited number of other textual resources, such as a few land registries and law books, the greater part of what makes up the Sagas as we now know them today derived from a collective social memory in the form of an oral tradition (Byock 2001; Sørensen 1992). The profession of bards spinning tales of obstacles and glorious triumph in Nordic and Germanic society has a long history, captured most infamously in the 8th-century text *Beowulf*. Just as *Beowulf* contains elements of its earlier oral form, the Sagas are also the palimpsestic recording of mnemonic devices; for example, the Sagas contain a number of standardized kennings, a common feature found in memorized speech events. Likewise, popular individuals make frequent appearances in several of the Sagas, but often under different names or variations on a name, precisely the kind of detail that research into oral tradition has shown are the more liable to undergo alterations; however, when writers use other texts as a source, names are likely to be transferred unchanged between works (G. Sigurðsson 2004: 27).

Likewise, Susan Niditch has argued that many of the books that make up the Bible were stories preserved in oral narratives, contending that 'large, perhaps dominant threads in Israelite culture were oral, and that literacy in ancient Israel must be understood in terms of its continuity and interaction with the oral world' (1996: 1). For both Israelite and Icelandic societies oral traditions are likely to have continued even after written traditions were established, so that the written and oral worlds were not separate, but were enmeshed within a continuum (Byock 2001: 143-45; Niditch 1996: 134). Critics are often skeptical about the ability of oral transmission accurately to maintain information. This view no doubt reflects our own logocentric world (Moreland 2001: 12, 33). Jack Goody (2000: 143) posits that writing has the ability to 'make the implicit explicit' and must be viewed as technology, a technology of the intellect. Technology can be defined as 'codified ways of deliberately manipulating the environment to achieve some material objective' (Adams 1996 [also Goody 2000: 132]). Goody posits that although technology is typically correlated with material objects, such as tools, communication is a form of technology, which can lead to changes in how individuals think and see the world, as well as inducing changes in social organization (2000: 133-35; 1986: 171). Manuel Castells's (2000a, 2000b, 2000c) masterful trilogy on *The Information Age: Economy, Society and Culture* illustrates the power of IT- (information technology-) based communication, as a technological revolution in the 20th century, and La Bianca and Scham's (2005) work has shown how this works in antiquity. However, Goody posits a sharp divide between literate and oral societies, suggesting that only in literate societies can one find documented histories (Goody 1986: 20). He suggests that histories can only be produced when one can trace the past through organized thought, achieved, he argues, through the processes of list making (1986: 37). Lacking the ability to make lists and then compare lists, oral societies, given the limitations of memory, can only preserve a generation of events (1986: 54-56). Goody is certainly correct when he asserts that literacy almost certainly develops because of the limitations and ambiguity of memory; however, he makes an unnecessary polarization between these 'kinds' of societies, without considering that even highly literate societies can still maintain an active oral tradition. Further, the polarization that Goody depicts is a rather new phenomenon (Moreland 2001: 35). Moreland suggests that in Medieval Europe, texts were meant to be read aloud; they were meant to be heard, not seen (2001: 36). 'Scribes were mediators between the spoken and written worlds; through their practice, they embedded the voices of the former in the latter' (Moreland 2001: 36). It is not until after the Protestant Reformation, which devalued the importance of objects, and the invention of the printing press, which allowed for a rapid dissemination of the printed word, that the hazy view of our now logocentric world comes into focus (Moreland 2001: 57). Prior to the 16th and 17th centuries, however, the oral and written narratives were not so sharply delineated. In Medieval Iceland, for example, one of the earliest written texts were the Grágás, or law codes. The Grágás stipulate that the laws must be maintained and enforced by law-speakers, who were chosen by chiefs to serve as arbitrators in the legal proceedings held at the national assembly or Althing (Anderson and Miller 1989; Bachrach and Nicholas 1989). Once a year, law-speakers would be tested on their ability to recite portions of the law codes. What gave these law-speakers their authority was not their ability to consult the Grágás, but to know them by memory and to possess the ability to recite the laws. As Niditch contends for ancient Israel, the majority of Medieval Icelanders were not literate and therefore they valued and assessed information through an individual's ability verbally to communicate ideas. Niditch posits that many of the historical events told through storytelling followed a specific organizational form that would have assisted individuals trying to memorize the stories, and would have allowed the audience to know if the orator was telling the story correctly (Niditch 1996: 20). This would perhaps explain some of the uniformity to how events are told in the Sagas, which seem to follow a fairly standard format. This loose standardization would have facilitated not only the telling of the story, but the remembering of the story, and may serve, as Ong suggests, as a cognitive tool for recalling memory, making it possible for us to suggest that historical events preserved in oral storytelling may have had the ability to last numerous generations (Ong 1982: 31-39).

Methodological Implications

The aim of this paper thus far has been to demonstrate that the challenges raised by the maximalist–minimalist debate can be addressed in a way that can produce new insights into how we can use texts to understand ancient societies better. The remainder of the discussion will take up one last challenge: the ability of anthropological archaeology to use both text and the material record to uncover the past lifeways of Iron Age southern Levant and the Settlement Period of Medieval Iceland. The methodology proposed here attempts to accomplish two tasks: first, to demonstrate that an anthropological methodology can prevent researchers from falling into earlier archaeological traps of proving or disproving texts, by integrating the two threads of evidence; and second to take the minimalist, postmodern, or book-prose challenge under advisement, illustrating, however, that despite the difficulties, one should not abandon the goal of striving to understand the past.

The conclusion often reached by those who challenge the historicity of texts like the Bible or the Sagas is that if these texts reflect any sort of historical image it is only a reflection of the elite members of the society; therefore, archaeology is left with the task of uncovering the patterns of everyday behavior, from everyday individuals. Moreland posits, however, that this a false dichotomy set between 'the Word and the dirt' (2001: 9-11). Moreland suggests that the discipline of archaeology has its own unique history from its origins as the 'handmaiden of history' to having the upper hand over history. We have seen this development in both South Levantine and Icelandic archaeology, where excavation and survey projects got their start because it was presumed that the material record could help to highlight the textual records. With the advent of New Archaeology (cf. Binford and Binford 1968), however, some archaeologists working in Iceland have opted to examine non-historical topics, such as environmental conditions, rather than tackle the thorny issue of the historicity of the Sagas. 'New Archaeology has minimized the impact of purposeful human thought and action in the creation of history and has neglected to examine human experience'

(Moreland 2001: 24). The view that somehow historians are the only ones in a position to examine elite activities, while archaeologists can get at the experience of non-elites, is yet another needless dichotomy. Archaeologists have successfully examined elite activities in societies that possessed no written documentation through analyses of monumental architecture, burials (Bloch-Smith 1992), prestige goods, trade networks, differences in diet, ritual and ideology (Zevit 2001), and the like. Dever (2001: 102-8) also rightly suggests that while it is typically the case that written records are controlled and produced by elites, there are often descriptions of specific *Sitze im Leben* or 'real-life settings'. While it may not have been the primary objective of the biblical writers, for example, to record mundane activities, such as the structure of households, they nevertheless have passed on those glimpses of the past, even if only in passing or in their set up for the story they purposefully sought to relay (King and Stager 2001; Stager 1985). While the archaeological record is traditionally viewed as an unintentional record of the past, and texts are seen as a purposeful recollection of the past, both material and textual remains contain elements of unintentional and intentional human action. For example, one could hardly claim that monuments are unintentional traces of human activity; these cultural materializations were often constructed with the goal of lasting into perpetuity. Therefore, we need not separate text from material remains to examine them singly, but rather both should be viewed in concert. Following a methodology that views text and the material record as two forms of independent, but not mutually exclusive, lines of evidence, one can then begin to address how we can uncover an anthropological view of the past. That is, we can begin to stretch the texts to their full potential, and to look not only at a chronology of events, but also at the everyday lived behavior of ancient societies. Likewise, we can begin to stretch the material record to its potential and move beyond typologies and environmental reconstructions, and begin to grasp a thicker, fuller view of the past. Having a firm historical chronology or material typology are absolutely essential and have rightly been the necessary starting points, but we can now begin the daunting task of moving forward and towards a more complex vision of past lifeways. This can only be done if we use all available sources of data.

To demonstrate the utility of this approach, we will conclude with a case study from Medieval Iceland that attempts to incorporate both text and anthropological archaeology. The social structure of the *Landnám* or Settlement Period (ca. 870–1000 CE) in Iceland has been viewed by some as unknowable, despite the fact that we have texts depicting the social structure, and have available anthropological and archaeological correlates that could help us come to understand the nature of the social configurations for this time period. Unfortunately, much of the debates surrounding the Sagas as well as the Bible have centered on proving or disproving whether or not individuals or specific events discussed in these texts can be proved archaeologically. Biblical scholar N.P. Lemche (1998) encapsulates this dialogue when discussing the possibility that Solomon may have been an actual king, and relates that the Bible 'reflects what we call a heroic society, heroic in the Greek sense. It's a kind of history you find in Norse tradition, among the Vikings, my forefathers. We love those stories, but we don't believe them to be true' (Dever *et al.* 1997: 32). Lemche neatly encapsulates the belief that the idea of a United Monarchy, a time of greatness and power for Israelites, is a form of what Thompson would call 'wish fulfillment' of marginalized writers; these writers made up, created, or invented the idea of a United Monarchy. Similarly, Lemche's statement alludes to a depiction of the Sagas as a time of heroism, honor, and friendship, where a system of checks and balances ensured that greed was quickly stamped out and no single individual could gain too much power, is a also nothing more a 'wish fulfillment' of a marginalized group of writers at the mercy of a distant king in Norway. Dever (2001: 106) has suggested that archaeology can be used to find 'convergences' between the text and the material remains in order to test the historicity of the Bible, and provides us with a reconstruction of the social structure of the United Monarchy (Iron Age IIA [ca. 1000–925 BCE]) in the southern Levant. We suggest here that Dever's methodology of convergences can serve as an analytical tool that can be applied cross-culturally and cross-temporally with the aim of uncovering social relationships. More than this, the recent boon in the application of high-precision radiocarbon dating and Bayesian statistical methods to the Iron Age of the southern Levant (cf. Bruins *et al.* 2003; Finkelstein and Piasetzky 2003; Levy *et al.* 2008; Levy and Higham 2005) demonstrates how researchers are able to examine textual evidence at the sub-century level, such as the campaign of the Egyptian Pharaoh Shoshanq or Shishik I in ancient Israel/Judah ca. 923 BCE, and highlights that even newer methods are being applied in the quest for objective methods for examining the relationship between text and the historical archaeology record.

If we can agree from the preceding sections of this paper, that written sources contain both intentional and unintentional reflections of human behavior, we should expect to find the text will converge harmoniously with some aspects of the archaeological record, and with dissonance in other respects. That is, texts, because they often wish to project specific messages, may not always jibe with the reality presented in the archaeological record; but it is here at these lines of both harmony and dissonance that we can begin to piece together the past.

Ethnography of the Sagas

At the end of the 9th century CE, with political upheaval in Norway (Graham-Campbell 2001: 78; Haywood 1995: 86-87, 117), and the lure of the discovery of islands in the North Atlantic (P. Sawyer 2001: 110), Norwegian farmers established a large colony in Iceland. According to Norwegian texts, such as *Heimskringla* (Sturlusson [1979]), the first settlers in Iceland consisted of two types of individuals: those who possessed no property in Norway and brought their fares to Iceland on cattle ships; and wealthy Norwegian chieftains, whose power waned with the creation of state monarchy under the rule of Harold Finehair (Bagge 1992: 70-75; Durrenberger 1992: 25-27). The *Landnámabók* reports that at least twenty-three *goðar* (chiefs) were part of the original settlement and that many of them had relatives already living in various Viking North Atlantic colonies, such as in the Hebrides, the Shetlands, and Orkney (Forte *et al.* 2005: 308-15). Medieval Iceland therefore presents scholars with the unique opportunity to study frontier colonization, social formation, and economic intensification all within the context of a previously uninhabited island. From a historical and anthropological perspective, early Iceland can serve as a fascinating social laboratory, where researchers can, through the interplay of the material record and text, witness the creation and the collapse of a polity. However, an inquiry from even a small sample of this vast cultural register cannot help but highlight countless contradictions in the portrayal of everyday life in Icelandic society. The documentary record itself is juxtaposed by the portrayal of two distinct Icelandic societies: one of a communal frontier society busy at work constructing a new social landscape centered on an agro-pastoral economy, as depicted in the Family Sagas, the other of a proto-aristocratic manorial society teetering on the edge of social attenuation, as described in the Contemporary Sagas of the 12th and 13th centuries CE. This discrepancy in societal portrayals has been a point of contention among Saga historians: on the one hand, these differences may reflect two different social realities separated by time (Durrenberger 1990b; W.I. Miller 1983, 1986); or these divergences may represent the use of allegorical devices in the Family Sagas in order to promote the Christian mores of the 13th century CE (Jochens 1980, 1995). From the methodology presented in this paper, one must ask if it is necessary for one to try and separate entirely these viewpoints in order to understand the lifeways of medieval Icelanders. That is, must we be able to conclude that the Family Sagas represent a distinct period of time without any trace of a 13th-century ethos or that these sagas are wholly the creation of a wistful society dreaming up a golden age that never was? Even if we can conclude that the Saga writers were not deliberating distorting the past, can we evaluate if these authors had any conception that the 13th century was different than the 9th and 10th centuries? Through an examination of economic transactions, Durrenberger was able to show a clear distinction between the Family Sagas and the Contemporary Sagas, concluding that 'if the Family Sagas were simply transpositions of contemporary events onto past locales and people, they would represent the same frequencies of types of events as the Sturlunga Sagas do… [T]hey do not, therefore we can conclude that they represent a different social reality, though it was as much as three centuries removed' (Durrenberger 1990b: 89). Likewise, Miller, who has used ethnographic comparisons to help understand feuding in Iceland, adds that the 'fictionalizing dialogue and chronology does not mean fictionalizing the process of exchange and feud…the negative judgment on saga historicity was too hastily extended to include matters not fully understood or satisfactorily disproved' (W.I. Miller 1986: 19).

Following the approaches of Durrenberger and Miller, one way out of this morass is to try and place the both the Family and Contemporary Sagas within a broader social and historical context, to read the Sagas as an ethnography, allowing us to uncover patterns of social behavior. Therefore, the question of whether there was ever a period in Icelandic history with greater social mobility than the proto-aristocratic manorial society of the 13th century can aptly be addressed by the model presented in this paper: examining social relationships within the synergetic union of text and archaeology rather than consigning the discussion to the impossible task of trying to prove or disprove the historicity of the text. The Sagas are embedded in history, but also transcend that history and are truthful of the Icelanders in their own fashion.

One significant area of dissonance between text and archaeology is the evidence revealed for how and why Iceland was settled in the 9th century CE. The Sagas suggest that major political and social changes in Norway resulted in the displacement of chiefs and their retainers, making the discovery of an uninhabited island, however distant, an attractive opportunity (Byock 2001; *Land-námabók* [Pálsson and Edwards] 1972; Fitzhugh and Ward 2000). Under such 'push' models for migration, rather than remain in Norway as marginalized elites, these chiefs pooled their resources and recruited individuals to form a new society, unsullied by taxation and kings. However, archaeologically we have little evidence of elite estates surrounded by the radii of small farms that would have housed a chief's retinue (Steindórsson *et al.* 1987) for the early medieval period. Instead, we have evidence for a fairly unstratified society, with the development of shared, multi-family farmsteads (Einarsson 1994; Herschend 1994; Vésteinsson 2000: 168). The texts do, however, describe situations that draw parallels to ethnographic (Cohen 1971; Curtain 1984; Hopkins and Wallerstein 1982; Wallerstein 1974) and historical archaeology accounts (Algaze 1989, 2005; Chase-Dunn and Hall 1997; Oates 1993; Orser 1998; Stein 1999, 2000a, 2000b, 2005) of diasporic communities. The Sagas may have slanted the original intent of the colony towards the personal aims of a minority of individuals, but they describe well the challenges and triumphs of a frontier society that had more on their minds than simply fleeing a king—they sought economic prosperity through continued trade throughout Scandinavia and the North Atlantic (Hodges and Whitehouse 1983; Moore 2000; Pirenne 1954; Rosedahl 1998). To situate both text and archaeology is to acknowledge that Iceland was part of a larger Scandinavian tradition of travel and trade that escalated to new heights during the Viking Age (Forte *et al.* 2005; Hodges and Whitehouse 1983) with the placement of trade colonies throughout the North Atlantic. The economic aim of the Viking Age was to acquire prestige goods that were not widely available, and then sell these goods at a high cost. This enterprise may in fact help explain the initial colonization of Iceland. Archaeological excavations in Iceland have begun to reveal that, consistent with medieval texts, the island was settled by large numbers of people between 870 and 900 CE, but there is also evidence a century before of small, seasonally occupied camps located near known walrus breeding areas (Perdikaris 1999; Perdikaris and McGovern 2007). Objects made of walrus ivory were known in Europe as long ago as the Roman Imperial period, and were, according to British medieval texts, a highly sought-after commodity in Western Europe during the Carolingian Dynasty (Rosedahl 2005, 2007). Likewise, archaeological sites during the same period in northern Norway have uncovered evidence supporting the processing of large numbers of walrus, presumably for their tusks and hides (Þorláksson 2007). The availability of a lucrative commodity in a period of widespread trade in the Norse world could have been a strong 'pull' towards establishing small trade diaspora colonies in Iceland. Over time, with the discovery of suitable grazing areas for livestock (Aðalsteinsson 1990; Sigurbjörnsson 2000; Smith 1995), larger planned settlements could be designed and enacted.

Under the parameters of a Viking Age economy, Iceland could not adequately compete on a global scale. Walrus ivory is not an easy resource to control, was not limitless, or even the closest source of ivory for the European market. By the 11th century, however, the Viking Age economy collapsed and was replaced by a 'medieval economy', an economy based on the bulk distribution of everyday subsistence goods that could be brought to the market at a low cost (Lopez 1976: 115-18). In a medieval economy, Iceland could compete with its one sustainable and renewable resource: wool. Throughout the 11th and 12th centuries, Iceland became a large producer of wool for European markets (Gelsinger 1981), which back home could fuel a chiefly economy of reciprocal gift exchange and redistribution at the local level. Wool production, unlike walrus ivory and hide extraction, was more readily controllable by an aristocratic class. All households needed land, so by controlling access to land, and perhaps even to livestock, through rent, aristocrats could control land use (J. Sigurðsson 1989, 1999), and in turn, they could control both the local and global markets. Likewise, while not every household could produce items for a Viking Age luxury market, they could and did in a medieval economy. All households produced wool for both their own domestic needs (Durrenberger 1990a), and a surplus that could be collected and used by elites in the global market. The shift in economy would have promoted a shift in household and labor organization (North 1982, 1990; Price 1977, 1984; Tilley 1998), two avenues of research compatible with the kinds of data found in the archaeological and textual records. Overtime, the need to protect and regulate trade networks can spark the need for state institutions, which in turn helps to support the interests of a growing aristocracy (Adams 1981).

While the Sagas do not focus on wool production, the archaeological record clearly does. Zooarchaeological remains demonstrate a shift in animal husbandry, from a focus on cattle in the early periods of colonization, towards an emphasis on sheep rearing beginning in the 11th century (Aðalsteinsson 1990; Ingimundarson 1992, 1995). These economic and subsequent social changes are likewise discernible in the archaeological record through shifting settlement patterns that reflect a heightened increase in sheep stocking and the creation of large manorial estates alongside a growing peasant class working and living on small tenant farms (Carter n.d.). The Sagas are, however, at their best depicting the politics of a chiefly economy with global dimensions, aptly illustrated through countless narratives on the ethics of honor, trust, and reciprocal relationships between chiefs and followers during the early settlement period as depicted in the Family Sagas, and the subsequent rupture in the society with the rise of an aristocratic class as seen in the Contemporary Sagas. The Sagas do not suggest a cause for this breakdown of reciprocal relationships, but by combining these texts with the archaeological record we can begin to piece together the processes of this social transformation.

It is not a matter of *either* the Family Sagas being more or less trustworthy than the later Contemporary Sagas, but is instead processes of social change writ large contained within the pages of these texts. While archaeological and textual examinations have identified a broad spectrum of influential factors, from environmental degradation (Amorosi *et al.* 1997; Buckland 2000 [cf. Guðbergsson 1975, 1996]; Buckland *et al.* 1992; S. Friðriksson 1972; Hallsdóttir 1987; Júlísson 2000; McGovern 1990; McGovern *et al.* 1988; Ogilvie 1984a, 1984b, 1990, 2000; Sveinbjarnardóttir 1991, 1992) to a calculated takeover by the Norwegian Crown (Finlay 1997; Gaskins 1998;

Hastrup 2004), it is only with the interplay of these datasets through an anthropological lens that we can begin to delve deeper to the roots of social processes at work during the settlement and subsequent formation of a new society in Medieval Iceland.

We argue here that the same sort of pattern can be seen in the Sagas, even though the Sagas rarely discuss trade or economic processes. To demonstrate the potential of this model presented in this paper, we have chosen to examine marriage and inheritance rights described in the Family and Contemporary Sagas (Frank 1973). This selection was not made arbitrarily, but was chosen as a tool for examining potential changes in social mobility and status over time. As a prime agent in forging social alliances, marriage practices allow a keen insight into the degree of social mobility within the society as well as garnering a gimpy into gender and class status. Cross-culturally, social mobility tends to decrease proportionately with the establishment of ascribed social status, limiting the viable number of potential marriage partners per class since alliances tend to be created between members sharing similar social positions only. Likewise, an increased control over matrimony corresponds with the higher tiers of social rank, with arguably more fluidity within marriage selection among the non-aristocratic members of society. The Sagas focus heavily on the conflicts and concords that only love and a desire for power can bring out in people, providing the modern reader with an ethnographic window into the developing social arrangements of a medieval society. A cursory examination of the Sagas reveals two distinct images of marriage and the status of women in Icelandic society, with women having a shrinking degree of freedom and influence in society over time. The goal here is to use the Family Sagas, which demonstrate marriage and inheritance practices for the early medieval period, and the contemporary Sturlunga Sagas, which illustrate the late 11th through 13th centuries, to see if there are any discernable patterns of behavior that can then be compared to the patterns emerging from archaeological data. Our hope here is that by using an interdisciplinary methodology we can begin to move our debates past the fixation with attempting to demonstrate that the culture and society described in the Family Sagas are either entirely accurate or are fictionalized accounts peppered with some historical elements depicting a social structure that in fact never existed. We will argue that the Sagas document a transformation of marriage practices, providing us with a vivid representation of the rise of an aristocratic class alongside shifting social identities for women, intimately tied, we posit, to changes in economy and household production seen in the archaeological record

Passions of the Free State:
Marriage, Love, and Economics in Medieval Iceland

Overall, from the textual information, the initial Norse-Icelandic society (ca. 850–1000 CE, a period known as the *Landnám* or land taking) is characterized as a time of prosperity. From the text, Iceland during this period can be characterized as a country in the making; as a time of relative cooperation between chiefs and independent farmers; as a time when the once empty fjords and valleys were being domesticated and transformed into a social landscape reminiscent of a Norwegian homeland. The first crucial step in this process was to recruit individuals motivated to take land on the island, who could then get to work building a society. The Book of Settlements 'shows us not only that large numbers of women were among the settlers of Iceland, but also that in certain circumstances they too could be primary settlers and not just a part of a man's bag and baggage, along with children, slaves and cattle' (Jesch 1991: 81). The wording of the Book of Settlements seems to suggest husband and wives were partners in the land-taking, describing husbands and wives as 'co-land takers'; this idea of a shared partnership fits well with earlier Norwegian conceptions of land ownership in the 8th century CE (B. Sawyer 1988).

In the chapter entitled 'most notable land takers' of the Book of Settlements, we find the chronicle of Aud the Deep Minded, whose story is also told in the first half of *Laxdœla saga*. From the Book of Settlements we learn that Aud was said to have been the daughter of Ketill flatnose, a Norwegian chieftain who moved his family to the Hebrides. After a series of deaths, Aud became the sole caretaker of her granddaughters and decided that she would have to marry these girls off since neither she nor they had a male guardian. From chapter 5 of Laxdœla saga, Aud is said to have planned to sail to Iceland, preparing a ship in secret, since it was against Norse law for a woman to travel without a male guardian, and that she was accompanied by her granddaughters and at least twenty male retainers. Along the way, she married off a granddaughter in Orkney and then one in the Faeroes before arriving in Iceland where two of her brothers were already living. One could argue that the existence of her brothers in Iceland is what spurred her immigration, but she does not take up residence with either brother, but instead claims land for herself and her retainers. The Book of Settlements reports that she settled in Breiðafjörður and established a farmstead at Hvammur. In the Breiðafjörður district she gave out land to her retainers (Herschend 1994: 182-85). In both Laxdœla saga and the Book of Settlements Aud is characterized as a deep thinker, a woman of intuition and intellect. Chapter 6 of Laxdœla saga portrays Aud as chief-like, as she fronted the costs of numerous commensality events and gave land grants to her loyal retainers. Ultimately, Aud opted for her followers 'to take part in an interlocking network, with both a horizontal and a vertical dimension, and to identify themselves with it' as members of a new society (Herschend 1994: 176). Aud, like any chief, is not content on establishing a lone farmstead for herself and grandchildren; she accepts nothing less than an alliance network, placing herself as a central hub in the channels of power and influence. Unlike other chiefs described in the Sagas, such as Skalagrim in *Egil's saga*, Aud accomplishes her goals not through violence but through persuasive speech and determination. The extent of Aud's power is depicted in the romanticized account of her death. After marrying off her remaining granddaughters, Aud decides to hold an elaborate three day feast. On the last night, she gave everyone gifts and good advice and then declared that this was not to be just a wedding feast, but a funeral feast as well for she had decided this was the right time to die. She then went to her bed, laid down, and was soon after dead.

In addition to claiming land, marriage was another mechanism for brokering wealth and social alliances in Medieval Iceland. In their Norwegian homeland, marriages were decided by a woman's male guardian and her potential suitor. For some time, even after the adoption of Christianity, the directive for the consent of a woman was often not legally enforced. However, the most striking feature of marriages depicted in the Family Sagas is the frequent mention of fathers asking for their daughters' consent to a marriage. In chapter 23 of Laxdœla saga, Egil assured his daughter Thorgerd that he would not answer the spokesman of her potential suitor until he was certain how she stood on the match. After the meeting, Egil concludes that the match seemed promising, but tells Thorgerd that 'I have left the matter for you to decide... [H]owever, I think it is easy to answer such a proposal for the match is a very credible one'. Thorgerd retorts: 'I have heard you say that you love me best of all your children, but now it seems you don't really mean it if you want to marry me off to a bondwoman's son, no matter how handsome and well decked out he is!' Egil tries to persuade her, but does not force her to marry, and instead ultimately rejects the proposal when it becomes clear that Thorgerd has no intention of being married off. Even once a proposal had been accepted by a male guardian, a woman still seemed able to persuade him to call off the wedding, as for example in chapter 97 of *Njal's saga* when Flosi's niece Hildigunnr does not wish to marry. Flosi assures Hildigunnr that 'it is sufficient for me to call off the negotiations if you do not want to get married'.

From these examples one can suggest that fathers often conferred with their daughters about potential marriage agreements, a suggestion strengthened by the anger and frustration of some women when they are not consulted (Jochens 1986a; 1986b: 37; 1993). One example comes from chapters 9 and 11 of Njal's saga, where Hallgerd is told that her father has, without conferring with her, accepted and performed a betrothal ceremony with Thorvald, a well-respected and good-natured man. Hallgerd was not pleased with the match or her father's actions and comments to him: 'now I am certain of what I have been suspecting for a long time, namely, that you do not love me as much as you have always said you did, since you do not think it necessary to discuss this proposal with me; besides, I do not find this marriage as prestigious as you had promised me'. Soon after the marriage, Hallgerd concocts a scheme to have Thorvald murdered. Hallgerd purposefully squandered away Thorvald's provisions of flour and dried fish, and then accused of him of being lazy and unable to provide aptly for his household. She continued to badger Thorvald until he became so enraged that he slapped her. In guilt, Thorvald conceded to Hallgerd's unreasonable wishes, and immediately assembled a crew of men and to set sail on a fishing expedition. Hallgerd seized the opportunity and runs to Thjostolf, her uncle who had supported Hallgerd's stance against marrying Thorvald, and tells him how her husband has dishonored her. Thjostolf promises to avenge her mistreatment and sets sail to find and murder Thorvald, which he does. Hallgerd then returns to her father's farm with the news, and after hearing the series of events concedes that the failure of her marriage was his fault since he had not consulted with her nor listened to Thjostolf's advice against forcing a daughter to marry.

While it is tempting to suggest that all women shared in Hildigunnr's advantage of having male guardians who conferred with them on marriage opportunities, or with Hallegerd's ability to end undesirable marriages, a fair number of marriages described in the Family Sagas seem to suggest that women frequently married at the behest of their guardians. In most cases the acceptance of a marriage is tacit and passive: 'the girl did not refuse' or 'did not say no on her behalf and asked her father to decide' or 'it was not against her will' (Jochens 1986b: 38). It is equally necessary to stress that the women described above all came from wealthy families, so it is likely that these fathers had a vested interest in being certain that a marriage alliance would be profitable and not end negatively. Further, the Family Sagas make implicit implications that girls of less wealthy families were often the prey of men seeking sexual gratification, not wives (Jochens 1991: 365-76). These 'illicit love visits' could involve either physical force or trickery, and if pregnancies resulted there was often little a woman could do if the man did not admit to the encounter. At the same time, however, social mobility was a feasible reality for some women of non-prestigious families, even for slaves. In Laxdœla saga, Hoskuldr, on a trip to Norway, buys a beautiful slave, Melkorka, who becomes a member of Hoskuldr's household and later the mother of his favorite son Óláfr, who inherits a considerable share in his father's land holdings. The saga suggests that Melkorka and Hoskuldr's wife get along well together, but this may not have been the norm. In Njal's saga, Njal takes a concubine, who is constantly at odds with his wife Bergthora. Njal has sons with both women who both stand to inherit adequately after his death; but unlike the case of Melkorka, Bergthora's sons challenge the right of Njal's illegitimate son to claim inheritance (see also Tulinius 1992).

What emerges from the preceding discussion on land holding, marriage, and divorce is a reality in which women could stake a claim in the Icelandic land rush and could stand to gain considerable wealth through marriage. A certain degree of social rigidity and fluidity is also present, where some women seem able to work the social system to their advantage and increase their status through marriage and alliances with wealthy men, while still others remain passive participants in their family's calculated social maneuverings. The image of women depicted in the Family Sagas is therefore multifaceted, with both the chance for positive opportunities and the malady of social restrictions.

Landnám: The Lifeways of Early Icelandic Society from Archaeological Evidence

The first task in understanding the lifeways of early Icelandic society is to recreate the natural and built environments of the 9th and 10th centuries CE. Climatological data suggest that an amelioration in average temperature, identified as the Little Climatic Optimum (ca. 800 CE), provided the first settlers of Iceland with a warmer and more moderate environment than the weather patterns today. From pollen and faunal analyses, we know that the settlers brought with them a transported landscape, one derived from their Norwegian homelands that centered on animal husbandry. Cattle, sheep, horses, goats, and pigs were immediately introduced by the Norse (Jóhannesson 1974: 288). These animals taken together form a 'Landnám package' that required substantial acres of rangelands (Amorosi *et al.* 1997: 501). Prior to Norse settlement, the landscape of Iceland consisted of a network of dense scrub birch and dwarf willow forests intersected with grassy meadows in the highlands, which were settled first, and a patchwork of wetlands and forests in the lowlands (Guðbergsson 1996; Smith 1995: 319). To meet the needs of their agro-pastoral economy, the Norse colonizers burned down large tracks of forests in the highlands and drained extensive networks of bogs that covered most of the lowlands. While grain could be grown in some areas in the south (Simpson *et al.* 2002: 423-43), Iceland quickly rallied its economy around cattle and sheep production. Therefore, the crucial agricultural component for all farms was grass that could be converted into fodder for animals (Aðalsteinsson 1990; S. Friðriksson 1972: 785).

An examination of settlement patterns and household size reveals that chiefs in the first half of the medieval period seem to have gained little economically by being leaders. Household data indicate that during the early medieval period there was little variation in house size and plan. Although a chieftain's longhouse (domestic structure) could be larger than some, the layout of the longhouse, as well as the farmstead itself, were not significantly different from other homesteads. Some independent farmers, too, had households as large as a chief's. Further, a characteristic in the settlement pattern of early Icelandic sites is the presence of more than one longhouse at each farmstead (Vésteinsson 2000: 168). At the sites of Bessastaðir, Reykjavík, and Herjólfsdalur two contemporaneous longhouses have been discovered; at Hvítarholt, three longhouses have been detected (Vésteinsson 2000: 168). The contemporaneity of these longhouses suggests that more than one family or group established a farmstead, inferring communal ownership of land. The challenge of costly labor investments necessary for creating a pastoral landscape were perhaps met by these shared, multihousehold farms.

While the Family Sagas described numerous instances of violence, such as Hallegerd plotting to have her husband murdered, evidence of warfare and violence are scarce in the archaeological record. Aside from grave goods, few weapons are found and skeletal remains rarely indicate pathological signs of violence. It would be inappropriate to conclude that violence therefore was infrequent in early Icelandic society; however, we can suggest from ethnographic comparison that often the threat of a feud was enough to serve as an efficient social-leveling mechanism, prohibiting a single individual from gaining ultimate control (Junker 1999: 345-49; W.I. Miller 1990: 186-90). Further, burial data indicate little social stratification. Most burials contain only modest grave offerings, with little variation in both the content of grave goods and burial construction. Some individuals were clearly wealthier than others; however, there is no direct evidence of political and economic power resting in the hands of a single individual or even among the twenty-three individuals noted as chiefs in the Book of Settlements, but was rather divided among many. The skeletal remains indicate that early Medieval Icelanders were characterized by overall good health, with little signs of malnutrition or infectious disease (Gestsdóttir 1998). The skeletal material infers that overall most Icelanders had the same diet and access to ample food resources.

When we examine the Family Sagas and the archaeological record in tandem, rather than in opposition, one can begin to piece together the range of possible social opportunities and constraints during the early Icelandic period. From the Sagas, Aud represents perhaps the maximum of what a woman could achieve in early medieval society. Counter to the gender rigidity of their Norwegian homelands, where women's roles were typically relegated to the household, women living in the settlement period of Iceland seem to have had greater opportunities for social advancement, for some time in that 'brief interval between leaving Norway and arriving in Iceland, some women clearly had to be more' (Jesch 1991: 83). There is no doubt that Aud took advantage of the greater opportunities and fewer social constraints of the Norse colonies in the North Atlantic and no matter how romanticized some of the images of her are, she embodied a true picture of the possibilities that opened up for women in the frenzied push of Viking colonization. The Family Sagas relate a situation in which Aud and her contemporaries entered both a vacant and unwritten physical and social landscapes, providing women with new innovative opportunities. From the Sagas, we see women as actively involved in shaping the economy of a new country, since women were energetic participants in the establishing of farmsteads. Through their labor, women, alongside men, created a new society.

Sturlunga: A Proto-Aristocratic Manorial Society

By the 13th century CE the social structure of Iceland was in peril, and the threat of a societal attenuation imminent. The *Sturlunga saga*, one of the Contemporary Sagas, depicts a society constantly at the edge of a sword. Documented in the Sturlunga saga is the civil war between members of the Sturlung family and of its rival, Gizur Þorvaldsson, a wealthy chieftain in Skagafjörður. Contained within the Sturlunga saga is a vivid tale of two chiefs vying for power and control over Iceland, with accounts of violent feuds, murder plots, and the burning of farmsteads found on nearly every page. These social changes are aptly reflected in the treatment of women in the Contemporary Sagas. Perhaps the most important line of evidence is the actual paucity of references to women in the Contemporary Sagas. While the Family Sagas often placed women like Aud and Hallegerd at the apex of situations, the Contemporary Sagas seem to lack an image of dynamic women.

A change in the treatment of women in the Contemporary Sagas is further correlated to changes in marriage alliances. In the settlement period, there were few restrictions on matrimony that involved property or wealth (Jochens 1995: 21). There was no restriction to marrying slaves for either a man or a woman; however, the child born to a free mother and a slave father, even if the woman had freed him in order to marry him, would not be allowed to inherit land. A child born to a free father and slave mother, as we saw in Laxdœla saga, by contrast could inherit land as long as a man admitted parentage (Karras 1988: 113; 1992). Unlike the settlement period, greater emphasis is placed on the concept of *jafnræði*, an equal match, which refers to both social prestige and to wealth. In fact, Grágás (K §148) states that 'if people join in marriage who own less property than 120 ounce-units in legal tender [silver], six ell ounce units [cloth], besides their everyday clothing and are without dependents [if they had dependents additional means were required] then their penalty is lesser outlawry, unless the woman is past childbearing'. If the couple did not agree to dissolve the union, they were forced to leave the country until they owned 120-ounce units or more or when the woman was past childbearing. While the Family Sagas describe the desire for prestigious marriage matches, the idea of a suitable match probably had more to do with wishing to ensure a marriage of equal social standing (free versus slave) was met. There is little indication to suggest that marriage alliances were confined by matters of wealth. The Grágás, however, demonstrate that wealth is a clear requirement for marriages during the Sturlunga period. The end result of this marriage regulation would have stymied social mobility since it prohibited marriage across wealth positions. Further, the proviso that a couple needed to have a certain basic level of wealth to even consider marriage would have further thwarted the creation of alliances and the making of economic networks, since marriage was, in both cases, the key means for fostering these kinds of relationships.

In contrast to the range of social opportunities available to women in the Family Sagas, the status of women depicted in the Contemporary Sagas is sharply prohibitive. A reading of either the documentary or material record singly will produce a muddled conclusion; however, if we examine the changing roles of women by placing the Sagas within a broader social and historical context that weaves together numerous lines of evidence, from texts to archaeology, the incongruence between the Family and Contemporary Sagas are both comprehensible and reasonable. Evidence from both text and archaeology suggests a shift in the social structure: from a loose configuration of many chiefs, to a hierarchical system with power vested in fewer and fewer hands. As the Viking Age economy rooted in luxury came to an end by 1050 CE, the local exchange economy likewise shifted to one grounded in weaving rather than in warring. A greater emphasis on sheep rearing and wool production created a different set of opportunities and limitations than had characterized the initial settlement period. By 1000 CE, Viking expansion had seen its limits. Attempts to colonize Greenland and Vínland were only mildly successful; Vínland only saw one colony, while Greenland's export-based economy of ivory and exotic animals garnered only a marginal position in European trade. As Viking ships stopped in ports back in Scandinavia and the colonies they had established across continental Europe, the British Isles, and islands in the North Atlantic, Norse populations transitioned their attention from conquest and expansion to a phase of consolidation. Iceland, too, moved into a period of consolidation, and away from an attitude of colonization, making alienable property an ever-greater concern. The penning of the Book of Settlements during this period reflects a need to document property rights, illustrating a social reality wherein property, through landownership, became the primary means of wealth and social status once the prospect of raiding and colonizing untapped lands ceased to be a profitable social and economic vehicle (Hastrup 1985: 192). Younger sons could no longer be appeased with the temptations of ship and sail, thus leading to the attenuation of conflict, especially, as the Sturlunga Sagas demonstrate, fraternal disputes. Likewise, Viking raids tapered off by the late 10th century CE, with the last raid reported around 1050 CE. Economies of loot and plunder were replaced with intensified agricultural production and a greater focus on craft specialization, both of which were used to generate surpluses that could be brought to the market. In Iceland, the production of *vaðmál* or fleece homespun cloth, produced by women in their households, became the principal export. *Vaðmál* was not traded extensively within Iceland; it was produced by every household for their own needs, but was also produced in surplus for the Icelandic-Norwegian market. Iceland became Norway's primary supplier of woolen cloth; in exchange, Norway provided Iceland with timber, grain, and embroidered clothing and tapestries—all items used by chiefs to gain and maintain allies. Without the ability to give gifts of land, chiefs began to rely more heavily on these imported goods to sustain their wealth and affluence in a community, which ultimately led to intense competition.

Increased wool production and the ability to accrue social power both rested on the ability of a household to produce high yields of grass to be converted into fodder for sheep. Pollen and geomorphological analyses have demonstrated that by the 12th century CE, overgrazing had severely eroded the highlands (Amorosi 1992; Buckland *et al.* 1990). This 'ovigenic landscape' initiated an erosional regime that removed highland topsoil that was then transported by wind action down-slope and dumped unevenly onto the lowlands (Dugmore and Buckland 1991: 499). The highlands, now denuded and suffering from severe erosion, became unproductive grazing land. However, with an increase in soil, the lowlands became more agriculturally productive, sharply circumscribing the island's resources as well as curtailing the ability of highland chiefs to maintain their political clout (Carter 2003). Likewise, sheep stocking, unlike walrus hunting, is far easier to control by local elites by controlling land use. All households need land, allowing elites to rent land, and even animals, in exchange for a percentage of the fodder and wool produced by that land through household labor. So, while not all households could contribute to producing luxury goods, they could all participate in the medieval economy. Correlated with this shift in household productivity is direct evidence of increased hostility and endemic warfare, presumably over land and labor rights. Weapons, such as daggers, axes, and swords, which had been scarcely found in sites dating to the settlement period, become frequently discovered artifacts in both household contexts as well as in graves. A group of burials found in southern Iceland that date to the Sturlunga period show clear evidence of violence (Byock and Walker 2003). One individual showed trauma to the head consistent with an axe blow that cut the top part of the skull in half. Pathological evidence suggests this was accomplished through two separate axe blows to the head, one from the front and one from behind. Another individual had a smashed skull resulting from a blunt force. Perhaps even more telling than the fatal wounds exhibited through the skeletal remains is how these individuals were buried. The group was placed in one large pit, with large stones positioned on the chests of each individual. This practice is commonplace in northern Europe and is often associated with a wrongful death and the fear of an angry soul rising up and seeking retribution. The violence of the Sturlunga Period was no doubt the mechanism used by chiefs to eliminate competition over land, prestige goods, and even more crucially, alliances. Beginning by the late 11th century CE, a process of consolidation in the number of chiefs sets in motion the emergence of the *stórgoðar* ('super chiefs'). No farmer was safe from their perdition, as these 'super chiefs' rapidly gobbled up the landscape, turning landowners into tenants and demanding tax payments.

While evidence from the settlement period suggests that leveling mechanisms would have curtailed the behavior of a super chief, archaeological evidence from the Sturlunga period suggests a society unable to thwart the ambitions of this new class of chiefs. Archaeologically, we find for the first time defensive wall constructions around large estates as well as a clear differentiation in size between the farmstead of a chieftain and that of an independent farmer, representing the beginnings of a manorial society. Chiefly households are not only larger, but they also demonstrate a division of space, with restricted access to some of the rooms as well a portion of the household devoted to specific economic activities, such as wool processing and the entrepreneurial production of cloth. The multihousehold farmsteads that once shared agricultural lands are replaced by single-family farmsteads indicating that communal land ownership was replaced with a concept of private or corporate-owned property during this period (Vésteinsson 2000: 169; 2005).

With a broader social context in place, let us now return to the issue of the status of women in the Sturlunga period. Weaving was the occupation of women, and given the high social and economic value assigned to cloth, one might expect the status of women to steadily rise along with the value of homespun. However, from the Grágás, we learn that while women may have been the primary producers of cloth, they were not the primary merchants and traders of their products; men became the brokers and public persona of the cloth industry. The Grágás (K §152) collaborates with this image of women being assigned to the household: 'When a man and a wife are in wedlock, he shall have charge of their property and all buying and selling. It is not required of a wife that she should own a share in the household, but if she has a share in the household with him, then she is to run the indoor household as she wishes and the dairying'. The Grágás (K §153) also state that: 'A woman is not permitted to sell goods at the assembly (marketplace), unless it involves joint money matters and her husband is unable to attend the assembly and has given her his permission to stand in his place. A woman can only buy household necessities if her husband is at the assembly'. Further, the Grágás (K §248) restrict a woman's ability to go on merchant voyages to Norway by enforcing: 'A woman can travel to Norway only if she is accompanied by her husband, father, brother, or son and if she pays three marks (Norwegian currency)'. Through ethnographic comparisons of chiefdom societies, one can suggest this pattern reflects an attempt commonly made by chiefs to regulate the redistribution of prestige goods, or in this case, to regulate the medium of exchange and transfer of cloth for prestige goods (Earle 1978: 19). Within a household, however, we might expect that women would have held considerable sway over the ambitions of her husband since she provided him with the social and economic currency of cloth that would dictate his ability to participate in the political economy. The Contemporary Sagas are woefully silent on the attitude toward women as weavers; however, Sturlunga saga does report some fifty cases of marriage, with wives often praised for their ability to suitably run the household (Damsholt 1984: 76; Jochens 1995: 153). We can therefore suggest that while women in the 11th century CE may not have enjoyed the public power of Aud, they did enjoy a considerable power over their own households. A woman could not only set the pace and tempo of the household economy, her labor and skill as a weaver were also an integral component of commensality and politics, since it was her cloth that provided men with the ability to finance the feasts necessary to broker alliances. Thus, while women may have been regulated to a more peripheral position in society, they wove not just cloth, but the social fabric that held Medieval Iceland together.

Taken together, we would posit that a clear shift in social structure is underway during the Sturlunga Period, as can be demonstrated through an increasingly complex set of marriage regulations, concerns over property rights, a shift in agricultural productivity, increased violence, the construction of larger and divided households, and the possible emergence of craft specialization.

Concluding Remarks

This paper began with a plea: a call to use the maximalist–minimalist dialogue productively, rather than to continue the onslaught of name-calling, jabs at professionalism, and attacks on personal credibility. Our aim has been to show that by framing the debate as a methodological issue, and by addressing the challenges raised, one can begin to sneak a meaningful glimpse of ancient societies. The applicability of the approach presented here is not confined to Biblical and Saga studies but can in fact be used in a broad range of social, geographical, and temporal contexts because the methodology centers on the reconstruction of a historical reality for past societies rather than on separating text and material records into opposing camps, where one record is correct while the other is a best misleading and at worst a lie. We have shown how the reticence among some Saga historians to treat the Family and Contemporary Sagas as distinct representations of historical periods within Iceland need not lead to a consensus that since the Family Sagas were written concurrently with the Contemporary Sagas both must solely reflect the psyche of 13th- and 14th-century Saga writers. The approach taken in this paper has demonstrated that the problem with debates focused on saga historicity is not the suggestion that a 13th-century ethos can or cannot be detected in the texts purporting to report on the 9th century; the problem arises from the creation of a false dichotomization of text and the archaeological record whereby one is *more* truthful than the other.

Our discussion on some of the events described in the Bible and the Sagas clearly reveals that these texts can at times both contradict and collaborate with the archaeological record, but we should not conclude from this disparity that the best course of action is simply to treat these datasets separately. The utility of an anthropological approach is that texts and the material record is that we need not nor should not expect these datasets to jibe perfectly but should instead focus on the interplay between the two. The space where text and the archaeological record intersect can be an insightful way to situate the past by allowing us to move our research and debates in new and more fertile directions.

Acknowledgments

Much of the research for this paper was done with the support of a Fulbright Dissertation Grant in Archaeology (Carter 2006–2007). The authors would like to thank Richard Elliott Friedman of the

University of Georgia, Athens, and William H.C. Propp of the University of California, San Diego, Gunnar Karlsson of the University of Iceland, and Ragnheiður Traustadóttir of Hólar University for their comments and suggestions. The authors, however, accept full responsibility for the views expressed here.

References

Aðalsteinsson, Stefán (1990) Importance of Sheep in Early Icelandic Agriculture. *Acta Archaeologica* 61: 285-91.

Adams, Robert Mccormick (1981) *Heartland of Cities: Surveys of Ancient Settlement and Land Use on the Central Floodplain of the Euphrates* (Chicago: University of Chicago Press).

—(1996) *Paths of Fire: An Anthropological Inquiry into Western Technology* (Princeton: Princeton University Press).

Ahlström, Gösta W. (1991) The Role of Archaeological and Literary Remains in Reconstructing Israel's History. In Edelman 1991: 116-42.

Alcock, Susan (2002) *Archaeologies of the Greek Past: Landscape, Monuments, and Memories* (New York: Cambridge University Press).

Algaze, Guillermo (1989) The Uruk Expansion. *CA* 30/5: 571-608.

—(1993) Expansionary Dynamics of Some Early Pristine States. *American Anthropologist* 95/2: 304-33.

—(2005) *The Uruk World System: The Dynamics of Expansion of Early Mesopotamian Civilization* (Chicago: University of Chicago Press).

Amorosi, Thomas (1992) Climate Impact and Human Response in Northeast Iceland: Archaeological Investigations at Svalbarð, 1986–1988. In Morris and Rackham 1992: 103-38.

Amorosi, Thomas, Paul Buckland, Andrew Dugmore, Jon Ingimundarson, and Thomas McGovern (1997) Raiding the Landscape: Human Impact in Scandinavian North Atlantic. *Human Ecology* 25/3: 491-518.

Anderson, Theodore, and William Ian Miller (1989) *Law and Literature in Medieval Iceland: Ljósvetninga Saga and Valla-Ljóts Saga* (Stanford: Stanford University Press).

Ando, Clifford (2000) *Imperial Ideology and Provincial Loyalty in the Roman Empire* (Berkeley: University of California Press).

Ankersmit, F. (1989) Historiography and Postmodernism. *History and Theory* 28: 137-53.

Avigad, N. (1972) Two Hebrew Inscriptions on Wine-Jars. *IEJ* 22: 1-9.

Avigad, N., and B. Sass (1997) *Corpus of West Semitic Stamp Seals* (Jerusalem: The Israel Academy of Sciences and Humanities, Israel Exploration Society, and The Institute of Archaeology, The Hebrew University).

Bachrach, Bernard, and David Nicholas (1989) *Law, Custom, and the Social Fabric in Medieval Europe* (Kalamazoo: Western Michigan University Press).

Bagge, Sverre (1992) From Sagas to Society: The Case of Heimskringla. In Pálsson 1992: 61-75.

Baker, David, V. Phillip Long, and Gordon Wenham (eds.) (2002) *Window into Old Testament History: Evidence, Argument, and the Crisis of 'Biblical Israel'* (Grand Rapids: Eerdmans): 111-30.

Barstad, Hans (1997) History and the Hebrew Bible. In Grabbe 1992: 37-64.

Binford, S.R., and L.R. Binford (eds.) (1968) *New Perspectives in Archaeology* (Chicago: Aldine).

Biran, A., and J. Naveh (1993) An Aramaic Stele Fragment from Tel Dan. *IEJ* 43: 81-98.

Blenkinsopp, Joseph (1992) *The Pentateuch: An Introduction to the First Five Books of the Bible* (New York: Doubleday).

Bloch-Smith, E (1992) *Judahite Burial Practices and Beliefs about the Dead* (Sheffield: JSOT Press).

Bruins, H.J., J. van der Plicht, and A. Mazar (2003) C-14 Dates from Tel Rehov: Iron-age Chronology, Pharaohs, and Hebrew Kings. *Science* 300: 315-18.

Brumfield, Elizabeth (2003) It's a Material World: History, Artifacts, and Anthropology. *ARA* 32: 205-23.

Buckland, Paul C. (2000) The North Atlantic Environment. In Fitzhugh and Ward 2000: 146-53.

Buckland, Paul C., Jon P. Sadler, and Guðrún Sveinbjarnardóttir (1992) Palaeoecological Investigations at Reykholt, Western Iceland. In Morris and Rackham 1992: 149-68.

Buckland, P., A. Dugmore, D. Perry, D. Savory, and G. Sveinbjarnardóttir (1990) Holt in Eyjafjallasveit, Iceland: A Paleoecological Study of the Impact of Landnám. *Acta Archaeologica* 61: 252-71.

Byock, Jesse (1988) *Medieval Iceland* (Berkeley: University of California Press).

—(1992) History and the Sagas: The Effect of Nationalism. In Pálsson 1992: 43-59.

—(2001) *Viking Age Iceland* (London: Penguin).

Byock, Jesse, and Phil Walker (2003) A Viking Age Farm, Church, and Cemetery at Hrísbrú, Mosfell Valley, Iceland. *Antiquity* 77(297): Project Gallery (http://antiquity.ac.uk/projgall/erlandson/erlandson.html).

Carter, Tara D. (2003) *Land Productivity and Social Collapse in Medieval Iceland* (M.A. thesis, California State University, Northridge).

—(n.d.) On the Edge of the Norse World: Economy and Secondary State Formation in Iceland (Ph.D. diss., in progress, University of California, San Diego).

Castells, M. (2000a) *The Rise of the Network Society*. Vol. 1, *The Information Age: Economy, Society and Culture* (2nd edn; Malden, MA: Blackwell).

—(2000b) *The Power of Identity*. Vol. 2, *The Information Age: Economy, Society and Culture* (Malden, MA: Blackwell).

—(2000c) *End of Millennium*. Vol. 3, *The Information Age: Economy, Society and Culture* (Malden, MA: Blackwell).

Chase-Dunn, C., and T.D. Hall (1997) *Rise and Demise: Comparing World-Systems* (Boulder: Westview Press).

Clines, David J.A. (1993) A World Established on Water (Psalm 24): Reader-Response, Deconstruction and Bespoke Interpretation. In Exum and Clines 1993: 79-90.

Clines, David J.A., and J. Cheryl Exum (1993) The New Literary Criticism. In Exum and Clines 1993: 11-25.

Clover, Carol (1982) *The Medieval Saga* (Ithaca: Cornell University Press).

—(1985) Icelandic Family Sagas (Íslendingasögur). In *Old Norse-Icelandic Literature: A Critical Guide*, edited by Carol Clover and John Lindow (Ithaca: Cornell University Press): 239-315.

Cohen, Abner (1971) Cultural Strategies in the Organization of Trading Diasporas. In *The Development of Indigenous Trade and Markets in West Africa*, edited by C. Meillassoux (London: Oxford University Press): 266-81.

Crabtree, Pam (1996) The Wool Trade and the Rise of Urbanism in Middle Saxon England. In *Craft Specialization and Social Evolution: In Memory of V. Gordon Childe*, edited by Bernard Wailes (Philadelphia: University of Pennsylvania Press): 99-105.

Cross, F.M. (1995) *The Ancient Library of Qumran* (3rd edn; Sheffield: Sheffield Academic Press).

Currid, John (1999) *Doing Archaeology in the Land of the Bible: A Basic Guide* (Grand Rapids: Baker Books).

Curtain, Philip (1984) *Cross-Cultural Trade in World History* (Cambridge: Cambridge University Press).

Damsholt, Nanna (1984) The Role of Icelandic Women in the Sagas and in the Role of the Production of Homespun Cloth. *Scandinavian Journal of History* 9/2: 75-90.

Davies, Philip (1992) *In Search of 'Ancient Israel'* (Sheffield: Sheffield Academic Press).

—(1995) *Whose Bible is it Anyway?* (Sheffield: Sheffield Academic Press).

—(1997) Whose History? Whose Israel? Whose Bible? Biblical Histories, Ancient and Modern. In Grabbe 1992: 104-22.

Davies, P.R., G.J. Brooke, and P.R. Callaway (2002) *The Complete World of the Dead Sea Scrolls* (London: Thames & Hudson).

Dennis, Andrew, Peter Foote, and Richard Perkins (1980) Introduction. In Dennis, Foote, and Perkins 1980: vii-xii.

Derrida, Jacques (1973) *Speech and Phenomena, and Other Essays on Husserl's Theory of Signs*, translated by David Allison (Evanston: Northwestern University Press).

Dever, William (1990) Of Myths and Methods. *BASOR* 277-78: 121-30.

—(1991) Archaeology, Material Culture and the Early Monarchical Period in Israel. In Edelman 1991: 103-15.

—(1995a) Will the Real Israel Please Stand Up? Part I. Archaeology and Israelite Historiography. *BASOR* 297: 61-80.

—(1995b) Will the Real Israel Please Stand Up? Part II: Archaeology and the Religions of Ancient Israel. *BASOR* 298: 37-58.

—(1997) Archaeology and the Age of Solomon: A Case Study in Archaeology and Historiograph. In *The Age of Solomon*, edited by Lowell K. Handy (Leiden: Brill): 217-51.

—(1999) Archaeology and the Ancient Israelite Cult: How the Kh. el-Qôm and Kuntillet 'Ajrûd 'Asherah' Texts have Changed the Picture. *Eretz-Israel* 26: 9-15.

—(2001) *What did the Biblical Writers Know and When Did they Know It? What Archaeology Can Tell Us about the Reality of Ancient Israel* (Grand Rapids: Eerdmans).

—(2003) *Who Were the Early Israelites and Where Did They Come From?* (Grand Rapids: Eerdmans).

Dever, William, Niels Peter Lemche, P. Kyle McCarter, and Thomas Thompson (1997) Biblical Minimalists Face their Challengers. *BAR* 23/4: 26-42, 66.

Drane, John (2000) *Introducing the Old Testament* (Oxford: Lion Publishing).

Dugmore, Andrew, and Paul Buckland (1991) Tephrochronology and Late Holocene Soil Erosion in South Iceland. In Maizels and Caseldine 1991: 147-60.

Durrenberger, E. Paul (1990a) Production in Medieval Iceland. *Acta Archaeologica* 61: 14-21.

—(1990b) Text and Transaction in Commonwealth Iceland. *Ethnos* 55(I-II): 74-91.

—(1992) *The Dynamics of Medieval Iceland* (Iowa City: University of Iowa Press).

Earle, Timothy (1978) *Economic and Social Organization of a Complex Chiefdom: The Halelea District, Kaua'i, Hawaii* (Ann Arbor: University of Michigan, Museum of Anthropology).

Edelman, Diana Vikander (1991) Doing History in Biblical Studies. In Edelman 1991: 13-25.

—(1993) *The New Literary Criticism and the Hebrew Bible* (Valley Forge: Trinity Press International).

Edelman, Diana Vikander (ed.) (1991) *The Fabric of History: Text, Artifact and Israel's Past* (Sheffield: Sheffield Academic Press).

Einarsson, Bjarni (1994) *The Settlement of Iceland: A Critical Approach* (Granastaðir and the Ecological Heritage, Gotarc, Series B; Gothenburg: Gothenburg University, Department of Anthropology).

Exum, J. Cheryl, and David J.A. Clines (eds.) (1993) *The New Literary Criticism and the Hebrew Bible* (Valley Forge: Trinity Press International)

Finkelstein, Israel (1996) Ethnicity and Origin of the Iron I Settlers in the Highlands of Canaan: Can the Real Israel Stand Up? *BA* 59: 198-212.

—(1998) *The Archaeology of Israelite Settlement* (Jerusalem: Israel Exploration Society).

Finkelstein, Israel, and E. Piasetzky (2003) Comment on 14C Dates from Tel Rehov: Iron Age Chronology, Pharaohs, and Hebrew Kings. *Science* 302: 568b.

Finkelstein, Israel, and Neil Asher Silberman (2001) *The Bible Unearthed: Archaeology's New Vision of Ancient Israel and the Origin of its Sacred Texts* (New York: Free Press).

—(2002) The Bible Unearthed: A Rejoinder. *BASOR* 327: 63-73.

—(2006) *David and Solomon: In Search of the Bible's Sacred Kings and the Roots of Western Tradition* (New York: Free Press).

Finlay, Alison (1997) Kings and Icelanders in Poet's Sagas and Þættir. In *Sagas and the Norwegian Experience* (reprints from the 10th International Saga Conference, Trondheim: Center for Middelalderstuder, NTNU): 159-68.

Fitzhugh, William, and Elisabeth I. Ward (eds.) (2000) *Vikings: The North Atlantic Saga* (Washington: Smithsonian Institution Press).

Forte, Angelo, Richard Oram, and Frederik Pedersen (2005) *Viking Empires* (Cambridge: Cambridge University Press).

Foucault, Michel (1977) *Discipline and Punish: The Birth of the Prison*, translated by Alan Sheridan (New York: Pantheon Books).

—(1978) *The History of Sexuality*, translated by Robert Hurley (New York: Pantheon Books).

Frank, Roberta (1973) Marriage in the Twelfth and Thirteenth Century Iceland. *VIATOR* 4: 473-84.

Freedman, D.N. (1980) *Pottery, Poetry, and Prophecy: Studies in Early Hebrew Poetry* (Winona Lake, IN: Eisenbrauns).

Friedman, R.E. (1988) *Who Wrote the Bible?* (London: Jonathan Cape).

Friðriksson, Adolf (1994) *Sagas and Popular Antiquarianism in Icelandic Archaeology* (Avebury: Ashgate Publishing).

Friðriksson, Adolf, and Orri Vésteinsson (2003) Creating a Past: A Historiography of the Settlement of Iceland. In *Contact, Continuity, and Collapse: The Norse Colonization of the North Atlantic*, edited by James Barrett (Turnhout: Brepols): 139-61.

Friðriksson, Sturla (1972) Grass and Grass Utilization in Iceland. *Ecology* 53/5: 785-96.

Gaskins, Richard (1998) Visions of Sovereignty in Snorri Sturlusson's *Heimskringla*. *Scandinavian Journal of History* 23(3-4): 173-88.

Geertz, Clifford (1973) *The Interpretation of Cultures: Selected Essays* (New York: Basic Books).

Gelinas, Margaret M. (1995) United Monarchy—Divided Monarchy: Fact or Fiction? In *The Pitcher is Broken*, edited by Steven Holloway and Lowell Handy (JSOTSup 190; Sheffield: Sheffield Academic Press): 227-37.

Gelsinger, Bruce E. (1981) *Icelandic Enterprise: Commerce and Economy in the Middle Ages* (Columbia: University of South Carolina Press).

Gestsdóttir, Hildur (1998) The Palaeopathological Diagnosis of Nutritional Disease: A Study of the Skeletal Material from Skeljastaðir, Iceland (M.A. Thesis, University of Bradford).

Goody, Jack (1986) *The Logic of Writing and the Organization of Society* (Cambridge: Cambridge University Press).

—(2000) *The Power of the Written Tradition* (Washington, DC: Smithsonian).

Grabbe, Lester L. (1997) Are Historians of Ancient Palestine Fellow Creatures—or Different Animals? In Grabbe 1997: 19-36.

Grabbe, Lester L. (ed.) (1997) *Can a History of Israel Be Written?* (Sheffield: Sheffield Academic Press).

Grágás (1980) *The Codex Regius of Grágás: Laws of Early Iceland*, vol. I, translated by Andrew Dennis, Peter Foote, and Richard Perkins (Winnipeg: University of Manitoba Press).

—(2000) *The Codex Regius of Grágás: Laws of Early Iceland*, vol. 2, translated by Andrew Dennis, Peter Foote, and Richard Perkins (Winnipeg: University of Manitoba Press).

Graham-Campbell, James (2001) *The Viking World* (London: Frances Lincoln).

Grettir's Saga (2005) Translated by Bernard Scudder (London: Penguin Press).

Grierson, Philip (1959) Commerce in the Dark Ages: A Critique of the Evidence. *Transactions of the Royal Historical Society* 9: 123-40.

Guðbergsson, Grétar (1975) Myndun Móajarðvegs í Skagafirði. *Íslenzkar landbúnaðar rannsóknir (Journal of Agricultural Research in Iceland)* 7: 20-45.

—(1996) Ì norðlenskri vist. Um gróður, jarðveg, búskaparlög og sögu. *Íslenzkar landbúnaðar rannsóknir* 10: 31-89.

Hallsdóttir, Margrét (1987) *Pollen Analytical Studies of Human Influence on Vegetation in Relation to the Landnám Tephra Layer in Southwest Iceland* (Lundqua Thesis 18; Lund: Lund University, Department of Quaternary Geology).

Halpern, Baruch (1988) *The First Historians: The Hebrew Bible and History* (San Francisco: Harper & Row).

—(1995) Erasing History: The Minimalist Assault on Ancient Israel. *Bible Review* 11/6: 26-35, 47.

—(1996) How Golden IS the Marshalltown, How Holy the Scripture? *The Jewish Quarterly Review* 87/1-2: 131-45.

Hanks, W.F. (1989) Text and Textuality. *ARA* 18: 95-127.

Hansen, Steffen Stummann (2001) Settlement Archaeology in Iceland: The Race for the Pan-Scandinavian Project in 1939. *Acta Archaeologica* 72/2: 115-27.

Hasel, M.G. (2003) Merenptah's Inscription and Reliefs and the Origins of Israel. In *The Near East in the Southwest: Essays in Honor of William G. Dever*, edited by B. Alpert Nakhai (Boston: American Schools of Oriental Research): 19-44.

Hastrup, Kirsten (1985) *Culture and History in Medieval Iceland: An Anthropological Analysis of Structure and Change* (Oxford: Clarendon Press).

—(1990) *Island of Anthropology: Studies in Past & Present Iceland* (Odense: Odense University Press).

—(1992) Uchronia and the Two Histories of Iceland, 1400–1800. In *Other Histories*, edited by Kirsten Hastrup (London: Rutledge): 102-20.

—(2004) Destined to Defeat: Old Icelandic Commercial Problems. In *Assyria and Beyond: Studies Presented to Mogens Trolle Larsen*, edited by J.G. Dercksen (Leiden: Nederlands Instituut Voor Het Nabije Oosten): 269-80.

Haywood, John (1995) *The Penguin Historical Atlas of the Vikings* (London: Penguin Press).

Heimskringla. [Snorri Sturlusson] (1979), translated by Bjarni Aðalbjarnarson (Reykjavík: Hið Íslenzka Fornritafélag).

Herschend, Frands (1994) Models of Petty Rulership: Two Early Settlements in Iceland. *TOR* 26: 163-91.

Hess, Richard (2002) Literacy in Iron Age Israel. In Baker, Phillip Long, and Wenham 2002: 82-102.

Heusler, Andreas (1908) *Die gelehrte Urgeschichte im isländischen Schrifttum* (Abhandlugen der Preußischen Akademie der Wissenschaften, Phil.-hist. Klasse 3; Berlin: Königl. Akademie der Wissenschaften).

—(1914) *Die Anfänge der isländischen Saga* (Abhandlugen der Preußischen Akademie der Wissenschaften, Phil.-hist. Klasse 9; Berlin: Königl. Akademie der Wissenschaften).

Hjálmarsson, Jón R. (1993) *History of Iceland: From Settlement to the Present Day* (Reykjavík: Iceland Review Press).

Hobsbawm, Eric, and Terrence Ranger (eds.) (1983) *The Invention of Tradition* (Cambridge: Cambridge University Press).

Hodges, Richard, and David Whitehouse (1983) *Mohammed, Charlemagne, and the Origins of Europe* (London: Duckworth Press).

Hopkins, Terence, and Immanuel Wallerstein (1982) *World-Systems Analysis: Theory and Methodology* (Beverly Hills: Sage Publications).

Hymes, Dell (1972) Models of the Interaction of Language and Social Life. In *Directions in Sociolinguistics: The Ethnography of Communication*, edited by John Gumperz and Dell Hymes (New York: Holt, Rinehart & Winston): 35-71.

Ingimundarson, Jón Haukur (1992) Spinning Goods and Tales: Market, Subsistence and Literary Productions. In Pálsson 1992: 217-30.

—(1995) Of Sagas and Sheep: Toward a Historical Anthropology of Social Change and Production for Market, Subsistence and Tribute in Early Iceland (10th to the 13th Century) (Ph.D. dissertation, University of Arizona).

Ingstad, Anne (1985) *The Norse Discovery of America*, translated by Elizabeth Seeberg (Oslo: Norwegian University Press).

Íslendingabók—The Book of the Icelanders [Ari Þorgilsson] (1980), translated by A. Boucher (Reykjavík: Iceland Review Saga Series).

Jesch, Judith (1991) *Women in the Viking Age* (Woodbridge: Boydell Press).

Jochens, Jenny (1980) The Church and Sexuality in Medieval Iceland. *Journal of Medieval History* 6: 377-92.

—(1986a) Consent in Marriage: Old Norse Law, Life, and Literature. *Scandinavian Studies* 58/2: 142-76.

—(1986b) The Medieval Icelandic Heroine: Fact or Fiction? *VIATOR* 17: 35-50.

—(1991) The Illicit Love Visit: An Archaeology of Old Norse Sexuality. *Journal of the History of Sexuality* 1/3: 357-92.

—(1993) Með Jákæði Hennar Sjálfrar: Consent as a Signifier in the Old Norse World. In *Consent and Coercion to Sex and Marriage in Ancient and Medieval Societies*, edited by Angeliki Laiou (Washington, DC: Dumbarton Oaks): 271-88.

—(1995) *Women in Old Norse Society* (Ithaca: Cornell University Press).

Jóhannesson, Jón (1974) *A History of the Old Icelandic Commonwealth: Íselendinga Saga*, translated by Haraldur Besson (Winnipeg: University of Manitoba Press).

Júlíusson, Árni Daníel (2000) The Environmental Effects of Icelandic Subsistence Farming in the Late Middle Ages and the Early Modern Period. In Sigurðsson and Skaptason 2000: 279-88.

Junker, Laura L. (1999) *Raiding, Trading, and Feasting: The Political Economy of Philippine Chiefdoms* (Honolulu: University of Hawaii Press).

Karlsson, Gunnar (2000) *Iceland's 1100 Years: A History of a Marginal Society* (Reykjavík: Mál og Menning Press).

Karras, Ruth Mazo (1988) *Slavery and Society in Medieval Scandinavia* (New Haven: Yale University Press).

—(1992) Servitude and Sexuality in Medieval Iceland. In Pálsson 1992: 289-304.

Kellogg, Robert (2000) Introduction. In *The Sagas of Icelanders: A Selection*, edited by R. Kellogg (New York: Viking Press): xv-lvii.

King, Philip, and Lawrence Stager (2001) *Life in Biblical Israel* (Louisville: Westminster John Knox Press).

Kitchen, Kenneth (2002) The Controlling Role of External Evidence in Assessing the Historical Status of the Israelite United Monarchy. In Baker, Phillip Long, and Wenham 2002: 111-30.

Knauf, Ernst Axel (1991) From History to Interpretation. In Edelman 1991: 26-64.

Kofoed, Jen Bruun (2002) Epistemology, Historiographical Method, and the Copenhagen School. In Baker, Phillip Long, and Wenham 2002: 23-43.

Kuznar, Lawrence (1997) *Reclaiming a Scientific Anthropology* (Walnut Creek: Altamira).

LaBianca, O., and S. Arnold Scham (eds.) (2005) *Connectivity in Antiquity—Globalization as a Long Term Historical Process* (Approaches in Anthropological Archaeology; London: Equinox).

Landnámabók—*The Book of Settlements* [Ari Þorgilsson] (1972), translated by H. Pálsson and P. Edwards (Winnipeg: University of Manitoba Press).

Laughlin, John (2000) *Archaeology and the Bible* (London: Routledge).

Laxdœla saga (1964), translated by A. Margaret Arent (Seattle: University of Washington Press).

Laxness, Halldór (1968) *Christianity at Glacier,* translated by Magnus Magnusson (Reykjavik: Helgafell).

Lemche, Niels Peter (1998) *The Israelites in History and Tradition* (Louisville: Westminster John Knox Press).

Levy, Thomas E. (ed.) (1995) *The Archaeology of Society in the Holy Land* (London: Leicester University Press).

Levy, T.E., and T. Higham (eds.) (2005) *The Bible and Radiocarbon Dating: Archaeology, Text and Science* (London: Equinox).

Levy, T.E., T. Higham, C. Bronk Ramsey, N.G. Smith, E. Ben-Yosef, M. Robinson, S. Munnger, K. Knabb, J. Schulze, P.M. Najjar, and L. Tauxe (2008) High-precision Radiocarbon Dating and Historical Biblical Archaeology in Southern Jordan. *Proceedings of the National Academy of Sciences* 105: 16460-65.

Lightfoot, Kent (1995) Culture Contact Studies: Redefining the Relationship between Prehistoric and Historic Archaeology. *AmAnt* 60/2: 199-217.

Lopez, Robert (1976) *The Commercial Revolution of the Middle Ages, 950–1350* (Cambridge: Cambridge University Press).

Maizels, J.K., and C. Caseldine (eds.) (1991) *Environmental Change in Iceland: Past and Present* (Netherlands: Kluwer Academic Publishers).

Marx, Karl (1981 [1852]) *The Eighteenth Brumaire of Louis Bonaparte* (New York: International Publishers).

Mazar, Amihai (1990) *Archaeology of the Land of the Bible, 10,000–586 B.C.E.* (New York: Doubleday).

McGovern, Thomas H. (1990) The Archaeology of the Norse North Atlantic. *ARA* 19: 331-51.

McGovern, T., G. Bigelow, T. Amorosi, and D. Russell (1988) Northern Islands, Human Error, and Environmental Degradation: A View of Social and Ecological Change in the Medieval North Atlantic. *Human Ecology* 16/3: 225-70.

McTurk, Rory (ed.) (2005) *A Companion to Old Norse-Icelandic Literature and Culture* (Oxford: Blackwell).

Meskell, Lynn (2003) Memory's Materiality: Ancestral Presence, Commemorative Practice and Disjunctive Locales. In Van Dyke and Alcock 2003: 34-55.

Miller, J. Maxwell (1974) The Moabite Stone as a Memorial Stele. *PEQ* 106: 9-18.

—(1993) Reading the Bible Historically: The Historian's Approach. In *To Each its Own: An Introduction to Biblical Criticisms and their Application,* edited by Steven Mckenzie and Stephen Haynes (Louisville: Westminster John Knox Press): 17-34.

Miller, William Ian (1983) Choosing the Avenger: Some Aspects of the Bloodfeud in Medieval Iceland and England. *Law and History Review* 1/2: 159-204.

—(1986) Gift, Sale, Payment, Raid: Case Studies in the Negotiation and Classification of Exchange in Medieval Iceland. *Speculum* 61.

—(1990) *Bloodtaking and Peacemaking: Feud, Law, and Society in Saga Iceland* (Chicago: University of Chicago Press).

Moore, R.I. (2000) *The First European Revolution, c. 970–1215* (Oxford: Blackwell).

Moorey, P.R.S. (1991) *A Century of Biblical Archaeology* (Louisville: Westminster John Knox Press).

Moreland, John (2001) *Archaeology and Text* (London: Duckworth).

Morris, Christopher, and D. James Rackham (eds.) (1992) *Norse and Later Settlement and Subsistence in the North Atlantic* (Glasgow: University of Glasgow Press).

Niditch, Susan (1996) *Oral World and Written Word* (Louisville: Westminster John Knox Press).

Njal's Saga (2000), translated by Robert Cook (London: Penguin Books).

Nordal, Sigurður (1940) *Hrafnkatla* (Studia Islandica 7; Reykjavik: H.Í.).

—(1953) Sagalitteraturen. *Nordisk kultur* 8b: 180-273.

North, Douglass C. (1982) *Structure and Change in Economic History* (New York: W.W. Norton & Co.).

—(1990) *Institutions, Institutional Change and Economic Performance* (Cambridge: Cambridge University Press).

Oates, Joan (1993) Trade and Power in the Fifth and Fourth Millennia BC: New Evidence from Northern Mesopotamia. *World Archaeology* 24/3: 403-22.

Ogilvie, Astrid E.J. (1984a) The Impact of Climate on Grass Grown and Hay Yield in Iceland: 1601 to 1780. In *Climatic Changes on a Yearly to Millennial Basis*, edited by N. Mörner and W. Karlén (Dordrecht: D. Reidel Publishing): 349-52.

—(1984b) The Past Climate and Sea-Ice Record from Iceland, Part I: Data to A.D. 1780. *Climatic Change* 6: 131-52.

—(1990) Climatic Changes in Iceland A.D. c. 865 to 1598. *Acta Archaeologica* 61: 233-51.

—(2000) Climate and Farming in Northern Iceland, ca. 1700–1850. In Sigurðsson and Skaptason 2000: 289-99.

Ólason, Vésteinn (1998) *Dialogues with the Viking Age* (Reykjavík: Heimskingla Press).

—(2005) Family Sagas. In McTurk 2005: 101-18.

Ong, Walter (1982) *Orality and Literacy: The Technologizing of the Word* (London: Routledge).

Orser, C.E. (1998) The Archaeology of African Diaspora. *ARA* 27: 63-82.

Pálsson, Gísli (1992) *Beyond Boundaries: Understanding, Translation and Anthropological Discourse* (Oxford: Berg).

—(1995) *The Textual Life of Savants* (Chur: Harwood Academic).

Pálsson, Gísli (ed.) (1992) *From Sagas to Society: Comparative Approaches to Early Iceland* (Middlesex: Hisarlik Press).

Pálsson, Hermann, and Paul Edwards (1972) Introduction to the *Landnámabók*. In *Landnámabók* 1972: 1-13.

Paynter, R. (2000) Historical and Anthropological Archaeology: Forging Alliances. *Journal of Archaeological Research* 8/1: 1-37.

Perdikaris, Sophia (1999) From Chiefly Provisioning to Commercial Fishery: Long-Term Economic Change in Arctic Norway. *World Archaeology* 30/3: 388-402.

Perdikaris, Sophia, and Thomas H. Mcgovern (2007) Chieftains, Cod Fish, and Walrus: Intensification in the North Atlantic. In *Seeking a Richer Harvest: The Archaeology of Subsistence, Intensification, and Change*, edited by Tina Thurston and Christopher Fisher (New York: Springer Science Press): 193-218.

Pirenne, Henri (1954) *Mohammed and Charlemagne* (London: George Allen Press).

Þorláksson, Helgi (1992) Social Ideals and the Concept of Profit in Thirteenth-Century Iceland. In Pálsson 1992: 231-45.

Price, Barbara (1977) Shifts in Production and Organization: A Cluster Interaction Model. *CA* 18/2: 209-33.

—(1984) Competition Productive Intensification and Ranked Society: Speculations from Evolutionary Theory. In *Warfare, Culture, and Environment*, edited by R. Brain Fergusson (Orlando: Academic Press): 209-40.

Propp, W.H.C. (1999) *Exodus 1–18: A New Translation with Introduction and Commentary* (New York: Doubleday).

Quinn, Judy (2000) From Orality to Literacy in Medieval Iceland. In Ross 2000: 30-60.

Rabinow, Paul (1983) *The Foucault Reader* (New York: Pantheon Books).

Renfrew, C., and P. Bahn (2004) *Archaeology: Theories, Methods, and Practice* (4th edn; New York: Thames & Hudson).

Robertshaw, Peter (2000) Sibling Rivalry? The Intersection of Archaeology and History. *History in Africa* 27: 261-86.

Robinson, E. (1867) *Biblical Researches in Palestine and Adjacent Regions* (1970 edn; London: J. Murray [reprint Jerusalem: Universitas]).

Roediger, H.L., and L.M. Goff (1998) Memory. In *A Companion to Cognitive Science*, edited by W. Bechtel and G. Graham (Oxford: Blackwell Press): 250-64.

Rosedahl, Else (1998 [1987]). *The Vikings* (2nd rev. edn; London: Penguin Books).

—(2005) Walrus Ivory: Demand, Supply, Workshops, and Greenland. In *Viking and Norse in the North Atlantic: Select Papers from the Proceedings of the 14th Viking Congress, Tórshavn 2001*, edited by Andras Mortensen and Símun (Annales Societatis Scientarium Faeroensis Supplementa 44; Tóshavn: Societatis Scientarium Faeroensis): 182-91.

—(2007) Walrus Ivory: On the Function and Economic Importance of Walrus Ivory around AD 900. In *A Late 9th-century Account of Voyages Along the Coasts of Norway and Denmark and its Cultural Context*, edited by Janet Bately and Anton Englert (Roskilde: The Viking Ship Museum in Roskilde Press): 92-93.

Ross, Margaret Clunies (ed.) (2000) *Old Icelandic Literature and Society* (Cambridge: Cambridge University Press).

Saussure, Ferdinand (1959) *Course in General Linguistics*, translated by Wade Baskin (New York: McGraw-Hill).

Sawyer, Birgit (1988) *Property and Inheritance in Viking Scandinavia: The Runic Evidence* (Occasional Papers on Medieval Topics 2; Alingsås, Sweden: Viktoria Bokförlag).

Sawyer, Peter (2001) *The Oxford Illustrated History of the Vikings* (Oxford: Oxford University Press).

Schacter, Daniel (1996) *Searching for Memory: The Brain, the Mind, and the Past* (New York: Basic Books).

Sigurbjörnsson, Björn (2000) Farming: Introduction. In Sigurðsson and Skaptason 2000: 102-25.

Sigurðsson, Gísli (2004) *The Medieval Icelandic Saga and Oral Tradition: A Discourse on Method* (Cambridge, MA: Harvard University Press).

Sigurðsson, Ingi, and Jón Skaptason (eds.) (2000) *Aspects of Arctic and Sub-Arctic History* (proceedings of the International Congress on the History of the Arctic and Sub-Arctic Region, Reykjavík, 18–21 June 1998; Reykjavík: University of Iceland Press).

Sigurðsson, Jón Viðar (1989) *Frá Goðorðum Til Ríkja* (Reykjavík: Bókaútgáfa Menningarsjóðs).

—(1999) *Chieftains and Power in the Icelandic Commonwealth*, translated by Jean Lundskær-Nielsen (Odense: Odense University Press).

Silberman, Neil Asher (1995) Power, Politics and the Past: The Construction of Antiquity in the Holy Land. In Levy 1995: 9-23.

Simpson, Ian, W. Paul Adderley, Garðar Guðmundsson, Margrét Hallsdóttir, Magnús Á. Sigurgeirsson, and Mjöll Snædóttir (2002) Soil Limitations to Agrarian Land Production in Premodern Iceland. *Human Ecology* 30/4: 423-43.

Sinopoli, Carla (2003) Echoes of Empire: Vijayanagara and Historical Memory, Vijayanagara as Historical Memory. In Van Dyke and Alcock 2003: 17-33.

Smith, Kevin (1995) *Landnám*: The Settlement of Iceland in Archaeological and Historical Perspective. *World Archaeology* 26/3: 329-47.

Sørensen, Preben Meulengracht (1992) Some Methodological Considerations in Connection with the Study of the Sagas. In Pálsson 1992: 27-41.

Stager, Lawrence (1985) The Archaeology of the Family in Ancient Israel. *BASOR* 260: 1-35.

Stein, Gil (1999) *Rethinking World-Systems: Diasporas, Colonies, and Interaction in Uruk Mesopotamia* (Tucson: Arizona University Press).

—(2002a) Colonies without Colonialism: A Trade Diaspora Model of Fourth Millennium B.C. Mesopotamian Enclaves in Anatolia. In *The Archaeology of Colonialism*, edited by C.L. Lyons and J.K. Papadopoulos (Los Angeles: Getty Research Institute): 27-64.

—(2002b) From Passive Periphery to Active Agents: Emerging Perspectives in the Archaeology of Interregional Interaction. *American Anthropologist* 104/3: 903-16.

—(2005) *The Archaeology of Colonial Encounters* (Santa Fe: School of American Research).

Steindórsson, Steindór, Þor Magnússon, and Ásgeir S. Björnsson (1987) *Daniel Bruun: Íslenskt Þjóðlíf íþúsund ár* (Reykjavík: Bókaútgáfan Örn Og Örlygur Hf).

Sturlunga saga (1970), translated by J. McGrew (New York: Twayne Publishers).

Sveinbjarnardóttir, Guðrún (1991) A Study of Farm Abandonment in Two Regions of Iceland. In Maizels and Caseldine 1991: 161-77.

—(1992) *Farm Abandonment in Medieval and Post-Medieval Iceland: An Interdisciplinary Study* (Oxbow Monograph 17; Oxford: Oxbow Books).

Tilley, Charles (1998) *Durable Inequality* (Berkeley: University of California Press).

Thompson, Thomas (1991) Text, Context, and Referent in Israelite Historiography. In Edelman 1991: 65-92.

—(1996) Historiography of Ancient Palestine and Early Jewish Historiography: W.G. Dever and the Not So New Biblical Archaeology. In *The Origins of the Ancient Israelite States*, edited by Volkmar Fritz and Philip Davies (JSOTSup 228; Sheffield: Sheffield Academic Press): 26-43.

—(1999) *The Mythic Past: Biblical Archaeology and the Myth of Israel* (London: Basic Books).

Trevor-Roper, Hugh (1983) The Invention of Tradition: The Highland Tradition of Scotland. In Hobsbawm and Ranger 1983: 15-41.

Tulinius, Torfi (1992) Inheritance, Ideology, and Literature: *Hervarar Saga ok Heiðreks*. In Pálsson 1992: 147-60.

Van Dyke, Ruth, and Susan Alcock (eds.) (2003) *Archaeologies of Memory* (Malden: Blackwell).

Vansina, Jan (1995) Historians, Are Archaeologists Your Siblings? *History in Africa* 22: 369-408.

Vésteinsson, Orri (2000) Early Settlement in Iceland. In Fitzhugh and Ward 2000: 164-74.

—(2005) Archaeology of Economy and Society. In McTurk 2005: 1-6.

Wallace, Birgitta (2000) The Viking Settlement at L'Anse aux Meadows. In Fitzhugh and Ward 2000: 208-16.

Wallerstein, Immanuel (1974) *The Modern World-System* (New York: Academic Press).

Wertsch, James V. (2002) *Voices of Collective Remembering* (Cambridge: Cambridge University Press).

Whaley, Diana (2000) A Useful Past: Historical Writing in Medieval Iceland. In Ross 2000: 161-202.

Würth, Stefanie (2005) Historiography and Pseudo-History. In McTurk 2005: 155-72.

Zevit, Z. (2001) *The Religions of Ancient Israel: A Synthesis of Parallactic Approaches* (London/New York: Continuum).

13 Excavating the Text of 1 Kings 9

In Search of the Gates of Solomon

William M. Schniedewind

Abstract

Biblical Archaeology first looked to 1 Kgs 9:15 as a literary correlate to the archaeological remains of gates at Gezer, Hazor, and Megiddo. More recently, archaeologists have critiqued this reliance on 1 Kgs 9:15. Neither the reliance upon this text nor the critique of this use of the text have seriously engaged the literary context and redactional history of the text. Verse 15 is actually part of a longer list that was interrupted by interpretative glosses of the deuteronomistic historian that relate to the deuteronomic 'law of the king'. Archaeologists need to reference the longer archival list in 1 Kgs 9:15, 17-18 rather than the truncated fragment in v. 15.

> *This is the account of the forced labor that King Solomon conscripted to build…Hazor, Megiddo, and Gezer.* (1 Kgs 9:15)

1 Kings 9:15 has been the source of naïve historical reconstructions for the Solomonic period as well as naïve dismissals of the historicity of Solomon. To be sure, the biblical text has too often been mined by the past generation of 'biblical' archaeologists and historians looking for archaeological clues. 1 Kings 9:15 in particular has been a poster child for critiques of such archaeological treasure hunts. At the same time, the backlash against Biblical Archaeology that has characterized the last few decades in Levantine Archaeology ironically is often no less naïve in its citation of 1 Kgs 9:15 and its focus on just the three cities of Hazor, Megiddo, and Gezer. This text reflects typical attributes of biblical historical literature. It is an edited text. Yet it is also based on an early—and recoverable—historical record that did not originally focus exclusively on just these three cities. The text has been put into the service of ideological and theological viewpoints, but at the same time it is derived from a pre-deuteronomic historical source that has been interpreted, misread, or misused from antiquity up until the most recent archaeological studies. 1 Kings 9:15 was originally a longer list of fortified cities that began with building projects in Jerusalem, continued with Hazor, Megiddo, and Gezer, and finally concluded with Lower Beth-Horon, Baalath, and Tamar.

In its edited form the biblical verse seems to only list three cities: Hazor, Megiddo, and Gezer. Gezer was excavated by the British archaeologist R.A.S. Macalister a century ago, who attributed little of significance to King Solomon. Megiddo in turn was excavated by teams from the University of Chicago in the 1930s. These teams found a major city, including buildings that they identified as the stables built by King Solomon for his chariots and horses. Finally, Yigael Yadin—the famous

Israeli general, politician, and archaeologist—excavated the city of Hazor in the 1950s and uncovered a large city with grand fortifications that he dated to King Solomon. Yadin was particularly struck by the monumental gate to the Solomonic city that included a pair of towers and three chambers on each side. Looking through excavation reports, Yadin made the observation that the gates at Hazor, Megiddo, and Gezer all seemed to be based on a similar tri-partite architectural plan (see Fig. 1).

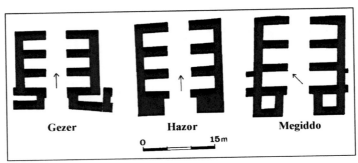

Figure 1. The Gates of Gezer, Hazor, and Megiddo

The dating and reconstruction of these gates, however, has been a subject of increasing archaeological scrutiny and even derision.[1] For example, this particular verse has been caricaturized in recent discussions of the period of Solomon by Israel Finkelstein who ridiculed the past generation of archaeologists claiming that their entire chronology is dependent on this single biblical verse. In his latest popular work, *David and Solomon: In Search of the Bible's Sacred Kings and the Roots of the Western Tradition*, co-authored with journalist Neil Silberman, Finkelstein heightens his rhetorical critique:

> The excavation of similar six-chambered gates at Hazor, Megiddo, and Gezer—linked with this single biblical verse and thus dated to the tenth century BCE—established the foundation for the traditional archaeology of Solomon and his united monarchy. Yet this interpretation has been conclusively disproved both on stratigraphic and chronological grounds. (Finkelstein and Silberman 2006: 159-60)

Whether this has actually been 'conclusively disproved' actually continues to be a matter of debate among archaeologists. But even the fact that archaeologists continue to debate this is troubling since it is a debate generated by the misreading of the Bible as an historical source.

Israel Finkelstein's ridicule is perhaps well taken because a previous generation of biblical archaeologists and biblical historians did uncritically use biblical literature in interpreting the archaeological record and reconstructing the history of Israel. The ridicule, however, is now a bit anachronistic and can even be counterproductive if it precludes a critical analysis of biblical narratives as potential historical sources. Using the tools of biblical criticism, we can analyze or 'excavate'—to use the archaeological metaphor—the text of 1 Kings 9 as an historical source.

Previous Excavations of 1 Kings 9

The Bible has literary layers, just like a tel has archaeological layers. Yet, it is noteworthy that most scholars who have appealed to 1 Kgs 9:15 have not employed any higher critical analysis of the

---

1.   See the survey and discussion in Halpern 2000.

biblical text—metaphorically, they have ignored the excavation of the biblical textual tel. As a result, the analysis of the strata of biblical texts by archaeologists can be as amateur as the use of archaeology by biblical scholars. This can be illustrated by two relatively recent excavations of 1 Kings 9. First, Hermann Michael Niemann, who has been excavating at Megiddo with Israel Finkelstein, published an investigation in the journal of the Institute of Archaeology at the Tel Aviv University. The article tries to use the archaeology of Megiddo 'for differentiating between the historical and the theological perception of Solomon' (Niemann 2000: 61). Niemann begins by calling attention to the 'scantiness and lack of clarity' in the texts concerning Megiddo, which he asserts 'is not typical of all the Solomonic traditions' (2000: 62). And, in the end, he concludes, 'Most likely 1 Kgs. 9:16-18 represents documentary information' (2000: 63), citing articles by Nadav Na'aman and Axel Knauf, whereas he feels that v. 15 is 'theologically oriented'. The truly unfortunate aspect of Niemann's opinion is that it is based on no objective criteria whatsoever. He simply opines that v. 15 'is idealistic and in general terms', whereas vv. 16-18 are 'tangibly historical'. Based on the content of the article, however, he presents his unsubstantiated assertion to support a particular historical and archaeological interpretation of the contentious stratigraphy of Megiddo. Perhaps that correlation is considered the argument itself. Yet, it is difficult to have confidence in this type of scholarship. To be sure, such reservations could be leveled at quite a bit of source and redaction criticism. Yet, there are critical and objective tools for understanding the redaction history of biblical texts.

A second recent example of the citation and analysis of 1 Kings 9 is Axel Knauf's critique: 'Solomon at Megiddo?' Knauf seems to prefer the objectivity of archaeology over the 'probabilistic generalizations' that characterize history generated from texts (Knauf 2001: 120-21). Knauf's analysis begins with questions about the traditional archaeological chronology for the Iron IIA period (i.e. 1000–925/900 BCE) that lead him to Solomon and the archaeology of Megiddo, Hazor, and Gezer. Depending largely on the archaeological conclusions of what might be termed the 'Tel Aviv School' (i.e. Finkelstein, Ussishkin, and their students), he concludes, 'The only king presently known to have built Hazor, Megiddo, and Gezer as cities of storage, chariots and horses is Jeroboam II' (Knauf 2001: 127). Knauf's analysis focuses both on the three cities and the notion that these were administrative cities for horses—both are questionable assumptions about 1 Kgs 9:15-19 as an early historical source. Knauf correctly notes that 1 Kgs 9:15-19 'is hardly what an archaeologist would call a "clean locus"' (2001: 123). He offers his own stratigraphy of the text that has four separate strata. Knauf sees the trio—Hazor, Megiddo, and Gezer—as 'the first insertion into the macrosyntatical and logical sequence 9.15, 20-21'. Verse 16 is another level of the redaction, adding a footnote to the history of Gezer. The second list of cities in vv. 17-18 is another layer to the text employing the 'catchword' of Gezer. While repetition is certainly an editorial technique, it is used for editorial insertions (as illustrated below with 1 Kgs 14 and 2 Chron. 12), which suggests that vv. 17-18 are a continuation of the author's source material. To be sure, Knauf's reading follows in the tradition of German source criticism and is sensitive to the editorial activity within the text. At the same time, his interpretation suffers from the typical fragmenting of the text among German source critics. The most disappointing aspect of Knauf's analysis is the apparent arbitrariness by which he separates these four layers. To further the archaeological metaphor, there is no correlation between the literary strata that Knauf identifies and strata elsewhere in the redaction of the book of Kings or other biblical literature. Thus, Knauf's analysis comes across as a subjective enterprise that has no coherence with the larger redactional activities in the book of Kings or biblical literature as a whole. I doubt that many archaeologists would tolerate this type of interpretation in archaeological excavations. The subjective nature of Knauf's analysis is underscored by a comparison with Niemann above, who gave a quite different analysis of 1 Kgs 9:15-18.

A striking archaeological misuse of 1 Kgs 9:15 is manifest in Finkelstein and Silberman's recent book *David and Solomon: In Search of the Bible's Sacred Kings and the Roots of the Western Tradition* (2006). After dismissing the historical implications that this passage has for Solomon, they apply the text to the Jeroboam II kingdom, which dates to a couple of centuries later. They begin their argument cautiously: 'But the specific mention in the Bible of Solmon's building of Hazor, Megiddo, and Gezer is significant in an entirely different respect. *All three cities* were located in the territory of the northern kingdom and were *probably* its most important administrative centers after its capital in Samaria. Hence, the historical reality behind 1 Kgs 9:15 should *probably* be sought in how the Solomonic tradition assimilated cherished memories from the history of the north' (Finkelstein and Silberman 2006: 160-61, emphasis added). After noting out how these cities flourished in the time of Jeroboam II, a more confident rhetoric ensues, '*There can be little doubt* that their mention in the Solomonic narrative represented an attempt both to enhance Solomon's stature and to further integrate the prestige of the northern and southern kingdoms by anachronistically attributing their architectural grandeur to him' (2006: 161, emphasis added). This vague correlation between the archaeology of the 8th century BCE and the Bible seems exactly the type of 'Biblical Archaeology' that Finkelstein and others have been railing against. Yet, Finkelstein and Silberman make no attempt to conduct a critical literary analysis of 1 Kgs 9:15 nor do they explain how the editor of the book of Kings (presumably another century later according to Finkelstein's argument) came to have this particular information about Jeroboam II's alleged building projects in the northern cities or why they would have seemed so important to him. As I shall argue, the very focus on the *three cities*—Hazor, Megiddo, and Gezer—which undergirds this new use of the Bible in the service of archaeological interpretation, is a misreading of the biblical text.

Method in Separating the Strata of 1 Kings 9

The excavation of 1 Kings 9 must begin with some discussion of our excavation methodology. There are objective tools for understanding the composition processes of biblical texts, and particularly biblical history. Indeed, in the case of biblical history, we have parallel texts in Samuel-Kings and Chronicles, and a simple comparison can give some insight into the composition processes of biblical literature that can then be applied elsewhere. Using redaction criticism along with the insights of inner-biblical interpretation, we can arrive at a more objective excavation of the biblical text and a history of its composition.

One good example of the compositional processes can be illustrated in the often discussed account of Pharaoh Shishak's invasion that we know about from Egyptian records. The example also provides the additional control of the parallel texts in 1 Kings 14 and the later literary stratum, 2 Chronicles 12. We can illustrate the compositional layers by a comparison of two accounts of the invasion of Pharaoh Shishak told in 1 Kings 14 and 2 Chronicles 12:

> In the fifth year of King Rehoboam, King Shishak of Egypt came up against Jerusalem; he took away the treasures of the house of YHWH and the treasures of the king's house; he took everything. He also took away all the shields of gold that Solomon had made; so King Rehoboam made shields of bronze instead, and committed them to the hands of the officers of the guard, who kept the door of the king's house. (1 Kgs 14:25-27)

> In the fifth year of King Rehoboam King Shishak of Egypt came up against Jerusalem, *because they had been unfaithful to YHWH*. Twelve hundred chariots, sixty thousand cavalry, and a countless army came with him from Egypt—Libyans, Sukkiim, and Ethiopians. He took the fortified cities of Judah and came as far as Jerusalem. Then the prophet Shemaiah came to Rehoboam and to the officers of Judah, who had gathered at Jerusalem because of Shishak, and said to them, 'Thus says YHWH: You

abandoned me, so I have abandoned you to the hand of Shishak'. Then the officers of Israel and the king humbled themselves and said, 'YHWH is in the right'. When YHWH saw that they humbled themselves, the word of YHWH came to Shemaiah, saying: 'They have humbled themselves; I will not destroy them, but I will grant them some deliverance, and my wrath shall not be poured out on Jerusalem by the hand of Shishak. Nevertheless they shall be his servants, so that they may know the difference between serving me and serving the kingdoms of other lands'. So King Shishak of Egypt came up against Jerusalem; he took away the treasures of the house of YHWH and the treasures of the king's house; he took everything. He also took away the shields of gold that Solomon had made. (2 Chron. 12:2-9)

The additional material that Chronicles adds to 1 Kings 14 is marked by a 'repetitive resumption', sometimes referred as a *Wiederaufnahme*.[2] This is a widely used editorial technique in the Hebrew Bible, in this case, the statement that 'Shishak came up against Jerusalem' frames the editorial addition. Once we know this technique, a critically trained scholar could identify the editorial insertion in 2 Chron. 12:2b-8 even without the Book of Kings—but in this case we have an objective control that confirms this technique.

We can push the analogy still further. Archaeology employs both relative and objective chronological methods. Relative chronology is understood by correlating the material culture from other sites. This is analogous in biblical literature to the comparison of literary motifs and languages among different corpora of biblical texts. Not surprisingly, the material in 2 Chron. 12:2b-8 picks up on important themes elsewhere in Chronicles such as being unfaithful to God (v. 2b), the use of prophetic speech to rebuke wayward kings (vv. 5-8), the importance of humility before God, and the significance of the exilic experience (v. 8). To use the archaeological metaphor, we can correlate the content of the editorial intrusion (vv. 2b-8) with the literary strata elsewhere in Chronicles. This approach allows us to correlate strata in the biblical text and distinguish between earlier strata (i.e. the sources) and the later strata (namely, the later editing and redaction).

Archaeology also employs objective methods like C-14 that, while not yielding an exact date, are based on objective scientific data. One source of objective data for source or redaction criticism of the biblical text is linguistic evidence.[3] For example, the term מעל (2 Chron. 12:2) with the meaning 'to be unfaithful (to God)' is characteristic of late Biblical Hebrew and the Book of Chronicles; the spelling of personal names like Shishak (with a *yod* in Chronicles instead of a *waw* as in Kings) is also more typical of late Biblical Hebrew. It is also worth noting that by most scholars' assessments the Book of Kings was first written down in the late 8th century at the very earliest, so these texts recall a campaign of Pharaoh Shishak from two or more centuries earlier. It is only the use of extrabiblical sources that allows the accurate historical placement of this story as attested by an Egyptian account of this campaign that was recorded by Pharaoh Shishak (or, Sheshonk) on a wall of the Temple at Karnak in Egypt (*ANET*, 263-64). Although there are various discussions that try to dismiss the historical accuracy in one manner or another,[4] these dismissals cannot ignore that fact that a much later author correctly identifies an Egyptian Pharaoh's campaign that took place centuries earlier. Thus, we have to account for both the later editorial framing of sources and the early scribal activity that preserved such an accurate chronological synchronism. This, I believe, is a sound and objective approach to excavating the biblical text for which there are numerous examples.

---

2.   For an outline of the editorial tools used in biblical literature for inner-biblical exegesis, see the discussion in Fishbane 1985: 44-65; see also Schniedewind 2005.

3.   See, e.g., Hurvitz 1999.

4.   See Finkelstein 2002; Knauf 2001: 131.

Excavating 1 Kings 9

With these methodological observations in hand, we can now make a few observations about the text of 1 Kings 9. Unfortunately, it is difficult to date precisely biblical texts, but we can identify the editorial hands in the text that represent different literary strata. We can also correlate the motifs in these strata with literary motifs elsewhere in the deuteronomic literary tradition.

Perhaps it is best to read 1 Kgs 9:15 in its wider context. The chapter as a whole relates to Solomon's building projects beginning with the royal palace and temple in Jerusalem. The building account gets sidetracked by several deuteronomic literary themes. In the following translation I have adapted the NRSV with a special attention to nuances and paragraphing and have added emphasis to highlight selected topics addressed below.

> When Solomon finished building the house of the LORD and the king's house and all that Solomon desired to build, the LORD appeared to Solomon a second time, as he had appeared to him at Gibeon. The LORD said to him, 'I have heard your prayer and your plea, which you made before me;[5] I have consecrated this house that you have built, and put my name there forever; my eyes and my heart will be there for all time. As for you, if you will walk before me, as David your father walked, with integrity of heart and uprightness, doing according to all that I have commanded you, and keeping my statutes and my ordinances, then I will establish your royal throne over Israel forever, as I promised your father David, saying, "There shall not fail you a successor on the throne of Israel".
>
> If you turn aside from following me, you or your children, and do not keep my commandments and my statutes that I have set before you, but go and serve other gods and worship them, then I will cut Israel off from the land that I have given them; and the house that I have consecrated for my name I will cast out of my sight; and Israel will become a proverb and a taunt among all peoples. This house will become a heap of ruins; everyone passing by it will be astonished, and will hiss; and they will say, 'Why has the LORD done such a thing to this land and to this house?' Then they will say, "Because they have forsaken the LORD their God, who brought their ancestors out of the land of Egypt, and embraced other gods, worshiping them and serving them; therefore the LORD has brought this disaster upon them.'
>
> At the end of twenty years, in which Solomon built the two houses, the house of the LORD and the king's house, King Hiram of Tyre supplied[6] Solomon with cedar and cypress timber and *gold, as much as he desired*, King Solomon gave to Hiram twenty cities in the land of Galilee. But when Hiram came from Tyre to see the cities that Solomon had given him, they did not please him. Therefore he said, 'What kind of cities are these that you have given me, my brother?' So they are called the land of Cabul to this day and Hiram sent to the king one hundred twenty talents of gold.
>
> This is the account of the forced labor that King Solomon conscripted to *build* the house of the LORD and his own house, the Millo and the wall of Jerusalem, Hazor, Megiddo, *Gezer*.
>
> (Now Pharaoh king of Egypt had gone up and captured Gezer and burned it down, had killed the Canaanites who lived in the city, and had given it as dowry to his daughter, Solomon's wife.)
>
> *so Solomon built Gezer* ['Gezer' is repetitive resumption/*Wiederaufnahme* of v. 15 that frames an editorial addition in paratheses], Lower Beth-horon, Baalath, Tamar in the wilderness, within the land, and all of Solomon's storage cities, that is, the cities for his chariots, the cities for his cavalry, and whatever Solomon desired to build, in Jerusalem, in Lebanon, and in all the land of his dominion.
>
> All the people who were left of the Amorites, the Hittites, the Perizzites, the Hivites, and the Jebusites, who were not of the people of Israel—their descendants who were still left in the land, whom the Israelites were unable to destroy completely—these Solomon conscripted for slave labor, and so they are to this day. But of the Israelites Solomon made no slaves; they were the soldiers, they were his officials, his commanders, his captains, and the commanders of his chariotry and cavalry.

---

5. This is a reference back to the content of Solomon's prayer in ch. 8; moreover, the content that follows is specifically related to the material in vv. 22ff. that alludes to the eventual exile of Judah and Jerusalem.

6. The verb 'supplied' translates the archaic *'az* preterite construction. On this construction, see Sáenz-Badillos 1993: 59; Waltke and O'Connor 1990: 513-14. Contrast 1 Kgs 9:24 discussed in n. 18.

These were the chief officials who were over Solomon's work: five hundred fifty, who had charge of the people who carried on the work.[7]

But[8] Pharaoh's daughter went up from the city of David to her own house that Solomon had built for her; then he built the Millo.[9] Three times a year Solomon used to offer up burnt offerings and sacrifices of well-being on the altar that he built for the LORD, offering incense before the LORD. So he completed the house.

King Solomon built a fleet of ships at Ezion-geber, which is near Elat on the shore of the Red Sea, in the land of Edom. Hiram sent his servants with the fleet, sailors who were familiar with the sea, together with the servants of Solomon. They went to Ophir, and imported from there four hundred twenty talents of gold, which they delivered to King Solomon.

There are three features that suggest the incorporation of an archival source into the narrative. First, the historical reference to Hiram is a shortened form of the Phoenician King 'Ahiram' (*'ạhiram*) whose name is found on an inscribed sarcophagus of a Phoenician king at Byblos (KAI 1). Our knowledge about this early period of Phoenician history is largely dependent on the later Jewish historian, Flavius Josephus, who claims to have used two earlier historians, Dius and Menander of Ephesus.[10] Josephus claims that the Phoenicians kept detailed chronicles (none of which have survived) and that Dius wrote the Histories of the Phoenicians 'after an accurate manner' (*Apion* 1.17.112; also see *Ant.* 8.147-49). In any case, a variety of historical sources suggest that Hiram (or, Ahiram) was roughly an historical contemporary of Solomon. Second, the list of cities, first in v. 15 but particularly its continuation in vv. 17-18, seems to be an archival fragment for three reasons. First, the beginning of v. 15, 'this is the account of the forced labor', is language typical of building inscriptions, which presumably derive from archival sources. Second, the Hebrew term for 'forced labor' (מס) is an early loanword known in the El-Amarna letters (EA 365:14, 23, 25) and Akkadian administrative texts (*massu*); thus, the building list would fit in a palace archival account. Third, the concern for the temple and its fate would be typical for temple or palace scribes. This concern creates the repetitive framework of the chapter in vv. 1, 10, 15, and 25b. Such repetition should be understood as later scribes employing framing repetitions (or, *Wiederaufnahme*) to add a literary and interpretative overlay to their source material. The first digression on this theme in the chapter is found in vv. 2-9, which begins by referring back to the prayer of Solomon in 1 Kings 8 and more specifically to the latter part of this prayer (vv. 22ff.) that foreshadows the destruction of the temple and the exile. From this evidence, it seems likely that the biblical narrative began with an archival source.

The signs of a specifically deuteronomic literary shaping of this source are also evident. To begin with, the deuteronomic law of the king provides the overriding literary themes in the chapter. The law of the king is concerned with the acquisition of gold, horses, and wives as detailed in Deut. 17:14-17:

When you have come into the land that the LORD your God is giving you, and have taken possession of it and settled in it, and you say, 'I will set a king over me, like all the nations that are around me'... Even so, he must not acquire many horses for himself, or return the people to Egypt in order to acquire more horses, since the LORD has said to you, 'You must never return that way again'. And he must not acquire many wives for himself, or else his heart will turn away; also silver and gold he must not acquire in great quantity for himself.

---

7. The actual list of names seems to be displaced, but can be found in 1 Kgs 4:1-19.

8. The particle, *'ak*, is commonly used by later editors for inserting comments. In this case, the additions about Pharaoh's daughter are all marked with editorial markers.

9. 'Then Solomon built', using the *'az* non-consecutive, which is later Hebrew. Note the contrast with v. 11 discussed in n. 15.

10. See the critical analysis of the sources by Katzenstein 1973: 75-115.

The narrative pointedly remarks that Solomon acquires gold from Hiram (v. 14) and goes on an expedition to the legendary Ophir with Hiram's men to acquire more gold (v. 28). The specific list of cities (1 Kgs 9:15, 17-18) is appended with a general note about storage cities for Solomon's horses and chariots (v. 19). This reference to cities for Solomon's horses and chariots is *general*, that is, it is not connected to Megiddo or any other city. From a linguistic perspective, it is worth noting that the word used for 'storage city'—מסכנות—is an Assyrian loanword (from *maškattu*, see *AHw* 626b), which suggests that this comment on chariot cities was added in a later period probably as part of deuteronomistic redaction or editing. Finally, the concern about Pharaoh's daughter, which appears in vv. 16 and 24, follows the deuteronomic concern about foreign wives. In sum, the narrative seems to be an implicit commentary on all three prohibitions in the law of the king. The other deuteronomistic literary theme in 1 Kings 9 is the promise to David (vv. 2-9), which is conditionalized and even abrogated by Solomonic behavior with regard to the law of the king. Another feature is the *topos* of Solomon's desires, which are mentioned in vv. 1b, 11b, and 19b. Indeed, it is these desires that lead the king astray into breaking the deuteronomic law, and these passages seem to be part of the core of the final literary shaping of the chapter.

But what can we recover of the earlier literary strata? The chapter begins with a note about Solomon's building activities (v. 1a) and repeatedly returns to this topic (vv. 10, 15, 17-18):

> When Solomon finished building the house of the LORD and the king's house...
> At the end of twenty years, in which Solomon built the two houses, the house of the LORD and the king's house...
> This is the account of the forced labor that King Solomon conscripted *to build* the house of the LORD and his own house, the Millo and the wall of Jerusalem, Hazor, Megiddo, Gezer...
> so Solomon built Gezer, Lower Beth-horon, Baalath, Tamar in the wilderness...

After each interruption, the building activities are resumed by repeating the place where the discussion left off. Thus, it becomes clear that the intervening material interrupts the account of the building activities. The account of the building activities becomes a point of departure for discussing the infractions of deuteronomic law. First, vv. 1b-9 begin with a digression from the Solomonic palace and temple to a discussion of the Promise to David that was centered on the notion of an eternal throne for the sons of David that was dependent on fidelity to the Yahwistic Temple. After the digression, the author returns to the palace and temple briefly before digressing into how Solomon used foreign workers and acquired gold from a foreign king. The account then returns again to the building of the temple and palace in v. 15, and the list continues with further building in Jerusalem and other cities, including Hazor, Megiddo, and Gezer. The mention of Gezer, however, serves as another point for digression as the author associates Gezer with Solomon's marriage to a foreign princess from Egypt (something explicitly forbidden by deuteronomic law). Verse 17 then resumes the account of Solomon's building activities. At the end of the list of cities in v. 18, the series of deuteronomistic digressions continues with a general commentary about Solomon building administrative cities for his horses and chariots (v. 19). What becomes clear in this excavation of the text is that the building activities are an earlier literary stratum around which the later deuteronomic critique of Solomon—gold, horse and foreign wives—is fashioned.

The exact date of the archival list of cities used by the Josianic historian is uncertain, but it would predate the deuteronomic editing of the narrative in the Josianic period (7th century BCE). There is no *a priori* reason to dismiss a 10th-century date. It is clear, however, that the archival list of cities included Hazor, Megiddo, Gezer, Lower Beth-Horon, Baalath, and Tamar. These were not necessarily connected with the stabling of horses or chariots. Moreover, as some archaeologists have pointed out, there is no reason to expect that this list of cities would have that same style of gates, even if they were all built by the venerable King Solomon.

More intriguing are the references to the second three cities that have barely received any attention at all from archaeologists. Lower Beth-Horon has yet to be properly excavated. Baalath has yet to be conclusively located. But Tamar 'in the wilderness' is almost certainly to be identified with Ein Hatzeva, which is located in the Arava Valley about 35 km south of the Dead Sea. It has been thought that the spring at Ein Hatzeva as well as its strategic position at the intersection of the north–south Arava road from Eilat and the Negev–Edom road were the reasons why several fortresses were built on this spot over the course of about 1000 years. More recently, the excavations by a team led by Thomas Levy at nearby Khirbet en-Nahas have uncovered extensive mining activities dating to the 11th through 9th centuries BCE, which would certainly have implications for the administrative role of the monarchy in this region (Levy *et al.* 2005, 2008). These discoveries should draw additional attention to the list in 1 Kgs 9:15, 17-18 and the ancient site of Tamar. They highlight the present literary analysis that demonstates that there was no list of three Solomonic cities—Hazor, Megiddo, and Gezer—but rather a longer archival list of towns and building projects that was interrupted and elaborated upon by the deuteronomistic scribes.

References

Finkelstein, I. (2002) The Campaign of Shoshenq I to Palestine: A Guide to the 10th Century BCE Polity. *ZDPV* 118: 109-35.

Finkelstein, Israel, and Neil Asher Siberman (2001) *The Bible Unearthed* (New York: Free Press).

—(2006) *David and Solomon: In Search of the Bible's Sacred Kings and the Roots of the Western Tradition* (New York: Free Press).

Fishbane, M. (1985) *Biblical Interpretation in Ancient Israel* (Oxford: Clarendon Press).

Halpern, B. (2000) The Gate of Megiddo and the Debate on the 10th Century. In *International Organization for the Study of the Old Testament: Congress Volume: Oslo, 1998* (VTSup 30; Leiden: Brill): 79-121.

Hurvitz, A. (1999) The Relevance of Biblical Hebrew Linguistics for the Historical Study of Ancient Israel. In *Proceedings of the Twelfth World Congress of Jewish Studies. Division A: The Bible and its World* (Jerusalem: World Union of Jewish Studies): 21*-33*.

Katzenstein, H.J. (1973) *The History of Tyre, from the Beginning of the Second Millennium B.C.E. until the Fall of the Neo-Babylonian Empire in 538 B.C.E.* (Jerusalem: Schocken Institute for Jewish Research of the Jewish Theological Seminary of America).

Knauf, A. (2001) Solomon at Megiddo? In *The Land that I Will Show You: Essays on the History and Archaeology of the Ancient Near East in Honour of J. Maxwell Miller*, edited by J.A. Dearman and M.P. Graham (JSOTSup 343; Sheffield: Sheffield Academic Press): 119-43.

Levy, T.E., T. Higham, C. Bronk Ramsey, N.G. Smith, E. Ben-Yosef, M. Robinson, S. Münger, K. Knabb, J. Schulze, P., M. Najjar, and L. Tauxe (2008) High-precision Radiocarbon Dating and Historical Biblical Archaeology in Southern Jordan. *Proceedings of the National Academy of Sciences* 105: 16460-65.

Levy, T.E., M. Najjar, J. van der Plicht, T. Higham, and H.J. Bruins (2005) Lowland Edom and the High and Low Chronologies: Edomite State Formation, the Bible and Recent Archaeological Research in Southern Jordan. In *The Bible and Radiocarbon Dating: Archaeology, Text and Science*, edited by T.E. Levy and T. Higham (London: Equinox): 129-63.

Niemann, H.M. (2000) Megiddo and Solomon: A Biblical Investigation in Relation to Archaeology. *Tel Aviv* 27: 61-74.

Sáenz-Badillos, A. (1993) *A History of the Hebrew Language*, translated by J. Elwolde (Cambridge: Cambridge University Press).

Schniedewind, W.M. (2005) Innerbiblical Exegesis. In *Dictionary of the Old Testament: Historical Books*, edited by B. Arnold and H.G.M. Williamson (Downers Grove, IL: InterVarsity Press): 502-9.

Waltke, B., and M. O'Connor (1990) *An Introduction to Biblical Hebrew Syntax* (Winona Lake, IN: Eisenbrauns).

14 Culture, Memory, and History

Reflections on Method in Biblical Studies

Ronald Hendel

Abstract

The historicist underpinnings of modern biblical scholarship have taken some hard hits in recent years. In this study I attempt to explore how recent theoretical work in various fields (anthropology, philosophy, literary criticism, historiography) impinge upon a renewed historical-critical method in biblical scholarship.

In his *Tractatus Theologico-Politicus* (1670), the apostate Jew and post-Cartesian philosopher Baruch (Benedictus) Spinoza proposed a new method of biblical interpretation. He argued that the meaning of biblical passages should be sought by contextual analysis, that is, by reading a passage within the semantic and conceptual horizons of its textual, cultural, and historical location. He argued that we should interpret Scripture 'in the light of its history', by which he means what we would call its historical horizons, including language, culture, etc. He famously distinguished the truth (or falsity) of a statement from its meaning, and argued that discerning the latter is the prime goal of the biblical interpreter (2001: 88):

> I term a pronouncement obscure or clear according to the degree of difficulty with which the meaning can be elicited from the context, and not according to the degree of difficulty with which its truth can be perceived by reason. For the point at issue is merely the meaning of the texts, not their truth.

By treating the Bible as an ancient book whose meanings can only be recovered responsibly by attention to its discursive, historical, and cultural contexts—and by granting that these meanings are in many cases unrecoverable—Spinoza scandalized his contemporaries and founded the method of modern biblical criticism (see Scholder 1990: 1-3, 138-42; Israel 2001: 275-85, 447-56). Through the influence of Richard Simon's *Histoire critique du Vieux Testament* (1685), which was in part a response and refinement of Spinoza's work, this method came to be called the historical-critical method.

It is salutary to recall Spinoza's insistence that the explication of meanings is the chief imperative of biblical interpretation. In our day the historical-critical method has too often devolved to tired debates about the dating or historicity of the biblical sources, or has balkanized itself into a variety of methods that take little cognizance of each other, each presuming conceptual autonomy. In my view the Spinozistic principle of the primacy of meaning can serve to recast some of these recent debates and revitalize the current practices of biblical criticism, particularly as it enhances our receptivity to critical reflections on such issues elsewhere in the humanities and social sciences.

The interpretive primacy of meaning over truth casts a critical light on a large swath of recent biblical scholarship whose criterion is all too often 'Is it true?' or 'When was it?' in a strictly historicist sense. It is certainly important to learn that the story of the conquest of Jericho in Joshua 6 is not historically factual (since Jericho was an uninhabited ruin at the time that the biblical text sets the story), or that the account of Pharaoh Shishak's invasion of Israel in 1 Kings 14 is more or less reliable (since we have Shishak's own account of his invasion, no doubt exaggerated in details), or that Solomon may not have built the fortifications at Hazor, Megiddo, and Gezer (as reported in 1 Kgs 9:15). All of these topics belong to the necessary context of biblical interpretation. But such questions are ultimately tangential to a more richly conceived historical method, which looks at how the biblical representations of the past are meaningful, not simply whether they are historically true or precisely dateable.

The emphasis on the exploration of meanings also cuts across another facile set of distinctions in contemporary biblical studies, that between historical, anthropological, and literary studies. All too often scholars claim that these are different types of inquiry, constituted by different, hermetically sealed methods. This too is puzzling and, to my mind, quite misleading. The objects of inquiry—texts, events, social institutions, etc.—are richly overlapping and intersignifying, and clearly belong within the coherent horizons of biblical interpretation. The methods one uses to explore these are varieties of the same method—the historical-critical method—adapted to the specific features of each set of data and frame of inquiry. Constructing a 'close reading' of history is not antithetical to constructing a 'close reading' of a text, though the range and interplay of interpretive skills may differ somewhat. To set imperial boundaries that separate the study of history, culture, and literature from each other is to sorely limit one's scope of inquiry and ultimately impoverishes the possibility of a rich understanding of any single aspect. A synthetic biblical interpretation involves an interwoven method, turning from historical to literary to anthropological questions at each bend, in a circulation of methods and meanings.

Such an approach is a natural consequence of the implications of the historical-critical method. It may involve some revision of habits, but it is not a radical departure or a new 'paradigm'. It attempts to reinvigorate biblical criticism and engages with relevant work in other scholarly fields. In my recent book, *Remembering Abraham: Culture, Memory, and History in the Hebrew Bible* (2005), I make some forays in the direction of a more robust historical-critical practice. Among the many sins of this book, it has been criticized for not clearly defining the terms in the subtitle—'culture', 'memory', and 'history'—and for not unpacking the implications of combining these concepts in a synthetic method. In part I avoided undertaking extensive terminological and theoretical discussion because of my preference for exploring the text rather than theorizing about exploring the text, and in part because I do not feel fully competent to tread in the relevant fields of social theory, literary theory, historiography, philosophy of knowledge, and so on. But I agree that it is important to unpack and explore one's terms and methods. In the following I attempt to lay out my understanding of these issues, beginning with further reflections on recent controversies concerning the historical-critical method, and then turning to the relevant domains of culture, memory, and history. But I should forewarn that my own understanding of these domains is partial, eclectic, and still in process.

Knowledge and Historical Criticism

The historical-critical method has come under attack from various quarters in recent years. Most prominent are the postmodernists who question the stability of any meanings, whether in texts or in language itself, and who therefore question whether we can gain any access to the past that is not wholly driven by our preconceptions and linguistic forms. The postmodern position usually presumes a radical relativism of cultural—and even individual—conceptualities. Partially diverging from the postmodernists are some feminists and other ideological critics who claim that the historical-critical method justifies male and/or bourgeois hegemony and its oppressive status quo. According to this position, critical inquiry is a mask of power relations and ideology. In my view both of these positions are partially true or revealing, but are overly simplistic—and even self-contradictory—when presented without qualification.[1]

On a somewhat different level, the legitimacy of the Spinozistic distinction between truth and meaning has been questioned, since the interpretation of meanings is always colored to some degree by the interpreter's own truth commitments. The bracketing of the question of truth is an ideal, but perhaps an impossible operation.

Another dimension of the problem is the word 'method' itself, which can convey a misleading impression of scientific accuracy, lawlike procedures, or assured results. To forestall this semantic confusion, I will use the word 'method' to mean simply a way of proceeding involving a set of intellectual criteria and skills, like the 'method' of a physician.[2]

In spite of the impossibility of pure objectivity—a condition that Hume and Kant exposed a century after Spinoza—it seems clear that a 'chastened' and self-reflective historical-critical method is still possible, and in fact is alive and well (see Iggers 1997; Dobbs-Allsopp 1999). The lively arguments about this method in biblical studies are, in my view, examples of the method in action. To put it simply, the critique of knowledge about texts and history is itself a part of the historical-critical method. The 'critical' aspect of the method goes all the way down, including the conditions and limitations of the method itself and the ways it is practiced in the lived world. The task of critique never ends, and is not immune to itself. In my view this is a good thing, and not at all a sign of the death-knell of critical inquiry.

As scholars of an ancient text we are always involved in a hermeneutic circle, attempting to understand discourses that operate in part by different principles than our own and impacted by different social and discursive forces than our own. Language and culture are difficulties not to be underestimated. Yet, although cross-cultural understanding of any kind is difficult, it is worth undertaking and, it seems to me, not at all foreclosed to us. An important consideration in this task is what the philosopher Donald Davidson calls 'the principle of charity', which illuminates the problem of communicating across differing conceptual schemes (1984, 2001). Davidson cogently argues that all humans have certain background knowledge and beliefs in common—especially those that impinge most directly on our interactions with the world—and hence the differences that do exist are a relatively small part of the whole, and do not warrant the concept of alternative or wholly incommensurate conceptual schemes. Richard Rorty unpacks this argument as follows:

> *many* more of our beliefs are the same as Greek beliefs than are different (e.g., our belief that barley is better than nettles and freedom than slavery, that red is a color, and that lightning often precedes thunder)… [This] point makes us remember, among other things, what a very small proportion of our beliefs are changed when our paradigms of physics, or poetry, or morals, change—and makes us realize how few of them *could* change. (1982: 8, 13)

With the principle of charity—which Davidson argues we already presume in our everyday interactions—we build up our communicative understanding from our shared background of beliefs. If we

---

1. See the judicious evaluations of these positions in Collins 2005.
2. Wittgenstein 1953: 51: 'There is not *a* philosophical method, though there are indeed methods, like different therapies'.

grant this principle, then not only is cross-cultural communication possible, but the essential difference or relativity of conceptual schemes is challenged and strongly qualified. In most respects we all inhabit and cope with a common world, and do not dwell in disjunctive monads or bubbles. Hence communication, foreign travel, and even historical inquiry are possible, based ultimately on our common fund of basic human experiences and beliefs.

There are other ways to justify formally inquiry into textual and historical meanings, such as the different but complementary emphases of Emmanuel Levinas (1989) and Jurgen Habermas (1989) on the primacy of human communication and intersubjectivity. But I wish merely to submit that such arguments are powerful and, in my view, compelling. The pronouncements from various corners concerning the death of the historical-critical method are, as Mark Twain said about the newspaper report of his death, greatly exaggerated.

Culture

In his classic essay, 'Thick Description: Toward an Interpretive Theory of Culture', Clifford Geertz presents an illuminating definition of culture:

> Believing, with Max Weber, that man is an animal suspended in webs of significance he himself has spun, I take culture to be those webs, and the analysis of it is to be therefore not an experimental science in search of law but an interpretive one in search of meaning. (1973: 5)

The interpretation of cultures, argues Geertz, is analogous to the interpretation of texts. Culture is an 'acted document', and its interpretation 'is like trying to read (in the sense of 'construct a reading of') a manuscript—foreign, faded, full of ellipses, incoherencies, suspicious emendations, and tendentious commentaries' (1973: 10). In other words, interpreting culture is like interpreting the Hebrew Bible, requiring attention, erudition, circumspection, and risking the constant danger of importing anachronistic or inaccurate concepts into the reading.

Like interpretation of texts, the interpretation of culture requires knowledge of its constituent features—its lexicon, grammar, and genres. The constituent features of culture consist of various interacting layers of institutions and social practices. For ancient Israel, these include the structures of kinship and marriage, gender roles and rules, codes of honor and shame, clan and tribal organization, kingship and royal administration, religious offices such as priests and prophets, rural and urban economies, etc. These topics have been explored extensively since the seminal works of Max Weber, Albrecht Alt, and Johannes Pedersen (see recently Perdue *et al.* 1997; King and Stager 2001), and our grasp of these matters continues to be refined. But our knowledge of the forms of Israelite culture needs to be more fully integrated into our interpretive practices. These constitute the language of the cultural text.

The analogy of cultures and texts only goes so far, however. Cultures also involve the powers of coercive force and discipline that are exerted by their institutions, and this has no direct textual analogy. As Mary Douglas (1973) and Michel Foucault (1984) have argued in different ways, the dialectic of institutional power and socially acceptable knowledge is a basic feature of human culture; it is a substratum of collective existence that shapes practices, self-conceptions, and beliefs. That is, culture involves forms of interaction and forms of coercion that create and enforce the rules of the system. The lines of authority are structured in various ways throughout a culture, yielding 'webs of force' that anchor and sustain the 'webs of significance' that Geertz defines as culture. The pervasive dimension of power/knowledge complicates the model of culture as an 'acted text' whose meanings are amenable to interpretation. The social text is itself shaped by relations of power and hierarchy.

From another angle, Pierre Bourdieu has emphasized that many cultural practices do not have consistent meanings. He speaks of the 'irregularities and even incoherences' of symbolic systems and social practices, since they 'implement, in the practical state, principles that are not only coherent...but also practical' (1990: 86). Bourdieu argues compellingly that 'the procedures of practical logic are rarely entirely coherent and rarely entirely incoherent' (1990: 12). On the basis of such arguments, culture is not wholly interpretable, since it includes features that are resistant to interpretation, including practices whose meanings are contradictory, incoherent, or forgotten.

The interpretation of culture is therefore both like and unlike the interpretation of texts. From another angle, texts are also a part of culture, in their genesis, their language, their conceptuality, and their reception. To interpret adequately the meanings of texts requires an intensive engagement with the cultural practices that the texts are themselves engaged with. A text may have various types of relationships with cultural structures and practices—as a charter, a model, a critique, or a complex layering of various modes—but it is inevitably enmeshed in culture. The text is a cultural discourse, with all the possibilities and limitations for our knowledge that this situation implies.

The interrelations of textual and cultural meanings have been the focus of a recent movement in literary studies that calls itself 'the new historicism' or 'cultural poetics'. Stephen Greenblatt, its most eloquent practitioner, traces its inspiration to the confluence of literary and cultural interests in the work of such scholars as Geertz and Erich Auerbach, among others. Greenblatt aptly describes the interrelatedness of the interpretation of cultures and texts:

> textuality—in its specificity, in its local knowledge, its buried network of assumptions—is not a system distinct from lived experience but an imitation of it, and 'imitation' (that is, representation) is the principal way human beings come to understand their existence and share it with others. (2000: 40)

Here we confront a complex dialectic between texts and culture: texts imitate lived experience in order to share and express particular understandings of it (this is Auerbach's thesis in his great work, *Mimesis* [1953]) Moreover, texts rely on the implicit assumptions and 'local knowledge' of culture (Geertz's phrase [1983]) for their symbolic codes, from language to literary conventions to politics, religion, gender, epistemology, etc. The critical discourse of new historicism provides a sophisticated model for the task of tracing the complex interplay of texts and culture.

In sum, to read a text richly requires reading it in relation to the larger world of circulating, conflicting, and sometimes uninterpretable practices, institutions, forces, and meanings that constitute culture. By attending to the nuances of culture in the text, and the text in culture, we enrich the path of the historical-critical method marked out by Spinoza.

Memory

Memory, wrote Augustine in his *Confessions*, is 'the present of things past' (9.20). The past exists for us only in our present memories, which may be themselves memories of previous memories. Our past selves, past events, past lives, all persist only to the extent that we remember them. But memories can also be of things that never happened, or of things that did not happen in quite the way we remember them. Memories recall the past in a way that recreates the past, foregrounding and embellishing certain parts and suppressing others. No one has total recall; our memories are always partial, meaning that they are both incomplete and biased, colored in various ways. Memory is unreliable, but it is also the foundation of our sense of who we are, and of our sense of the past.[3]

Cultures also have what we can call memories, a body of collective memories that individuals are initiated into as part of the process of acculturation, and that comprise an essential ingredient and

---

3. See the wide-ranging treatment in Lowenthal 1985: 193-210.

causative agent of cultural identity. The shared memories of a culture and of its nested subsets—families, tribes, religious communities, etc.—are subject to the same kinds of changes as individual memory. They are a blend of historical details and imaginative embellishments, elements of history, legend, and myth, blending and crystallizing differently according to the concerns and experiences of each generation. As Maurice Halbwachs observed in his classic study, *Les cadres sociaux de la memoire*:

> the collective frameworks of memory [viz. in the family, the religion, social classes] are not constructed after the fact by the combination of individual recollections; nor are they empty forms where recollections coming from elsewhere would insert themselves. Collective frameworks are, to the contrary, precisely the instruments used by the collective memory to reconstruct an image of the past which is in accord, in each epoch, with the predominant thoughts of the society. (1992: 40)

The collective memories of a culture recall and recreate a past that is relevant for the present. It is not the past of the historian, nor is it a wholly fictional past. It is a representation of the past that serves as a foundation and charter for collective values and identity, and as such is true existentially and morally, if not entirely true historically.

The aspects of the past that are not in harmony with the present are forgotten in collective memory. For example, the American collective memory of the Pilgrims, to which young children are dutifully initiated at school and in the family feast of Thanksgiving, is heroic and morally uplifting. The features foregrounded are prototypically American—brave pioneer immigrants who left behind the corrupt Old World and risked their lives to find freedom, living in harmony with nature and their neighbors, God-fearing, modest, and blessed. The historical realities of the early Puritan colonists—who may be fairly described as a sect of radical zealots—are rightly forgotten in this cultural portrait of the foundational past. The collective memories of the past are perennially filtered through the frameworks of a culture's moral ideals and self-representation.

Jan Assmann has recently explored the dynamics of cultural memory in several works, most comprehensively in *Das kulturelle Gedächtnis* (1997). Not surprisingly, he describes ancient Israel as the prototype of a 'memory culture' (*Erinnerungskultur*), since 'Israel as a people was constituted and continued under the imperative, "Keep and remember"' (שמור וזכור) (1997: 78). This characterization alludes to and acknowledges Yosef Yerushalmi's important book, *Zakhor* (1989), which elegantly explores the nature of biblical memory. Assmann (and to a lesser extent Yerushalmi) emphasizes that in ancient cultures cultural memory is often recited or performed in ritual contexts, involving the twin processes of repetition and actualization in the present. The ritual performances of cultural memories in ancient Israel—such as in the Passover ceremony ('Remember this day…', Exod. 13:3), the rites of the first fruits ('My father was a wandering Aramean…', Deut. 26:5), and pan-tribal festivals ('In olden times your forefathers…', Josh. 24)—provided an essential 'connective structure' for Israelite society and for its cultural and religious self-definition. In such rituals, as Yerushalmi observes:

> the language and the gesture are geared to spur, not so much a leap of memory as a fusion of past and present. Memory here is no longer recollection, which still preserves a sense of distance, but reactualization. (1989: 44)

Hence the Passover ritual and the appeals to memory in Deuteronomy continually stress the contemporary or existential quality of the past events: 'And you will tell your son on that day, "It is because of what Yahweh did *for me* when *I* went out from Egypt"' (Exod. 13:8). The constitutive and sacred events of the past are still alive in the present, particularly in the evocative and performative context of ritual.

The appeal to Israel's cultural memories also served a variety of other social functions, including justification of legal and moral norms, providing charters for religious institutions, and enabling cultural critique. For example, the cultural memory of Egyptian bondage serves as a warrant for the compassionate treatment of slaves, resident aliens, and even Egyptians (Exod. 22:20; 23:9; Deut. 15:15; 23:8). This memory serves not only as a charter and focus for the festival of Passover, it also serves as a charter for the observance of the Sabbath. In the Deuteronomic version of the Decalogue, the Sabbath is a day of recollection and actualization in the present (Assmann's *Wiederholung* and *Vergegenwärtigung*) of deliverance from bondage:

> Remember that you were slaves in the land of Egypt, and Yahweh your God brought you out from there with a strong hand and outstretched arm; therefore Yahweh your God has commanded you to observe the Sabbath day. (Deut. 5:15)

As Brevard Childs comments (1962: 53), 'Israel observes the Sabbath *in order* to remember her slavery and deliverance'. The Sabbath, in this sense, enacts a weekly Exodus, and the work-week is a metaphorical model of Egyptian bondage. (This contrasts with the version of the Sabbath command in Exod. 20:11, where the Sabbath is motivated by God's rest on the seventh day.)

The appeal to the cultural memory of the Exodus also served as a resource for cultural critique. In the story of the division of the kingdom (1 Kgs 12) there are several indications that secession of the northern tribes, under their leader Jeroboam, was figured as a new Exodus from the slavery imposed by Solomon. Rainer Albertz argues that 'the battle against Solomon's forced labor by Jeroboam and the northern tribes was fought with an appeal to the liberation of their forefathers from Egyptian forced labor' (1994: 142). The traces of this appeal to the Exodus are overwritten to some degree in the Deuteronomistic edition of this text, but the emphasis on the harsh burden of forced labor (recalling the hard labor imposed by Pharaoh), Jeroboam's flight and return from Egypt (recalling Moses' flight and return to Egypt), and Jeroboam's appeal to 'your god(s), O Israel, who brought you out of the land of Egypt' (1 Kgs 12:28) make this set of allusions to the Exodus recognizable.[4]

Ultimately the locus of Israelite collective memory was transposed from domestic and ritual recitations to authoritative texts. Assmann describes the new connective structure that arose from this process:

> In connection with the textualization of traditions a gradual transition took place from the dominance of repetition to the dominance of actualization, from 'ritual' to 'textual' coherence. With this a new connective structure emerged. Its binding power consisted not of imitation and preservation, but of interpretation and remembering. In the place of liturgy came hermeneutics. (1997: 18)

Israel's cultural memories were transposed into a collection of authoritative texts, which themselves came to require authoritative commentary. This transposition eventually entailed a new form of ritual coherence, as the central canonical text—the Pentateuch—came to be recited in annual (or triennial) cycles of weekly readings. This created a new ritual context of repetition and actualization in the synagogue and study house, with the text as the focus of ritual coherence.

This transition to textuality also created a new model for critical revisions of cultural memory, since textual compositions could be attributed to ancient figures. Such critical revisions can be called countermemories, counterhistories, or invented traditions (see Funkenstein 1993: 36-49; Hobsbawm and Ranger 1984; and in a slightly different sense, Foucault 1977: 160). Ironically, Assmann's

---

4.   Note the phrase, 'the hard labor of your father' (עבדת אביך הקשה, 1 Kgs 12:4), which evokes the 'hard labor' of Pharaoh (עבדה קשה in Exod. 1:14; 6:9; Deut. 26:6); see further Zakovitch 1991: 87-97; Frisch 2000: 13-17.

paradigm for a book of memory, Deuteronomy (1997: 212-28), is better described as such a countermemory or invented tradition. The book that most dramatically thematizes the topic of memory—God's command to 'remember' occurs most often in this book—is aptly described by Bernard Levinson as a work of 'transformative exegesis, the deliberate attempt to rework prestigious texts in the light of the innovation of centralization' (1997: 6). He observes that 'the authors camouflaged the radical and often subversive nature of their innovations [by] using the terms of the older dispensation' (1997: 6). The rhetoric of memory is one of the ways that Deuteronomy masks and authorizes its radical revision, asserting itself through Moses' voice as the authoritative memory of God's revelation. Deuteronomy is a book of cultural memory precisely as a countermemory—a remarkable discourse of power/knowledge asserting the legitimacy of a centralized and purified cult[5]—which substitutes its revised or reinterpreted memories for the cultural memories embodied in the earlier traditions and sources (especially J and E).

The analysis of the biblical narratives of Israel's foundational past—its ethnogenesis—as literary transpositions of cultural memory is powerful and apt. It helps to untangle some of the difficult questions of the relationship between the biblical narratives and Israelite culture and history, and provides a way to explore their meanings as simultaneously literary, cultural, and (in varying degrees) historical. In the ancient world, as in the modern, the forms of cultural memory and countermemory are more pervasive and important than the related practice of historical writing, which itself is a child of memory.

History

The word 'history' has two different but interrelated meanings: what happened in the past, and an account or inquiry of what happened in the past. Hegel commented on this duality in his *Philosophie der Geschichte*, concluding that there is an inner connection between history's 'objective' side (viz. the things that happened) and its 'subjective' side (viz. the narration of the things that happened), such that the transcendent World-Spirit manifests itself through both (see Funkenstein 1993: 3-5). In recent years scholars have seen that the relationship between these two sides of history is more problematic. In particular, a number of scholars—particularly Paul Veyne (1984) and Hayden White (1978, 1987)—have argued that the subjective side (the narration) shapes and constrains our conception of the objective side (the things that happened). In part this is an extension of the Kantian principle that our perception of reality is necessarily mediated through our perceptual and conceptual forms, but this principle now extends to the representational forms of narrative discourse. As Veyne argues, 'history is what the conventions of the genre make of it, unknown to us' (1984: 289). Since it uses narrative forms but focuses on actual events, Veyne elegantly describes the genre of history as 'a true novel' (1984: x). White similarly argues that 'interpretation in history consists of the provisions of a plot-structure for a sequence of events so that their nature as a comprehensible process is revealed by their figuration as a story of a particular kind' (1978: 58). The imaginative processes of figuration and narrative representation necessarily shape our historical understanding.

In this way the boundary between objective history (the things that happened) and the subjective practice of historical inquiry has become problematized. Our histories of the past impose various kinds of plots and discursive structures on the past, and even determine what counts as a significant (because narratable) historical fact. Michel de Certeau describes this situation as 'the paradox—almost an oxymoron—of a relation established between two antinomic terms, between the real and discourse'. Yet, he adds, the task of writing history is to work '*as if* the two were being joined'

---

5. Note that this discourse was enforced by bloodshed (2 Kgs 23:20).

(1988: xxvii). Once again, we must work within the horizons of a pragmatic and 'chastened' method, one whose goal—comprehending the past—is achievable to a lesser degree than its founding fathers imagined, since our tools have their own perceptual features. Yet I would add that, in principle, understanding the discourses of past others is not differently constituted than understanding others in the present—it requires charity and effort, but it is certainly possible—and we engage in understanding others all the time, usually with felicity.

Another distinction needs to be inserted here, that between our modern analytical category of history and the concepts and practices that are native to our ancient source, the Hebrew Bible. We need to examine the relationships between our categories and theirs, between our senses of history and the Bible's senses of the past. Recent discussions often blur these distinctions, either subsuming modern history-writing and the biblical writings about the past under the same rubric of 'history',[6] which ignores the distinctive features and internal differentiations of the biblical practices and our practices, or denying that the Bible has a historical sense at all, figuring the biblical writers as pre-logical or romantic primitives.[7] What we need is a more detailed and layered sense of the similarities and the differences between our views and practices and theirs, and the differences among the biblical practices.

B. Halpern has made some strides toward a more nuanced picture by contrasting the procedures of the Deuteronomic historian (DtrH, the Josianic editor/author of the Deuteronomistic History) with those of his written sources (1988: esp. 205-80). For example, Halpern notes that the prose narrative of Judges 4, which relies upon and interprets the older poetic text of Judges 5, offers a naturalistic interpretation of events, omitting the miraculous events and language of Judges 5. The divine hand is still present in the overall picture—the text concludes: 'On that day God defeated Jabin king of Canaan before the Israelites' (Judg. 4:23)—but God's agency works through human agency in a kind of complementary causality, eschewing direct divine intervention. This approach yields, as Halpern notes, 'supernatural causation' but natural events, in contrast with the focus on supernatural events in the poetry (1988: 271).

Halpern observes that different types of description of past events in the Bible correspond to different social locations. He draws a distinction between cultic and non-cultic discourses, the former localized in ritual sites and occasions, the latter found in such settings as public administration, law, etc.:

> Myth and history belonged not just to different intellectual or economic realms, but to different spatial ones as well: they were local, restricted, genres of thought and literature. (1988: 270)

The genre of history begins in earnest, in Halpern's view, after the era of cultic-related events has ended. Interestingly, this transition in narrative modes transpires after the dramatic recital of collective memory by Joshua at the all-Israel ceremony at Shechem (Josh. 24). There Joshua recounts *in nuce* the story of Yahweh's promises and covenant from the call of Abraham to the settlement of the Promised Land. This covenant renewal ceremony in the Land itself is a decisive

---

6. E.g. Van Seters 1992: 35: 'there may be a great many inherited images of the past—traditions of almost infinite variety. But their selective collection and organization according to chronological and thematic or "causal" relationships is the intellectual activity of historiography'. Van Seters thereby lumps together Genesis and Kings, Hesiod and Herodotus. This approach seems to conflate categories rather than analyze them. A similar criticism applies to Brettler's more narrowly focused proposal for 'defining a historical narrative within biblical studies as "a narrative that presents a past"' (1995: 12). B. Halpern's approach usefully incorporates historiographical intention—'histories purport to be true, or probable, representations of events and relationships in the past' (1988: 6)—but underemphasizes the historiographic role of documentary and evidential critique (see below).

7. See the critical discussion in Halpern 1988: 266-71 ('A Poet and Not a Historian').

scene of *Wiederholung* and *Vergegenwärtigung*. After this, Halpern observes, 'starting from the era of the Judges…there is no spectacle, no suns standing still, no seas hurled about' (1988: 276). The period that we may, with some qualifications, count as historical commences after the ritual recitation and summing up of the constitutive and most sacred past, the era of cultural memory.

After the divine promises of land, offspring, and blessing are fulfilled by the conquest and settlement of the Promised Land, subsequent time is not so valorized, and is subjected to a more naturalistic analysis and presentation. The former era is repeated and actualized in ritual contexts, while the latter era is the object of discourse in non-cultic contexts. These histories are still infused with theological forms of causality, and interspersed with traditional material (such as the Samson and the Elijah/Elisha cycles), which reverts to the miracles of ancestral times. But a distinction between ritual and non-ritual genres—or discourses that are amenable to ritual recitation and those that are not—seems to hold.[8]

The biblical writings may be fairly described as operating on various points of a continuum involving myth, memory, and history. But the biblical writers are not historians in the modern sense, since they do not question the veracity of their sources, which since Herodotus and Thucydides has been a prerequisite for critical history-writing. The biblical writings that address Israel's political history evince a practice that has a family relationship to critical history without entering it completely. To revert to Spinoza's diction, there is as yet no conceptual distinction between a text's (or tradition's) truth and its meaning. There are historical facts in these books, but history-writing must be critical in order to be itself.[9] On the other hand, the absence of documentary critique perhaps allowed the biblical writers to imagine the past more richly, without the burden of methodological doubt.

If the history-like writings of the Bible present a relatively disenchanted account of the era of tribes and kings, the texts before and outside this world of prose belong to the domain of sacred time, where the discourse performs its own alchemy. These are the narratives most rooted in cultural memory, which includes and transforms history without being bound to it. Their meanings are perhaps more durable than history, since they do not depend on the mere successiveness of events.[10] They have their own reasons and meanings, a dense and deceptive simplicity, to which the writing of history—in its various modalities—can only aspire.

References

Albertz, R. (1994) *A History of Israelite Religion in the Old Testament Period.* Vol. 1, *From the Beginnings to the End of the Monarchy* (Louisville, KY: Westminster John Knox Press).

Assmann, J. (1997) *Das kulturelle Gedächtnis: Schrift, Erinnerung und politische Identität in frühen Hochkulturen* (Munich: Beck).

Auerbach, E. (1953) *Mimesis: The Representation of Reality in Western Literature* (Princeton, NJ: Princeton University Press).

Bourdieu, P. (1990) *The Logic of Practice* (Stanford: Stanford University Press).

---

8. Note that the royal psalms, which were presumably recited in ritual contexts, never address historical events, only the mythic or paradigmatic past. The only seeming exception, Ps. 132, describes David bringing the Ark to Jerusalem, which is a paradigmatic cultic event, and is often argued to have been reactualized in ritual performances; see, e.g., Kraus 1993: 475-79.

9. A similar distinction is made by Knauf 1991: 62-63: 'Ancient [Near Eastern] histories, like their modern counterparts, are theoretical constructs that incorporate empirical data. However, they are closed systems that allow for the criticism of persons acting in history, but not for the criticism of the system's theoretical presuppositions.'

10. See Aristotle, *Poetics* 51b.6-8; and Hendel 1995: 36-37.

Brettler, M.Z. (1995) *The Creation of History in Ancient Israel* (London: Routledge).

Certeau, M. de (1988) *The Writing of History* (New York: Columbia University Press).

Childs, B.S. (1962) *Memory and Tradition in Israel* (London: SCM Press).

Collins, J.J. (2005) *The Bible After Babel: Historical Criticism in a Postmodern Age* (Grand Rapids: Eerdmans).

Davidson, D. (1984) On the Very Idea of a Conceptual Scheme. In *Inquiries into Truth and Interpretation* (Oxford: Clarendon Press): 183-98.

—(2001) Three Varieties of Knowledge. In *Subjective, Intersubjective, Objective* (Oxford: Clarendon Press): 205-20.

Dobbs-Allsopp, F.W. (1999) Rethinking Historical Criticism. *Biblical Interpretation* 7: 235-71.

Douglas, M. (1973) *Natural Symbols: Explorations in Cosmology* (2nd edn; New York: Random House).

Foucault, M. (1977) *Language, Counter-memory, Practice: Selected Essays and Interviews*, edited by D.F. Bouchard (Ithaca: Cornell University Press).

—(1984) *The Foucault Reader*, edited by P. Rabinow (New York: Pantheon).

Frisch, A. (2000) The Exodus Motif in 1 Kings 1–14. *JSOT* 87: 3-21.

Funkenstein, A. (1993) *Perceptions of Jewish History* (Berkeley: University of California Press).

Geertz, C. (1973) *The Interpretation of Cultures* (New York: Basic Books).

—(1983) *Local Knowledge* (New York: Basic Books).

Greenblatt, S. (2000) The Touch of the Real. In C. Gallagher and S. Greenblatt, *Practicing New Historicism* (Chicago: University of Chicago Press): 20-48.

Habermas, J. (1989) *Communication and the Evolution of Society* (Boston: Beacon Press).

Halbwachs, M. (1992) The Social Frameworks of Memory. In *On Collective Memory*, edited by L.A. Coser (Chicago: University of Chicago Press): 35-189.

Halpern, B. (1988) *The First Historians: The Hebrew Bible and History* (San Francisco: Harper & Row).

Hegel, G.W.F. (1975) *Lectures on the Philosophy of World History: Introduction*, translated by H.B. Nisbet (Cambridge: Cambridge University Press).

Hendel, R. (1995) Tangled Plots in Genesis. In *Fortunate the Eyes that See: Essays in Honor of David Noel Freedman*, edited by A.B. Beck *et al.* (Grand Rapids: Eerdmans): 35-51.

—(2005) *Remembering Abraham: Culture, Memory, and History in the Hebrew Bible* (New York: Oxford University Press).

Hobsbawm, E., and T. Ranger (eds.) (1984) *The Invention of Tradition* (Cambridge: Cambridge University Press).

Iggers, G.G. (1997) *Historiography in the Twentieth Century: From Scientific Objectivity to the Postmodern Challenge* (Hanover, NH: Wesleyan University Press).

Israel, J.I. (2001) *Radical Enlightenment: Philosophy and the Making of Modernity 1650–1750* (Oxford: Oxford University Press).

King, P.J., and L.E. Stager (2001) *Life in Biblical Israel* (Louisville: Westminster John Knox Press).

Knauf, E.A. (1991) From History to Interpretation. In *The Fabric of History: Text, Artifact and Israel's Past*, edited by D.V. Edelman (Sheffield: JSOT Press): 26-64.

Kraus, H.-J. (1993) *Psalms 60–150* (Minneapolis: Fortress Press).

Levinas, E. (1989) *The Levinas Reader*, edited by S. Hand (Oxford: Blackwell).

Levinson, B.M. (1997) *Deuteronomy and the Hermeneutics of Legal Innovation* (New York: Oxford University Press).

Lowenthal, D. (1985) *The Past is a Foreign Country* (Cambridge: Cambridge University Press).

Perdue, L.G., J. Blenkinsopp, J.J. Collins, and C. Meyers (1997) *Families in Ancient Israel* (Louisville, KY: Westminster John Knox Press)

Rorty, R. (1982) The World Well Lost. In *Consequences of Pragmatism* (Minneapolis: University of Minnesota Press): 3-18.

Scholder, K. (1990) *The Birth of Modern Critical Theology: Origins and Problems of Biblical Criticism in the Seventeenth Century* (London: SCM Press).

Simon, R. (1685) *Histoire critique du Vieux Testament* (Rotterdam: Reinier Leers).

Spinoza, B. (2001) *Theological-Political Treatise*, translated by S. Shirley (2nd edn; Indianapolis: Hackett).

Van Seters, J. (1992) *Prologue to History: The Yahwist as Historian in Genesis* (Louisville, KY: Westminster John Knox Press).

Veyne, P. (1984) *Writing History: Essay on Epistemology* (Middletown, CT: Wesleyan University Press).

White, H. (1978) *Tropics of Discourse: Essays in Cultural Criticism* (Baltimore: The Johns Hopkins University Press).

—(1987) *The Content of the Form: Narrative Discourse and Historical Representation* (Baltimore: The Johns Hopkins University Press).

Wittgenstein, L. (1953) *Philosophical Investigations* (New York: Macmillan).

Yerushalmi, Y.H. (1989) *Zakhor: Jewish History and Jewish Memory* (2nd edn; New York: Schocken).

Zakovitch, Y. (1991) *'And You Shall Tell Your Son...': The Concept of the Exodus in the Bible* (Jerusalem: Magnes Press).

15 Archaeology, the Bible and History

The Fall of the House of Omri—and the Origins of the Israelite State

Baruch Halpern

Abstract

Specialized isolation of corpora of evidence for individual evaluation is the basis on which historical reconstruction must proceed. But the evaluators must exhibit cognizance of the range of likely implications, and even possible ones, for each corpus. Only in that context can one consider the sources as a web, or tapestry, or information. Here, the combination of data for the 9th century from Mesopotamia to the West exposes literary slants and archaeological shortcomings. The results shed light on the rise of the Israelite state to its apogees in the mid-9th and early 8th centuries, and raise a series of questions about isolating indications from historical archaeology.

Introduction

In 1998, excavators at Megiddo encountered anew the stables of Solomon. Chicago identified these buildings as stables in the 1920s, because they had troughs between pillars that notionally defined stalls. They were Solomonic because the Bible tied stables as well as Megiddo to that king, but mentioned stables of no other king.

They weren't Solomonic. Hindsight showed that the stratum (IVA) was later. Ahab, Shalmaneser III says, sent 2000 chariots to central Syria in 853. So, remaining stables, the buildings moved to Ahab. Still, perhaps Shalmaneser was exaggerating a contingent of 200 chariots, or 20. So maybe the stables' proprietor was Jeroboam II: not long after him, Sargon incorporated a division of 50 or more Israelite chariots as an intact unit into the Assyrian cavalry, an exception to standard Assyrian military practice (Dalley 1985).

And we don't have stables. This issue is in dispute, since identifiable stables do not have troughs (although field troughs did exist; for the history of discussion, see Holladay 1986; Herr 1988; latterly, Cantrell and Finkelstein 2006). And Megiddo has disgorged no stratified horse bones in this period; the buildings are in the wrong location, too far from the city gates; the drainage is inadequate given equine liquid discharge, versus extensive collection facilities at Per-Ramesses, for tanning;[1] hauling fodder, feed, water and bedding would be little short of Herculean; the Assyrians deliberately robbed and buried, rather than reusing, the facilities using the old pillars and troughs as general building materials, although they had horses on site; and so on.

Soil tests were inconclusive. Even a minor shift in PH level can dramatically affect phosphorus concentrations. Phytolith count was pretty even around the site—there are a lot of calling cards in the soil of the tell. The answers may not involve horses: my money is on opium and on fatted sheep. But a better theory will crop up. The state did not devote 15–20% of a walled administrative center to unnecessary consumption, or even to production or mercantile activity that was not lucrative.

The argument about the stables, dragging on for 80 years, is a snapshot of our field. Inside any discipline, we cannot for the life of us agree. Is a pottery assemblage 10th century, or is it 9th? Is the building a stable, a barracks, a market, a depot, an opium factory? Assuming that Solomon lived, does Kings even claim that he stabled horses at Megiddo? Did Ahab have thousands or dozens of horses?

Our structures may not be stables. But every scholar who deals with the issue appeals to results from neighboring fields in order to validate his or her view. Colleagues with whom we have the expertise to disagree are in error. But on colleagues in other fields, we may implicitly rely. The same is true of natural scientists who rely on archaeological or historical results. How, in sum, do we cross fields?

The basis is chronology. In the Iron Age, Assyria connected a solar eclipse report to lists of annual eponyms, or *limmu*s, inside of reliable kinglists.[2] Assyrian kings sometimes detailed their reigns in proper annals, so that sporadically we have a year-by-year window on some events. Down a level on the scales of granularity and probability, we have probable reference to a 7th-century eclipse abroad in Egyptian sources, and other textual sources which, taken at face value, move the chronology from this point into the classical era. Down another level on our scale, we have stratigraphy, and then typologies: pottery, orthography, paleography, artistic technique; down a level from that, dating texts or their sources by their relation to realia (or, sometimes naively, *vice versa*), down another level, texts in relation to one another. Down another level, dating texts by the way their ideology or form can be construed to belong to a period one reconstructs, the last being the dominant form of dating in biblical scholarship.[3]

The history of the 9th century offers an example. Here, we have *limmu*s and the annals and monuments of Asshurnasirpal II, Shalmaneser III, Adad-Narari III, Shamshi-Adad V and even

---

1.   Reported by Reuters in October, 1999 (BBC, 14 October) and excavated by Edgar Pusch; notably the stable units are more than double the length of the 'stalls' at Megiddo.

2.   See Millard 1994: 41, in Sivan. Only one such eclipse fits, that of June 15, 763, whose path of totality reached Assyria ca. 8:20 AM, and which was near total in Israel, where it began just before 6 and ended at around 9:30, about 17 minutes earlier. It may be referred to in Amos 4:13 ('who makes dawn darkness') 5:8 ('who makes morning into pitch darkness'). From there, we extrapolate on the basis of synchronisms, but also of kinglists in Egypt, Babylon, Judah, Israel and Tyre, to build a chronology. The consistency with the external material, especially of the kinglists of Israel and Judah, is part of the argument to their reliability. Logically, the same is true of the materials from other regions—that is, the argument to reliability in the retailing of succession hinges on synchronisms.

3.   In its Pyrrhonism regarding sources, this method ignores the principle that texts, like oral recitations, are renegotiated with each audience to which they are directed, such that any inherited information is liable to be glossed, without, however, forfeiting entirely its historical value. See Vansina 1965, 1985. With attention to the role of objects in preserving and in inspiring accounts of the past, see David 2006.

Marduk-zakir-shumi I, plus records in chronicles. In the west, we have a plethora of royal inscriptions.[4] Kings devotes seventeen chapters to the Omrides, and Jehu's successors continue for five, with a reference to 841 in Hosea. The sources weave a web of synchronisms. And the pertinence of some of our remains (at Lachish, Ashdod, Jezreel) is not yet in question. Altogether, the 9th century is remarkably well illuminated.

Of all this, what is securely and finely dated? Not the archaeological layers.[5] Archaeological derivates come from gross, but robust data. The bigger town, with the more monumental structures, for example, is the capital—historically a statistically probable conclusion over spans of many years, but far from a foregone one. And which 'time' is under discussion? Assemblages differ within and across sites: comparability is rough, except in short-lived contemporary strata with common imports. And even imports *survive* differentially, affecting the limits of ceramic synchroneity. The presence of Philistine monochrome and bichrome or of bichrome and red slip in a stratum has no implication for times of any given pot's production, for example. Rarely considered, but important, is also the fact that a stratum is not a snapshot in time, but reflects time depth: in the same way that one cannot take a snapshot of the universe at a single moment, one cannot do so for an excavated culture, as opposed to a landscape (if one excavates a complete destruction perfectly, a rarity in compound sites).

Text, by contrast, leads to fine inferences from fragile data. Text codes intention, sometimes veiled: it is tricky to identify blunders and lies. Relating a web of sites to history turns always on which evidence is strongest. Often, archaeology must guide interpretation. One cannot construct a Davidic empire on the Euphrates, with no public works outside Jerusalem (E. Mazar 2006; likely, the stepped stone structure ca. 1000–970), or project leveraged olive presses into LB. Conversely, it would be foolhardy to deny 9th-century Assyrian expansion, regardless of its absence in local archaeological records, latterly more and more supplemented by epigraphs.

The strongest archaeological correlation is with the world behind texts—on organization, on stratification in the village; on daily and elite life, on topography, on trade. This is also the information many texts presuppose, and so least distort. In the 7th century, both sources evince growing state intrusiveness into the life of the family, marginalization of intermediary kinship structures, increasing individuation accompanied by the universalization of norms, industrialization, central planning and autocracy. This comes with a missionary self-righteousness bent on tearing out the traditional culture by its roots and replacing it with philosophical monotheism of one or another stripe (as Halpern 1996b, 2003).

The 9th-Century Sources

Mesha can be dated only by Kings or paleography.[6] But Assyrian texts, datable within a span of a few years, securely limit the transition from Hadadezer to Hazael in Damascus—and the dates of contemporary Israelite kings; Josephus's sources include a Tyrian kinglist (see *Ap.* 1.106-127; *Ant.* 8.55-56, 61-62). We have a fixed date in 853 for the confrontation at Qarqar, along with the names

---

4. E.g., Zincirli, Karatepe, Zakur, Bredsch, the Hazael booty inscriptions, the Dan stela and Mesha. See below.

5. See Finkelstein 1996a, 1996b, 1998a, 1998b, 1999, 2000a, 2000b, 2001, 2002 versus Ben-Tor and Ben-Ami 1998; Ben-Tor 2001, 2002; Dever 2001; Gal and Alexandre 2000; Gal 2003; A. Mazar 2005; Routledge 2003.

6. There is some chronological significance to the fact that Mesha participates in the 9th-century feeding frenzy of the erection of stelae in the west, as at Dan, Afis (Zakur) and so on, and the border markers of Adad-Narari III. All these texts date to the last part of the 9th century and the early part of the 8th.

of several participants. For the eruption in 841, Kings complements Assyrian claims and those of the Dan stela. Mesha, too, celebrates 841: 'I saw [the son of Omri] humiliated and all his dynasty'.[7] Adad-Narari mentions both Joash of Israel and Zakur of Hamath and Luash, along with Atarshumki of Arpad, a Mari' of Damascus and kings of Kummuh and Gurgum.[8] Zakur (*KAI* 202) and Joash's regnal account (2 Kgs 13:10-25 + 14:8-14) forefront Bar-Hadad, Adad-Narari's Mari', a title the king of Damascus inherited from Hazael, his father. Zakur's chief antagonist after Bar-Hadad was Atarshumki of Arpad[9]—this 'king of Aram' sired the Melqart stele's donor[10] and Matiel, the junior partner in the Sefire treaty and leader of Aram after the circumscription of Damascene influence. Adad-Narari relates that Atarshumki led a coalition of 8 kings against him in the north, around Gaziantepe; to this campaign, he regularly reverts.[11] Zakur mentions the same coalition, of seven or ten kings, led by Bar-Hadad, king of Aram.[12] The besiegers of Hazrach include Arpad,

7.   *w'r'h bh wbbth* in *KAI* 181:7, *hr'ny b-* in 181:4; cf. Cowley 1923: 30:17, 31:16 = Porten and Yardeni 1986: 7:17, 8:16, *bzyn bhwn*; Cowley 1923: 30 [Porten and Yardeni 1986: 7]: 16 (*hhwyn' bwydrng*); 31:15 [Porten and Yardeni 1986: 8] (*hwyn' bwyddrng*); probably related to Ahiqar 106, 'death, which is/can not be seen (*mthzh*). The sense of the idiom, {[verb meaning: see] + b-} is clear in all these instances, namely, to see one's opponent humbled (i.e. naked, stripped physically or metaphorically) or, perhaps more specifically, dead. Compare the use of *glh 'rwh* in P and Exod. 20:26 (E); Deut. 27:20; Ezek. 22:10; and, *glh*, N, as in 2 Sam. 6:20-22; Jer. 13:22; 23:29. Exposure of the body, but especially of the corpse, was anathema.

8.   Grayson 1996: A.0.104.2 (Antakya stele with the Orontes as border between Zakur and Atarshumki, protecting the latter); 3:7-22 (Pazarcik stele, intervening at the invitation of Ushpilulume of Kummuh against Atarshumki and eight allied kings at Paqarahubunu, and establishing a border between Kummuh and Gurgum, protecting the former); 4:8-9 (tribute from Atarshumki, and probably allies along a river, likely, the Euphrates); 5:5-8 (Sheikh Hammad, one year conquest of Atarshumki and allies, kings of land of Hatti); 6:11-20 (Saba'a stele, 797 or later, detailing the submission of kings of Hatti who had withheld tribute starting under Shamshi-Adad V in 5th year, and a possibly later march on Damascus and Mari'); 7:4-12 (Rimah stele, 797 or later, subduing Amurru, Hatti in one year, receiving, possibly later, tribute from Mari', Joash the Samarian, Tyre and Sidon, plus erecting a statue in Arwad, logging cedars and receiving tribute from the kings of Nairi); 8:11-21 (Calah, summary, subjecting Hatti, Amurru entirely, and, perhaps later, Tyre, Sidon, Omri [= Israel], Edom and Philistia, and march on Damascus, submission of Mari'); 1003 (fragment mentioning Zakur). See further Grayson 1975: 169 iv 19-22, presumably referring to inroads against Shalmaneser III, Shamshi-Adad V, Shalmaneser IV and Asshur-Dan III, but reflecting the same concerns for fixing borders as the royal inscriptions (and 169 iv 23 - 171 iv 30 may stem from such an inscription).

9.   Grayson 1996: A.0.104.2:5, 9 (son of Adramu); 3:11-13 (son of Adramu of the town, Arpad); 4:9 (son of Arame, in a fragmentary context); = *br gš*, 'the scion of Agusi', named second in *KAI* 202:5.

10.   *KAI* 201; see further Pitard 1987: 141; 1988, for the reading *'trhmk*. The traces of the letter Pitard reads as -*h*-, however, are at least equally and perhaps more compatible with the reading, *samekh*. See Pitard 1988: 4 Fig. 1; 6 Fig. 7, and the breakthrough to the right of the lowest horizontal stroke on the letter. Pitard entertains but rejects this possibility (1988: 12). Even were Pitard's reading correct—improbably for historical and linguistic reasons—the result would be a phoneme /h/ for */s/, Assyrian /š/, not an impossibility in its own right.

11.   See above, n. 8, for summaries of the relevant texts, which, unlike annals, in several cases run the campaign of 805 together with later accomplishments.

12.   So Arpad and Damascus both have a 'king of Aram', meaning 'Aramean king' (cf. 1 Kgs 15:18, king of Aram who dwelt in Damascus); in self-designation, the phrase suggests, without necessarily claiming, kingship over all of inland Syria. Both Bar-Hadad of Damascus and Atarshumki (*br gš* in the Zakur stela) may have claimed it. Alternatively, Bar-Hadad of Arpad may have adopted it after the defeat of Bar-Hadad of Damascus, around 796: see Millard 1994: 35. Against Pitard 1988: 12-13, the Aramu of Shalmaneser III's annals is probably identical with the Adramu whom Adad-Narari identifies as the father of Atarshumki (with /dr/ reflecting a slight trilling of the /r/ rather than differing roots: see Grayson 1996: A.0.102.4:11). Bar-Hadad son of Atarsamek may thus have been succeeded by Mati'el of the Sefire treaty. Bar-Hadad styles himself 'king of Aram' and the Sefire treaty, slightly later, implies the same of Matiel (as *KAI* 222A:4-6; B:1-4)—*ktk* at Sefire is most probably Kashku, despite the philological objection that the Old Aramaic phoneme,

Que, Unqi, Gurgum, Sam'al and Melid (*KAI* 202:5-7), whose kings probably joined Atarshumki and Gurgum against Adad-Narari and Kummuh at Paqarahubunu in 805. This same redoubt had been contested by Shalmaneser III (as Grayson 1996: A.0.102.6.iii.17-20; 8:42'-43'; 10.iii.7-10; 14:90). Such conflicts eventually led to Gurgum's incorporation into Kummuh to the east and Que to the west.

Kings also reports Bar-Hadad's succession to the throne of his father, Hazael (2 Kgs 13:24). 2 Kgs 13:3-4, placing Jehoahaz with both (contrast 13:22-24, where Bar-Hadad is related only to Joash), and the Zakur inscription (*KAI* 202A:11ff.) even treat Adad-Narari's intervention against Bar-Hadad identically: in both, Assyria was literally the answer to a prayer, and in neither is Assyria identified. The other trope for justifying foreign assistance is purchasing it cheap, as with Asa, Kilamuwa of Zincirli, and Ahaz.[13] When Menahem does the same (2 Kgs 15:19-20), the same procedure (pay-off) is treated negatively, without the term 'bribe'. Permanent imperial presence rendered these apologies unusable. The coincidence between Jehoahaz's regnal account and Zakur's reflects an alliance of Israel and Hamath in the early 8th century, when Adad-Narari moved against Damascus (Lemaire 1993).

By the end of the century, then, Hazael had rewoven and Bar-Hadad inherited a fabric of alliances, a variant of which had confronted Shalmaneser III at Qarqar and thereafter. Damascus and Arpad dominated Syria. At some point, Hazael conquered Hamath and crossed the Orontes to dominate Unqi (Eph'al and Naveh 1989; Halpern 1996a; cf. Na'aman 1995 and especially Yamada 2000: 159-61). This followed or, more likely, occasioned defection in Patina sometime before 831 (Grayson 1996: A.0.102.16:268'-286'): after three years' campaigning in Que; in 829, the Assyrian army was back in Unqi (Millard 1994: 30).

Hazael's success led to revolt in Assyria, occupying Shalmaneser's last four years and the first three of Shamshi-Adad V (827–821). Bar-Hadad later claimed his titles. In 805–802, Adad-Narari fractured the coalition, restricted Arpad to the east of the Orontes and gave Hamath to Zakur, probably king of Luash (Luhuti) and a usurper. In 796, Adad-Narari received tribute in Damascus. His successors camped at Damascus in 773, and at Hadrach in 772, 765 and 755 (Millard 1994: 30-34, 39-42). Indicating steadiness in policy, the 773 campaign, conducted against Bar-Hadad's successor Hadyanu (a name related to Hazael's, and identical with that of Hezyon in 1 Kgs 15:18) for Shalmaneser IV by Shamshi-Ilu, resulted in yet another benefice to Kummuh, presumably against Gurgum (Grayson 1996: A.0.105.1). These forays, and Tiglath-Pileser's annexation of Damascus, explain the appearance of Hazael's tribute at the Samian Heraion, Arslan Tash and Kalah in the 8th–7th centuries.[14] Probably, Adad-Narari or Shalmaneser IV transferred the Beqa to Israel (cf. Amos 1:5). Hence the taking of territory to Lebo-Hamath by Jeroboam II (Halpern 2001a).

All these developments have a prehistory, in the time of Shalmaneser III. That king confronted a coalition of Western states, in which the lead players were Damascus, under Hadadezer, Hamath, under Irhuleni and Israel, under Ahab and his sons (probably, only Joram). Eventually, he broke through, cowing Damascus in 841 and 838, and encountering new kings at the time: Hazael in

---

/ṭ/, should be reflected in the letter, /t/, in Assyrian reports, an argument that depends on the absence of dialect geography from the region. See Tadmor 1994: 68:14*.1; 89:27:6; 108:15; Fuchs 1994: 33:15; 63:21; 76:16; 128:220; 262:36, with the probable location of Kashku on p. 392 (#22), on the plateau north of Melid. It is possible that in this location, */ṭ/ had merged with /š/. On transformations of the original phoneme, see Garr 1985: 28-30.

13. 1 Kgs 15:18-22; *KAI* 24:7-8; 2 Kgs 16:5-9; cf. Tadmor and Cogan 1979; Lemaire 1993, 2001.

14. Eph'al and Naveh 1989; *KAI* 311. See Thureau-Dangin 1931: 135-38 for the ivory inscribed 'for our lord, Hazael', now *KAI* 232, probably on the same occasion; and Mallowan 1966: 598 for the Calah instance. These pieces probably come from the palace of Tiglath-Pileser III there, at Hadattu, suggesting an Assyrian donation to the Samian Heraion.

Damascus ('the son of no one', a term also applied once by Asshurnasirpal II) and Jehu, founder of the Nimshide dynasty, in Israel. Something is omitted.

In royal inscriptions, silence is meaningful: if the king does not claim an accomplishment, he does not deserve credit for it; this is the contrapositive of the Tiglath-Pileser Principle that royal inscriptions exaggerate the king's achievements to the limits of verisimilitude.[15] Shalmaneser fights in the West, sometimes in northern Hamath, in 853, 849 and 848. In 845, Shalmaneser fights at the Euphrates. Had we an Aramean source, it would claim that their forces crossed the Euphrates to the east. In 841, however, Shalmaneser III is at Damascus.

Yet, between 844 and 841, he never mentions Hamath. Its absence in the annals indicates that Shalmaneser could not take credit for its apparent inaction: that it does not submit in 841 or in 838, when other vassals are named and Damascus is ravaged is especially suspicious, not least as the *limmu* lists suggest further action in Damascene territory in 837. Similarly, in the Adventure of Silver Blaize, Sherlock Holmes responds to a policeman's request for guidance by commending to his attention 'this singular epidemic among the sheep' and 'the curious incident of the dog in the night-time.' 'But the dog did nothing in the night-time', comes the reply. 'That was the curious incident.'[16]

Hamath was the dog in the night-time of the 9th century. Its submission leaves no mark until Sargon, a century later, mentions an imposition on its king (from 853 to 845), Irhuleni. Sargon claims that his royal 'fathers'[17] had imposed tribute, tax, corvée and, *most markedly* and perhaps originally only, the obligation to participate in Assyrian campaigns (Lambert 1981: 83; cf. Yamada 2000: 182-83); this last probably covers the other obligations. That is, Hamath joined a possibly junior Assyria in its battles with Damascus in 841, 838 and 837 (note Hawkins 1976–80; Millard 1994: 29); hence Sargon's assertion of earlier suzerainty over it, with the implication that this was won by Shalmaneser, though it was probably never ratified until the time of Adad-Narari, and even then on apparently generous terms.

The History of the 9th Century

A course of events can be inferred. Omri (885–874) established himself by 880, conquered Moab and dominated Ammon. He disembedded and planned the ashlar capital. He also participated in a network of local alliances, marrying his heir to a Tyrian princess, and lent his name to the kingdom. His five verses in 1 Kings 16 deny him territorial gain. This is of a piece with Kings' Israelite history.

Ahab (874–853) finished Omri's acropolis, and arranged a diplomatic marriage with Judah— Israel's ally in the Dan stela (Biran and Naveh 1995)—by 864.[18] He collaborated with Damascus and Hamath against Assyria from early on (Tyre stayed in the background). His sons pursued his policies. After 853, Shalmaneser next ventured west in 849, razing towns near the Euphrates; the

---

15. The 'Tiglath-Pileser principle'—Halpern 2001b—which continues to apply to communiques today, also underlies the LB mindset explored by Liverani 1990: 44-65; Westbrook 1999.

16. *Strand*, Dec., 1892; collected in *Memoirs*.

17. Sargon having himself usurped the throne, this text exhibits the usage ('father' meaning 'predecessor') that Lemaire posits (1994a, 1998a), perhaps rightly, in order to attribute the Dan stela to Hazael.

18. 2 Kgs 8:26: Ahazyahu of Judah dies in 841, his single year of reign, at the age of 22. Ahazyahu was therefore born in 863, when his father was 18. His mother was Athalyah, usually identified as Ahab's young daughter (2 Kgs 8:18 + 25; contrast 8:26-27). Allow Athaliah to be in the vicinity of 16 in 863, and she is born around 879, so Ahab's birth dates back at least to the mid-890s. Since Omri is hardly likely to have won for his son the daughter of a Tyrian king, or even a senior priest, before 885, the likelihood is that the marriage of Ahab and Jezebel was arranged in the 870s unless Jezebel's father had not yet usurped the throne at the time of the marriage. On the internal chronological implications, further below n. 24.

Syro-Phoenician coalition opposed him. In 848, he reached Hamath's territory, and took trophies from 89 settlements: he burns nothing down, however; the gain is ephemeral.[19] His campaigns of 847 and 846 in the north entailed light fighting.

Irhuleni of Hamath and Hadadezer of Damascus last appear in 845. 'I crossed the Euphrates in flood with 120,000 troops', says Shalmaneser.[20] He doesn't traverse physical obstacles, or take territory or towns or enumerate booty: he took away (vague) equipment from the horse arm.[21] He states that the Western allies attacked him (8:45'-46'). He doesn't even say where the battle took place! He retires, and fords the Euphrates only four years later. An army of 120,000, and nothing to show for it but a mortifying defeat. His accomplishment was the fording. There was nothing else he could relate. He may have lost territory east of the Euphrates.

Shalmaneser spent 844 and 843 in the north and east (as Grayson 1996: A.0.102.6 iii 45 - iv 7), probably quelling light resistance and intending to intimidate vassals to the south. In 842, he skirted Aram's northern edge to the Amanus between Sam'al and Gurgum; he staged a ritual hunt at the Euphrates on his return.[22] But in 841, the usurpers Hazael and Jehu appear in his annals, and Hadadezer and Irhuleni and Hamath vanish. The Western alliance collapsed in Shalmaneser's absence. Beaten back across the Euphrates in 845, Shalmaneser in 841 and in 838 materialized at the gates of Damascus.[23] And, Israel and Damascus were at war before Jehu's coup in 841, as Joram of Israel was wounded in a fight with Hazael and had repaired to Jezreel to recuperate when Jehu cut him down.[24]

Astour (1971) argued that Jehu joined Assyria against Damascus. But Jehu sundered Israel's relations with Judah and Tyre, and Israel suffered forty years of subjection: did Jehu grossly

---

19. Cf. Grayson 1996: A.0.102.82, in which KUR-*ud*, as in 102.76, should be translated, literally, 'I reached [Ashtammaku]'; for the events of 849–848, see, for example, Grayson 1996: A.0.102.6 ii 55 - iii 15.

20. See Grayson 1996: A.0.102.6 iii 24-26; 8:44'-45'; 10.iii.14-17; 14:91-92; 16:85'-88'; but 23:21-27; 24:14-17; 30:22-25 (which is emplaced right after Ahuni's deportation, as they do not reflect the events of 841); cf. the claims about 844 and reaching 'the Great Sea' and Amanus in 29-33; 35-36, which do not follow chronology and deliberately suggest that the confrontation occurred in 844 or later: Shalmaneser is boasting about surviving the onslaught of 845. For achronological elements, note, for example, 29:8-12 (the inclusion of Anum-Hirbe's statue on Mount Lallar in 29:24-25; 28:22-24 really reflects events of 858 in 2 ii 9-10; 3:89-92, and on Mount Atalur; to be distinguished from 2 [i 49-51 = 1:63-64] ii 8 [and ii 44]; 3:87-88; no later text mentions two statues in this year—5 i 3; 6 i 42-45; 10 i 23-30; 14:26-31; 16:8-11—but cf. 28:13 and 28:22-24; the statue erected in 844, as in 6:34-38; 8:47'-49'; 10 iii 26-28; 14:92-93, may have led writers of display texts to collapse these episodes); 30:20-21; 34:6-7 on deporting Ahunu 'at that time', which in reality occurred in 855 (as 2:74-75; 5 iii 5-6; 6 ii 7-9; 10 ii 2-6; 14:48-50; 16:22-23).

21. The application of terms distinguishing the fate of the cavalry and the 'goods', the latter being taken, the former attacked, in 6 iii 31-33; 8:47, is forgone in 10:23-24, implying capture of all without truly asserting it—'I deprived them of', which is not quite the same as stating that he actually acquired these things.

22. He would stage another hunt in the same place in 840, probably reflecting the fulfillment of a vow regarding success in 841: Grayson 1996: A.0.102.10 iii 37-45; iv 15-22. On the ritual hunt, in connection with the *akītu* and Asshurbanipal, see Weissert 1997; on hunting in the Middle Assyrian annals, Halpern 2001b: 113-24.

23. Grayson 1996: A.0.102.8:1'-27'; 9:1'-13'; 10 iii 45 - iv 15 (with another statue, this time in the company of one of Tiglath-Pileser I); 12:21-30; 14:97-99; 16:122'-137'; 40 i 25 - ii 1.

24. 2 Kgs 8:28-29; 9:14-15; note the statement that Jehu conspired against Joram, who had been guarding Ramoth Gilead against Hazael, suggesting, though not stating outright, the conclusions reached below. The story of Joram's retreat, wounded, from Ramoth Gilead has certainly inspired the story in 1 Kgs 22, of Ahab's alleged death in battle. 1 Kgs 22 is later than the account of Jehu's coup, and therefore than the Nimshide apology (see Miller 1966), but how much later is a question. It is also first inserted into the history in the Josianic edition of Kings. The death in battle is contradicted by 1 Kgs 22:40, which tells us that Ahab died

underestimate the power he had been fighting? More likely, Hazael's coup, between 845 and 841, led to resistance from and pressure on other coalition partners, including both Hamath and Israel, and to the unseating of Baasha in Ammon.[25] Hamath and Assyria linked arms. Jehu blinked.

Kings condemns Omri and Ahab based on Jehu's apology, defending the usurpation that Hosea (1:3-5) continues to attack. Jehu's heirs demonized Ahab and Jezebel, and the deuteronomistic historian (H[Dtr]) cheerily followed suit.[26] Yet in 841, Ramoth Gilead was the border (2 Kgs 8:28-29; 9:1-15; KAI 310). Likewise, the Jezreel was secure: Ahazyahu of Judah flees from Jezreel via Yibleam to Megiddo; his body is transported to Judah.[27] The text presents Megiddo as an Omride safe haven: the fortification of Stratum IVA predates 841.

Before Jehu, the north is intact. The historian, and his sources, would gladly have attributed losses in Transjordan to the Omrides. Instead, the regnant hypothesis asserts the translation of a few battles from Jehu and his heirs to the Omrides—which they win![28] Yet the territorial loss remains Nimshide.

Jehu ceded Transjordan all the way to Aroer on the Arnon (2 Kgs 10:32-33), which appears in Mesha's inscription—in almost those words: 'I built Aroer, and I made the "highway" on the Arnon'.[29] What Mesha forgets to mention is that, like Jehu, he was Hazael's creature. Jehu folded under Damascene pressure, and let loose Moab with the rest of Transjordan. Mesha's revolt starts in earnest under Joram, 2 Kgs 3:4-27 coordinating a foray against southern Moab, which is to say, before Mesha's expansion, with Ahab's death.[30] If Omri secured northern Moab toward the start of his reign, Mesha's claim that Israel occupied Madeba and Ataroth for forty years, up to the Arnon, intimates an end close to 841. This suggests that his revolt gathered momentum after Hazael's

---

in peace. See Halpern and Vanderhooft (1991) on the expression, and on the literary and literary-historical issues. Note that if Ahab had a marriageable daughter in say 865, who could bear a child in 863, then if she was no younger than 15 at the time of the birth, he was no younger than about 15 or 16, and perhaps a good deal older, in 878. This places his birth before 892, and probably a good deal earlier, so that his death 'in peace' in the original edition of Kings, which presupposes perhaps a birth ca. 903–908, makes sense. Certainly, Omri in 885, at the start of the civil war, was no spring chicken, but as commander of a royal army certainly in his 30s, perhaps in his 40s or even 50s, which also explains his death 'in peace' in 874.

25. Ammon, not Amanus, since Shalmaneser always spells the latter Hamana. For other cases of RN son of RN king of GN, see Adad-Narari III's Pazarcik stela (Atarshumki son of Adramu of the city Arpad—Grayson 1996: A.0.104.3:11); Zakur's (KAI 202) Brhdd bn hz'l mlk 'rm; 1 Kgs 15:18-20 Ben-Hadad ben Tabrimmon ben Hezyon king of Aram who dwelt in Damascus; KAI 201, the Melqart stela, Bar-Hadad bar 'Atarsamk king of Aram; KAI 181, Mesha son of Kemoshayat, king of Moab, the Dibonite; and any Assyrian inscription by a king with a royal predecessor. The formulation is used in self-description as well as, as in the first two citations above, in describing some foreign kings. Baasha son of Ruhubi of Ammon is merely the only one so named by Shalmaneser, as Atarshumki is the only one so named by Adad-Narari, and Bar-Hadad by Zakur (cf. Na'aman 1995).

26. My student, John Hodgson, suggests, in my view correctly, that Pekah's reign is antedated to the end of the Nimshide dynasty, and so includes the years of Menahem and Pekahiah. Since Pekah was resisting Assyria in 834 and possibly later, the continuity is an index of what the latest edition of the Israelite royal chronicles may have looked like to H(Dtr).

27. 2 Kgs 9:27-28. Note the omission of Taanach, unoccupied at the time.

28. 1 Kgs 20; 22: see Miller 1966; and, possibly 2 Kgs 6–7, if this has any historical kernel; see below.

29. 'nk bnty 'r'r w'nk 'šty hmslt b'rnn, KAI 181:26. On the 'highway', see Tidwell 1999, with bibliography.

30. Taking the combination of Jehoshaphat with Joram and Edom in the chapter seriously would date the expedition to 853–849. But as Elisha is active in the account, its route of transmission is uncertain. Cf. Smelik 1992: 81, taking 'half' in Mesha too literally, and 'his sons', bnh, as a singular.

accession in Damascus, with Israel then engaged in northern Transjordan. Hazael probably took control of Ammon, and assigned territory north of the Arnon, such as the Madeba Plain, to Mesha, his vassal.[31]

In 2 Kgs 12:18-19, Hazael reaches Gath and Jerusalem without campaigning in Israel: Jehu's overlord probably enlisted him in the attack. Thus, Adad-Narari III is the first Assyrian king to mention Judah, Philistia or Edom as vassals. Hazael controlled the whole region until his death.

Victory in 845 raised the prospect of Western expansion across the Euphrates. Hamath stood to benefit most. (Bit-Adini remained subordinate in 844, and Arpad seems to have blown with the wind.) Hazael saw Aram as an empire to be consolidated, however. By 842, he killed his predecessor and took the throne. Shalmaneser refers to him as the 'son of no one' (Grayson 1996: 40 i 26; the same phrase appears in another connection in Asshurnasirpal's annals); Kings describes him as a usurper, albeit with a divine commission (1 Kgs 19:15-18; 2 Kgs 8:9-15). The asperity of these descriptions is unusual for a foreign king in either source, and the coincidence of the negative references is unparalleled.[32] Treating the usurper Jehu as a tributary, Shalmaneser does *not* apply similar terminology.

Hazael took the throne before Jehu's succession (*KAI* 310; 2 Kgs 8:9-15, 28-29; 9:1-15). The indications are that his coup was not complete, as he incurred opposition from Israel and Hamath. Irhuleni, and possibly Joram, treated with Shalmaneser.[33]

Soon, Hazael turned militarily on Israel. By 841, he had induced panic in Jehu, who faced an unrestrained Damascus, as well as the gadfly, Mesha, in the south. Jehu killed Israel's and a Judahite king, plus Israel's royal Tyrian queen. In one annals edition, Shalmaneser implies that he himself killed Giammu, a king on the Balih, in 853; other versions indicate the locals killed Giammu to sue for peace. The Dan stone likewise implies that Hazael killed, rather than bested, Joram of Israel and Ahazyahu of Judah (see generally Lemaire 1998a). The configuration is unmistakable: Damascus and Moab squeezed Israel until, in 841 (Mesha: 'Israel has perished, perished forever'), Jehu exchanged Transjordan for support in overthrowing the Omrides. Mesha retook Madeba after 40 years of Israelite occupation from the time of Omri: his revolt depended on Hazael for its success after 841.

But, while Hazael was still securing his territorial accessions, Shalmaneser turned up, at Irhuleni's bidding, and perhaps Joram's. Shalmaneser claims to have 'deprived' Hazael of much chariotry. Jehu paid Shalmaneser, but remained Hazael's vassal. In 838 there was a recurrence, but Hamath and Shalmaneser again returned home after shutting Hazael up temporarily in Damascus and ravaging the countryside. In the accounts of the campaign of 838, there is no further indication of tribute from Jehu or Tyre. By the mid-830s, Hazael had secured his flanks and resumed his expansion northward, In the time of his son, Bar-Hadad, only Hamath resisted membership in the alliance, led by Damascus against Hamath, and by Arpad against the neo-Hittite states to the north, especially Kummuh. The Eponym Chronicle relates an Assyrian return to Damascus in 773 and, likely in the same connection, to Hadrach in 772 and 765.

---

31. On Aroer, see 2 Kgs 10:32-33; *KAI* 181:26. Mesha's stela does not necessarily follow a chronological order, as it is in large measure a record of his building and garrisoning activities. For geographical analysis in light of texts and archaeological data, see Dearman 1989; Smelik 1992: 72-79. See generally Routledge 2000.

32. Contrast Na'aman 1995, identifying Hazael as a king of a kingdom, Amki, in the anti-Lebanon. This depends on a web of identifications, including of Baasha in the Kurkh stela as a predecessor in 'Bet Rehob' (contrast n. 25 above), that is brilliant, to be sure, but overly complex. Cf. Yamada 2000: 159-61.

33. Local hieroglyphic inscriptions attest Irhuleni's son's (I[r]tames's) succession, as well as his father's name, Etas(?) (Hawkins 1976–80).

The Sources of Kings

So, concerning public events, Kings is reasonably robust. Shoshenq, for example, is dated partly by his synchronism with Rehoboam. But Egyptian data support the reliability of the king list underlying Kings and its transmission (Shortland 2005). Shalmaneser's texts confirm the sequence from Ahab to Jehu.[34] True, Kings names Hazael's predecessor as Ben-Hadad, rather than Hadadezer. But it places Mesha's first success after Ahab's death, and makes Hazael Israel's opponent before Jehu's coup. It correctly places an Ethbaal on the Tyrian throne. It knows the sequence of reigns, and such details as the nature of kings' deaths[35] and the locations of capitals. It also reflects, in the marriage alliances of the Omrides with Tyre and Judah, the same pattern of Western relations that Shalmaneser reports, to be replaced in 841 by Hazael's hegemony. Inaccuracy in the record is mainly bound up with the stories about prophets—and even those sometimes contain reflections of historical reality.[36] Thus, when Kings relates that Jehu rather than Ahab lost Transjordan, that Jehoshaphat and Ahaziah of Israel contemplated a joint naval venture in the south, or that Edom and Libnah revolted against Jehoram of Judah, outside of the context of an ongoing narrative, it probably depends on written sources.

But much of the material originates in apologetic. The story of Naboth's vineyard furnishes a model (1 Kgs 21). Ahab negotiates with Naboth, asking for his vineyard. After the refusal, Ahab comes home to sulk. Jezebel writes letters, in his name, sealed with his seal, to order the elders of Jezreel to suborn perjury from two witnesses; they kill Naboth and his family. So who are the whistleblowers? Jezebel, the witnesses, the elders of Jezreel who suborn the witnesses: who is talking? The same holds for the case of Uriah, in which only David and Joab, and probably a scribe, are in the know, and it takes a divine revelation to unravel the crime.[37] Such demonization of rulers is common. But in this case, Jezebel, rather than Ahab, is its object. The story justifies her defenestration.

An attorney for Ahab would argue that Naboth was a loutish clod, who left dead donkeys and other detritus on his property upwind from the winter palace. Desperate, Ahab approached him, with the intention of creating a royal park on the Assyrian, or a Phoenician, model. Naboth not

34. The principal tinkering reflected in the Greek was with synchronisms—hence the Old Greek chronology precisely in the Omride period. Cf. Shenkel 1968.

35. Ahab being a complex case—1 Kgs 22:40 reports that he died peacefully, but 1 Kgs 22:1-39 presents a later story involving prophets about his death in battle. See above, n. 24.

36. Note that the story of Mesha in 2 Kgs 3:4-27 and the southern invasion is also highly plausible, and set in the right period, despite having a prophetic element attached to it. The background of 1 Kgs 20 may lie in the reign of Joash—with the capture of a Ben-Hadad before Hazael in the displaced account, this name may have been displaced (see below) onto that of Hadadezer (who perhaps never engaged Ahab in reality). And the displaced story becomes an occasion to castigate Ahab (compare Joash in 2 Kgs 13:14-25). When was there, if there was, a siege of Samaria (1 Kgs 6–7)? That material is not Omride either.

37. Listeners to classic comedy routines from stand-up venues are probably familiar with Bill Cosby's reminiscences about his days as a fullback when Temple played Syracuse in football. He describes the physical mismatch—Syracuse is a team of Goliaths. But David does not triumph: the main play on the Temple offense is 'Cosby up the middle and the rest of the team off the end of the field.' That's the Uriah story. It has often been argued that Nathan's references to Uriah's murder in 2 Sam. 12:9 have no real parallel in the juridical parable with which Nathan induces David to condemn himself in 2 Sam. 12:1-4. In the twin references in 12:9, the first speaks of David smiting Uriah by the sword, the second by the sword of the Ammonites—the first being parallel to the Giammu and Dan claims. Whatever view one takes of the verse's development, it is the violation of Bathsheba that exhibits the parallel, and the treatment of Uriah is almost secondary. But all this is of a piece: one could see that Bathsheba had later moved to the palace; one could not know positively, other than through revelation, that David had ordered Uriah's murder.

only refused, despite increases in the original offer, but cast aspersions on Ahab's parentage. Ahab documented the incident, and attainted Naboth. But Jehu's apologists turned this into a *cause célèbre*. They directed their ire at the woman and children whom Jehu actually killed, since Ahab had been dead for a dozen years.

Other texts fulfill a like function. 1 Kings 20, which cannot be direct from annals, now justifies a condemnation of Ahab (cf. Joash in 2 Kgs 13:14-25). But the story itself is probably displaced from the reign of Joash, who did confront a Bar-Hadad of Damascus (including a motif of incomplete victory, 2 Kgs 13:14-25). 1 Kings 22 is a version of Joram's death displaced onto Ahab (and, in the film, onto *El Cid*) late and orally. The events in 2 Kings 6–7 postdate 841, when the border was secure. But the narrative relates a siege of Samaria, suggesting a possible episode under Jehu, or, more likely, Jehoahaz, when Hazael's demands may have inspired a revolt in Israel. Placing Mesha's revolt in 2 Kings 3 under the Omrides relieves the historian of the responsibility of reporting that his real territorial gains occurred only after Jehu came to power. These stories involve apologetic, particularly in the involvement of prophets, and yet reflect one or another historical background. Our prophetic stories may therefore not be so much 'oral', although the story of Gehazi's relations (2 Kgs 8:4) may suggest this, as literary imitations of the oral. They are the apparatus of justification for the Nimshide dynasty.

But where does this material come from? Much of it has to do with the prophets, Elijah and Elisha. And their relationship is the prototype for the description of John the Baptist's relationship to Jesus in the New Testament.

Elijah condemns Ahab, then Jezebel, and commissions Elisha. Then the stories about Elisha recapitulate many of the *private* miracles in the cycle about Elijah—feeding the hungry (siege of Samaria), resurrection, amazing the sons of the prophets, dealing with an Aramaean leader and so on. The stories do not duplicate the revelations and public miracles of Elijah, as in 1 Kings 18–19. But it is Elijah's commission that Elisha executes in inciting the coups of Jehu and Hazael. All of this invites suspicion about Elisha's real status, in that he required narrative legitimation and authority from Elijah's inspiration. The reasons for that may be purely chronological, or may be geared to justify Elisha's alignment with Nimshide policy. Probably, Elisha embraced Elijah in an attempt to recruit particular communities to Jehu's cause. One of these was the Rechabites, a primitivist pastoral group who, like the Qenites, might be useful in policing areas between settlements and in preventing the coordination of uprisings across settlements. Elijah lay far enough in the past, too, to spin his accomplishments as public miracles.

Elisha has a deathbed scene with Joash of Israel, sometime around 800 BCE (2 Kgs 13:14-25). That is, the narrative asserts that he died as a chief mantic advisor to Jehu's great-grandson. The care taken to connect him with Elijah means that Elijah was a powerful anti-Omride figure in popular consciousness, the inspiration perhaps for the movement that swept the army into Jehu's camp. Just as Gehazi (2 Kgs 8:4-6) retails 'all the great things that Elisha did', the retailing of Elijah's deeds justifies the overthrow of the Omrides, what Hosea calls 'the day of Jezreel'. And Elisha's deeds include Hazael's accession—by a self-working prophecy, as in Macbeth—an act of divine manipulation that leads to the harrowing of Israel, but under Jehu and his heirs. The failure of Jehu's policy, and Israel's dismemberment, were foreordained (2 Kgs 8:12).

This all justifies Jehu's coup and his bargain with Hazael. And Elisha's longevity, from 841 or earlier into the reign of Joash, and his prominence in our literature, suggest he served as chief ideological exponent and propagandist for the Nimshide dynasty. We should not underestimate the impact of prophets of whom we know, versus the vast majority of whom we do not know, on support for or opposition to Israelite kings. The ones of whom we know were successful factional spokesmen.

The Importance of the Omride State

Overall, four corpora attest the importance of the Omrides: Shalmaneser, who encounters Ahab in 853 and Jehu in 841; Mesha, where Chemosh takes credit for 841; Dan, in which Hazael gets credit for 841; and Kings, reluctantly, but decisively. All four know the kingdom as Israel. Shalmaneser is the first to use '(son of) Omri' as a dynastic denomination for the land.[38] But Dan, and probably Mesha, refer to Judah as 'the house of David' (Lemaire 1994b, 1994c; Puech 1994), a term that does not recur abroad after the late 9th century. 'House of David' appears in Kings and elsewhere as a designation for Judah; but Kings, with its Nimshide bias, eschews the term 'Omri' as a dynastic designation. In HB, the dynasty is called 'the House of Ahab'; only Mic. 6:16, who adopts the Jerusalemite, or perhaps factional, view blaming the Assyrian conquest and deportations on the Omrides (against Hosea), sets the 'inscribings of Omri' into parallelism with 'the House of Ahab'.[39] The variance with Assyria's impression, and Mesha's, smacks of local apologetic.

Shalmaneser names Israel third, after two states, Hamath and Damascus, nearer Assyria, as a partner in the Western coalition. Omri and his heirs colonized Transjordan to the Arnon—which David never did. They probably dominated Ammon. Omri, like David, disembedded the capital city. And he arranged marriage alliances with Tyre and Judah, resurrecting the Davido-Solomonic trade network from Edom to Phoenicia. The Omrides (though Omri is the only Israelite king without a patronym, excepting Zimri) were welcomed into the lodge of Western kings.

The scarped, ashlar and ivory-inlaid capital and the ashlar Jezreel enclosure attest Omride wealth.[40] And the lavish first stage of Megiddo IVA, including the city wall, the southern stables and Building 339, was in their hands (above). Only inherited wealth, little of it extracted through conquest, could make all this possible. There was a potent Israelite state, for thirty years, which Damascus afterward dominated; a period of prosperity followed, and lasted until Tiglath-Pileser. Here, Hazor IX and VIII and Megiddo IVA fit well. Correlating phasing to the historical framework might actually tie the Omrides to Hazor IXA, although Hazor VIII's public architecture better matches Megiddo IVA. But Hazor, probably like Dan, may have changed hands more than once in this period without undergoing destruction—it was an era of fluid, field combat, and lines may often have passed the fortress by.

In the same vein, a set of mature states in Tyre, Damascus, Israel, Judah, Ammon and Moab, with connections to one another and to allies at least as far north as Que, did not emerge overnight. The marital alliances included commercial development, such as that at Horvat Rosh Zayit (Gal and Alexandre 2000; cf. 1 Kgs 22:48-50). These powers saw a common interest and protected it aggressively.

---

38. See Grayson 1996: 213:12 for Adad-Narari III's use of 'the land of Omri'; Tadmor 1994: 138:6'; 140:15'; 186 r 4 for Tiglath-Pileser III's usage, 'the land of the house of Omri'; Fuchs 1994: 34:19, 20; 63:21; 76:15; 261:32 for Sargon's identical usage. With the fall of the Israelite state, the dynastic term falls into desuetude.

39. Mesha's reference to the Omride dynasty, in parallel to 'Israel', seems most proximately to equate 'his house' with that of Omri's son as well: *KAI* 181:7. Athaliah's identification with Omri (2 Kgs 8:26) may be another instance.

40. The construction of the Jezreel enclosure antedates the Naboth story, Jehu's apology for defenstrating Jezebel and probably Naboth's death. The pre-enclosure fills at Jezreel arguably reflect the state of the village ceramic repertoire before the introduction of a royal residence there. On the enclosure, see Ussishkin and Woodhead 1997; Ussishkin 1996, 2000; and, on the fills, Zimhoni 1997. Note that Jezreel is allegedly occupied in Saul's time (1 Sam. 25:43; 27:3; 30:5; 2 Sam. 2:2; 3:2; 4:4). On Samaria, see Tappy 1992; Franklin 2003, 2004 (but note that a palace in Jezreel is presupposed in 2 Kgs 9).

By 853, Ahab's chariots had a distinctive tactical tradition, unsupported by cavalry (see Dalley 1985; cf. Lemaire 1998b). His chariot arm was bigger than his allies' contingents combined, rivaling the Assyrian arm in number. 2000 chariots imply the presence of 6000 warhorses, in addition to breeding stock, the brood to perpetuate it, horses not fielded or in other use and young horses in training.

The prehistory of the expedition involved acquiring stock and training trainers, breeders, drivers and grooms, breeding horses, training horses to work in tandem, drilling the chariotry in units, and drilling chariotry, infantry and ballistics arms to combine together (as well as schooling an officer corps in combined tactics). The whole investment presupposes an advanced system of taxation producing a reliable and within limits predictable revenue stream.

So, at the very start of the process, there was a state with a stake to invest. This takes the state's beginnings easily to the 890s, and, in light of its periodic disruptions, probably decades earlier.[41] Israel is a creature of the 10th century, and not necessarily late in the century.

Israel's United Monarchy was a culmination of secular trends, such as an exploding highland population (Zertal 1988; Gal 1992; Finkelstein and Magen 1993; Finkelstein, Lederman and Bunimovitz 1997; Frankel *et al.* 2001; Alt 1953). It also reflects first, 20th-Dynasty diversion of Arabian trade from the southern coastlands, into the second half of the 12th century (and hence the *cordon sanitaire* around Philistia—Stager 1995); on this followed renewed inland traffic in the 10th century, diverting Arabian trade from Egypt toward Tyre. Not least, exploitation of mineral wealth in Edom, probably traded in part for the rare earths of the Arabian peninsula and east Africa, contributed to the burgeoning conflict between erstwhile states in the Israelite ecumene (see Levy, this volume). As I have noted elsewhere, smelting in this period reaches and sustains an increased curve of production.

Wealth in the highlands and the increasing circumvallation of towns are signs of government and of infrastructure even outside elite zones of clan section shrines and residences. Possibly, our strange little corpus of inscribed arrowheads belongs to or just before this period (Deutsch and Heltzer 1997: 1-25). Some of these are authentic, and suggest either belomancy or ritual group hunts. In either case, increasing professionalization and stratification again underlie the development. The arrowheads distinguish themselves by script, not pictures. They are the first indices we have for the social role of writing in the local Iron Age.

Anepigraphic Iron Age seals appear in the lowlands in Iron I. But in the highlands, anepigraphic seals are more common in Iron II than in Iron I—only in Iron II does state regulation create the political framework for a mercantilizing economy. Even such a small increment in efficiency as signed seals, versus anepigraphic, has a significant impact on economic efficiency. This is, in fact, the first step in the direction of coinage warranted by the issuer. One does not implicitly trust the issuer, or the sealer; but regular relations and honorable dealing quiet the distrust over time.

Some seals seem to wed iconography with epigraphs in the 9th, or surely the mid-8th century (cf. the later *lmlk*-stamps). 7th-century seals shift from solar to lunistellar imagery, and in Judah toward aniconism, as bureaucrats' literacy increased.[42] The inscribed seals in the 9th/8th centuries indicate that the state was recording provenance by writing, as in the early-8th-century Samaria

---

41. 2 Kgs 16:9 already characterizes Zimri, Omri's predecessor, as a chariotry division commander, for no obvious reason aside from the fact that Zimri lacks a patronym (Omri being identified as an 'army commander' in 2 Kgs 16:16). That is, around 885, Israel had a developed chariot arm, reflecting a period of capital accumulation followed by long development.

42. For 9th-century seals, Hestrin and Dayagi-Mendels 1979: #31 = Avigad 1997: 740; 1 Kgs 21:8. For mid-8th century, e.g., Avigad 1997: 2-5, 29 face B, 85, 160. For the date and significance of lunistellar seal iconography, Keel and Uehlinger 1992: 340-69; Uehlinger 1993; Ornan 1993, 2005; Halpern 2003.

ostraca. By the late 9th century, when royal monuments and inscribed objects proliferate, Western states were mature, even in peripheries such as Moab. The fact that Adad-Narari III mentions Edom among his distant tributaries testifies to the same phenomenon (and may, incidentally, indicate ongoing copper smelting, if in diminished quantity, at Khirbet en-Nahas). It also underscores Edom's importance as a trade conduit to Judah and Philistia, and thence to major markets.

Cultural Transformation and Chronology

In historical archaeology, inquiry into social change leads to different conclusions from textual: two different forms of evidence and logics of analysis are operating. The question is always, what is the most robust correlation? The rules of archaeological argument—comparison of ceramic assemblages, for example—dictate that destructions willy-nilly be considered simultaneous, when decades may divide them. Nor is it safe to proceed from a picture of society to historical causation. For example, Izbet Sartah II is a poster boy for the argument for social stratification (see Finkelstein 1986). Does this reflect conditions that led to monarchy or conditions that monarchy produced (cf. Far'a VIIb)? Likewise, the Solomonic towns at Gezer, Hazor and Megiddo are highly stratified—with a common dearth of domestic architecture. The rise of the central state—in Israel and Judah before the mid-9th century (cf. Jamieson-Drake 1991; Finkelstein and Silberman 2006)—begs us to ask, what would we need to know in order to know what we seek to know?

The most robust anchor for correlation lies in the Negev. Shoshenq uprooted an extensive network of what he in nine cases describes as 'enclosures' (*ḥqr*, probably the Egyptian reception of a local pronunciation of /hdr/, Hebrew *ḥṣr*)[43] and in others presupposes are settlements. The correlatives are the 10th-century Negev outposts containing much handmade ware and Iron II burnished red-slip pottery (Cohen and Cohen-Amin 2004).

At Megiddo this ware appears in VB loci, and plentifully in VA–IVB. At Hazor and Gezer, its arrival is coterminous with other six-chambered gates and with attached casemate walls, though the presence of the latter in Megiddo's gate area is doubtful. The combination of Kings with the pottery and the architecture is inviting. A lower chronology implies burnished red slip reached the fortresses only after reaching Solomon's Negev; that the Solomonic towns in 1 Kgs 9:17-18 did not resemble one another, but the Omride towns did; and the Omride gates resembled those of non-Israelite sites.[44]

The three fortresses share common elite pottery and architecture (degenerate bichrome occurs in Megiddo VIA and Gezer IX, but less at Hazor XII–XI). Without Shishaq, the correlation depends on a vision of what summoned the texts into being, a question rarely asked in Biblical Studies. Even

---

43.   So Halpern 2001b: 462-63; note the coincidences not just of Arad and Hazar-Gaddah (Haqar-'rgd in Shishaq) with Shishaq's list, but also of Shishaq's Haqar-Tolon with the Ketib Tolon in 1 Chron. 4:20; and the whole practice of naming southern settlements of the 7th century 'Enclosure' or 'Enclosures' or 'Enclosure of PN', a practice reflecting the character of those settlements, the tradition of building them as enclosures in the region along routes of transit, and it would seem the continuity of naming practice from the 10th to the 8th–7th centuries. Ryan Byrne and I plan a new treatment of the Shishaq list in the near future. Note the phonological sequence /hdr/ > /ḥṣr/ḥqr/ > /hgr/ > /ḥgr/, compare *KAI* 215:16, *šmrg*, from *mrd. Further, note the mention of *tyrq'y'r*, Tirqa-'el, in Pap. Anast. I 22:8, near Bet-Shan, and thus probably Tirzah (< *rdy), and the Trq in Thutmosis III's list. Contrast Aḥituv 1984: 189-90.

44.   10th century at 'En Hazeva (identified with Tamar in Cohen and Yisrael 1995), late 10th or early 9th century at Ashdod IX (in the stratum after the introduction of burnished red slip, found with degenerate bichrome in X); 9th century at Lachish IV (on Lachish, see Ussishkin 2004). Six-chambered gates at Khirbet Mudayna and Tel Ira date to the early and late 8th century, respectively. But once the plans were available, later adaptations could be made of them.

if Finkelstein is right to push Philistine bichrome down in time, however, the duration of ceramic phases is unclear. The one solid correlation is in a periphery with burnished red slip and without bichrome. Absence can indicate symbolic charge, a *cordon* succeeding that of the 20th Dynasty. Admittedly, argument from absence, as in Jerusalem (latterly E. Mazar 2006), would preclude finding an Alexander or a dominant 5th-century Sparta. Still, Arad XII and the Negev are later than Megiddo VIA (A. Mazar 2005).

Shoshenq expected to consolidate his dynasty; to enrich himself with booty; to capture an income from foreign provinces. At Megiddo he left a monument to bear comparison with those of his most illustrious predecessor. Megiddo's name resounded on temple walls as the keystone of empire. It was the intended endpoint of the campaign, which is why it is the northernmost major settlement in his itinerary, whose name physically occupies the center of his list.[45] Only at Megiddo, among sites on Shoshenq's list, has a monument been found.[46] It represents his northernmost thrust, and occupies the central point, and turning-point, in the inscription of his itinerary. Ideologically, the emphasis has the effect of reinforcing comparison of Shoshenq to Thutmosis III. But what was its practical value?

Shoshenq's movements are all within Judah and Israel. The United Monarchy was his target, softened up, if we rely on Kings, by Jeroboam. This schism it can only have been Shoshenq's intention to ratify.[47] Stopping on the border, Shoshenq also signaled an interest in cowing Tyre, whereas he made no such statement in Damascus's direction. This brings us back to the Negev.

The dozens of flimsy enclosures here have one strategic valence: they represent the tendrils of a Tyrian connection with Arabia bypassing the Bubastite Delta. This network ran, as it would in the 9th century, through Israel's allied hinterland. Shoshenq eliminated Judah from the competition for Red Sea traffic. Jeroboam's return at Solomon's death, after 16 years in Egypt, also disrupted the nexus with Tyre. And Shoshenq's decision to park at Megiddo semaphored the Phoenician end of the conduit. Not coincidentally, one of Solomon's early Egyptian-sponsored foes is Hadad the Edomite, whose revolt is suppressed (1 Kgs 11:14-22).[48] Nor is it coincidental that Byblian royal inscriptions appear on pharaonic statues of just this era (Lemaire 2006): southern Phoenicia was effectively bookended by Egyptian allies.

The southern trade represents a focus of international conflict from the 20th Dynasty forward. Damascus regularly attempted to seize it. The Assyrians in the 8th–7th centuries directed traffic through Judah. It was a factor in Necho's conflict with Josiah, and clearly in the 6th century, when Necho dug a canal down the Wadi Tumeilat, and when Nabunaid relocated for 10 years to Teima. Judah never flourished without exploiting transport south. But this confirms that Shoshenq's Megiddo had been Solomon's center.

---

45.   He may have sent raiders north from Megiddo, as Kitchen (1986: 299) speculates, but to the near north if at all. The following three terms in the list (*'dr, ydhmrk, hnm*) may all refer to the vicinity of Megiddo: the first meaning 'great', the second referring to a stela or carving, and the third to a military camp or camps.

46.   Excavated sites include a number in the Negev, including Arad, Aroer and Tel Milh, plus Gibeon, Tel Fara North, Rehob, Bet Shan, Taanach and Megiddo, and probably a number of others not plainly identified (e.g. Bet Shemesh, if it is Rubuti). Robbed sites include Aruna and probably any number of others. For the stela, originally three meters high, see Fisher 1929: 12-16 figs 7-9; Lamon and Shipton 1939: 60f. fig 70. Fisher estimates its original size at about 10 feet high. The other stela of Shishaq outside Egypt was sent to Abibaal's Byblos, but possibly later.

47.   Shoshenq names no kingdoms other than the traditional Nine Bows. He denied recognition of Canaanite polities larger than a city-state, perhaps polemically, perhaps to refrain from mentioning the disintegration of the great state that he attacked, perhaps to imitate Thutmosis III's lists. For Jeroboam, see 1 Kgs 11:26-40; for Shishaq's intentions as above, Wilson 2005; as below, Halpern 1974.

48.   On the date of Solomon's construction programme, see Halpern 1974.

The ashlar, Phoenicianizing Megiddo VA–IVB was probably a facade. Here, Shoshenq's call on Tyre has a reflex, not in the mudbrick VIA. No circumvallation was completed: only around Palaces 6000 and 1723 are casemates found. The gate, however, and especially the gate towers imply that a wall was planned, and probably bonded into the gate (2156).[49] Megiddo was Solomon's only fortress on a friendly border. The text puts its construction late in his reign, and Ussishkin (1980, 1990), Finkelstein (2000b) and Holladay (1990) downdate it or elements of it, if differentially. But both the Solomonic VA–IVB and IVA mediated exchange with Tyre.

Are all destructions of sites with recently introduced burnished red slip to be ascribed to Shoshenq? Some sites may have surrendered and survived intact (Megiddo VA–IVB). Still others are destroyed and rebuilt (e.g. Rehov, Gezer). And in light of their trade role, it is hardly a surprise that the Negev sites have no near-term successors.

In the United Monarchy, in early texts, lowland fortifications are government centers; on the ground, they lack concentrated intramural domestic population, probably to keep them from defecting. These centers feature display, reflecting a new urge to play the international stage. They lack temples, so the royal capital is elsewhere. And they are partly devoted to trade or industry—Blakely (2002) observes a coincidence of 'tripartite buildings' such as the later 'stables' (cf. Davies 1988), with Solomon's borders: those with Tyre, Philistia, Damascus and the Negev indicate control of trade; similar control appears in the highlands and Shephela (as the Far`a N gate area and Beit Mirsim West Gate and Tower).

Unlike its (Philistine or imported) Iron I counterparts, Iron IIA formal service evinces a repetitive, efficient surface treatment. The difference between display and daily wares is muted; but the difference now appears in the highlands, and in the Negev (Holladay 1990). Homogeneity in large pillared house forms in the Israelite region is on the wax, from the 10th to the 8th century (Braemer 1982). More elaborate burials appear especially in Judah (Bloch-Smith 1992; cf. Halpern 2003). For other reasons, Philistine consumption tilts from pig toward caprovids (Hesse 1986; on Dan, Wapnish and Hesse 1991). The local economy, in short, is more integrated. So is the culture. Wealth is reaching the highlands, partly through the enforcement of debt mechanisms across sites; stratification diminishes in the plain. While the beginnings are earlier (Finkelstein 1986), there is ongoing development in the 9th century (as Lachish IV, Jezreel, Samaria, Far`a, Rehov; Gath; Ashdod).

Israel and Judah have their roots in the period roughly of the United Monarchy. After Shoshenq's conquest, these states invested in administration, which is what the fortresses reflect. Severally, they inherited the territory and bureaucrats of the United Monarchy. They also inherited the fine ware tradition (A. Mazar 2003, 2005). And the architectural enrichment of the region expresses itself, for example, in the first phase of Megiddo IVA, starting with the outer fortifications; here, too, the early phase probably did not incorporate the northern 'stables'. Similarly, the construction of Hazor VIII, in the same period, reflects a new function—still—controlled from a remote central authority. These towns are not merely fortifications, but commercial centers. At Megiddo (final phases of IVA) and Hazor (IX–VIII), this led ultimately to the increasing devotion of space to state mercantile structures. Effectively, these sites were ports serving a center in the central hills (see Blakely 2002: 52-53).

The continuing operation into the mid-9th century of a trade network, and the wealth with which the period ends in the mid-8th century, reflects the circumstances in which Western alliances flourished. So the pre-Assyrian layers in question (except, indirectly, Tel Dan) do not so much reflect Hazael's and Ben-Hadad's proximate sovereignty as the extent of their control and the

---

49.   Israel Finkelstein suggests that the casemate of 6000 enclosed only that palace (in conversation). On the stratigraphy and bonding of Gate 2156, see Halpern 2000. The bonding of the front pairs of piers of the gate indicates bonding to the wall as well. The rear piers of the gate were not bonded, and may be secondary.

suddenness with which it was ended. Assyria, too, exploited traditional routes of trade even in the period of empire.

For about forty years after 841, Hazael and his son, Bar-Hadad, dominated politics in Syria, reaching Amqi physically, and possibly extending their reach northward in concert with Arpad. It is no coincidence, thus, that Amos's oracle against Damascus includes punishment of the dynasty founded by Hazael ('I will send fire against the House of Hazael'), of the 'palaces of Ben-Hadad', but is completed only with the liberation of Bit-Adini (Amos 1:4-5). Zakur and Jehoahaz, then Joash, resisted Hazael's son, and Adad-Narari III mastered and fixed the territories of the north Syrian states sometime between 810 and 803. He fought Arpad and its eight allies at Paqarahubunu in 808, and fought Arpad again, probably on Zakur's account, in 805. In conjunction with his, or Shamshi-Ilu's, campaign against Damascus, he mentions as (alleged) tributaries Tyre, Sidon, Joash of Israel, Edom and Philistia. He is the first to mention either of the latter two, formerly in Hazael's ambit. The trading powers of the southern Levant evidently joined Hamath in opposing Damascene-Arpadite hegemony. The prosperity of long-distance exchange evidently diminished when Damascus led the West.

Adad-Narari restored the balance of power in the West to an earlier state. Asshur's development in the 8th century would determine the fates of many states. But, force aside, it also established a free trade zone. Assyria did not neglect science, in omenology or in the sky. It brought in the dawn of western consciousness on the peripheries of its empire. One could say, therefore, that Western civilization is the deep penetration agent of Assyrian imperial ambition. Or one could say that the Assyrians ultimately carved out the mercantile and individualizing identity that midwived literacy and monotheism in Judah, and science in Ionia (see Wilkinson *et al.* 2005; Halpern 1996b, 2005). The Egyptian unification of Levantine long-distance trade was inevitably recapitulated, but differently, in later times, and the process quickened mutual elite adaptation to alien cultural exchange models and values. When Joash and Jeroboam II of Israel recouped and expanded their kingdom's territories, the latter to the border of Hamath, they cemented a trade connection that was fitfully active under Solomon and Hiram, and under Jehoshaphat, the Omrides and Tyre, once again. It bears note that coastal areas inured by obstacles or distance to direct Arpadite control, such as Que (Kaufman 2007) and Byblos (Grayson 1996: A.0.103.2001), at least appear to have pursued a policy in the 8th century of dealing with Assyria rather than with the Tyrian bloc.

Questions

Late Solomonic trade patterns should reiterate those of the Omrides, who, liberating Israel from Egyptian overlordship,[50] recreated the linkage between Tyre in the north and the Red Sea in the south that Shoshenq had been at such pains to uncouple. Is the economy of Megiddo VIA, then, closer to that of Megiddo VA–IVB than is the economy of the earliest phase of IVA? Is that of Hazor X closer to Hazor VIII or to Hazor XI? Have we evidence of resources being drawn south after Shoshenq, north in the last phases of Megiddo IVA? What turns up abroad, or what was in laden shipping jars?

---

50. Note that Baasha is apparently allied with Egypt, against Judah and Damascus. Judah after Shoshenq will have been neglected by Egypt, since it lacked the agricultural development to be of any further interest (and see on Megiddo above). One should consider the possibility that Jerusalem was in this era a vassal kingdom of Israel, though, based on the Dan stela, an independent one. The politics of the Philistine city-states is less perspicuous: Ashdod seems to have contended against Israel, during a period of competition with Damascus, for Gibbethon; and Hazael of Damascus eventually strikes, not at this party, but at Gath on his way to a now-independent Judah. The public historical framework in Kings, even that interspersed with the Elijah-Elisha materials, fits the 9th-century framework closely.

The impact of each successive form of state organization registers in the disposition and character of fortifications. But architecture aside, evidence for intra-site differentiation in the 10th century is scarce ('Ein Zippori may confound the issue). The same holds for later sites. Yet texts indicate that the trade networks of each of these periods differed in state organization. Some reflex in social organization and especially in specialization is to be expected. The commercial structures at Megiddo, Hazor and elsewhere are evidence of such exploitation. Indeed, the proliferation and distribution of olive presses in the 9th and 8th centuries would seem to suggest a consolidation of that industry, too, under state regulation rather than direct control (as the Samaria ostraca suggest). State control of distribution, however, clearly characterizes the Assyrian period as represented at Eqron. Likewise, brick production was standardized and even specialized (SAA 5.291). Can we at the same time locate social differentiation in Judah? In burials, certainly (see Faust and Bunimovitz 2008 for a recent interpretation), but also in the size of cooking pots, and in the virtual disappearance of kin-based residence patterns, and in other ways as well, including the 8th-century standardization of weights, a precursor, along with increasingly abundant chunks of silver, of the economic efficiencies that would lead to coinage (Halpern 1996b).

What intra-site data might confirm such a hypothesis? The cult of Jeroboam is archaeologically inaccessible. But a differential change in foodways is (e.g. the Dan temenos, Wapnish and Hesse 1991). If an Iron I highland village or at least region was almost autarkic, do storage containers indicate imports in Iron II? What is the distribution of fine closed vessels, relative to fine open vessels and to storage assemblages, within regions and within sites? Similarly, given a state, and debt enforcement mechanisms witnessed by seals and receipts, what changes in herding strategies register in the age profile of the zoological sample? Are elite quarters, like the big house at Izbet Sartah, more characterized by younger sheep than other dwellings? Where are the deer, where the imported fish? Are we chiefly encountering smaller skeletal units in domestic processing areas, and thus evidence of commercial differentiation, an index of social hierarchy? As the trading zone expanded, recombined, and expanded again, an increase in specialization and in imports should logically have progressed, if saccadicly. Such a hypothesis can only be formed from text, and ethnographic comparison.

Separately, text and historical archaeology are inseparable. Did Damascus destroy, occupy or dominate Israelite centers? Texts offer alternatives, as does the dirt. The object is always to sift both, and then to arrive at a conclusion that explains both cogently. It is in the nature of the field that this can never be persuasive even to a sizeable majority of professionals.

But to judge scholars by their conclusions is to misprise scholarship. We rely on one another's readings of texts, or dating of eclipses, or stratifying sites and seriating ceramic assemblages, or imagining general cultural frameworks. Yet we inevitably err in our own work. Our job in the end is to advance discussion, maintain critical distance and minimize distraction from the center of the issues. We never teach anyone the truth, but, at our very best, how to address the evidence. With no technique for fine dating, neither textual arguments—even regarding the little-charged 9th century—nor archaeological can achieve the sort of consensus that deflects scholarly attention down more productive specialized channels, without reference to one another. Yet, after some years, our discussion of textual-archaeological correlations, as in the case of the Settlement, grows sterile, or stale. Of course, I've been wrong about much in the past, and hope to be wrong again in the future. But in those matters carrying scholarly charge, such as the correlations with the early monarchy in the last decade, a fallow period can prove a powerful tonic to new inventiveness. All we can do in the meantime is to ask one another: What is it we need to know in order to know what we would like to know? That, in the end, is an argument about method that can only improve our students' contributions to the field.

References

Ahituv, Shmuel (1984) *Canaanite Toponyms in Ancient Egyptian Documents* (Jerusalem: Magnes Press).

Alt, Albrecht (1953 [1926]). Die Landnahme der Israeliten in Palästina. In vol. 1 of *Kleine Schriften zur Geschichte des Volkes Israel* (Munich: C.H. Beck): 126-75.

Astour, Michael (1971) 841 BC: The First Assyrian Invasion of Israel. *Journal of the American Oriental Society* 91: 383-89.

Avigad, Nachman (1997) *A Corpus of Northwest Semitic Seals*, edited by Benjamin Sass (Jerusalem: Israel Academy of Sciences and Humanities, Israel Exploration Society, and Institute of Archaeology, Hebrew University of Jerusalem).

Ben-Tor, Amnon (2001) Responding to Finkelstein's Addendum (On the Dating of Hazor X–VII). *Tel Aviv* 27: 231-47.

—(2002) Hazor and the Chronology of Northern Israel: A Reply to Israel Finkelstein. *BASOR* 317: 9-15.

Ben-Tor, Amnon, and David Ben-Ami (1998) Hazor and the Archaeology of the Tenth Century BCE. *IEJ* 48: 1-37.

Biran, Avraham, and Joseph Naveh (1995) The Tel Dan Inscription: A New Fragment. *IEJ* 45: 1-18.

Blakely, Jeffrey A. (2002) Reconciling Two Maps: Archaeological Evidence for the Kingdoms of David and Solomon. *BASOR* 327: 49-54.

Bloch-Smith, Elizabeth (1992) *Judahite Burial Practices and Beliefs about the Dead* (JSOTSup 123; JSOT/ASOR Monographs 7; Sheffield: Sheffield Academic Press).

Braemer, Frank (1982) L'architecture domestique du Levant a l'Age du Fer (Paris: Éditions Recherche sur les civilisations).

Cantrell, Deborah, and Israel Finkelstein (2006) A Kingdom for a Horse: The Megiddo Stables and Eighth Century Israel. In *Megiddo IV: Seasons 1996, 1998 and 2000*, edited by Israel Finkelstein, David Ussishkin and Baruch Halpern (Tel Aviv: Institute of Archaeology): 643-65.

Cohen, Rudolph, and Rebecca Cohen-Amin (2004) *Ancient Settlement of the Negev Highlands*. II. *The Iron Age and Persian Period* (IAA Reports 20; Jerusalem: Israel Antiquities Authority).

Cohen, Rudolph, and Yigal Yisrael (1995) The Iron Age Fortresses at 'En Haseva. *BA* 58: 223-35.

Cowley, A.E. (1923) *Aramaic Papyri of the Fifth Century B.C.* (Oxford: Clarendon Press).

Dalley, Stephanie (1985) Foreign Chariotry in the Armies of Tiglath-Pileser III and Sargon II. *Iraq* 47: 31-48.

Daviau, P.M. Michèle, John W. Wevers and Michael Weigl (eds.) (2001) *The World of the Aramaeans*, vol. 1 (JSOTSup 324; Sheffield: Sheffield Academic Press).

David, Jonathan (2006) Iconatrophy, Propaganda, and 'Folk-Tale' in Herodotus' Barbarian Logoi (Ph.D. diss., Pennsylvania State University).

Davies, Graham I. (1988) Solomonic Stables at Megiddo after all? *PEQ* 120: 130-41.

Dearman, Andrew (1989) Historical Reconstruction and the Mesha' Inscription. In *Studies in the Mesha Inscription and Moab*, edited by Andrew Dearman (Archaeology and Biblical Studies 2; Atlanta: Scholars Press): 155-210.

Deutsch, Robert, and Michael Heltzer (1997) *Windows to the Past* (Tel Aviv-Jaffa: Archaeological Publications).

Dever, William G. (2001) Excavating the Hebrew Bible, or Burying It Again? *BASOR* 322: 67-77.

Eph'al, Israel, and Joseph Naveh (1989) Hazael's Booty Inscriptions. *IEJ* 39: 192-200.

Faust, Avraham, and Shlomo Bunimovitz (2008) The Judahite Rock-Cut Tomb: Family Response at a Time of Change. *IEJ* 58: 150-70.

Finkelstein, I. (1986) *'Izbet _ar_ah. An Early Iron Age Site near Rosh Ha'ayin, Israel* (BAR International Series 299; London: British Archaeological Society).

—(1996a) The Archaeology of the United Monarchy: An Alternative View. *Levant* 28: 177-87.

—(1996b) The Stratigraphy and Chronology of Megiddo and Beth-Shan in the 12th–11th Centuries B.C.E. *Tel Aviv* 23: 170-84.

—(1998a) Philistine Chronology: High, Middle or Low? In *Mediterranean Peoples in Transition Thirteenth to Early Tenth Centuries BCE*, Fs. Trude Dothan, edited by Seymour Gitin, Amihai Mazar and Ephraim Stern (Jerusalem: Israel Exploration Society): 140-47.

—(1998b) Notes on the Stratigraphy and Chronology of Iron Age Taanach. *Tel Aviv* 25: 208-18.

—(1999) Hazor and the North in the Iron Age: A Low Chronology Perspective. *BASOR* 314: 55-70.

—(2000a) Hazor XII–XI with an Addendum on Ben-Tor's Dating of Hazor X–VII. *Tel Aviv* 27: 231-47.

—(2000b) Omride Architecture. *ZDPV* 116: 114-38.

—(2001) The Rise of Jerusalem and Judah: The Missing Link. *Levant* 33: 105-15.

—(2002) Gezer Revisited and Revised. *Tel Aviv* 29: 262-96.

Finkelstein, Israel, Z. Lederman and S. Bunimovitz (1997) *Highlands of Many Cultures: The Southern Samaria Survey. The Sites* (Sonia and Marco Nadler Institute of Archaeology Monographs 14; Tel Aviv: Institute of Archaeology).

Finkelstein, Israel, and Yitzhaq Magen (eds.) (1993) *Archaeological Survey of the Hill Country of Benjamin* (Jerusalem: Israel Antiquities Authority).

Finkelstein, Israel, and Neil H. Silberman (2006) *David and Solomon: In Search of the Bible's Sacred Kings and the Roots of the Western Tradition* (New York: Free Press).

Fisher, Clarence S. (1929) *The Excavation of Armageddon* (Oriental Institute Communications 4; Chicago: Oriental Institute).

Frankel, Rafael, Nimrod Getzov, Mordechai Aviam and Avi Degani (2001) *Settlement Dynamics and Regional Diversity in Ancient Upper Galilee: Archaeological Survey of Upper Galilee* (IAA Reports 14; Jerusalem: Israel Antiquities Authority).

Franklin, Norma (2003) The Tombs of the Kings of Israel. *ZDPV* 119: 1-11.

—(2004) Samaria: from the Bedrock to the Omride Palace. *Levant* 36: 189-202.

Fuchs, Andreas (1994) *Die Inschriften Sargons II. aus Khorsabad* (Göttingen: Cuvillier).

Gal, Zvi (1992) *Lower Galilee during the Iron Age* (American Schools of Oriental Research Dissertations 8; Winona Lake, IN: Eisenbrauns).

—(2003) The Iron Age 'Low Chronology' in Light of the Excavations at Ḥorvat Rosh Zayit. *IEJ* 53: 147-50.

Gal, Zvi, and Yardenna Alexandre (2000) *Ḥorbat Rosh Zayit. An Iron Age Storage Fort and Village* (IAA Reports 8; Jerusalem: Israel Antiquities Authority).

Garr, W. Randall (1985) *Dialect Geography of Syria-Palestine, 1000–586 B.C.E.* (Philadelphia: University of Pennsylvania Press).

Gibson, J.C.L. (1971) *Textbook of Syrian Semitic Inscriptions*. Vol. 1, *Hebrew and Moabite Inscriptions* (Oxford: Clarendon).

Grayson, A. Kirk (1996) *Assyrian Rulers of the Early First Millennium BC. II (858–745 BC)* (Royal Inscriptions of Mesopotamia Assyrian Periods 3; Toronto: University of Toronto Press).

Halpern, B. (1974) Sectionalism and the Schism. *JBL* 94: 519-32.

—(1996a) The Construction of the Davidic State: An Exercise in Historiography. In *The Origins of the Ancient Israelite States*, edited by Volkmar Fritz and Philip Davies (JSOTSup 228; Sheffield: Sheffield Academic Press): 44-75.

—(1996b) 'Sybil, or the Two Nations': Archaism, Alienation and the Elite Redefinition of Traditional Culture in Judah in the 8th–7th Centuries B.C.E. In *The Study of the Near East in the 21st Century: The William Foxwell Albright Centennial Conference*, edited by Jerrold S. Cooper and Glenn M. Schwartz (Winona Lake, IN: Eisenbrauns): 291-338.

—(2000) The Gate of Megiddo and the Debate on the 10th Century. In *Congress Volume, 1998*, edited by André Lemaire and M. Sæbø (VTSup 80; Leiden: Brill): 79-121.

—(2001a) The Taking of Nothing: 2 Kings 14.25, Amos 6.14 and the Geography of the Deuteronomistic History. In Daviau, Wevers and Weigl 2001: 186-204.

—(2001b) *David's Secret Demons* (Grand Rapids: Eerdmans).

—(2003) Late Israelite Astronomy and the Early Greeks. In *Symbiosis, Symbolism and the Power of the Past: Canaan, ancient Israel, and their Neighbors from the Late Bronze Age through Roman Palaestina*, edited by William G. Dever and Seymour Gitin (Albright Institute Centennial Symposium; Winona Lake, IN: Eisenbrauns): 323-52.

—(2005) Biblical and Greek Historiography: A Comparison. In *Das Alte Testament—ein Geschichtsbuch?*, edited by Erhard Blum, William Johnstone and Christoph Marschies (Altes Testament und Moderne 8; Münster: Lit): 101-27.

Halpern, B., and David Vanderhooft (1991) The Editions of Kings in the 7th–6th Centuries BCE. *Hebrew Union College Annual* 62: 179-244.

Hawkins, J.D. (1976–80) Irhuleni. In vol. 5 of *Reallexicon der Assyriologie und Vorderasiatischen Archäologie*, edited by D.O. Edzard (Berlin: W. de Gruyter): 162.

Herr, Larry G. (1988) Tripartite Pillared Buildings and the Market Place in Iron Age Israel. *BASOR* 272: 47-67.

Hesse, Brian (1986) Animal Use at Tel Miqne-Ekron in the Bronze Age and Iron Age. *BASOR* 286: 17-27.

Hestrin, Ruth, and Michal Dayagi-Mendels (1979) *Inscribed Seals: First Temple Period* (Jerusalem: Israel Museum).

Holladay, J.S. (1986) The Stables of Ancient Israel: Functional Determinants of Stable Construction and the Interpretation of Pillared Building Remains of the Palestinian Iron Age. In *The Archaeology of Jordan and Other Studies Presented to Siegfried H. Horn*, edited by Lawrence T. Geraty and Larry G. Herr (Berrien Springs, MI: Andrews University Press): 103-65.

—(1990) Red Slip, Burnish, and the Solomonic Gateway at Gezer. *BASOR* 277/278: 23-70.

Jamieson-Drake, David (1991) *Scribes and Schools in Monarchic Judah* (Sheffield: Almond Press).

KAI. Donner, Herbert and Wolfgang Röllig (2002) *Kanaanäische und Aramäische Inschriften*, vol.1 (5th edn; Wiesbaden: Harrassowitz).

Kaufman, Stephen A. (2007) The Phoenician Inscription of the Incirli Trilingual: A Tentative Reconstruction and Translation. *MAARAV* 14.2: 7-26.

Keel, Othmar, and Christoph Uehlinger (1992) *Göttinnen, Götter und Gottessymbole. Neue Erkenntnisse zur Religionsgeschichte Kanaans und Israels aufgrund bislang unerschlossener ikonographischer Quellen* (Quaestiones disputatae 134; Freiburg: Herder).

Kitchen, Kenneth A. (1986) *The Third Intermediate Period in Egypt (1100–650 B.C.)* (Warminster: Aris & Phillips).

Lambert, W.G. (1981) Portion of Inscribed Stela of Sargon II. In *Ladders to Heaven: Art Treasures from Lands of the Bible*, edited by O.W. Muscarella (Toronto: McClellan & Stewart): 83.

Lemaire, Andre (1993) Joas de Samarie, Barhadad de Damas, Zakkur de Hamat: la Syrie-Palestine vers 800 av. J.-C. *Eretz-Israel* 24: 148*-57*.

—(1994a) Epigraphie Palestinienne: Nouveaux Documents. I. Fragment de Stele Arameenne de Tell Dan (Ixe s. av. J.-C.). *Henoch* 16: 87-93.

—(1994b) La dynastie davidique (*byt dwd*) dans deux inscriptions Ouest-Sémitiques du Ixe s. av. J.-C. *SEL* 11: 17-19.

—(1994c) 'House of David' Restored in Moabite Inscription. *BAR* 20/3: 30-37.

—(1998a) The Tel Dan Stela as a Piece of Royal Historiography. *JSOT* 81: 3-14.

—(1998b) Chars et cavaliers dans l'ancien Israël. *Transeuphratène* 15: 165-82.

—(2001) Les premiers rois araméens dans la tradition biblique. In Daviau, Wevers and Weigl 2001: 113-43.

—(2006) La datation des rois de Byblos Abibaal et Élibaal et les relations entre l'Égypte et le Levant au Xe siècle av. Notre ère (*Académie des Insriptions & Belles-Lettres. Comptes Rendus*): 1697-16.

Lamon, Rober S., and Geoffrey M. Shipton (1939) *Megiddo. I. Seasons of 1925–34, Strata 1–4* (Oriental Institute Publications 42; Chicago: University of Chicago Press).

Levy, Thomas E., and Thomas Higham (eds.) (2005) *The Bible and Radiocarbon Dating: Archaeology, Text and Science* (London: Equinox).

Liverani, Mario (1990) *Prestige and Interest: International Relations in the Near East ca. 1600–1100 B.C.* (History of the Ancient Near East Studies 3/3; Padova: Sargon).

Mallowan, M.E.L. (1966) *Nimrud and its Remains* (New York: Dodd, Mead).

Mazar, Amihai (2003) The Excavations at Tel Rehov and their Significance for the Study of the Iron Age in Israel. *Eretz-Israel* 27: 143-60.

—(2005) The Debate over the Chronology of the Iron Age in the Southern Levant: Its History, the Current Situation, and a Suggested Resolution. In Levy and Higham 2005: 15-30.

Mazar, E. (2006) Did I Find King David's Palace? *BAR* 32/1: 16-27, 70.

Millard, Alan (1994) *The Eponyms of the Assyrian Empire 910–612 BC* (State Archives of Assyria Studies 2; Helsinki: Neo-Assyrian Text Corpus Project, Dept. of Asian and African Studies, University of Helsinki).

Miller, J. Maxwell (1966) The Elisha Cycle and the Accounts of the Omride Wars. *JBL* 85: 441-55.

Na'aman, Nadav (1995) Hazael of 'Amqi and Hadadezer of Beth-rehob. *Ugarit-Forschungen* 27: 381-94.

Ornan, Tallay (1993) The Transition from Figured to Non-Figured Representation in First Millennium Mesopotamian Glyptic. In *Seals and Sealings in the Ancient Near East*, edited by Joan Goodnick Westenholz (Jerusalem: Bible Lands Museum): 39-56.

—(2005) *The Triumph of the Symbol: Pictorial Representations of Deities in Mesopotamia and the Biblical Image Ban* (Orbis Biblicus et Orientalis 213; Fribourg: University of Fribourg Press).

Pitard, Wayne T. (1987) *Ancient Damascus: A Historical Study of the Syrian City-State from Earliest Times until its Fall to the Assyrians in 732 B.C.E.* (Winona Lake, IN: Eisenbrauns).

—(1988) The Identity of the Bir-Hadad of the Melqart Stela. *BASOR* 272: 3-21.

Porten, Bezalel, and Ada Yardeni (1986) *Textbook of Aramaic Documents from Egypt*. Vol. 1, *Letters* (Jerusalem: Department of the History of the Jewish People, Hebrew University).

Puech, Emile (1994) La stèle araméene de Dan: Bar Hadad II et la coalition des Omrides et de la maison de David. *Revue Biblique* 101: 415-421.

Routledge, Bruce (2000) The Politics of Mesha: Segmented Identities and State Formation in Iron Age Moab. *Journal of the Economic and Social History of the Orient* 43: 221-56.

—(2003) A Comment on A.F. Rainey's 'The New Inscription from Khirbet el-Mudeiyineh'. *IEJ* 53: 192-95.

Shenkel, J.D. (1968) *Chronology and Recensional Development in the Greek Text of Kings* (Harvard Semitic Monographs 1: Cambridge, MA: Harvard University Press).

Shortland, A.J. (2005) Shishaq, King of Egypt: The Challenges of Egyptian Calendrical Chronology. In Levy and Higham 2005: 43-54.

Smelik, Klaas A.D. (1992) *Converting the Past: Studies in Ancient Israelite and Moabite Historiography* (Oudtestamentische Studiën 28; Leiden: Brill).

Stager, L.E. (1995) The Impact of the Sea Peoples in Canaan (1185–1050 BCE). In *The Archaeology of Society in the Holy Land*, edited by T.E. Levy (London: Facts on File, Leicester University Press): 332-48.

Tadmor, Hayim (1994) *The Inscriptions of Tiglath-Pileser III King of Assyria: Critical Edition, with Introductions, Translations and Commentary* (Jerusalem: Israel Academy of Sciences and Humanities).

Tadmor, Hayim, and Mordechai Cogan (1979) Ahaz and Tiglath-Pileser in the Book of Kings: Historiographic Considerations. *Biblica* 61: 491-508.

Tappy, Ron E. (1992) *The Archaeology of Israelite Samaria*. I. *Early Iron Age through the Ninth Century* BCE (Harvard Semitic Studies 44; Atlanta: Scholars Press).

Thureau-Dangin, F. (1931) *Arslan Tash* (Bibliothèque archéologique et historique 16; Paris: Geuthner).

Tidwell, N.L. (1999) A Further Note on Mesha's *hmslt b'rnn*. *VT* 49: 132-34.

Uehlinger, Christoph (1993) Northwest Semitic Inscribed Seals, Iconography and Syro-Palestinian Religions of Iron Age II: Some Afterthoughts and Conclusions. In *Studies in the Iconography of Northwest Semitic Inscribed Seals*, edited by Benjamin Sass and Christoph Uehlinger (Orbis Biblicus et Orientalis 125; Fribourg: University of Fribourg Press): 257-88.

Ussishkin, David (1980) Was the 'Solomonic' City Gate at Megiddo Built by King Solomon? *BASOR* 239: 1-18.

—(1990) Notes on Megiddo, Gezer, Ashdod, and Tel Batash in the Tenth to Ninth Centuries B.C. *BASOR* 277/278: 71-91.

—(1996) The Fortified Enclosure of the Kings of the House of Omri at Jezreel. *Eretz-Israel* 25: 1-14.

—(2000) The Credibility of the Tel Jezreel Excavations: A Rejoinder to Amnon Ben-Tor. *Tel Aviv* 27: 248-56.

Ussishkin, David (ed.) (2004) *The Renewed Archaeological Excavations at Lachish (1973–1994)* (Sonia and Marco Nadler Institute of Archaeology Monographs 22; Tel Aviv: Emery and Claire Yass Publications in Archaeology).

Ussishkin, David, and John Woodhead (1997) Excavations at Tel Jezreel 1994–1996: Third Preliminary Report. *Tel Aviv* 24: 6-72.

Vansina, Jan (1965) *Oral Tradition: A Study in Historical Methodology* (Madison: University of Wisconsin Press).

—(1985) *Oral Tradition as History* (Madison: University of Wisconsin Press).

Wapnish, Paula, and Brian Hesse (1991) Faunal Remains from Tel Dan: Perspectives on Animal Production at a Village, Urban and Ritual Center. *ArchaeoZoologia* 4: 9-86.

Weissert, Elnathan (1997) Royal Hunt and Royal Triumph in a Prism Fragment of Ashurbanipal (82-5-22,2). In *Assyria 1995: Proceedings of the 10th Anniversary Symposium of the Neo-Assyrian Text Corpus Project. Helsinki, September 7–11, 1995*, edited by S. Parpola and R.M. Whiting (Helsinki: The Neo-Assyrian Text Project): 339-38.

Westbrook, R. (1999) Codex Hammurabi and the Ends of the Earth. In *Landscapes, Territories, Frontiers and Horizons in the Ancient Near East. III. Landscape in Ideology, Religion, Literature and Art*, edited by L. Milano, S. de Martino, F.M. Fales and G.B. Lanfranchi (44th Rencontre Assyriologique; History of the Ancient Near East Monographs 3/3; Padova: Sargon): 101-3.

Wilkinson, T.J., Eleanor Barbanes Wilkinson, Jason Ur and Mark Altaweel (2005) Landscape and Settlement in the Neo-Assyrian Empire. *BASOR* 340: 23-56.

Wilson, Kevin A. (2005) *The Campaign of the Pharaoh Shoshenq I into Palestine* (Forschungen zum Alten Testament 2/9; Tübingen: Mohr Siebeck).

Yamada, Shigeo (2000) *The Construction of the Assyrian Empire: A Historical Study of the Inscriptions of Shalmanesar III (859–824 B.C.) Relating to his Campaigns to the West* (Culture and History of the Ancient Near East 3; Leiden: Brill).

Zertal, Adam (1988) *The Israelite Settlement in the Hill-Country of Manasseh* (Haifa: Haifa University Press).

Zimhoni, Orna (1997) Clues from the Enclosure-fills: Pre-Omride Settlement at Tel Jezreel. *Tel Aviv* 24: 83-109.

16 Integrating Archaeology and Texts

The Example of the Qumran Toilet

Jodi Magness

Abstract

The nature of the Qumran settlement is an ongoing subject of scholarly debate and controversy. Whereas the site's original excavator, Roland de Vaux, identified Qumran as a sectarian settlement, other scholars have proposed that it was something else (e.g. a villa, manor house, fort, commercial entrepot, or pottery manufacturing center). Scholars who identify Qumran as anything but a sectarian settlement must argue that there is no connection between the site and the Dead Sea Scrolls, which were found in the nearby caves. This paper is a case study of a toilet excavated by de Vaux at Qumran, which illustrates how archaeological and literary sources can be used together to gain a more complete understanding of the past.

Introduction

2007 marked the 60th anniversary of the discovery of the first Dead Sea Scrolls. Five years after that discovery, excavations were undertaken at the site of Qumran. This small, unimpressive ruin has attracted more than its share of scholarly and media attention. This is a result of the site's association with the Dead Sea Scrolls, which were found in the nearby caves. Ironically, some archaeologists seem determined to deny any link between Qumran and the scrolls. Was Qumran a sectarian (and specifically, Essene) settlement, as the original excavator, Roland de Vaux, proposed (and as I believe, following de Vaux), or was it something else—a villa, manor house, fort, commercial entrepot, or pottery manufacturing center—as others have suggested?

The interpretation of Qumran as a sectarian settlement depends on whether one accepts or rejects the association of the scrolls with the site. Simply put, scholars who accept the connection between the scrolls and the site identify Qumran as a sectarian settlement (this is true regardless of whether these scholars identify the sectarians as Essenes). Scholars who reject the identification of Qumran as a sectarian settlement argue that there is no connection between the scrolls and the site. According to this view, the inhabitants of Qumran did not own and use the scrolls or deposit them in the nearby caves. In this paper I discuss the toilet at Qumran as an example of how integrating archaeology and texts can help us to understand better the lifestyle and beliefs of this community.

The Qumran Community

The settlement at Qumran was established by a group of Jewish sectarians, apparently around 80 BCE (see Magness 2003: 422; Bar-Nathan 2006: 264 n. 8, now seems to concur). Dispossessed Zadokite priests seem to have played a central role in the initial foundation of this sect, although not all members (or even leaders) were Zadokites (Magness 2002: 36-37). The sectarians called themselves by various names including the *yahad* and Sons of Light. Others referred to them as Essenes, a Greek and Latin term (Magness 2002: 37-38, 41-42). Members of the sect lived in towns and villages around the country, including in Jerusalem, and some practiced desert separatism. Qumran was one such community; we do not know whether there were others (Magness 2002: 37). After Qumran's destruction in 68 CE during the First Jewish Revolt against the Romans, the sectarians disappear from the stage of history (see Magness 2002: 62).

Because the sect was established by dispossessed Zadokite priests, they did not recognize the current Jerusalem priesthood as legitimate. They believed those priests were impure and unfit to serve. They considered the temple polluted and constituted their community as a substitute temple, with each full member living in imitation of the priests serving in the Jerusalem temple. This meant maintaining the highest level of purity required in Judaism, which required avoiding contact with anything or anyone at a lower level of purity and frequent immersion in miqva'ot (Jewish ritual baths). To be admitted as a full member, one had to pass through a series of stages of initiation, attaining with each stage a higher and higher level of purity (Magness 2002: 37-38). The sect universalized a priestly lifestyle to full members, who consumed only pure food and drink and wore white linen garments like priests in the temple (Magness 2002: 113, 206).

The sectarian settlement at Qumran is characterized by the large number of miqva'ot (and their large sizes), communal dining rooms with pantries containing hundreds of dishes, animal bone deposits, and an unusual ceramic assemblage with hundreds of cylindrical jars. These features are physical expressions of this community's priestly lifestyle and peculiar halakhah, which involved maintaining the highest possible level of ritual purity. This is why these features are unparalleled at other sites. Rarely does archaeology so clearly reflect a system of religious beliefs and practices (see Magness 2002, 2005).

The Toilet at Qumran: Archaeological Evidence

The sect's purity concerns impacted even their toilet habits. At Qumran de Vaux found a toilet in Locus 51, a room on the eastern side of the settlement. A terracotta pipe surrounded by stones was set into a mud-lined pit that was filled with layers of foul, dirty soil (*terre sale*) (Humbert and Chambon 1994: 309; Photos 148-51; the caption to Photo 150 erroneously describes the dried mud lining of the pit as a *jarre receptacle*).

Perhaps the best-known examples of ancient toilets are Roman luxury latrines, which were equipped with stone or wooden seats pierced with holes mounted along the walls of a room. The arrangement of side-by-side seats means that there was no toilet privacy. A constantly running stream of water below the seats carried the sewage away from the bathhouse. Since luxury latrines relied on a constant supply of fresh water piped in by aqueduct, they are rarely found outside Roman civic bathhouses or other public establishments (see Neudecker 1994; Hodge 1992: 270-71).

Sanitary arrangements otherwise varied greatly in the ancient Mediterranean world, even during the time of the Roman Empire (Hodge 1992: 337). Because many private homes in Roman cities lacked any toilet facilities, residents either had to use a chamber pot (such as the bottom half of a broken amphora), or relieved themselves outdoors (Hodge 1992: 336; Scobie 1986: 421; Bodel 1986: 32). The contents of chamber pots were emptied from the windows of houses onto the street below (Scobie 1986: 417). This is why better-designed Roman cities such as Pompeii have high curbs with stepping-stones across the streets. The waste was washed away by the overflow from public fountains, which ran through gutters into underground sewers (Hodge 1992: 334-35; Scobie 1986: 411, but see the qualification on p. 418). The lack of concern with toilet privacy is indicated by notices posted outside shops at Pompeii requesting that individuals relieve themselves elsewhere (Hodge 1992: 337; also see Scobie 1986: 429). As John Bodel observed, 'streets, public reservoirs, doorways, statues, even public and private buildings, not to mention tombs—virtually any outdoor place accessible to the public seems to have been liable to the danger of being fouled with ordure...' (Bodel 1986: 33; also see Scobie 1986: 416 for an inscription at Pompeii prohibiting the fouling of a public water basin with excrement).

When toilet installations are found in Roman houses, they usually consist of a stone or wooden seat built over a cesspit. Cesspits were emptied by manure merchants, who sold the contents as fertilizer (Hodge 1992: 336-37; Scobie 1986: 409, 413-14; Bodel 1986: 32). A close parallel to the toilet at Qumran comes from the late Iron Age House of Ahiel in the City of David in Jerusalem, where a square stone toilet seat pierced by a hole was found in its original position over a cesspit (see Cahill *et al.* 1991: 65; for other examples, see Magness 2004: 64-65). The installation at Qumran appears to represent a toilet of this type. Since no seat was found in L51 at Qumran, it might have been made of wood. However, a pierced stone block that de Vaux found in L44, which is adjacent to and east of L51, could be the toilet seat. There are no published illustrations of this object, which de Vaux tentatively identified as part of a conduit or chimney flue (see Humbert and Chambon 1994: 307).

Ancient Literary Sources on Sectarian Toilets and Toilet Habits

The Temple Scroll, War Scroll, and Josephus provide valuable information on sectarian toilets and toilet practices. In the scrolls, toilets are referred to by the Biblical Hebrew term the hand or the place for a hand. In Qumranic Hebrew the term hand (*yad*) means penis. The War Scroll mandates the placement of toilets at a distance of 2000 cubits from the camps:

> And there will be a space between all their camps and 'the place of the hand' of about two thousand cubits. And no immodest nakedness will be seen in the surroundings of all their camps. (1QM 7:6-7; from Martínez and Tigchelaar 1997: 125; see also Yadin 1983: 295)

The relevant passage from the Temple Scroll reads:

> And you shall make them a place for a hand outside the city, to which they shall go out, to the north-west of the city—roofed houses with pits within them into which the excrement will descend, so that it will not be visible at any distance from the city, 3000 cubits. (11Q 46:13-16; from Yadin 1983: 294)

The sectarians' concern with covering or concealing excrement is based on their understanding of Deut. 23:9-14:

> When you are encamped against your enemies you shall guard against any impropriety. If one of you becomes unclean (impure) because of a nocturnal emission, then he shall go outside the camp; he must not come within the camp. When evening comes, he shall wash himself with water, and when the sun has set, he may come back into the camp. You shall have a designated area outside the camp to which you shall go. With your utensils you shall have a trowel (*yeted*); when you relieve yourself outside, you shall dig a hole with it and then cover up your excrement. Because the Lord your God travels along with your camp, to save you and to hand over your enemies to you, therefore your camp must be holy, so that he may not see anything indecent among you and turn away from you.[1]

---

1.   The biblical passages cited here are from the *Harper Collins Study Bible*, NRSV translation.

Josephus describes as follows the sanitation practices of the Essenes:

> (On the Sabbath they do not) even go to stool. On other days they dig a trench a foot deep with a mattock (*skalidi*)—such is the nature of the hatchet which they present to neophytes—and wrapping their mantle about them, that they may not offend the rays of the deity, sit above it. They then replace the excavated soil in the trench. For this purpose they select the more retired spots. And though this discharge of the excrements is a natural function, they make it a rule to wash themselves after it, as if defiled. (*War* 2:147-49; Loeb edition)

The literary evidence combined with the presence of a toilet at Qumran indicate that the sectarians attended to their bodily functions in various ways. When they did not have access to built toilet facilities in permanent settlements, they relieved themselves in the manner described by Josephus. The location of the toilet in L51 on the eastern side of the main building suggests that the distance regulations mandated for toilets in the War Scroll and the Temple Scroll did not apply to the settlement at Qumran. These sources make a point of requiring the placement of toilets at minimum distances from the war camps at the end of days and from the ideal city of Jerusalem. However, the fact that the toilet in L51 does not seem to have been replaced after the earthquake of 31 BCE suggests that the sectarians reorganized the settlement at Qumran along the lines of their ideal Jerusalem (see Magness 2004: 111). Even before 31 the toilet in L51 could not have served the needs of the entire community. Therefore most of the members (before 31) must have relieved themselves outside the settlement (and after 31 all members did), in built facilities and in the manner described by Josephus (Magness 2004: 111).

The silence of ancient Roman sources concerning the placement and construction of domestic latrines reflects a lack of regulation or concern, in contrast to the Qumran community (see Scobie 1986: 409). Similarly, Josephus was struck by the fact that the Essenes secluded themselves when defecating outdoors, in contrast to the contemporary practice of openly relieving oneself. This corresponds with the Temple Scroll's requirement that the toilets be located within an enclosed, roofed building, thereby ensuring privacy.

The sectarian concern for toilet privacy reflected in the Temple Scroll's legislation and Josephus's testimony was exceptional in the Roman world. The Temple Scroll describes the type of toilet found at Qumran and undoubtedly in other permanent settlements, but it and the War Scroll added a distance regulation because of the state of purity required in the ideal holy city or during the war at the end of days, to ensure that nothing indecent would be visible.

Yigael Yadin noted that the distances mandated by the Temple Scroll and War Scroll would have placed the toilets beyond the Sabbath limits (Yadin 1983: 300-301). Similarly, Josephus observed that the Essenes did not defecate on the Sabbath. If this regulation was observed at Qumran, the inhabitants presumably refrained from using the toilet in L51 on the Sabbath. In addition, the passages from the Temple Scroll and from Josephus attest to a sectarian concern that excrement be concealed in a pit. This concern stems from the sectarians' understanding of Deut. 23:12-14:

> You shall have a designated area outside the camp to which you shall go. With your utensils you shall have a trowel (*yeted*); when you relieve yourself outside, you shall dig a hole with it and then cover up your excrement. Because the Lord your God travels along with your camp, to save you and to hand over your enemies to you, therefore your camp must be holy, so that he may not see anything indecent among you and turn away from you.

The sectarians differed from other Jews in regarding defecation as a polluting activity, and therefore required immersion afterwards as Josephus describes. I do not believe it is a coincidence that the only doorway in the room with the toilet at Qumran opens onto a miqveh (L48-49; see Humbert and Chambon 1994: Fig. XII). Another miqveh located by the entrance at the northwest side of the settlement might have been used by members who exited in that direction to relieve themselves, if we assume that toilets were located to the northwest as mandated for Jerusalem in the Temple Scroll (L138; see Humbert and Chambon 1994: Fig. XIX; Magness 2002: 147-48).

Rabbinic Legislation Concerning Toilets and Excrement

In contrast to the sectarian view, rabbinic Judaism does not associate excrement and defecation with impurity:

> These do not become unclean and do not impart susceptibility to uncleanness: 1) sweat, 2) stinking pus, 3) excrement, 4) blood which exudes with them, and 5) liquid [which is excreted with a stillborn child] at the eighth month. (*m. Makh.* 6:7; from Neusner 1988: 1107)

According to the Mishnah (*Kel.* 10:2), excrement can be used to seal a clay vessel.

In the Palestinian Talmud, Rabbi Jose ruled that defecation is associated with purity instead of impurity:

> And is excrement [a matter of ritual] impurity; is it not merely [rather a matter of] cleanliness [being considered filth]? (*y. Pes.* 7:12; from Bokser and Schiffman 1994: 378)

By this he meant that the evacuation of excrement from the body leaves it clean, whereas the emission of semen (for example) makes it impure.

A similar view is expressed in the Babylonian Talmud:

> R. Papa said: If there be excrement in its place [in the anus; *bemkomah*], he must not read the Shema'. How shall we imagine this case? If to say that it is invisible, that is self-evident: if to say that it is unseen—surely 'The Torah was not given to the ministering angels!'—This has but reference to a situation in which it is obvious when he sits and invisible when he stands. But what is the difference between this and one who has filth (excrement; *tso'ah*) on his body, for it has been stated: Where one who has filth on his body, or whose hands are in a privy. R. Huna permits the reading of the Shema' and R. Hisda forbids it?—In its place filth is most execrable (*nafish zohama*), away from it, it is less so (*lo nafish zohama*). (*b. Yom.* 30a:4-9; Soncino edition)

In other words, if excrement is visible in the anus when a person sits or squats, he is not allowed to recite the Shema'. Although the rabbis did not associate excrement with impurity, like the Qumran sectarians they understood the passage from Deuteronomy as meaning that excrement is indecent and should be hidden from God's view. For this reason the rabbis prohibited the reciting of the Shema' in the vicinity of human and animal excrement, urine, and other sources of foul odors. Effectively this means that the Shema' cannot be recited while one is defecating or in a toilet, as the following passages from the Palestinian Talmud (*Ber.* 3:5) indicate:

> It is stated: One removes himself [in order to pray or recite the Shema'] from human excrement four cubits and from dog's excrement four cubits..
>
> Rebbi Yose bar Hanina said: One removes himself four cubits from animal dung...
>
> It is stated: One removes himself four cubits from a bad smell...
>
> It is stated: One must remove himself four cubits from a chamber pot, be it used for excrement or for urine... (from Guggenheimer 2000: 312-15).

I believe the Mishnah provides the key to understanding why the Qumran sectarians differed from other Jews in associating excrement with impurity: 'This governing principle applied in the temple: Whoever covers his feet [and defecates] requires immersion' (*m. Yom.* 3:2; from Neusner 1988: 268). This passage refers to the toilet used by the priests in the Jerusalem temple. After using the toilet, the priests were required to immerse themselves in a miqveh. Because the sect extended the temple purity laws to its members, they viewed defecation as a polluting activity and required immersion afterwards.

The sectarian association of excrement with impurity is expressed in other ways. For example, the Damascus Document prohibits ritual immersion in *mayim tso'im*, which is usually translated 'dirty water' but must refer to water containing excrement:

> Concerning purification with water. No one should bathe in water which is dirty (*mayim tso'im*) or which is less than the amount which covers a man. No one should purify a vessel in it. (CD-A 10:10-12; from Martínez and Tigchelaar 1997: 567-69)

A few lines below this the Damascus Document forbids wearing clothes soiled with excrement on the Sabbath:

> No one is to wear dirty clothes (*begadim tso'im*)... (CD 11:3; from Martínez and Tigchelaar 1997: 569)

In contrast, rabbinic discussions about ritual immersion focus on the color and odor of the water but do not refer to *mayim tso'im*. For example:

> Three *logs* of [drawn] water—and into them fell a *qartob* of wine—and lo, their color is the color of wine—and they fell into the immersion pool—they have not rendered it unfit. Three *logs* of water, lacking a *qartob*—and a *qartob* of milk fell into them, and lo, their color is the color of the water—and they fell into immersion pool—they have not rendered it unfit. R. Yohanan b. Nuri says, 'All follows the color (*hakol holech ahar hamar'eh*)'. (*m. Miq.* 7:5; from Neusner 1988: 1071)

> He [a *zab*] should not cover himself with foul water (*bamayim ha-ra'im*) or water used for soaking [flax] (*bimai ha- mishrah*) unless he has poured into it [some fresh] water. And how far should one distance himself from them [from foul water] and from excrement [before he may recite]? Four cubits (*m. Ber.* 3:5; from Neusner 1988: 7; this is necessary because a zab recites the Shema' while immersing; see Danby 1933: 4)

A passage in the Mishnah sheds light on why the Temple Scroll mandates the placement of the toilets to the northwest of Jerusalem. The miqveh associated with the toilet used by the priests in the temple was located in the Chamber of Immersion. The toilet and immersion facilities were located in underground rooms on the northwest side of the temple courtyard: 'Through that [room in the Beit Hamoked, the Chamber of the Hearth] on the northwestern side do they go down to the room for immersion' (*m. Mid.* 1:6, from Neusner 1988: 874). The Temple Scroll mandates the placement of toilets in the ideal city of Jerusalem to the northwest of the city because the toilet facilities within the Second Temple were located on the northwest side.

Similarly, the sectarian concern with toilet privacy or modesty can be understood in light of the temple arrangements described in the Mishnah:

> [If] one of them should have a nocturnal emission of semen, he goes out, proceeding along the passage that leads below the building—and lamps flicker on this side and on that—and he reaches the immersion room, and there was a fire there, and a privy in good taste. And this was its good taste: [if] he found it locked, he knows that someone is there; [if he found it] open, he know that no one is there. He went down and immersed and came up and dried off, and warmed himself by the fire. (*m. Tam.* 1:1; from Neusner 1988: 863)

In other words, the room containing the toilet used by the priests serving in the temple had a door that could be closed or locked to ensure privacy. This concern for toilet privacy explains the placement of the toilet at Qumran in a room at the eastern edge of the settlement and at the extreme western end of the room. Not only was this toilet located in a roofed house like the toilets mandated by the Temple Scroll but it would not have been visible to passersby. In fact, the only way to view the toilet from outside L51 would be from the eastern wall of L52, a spot that no one was likely to pass by casually. Furthermore, de Vaux found evidence that the doorway in L51 was closed by a wooden door, as indicated by a wooden beam and iron nails lying in and around the threshold (see Humbert and Chambon 1994: 309).

The placement of the doorway on the south side of L51 might reflect a custom that was also observed outside sectarian circles, as suggested by a passage in the Babylonian Talmud:

> Our Rabbis taught: One who defecates (*ha-nefaneh*) in Judea should not do so east and west but north and south. In Galilee he should do so only east and west. (*Ber.* 61b:3-4; Soncino edition)

Jesus' Position on the Impurity of Excrement

An episode described in the Gospels might provide evidence for Jesus' position on the impurity of excrement. Mark 7:1-23 records a dispute between Jesus and the scribes and Pharisees over the need to wash the hands before eating, to which Jesus responds: 'there is nothing outside a person that by going in can defile, but the things that come out are what defile' (Mk 7:15). The parallel passage in Matthew (15:11) reads: 'it is not what goes into the mouth that defiles a person, but it is what comes out of the mouth that defiles'. Notice that Matthew has clarified the Markan statement by adding that it is what goes in and out *of the mouth* that does or does not defile.

In the following passage in Mark, Jesus reiterates his position:

> When he had left the crowd and entered the house, his disciples asked him about the parable. He said to them, 'Then do you also fail to understand? Do you not see that whatever goes into a person from outside cannot defile, since it enters, not the heart, but the stomach, and goes out into the sewer?' (Thus he declared all foods clean.) And he said, 'It is what comes out from a person that defiles. For it is from within, from the human heart, that evil intentions come; fornication, theft, murder, adultery, avarice, wickedness, deceit, licentiousness, envy, slander, pride, folly. All these evil things come from within, and they defile a person'. (Mk 7:17-23)

These passages suggest that like the rabbis but unlike the Qumran sectarians, Jesus did not consider excrement—that is, what passes through the stomach and into the sewer—to be impure (assuming these passages reflect Jesus' views).

Conclusion

Because the Qumran sectarians viewed themselves as a replacement for the temple and created by means of the sect a substitute for the sacrificial cult, temple purity laws were applied to the lives of all full members. The requirement of immersion after defecation and concern for toilet privacy among priests serving in the temple were therefore made universal among the sectarians.

This review of the sect's toilets and toilet habits illustrates how information gleaned from archaeological and literary sources can be used to gain a more complete understanding of the past. I began this paper by describing the physical (archaeological) remains of the toilet at Qumran, which were examined and compared with facilities at other sites in Palestine and the Roman world. This was followed by a consideration of Roman toilet habits, and a review of the literary evidence for sectarian and rabbinic toilets and toilet habits, as well as possible evidence for Jesus' views. These comparisons reveal that because of their unique purity concerns, sectarian toilets and toilet habits differed from those of their Jewish and non-Jewish contemporaries. I believe that archaeologists can use a similar methodology to advance our understanding of other aspects of the Qumran settlement. The future of Qumran archaeology, like its past, lies in the careful study of the intersection of texts and artifacts.

References

Bar-Nathan, R. (2006) Qumran and the Hasmonean and Herodian Winter Palaces of Jericho: The Implication of the Pottery Finds on the Interpretation of the Settlement at Qumran. In *Qumran, the Site of the Dead Sea Scrolls: Archaeological Interpretations and Debates*, edited by K. Galor, J.-B. Humbert, and J. Zangenberg (Boston: Brill): 263-77.

Bodel, J. (1986 [1994]) Graveyards and Groves: A Study of the *Lex Lucerina*. *American Journal of Ancient History* 11.

Bokser, B.M., and L.H. Schiffman (1994) *The Talmud of the Land of Israel: A Preliminary Translation and Explanation*. Vol. 13, *Yerushalmi Pesahim* (Chicago: University of Chicago Press).

Cahill, J., K. Reinhard, D. Tarler, and P. Warnock (1991) It Had to Happen: Scientists Examine Remains of Ancient Bathroom. *BAR* 17/3 (1991): 64-69.

Danby, H. (1933) *The Mishnah, Translated from the Hebrew with Introduction and Brief Explanatory Notes* (Oxford: Clarendon Press).

Guggenheimer, H.W. (2000) *The Jerusalem Talmud*. XVIII, *First Order: Zeraim, Tractate Berakhot* (Berlin: W. de Gruyter).

Hodge, A.T. (1992) *Roman Aqueducts and Water Supply* (London: Duckworth).

Humbert, J-B., and A. Chambon (1994) *Fouilles de Khirbet Qumrân et de Aïn Feshkha I* (Fribourg: Édition Universitaires).

Magness, J. (2002) *The Archaeology of Qumran and the Dead Sea Scrolls* (Grand Rapids: Eerdmans).

—(2003) Review of *Hasmonean and Herodian Palaces at Jericho: Final Reports of the 1973–1987 Excavations*. Vol. 3, *The Pottery*, by R. Bar-Nathan. *Dead Sea Discoveries* 10.3: 420-28.

—(2004) *Debating Qumran: Collected Essays on its Archaeology* (Leuven: Peeters).

—(2005) Review of *Qumran in Context: Reassessing the Archaeological Evidence*, by Y. Hirschfeld. *Review of Biblical Literature*. Online: http://www.bookreviews.org (accessed 27 August 2005).

Martínez, F.G., and E.J.C. Tigchelaar (1997) *The Dead Sea Scrolls Study Edition*, vol. 1 (Leiden: Brill).

Neudecker, R. (1994) *Die Pracht der Latrine, Zum Wandel Öffentlicher Bedürfnisanstalten in der kaiserzeitlichen Stadt* (Munich: Dr. Friedrich Pfeil).

Neusner, J. (1988) *The Mishnah: A New Translation* (New Haven: Yale University Press).

Scobie, A. (1986) Slums, Sanitation, and Mortality in the Roman World. *Klio* 68: 409-17.

Yadin, Y. (1983) *The Temple Scroll*, vol. 1 (Jerusalem: Israel Exploration Society).

IV.
IN PERSPECTIVE

17 Stones, Bones, Texts and Relevance

Or, How I Lost my Fear of Biblical Archaeology and Started Enjoying It

Aren Maeir

Abstract

Biblical Archaeology is seen by many as being an outdated and outmoded practice of archaeology, so much so that many have proposed dropping this term altogether. In this brief contribution, while acknowledging some of the past problems of Biblical Archaeology, I attempt to demonstrate how mainstream Biblical Archaeology is still a vibrant, cutting edge and important professional endeavor, one which unabashedly can stand at the forefront of archaeological research, in comparison with any of the other many subsets of the archaeological profession throughout the world today. In fact, I argue that not only should the title Biblical Archaeologist not be abandoned—but rather, as I do—be professed with pride!

Introduction

During one of the first classes of my freshman year at the Institute of Archaeology at the Hebrew University, in the fall of 1982, the professor who gave the introductory class to 'Biblical Archaeology' presented an overview of the history of the archaeological research in the Land of Israel. Having reviewed research in pre-State of Israel times, he then went on to categorize the archaeological research in the State of Israel. One of the points that he stressed was that Israeli archaeology is a distinctly secular endeavor, and that none of the past, and present, practicing archaeologists in Israel came from a Jewish religiously observant background and orientation. This he interpreted as being a direct influence of the British archaeological tradition in this region (which he defined as largely secularly oriented), as opposed to the American tradition, which, at least until recently, he saw as being a predominantly theologically oriented tradition. As a person who identified himself as being oriented towards traditional Judaism (so-called 'Modern Orthodox'), such a statement clearly excluded me from the 'gang'.[1]

---

1.   Somewhat ironically, of the seventy or so students that had been sitting in that particular class, only three currently have tenured positions in archaeology at academic institutions in Israel (H. Eshel, Z. Weiss and

In other words, a predominant feeling among practicing Israeli archaeologists during the early '80s was that Israeli archaeology was a professional venue with little religious connections, and, as such, it continued the European, and not the American tradition, of secular-based archaeological scientific research. More or less at the very same time, American archaeologists working in the Levant were going through a similar reassessment of the methodological and theoretical background of the practice of archaeology in the Near East, attempting to realign it from being identified as 'Biblical Archaeology' to a more 'scientifically sounding', 'Syro-Palestinian' archaeology (e.g. Dever 1981; see Zevit 2004).

It would appear that the attempt to distance the practice of archaeology of the Near East from religious and/or sectarian interests was a central motif among the practitioners of this profession over the last several decades. It was felt, and I believe justifiably so, that in the past, all-too-often, the fields of interest, research agendas and strategies, as well as conclusions, were heavily influenced by contemporary religious, ideological and other agendas. Needless to say, this aspect has been thoroughly and extensively discussed, and need not be repeated here (e.g. Silberman 1990; Ben-Yehuda 2001; Meyers 2006).[2]

One of the most strongly felt currents in contemporary ancient Near Eastern archaeology is an almost automatic aversion on the part of most practitioners in the field to the very term 'Biblical Archaeology'. So much so, very few practicing archaeologists are willing to identify themselves as 'biblical archaeologists', in light of feeling that the very name denotes an antiquated, parochial and ideologically driven endeavor. Thus, for example, several years ago, the editors of the journal *Biblical Archaeology* expressed a wish to change the name of the journal to a more 'modern' and up-to-date name (*Near Eastern Archaeology*) and held a poll among their readers. Despite the fact that there was an overall majority among the readers (of which, clearly, many are not professional archaeologists) to *retain* the old name, the editors changed the name to the suggested (and currently used) name.

It would seem then that the very term Biblical Archaeology and what it represents has been undermined, and in many circles is viewed in a very negative manner. In the following pages I would like to argue that this, in my opinion, is a faulty approach, which is derived from several misconceptions:

1. A misunderstanding of what Biblical Archaeology is and should be.
2. A strong influence that is/was exerted (implicitly or explicitly) on the practitioners of Near Eastern archaeology (who deal with cultures that produced texts) by the paradigms of archaeologists who work in text-less cultures.
3. Due to the major changes and fluctuations that the study of the biblical text has undergone in the last decades, archaeologists are hesitant to grapple with a less-than-naïve interface between 'spade' and 'text'. Since the biblical text cannot be read as a uniform and univocal 'artifact', they prefer not reading it at all, particularly vis-à-vis its relationship to the archaeological evidence.
4. There is a 'fear' among many practitioners of Near Eastern archaeology of dealing with the biblical text in the context of archaeological research since in their opinion it mirrors old-fashioned, parochial worldviews, inappropriate in a post-modern world.

---

the current writer)—all three of which profess a orthodox-oriented Jewish perspective. Perhaps this can serve as a warning against making wide-ranging generalizations, or, perchance, it can inform us of the many changes that have occurred in Israeli society, and the archaeological profession in particular, over the last several decades.

2.   Nevertheless, it should be stressed that the belief that an ideologically driven agenda is the primary agency behind the practice of archaeology in Israel to this day and age (as, for example, Abu el-Haj 2001 claims) is simply a gross misrepresentation of the current state of affairs (see, e.g., Maeir 2004a).

I believe that this approach is not only a very basic methodological mistake, but that it has the potential to miss out on one of the central roles that the professional archaeologist has—to serve as a steward of the past, in a manner that evokes interest and meaning for the general public. A modern and updated approach to Biblical Archaeology (with capital B and A) can insure both a cutting-edge scientific approach to the study of the ancient Near East, and at the same time, it can spark the interest, fascination and imagination of the public—the true constituency of our work!

I firmly believe that:

1. Biblical Archaeology is a vibrant and forward looking endeavor with a wide perspective and a cutting-edge, sophisticated outlook on the cultures of the Ancient Near East.
2. One must grapple with the interface between the archaeological finds and the biblical text (and related literatures)—even if this is not a straightforward and simple task.
3. Shying away from this is a haven for a narrow-minded, simplistic understanding of the relevant cultures and periods.

Some Background

If you would conduct a poll on the streets, asking lay people their opinion on 'Biblical Archaeology', this is what you would probably hear: (1) Either that they are very excited—thinking about the biblical stories that they learnt in their childhood, with images of Bedouins, shepherds and camels, and of course, 'Indiana Jones and the Raiders of the Lost Ark'; (2) Alternatively, this profession would be seen as an old fashioned, parochial and ideologically (mis)guided pursuit, very much 'passé' in today's postmodern world, and perhaps even a tool of unacceptable, colonialist practices!

Clearly, these are very different perspectives, each deriving from very different places. Which perspective is correct? Apparently, neither...

The field of Biblical Archaeology suffers from a bad public image (in some quarters) due to the practices of scholars of decades ago. In fact, early biblical, historical, archaeological and geographical scholars of the Near East often did produce one-dimensional and strongly biased attempts to connect the biblical text and the archaeological finds. Whether following extremely simplistic patterns (such as the famous 'Babel und Bibel' controversy—see, e.g., Liwag 1998; Shavit and Eran 2003) or more evidence-based ones (such as regarding the historical and archaeological evidence for the Patriarchs [e.g. Albright 1941], the Israelite conquest [e.g. Yadin 1982], the 'United Monarchy' [e.g. Malamat 1982], etc.), nevertheless rather naïve interpretations of the relationship between the archaeological evidence and the biblical text were suggested. Over time, these, and other, approaches were critiqued (e.g. Thompson 1974; Finkelstein 1988; Handy 1997), and they do not represent the paradigmatic approach in use today.

Parallel to this, time and again, the archaeological evidence was enlisted to 'prove' religious beliefs (e.g. Marston 1934). A well-known example is the reasoning behind the founding of the Palestine Exploration Fund, which was created to provide 'biblical illustration' based on the study of various aspects of Palestine (Grove 1869); and this may have been a central factor in many of the early archaeological endeavors, whether stated explicitly or not.[3]

Without a doubt, many of the founding fathers of Biblical Archaeology were astounding scholars with control of an extremely wide range of materials—ranging from the archaeological, historical and ethnographic, to mention a few. In fact, their breadth of knowledge enabled them to form a truly synthetic view of the biblical world. Nevertheless, one should not forget that their knowledge

---

3. Unfortunately, the need to 'prove' or 'disprove' is still an issue with the understanding of various lay persons (and some archaeologists) on the relationship between archaeology and the Bible. See, e.g., Kitchen 2003; Meitlis 2006.

base, and worldview, was based on a 19th-century/early 20th-century perspective, which needless to say was at times both naïve and close-minded, and, to a large extent, quite conservative. As such, they placed too much emphasis, or rather, prominence, on DIRECTLY and UNCRITICALLY connecting between the archaeological remains and the biblical text.[4]

In addition, as is the case with many national narratives (e.g. Kohl 1998), biblical archaeology was used within the context of the conflicting national narratives of the Near East, most often by people who were not professional archaeologists. This too was strongly critiqued in recent decades, often justifiably so (see, e.g., Silberman 1990; Meyers 2006).[5]

It is these aspects which gave Biblical Archaeology a 'bad name' (at least among some groups)! It is the misconception that this endeavor can 'prove', or for that matter 'disprove', the theological underpinnings of the biblical text that has so strongly handicapped the image of this profession. And it is with this type of image in mind that some have claimed that this profession had met its ultimate demise (e.g. Davis 2004a).

This being the case, then what is Biblical Archaeology, or rather, how should we define it in this day and age?

I would suggest the following definitions:

1.   It is the scientific endeavor in which archaeologists study the material culture remains (utilizing modern archaeological methods) of the regions, periods and cultures from which the biblical corpus grew.[6]

2.   Although the main focus lies in the immediate region of the Land of Israel, interest also extends to other areas, including major parts of the Mediterranean, Mesopotamia and beyond, Egypt and Nubia, etc.

3.   Time wise, since it does not deal solely with the specific time-frame of this or that biblical book, but rather the cultural background in which these books were formed, one has to take an interest from the late Prehistoric periods when sedentary lifestyles and domesticated agriculture appeared (and were a basic requirement for the appearance of the hierarchic societies in which the foundations for the biblical text were laid) until the Roman and Byzantine period, when the last biblical texts and their immediate successors emerged.

4.   It is absolutely necessary that the research agendas be set by archaeological perspectives and priorities—even if the results can shed light on the biblical text and its understanding.

5.   Once again, Biblical Archaeology is not meant to prove, or for that matter, to disprove the Bible! 'Proving' or 'disproving' the Bible (whatever that means...) is for theologians.

6.   But, not to utilize the archaeological evidence as a possible tool to understand further aspects of the biblical text is foolish. Clearly, the biblical text was formed within the wide time-frame defined above, and there is no doubt that the text was formed within given cultural milieus. Archaeology, and in this case Biblical Archaeology, offers a unique window through which one can learn of the cultural *zeitgeist* of these periods. Not to use this is simply foolish! Thus, scholars who suggest divorcing archaeology from any relationship with textual studies (e.g. Ussishkin 2007)[7] are making a foolhardy decision.

---

4.   See Zevit (2004) for a review of the controversy of Biblical versus Syro-Palestinian Archaeology. It is his conclusions (pp. 18-19) which are unfortunate (and I do not agree with)—that biblical scholars and archaeologists have parted company.

5.   Unfortunately, this issue, and its relationship to the contemporary Middle East and to the practice of archaeology in present-day Israel, has often been grossly misunderstood. See, e.g., Abu el-Haj 2001; Marcus 2000.

6.   As Fritz (1994: 11-12) has so succinctly stated.

7.   Ussishkin (2007: 132) has suggested that professional archaeologists should see *Hercule Poirot* and *Sherlock Holmes* as their mentors. If one is already choosing imaginary detective figures as role models, I

7.   Bottom line—the dialogue between 'Tell' and 'Text' can provide important insights for the archaeologist, the historian, and the biblical scholar.

If one defines the scope of Biblical Archaeology over such a wide temporal and geographic span, clearly the question arises: How can one possible study such an enormous body of knowledge? Does this wide scope, by definition, mean that Biblical Archaeologists 'spread themselves too thin' (Zevit 2004: 5)?

Clearly, one cannot study it all! Scholars must focus on different aspects within this large world—although always being aware of the connections. Thus, for example, I focus on the Bronze and Iron Age of Canaan/Palestine/Israel, but always 'keep my eyes open' for the explicit and implicit connections with the other facets mentioned above. One cannot study the archaeology of ancient Israel (or for that matter, any ancient culture) without an in-depth knowledge of what is 'going on' in neighboring cultures. This is not only the case for Biblical Archaeology—this is how archaeology should be done all over![8]

So What Does a Modern Biblical Archaeologist Do?

First of all—we dig! If you don't conduct new, updated excavations, you are simply rehashing old materials, excavated, documented and analyzed using older perspectives! All too often, discussions on and about Biblical Archaeology are conducted by archaeologists and/or people in related disciplines who are not active FIELD archaeologists. What is done in the field today is very different from a lot of what many very-well-read scholars remember from either introductory courses in archaeology that they took during their education, or from the limited field experience of yester-year.[9] The very notion that is sometimes heard that enough excavations have been conducted, and now we should only publish and analyze the existing finds (e.g. Kletter and De-Groot 2001; cf. Maeir 2001) is a major misconception! We are not excavating for the sake of it, or simply because we enjoy it (which, I for one, truly do!). Rather, we now conduct excavations with focused research questions in mind, utilizing a panoply of methods that enable us to answer these questions. The information that is discovered in modern, scientifically oriented excavation was not available from older excavations. If we want to deal with cutting-edge research questions and topics, one cannot base our discussions on the results of older excavations from which the data on which we can base our discussions was not presented! Thus, for example, if I'm interested in discussing the development, change and relationship between the Philistine and Israelite diet and cooking traditions (e.g. Ben-Shlomo *et al.* 2008), this can only be done based on data from excavations where relevant, and sufficient, information relating to these issues was retrieved. Data from older excavations, which often provide only aspects of typology and stratigraphy, are simply not enough!

Biblical Archaeologists, like professionals in all fields, range from very good practitioners to those that are less proficient.[10] Those that lead the field use excavation techniques and methods,

---

suggest that we go for *Tintin* and the *Hardy Boys*—they seem to regularly successfully 'get their man' and at the same time have much more fun.

8.   See Kristiansen and Larsson (2005) for a truly expansive view of how to understand European Bronze Age archaeology—from the Mediterranean and its environs, to the farthest corners of Northern and Western Europe.

9.   For example, in the recent volume *The Future of Biblical Archaeology* (Hoffmeier and Millard 2004), less than a third of the contributions were written by practicing field archaeologists!

10.   By and large, most examples of 'Old Fashioned' Biblical Archaeology (with naïve connections between Bible and Archaeology) that one still finds today are put out by scholars who are often quite marginal; e.g. Rohl 1995; van der Veen and Zerbst 2002; Meitlis 2006.

along with analytic perspectives, that can compete with the best in the world. If one checks in the field today, most Biblical Archaeological excavations use meticulous field methods for excavation, recording and analysis.[11]

In addition, there is extensive and intensive utilization of inter- and multi-disciplinary studies, as a perusal of the relevant literature will reveal (for example, any of the issues of journals such as *Journal of Archaeological Science, Bulletin of the American Schools of Oriental Research*, etc.).

It is only once the archaeological finds are excavated, recorded and analyzed from *an archaeological perspective* that one must then be open to look at them from other viewpoints. Thus, one must also incorporate insights from the various textual corpuses, whether ancient sources, biblical or other. Clearly, one should not make automatic, and senseless, connections between the archaeological remains and the textual evidence—but on the other hand, one should not be frightened to search for such connections!

But Nevertheless—Biblical Archaeology!

Despite the reservations that some have sounded against this profession, Biblical Archaeology can, and should, continue, and it can, and must, be accessible and interesting to the lay public.

What is needed is a sophisticated, non-parochial viewpoint, combined with the most modern analytic techniques. At the same time, there is no reason to shy away from looking for explicit or implicit connections between the material remains (the archaeological evidence) and the cultural and historical *realia* imbedded in the biblical text, while being very much aware of the multi-vocality and multi-layered structure of the biblical text. Just as one relates to an archaeological site as a multi-faceted 'artifact', representing the actions of different cultures and the effect of different periods and processes, thus the biblical text, to a large extent, can be compared to a multi-period archaeological site.[12] Only if one relates to both sources of data (archaeological and biblical) as being of (a) diverse and complex character(s), can one truly study and integrate the two. If one does, then one can form a sophisticated dove-tailing of the biblical and archaeological evidence, which can provide important insights for both fields of research.

Choosing a cautious and judicious approach to the problem of 'text and spade', whatever the results are, can produce very interesting and revealing aspects of the relationship between these studies. Even if this results in quite different approaches (e.g. Finkelstein and Silberman 2006 as

---

11.   Thus, for example, perhaps one of the world's most advanced integrations of 'plain vanilla' archaeology and archaeological science is carried out at the Tell es-Safi/Gath Excavations (which I have the good fortune to direct), where a ten-person team of 'archaeological scientists' (members of the Bar-Ilan University/Weizmann Institute of Science Joint Program in Archaeological Sciences; see http://www.weizmann.ac.il/kimmel-arch/iuprogram.html) are fully integrated, in the field, with the excavation team. This robustly harnesses the analytic ability of cutting-edge science, and allows new perspectives, understanding and analyses on the one hand, but opens up new vistas for in-the-field planning of excavation strategies.

12.   Recently, Zevit (2007) has argued that archaeology has not contributed to the dating of biblical texts. Clearly, this is a misconception. If one expects to be able to date the entire biblical corpus, or even a specific book, on the basis of the archaeological finds, one in fact is doomed to despair. On the other hand, if one relates to the biblical text as a multi-faceted, multi-layered 'site', then archaeology can, and has, provided dating for specific aspects within the biblical text (= layers and/or artifacts at a 'site'). Thus, archaeological finds have provided the chronological context of the reference to unique, datable, Iron Age artifacts in the biblical text (such as the famous case of the *pym* weights in 1 Sam. 31:21; see, e.g., Dever 2001: 227). Or, archaeological evidence of specific events can provide the chronological context of events alluded to in the biblical text (see, e.g., the dating of Amos 6:2—Maeir 2004b).

opposed to Mazar 2007), both attempt to grapple with, and distill, the significance of the relationship between the archaeological evidence and the biblical text(s).

Such a relationship can be exemplified in many studies that combine the various data sets, whether relating to more extensive 'overviews' (e.g. Dever 2001; Finkelstein and Silberstein 2006; Mazar 2007), or as seen with more limited cases studies as well (e.g Stager 1988; Dever 1994; Maeir 2004b, 2007; Smith 2007; etc.). These, and many others, are examples of 'how it should be done'.

Even if this is not always popular in the 'postmodern' world in which we live—to connect the archaeological remains and the cultural traditions of contemporary cultures (Jews, Christians, Muslims, etc.)—there is no reason to be hesitant to do this, as long as this is based on sound research, and, it does not negate the rights of others.

Summary: What's the Difference between New and Old Biblical Archaeology?

The new Biblical Archaeology is a scientific endeavor that harnesses the newest, most 'cutting-edge' methods to study the past. Only a truly inter- and multi-disciplinary approach to the study of the past can be accepted!

The new Biblical Archaeology utilizes a less naïve perspective on the relationship between text and archaeology. Although the relationship does exist in many cases, it is not always a direct and simplistic one.

The new Biblical Archaeology must display willingness, nay necessity, to engage the interface between 'Bible and Spade'—despite the fact that the interface is not always simple. This also includes a willingness to find the connections between the past, the present and the future, so that archaeology has a meaningful impact on society![13]

Only by combining state-of-the-art archaeological methodology and analysis, along with an openness to explore the relevancy of the finds to the study of the biblical text, can Biblical Archaeology remain a vibrant scientific endeavor, and at the same time, still retain and expand the general public's fascination in its results. Although we must aim to be scientifically sound and as 'objective' as possible, there is no need to quake with fear at the very possibility that any aspect of modern ideologies will effect, and distort, our interpretations. First of all, nobody is completely objective—all we can do is make an effort to be as objective as possible. Secondly, if we don't find relevance between the past, the present and the future, within the constraints of 'good scientific practice' (which is defined by the scientific paradigms of these times), then we are missing out on our primary calling—as stewards and 'carriers' of the past for the general public![14] The understanding of the past, within the context of contemporary life, is possible, even if at times it is not easy to attain. Whether the 'Past is a Foreign Country' (e.g. Lowenthal 1985) or not (e.g. Shapira 1999), it is attainable, and relevant. This is contrary to the feeling that one can get from following the work of some scholars of Ancient Israel, those who divorce the archaeological evidence from the biblical text, and refuse to utilize a wide range of data to interpret the past (e.g. Davies 1992; Thompson 1999). In fact, at times one wonders whether the past for them is an unattainable entity—perhaps even that the past is viewed as an 'enemy country'...

13. By and large, I tend to agree with Davis' (2004b: 26-28) summary of what he sees as 'good' practice in Biblical Archaeology.

14. For debates on similar issues within the context of historical studies, see, e.g., Bagby 1976; Baron 1986; Haskell 1998.

So, despite the fact that many of my colleagues, who in the past would have defined themselves as Biblical Archaeologists, now hesitate to do so, I proudly wear the badge of 'The New Biblical Archaeology'. I lost my fear of being a 'Biblical Archaeologist'—in fact, I enjoy stating emphatically that Biblical Archaeology is my professional calling!

References

Abu el-Haj, N. (2001) *Facts on the Ground: Archaeological Practice and Territorial Self-Fashioning in Israeli Society* (Chicago: University of Chicago Press).

Albright, W.F. (1941) New Egyptian Data on Palestine in the Patriarchal Age. *BASOR* 81:16-21.

Bagby, P. (1976) *Culture and History: Prolegomena to the Comparative Study of Civilizations* (Westport, CO: Greenwood Press).

Baron, S. (1986) *The Contemporary Relevance of History: A Study of Approaches and Methods* (New York: Columbia University Press).

Ben-Shlomo, D., I. Shai, A. Zukerman, and A. Maeir (2008) Cooking Identities: Aegean-Style and Philistine Cooking Jugs and Cultural Interaction in the Southern Levant during the Iron Age. *American Journal of Archaeology* 112/2: 225-46.

Ben-Yehuda, N. (2001) *Sacrificing Truth: Archaeology and the Myth of Masada* (Amherst, NY: Humanity Books).

Davies, P. (1992) *In Search of 'Ancient Israel'* (Sheffield: JSOT Press).

Davis, T. (2004a) *Shifting Sands: The Rise and Fall of Biblical Archaeology* (Oxford: Oxford University Press).

—(2004b) Theory and Method in Biblical Archaeology. In Hoffmeier and Millard 2004: 20-28.

Dever, W.G. (1981) The Impact of the 'New Archaeology' on Syro-Palestinian Archaeology. *BASOR* 242: 15-29.

—(1994) The Silence of the Text: An Archaeological Commentary on 2 Kings 23. In *Scripture and Other Artifacts: Essays on the Bible and Archaeology in Honor of Philip J. King*, edited by M.D. Coogan, J.C. Exum and L.E. Stager (Louisville, KY: Westminster Press): 143-68.

—(2001) *What Did the Biblical Writers Know, and When Did They Know It? What Archaeology Can Tell Us about the Reality of Ancient Israel* (Grand Rapids: Eerdmans).

Finkelstein, I. (1988) *The Archaeology of the Israelite Settlement* (Jerusalem: Israel Exploration Society).

Finkelstein, I., and N. Silberman (2006) *David and Solomon: In Search of the Bible's Sacred Kings and the Roots of the Western Tradition* (New York: Free Press).

Fritz, V. (1994) *An Introduction to Biblical Archaeology* (JSOTSup 172; Sheffield: Sheffield Academic Press).

Gitin, S., J. Wright and J. Dessel (eds.) (2006) *Confronting the Past: Archaeological and Historical Essays on Ancient Israel in Honor of W.G. Dever* (Winona Lake, IN: Eisenbrauns).

Grove, C. (1869) From the Original Prospectus. *Palestine Exploration Fund Quarterly Statement* 1: 1-2.

Handy, L. (ed.) (1997) *The Age of Solomon: Scholarship at the Turn of the Millennium* (Studies in the History and Culture of the Ancient Near East 11; Brill: Leiden).

Haskell, T. (1998) Objectivity is Not Neutrality: Rhetoric versus Practice in Peter Novick's 'That Noble Dream'. In *History and Theory: Contemporary Readings*, edited by B. Fay, P. Pomper and R. Vann (Oxford: Blackwell): 299-319.

Hoffmeier, J., and A. Millard (eds.) (2004) *The Future of Biblical Archaeology: Reassessing Methodologies and Assumptions* (Grand Rapids: Eerdmans).

Kitchen, K. (2003) *The Reliability of the Old Testament* (Grand Rapids: Eerdmans).

Kletter, R., and A. De-Groot (2001) Excavating to Excess? Implications of the Last Decade of Archaeology in Israel. *Journal of Mediterranean Archaeology* 14/1: 76-85.

Kohl, P. (1998) Nationalism and Archaeology: On the Constructions of Nations and the Reconstructions of the Remote Past. *ARA* 27: 223-46.

Kristiansen, K., and T. Larsson (2005) *The Rise of Bronze Age Society: Travels, Transmissions and Transformations* (Cambridge: Cambridge University Press).

Liwag, R. (1998) Bible und Babel. *Berliner Theologische Zeitschrift* 15/1: 206-89.

Lowenthal, D. (1985) *The Past is a Foreign Country* (Cambridge: Cambridge University Press).

Maeir, A. (2001) The Baby, the Bathwater or Both: A Reaction to Kletter and De-Groot's Proposal. *Journal of Mediterranean Archaeology* 14/1: 90-92.

—(2004a) Review of: Nadia Abu el-Haj, *Facts on the Ground: Archaeological Practice and Territorial Self-Fashioning in Israeli Society. Isis* 95/3: 523-24.

—(2004b) The Historical Background and Dating of Amos VI 2: An Archaeological Perspective from Tell es-Safi/Gath. *VT* 54/3: 319-34.

—(2007) A New Interpretation of the Term 'opalim (עפלים) in Light of Recent Archaeological Finds from Philistia. *JSOT* 32: 23-40.

Malamat, A. (1982) A Political Look at the Kingdom of David and Solomon and its Relations with Egypt. In *Studies in the Period of David and Solomon and Other Essays*, edited by T. Ishida (Winona Lake, IN: Eisenbrauns): 189-204.

Marcus, A. (2000) *The View from Nebo: How Archaeology is Rewriting the Bible and Reshaping the Middle East* (Boston: Little, Brown & Co.).

Marston, C. (1934) *The Bible is True* (London: Eyre & Spottiswoode).

Mazar, A. (2007) The Spade and the Text: The Interaction between Archaeology and Israelite History Relating to the Tenth–Ninth Centuries BCE. In Williamson 2007: 143-71.

Meitlis, Y. (2006) *Digging the Bible* (Jerusalem: Rubin Mass [Hebrew with English summary]).

Meyers, E. (2006) Israel and its Neighbors Then and Now: Revisionist History and the Quest for History in the Middle East Today. In Gitin, Wright and Dessel 2006: 255-64.

Rohl, D. (1995) *Pharaohs and Kings: A Biblical Quest* (New York: Crown).

Shapira, A. (1999) The Past is not a Foreign Country. *The New Republic* 29 (November): 26-36.

Shavit, Y., and M. Eran (2003) *The War of the Tablets: The Defense of the Bible in the 19th Century Babel–Bibel Controversy* (Tel Aviv: Am Oved [Hebrew]).

Silberman, N.A. (1990) *Between Past and Present: Archaeology, Ideology, and Nationalism in the Modern Middle East* (New York: Doubleday).

Smith, M. (2006) In Solomon's Temple (1 Kings 6–7): Between Text and Archaeology. In Gitin, Wright and Dessel 2006: 275-82.

Stager, L. (1988) Archaeology, Ecology, and Social History: Background Themes to the Song of Deborah. *VTSup* 40: 221-34.

Thompson, T. (1974) *The Historicity of the Patriarchal Narratives: The Quest for the Historical Abraham* (Beiheft zur Zeitschrift für die alttestamentliche Wissenschaft 133; Berlin: W. de Gruyter).

—(1999) *The Mythic Past: Biblical Archaeology and the Myth of Israel* (London: Basic Books).

Ussishkin, D. (2007) Archaeology of the Biblical Period: On Some Questions of Methodology and Chronology of the Iron Age. In Williamson 2007: 131-41.

Veen, P. van der, and U. Zerbst (eds.) (2002) *Biblische Archäologie am Scheideweg? Für und Wider einer Neudatierung archäologischer Epochen im alttestamentlichen Palästina* (Studium Intergrale Archäologie; Holzgerlingen: Hänssler).

Williamson, H.G.M. (ed.) (2007) *Understanding the History of Ancient Israel* (Oxford: British Academy).

Yadin, Y. (1982) Is the Biblical Conquest of Canaan Historically Reliable? *BAR* 8/2: 16-23.

Zevit, Z. 2004. The Biblical Archaeology versus Syro-Palestinian Archaeology Debate in its American Institutional and Intellectual Contexts. In Hoffmeier and Millard 2004: 3-19.

—(2007) Scratched Silver and Painted Walls: Can we Date Biblical Texts Archaeologically? *Hebrew Studies* 48: 23-37.

18 A Bible Scholar in the City of David

Richard Elliott Friedman

Abstract

Connecting Bible study closely with archaeological study means recognizing what our culture's and our communities' greatest interest in this enterprise is, namely the Bible. One can be an able literary analyst of text and still get the story wrong if one cannot deal with archaeology. One can be an able archaeologist and still make serious errors if one cannot deal with the issues of the text. Much of the low estimation of the work of members of our field who are called by the names 'minimalist' and 'revisionist' is due precisely to their inability to deal with the two sides of our field—the biblical and the archaeological—with the necessary skills of the trade. Ernest Wright was known as a biblical theologian alongside his distinction as an archaeologist, but the explosion of knowledge and of graphomania has made it practically impossible for anyone to control it all anymore (with a couple of notable exceptions). So for the future of these fields the natural solution to this has to be teamwork. It means a high level of cooperation and sharing credit. This article considers the value, as an exercise, of thinking of the Bible as having been discovered later than our archaeological evidence. We thought of archaeology in service of the Bible—as needing to prove the Bible—for so long because we had the Bible first. Looking at these two sources in the reverse order serves to remind us that the two should rather be studied in balance and that the relationship between the two is dialectical.

Among the best things that occurred for me in the thirty years that I spent at the University of California was my acquaintance and collaboration with Yigal Shiloh, *zikrônô lĭbĕrākâ*, who came as a Visiting Professor in 1980. We became good friends, and this led to my participation in his City of David Project excavations of biblical Jerusalem with my students for four seasons.

I therefore write as a Bible scholar with special experience with archaeology: for those four seasons, I arrived on the site every day in time for lunch, occasionally wearing a white shirt which never got dirty. I never found anything until, on the last day, I uncovered a coin, which turned out to be a quarter that I had dropped on the first day. But those were invaluable seasons of learning for me because I came to appreciate archaeological method when practiced by a superior archaeologist in the field. (I recall one lesson from Yigal one day when he picked up a shard and tossed it to the bottom of a hill and said, 'See, I change history'.) And my students, meanwhile, learned the joy of the archaeological enterprise.

Yigal and I doubled the experience of those students by pairing his direction of them on the site with my instructing them in biblical text and history in an informal classroom setting. That model of introducing undergraduate students to Bible and archaeology together is the paradigm for my discussion here.

Now, in connecting Bible study so closely with archaeological study, I realize that I am already taking a position in a dialogue that has a history. I am one of those who are still comfortable with the phrase 'Biblical Archaeology'. It does not mean that if we uncover a non-biblical artifact on an excavation we have to throw it away. And it does not mean that we are there in the field to prove that the Bible is true. It does not even mean that our purpose and interest in the work is entirely biblical. Rather, it is recognizing what our culture's and our communities' greatest interest in this enterprise is. Most of the questions we are asked in our public lectures are biblical. Likewise most of the questions our own students ask us are biblical. That is also the interest of most of our colleagues from other fields on university faculties. And we know in our hearts that it is our own interest as well. Avraham Biran said that what excited him most about his excavations one summer at Tel Dan was the discovery of how a gate's doorpost structure—a pintel—worked, but no one on earth thought that that pintel of the lintel was more exciting than the 'House of David' inscription that he uncovered that same season. I submit that calling our enterprise by other names like 'Syro-Palestinian archaeology' for a few years was a useful and significant declaration of independence by archaeologists. But that battle has been won. To dig sites in Israel from the world of the 12th to the 2nd centuries BCE now and say that what we are doing is not about the Bible is pointless.

Even those sadly misled and misleading members of our field who are called by the names 'minimalist' and 'revisionist' (among other names), who deny the very existence of much of the biblical world, know perfectly well that whatever attention or notoriety they receive is due to their denial of much of the Bible. If, instead of the Bible, they denied any historicity to the *Iliad* and the *Odyssey*, and they dated Homer centuries later, their book sales would be significantly reduced—and so would their arrogance. They denigrate the Bible as a reliable source in a burst of joyous post-modern carpet-pulling from under absolutely everyone who ever came before them. They cry, 'Notice me', and that is just what people do. Whether one's works are an affirmation of the Bible or a negation of the Bible, the fact remains that what everyone wants to hear about is: *the Bible*. Those revisionist, minimalist, post-modern writers frequently express their chagrin over the low regard in which they are held by many scholars, but much of that low estimation of their work is due precisely to their inability to deal with the two sides of our field—the biblical and the archaeological—with the necessary skills of the trade. These writers include teachers of Bible who make claims about the authenticity of inscriptions when they do not have sufficient training in epigraphy to justify this. They deal with excavated Hebrew inscriptions ineptly and then complain that people question their competence. They arrive at conclusions about dates of texts without taking into account whole bodies of evidence like: *Hebrew!* And then they protest that other scholars do not give them a fair shake. When this is pointed out to their faces, they promise that they will fill in these gaps, but then they fail to do so, and, when their silence is pointed out publicly in their presence, they sit and chuckle as if nothing concerning them has been said. And then they are annoyed that they are not taken seriously. When scholars who oppose them still invite them to a forum, they give inept answers to serious challenging questions. And then they question the ethics of those who hold forums and do not invite them. They come to positions at which no one would ever arrive simply by following the evidence. And then they complain that people question their motives. They behave rudely and disrespectfully to colleagues. And then they protest that they are treated with disrespect. They write things that are irresponsible, outrageous, poorly defended. And then the scholars in the field have two choices: (1) treat them the same as any other scholars, pretending not to notice the poor quality of the work and the misrepresentations and the ignoring of evidence and how the conclusions appear to have preceded the arguments, or (2) treat them with the disdain they provoke. If you do (1) then you grant them legitimacy. If you do (2) then they attack you for being unfair, for being *threatened*, for using personal attack because you cannot defeat their arguments.

Meanwhile, there are scholars who make the error of thinking that focusing on literary studies excuses them from having to know what we have learned from archaeology. It seems alright to those outside the field; and scholars in our field, too, have been quite welcoming to such studies, both by specialists and even by literary scholars who are not trained in this field. But, in fact, even some of the best of such studies go wrong because of a lack of archaeological knowledge of the biblical world. They are reading narratives and poetry whose scene they cannot picture. Our colleague Robert Alter, in a well-intentioned and interesting piece about the biblical judge Ehud's assassination of King Eglon in Judges 3, wrote:

> Each of the details contributes to a clear understanding of just how the thing was done—clearer, of course, for the ancient audience than for us because we no longer have a coherent picture of the floor plan of the sort of Canaanite summer residence favored by Moabite kings and so we may have a little difficulty in reconstructing Ehud's entrances and exits.[1]

Compare Baruch Halpern's treatment of the same story. Halpern did in fact establish a coherent picture of the floor plan of ancient Near Eastern kings' *bit hilani* from texts and remains, from Assyria to the West. He thus reconstructed Ehud's assassination of Eglon as taking place in the king's *ʿăliyat hammĕqērâ*, an upper room constructed over beams, where the king could privately relieve himself into a receptacle area below, a *misdĕrôn*. (We uncovered two such 'bathrooms' in the City of David [Shiloh 1984: 10, 18].) This explained numerous enigmas of the story: This is how Ehud escapes from the king's room when it was locked from the *inside*. He makes a clandestine escape through that unpleasant place. This explained why the narrator included the detail of the king's release of waste at the time of his death: so that the king's servants then find him in this condition and thus assume a death by natural causes, not by assassination. This explained why Ehud leaves a hilt-less sword buried unseen in Eglon's fat body: to coincide with the servants' assumption of death by natural causes (Halpern 1988).

Alter, unaware of such archaeological evidence, wrote: 'perhaps Ehud leaves the weapon buried in the flesh in order not to splatter blood on himself, so that he can walk out through the vestibule unsuspected and make his escape'. But in the text there is no hint of concern about any blood spattering, and Ehud's scatological path out is no 'vestibule'.

Lawrence Stager challenged Halpern's reading in a study of evidence of how locks and keys functioned at that time (Stager 2003). I still find Halpern's picture the more probable, but my point at present is not to weigh Halpern versus Stager. It is rather to convey that Alter attempted to interpret the story unaware of what was involved and what it is possible to know, and so he misread the story.

Nor do I mean to denigrate Alter here. On the contrary, he was a congenial colleague to us in the University of California for decades, and I think that he is the most able of the literary scholars who have sought to engage biblical scholars in matters of artistry. My point rather is precisely that one can be an able literary analyst of text and still get the story wrong if one cannot deal with archaeology. In Halpern's reading, the Ehud episode is an early (the first?) example of the genre of the locked-door mystery. Without the archaeology, even a good literary scholar can mistake the details and miss the genre. Those scholars from other fields of literature who are attracted to the literary study of the Bible but who are not prepared to take on the archaeological and historical

---

1. Alter 1981. This also appears in Alter 1983.

aspect of the field are a further demonstration of the fact that we are kidding ourselves if we deny that it is the fascination with the Bible that makes our vehicle run: when scholars of French and English and comparative literature go outside their fields of expertise, they do not take on Dante to make a name for themselves. They do not go into George Eliot studies to achieve notoriety. And they do not seek new insights into *Beowulf* to get big book sales. Whether it is the text on the page or the spade in the soil of Israel, we all know what people want to hear about.

I am not just talking about the need for those who do Bible to pay due attention to archaeology. The same applies to archaeologists who write about the Bible without a sufficient footing in the biblical scholarship. Israel Finkelstein, whose skills as an archaeologist I respect, still is unfortunately lost in the sources of the biblical narrative, arguing that the very same texts are both early and late, not dealing with or acknowledging the existence of the vast work that has been done by Bible scholars, with which he is not familiar (Finkelstein and Silberman 2001). He and other archaeologists have understood stories from the texts known as J and E to derive from the 7th century, from the time of King Josiah; but that archaeological conclusion is an impossibility in the light of the textual evidence in the Bible, which establishes that both of those texts had to have been composed during the era of the divided kingdoms of Israel and Judah.[2] That is, they are from a time at least a hundred years before Josiah. Another archaeologist whose skills I respect wrote an archaeological work on biblical Israel which came out on two levels: when this colleague treated the archaeological material, it was with learning and rigor, but, when writing history, he frequently paraphrased the Bible's report uncritically, just converting it into contemporary historical terminology. Still another leading archaeologist likewise may have overestimated his skill with the text when he heard me read a paper on the phenomenon of the evolving hiddenness of God through the Hebrew Bible, and he countered, 'I've been reading the Bible all my life. How could it be that there's something this significant running through the text, and *I* haven't seen it?'

Now the point of this was not to criticize these colleagues. On the contrary, my point is precisely that the most skillful of archaeologists and the most skillful of literary critics are severely restricted when they do biblical research beyond their area.

The Albrightian ideal of those who could master both Bible and archaeology was fine in Albright's generation and in my teacher Ernest Wright's. Wright was known as a biblical theologian alongside his distinction as an archaeologist. But the explosion of knowledge and of graphomania has made it practically impossible for anyone to control it all anymore (with a couple of notable exceptions). So for the rest of us, and for the future of these fields, it seems to me that the natural solution to this has to be teamwork. It means a high level of things for which we scholars are not exactly well known: Cooperation. Sharing credit. Back in the City of David, Yigal Shiloh proposed that he and I write a book together in which, in each chapter, I would first write about the picture we would have of Jerusalem in a given period if we had only the Bible as a source. Then he would write about that picture in the light of the archaeology of Jerusalem. I think he had the right idea for the future and Biblical Archaeology: that we might do best to have collaborations by an archaeologist and a Bible scholar. In my years at the University of California, San Diego, my colleagues and I tried to do that, with many of our students learning both the text and the field, and with some students writing dissertations directed jointly by William Propp and Thomas Levy—plus the fact that we put on conferences like the one that led to this volume. Pennsylvania State and Harvard stand out as centers that do this as well. On one occasion William Dever and I did a back-to-back program in which he spoke under the title 'An Archaeologist Looks at the Bible', and I spoke under

---

2.   I listed and summarized the evidence in Friedman 2003: 18-21. See also Friedman and Dolansky 2007.

the title 'A Biblical Scholar Looks at Archaeology'. Again, the conclusion was the necessity for merger and cooperation.

Shiloh's idea of first looking at the biblical picture and then seeing what the excavations reveal about it was a good one. And it fits with what I have been claiming here about what almost everyone's real interest in the archaeology of Israel is. But, as an exercise, I propose that we imagine the opposite scenario: *What if we had only archaeology for hundreds of years, and then someone discovered the Bible?* Front page New York Times! (Page 5 in the Copenhagen press.) Now, with the discovery of this book, we would know more about who those mysterious *benê qorah* are at Arad. Now we would have a great new story about that enigmatic Balaam ben Beor at Deir Alla. Now we would have an idea of what the elusive meaning of that reference to a House of David was in the Tel Dan inscription, and we would have substantial evidence that those who had thought it read 'House of the Beloved' were wrong. Now we would have the Jews' own version of what happened when Sennacherib came to Jerusalem, confirming much of what is claimed in the Sennacherib prism stele, and challenging parts of it. What would be the response to this discovery? Some would say that this newly discovered book was a forgery. But it would in fact be the greatest literary, archaeological, historical, religious, discovery of all time. To the religious it would be a revelation. To the secular it would be the stuff dissertations are made of. To *Reader's Digest* it would cry out for an abridgement.

Just as there is excitement over a new archaeological find that sheds light on some aspect of the Bible, there would be excitement over this new lengthy text that sheds light on our excavated artifacts. In fact, this latter excitement would be greater. Now the references to a King Omri and his dynasty in inscriptions from Mesha and Adad-Nirari III and the Black Obelisk would come alive in stories of Omri and especially of Ahab and Jehu. To return to the *byt dwd* inscription, imagine having only the inscription first and then getting the Court History! It would put flesh on the archaeological bones. Most of all, this book would give us connections, continuity, chronology. In other words: it would give us history.

As a case in point, in my work on the biblical Tabernacle, the *miškān*, I derived a different set of measurements from those that most scholars had determined. Rather than the standard 10 by 30 cubits, I argued that it was 6 to 8 by 20 cubits (Friedman 1980, 1992). And then I learned that the measurements of the temple that Aharoni had excavated at Arad were just that: 6 by 20 cubits. I had the thrill of a Bible scholar who is lucky enough to get a piece of confirming evidence from archaeology. When Aharoni uncovered that Arad sanctuary he had noted some parallels that indicated a connection between it and the Tabernacle, but those measurements meant nothing to him or to those who read his reports (Aharoni 1973). So there was the possibility of the reverse thrill as well: finding a structure archaeologically and then discovering the biblical evidence that would confirm what the discovery was all about and open other doors concerning its history. Our exercise of thinking of the Bible as having been discovered later than our archaeological evidence would mean taking this one example and multiplying it ten thousandfold.

For most of us, we would neither take that newly discovered work as entirely factual nor write it off as entirely fiction. When some claimed—as they surely would—that none of it was true, how would we respond? When others claimed that it was a medieval composition—as was claimed about the Dead Sea Scrolls, after all—or that it was fraudulently composed based on the facts that had already become known archaeologically, how would we set out to test its historicity? But, above all, would we regard it as any less significant than what we had already established from excavations? Would the situation not be just the opposite: we would stand in awe before this wondrous new source that gave us far more detail, history, psychological insight, understanding of the development of the Hebrew language, techniques of scribes, theology, wisdom, and law than we had ever had before, together with a previously unimaginable trove of some of the finest prose and poetry our species has produced.

We thought of archaeology in service of the Bible—as needing to prove the Bible—for so long because we had the Bible first. Looking at these two sources in the reverse order serves to remind us that the two should rather be studied in balance and that the relationship between the two is dialectical. The insights derived from each influence the interpretations of the data from the other. There is a sense that archaeology is more objective, more reliable than textual scholarship. My main point here is to indicate that this sense is wrong. Both text and artifact have the possibility of producing concrete, verifiable facts. Both text and artifact are subject to interpretation. And best of all: when both text and artifact are analyzed together, they provide the kind of controls that we desire and require in all fields of science: verification, independent sources, means of negation. My work was improved and refined by my acquaintance with Yigal Shiloh, first as a visiting colleague at UCSD and later in the City of David, and then my work benefited further by my acquaintance with Tom Levy as a colleague for many years at UCSD. My sincere wish is that the cooperation and collegiality among us can be a model for others of what can be accomplished when scholars who respect each other get together.

References

Aharoni, Y. (1973) The Solomonic Temple, the Tabernacle, and the Arad Sanctuary. In *Orient and Occident*, edited by H.A. Hoffman Jr (Festschrift Cyrus Gordon: Neukirchen–Vluyn: Neukirchener Verlag): 1-8.

Alter, R. (1981) Sacred History and Prose Fiction. In *The Creation of Sacred Literature*, edited by Richard Elliott Friedman (Berkeley: University of California Press): 7-24

—(1983) *The Art of Biblical Narrative* (New York: Basic Books).

Finkelstein, I., and N.A. Silberman (2001) *The Bible Unearthed* (New York: Free Press).

Friedman, R.E. (1980) The Tabernacle in the Temple. *BA* 43: 241-48.

—(1992) Tabernacle. *ABD* 6: 292-300.

—(2003) *The Bible with Sources Revealed* (San Francisco: HarperCollins).

Friedman, R.E., and S. Dolansky (2007). Pentateuch. *Encyclopedia Judaica* 15: 730-53.

Halpern, B. (1988) *The First Historians* (San Francisco: Harper).

Shiloh, Y. (1984) *Excavations at the City of David*, vol. 1 (Qedem 19; Jerusalem: Institute of Archaeology, Hebrew University of Jerusalem).

Stager, L. (2003) Key Passages. *Eretz-Israel* 27 (Hayim and Miriam Tadmor Volume): 240-45.

19 Books and Stones and Ancient Jewish History

A View from Camp David[*]

David Goodblatt

Abstract

Archaeological evidence is often invoked to confirm or refute claims made by ancient authors. For example, many scholars assert that the archaeological record does not support the biblical account of the conquest of Canaan by Joshua or the extent of the united monarchy under David and Solomon. The question at issue in this paper turns the tables and has ancient authors resolve the uncertainties of the archaeological record. The expansion and renovation by Herod of the temple to the God of Israel in Jerusalem left many physical remains. Some, above all the Western Wall, have been know for centuries. Others were uncovered in excavations over the past few decades. In all cases archaeology by itself cannot prove that these remains come from the Jewish temple. Only the testimony of the ancient authors provides definitive confirmation that the surviving architectural features, fragments and inscriptions come from the temple built by Herod. The conclusion is that neither archaeology nor history should be 'privileged' over the other. Dialogue between the two disciplines brings the best results.

I want to begin by thanking Professor Levy for inviting me to participate in this symposium marking the inauguration of the Kershaw Chair in the Archaeology of Ancient Israel and Neighboring Lands. It is an honor to appear on the same program with such a distinguished roster of archaeologists and Bible scholars. As I thought about what I might contribute to the program, I felt a certain amount of envy for my colleagues in those two fields. Both archaeology and Bible attract considerable interest from the general public. In fact, my UCSD colleagues in each of those fields have appeared in the mass media. In contrast my field, Ancient History, has become a synonym for irrelevant. Every so often, however, the obscure topics that I study make the news. It was only a few years ago that Mel Gibson's *The Passion of the Christ* inspired public debates about such abstruse issues as the jurisdictional competence of the Jerusalem Sanhedrin in the Roman province of Iudaea. Here was a topic on which I had some expertise, indeed one about which I had published. Not that anyone in the media bothered to ask my opinion, but at least I experienced what it felt like to have the general public interested in the subjects of one's research.

---

[*] This study reproduces a talk given April 30, 2006 at a public forum for a general audience.

Another case where ancient Jewish history suddenly became relevant is alluded to in the title of this article. It involves events that many in this audience remember, at least in a general way. Let's go back some six years, to the summer of 2000. The location is the Catoctin Mountains of Maryland, the site of the presidential retreat of Camp David. In July of that year President Bill Clinton hosted negotiations between the Israelis and the Palestinians in an attempt to fulfill the promise of the Oslo Accords and bring peace to the region. As Ehud Barak and Yasser Arafat and their advisers tried to resolve their differences, President Clinton and his aides worked to bridge the disagreements. One particularly thorny issue was the fate of Jerusalem. And the most difficult part of that issue concerned control of the semi-artificial elevation on the eastern edge of the Old City known to the Jews as *har habayit*, or the Temple Mount, and to the Muslims as *haram al-sharif*, or the Noble Sanctuary (Eliav 2005; Grabar 1996). Since the site was holy to both faiths, the question of who would control it—in whole or in part—was a potential deal breaker for each side. This was the background for an attempt by the Americans to propose a way out. If agreement could be reached on the other issues, why not defer resolution of the question of Jerusalem. On July 19 President Clinton met privately with Arafat to present the American suggestion. Apparently at this meeting he tried explaining to Arafat Jewish sensitivities about the site of their ancient temple. As was widely reported at the time, Arafat's response was to deny that there had been a Jewish temple on the site.

Recalling the line about newspapers being 'the first draft of history', I realized that I needed to consult subsequent drafts if I wanted to know what was actually said at Camp David. I began with Dennis Ross's book *The Missing Peace*. Describing the incident in question, he reports that Arafat exclaimed, 'Solomon's Temple was not in Jerusalem, but Nablus' (Ross 2004: 694). Now I wasn't sure whether I could rely on Ross's account. Granted, Ross was actually at Camp David and played a central role in the negotiations. However, he is Jewish and, still more problematic, he actually believes Israel has a right to exist. So I looked for another source where this bias would not be a concern. I discovered that The Nation Press had published a book about the negotiations entitled *The Truth about Camp David* by Clayton E. Swisher. Since *The Nation* was behind this publication, we need not worry about such pro-Israeli prejudices as believing the Jewish state has the right to exist. Now according to Swisher, at the meeting in question Clinton began to lose patience with Arafat and almost shouted at him, 'It is impossible...to ignore the rights of Jews on the Temple Mount'. To which Arafat responded that 'the Temple Mount was not in Jerusalem, it was in Nablus' (Swisher 2004: 305).

As a person trained in reading texts I immediately noted the difference between the two accounts. According to Ross it was the existence of the temple in Jerusalem built by Solomon that Arafat denied. According to Swisher he referred to the Temple Mount. Using the skills I had been taught as a graduate student, I pursued the matter further. Supporting Swisher's version was an interview he conducted with Gemal Helal, an Egyptian born American citizen who became a State Department employee and was the chief Arabic translator under President Clinton. Like Denis Ross, Helal took part in the negotiations at Camp David in July 2000. Helal is quoted as saying, 'It was a huge Palestinian mistake to not recognize the holy status of the Temple Mount. They never recognized this. In fact, Arafat said the Temple Mount was in Nablus, then in Northern Yemen and then Saudi Arabia. Arafat will never recognize their temple. Some Palestinian negotiators have in the past confided in me that, if they were to accept this, it would mean that their religion, Islam, is wrong. They could never do this' (Swisher 2004: 305).

As an aside, I have to admit this is very puzzling to me. Why would the existence of an ancient Jewish temple in Jerusalem, that was *destroyed* 1200 years before the beginning of the Muslim era (if we talk of the temple built by Solomon) or 500 years before the birth of Muhammed (if we talk of the Second Temple—see below), falsify Islam? Indeed, what seems to this outsider to be quite orthodox Muslim tradition affirms the existence of a Jewish temple in Jerusalem. According to Oleg

Grabar (1986: 322; compare Friedman 1992: 144) in early Islam Jerusalem was called *madinat bayt al-maqdis*, 'the city of the temple', echoing the Hebrew term for 'temple' *bêt hammiqdash*. And the early 10th century historian al-Tabari, who relied on older sources, reports how the Caliph 'Umar personally led the clearing of 'the rubbish in which the Romans had buried the temple [*bayt al-maqdis*] of the sons of Israel' (trans. Friedman 1992: 195; compare Gil 1992: 65-68). Calling Jerusalem 'the city of the temple' could be based on the ancient sanctuary attributed to Solomon by biblical tradition. The story about 'Umar, however, makes better sense with regard to the Second Temple. Jewish tradition and historiography calls the one built by Solomon and destroyed by the Babylonians when they captured Jerusalem in 586 BCE the First Temple. The term Second Temple refers to the one built after the return from the Babylonian exile and dedicated in 515 BCE according to the biblical account. This building was refurbished by Judah the Maccabee in 164 BCE and probably expanded by his successors from the Hasmonean dynasty (B. Mazar 1985). It was certainly expanded by King Herod who was responsible for creating the artificial extension of the Temple Mount and rebuilding the temple on a grand scale late in the last century BCE. It was Herod's temple that was destroyed by the Romans when they took Jerusalem in August of the year 70 (Meyers 1992). Both temples may be mentioned in Sura 17 of the Qur'an, the chapter known *inter alia* as *Bani Isra'il* or 'the sons of Israel/the Israelites'. According to several commentators, both traditionalist Muslim interpreters and modern scholars, vv. 4-8 allude to the destruction of both the first and second Jewish temples in Jerusalem (Grabar 1986: 323; Neuwirth 2003: 382, 389; *Holy Qur'an* 1991: 545; 1994: 775). In light of all these traditions, the apparent refusal of (some) contemporary Muslims to concede the existence of Jewish temples in Jerusalem is truly puzzling. But this issue is not our concern here.

Let us return to the question of exactly what Arafat did have in mind. Swisher's version allows me to claim that the site whose location in Jerusalem Arafat denied was not Solomon's Temple but the Temple Mount. What's the difference? Well, if what he denied was the presence or existence of Solomon's Temple, then I have to leave any further discussion to my colleagues who work on the Bible. But if he referred to the Temple Mount then he may also, or perhaps even primarily, have denied the existence in Jerusalem of the Second Temple. And if so, then this is a subject that I know—or at least am expected to know—something about. One of my areas of specialization is called Second Temple history. In light of my involvement in this field, I was especially interested in the aftermath of Arafat's denial of the existence of the Temple Mount in Jerusalem. I recall at the time reading how some of Clinton's aides went running to the Encyclopedia Britannica to try to find material that might convince Arafat that there really had been a Jewish temple there. Alas, neither Ross nor Swisher says anything about this aftermath. I did take a look at the Encyclopedia Britannica, and I found that both the article in the Micropedia and the one in the Macropedia were academically respectable (Jerusalem 2005; Perowne and Prawer 2005 [both originally appeared in the 1974 edition]). But, as I said, I could not confirm that the Britannica was consulted during this crisis at Camp David. And that got me thinking. Before coming to UCSD I taught at the University of Maryland, College Park on the outskirts of Washington, DC and only about an hour's drive from the Catoctins. Suppose, I fantasized, I had received a call from presidential aides asking me how I could convince a skeptic that there had once been a Jewish temple in Jerusalem, especially the second one that lasted until 70 CE.

At this point, some of you may be asking yourselves what is the problem? Open any one of a number of books, and you can find illustrations of the Second Temple (for example, E. Mazar 2002: 25, 28 and Ritmeyer and Ritmeyer 2004: 12, 14-15). Of course these are artists' reconstructions. But much of those reconstructions is based on physical remains. In fact, a surprising amount of what one sees in those pictures is actually still there in Jerusalem and is accessible to visitors. To begin with, the retaining walls on the western and southern end of the Temple Mount survive.

These walls hold in the fill and infrastructure (of vaults) that Herod's engineers used to extend the Temple Mount to the south and create the large esplanade that still exists today. The western retaining wall has been famous for centuries as the last remnant of the temple, known in Hebrew as the Western Wall (and in European languages as the Wailing Wall because it was the site of Jews mourning the destruction of the temple). Further, parts of the arches that supported a bridge and a staircase from the western side of the esplanade survive, as does the street that ran under the arches—on which you can walk today. The Hulda gates in the southern wall and the steps that lead up to them survive. Some architectural fragments of the royal stoa or basilica on the southern edge of the esplanade also survive, including pieces of columns, capitals, friezes, cornices and so forth (Geva 1993: 736-44; E. Mazar 2002: 24-61). In light of all this, how can one deny the existence of the Second Temple in Jerusalem?

The problem is that while a there are lots of architectural remains, those remains do not tell us exactly what they come from. What I mean is that clearly someone built a large, elevated esplanade on the eastern edge of the city with monumental buildings on it, walkways leading off it, and steps and gates leading onto it. But how do we know what all that construction was for? Maybe it was just palaces and public buildings. What we would really like is a gateway with a nice, informative inscription such as 'Welcome to the Temple of the God of Israel'. Or perhaps a cornerstone inscription that reads, 'This temple was built by King Herod and dedicated in the 20th year [say] of his reign'. Hoping to find such an inscription is not impossible. Possibly right down the street from the temple in Jerusalem, certainly in the shadow of the Temple Mount and within sight of the temple, there was a synagogue. And we have a dedication inscription in Greek from that synagogue. The attendees of this synagogue apparently were Greek speakers, possibly people from the Diaspora who settled in Jerusalem. Here is what the inscription says in part (Verbin 2000):

> Theodotos son of Vettenos, priest and head of the synagogue…built this synagogue for reading of the torah and for teaching the commandments etc.

The synagogue itself has unfortunately not survived, only the dedication inscription. (By the way, I have told rabbis what a great sales pitch this is to potential donors. You can tell them that 2000 years from now the congregation will be long gone, the building will have disappeared, but the plaque with your name on it will survive and be prominently displayed in some museum.) While the building has not survived, the inscription tells us exactly what the building was and what it was used for. The only thing this text lacks is a date, like the ones we occasionally find in other ancient synagogue inscriptions. For example there is the inscription from the Dura Europos synagogue on the Middle Euphrates, today in Syria, 'This house was built in year 556 [Seleucid era] which is year two of Philip Caesar when Samuel the Priest son of Yedayah the archon was serving as elder…' Here we have a triple date. While we wouldn't know when Samuel served as elder we do know the other dates, which correspond to 245 CE (Kraeling 1956: 261-68).

If only we had inscriptions like these, we could be sure that the buildings on the esplanade comprised the Jewish temple. Without such texts, physical remains like the ones we have from in and around the Temple Mount are not self-explanatory. Without written evidence we are left guessing about the function of the construction from which the remains come. So do we have any inscriptions from on or around the esplanade that unambiguously identify the site as the location of the Jewish temple? It depends on how we define 'unambiguous'. Take for example an inscription with a date found about 100 yards south of the southern retaining wall in a pile of debris dumped in a pool. Only a small fragment survives of what once was a monumental inscription in Greek. However, enough survives to give us a good idea what it was about (Isaac 1983).

Year] 20 under the high priest[
]Paris [son of] Akesonos
]in Rhodes
]pavement
d]rachmas

Apparently the inscription commemorates the person, one Paris from the Island of Rhodes, who contributed the funds for a pavement—most probably the pavement at the southern end of the esplanade, north of the royal stoa. The date must be the 20th year of King Herod—either 21/20 or 18/17 BCE depending on when Herod began his regnal era. Of course, what is missing is any specification of the nature of the complex that the pavement was part of.

Another example of the ambiguities of potentially Temple-related inscriptions was found in a burial cave in the Giv'at Hamivtar neighborhood well to the north of the Temple Mount. One of the ossuaries found in the cave had the following Aramaic inscription incised on it twice 'Simon builder of the Temple (*ḥêkhlah*)' (Naveh 1970: 32-33; Geva 1993: 754). The word *ḥêkhlah* is cognate to the Hebrew *ḥêkhal*, which is used to refer to the Jerusalem Temple (both first and second) throughout the Bible. The word is also used for palaces of humans, but the meaning 'temple' predominates. The Aramaic form also appears in the Bible, both with reference to the Jerusalem Temple and to palaces of Babylonian and Persian kings (Meyers 1992: 351-52). The scholarly consensus views the inscription as the epitaph of someone who worked on Herod's reconstruction of the Temple. Of course, what is missing in the inscription is the location of the *ḥêkhlah* on which Simon worked. In theory, Arafat could have argued that Simon commuted from Jerusalem to work on the Jewish temple allegedly existing in Nablus. Alternatively, the building in question was one of the royal or high priestly palaces in late Second Temple Jerusalem. Granted, the most likely interpretation is in fact that Simon worked on the Jerusalem Temple. But even then, nothing requires us to assume that the building in question was located on the elevated esplanade on the eastern edge of the old city. In sum, the inscription of Simon is not sufficient to rebut those who deny the existence of a Jewish temple on the Temple Mount.

Other inscriptions are more helpful. In 1870 a stone slab was found north of the Temple Mount with the following Greek inscription (Geva 1993: 744),

> No foreigner (*allogenes*) shall enter within the balustrade of the Temple (*hieron*), or within the precinct and whosoever shall be caught shall be responsible for (his) death that will follow in consequence (of his trespassing).

A second example of the inscription was found in 1938 outside the Lions Gate, also know as St. Stephen's Gate, again to the north of the Temple Mount. The Greek word translated 'Temple' could indeed refer to the sanctuary built by Herod. But there is still room for uncertainty, since the inscriptions were not found in their original location. And inscriptions like these can be paralleled from non-Jewish temples (Bickerman 1946–47). In theory the inscriptions could come from a pagan temple in the city of Aelia Capitolina, built on the site of Jerusalem by Hadrian.

What gives us confidence that these inscription come from the Jewish temple is what we find not in the stones, not even on the ones engraved with inscriptions, but in books. I refer in this case to the books written by the Jerusalem priest and historian Joseph the son of Mattathias, born in 37 CE and better known by the name he took on becoming a Roman citizen, Flavius Josephus (Rajak 1983; Bilde 1988). In his account (usually titled the *Bellum Iudaicum, The Judean War*) of the Judean revolt against Rome that culminated in the destruction of the Jerusalem Temple, Josephus describes the buildings on the Temple Mount. He describes a series of courtyards surrounding the temple, one inside the other. According to Josephus non-Israelites were permitted access to the outermost courtyard. Josephus continues that separating the outer courtyard from the inner ones was a stone balustrade or railing about 5 feet high. In this railing at regular intervals were slabs with inscriptions, some in Latin and some in Greek, warning that no foreigner (*allophulos*) was permitted to enter any farther (*War* 5:194; and see the reconstruction in Ben-Dov 1985: 102). In another of Josephus's books, the *Jewish Antiquities* he adds that the inscription warned that the penalty for foreigners (*alloethnos*) who entered was death (*Ant.* 15:417). So it is thanks to these books that we can explain the inscription, which may be the best archaeological evidence that the esplanade was the site of the Jewish temple.

A similar situation prevails with another inscription, this one in Hebrew, discovered in the 1970s among the debris fallen into the street that ran alongside the bottom of the western retaining wall, under the walkways supported by the arches. Inscribed on a dressed block of stone were the words 'to the place of the sounding [of the horn/trumpet]...' (Geva 1993: 740; E. Mazar 2002: 44). By itself, the inscription means little. Before modern times wind instruments were used to give signals. Even today bugle calls are used for reveille and taps. The ancient Jews used metal trumpets or rams' horns for several forms of communication including military and civilian ones. So if all we had was the inscription, we might not think it had any connection to the Temple. Again it is a book that helps make that connection, and once again the author of the book is Josephus. While describing the fortifications erected in the Temple by the Jewish rebels during the revolt against Rome, he tells how they built high towers from which they could shoot their missiles more effectively. En passant he mentions that one of these towers was built above the place where it was the custom for a priest to stand and sound the trumpet to announce the onset of the Sabbath on Friday afternoon and then the end of the Sabbath on Saturday evening (*War* 4:582). This is in all likelihood the place of sounding the horn/trumpet that our inscription alludes to, in which case the inscription does come from the Temple (see a reconstruction of the site in E. Mazar 2002: 42). Once again it was not the mute stone that told us anything, but an inscription. And even the inscription would not have been informative were it not for information we gleaned from a book.

The point should be clear by now. If we want to prove that the esplanade the Muslims call the *haram al-sharif* was the site of an ancient Jewish temple, archaeology by itself is not enough. Ultimately it is written sources that nail down the identification. When all is said and done, it is the descriptions by Josephus, who spent the first 30 years or so of his life in Jerusalem while the temple stood, which are our best source. But Josephus is not our only source. Many other ancient authors add to the evidence, and not just Jewish authors. The Gospels and the book of Acts in the New Testament include references to and descriptions of the Jerusalem Temple. (See, for example, Mk 11:15-19 // Mt. 21:12-13 // Luke 19:45-48 // John 2:13-17; Mk 13:1-4 // Mt. 24:1-3 // Luke 21:5-7; Acts 3:1-4, 11.) The authors of these books wrote at roughly the same time as Josephus, within a generation of the destruction of the Temple. Later Christian sources, from the 4th through the 7th centuries, contain eyewitness descriptions of the site of Herod's Temple and the ruins there. These sources are likely to reflect Christian theological interpretations, such as the view that the destruction of the Jewish temple was a punishment for the killing of Jesus by the Jews. This need not diminish the accuracy of the descriptions, which attest that a temple once stood on that site (Eliav 2005: 135-46). In any case we can also adduce pagan authors, innocent of any biblically based preconceptions, who mention the Jerusalem Temple. One good example is the Roman historian Tacitus who was about a generation younger than Josephus. Tacitus is a good witness not just because he wasn't Jewish, but because he didn't like the Jews very much. He famously observed, 'The Jews regard as profane all that we hold sacred...they permit all that we abhor' (*Historiae* V.4; Stern 1980: 25). And he adds that their customs are 'base and abominable'. 'The Jews are loyal to one another...but toward every other people they feel only hate and enmity' (*Historiae* V.5; Stern 1980: 26). Having established that Tacitus is a hostile witness, we can all the more readily accept his testimony about the Jewish temple. Thus he writes, 'Jerusalem is the capital of Jews. In it was a temple (*templum*) possessing enormous riches. Only a Jew might approach its doors'—think of the warning inscriptions—'and all except the priests were forbidden to cross the threshold' (*Historiae* V.8; Stern 1980: 28). He continues, 'The temple was built like a citadel, with walls of its own, which were constructed with more care and effort than any of the rest; the very colonnades around the temple made a splendid defense' (*Historiae* V.12; Stern 1980: 30). Possibly also from the pen of Tacitus is the account of the Roman war council at which it was decided to destroy the Jewish temple in Jerusalem. The account is preserved by the Christian chronicler Sulpicius Severus (*Chronica* II, 30; Stern 1980: 64). According to this account the Roman commander Titus, son of the emperor Vespasian and himself eventually emperor, convened his generals to address the following question.

> Whether he should overthrow a sanctuary (*templum*) of such workmanship, since it seemed to many that a sacred building, one more remarkable than any other human work, should not be destroyed. And if preserved it would testify to the moderation of the Romans, while if demolished it would be a perpetual sign of cruelty. On the other hand, others...expressed the opinion that the temple (*templum*) should be destroyed without delay in order that the religion of the Jews...should be more completely exterminated.

Let me cite one more pagan author, another Roman though he wrote in Greek. This is the Roman official and historian Cassius Dio (about 160–230) who wrote around the year 200. In his *Historia Romana* he recounts the conquest of Jerusalem by Pompey in 63 BCE. Dio tells us that Pompey had trouble in besieging Jerusalem. To be precise, 'Most of the city, to be sure, he took without any trouble...; but the temple (*hieron*) itself...he captured only with difficulty. For it was on high ground with a wall of its own...' (*Historia Romana* 37:15-16; Stern 1980: 350) A little later he describes that temple as 'extremely large and beautiful' (*Historia Romana* 37:17; Stern 1980: 351). Among the most impressive passages in Dio is a very dramatic account of the fall of the Jerusalem Temple to the Romans (*Historia Romana* 66:6-7; Stern 1980: 374-75). And this will be the last source I cite.

Dio writes how the Jewish defenders, amidst heavy fighting, tried to stop the Romans by setting fire to some outbuildings. This fire accidentally engulfed the barrier around the sacred precinct, and the entrance to the temple now lay open to the Roman troops. The Roman soldiers at first were afraid to enter the temple courtyard because of what Dio calls superstition. That is, they feared that the god who lived in the temple would punish them for trespassing by killing them. Dio doesn't say this, but we can imagine the literate soldiers reading the warnings in Greek and Latin that were referred to above. In any case, Titus finally forced his men to enter. Here is Dio's account of what followed:

> Then the Jews defended themselves much more vigorously than before, as if they had discovered a piece of rare good fortune in being able to fight near the temple (*naos*) and fall in its defense. The populace (*demos*) was stationed below in the courtyard, the councilors (*bouleutai*) on the steps, and the priests in the sanctuary itself. And though they were but a handful fighting against a far superior force, they were not conquered until a part of the temple was set on fire. Then they met death willingly, some throwing themselves on the swords of the Romans, some slaying one another, others taking their own lives, and still others leaping into the flames. And it seemed to everybody, and especially to them, that so far from being destruction, it was victory and salvation and happiness to them that they perished along with the temple (*naos*).

Let me conclude now by returning to my fantasy. If President Clinton's aides had asked me how to prove there was an ancient Jewish temple on that elevated esplanade on the eastern edge of the old city of Jerusalem, I would have sent them first of all not to stones, but to books. And not to the Britannica, even though its articles are reliable. I would have sent them to ancient authors whose books have survived, to the books studied by historians of antiquity. Certainly Josephus would have been my first choice, for he is the source of the most detailed account. I might also have sent them to the Mishnah of the rabbis, a document compiled in the early 3rd century that devotes an entire tractate, Tractate *Middot*, to a physical description of the temple. Then I would have added the New Testament, a source contemporaneous with Josephus. Next I would send them to the ancient anti-Jewish Roman historian Tacitus, and finally to another pagan Roman historian from a century later, Cassius Dio. Only after these books, the materials that historians work on, had been consulted would I direct them to the inscriptions and the physical remains unearthed by the archaeologists. It is thanks to the literary evidence that we are able to interpret the physical remains and the inscriptions and identify them as the rock solid evidence for the existence of a Jewish temple in Jerusalem. As I tried to demonstrate, without the literary evidence the physical remains remain mute, ambiguous and uninformative. In other words, without the books, all we have are stones.

Bibliography

Ben-Dov, M. (1985) *In The Shadow of the Temple: The Discovery of Ancient Jerusalem* (New York: Harper & Row).

Bickerman, E. (1946–47) The Warning Inscription of Herod's Temple. *Jewish Quarterly Review* 37: 387-405.

Bilde, P. (1988) *Flavius Josephus between Jerusalem and Rome: His Life, his Works, and their Importance* (Sheffield: JSOT Press).

Eliav, Y.Z. (2005) *God's Mountain: The Temple Mount in Time, Place and Memory* (Baltimore: The Johns Hopkins University Press).

Friedman, Y. (1992) *The History of al-Tabari*. Vol. 12, *The Battle of al-Qadisiyyah and the Conquest of Syria and Palestine* (Albany: State University of New York Press).

Geva, H. (1993) Jerusalem: Second Temple Period. In *The New Encyclopaedia of Archaeological Excavations in the Holy Land*, vol. 2 (Jerusalem: Israel Exploration Society/Carta): 717-57.

Gil, M. (1992) *A History of Palestine, 634–1099* (Cambridge: Cambridge University Press).

Grabar, O. (1986) Al-Kuds. In *Encyclopedia of Islam*, vol. 5, edited by C.E. Bosworth, E. van Donzel, B. Lewis and C. Pellat (Leiden: E.J. Brill): 322-44.

—(1996) *The Shape of the Holy: Early Islamic Jerusalem* (Princeton, NJ: Princeton University Press).

Holy Qur'an (1991) *The Holy Qur'an: Arabic Text, English Translation and Commentary by Maulana Muhammad Ali, Seventh Edition* (Columbus, OH: Ahmadiyyah Anjuman Insha'at Islam Lahore Inc. U.S.A.).

— (1994) *The Holy Qur-an: English Translation of the meanings and Commentary Revised and Edited by the Presidency of Islamic Researches, IFTA, Call and Guidance* (Al-Madinah al-Munawarah: King Fahd Holy Qur-an Printing Complex).

Isaac, B. (1983) A Donation for Herod's Temple in Jerusalem. *IEJ* 33: 86-92.

Jerusalem (2005) Jerusalem. In *The New Encyclopaedia Britannica*, vol. 6 (15th edn; Chicago: Encyclopaedia Britannica): 539.

Kraeling, C.H. (1956) *The Excavations at Dura-Europos-Final Report*. Vol. 8, *The Synagogue* (New Haven: Yale University Press).

Mazar, B. (1985) The Temple Mount. In *Biblical Archaeology Today: Proceedings of the International Congress of Biblical Archaeology—Jerusalem, April 1984* (Jerusalem: Israel Exploration Society, Israel Academy of Sciences and Humanities, American Schools of Oriental Research): 463-68.

Mazar, E. (2002) *The Complete Guide to the Temple Mount Excavations* (Jerusalem: Shoham Academic Research and Publications).

Meyers, C. (1992) Temple, Jerusalem. In *The Anchor Bible Dictionary*, vol. 6, edited by David Noel Freedman (New York: Doubleday): 350-69.

Naveh, J. (1970) The Ossuary Inscriptions from Giv'at Hamivtar. *IEJ* 20: 33-37.

Neuwirth, A. (2003) From the Sacred Mosque to the Remote Temple: Surat al-Isra' between Text and Commentary. In *With Reverence for the Word: Medieval Scriptural Exegesis in Judaism, Christianity, and Islam*, edited by J.D. McAuliffe, B.D. Walfish and J.W. Goering (Oxford: Oxford University Press): 376-407.

Perowne, S.H., and J. Prawer (2005) Jerusalem. In *The New Encyclopaedia Britannica*, vol. 22 (15th edn; Chicago: Encyclopaedia Britannica): 328-35.

Rajak, T. (1983) *Josephus: The Historian and his Society* (London: Duckworth).

Ritmeyer, L., and K. Ritmeyer (2004) *Jerusalem in the Year 30 A.D.* (Jerusalem: Carta).

Ross, D. (2004) *The Missing Peace: The Inside Story of the Fight for Middle East Peace* (New York: Farrar, Strauss & Giroux).

Stern, M. (1980) *Greek and Latin Authors on Jews and Judaism*, vol. 2 (Jerusalem: Israel Academy of Sciences and Humanities).

Swisher, C.E. (2004) *The Truth About Camp David* (New York: Nation Books).

Verbin, J.S.K. (2000) Dating Theodotus. *Journal of Jewish Studies* 51: 243-80.

20 The Archaeology of Palestine in the Post-Biblical Periods

The Intersection of Text and Artifact

Jodi Magness

Abstract

In this paper I review the present state and future prospects of the archaeology of Palestine in the post-biblical periods, a sub-discipline of Biblical Archaeology that is marginalized in the American academic setting. The controversies surrounding Qumran, the site where the Dead Sea Scrolls were found, illustrate what happens when archaeological remains are interpreted without taking into account the historical context and literary sources. Postmodernism and sensationalism as well as academic over-specialization and isolation have contributed to the development of these polarizing controversies. I conclude by suggesting ways in which graduate students in biblical and post-Biblical Archaeology might be trained in order to ensure the future life and vitality of the field.

Introduction

In this paper I review the present state and future prospects of the archaeology of Palestine in the post-biblical periods (post-586 BCE), a sub-discipline of Biblical Archaeology that includes the late Second Temple or New Testament period (first century BCE—first century CE). The late Second Temple period is extraordinarily rich in archaeological remains and literary sources, including the testimony of Flavius Josephus, the Dead Sea Scrolls, and the Mishnah (which was edited later but incorporates earlier traditions). The current controversies surrounding Qumran, the site where the Dead Sea Scrolls were found, illustrate what happens when scholars fail to consider both archaeological and literary evidence in order to obtain a balanced and accurate understanding of the past. I begin by describing my own educational background by way of an introduction.

I earned a B.A. in Archaeology and History at the Hebrew University of Jerusalem and a Ph.D. in Classical Archaeology at the University of Pennsylvania. My field of expertise, the archaeology of Palestine in the post-biblical periods, does not exist as an independent discipline in the American academic framework. This is reflected in the ways I describe myself to other archaeologists: as a classical archaeologist who specializes in ancient Palestine or as a Syro-Palestinian (or biblical) archaeologist who specializes in the Roman, Byzantine, and early Islamic periods. I barely appear on the radar of most classical archaeologists, who consider anything east of Greece outside the realm of the classical world. And many of my biblical archaeologist colleagues regard everything that happened after 586 BCE (where most textbooks end) as modern history.

When I first arrived at the University of North Carolina at Chapel Hill in 2002, the archaeologists in the Department of Anthropology were astonished to learn that my appointment was in the Department of Religious Studies. Their surprise is understandable. As far as I can tell, I am the only classical archaeologist in the United States (that is, holding a Ph.D. in classical archaeology) with a full-time appointment in a Department of Religious Studies (as opposed to a combined Department of Classics and Religion or Classics and Near Eastern Studies). Therefore, my experience is not normal or normative, nor do I believe that positions like mine will become more common in the future. In fact, I think that my position is due to an unusual and highly specific set of circumstances.

Nevertheless, the fact that a classical archaeologist can wind up in a Department of Religious Studies highlights the unique position of archaeology within the American academic setting. Unlike Europe, where archaeologists are usually housed in institutes or departments of archaeology, no such thing exists in the U.S. In Europe archaeology has a long and well-established history as an academic discipline going back to the time of the Renaissance, and European countries have rich archaeological heritages relating to the classical past. In contrast, New World archaeology developed later as a discipline, long after academic departments had crystallized in North American universities.

Biblical and Post-Biblical Archaeology in Academia

Students in North America who wish to pursue graduate studies in Biblical Archaeology (that is, the archaeology of Palestine in the Bronze and Iron Age) have only a handful of programs to choose from, including Harvard University, the University of Chicago, the University of Toronto, and the University of California at San Diego. These programs typically are housed within departments of Near Eastern Languages and Civilizations. But *no* graduate programs exist for students who wish to specialize in the archaeology of Palestine in the post-biblical periods. There is not a single endowed chair in the archaeology of Palestine in the post-biblical periods in the U.S.; my own chair is in early Judaism, not archaeology. Students must choose between pursuing a Ph.D. in classical archaeology with a concentration in the Near East or enter a Ph.D. program in religious studies that includes an archaeological component. The first option is offered, for example, at the University of Michigan (Sharon Herbert) and the University of Minnesota (Andrea Berlin). The second option is available at Duke University (Eric Meyers) and the University of North Carolina at Chapel Hill (me). The archaeology of Palestine in the post-biblical periods exists as an independent field of study only at Israeli universities.

I am not suggesting that we develop programs in the archaeology of Palestine in the post-biblical periods in the U.S. but am merely pointing out that any discussion about the future of this field will be different from others, including Biblical Archaeology. It is ironic that the archaeology of Roman Palestine—a discipline that does not exist within the American academic setting—often has greater popular appeal than biblical and classical archaeology, as demonstrated by the public fascination with the Dead Sea Scrolls, the so-called James ossuary, and indeed any archaeological artifact that might have been associated with Jesus (the situation of Egyptology in the U.S. is similar). I also find it ironic that, in general, archaeology—the poster child for interdisciplinary studies—struggles to survive in the same American academic system that pays so much lip service to interdisciplinarity and multi-culturalism.

It might be nice to have institutes of archaeology in the U.S. like in Europe and Israel. Imagine teaching in a setting where archaeology and archaeological methodology are the focus, and where one always has a full complement of colleagues who are archaeologists. If there were institutes of archaeology in the U.S., it would undoubtedly affect not only the way we teach and interact in the university setting but also the way we advise and train our students. On the other hand, the European model also produces academic isolation and over-specialization.

Although archaeology is disadvantaged in the U.S. by not having independent departments (and therefore lacks the power of advocacy), offering archaeology in different departmental settings benefits students. Some of the graduate students in religious studies at the University of North Carolina have been exposed to archaeology in my classes, and several have participated on my excavation in Israel. Hopefully these students not only gain an appreciation of archaeology but also an understanding of its methodologies and limitations. What happens when the study of archaeology is divorced from its historical context is illustrated vividly by the case of Qumran and the Dead Sea Scrolls. The settlement at Qumran as understood by archaeologists who ignore the Dead Sea Scrolls and ancient sources such as Josephus bears no resemblance to Qumran as understood by scholars who incorporate the literary evidence. And scholars on both sides of the issue (archaeologists and text specialists) express an inability or unwillingness to evaluate critically arguments and interpretations outside their own fields of expertise.

The Controversies Surrounding Qumran

In the last decade, the interpretation of the site of Qumran has become one of the most hotly debated issues in the field of Second Temple period archaeology. Was Qumran a sectarian (and specifically, Essene) settlement, as the original excavator, Roland de Vaux proposed (and as I believe, following de Vaux) or was it something else—a villa, manor house, fort, commercial entrepot, or pottery manufacturing center—as others have suggested? (for the former opinion see Magness 2002; for examples of the latter see Galor, Humbert, and Zangenberg 2006). In his book *Qumran in Context* (2004), Yizhar Hirschfeld presents a sweeping revisionist interpretation, identifying Qumran as a field fort and road station in the Hasmonean period and as a manor house in the Herodian period.

As John Collins notes in his endorsement on the dust jacket: 'Hirschfeld's description of the archaeology of Qumran is so different from the influential accounts of de Vaux and Magness that it is sure to be controversial' (Hirschfeld 2004). The alternative interpretations of Qumran proposed by Hirschfeld and others have caused a great deal of confusion among archaeologists, Dead Sea Scrolls scholars, and the general public. For how can anyone—and especially those who do not specialize in archaeology—judge the validity of the various interpretations when the same evidence is interpreted so differently?

The interpretation of Qumran as a sectarian settlement depends on whether one accepts or rejects the association of the scrolls with the site. Simply put, scholars who accept the connection between the scrolls and the site identify Qumran as a sectarian settlement (this is true regardless of whether or not these scholars identify the sectarians as Essenes). This school of thought is sometimes described as consensual (or consensus). Scholars who reject the identification of Qumran as a sectarian settlement (the non-consensual or non-consensus school of thought) argue that there is no connection between the scrolls and the site. According to this view, the inhabitants of Qumran did not own and use the scrolls or deposit them in the nearby caves.

The rejection of any connection between the scrolls and the site of Qumran might seem to be a simple matter of prioritizing the archaeological evidence over literary sources—a question of how to weight the evidence. As Jürgen Zangenberg writes, Hirschfeld's book is distinguished by 'following a strictly archaeological agenda...[showing] how to read the archaeology of Qumran as *archaeology* for the first time' (Hirschfeld 2004: xiii). In fact, Hirschfeld can support his identification of

Qumran as a manor house only by ignoring the information the scrolls provide about the community that deposited them in the caves.

The prioritizing of archaeological evidence over literary sources might seem to be innocent and even laudable. Why not let the archaeological evidence speak for itself? As Zangenberg puts it: 'In the "Qumran-Essene-Theory" the role of archaeology is largely affirmative and illustrative... The so-called "consensus" never really took the archaeology of the site seriously as an independent source of information and knowledge, but rather, concurred with a widespread tendency of scholars who mainly deal with texts to deny archeology its very own power to formulate concepts and ideas about the past' (Hirschfeld 2004: xii). Zangenberg's claim that scholars who identify Qumran as a sectarian settlement have not seriously considered the archaeological evidence belittles the contributions made by such scholars as Roland de Vaux, Yigael Yadin, and Magen Broshi. More importantly, Zangenberg and Hirschfeld do not just prioritize the archaeological evidence but dismiss the literary evidence altogether. Why should one type of evidence (archaeological) have priority over another (literary)? Why not use both types of evidence together, to complement each other? Qumran represents an extraordinary discovery that provides an opportunity to use archaeological and literary evidence to understand the lifestyle and beliefs of this community. For example, archaeologically we can identify ten miqva'ot (ritual baths) at Qumran, while literary sources (the scrolls and Josephus) describe the purification rituals of this community. Taken together these two types of evidence are complementary. In fact, Qumran is an excellent example of a site that provides physical, archaeological evidence for the religious beliefs and practices of its inhabitants. Why would anyone want to disregard or prioritize one type of evidence over another? Of course, the answer is that this is necessary if that evidence does not support one's interpretation.

A comparison between Qumran and other sites—that is, a consideration of Qumran within its larger regional context—reveals just how different it is. In de Vaux's time Qumran appeared to be unique because few sites had been excavated in the Dead Sea region. The fact that many more sites have been excavated and published since then—including Herodian Jericho, Ein Boqeq, Ein Gedi, Herodium, Masada, Kallirrhoe, and Machaerus—only highlights the unique nature of the settlement at Qumran. None of the anomalous features at Qumran is paralleled at any other site. These include the large number of miqva'ot (and their large sizes), the animal bone deposits, the large adjacent cemetery, the communal dining rooms with adjacent pantries containing hundreds of dishes, the numerous workshops, and an unusual ceramic repertoire (see Magness 2002). Examining Qumran within a larger regional context actually works against Hirschfeld and Zangenberg by showing just how unique it is. In other words, the alternative interpretations of Qumran are clearly contradicted by the archaeological evidence, even without taking the scrolls into account.

The Effects of Postmodernism on Qumran Archaeology

A pronounced element of postmodernism underlies the non-consensual school's interpretation of Qumran. This is evident in the prioritizing of the archaeological evidence and the rejection of any connection between the scrolls and the site. As a result Qumran is ripped from its social-religious-historical context, leaving us with the archaeological remains alone—stones, potsherds, coins, glass. Although these remains provide certain types of information (for example, the large number of miqva'ot suggests a concern with ritual purity), they cannot inform us about the religious beliefs and ideology of the inhabitants (for example, only from the scrolls do we learn that the sect was concerned with ritual purity because they conceived of their community as a substitute temple) (see Magness 2002: 158). In other words, without the scrolls the archaeological remains are ambiguous enough to support a variety of possible interpretations—that Qumran was a villa, manor house, fort, commercial entrepot, pottery manufacturing center, and so on. As Hirschfeld states: 'Qumran has been variously defined as a fortress, a road station, or the center of an agricultural estate…these interpretations are not necessarily mutually exclusive' (Hirschfeld 2004: xv).

Denying any connection between Qumran and the scrolls automatically creates ambiguity—a situation in which Qumran can be interpreted in any one of a number of ways and all interpretations are equally valid. This is another reflection of postmodernism, according to which no one interpretation is correct and all interpretations have equal value. I would argue that the exact opposite is the case. Qumran could not have been a sectarian settlement, a villa, a fort, and a commercial entrepot—at least, not all at the same time. Only one interpretation can be correct, and not all interpretations carry the same weight or are equally legitimate. Although it is possible to interpret both the literary and archaeological evidence in different ways, only one interpretation is supported by a majority of the evidence and creates a minimum number of problems. For example, scholars who reject the connection between Qumran and the scrolls must explain how the scrolls came to be deposited in caves immediately below the settlement at the same time the site was occupied.

Similar postmodern tendencies underlie the minimalist–maximalist debate raging over the origins of the Israelites and the nature of the United Kingdom. The minimalists reject any element of historicity in the biblical accounts. This removes the archaeological remains from their historical and religious context, making it possible to argue for different ranges of dates and for different interpretations (for example, the kingdom of David and Solomon was just a small chiefdom, and the monumental building remains traditionally associated with them date to a later period) (for examples of opposing views see Dever 2001; Finkelstein and Silberman 2001).

Sensationalism in Archaeology

Magen Broshi (2005) recently pointed out the sensationalistic aspects of the Qumran controversy. He notes that whereas many highly respected scrolls specialists have never received media attention, a new and different interpretation of Qumran is almost certain to make the news. After all, everyone has heard of the Dead Sea Scrolls, even if most people do not understand what they are. I am not suggesting that all advocates of alternative interpretations seek to grab headlines. But there is no denying that scholars who challenge the consensus by proposing alternative theories generally get more media attention, whatever their motivation.

In fact, a number of sensational archaeological finds recently made headlines around the world—from a small stone box that supposedly contained the remains of Jesus' brother James to the world's earliest church to a cave allegedly associated with John the Baptist (for the ossuary see Lemaire 2002; for the church see Tepper 2006; for the cave of John the Baptist see Gibson 2004). On the one hand, archaeologists exploit the media to enhance their own fame and fortune, since the excavation of a site associated with a famous biblical figure is more likely to attract funding. On the other hand, the discovery of sensational relics plays on the public's inability to evaluate the credibility and legitimacy of these claims. And these discoveries, whether they are announced by archaeologists or collectors, gain legitimization (at least in the eyes of the public) once they have been publicized by the media.

Of course there have always been unscrupulous dealers, as illustrated by the Shapira affair (see Allegro 1965), and unscrupulous archaeologists such as Heinrich Schliemann, who apparently salted his excavations at Hissarlik (Troy) with gold objects purchased on the antiquities market (see Traill 1995). Sooner or later these fraudulent acts and claims are revealed and the discoveries (and discoverers) are discredited.

In my opinion, sensational finds or theories that exploit the public's ignorance make a mockery of our discipline. They feed into the popular perception that archaeologists are treasure hunters like Indiana Jones. And these controversies only detract from productive and legitimate scholarly discourse. For example, allegations of Vatican conspiracies contributed nothing to the field of Dead Sea Scrolls studies (see, e.g., Baigent and Leigh 1991). Once all of the Dead Sea Scrolls were published and made fully accessible, claims of secrets that undermine the Catholic Church and its teachings disappeared. Although the allegations of Vatican conspiracies were widely publicized, today they are nothing but a footnote in the history of Dead Sea Scrolls studies.

I believe that the recently completed publication of the Dead Sea Scrolls marks the beginning, not the end of a long process. Scholars have barely scratched the surface in terms of understanding and appreciating the wealth of information contained in the scrolls, which shed light not only on the Qumran sect but on Second Temple period and rabbinic Judaism, the Hebrew Bible and related literature, apocalyptic anxieties and expectations, and yes, even Jesus and his movement. If you are a student or if you have students looking for a field of study or thesis topic, you need look no further. Specialists will spend the foreseeable future digesting and studying the contents of the scrolls. Archaeologists can advance our understanding of Qumran by examining the physical remains in light of this wealth of newly published information. The future of Qumran archaeology, like its past, lies in the careful study of the intersection of texts and artifacts.

The Consequences of Academic Over-Specialization

Aside from the effects of sensationalism and postmodernism, the refusal of some scholars to consider the literary and archaeological evidence from Qumran as part of an integrated whole is also a result of an increasing degree of specialization in academic circles. Previous generations of scholars, such as William Foxwell Albright and Yigael Yadin, worked easily with different kinds of evidence (literary, archaeological, and epigraphic), mastered multiple ancient languages, and displayed a healthy intellectual curiosity and interest in broadly defined periods and fields. For example, Yadin excavated Hazor, Masada, and the Bar Kokhba caves in Nahal Hever, and his publications of the War Scroll and Temple Scroll from Qumran remain the definitive studies of those documents (for a biography of Yadin see Silberman 1993; for a recent retrospective of Yadin's scholarship see *In Memory of Yigael Yadin* 2004). Few if any scholars today have the breadth, depth, and brilliance of these giants. To be fair, the current situation is at least partly due to technology and the information explosion. The web has made scholarship more easily and widely accessible, but it has also multiplied exponentially the amount of information that is published in print and electronically. It is nearly impossible for any one person today to keep abreast of all developments and publications even in a single narrow field of specialization. Small wonder that some archaeologists ignore or misrepresent the contents of the Dead Sea Scrolls and the testimony of ancient authors when considering the nature of the settlement at Qumran.

Ensuring the Future of Biblical (and Post-Biblical) Archaeology

Qumran illustrates the importance of integrating archaeological and literary evidence, especially in the historically rich setting of post-biblical Palestine. Our graduate students must be prepared accordingly, so that they can deal competently with different kinds of evidence even if they choose to specialize in archaeology. How can we ensure their futures and the future of the discipline?

(1) We need to create and maintain contacts and connections with our non-archaeologist colleagues, so that they are not only aware of what we do but appreciate the importance and relevance of archaeology to their disciplines. This is why I have opposed the split between the American Schools of Oriental Research (ASOR) and the Society of Biblical Literature (SBL). Its not just that the main job markets (with job interviews for graduate students) are at the SBL meetings, but that we have a responsibility to ensure the future of our discipline by keeping archaeology in front of the

noses of philologists and text scholars, many of whom have little knowledge of or interest in archaeology. Since they are the ones who control university departments and decide on the formulation of job descriptions and positions, they need to be educated about the relevance of archaeology to their own disciplines.

(2) We need to advise and train our students so they are competitive on the job market. Students who decide to pursue a career in archaeology must be advised and mentored closely, probably more so than in other disciplines. The realities of the job market mean that a student trained purely as an archaeologist will have a hard time finding a job anywhere but in contract archaeology or cultural resource management (CRM). Most of our graduate students end up finding jobs in small universities, colleges, and seminaries where they are expected to teach a broad range of courses (including surveys of Western art or civilization) instead of upper-level courses in their field of research specialization. To be competitive for positions in anthropology, students must have a solid grounding in socio-cultural and biological anthropology and theory. For positions in departments of classics or religious studies, archaeology students must be proficient in the relevant languages—Greek, Latin, Biblical Hebrew, etc., as well as in ancient texts—since in many cases they will be competing for the same positions as textually oriented students. For positions in art history and history, archaeology students must be trained in the relevant theories and methodologies and be able to teach general surveys including modern periods. In nearly all of these cases archaeologists are at a disadvantage. They find themselves competing for the same jobs as philologists (who are better trained in the languages and literature) or art historians/historians (with few positions only in ancient art or history, students often apply for positions that are either for generalists or perhaps ancient *and* medieval art or history), or anthropologists (which is a hard sell for archaeologists specializing in historical periods in the classical world or Near East).

Teaching Biblical and Post-Biblical Archaeology in the American Academic Setting

One consequence of the situation of archaeology in the American academic setting is that we are forced to learn about different disciplines to a much greater degree than in Europe or Israel, for example. Whether we are in departments of religious studies, classics, art history, history, or anthropology, most archaeologists have found ourselves in positions of having to teach material outside our field of expertise. I myself have taught, at one time or another, courses on Principles of Archaeology (in the Department of Anthropology at the University of Miami), Art History 1 ('Cavemen to Cathedrals' in the Department of Visual Arts at Florida International University), Classics of Greece (ancient Greek literature in the Department of Classics at Tufts), Bronze Age Aegean archaeology, Etruscan archaeology, and Greek and Roman art and archaeology (in the Departments of Art History and Classics at Tufts), and now Introduction to Early Judaism (in the Department of Religious Studies at the University of North Carolina). Teaching a range of courses is both a blessing and a curse. It's a curse when we have to prepare to teach something we know almost nothing about. But after we're done it's almost always a blessing, an enriching experience that adds a new dimension to our scholarship. Teaching early Judaism in a Department of Religious Studies has given me new knowledge, perspectives, and insights on familiar archaeological material. I'm sure others have had similar experiences in different contexts.

Having to teach different kinds of courses is not the only enriching aspect of being in a non-archaeological academic setting. There's also the interaction with our colleagues, both in the departmental setting and at professional meetings. And I've learned along the way that there are divisions in the field of (and in departments of) religious studies that mirror what we see in archaeology. For example, until recently the American Academy of Religion (AAR) and SBL held their annual meeting together. This was a gigantic meeting with about 10,000 attendees. A few years ago the AAR announced that it would split from the SBL and hold its annual meeting separately. This has generated a crisis in religious studies departments and will undoubtedly affect the job market. I now realize that this split reflects an existing schism between scholars of religion who are more theoretical in their approach (AAR) and those who are more historically and textually oriented (SBL). Of course the same sort of postmodern schism exists in art history and other disciplines (see Cheney 1995).

Conclusion: The Future of Biblical and Post-Biblical Archaeology

It seems nearly impossible to envision the future of the archaeology of Palestine in the biblical and post-biblical periods in the U.S. because there are so many unknown factors. When I was a graduate student in the 1980s, it was predicted that beginning in 1990 (about the time I graduated) there would be a shortage of Ph.D.s in the humanities due to a wave of retirements. However, these predictions never came to pass. In fact, the exact opposite happened, thanks largely to two unforeseen events: (1) a recession hit the U.S. in the early 1990s; and (2) the laws were changed so that retirement at age 65 was no longer mandatory. This means that the wave of retirements never came, and when individual members of the older generation did retire, their lines were eliminated or were allocated to other departments. For this reason I hesitate to make any predictions about the future of biblical and post-Biblical Archaeology in the U.S. However, I hope we can ensure the future of the discipline by training students as broadly as possible (without compromising their competence in a specific field), so they will be competitive for jobs in religious studies, history, art history, classics, and anthropology.

Finally, we must seek to promote education and dialogue across national and international as well as disciplinary boundaries. If Biblical Archaeology disappears from American universities, we shall be ceding the field to the Israelis, who already dominate it. American involvement in archaeology benefits Israelis too by counterbalancing academic isolation, inbreeding, and over-specialization. Continued interaction and dialogue between Americans, Israelis, and Europeans is vital to keep the discipline healthy.

Acknowledgments

It is a pleasure to honor Tom Levy with this paper on the occasion of the establishment of his endowed chair. I also wish to acknowledge the generosity of Norma Kershaw, who has helped to secure the future of Biblical Archaeology in the American academic setting by endowing this chair.

References

Allegro, J.M. (1965) *The Shapira Affair: The Mystery of a Nineteenth-Century Discovery of a Dead Sea Manuscript; A Forgery or the Oldest Bible in the World?* (Garden City, NY: Doubleday).
Baigent, M., and R. Leigh (1991) *The Dead Sea Scrolls Deception* (London: Cape).
Broshi, M. (2005) 'The Man Who Found the Cult of the Mushroom in the New Testament'. Review of A. Brown, *John Marco Allegro: The Maverick of the Dead Sea Scrolls* (Grand Rapids: Eerdmans, 2005). *Haaretz* 06/10/2005 (Hebrew).
Cheney, L.V. (1995) *Telling the Truth: Why Our Culture and Our Country Have Stopped Making Sense—and What We Can Do About It* (New York: Simon & Schuster).
Dever, W.G. (2001) *What Did the Biblical Writers Know and When Did They Know It?* (Grand Rapids: Eerdmans).

Finkelstein, I., and N.A. Silberman (2001) *The Bible Unearthed: Archaeology's New Vision of Ancient Israel and the Origin of its Sacred Texts* (New York: Simon & Schuster).

Galor, K., J.-B. Humbert, and J. Zangenberg (eds.) (2006) *Qumran, the Site of the Dead Sea Scrolls: Archaeological Interpretations and Debates—Proceedings of a Conference held at Brown University, November 17–19, 2002* (Leiden: Brill).

Gibson, S. (2004) *The Cave of John the Baptist* (London: Century).

Hirschfeld, Y. (2004) *Qumran in Context: Reassessing the Archaeological Evidence* (Peabody, MA: Hendrickson).

In Memory of Yigael Yadin (1917–1984), Lectures Presented at the Symposium on the Twentieth Anniversary of his Death, Thursday, October 28, 2004 (Jerusalem: Hebrew University).

Lemaire, A. (2002) Burial Box of James the Brother of Jesus. *BAR* 28.6: 24-33, 70.

Magness, J. (2002) *The Archaeology of Qumran and the Dead Sea Scrolls* (Grand Rapids: Eerdmans).

Silberman, N.A. (1993) *A Prophet from Amongst You: The Life of Yigael Yadin: Soldier, Scholar, and Mythmaker of Modern Israel* (Reading, MA: Addison-Wesley).

Tepper, Y. (2006) Legio, Kefar 'Otnay. *ESI* 118. Online: http://www.hadashot esi.org.il/report_detail_ eng.asp?id=363&mag_id=111 (accessed 4 March 2010).

Traill, D.A. (1995) *Schliemann of Troy: Treasure and Deceit* (London: John Murray).

21 The Changing Place of Biblical Archaeology

Exceptionalism or Normal Science?*

Alexander H. Joffe

Abstract

The physical, socio-intellectual, and political environments of Biblical Archaeology are reviewed, along with the role of religion in the 21st century. Changes in the political economy of universities and the various media used to disseminate archaeological results are also discussed. It is concluded that while Biblical Archaeology is scientific in practice and subject to many of the same constraints as archaeology worldwide, special constraints remain which make it exceptional.

Introduction

Biblical Archaeology is a comparatively old and well-developed branch of world archaeology, with an extraordinarily large and detailed database. The era of primary or basic research into time–space systematics is long over and a secondary or applied phase is well underway. Biblical Archaeology is also an international enterprise that draws researchers from many countries, is deeply inter-disciplinary, and addresses methodological and certain theoretical questions at high levels. As in the West, archaeology in Israel, Jordan, and the Palestinian territories is incorporated into local law and custom and enjoys governmental and private funding, and the enterprise has a nominal place in society.

But regardless of the theoretical, methodological, and thematic commonalities with other branches of archaeology, Biblical Archaeology's subject matter also stands at the center of two, or possibly three, world religions. If nothing else, the positive and negative expectations of the public and fellow professionals are strongly shaped by this fact.

Since the very beginning the essential question facing the discipline is how or whether to shape a branch of archaeology around a particular series of Iron Age political and literary developments.

---

*   I express my thanks to Tom Levy for his repeated invitations to contribute to this volume, and to Sam Wolff for his comments.

These occurred across less than a millennium in an area of a few thousand square kilometers. In geographical terms this represents a relatively small part of the integral unit of the Levant. In temporal terms it comprises not even 1% of the overall span during which biologically modern humans resided in this portion of West Asia. And yet the question remains.

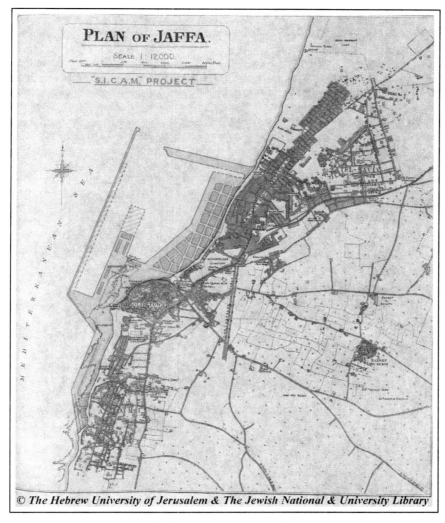

Map of Jaffa 1923. Online: http://historic-
cities.huji.ac.il/israel/tel_aviv/maps/palmer_1923_tel_aviv_d.html
(retrieved 4 February 2009)

That said, everything else about Biblical Archaeology is changing. The discipline's evolving sense of self, represented in its various names, 'Biblical Archaeology', 'biblical archaeology', 'Holy Land archaeology', 'Syro-Palestinian archaeology', 'Palestinian archaeology', and the 'New Biblical Archaeology' has been discussed elsewhere (e.g. Zevit 2004).[1] Rather than look at history, this paper examines the future of Biblical Archaeology in the 21st century through four broad lenses of change; the Near East environment, the university, the place of religion in the West and East, and communications. More facets could certainly be examined but each of these is helping to shape new conditions and expectations for archaeology generally and Biblical Archaeology specifically.

But the more some things change, the more others stay the same. If the discipline itself is different, along with its operating environment, it will never expunge religion from its core. Nor should it.

Changes in the Near Eastern Environment

The Physical Environment

Biblical Archaeology came of age professionally at a propitious time since it coincided with the transition to modernity generally in the region and the transformation of the Near Eastern, particularly Levantine, landscape. Since the mid-20th century and the emergence of independent nation-states population densities have exploded, urban areas have expanded, along with road systems and other infrastructure, and land use has become intense in all ways. In 1914, the population of Ottoman Palestine west of the Jordan River was estimated at 689,000 (Luke and Keith-Roach 1934: 39). Today the population is more that ten times that figure. When the British captured Palestine from the Turks in 1918 there were neither private automobiles nor any all-weather roads in the entire country (Biger 1994: 33-34, 133). Between 1918 and 2002 the urban area of Amman increased by $162km^2$ or 509 times (Al Rawashdeh and Saleh 2006). Now one need only fly into Tel Aviv, Amman, or Beirut to see urban sprawl, superhighways, industrial, and agricultural development. The speed and depth of these changes are easily measured. While the study of collapse warns us that the social and spatial manifestations of civilizational rise are reversible, their impacts on the archaeological record are not.

The implications for archaeology are clear. Whole, intact landscapes as objects of study are becoming a thing of the past, certainly within Mediterranean zones. Regions around sites are pervasively disrupted by development of one sort or another. Deep plowing even destroys buried sites and soil horizons. The non-site aspects of the archaeological record are being swept away along with not a few sites, mostly small or buried ones. This is of course the inevitable encroachment of the modern world. Archaeologists may lament these changes but residents who can grow their own food, take advantage of modern infrastructure, employment, and lifestyles, and live with a roof over their heads, are unlikely to agree.

---

1.   For the record, this writer has endorsed the position that the discipline should be Levantine Archaeology. This concept unites (1) the westward facing Mediterranean complex of coast, foothills, mountains, and desert or steppe, comparable in terms of resources and climate to relatively few other places including western Spain and coastal California, (2) related West Semitic cultural and linguistic areas, and (3) defies arbitrary modern political boundaries. Perhaps for these reasons it has not been embraced.

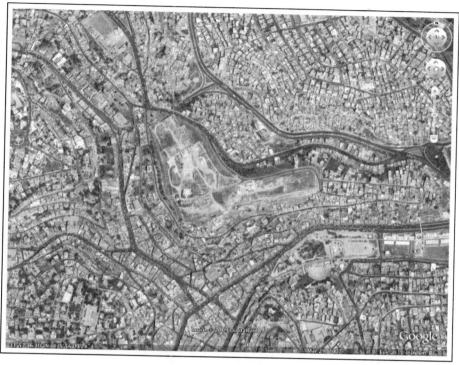

Aerial view of Amman Citadel, Google Earth
(retrieved 4 February 2009)

The mass archaeological extinction event of the 21st century is underway. Archaeologists find themselves powerless to stop it. The Levantine landscape is swiftly being transformed in ways familiar to North Americans and Europeans, and with it the practice of archaeology itself. For one thing, at the practical and experiential levels, no longer does archaeology take place *out* there, in the wide-open spaces, far away from civilization. Rather, to a large degree it is now done in the interstices between modernity, just at the end of the road. The impact of archaeology being done *right here* is equally obvious. Archaeological survey has developed into a robust field not only requiring good eyes and strong boots but statistical acumen (Banning 2004). Major sites are penned up in parks or reserves, reconstructed beyond recognition, and the better known are visited in season by busloads of tourists, who may also stop to gape at archaeologists at work. Only the deserts are still at a remove, but even these are now routinely penetrated by a new breed of tourists. This development can be good for locals and bad for archaeological sites and the environment (Chatelard 2005).

For those archaeologists who have worked in other tourism heavy areas of the Old and New Worlds, the situation is depressingly familiar. Megiddo has much in common now with Stonehenge.[1] Results must be interpreted for audiences with preconceived agendas, and archaeologists must work alongside transportation planners and marketing specialists to ensure that sites are protected yet accessible. This is 'heritage management'. But inevitable laments over the loss of authenticity notwithstanding, the idea that the archaeological profession generates results that are then incorporated into nationalist, capitalist, or 'post-capitalist' fields is an old one (cf. Baram and Rowan 2004; Baram 2007). The fact remains that archaeology is and always will be a kind of service industry. But making effective arguments that contribute to the equally inevitable cost–benefit analyses that decide the fate of site and landscapes is the challenge for archaeologists everywhere. In general, those unfortunate enough to live near a profitable archaeological site will be removed while those living near less profitable ones will simply overwhelm them. Ironically, archaeological sites in unfree societies sometimes fare better than those in free societies, thanks to the whims of the powerful. The larger and more important question than the fate of archaeological sites is what sorts of political values and institutions prevail for the living, which in turn create the conditions in which history can be meaningfully studied (Joffe forthcoming a).

Aerial view of Tel Balata, ancient Shechem,
Google Earth (retrieved 4 February 2009)

The physical shape of the future is unknown. Rates of population, urban, and other growth in Levantine countries can be roughly estimated. One estimate for Israel sees a population density of 400 persons per square kilometer by 2020, roughly equal to the Netherlands, the most densely populated country in Europe (http://www.cbs.gov.il/mifkad/popul00_000_e.htm). Levantine archaeologists are unlikely to encounter a landscape bereft of sites (as Albright himself feared almost a century ago), but the archaeological record will be substantially degraded (cf. Kletter and de Groot 2001). At some point in the future the number and types of remaining sites will no longer warrant a robust archaeological industry and a spasm of contraction should be expected. This is what is likely to occur in the United States (Moore 2006a). At the same time the landscape effects will likely force even greater emphasis on large sites when creating reconstructions, at the same time as more small sites are being excavated.

Social and Intellectual Environments

One result of landscape changes is that the number of salvage and rescue projects have begun to predominate over research projects. Such exigencies have always been present in Biblical Archaeology and have produced important discoveries; witness R.W. Hamilton's excavations at Tell Abu Hawwam that opened new dimensions regarding Late Bronze Age Mediterranean connections, impelled by the use of the site as a gravel quarry (Hamilton 1935). But the demands of road and construction projects now drive survey and excavation as never before. These range from large-scale, multi-year projects prior to the construction of new infrastructure (e.g. 'En Esur, Yannai and Ariel 2006) and towns (e.g. Shoham, van den Brink, Gophna, and Carmi 2005) to soundings conducted in a matter of days under the shadow of bulldozers. Finds similarly range from entire ancient settlements to tiny snips of walls, surfaces, or pits. Construction projects like Israel's Highway Six and Jerusalem Light Rail project have been a boon for 'cultural resource management' or 'heritage' style archaeology long familiar in Europe and North America, where firms bid for contracts from engineering and construction firms that must set aside a small percentage of their government contracts to 'mitigate' archaeological remains. Immense geo-engineering projects such as the 'Dead-Med' or 'Dead-Red' canals or tunnels intended to replenish the Dead Sea and provide hydropower (Murakami 1998) or vast infrastructure connected with a future Palestinian state (Suisman *et al.* 2005) would require international funding and commensurate archaeological mitigation.

At least some of these changes in the organization of archaeology, whatever their scale or structure, are inevitable and have begun to change the nature of research. Thanks to the British Mandate, local custom and law dictate that excavations and surveys be done, whether there are large questions or not. Historic preservation and planning are similarly required (see El-Eini 2006: 59, 73). Whatever research agendas may be designed before or after the fact, they are unlike large-site, regional, or landscape projects, where long-term research is carefully structured beforehand. To be sure, new and interesting things are being found (e.g. Milevski 2002). But salvage and rescue projects are not typically problem-driven or pioneering (cf. Braun 1992). Results have the benefit of being fitted into already well-established chronologies and regional pictures. But that does not necessarily make them accessible or understandable. Research agendas continue to be set by large-scale projects pursuing the core problems defined at or near the discipline's beginning; the emergence of food production and sedentism, village and town life, the nature of society under imperial domination, and, above all, the nature of Iron Age polities, all defined mostly in 'historical' rather than processual terms (Dessel and Joffe 2000).

In Israel, Jordan, and the Palestinian territories, rescue and salvage projects usually go unpublished, or when published (in M.A. and Ph.D. theses, conference proceedings, or reports to funding or licensing agencies), the results are neither well disseminated nor fully incorporated into subsequent analyses. These problems are deeply familiar to European and North American archaeologists. At one extreme there is simply non-publication. Hence the Levy/White Program for Archaeological Publication, designed to coax at least a few projects out of the darkness, whether or not the excavators had the initial foresight to budget for publication or not (http://www.fas.harvard.edu/~semitic/wl/application.html). At that same end of the spectrum there are projects whose publications are promised (rather like vaporware, to use a software term). When and if they appear it is so long after the project's end (if at all) that anything new and interesting is inevitably lost. Others, including flagship projects at Megiddo, Beth Shan, and Hazor, have produced either final or detailed preliminary reports with admirable speed (e.g. Megiddo, Finkelstein and Ussishkin 2006).

But even when publications really do appear they form an increasingly intractable domain. Part of the problem is simply access. The number of journals, books, festschriften, conference volumes, doctorates and theses, and other publications has increased vastly. Most 'grey literature' is simply not accessible even in good university collections. Only a few well-heeled universities and research centers can afford to try to keep up, thus restricting the number of scholars who can participate effectively in the enterprise. Although important digital repositories have been created in some countries (e.g. England, see http://ads.ahds.ac.uk/catalogue/library/greylit/index.cfm) efforts in the Levant have been uneven. One notable development is the online availability of the Israel Antiquities Authority series Hadashot Arkheologiyot—Excavations and Surveys in Israel (http://www.hadashot-esi.org.il/index_eng.asp). This day may well come for Biblical Archaeology, and it cannot be too soon, since books have now run their course as a means for information storage and transmission.

But the actual doing of archaeology is also vastly different from even ten or fifteen years ago. Once it was possible to apprehend a period or a question by reading a dozen or two books and journals, visiting sites, and examining study collections. This is impossible today. The numbers of excavated sites are so extraordinary that examining relevant collections is nearly a full-time task. Reconstructing temporal or regional processes beyond one's own site is harder than ever. Only a few decades ago Kathleen Kenyon could confidently take her soundings at Jericho as representative of the entire Southern Levant or the entire Neolithic period. Today—knowing as much as we know—it is difficult to correlate confidently material culture from one site to another at a remove of even a few kilometers, much less reconstruct social processes. The awareness of inter-site and inter-regional variability that has come as a function of sheer data density is an impediment to larger questions, although these still seem to be answered with alarming confidence.

Another upshot of the data problem is that it is increasingly difficult to understand the archaeology without being a full-time resident of the country in question. And indeed, this is what is happening. Scholars have always gone out from their home institutions to study and work in the Middle East, sometimes for years. There is no substitute for learning the landscape, the material, and becoming part of the social enterprise of archaeology. But those who generate and then sit on the data have the advantage, both in terms of simple familiarity and with respect to the wider conversation. This has coincided with the dramatic shift of intellectual leadership away from Western scholars and institutions to those in host countries.

But the data explosion is not easily dealt with even by those who live close at hand. Computerized site and collection inventories have been established as part of cultural resource management (e.g. JADIS, see Palumbo *et al.* 1994). Numerous projects seek to archive or standardize excavation data, and virtual communities are being created to give easier access to dispersed digital collections (e.g. http://daahl.ucsd.edu/DAAHL/). Efforts are also afoot to employ digital means to record continuously excavations in four dimensions (http://news.brown.edu/pressreleases/2008/12/archaeology). The goal of recording and recreating excavations at the scale of 1:1 is not far off. The ability to record and represent more data has begun to outstrip the ability to create narratives for professionals and the public alike. Problems related to digital media and communication with the public are discussed further below.

Political Environment

Finally, a discussion of the Near Eastern environment for archaeology would not be complete without looking at the impact of politics on archaeology. One dimension is political economics. Where does funding come from for excavations? Where among myriad budgetary priorities of Israel, Jordan, and the Palestinian Authority is archaeology? Governmental transparency is not the norm in the region and the readily available figures, such as those for the Israel Antiquities Authority budget (http://www.antiquities.org.il/about_eng.asp?Modul_id=4) tell only part of the story. As a proxy, the parlous condition of universities in these states is one indication that applied research such as archaeology is not healthy. Enrollment figures for various programs are difficult to come by but it seems unlikely that the discipline is experiencing growth. At the same time, it is only realistic to think that dire straits have always been the norm for archaeology.

More threatening to Biblical or any archaeology is the rise of religious fundamentalism, Muslim and to a lesser extent Jewish. The anti-Western, anti-scientific, and anti-semitic force of Hamas, an offshoot of the Sunni Egyptian Muslim Brotherhood paradoxically supported by Shia Iran, is ascendant in Gaza (see generally Mishal and Sela 2006). In the West Bank the Fatah-run Palestinian Authority is corrupt and ineffective and Hamas is kept at bay largely by Israeli forces. There is little reason to think that Hamas would be favorably inclined toward Biblical Archaeology as such, although its attitude toward other forms seems fairly indifferent (see Armaly *et al.* 2007). Indeed, its propaganda is largely consonant with that of the Palestinian Authority and sees Jews as existential enemies of Islam, forgers of Scripture, and usurpers of Muslim land, whose claim that there was a Temple in Jerusalem is a paramount example of Jewish perfidy (Maissy-Noy 2006; Reiter 2008). Hezbollah expresses similar themes, as does the Muslim Brotherhood-linked opposition in Jordan.

The 'liminality' of Palestinian heritage notwithstanding (Sauders 2008), larger problems remain. Collective or national identity based on 'resistance' (Khalidi 1997) or emphasizing linkages to the premodern past, as suggested by Glock (1994), seem unlikely to promote a scientific approach to the past. Using archaeology as a confidence-building measure between communities, as suggested by other contributors in this volume, has more immediate utility but does not address the issues at a societal level. As a whole, secular and religious narratives compete for paramount status in Palestinian society. The contradiction between the local (in this case Palestinian) and general (pan-Arab and pan-Islamic) 'narratives' with respect to authenticity have also been played out elsewhere in the region (e.g. Zisser 2003). Another factor that will affect archaeology is Islamic religious attitudes toward the Other as well as the *jahilliya* or 'age of ignorance' before the coming of Islam (e.g. Vajda 1937; Ben-Shammai 1988). Given the weakness of civil society in the West Bank and the tenuous hold of what might be called secularism and secular institutions, it is difficult to see how archaeology will take hold, socially or institutionally. It may be that the 'fuzziness' of Jordanian national identity, and the adept manipulations of the ruling monarchy, are factors that have partially elided such problems in that country (Frisch 2002). On the other hand, there is every reason to think that Islamic Archaeology of the Levant, emphasizing a more recent millennium than that held dear by 'classical' Biblical Archaeology, is finding some type of home at Palestinian and Jordanian institutions. The foreign projects undertaken in the Palestinian territories include Jericho, which has a strong preservation and heritage component (Nigro and Taha 2006), and Early Bronze Age Tell es-Sakkan in Gaza (Tengberg *et al.* 2001), neither of which are especially Biblical. Nothing suggests that Biblical Archaeology as such would find a comfortable place in a secular Palestinian state or any place at all in an Islamic one.

In contrast, the role of archaeology for Israelis was once central but has diminished considerably (Hallote and Joffe 2002). An instinctive interest in and reflex to the past has been reignited by the post-Zionism debates of the 1990s as well as by the secular–religious divide. This latter divide is also characterized by dichotomous communal attitudes between the secular emphasis on sovereign space and the religious emphasis on sacred space (Shilhav 2007; cf. Cohen 2007). Jewish fundamentalism, represented on the one hand by Haredi political parties such as Shas, and on the other by the settler movement, treats archaeology in different ways. The former has little place for secular studies or science, although economic forces have prompted accommodations to an anti-modern view. Haredi fundamentalism threatens archaeology primarily through the mechanism of coalition politics, educational curricula, and funding decisions. Settler fundamentalism, however, selects archaeological results to harmonize with the biblical accounts and validate settlement activities, in contravention of Israeli law and public opinion. Its defense of biblically ordained 'sacred space' simultaneously exerts maximalist pressure on political coalitions and threatens the integrity of the archaeological enterprise as a whole through selective and anti-scientific readings of data, in effect radically privileging text over artifact (Feige 2007; Sasson and Kelner 2008). Both trends, however, exist within a democratic polity that, by and large, has less and less recourse to the 'past' as a tool for mobilization or legitimation, and which seems relatively uninterested in the mundane work of archaeology. But the Israeli public, like other publics in the West, continue to be stimulated by 'Biblical' discoveries, such as 'David's Palace' in the City of David and the 'James Ossuary', since they suggest linkages to intertwined religious and national identities (Hallote 2009). The role of archaeology in individual and collective identify-formation underlies much of the rationale for archaeology everywhere. Some thoughts on this problem are offered below.

Finally, in terms of politics, there is the large context of the Arab–Israeli conflict. All indications are that Israelis are willing to accept a Palestinian state, with which they want nothing to do. By and large Palestinians feel the same way about Israel, with a core of rejectionists that reliably act as spoilers (http://www.pcpsr.org/survey/polls/2008/p27ejoint.html; cf. Maddy-Weitzman 2003). After that, nothing is resolved, nor is it likely to be. Archaeology will be dragged along as facilitator of national narratives as well as proposed as a diplomatic and therapeutic mechanism. Explicit politicization of archaeology is apparently acceptable when done for 'correct' ends. It will be excoriated from within and without all along the way (Scham and Yahya 2003; Israeli–Palestinian Archaeology Working Group 2007; cf. Joffe forthcoming b). But given the religious antipathy displayed by at least some Muslims locally and worldwide to the very concepts of Jewish sovereignty and the Jewish past, and their ability to exercise a veto on Palestinian willingness to negotiate, there is no reason to think that any peace agreements between Israel and Palestine will be made in the foreseeable future. To deem this situation for archaeology 'overtly contested' and call for 'polyvocality' as a means of conflict resolution seems remarkably understated (Killebrew 2006; Killebrew et al. 2006; Dodd 2007).

In this grim scenario, archaeological sites and landscapes will continue to suffer. Mining of sites in the West Bank for artifacts and their transport and sale through Israel will likely continue, since it is in the economic interest of all participants and since the political will to stop it is lacking on all sides (Kersel 2008).

The Changing Place of Religion in West and East

Biblical Literacy and Religion in the Public Square
As indicated at the outset of this paper, the essential fact of Biblical Archaeology is the Bible, the original concern for all archaeology in the Middle East and that in the Levant specifically. Many have discussed precisely how the concerns and agendas of religion have shaped Biblical Archaeology. The ability of Biblical Archaeology, in its narrow sense, to provide evidence that complements (or 'confirms' or 'illustrates') religious narratives and hence individual and communal senses of place and worldviews, continues to be a powerful attraction for the public.

But the religious landscape of the world is being radically transformed in the 21st century. The place of religion in the public and private spheres in Western nation-states would be unrecognizable to visitors from even a half century ago, much less from 100 or more years ago. In the United States religion has been aggressively pushed into the private sphere. Religious and Biblical language no longer infuses public discourse, and even less so political discourse. Religious discourse is virtually absent from Europe, where official churches remain, and even there it is usually the purvey of the right and far right. The dechristianization of Europe is particularly glaring. Surveys demonstrate that church attendance has dropped dramatically in recent years: only 6% of French and 13% of British individuals 18 or older report attending a religious service at least once a week (http://www. eurofound.europa.eu/areas/qualityoflife/eurlife/index.php?template=3&radioindic =69&idDomain=6). Nowhere are the elite educated in religion or the Bible, even in a didactic or homiletic sense. Abraham Lincoln, whose entire morality, worldview, and rhetoric were shaped by the Bible (and Aesop's Fables), would be unthinkable as a political leader today. He would, in turn, not recognize our world.

The reasons for this are complex. The rise of the technocratic state, official multiculturalism in Europe, and unofficially in the United States, the tandem rise of litigious and therapeutic cultures, the secularization of opinion-shaping elites, the assimilation of Jews, and a host of other factors played roles. The removal of religious texts from the public sphere is a manifestation, and Biblical literacy has reached such a parlous state that sectarian and mainstream universities alike offer courses introducing essential Biblical characters (e.g. http://home.snu.edu/~hculbert/biblit.htm). All these factors bode ill for Biblical Archaeology, since global intelligentsia and idea-forming elites actively reject and disdain religion and the Bible. At the same time, however, there are demographic factors that will have an equally profound influence on the place of the Bible and religion on Earth.

Demographics

Traditional Biblical Archaeology had a particular appeal to the Anglican and Lutheran communities of Europe, while Catholics perceived it rather differently (e.g. Humbert in Armaly 2007). Questions of sectarian appeal, however, now seem quite beside the point. The dechristianization of Europe has been accompanied by a drop in European birth rates (Kohler, Billari, and Ortega 2006). Most are well below replacement rates and imply a halving of populations within 45 years. These declines are strongly correlated with reductions in religious belief and observance (Frejka and Westoff 2006).

But these developments in the global north are made more paradoxical by the equally evident explosion of pentacostal and charismatic Christianity in the Southern Hemisphere (Jenkins 2007, 2008). In Africa alone there are now over 400 million Christians, comprising over 46% of the population (http://pewforum.org/surveys/pentecostal/africa/). Similar trends are underway in Central and South America, as well as China, where there are estimated to be between 70 and 130 million Christians (http://www.economist.com/world/asia/displaystory.cfm?story_id=12342509). Indeed, even in Europe itself, mainline Protestant denominations and Catholicism are being outstripped by rapidly growing evangelical mega-churches.

Clearly the religious audience for Biblical Archaeology is changing, and may, in fact, be growing in terms of absolute numbers. But the cultural influence and receptiveness to Biblical Archaeology in the Southern Hemisphere has yet to be felt. Purely from a marketing perspective there is huge potential, albeit for a traditional or narrow form of Biblical Archaeology, but it remains difficult to reach audiences in regions with weak middle classes, institutions, and infrastructure. The potential for globalizing Biblical Archaeology, of the traditional and perhaps even modern sort, should not be underestimated.

Two other demographic dimensions will have an impact on Biblical Archaeology. One is the gradual shrinking of the Western Jewish community. The reasons are complex but the trajectory is clear; there are fewer identifying Jews, with a Jewish education and sense of affiliation, and they are distanced increasingly from the modern state of Israel and fellow Jews (Joffe 2006a; Della Pergola, Rebhun, and Tolts 2005). The only segment of the Jewish community that is growing in number or proportion is ultra-Orthodoxy, which does not value engagement with the modern world or with secular learning.

Most Jews do not engage with the Bible or with archaeology any more than Christians or secularists. And most are unlikely to support Biblical Archaeology directly or indirectly in the same way as in previous decades. Ungeleider Mayerson, Scheur, Levy/White, Kershaw, and others were central philanthropic figures who have not been replaced. Roger Hertog's support of the Shalem Center excavations at the City of David and the Foundation Stone's of the Khirbet Qeiyafa project cannot yet compare with that provided over decades by others. Picking winners is always a good strategy, for archaeologists and philanthropists. But overall a reduction of Jewish support for Biblical Archaeology should be expected.

The implications of these profound demographic, attitudinal, and generational changes in Western Jews of course go far beyond archaeology. The outer-directedness of Jewish philanthropy, along with that of WASPs, was central to building the modern American infrastructures of higher education, culture, the arts, and medicine (Goodwin 1998a, 1998b; Tobin 2001). In the modern era of philanthropy, names like Annenberg, Weill, Levy, and Tisch rank with Gates, Rockefeller, Pickens, Hewlett, and Packard for mega-giving in the billions. Jews in the future are unlikely to have so much money to lavish on projects that demonstrate, among other things, their dedication to the American project and its ideals of civic and democratic engagement, rule of law, free markets, and free speech. If trends at universities are any indication, they are already outspent by Arab and Muslim donors with far more narrow interests, mostly the promotion of mechanisms for the defense of the faith. That said, the university itself will likely be transformed beyond recognition as the 21st century progresses, by forces far beyond the control of any individual faith community or nation-state.

Changes in the University

The Price of Respectability

The emergence of the research university at the end of the 19th century gave the nascent field of Biblical Archaeology an ideal home. Arcane knowledge and specialized skills that were once the exclusive remit of the wealthy now had a new venue (e.g. Breasted 1977). Since then the university has been the intellectual center for archaeology and its allied fields, both in the West and in the Middle East. Albright at Johns Hopkins, Yadin at Hebrew University, and other lesser lights shone brightly, along with those at various seminaries. Excavations were mounted and new students were trained, in a process that conveyed knowledge and pedigree across the generations.

In general, post-World War II expansion and specialization was coupled to a process by which universities became, on the one hand, the symbol of middle-class respectability and upward socioeconomic mobility, and on the other, a training and certification service for capitalism. In the process they became, if nothing else, predictably Brobdignasian bureaucracies dedicated above all to their own preservation. Expansionary pressures, however, were a mixed blessing, especially for smaller disciplines (cf. Geiger 1993).

The university of plenty, which coincided with gradual American and European deindustrialization, gradually became a mechanism of social engineering. The ethos of inclusion was extended to those who were unprepared for college-level education. This was to some extent merely a function of democratization, opening previously closed doors to participation and advancement. But a more analytical view sees it as expanding market share to new demographics of consumers and adapting the product in the process. In pursuit of ever-larger markets, the standards and practices of the industry were necessarily defined downward. Vast remediation was necessary to bring the new consumers up to the minimally tolerable levels of skills and knowledge, which in turn helped create enormous new infrastructures in the universities. Since consumers cannot be permitted to be disappointed with the product, failure was no longer an option.

Predictably, compensatory post-graduate mechanisms for assessment and retraining also developed outside academia (Fallows 1985). The need to service large numbers of unqualified consumers meant that pedagogy was transformed. First large lectures courses were instituted and then new means of 'content delivery' had to be developed, again at the expense of the more specialized disciplines and smaller classes. With its foundation in material culture, archaeology generally is well suited to the image and mass presentation. But while Biblical Archaeology might provide a popular lecture class, beyond the introductory level the prospects are grim. It is more likely that Biblical Archaeology will be sacrificed on the altar of trendiness and 'relevance' (that is, consumer preferences) than will courses on the semiotics of Harry Potter.

Higher education's primary problem was that even though they were providers of consumer products in a highly competitive mass market, they continued to price themselves as luxury goods. Universities have successfully marketed the idea that their product conveys respectability and propels upward class mobility (and indeed, both of these propositions are to some extent true, see U.S. Census Bureau 2002). But the price equations are becoming unsustainable. Operating costs skyrocketed as middle-level bureaucrats proliferated in order to attend to unfunded mandates and to provide ever more elaborate support services to consumers. College and university infrastructures have come to resemble luxury resorts. Though endowments have grown (some to titanic proportions), operating expenses are mostly covered by a combination of Federal and state allocations, research grants, and other means, including student tuition. And to fund the students, there emerged an enabling range of legislation and institutions dedicated to lending the money to achieve the dreams. Much of this is now at an end.

Ironically, though universities have been its home since the beginning, it is beginning to become too expensive to support niche products like lesser-taught languages or arcane subjects such as archaeology. Cutbacks in these and other areas continue as disciplines are forced to justify their funding and existence through body counts of enrolled students. But even these adaptations seem unsustainable. The economic crisis of 2008 and beyond will be felt disproportionately by universities, and die back should be expected. The closure of Antioch College in 2007 and the near bankruptcy of Brandeis University in 2009 (resulting in the closing and sale of the Rose Art Museum, http://www.thedailybeast.com/blogs-and-stories/2009-01-28/did-bernie-bankrupt-brandeis) are merely examples of what will likely be a long series of crises that will diminish the number and variety of colleges and universities. Course cutbacks and faculty reductions are already following hard on hiring freezes and increased reliance on part-time teachers. In short, the higher education industry will contract and will take archaeology with it (http://www.insidehighered.com/views/2008/09/29/burke). Biblical Archaeology, which typically finds itself in classics, history, Middle East studies, or religion departments, is unlikely to be spared. The inability to retain existing positions in Biblical Archaeology has long been a problem. Senior professors, now at or approaching retirement, have failed to institutionalize their own positions and a net loss is to be expected. Arguments that Biblical Archaeology, or any archaeology, should be exempted from contraction and rationalization will be difficult to come by. Faculty members are unlikely to help themselves on this point.

Complementing the mass marketing of the universities was an ironic process of faculty specialization and political extremism. The mass economics of the university engendered an antinomian intellectual culture that reveled in obscurantism and a juvenile obsession with tweaking the middle-class sensibilities that underpinned the foundations of higher education. This alienation from its roots produced among other things a queer sort of high-brow populism and cheering for non-Western culture and anti-Western politics that veered into self-abnegation. While some archaeologists decry the politicization of the discipline, others embrace it as a tool of social liberation: anti-capitalist, anti-nationalist, and anti-capitalist (e.g. McGuire 2008). Western colonialism and nationalism are regarded as uniquely evil and irredeemable, rather than simply iterations of the human realities of power and identity, respectively. Objectivity and science are tools for false consciousness. And archaeology, particularly in the Middle East, is either a tool for domination or therapy (Scham 2008). Faced with such Manichean choices it is little wonder archaeology is being split between scientism and politics. This sees archaeology divided between adaptive strategies that explicitly align it with the hard sciences (and their funding sources) and others that stress (like a broad swath of the humanities) the discipline as a tool for correct political engagement (Joffe 2003). Such mixed and negative messages are unlikely to persuade either bourgeois consumers or education managers that Biblical Archaeology (or any archaeology) is particularly worth having around in the future. In the broader sense, however, archaeology mirrors academia's 'Two Culture' problem, the bifurcation of the sciences and humanities (Snow 1959).

The distancing of the middle class from the universities is difficult to quantify but it will be intensified by purely materialist factors, namely expense. The credit crisis of 2008 was founded on the collapse of a housing bubble; in 2009 voices are already pointing at an education credit bubble (Kristof 2009). The very concept of higher education as a sign of middle-class respectability is now threatened as never before. To compound the irony, all this comes at a time when mass and hyper-media challenge the authority of academia in new ways, and force changes in the very ways in which humans cognize information.

Changes in Media and Dissemination

Words

Biblical Archaeology has always had a strong sense of public engagement, both as a means of self-promotion and in the dissemination of quasi-religious findings. In the late 19th and first half of the 20th century a series of volumes like Albright's *The Archaeology of Palestine* (1932) or Barton's *Archaeology and the Bible* (1916) self-consciously summarized results to the lay public and attempted to chart the future of the discipline. During the discipline's heyday its chief practitioners generously presented interpretation for lay and professional audiences. Yigael Yadin mastered this with popular books on the excavations at Hazor and Masada (Yadin 1966, 1975). Dramatic advances in literacy and print technology facilitated this information explosion. Linear exposition that made reference to the shared cultural resource of the Bible, illustrated by photographs and drawings, connected Biblical Archaeology with the lay public.

But it is a sad fact that in the 21st century the book is doomed (Kachka 2008). The Western publishing industry is in crisis as economies of scale fail to stem rising costs of production and distribution and the loss of readers to digital media. For archaeology this is doubly tragic. The large and beautiful books that were the final product of archaeological projects are anachronisms. They are expensive and time-consuming to produce, narrowly distributed, and have structural limitations. Only so much data can be included, in static formats that are completely at odds with the current thrall to hyperlinked connectivity between materials, sources, and ideas, and where text and image are seamlessly integrated. Books like *Megiddo II* that were once the foundation of the discipline (and the grail of bibliophilic students) are the illuminated manuscripts of the new information age, artifacts in themselves.

But there are also decided positives. With the vast digitizing project undertaken by Google, paper itself is no longer even necessary (Darnton 2009). Digital libraries such as ETANA already make much classic literature in ancient Near Eastern studies available (http://etana.org/). Eventually most classical literature in archaeology will be available, and perhaps after that much of the grey literature. Although the economics of producing books at a profit has yet to be established, the necessity to present large data sets and narratives will remain, regardless of format. Theoretically, global access to 'all' information will make it possible for a researcher in Kinshasa to undertake research as if he or she were in Cambridge or Jerusalem, provided of course there is an adequate internet connection. And with enough hard drive space, texts can be searched and indexed to produce new connections and insights. For archaeology this is a mostly positive development. Words and images can be produced, analyzed, and disseminated more cheaply and effectively, but the aesthetic appreciation that comes from using paper is lost.

If books are dying then newspapers are near dead (Epstein 2006). Once the primary mechanism for reaching the public, newspapers are too slow and too expensive to compete with the Internet as sources of information or generators of revenue. That the American newspaper of record, the *New York Times*, has been forced to obtain a loan from a Mexican billionaire at usurious terms, after seeing its stock price fall from over $50 to less than the price of a Sunday paper, speaks to both an astonishing lack of business acumen and a larger industry crisis. Dozens of metropolitan dailies and local weeklies have closed and more, including flagships like the *Miami Herald*, are likely to go under. At the same time, polls indicate that public trust in the media has reached a new low (http://www.reuters.com/article/pressRelease/idUS160770+08-Jan-2008+PRN20080108). Similar trends exist worldwide.

For archaeology, reaching the public through newspapers as a means of public relations has always had utility. Being covered by the *New York Times'* John Noble Wilford (http://topics.nytimes.com/top/reference/timestopics/people/w/john_noble_wilford/index.html) was a sign that scholars and issues were being taken seriously by an arbiter of intellect and respectability. But the rise of television, in particular cable television programs on networks like Discovery or the History Channel which reliably reach a few million viewers, has begun to supplant the PR value of newspapers. Shows such as *Mysteries of the Bible* (1994–98), *The Naked Archaeologist* (2005–present), and *Digging for the Truth* (2005–present) have reliably emphasized the adventurousness of archaeology and the unveiling of mysteries. As such they complement the popular figures of Indiana Jones and Lara Croft, so hated by professional archaeologists but so loved by the public eager to 'participate' vicariously in a fundamentally alien realm of experience (Holtof 2006).

As with *Biblical Archaeology Review*, and the larger philanthropic and PR role of the National Geographic Society, the agenda-setting function of these venues must be questioned (Joffe 2006b). Shaping projects and presenting finds in ways that suit funders may not be new, but the deliberate conflation of information and entertainment is. Even more dramatic are changes in the visual and indeed cognitive aspects of archaeology.

Archaeological Cognitions

How archaeology is cognized by the lay public and professionals thanks to technology is a relatively new area of inquiry. From a social perspective, cable TV and above all the Internet have dramatically shifted authority away from academics to anyone with the ability to create a website. The loss of authority has been so alarming that academics have been forced to mount defenses of their own roles (e.g. Scham 2006) in the face of a plethora of sites that claim to present the hidden truths and unseen connections on pyramids, goddesses, the Nazi base on the moon, and everything in between. Mounting a spirited defense of archaeology's intellectual, professional, and social authority (and hierarchy generally) is a good thing (Joffe 2008) but is completely out of character for academic disciplines that have developed deep tendencies toward apology as part of their larger therapeutic orientations. It may also be too little too late. Authority lost is not easily regained simply by resort to credentialism, particularly when accompanied by condescension. The growing role of Wikipedia as a credible source, whose authority is derived from the least common denominator of mass participation, is alarming.

The inability of the Internet create to a common, shared culture has intensified the social partitioning ignited by the breakdown of monolithic mass media such as newspapers and television networks. There are too many websites directed at narrow audiences for there to be a common fund of shared knowledge or common conversation. Even in as tiny a domain as Biblical Archaeology there are more sites that present tendentious religious or political interpretations than there are academic ones (e.g. http://www.baseinstitute.org/). How are lay people to distinguish what is 'reliable' from what is not? And by what authority do academics arrogate to themselves the right to make such determinations? The exemptions academics granted themselves under the doctrine of antinomianism no longer pertain. Sadly, the incentives for public engagement (as opposed to purely self-serving public relations) have never been high in academia. How this aspect will be realized in an age of shrinking budgets and positions is entirely unclear. A successful book like *The Bible Unearthed* (Finkelstein and Silberman 2001) could not have been produced by junior faculty, busily chasing after grants and other forms of professional validation. At the same time, information overload overwhelms consumers with too many choices and consumes too much worker time and energy (BASEX 2007).

But the deepest level of change is cognition. The hyperlinked structure of knowledge of the Internet (questions of authority notwithstanding) has supplanted the linearity of previous ages (Guertin 2004)). The structure provided by narratives presented in books with chapters arranged one after the other, as the author intended, is being replaced with ad hoc structures created by the reader on the fly, following links or Googling items of interest. Statements of fact and opinion, evidence and proofs, arguments, are now mashed-up, with the reader as the author of the 'post-narrative'.

The ability to incorporate images of all sorts is of course a major advantage of computer-based sources. The ability to search records, and now text and image, in search of new connections, is an important leap forward. New patterns will be recognized as larger data sets are manipulated. Archaeology has also long pioneered visualization and multimedia approaches to representing data, both professionally and for the lay public. But here, as in many areas, images have begun to supplant words (e.g. http://www.archatlas.dept.shef.ac.uk/Home.php), and scholars have begun to grasp for means to configure their products for effective pedagogy and to retain authorial structure, intent, and authority (e.g. Kensek, Swartz Dodd, and Cipolla 2004). Whether this will be successful remains to be seen, particularly for audiences accustomed to controlling game play on consoles and computers. But fundamentally, experiencing the image via screens is replacing the effort required to interpret words and arguments with sensations. Authorial intent is reduced still further. The resulting cognitive changes from all this are unclear. Observationally it appears that a profound generational shift is underway and that shortened attention spans are one manifestation, along with the unwillingness and inability to follow complex arguments. If the results of the Powerpoint revolution are any indication, the results will be more superficiality, a mistaken and implied sense of causality, and an undeserved sense of mastery among both those who teach and are taught with such tools (Tufte 2003). Biblical Archaeology will surely survive, but it will be understood in new ways by brains that are wired quite differently.

Conclusions

Biblical Archaeology stands in an odd place between normal science and exceptionalism. Organizationally and thematically it is almost exactly like every other form of archaeology found in the Mediterranean, Europe, or the Americas. While the antiquated terminology of the Three Age System endures, rather than equally misleading developmental terms used in the New World, the same types of questions are asked, data gathered and analyzed, and financial and other challenges faced. Biblical Archaeology offers a particularly wide range of physical and depositional environments, from Mediterranean to hyperarid and underwater to deserts, which make it a valuable training ground for students and a challenging environment for scholars. Data density has been discussed earlier; the necessity to engage with earlier research is, again, a valuable exercise and training ground.

Biblical Archaeology also faces distinct intellectual challenges. One is to tack between artifact and text to create 'historical' archaeology (Joffe 2002). The second is to tack between 'prehistory' and 'history' to understand contexts and create truly *longue durée* reconstructions (Joffe 2003). Above all, there is the need to engage with texts, and one, the Greatest Text Ever Written, above all. A more challenging archaeological enterprise can hardly be imagined. And yet the field remains marginal. Why?

For some three decades Biblical Archaeology has strived to be accepted as another branch of world archaeology. This has failed. Efforts assertively to link the field with anthropology have largely floundered, as have those intended to reunite the Southern Levant with the rest of that region and with Western Asia as a whole. The reasons have more to do with the clash of parochialisms, egos, and unrealistic expectations than they do with materials and methods. With respect to Western Asia, the offshoots reject the parent for fear of being smothered. The Bible, and religion as a whole, are seemingly insurmountable obstacles for regional non-Biblical archaeologists. Interactions are rare except for prehistorians and perhaps 'historical archaeologists' addressing the past few hundred years (Baram 2002). For the remainder of world archaeology, many of the prejudices of secular intellectuals appear to be at work. While collegial relations may be quite warm, and individual research prized, Biblical Archaeology is regarded as theology. Changing the name of the enterprise has not helped.

So be it. Biblical Archaeology's own shortcomings are well known and many have been recited above. Those of archaeology as a whole are less frequently analyzed. But part of the pernicious legacy of the 1960s was the notion that 'archaeology is anthropology'. Nothing could have been more wrong and misleading. Archaeology was, is, and will always be archaeology, a domain that has no theory of its own but which is uniquely interdisciplinary (Joffe 2003). The limitations of the former approach in the New World have been increasingly apparent. The split between politics and scientism has been noted above. With that came distancing from the public, despite the growth of 'public archaeology', and the discipline is as dependent on highway projects, theme parks, and the occasional gold-encrusted tomb as Old World archaeology. Public engagement dropped, the discipline bifurcated into academic and service components, funding has peaked, and many fear its survival is threatened. Even professionals are rejecting preexisting terms and calling for engagement with bourgeois consumers in order to ensure disciplinary survival (Moore 2006b).

A few tentative conclusions may be offered with respect to the present and future of Biblical Archaeology.

1. The practice of Biblical Archaeology is that of normal science, with professional organization and standards. While there may not be a full self-image as a 'science', practice is 'scientific' and certainly multidisciplinary. In narrative terms the structure is linear and historical, features found, for example, in European archaeology. But at the center there remains the Bible and the inevitability of engaging with the question of the transcendent. What is normal for Biblical Archaeology is therefore quite exceptional for all others.

2. As is the case globally, the practical constraints for doing any archaeology at all are increasing in the 'Biblical' world, in terms of landscape destruction, funding problems, the emphasis on salvage rather than research, public disinterest, and religious fundamentalism. These are now normal factors everywhere.

3. Public expectations for religiously oriented discoveries are still high, as shown by the continued popularity of *BAR*, cable TV shows, and of course tourism. In the sense that archaeo-tourism and other forms of consumption are the norm for globalizing middle classes, these developments are not unusual. But the attraction to Biblical Archaeology remains intense. The potential contribution of Biblical Archaeology to individual identity-formation has unique characteristics in that the religious sensibilities informed are not modern constructs but rather ancient ones.

4. The religion problem, including fundamentalisms among Christians, Muslims, Jews, and atheists, threaten the enterprise in different ways ranging from disinterest to active attacks. While religious attempts to lower education standards and political manipulations are quite normal, the mix of features facing Biblical Archaeology is greater than ever before and must be considered exceptional. In cost–benefit terms, however, it seems unlikely that any Middle Eastern state would forsake the tourist revenue stream for the sake of strict ideology. Rationalism, however, has never been the region's strong point. Biblical and other archaeologies will continue to navigate uneasily in these waters and to the dissatisfaction of most.

5. Biblical Archaeology must continue to adapt to the changing political, research, funding, physical, and social environments, which means continued interdisciplinary and traditional text-oriented training plus training on how to be funding and media savvy. These are hardly new suggestions but the latter are rarely incorporated into high-brow graduate training.

6. Finally, Biblical Archaeology has always stood in a dialectic with religion. The situation is not entirely unique; witness the encounters between British archaeologists and 'Druids' or more pointedly, between Southwest U.S. archaeologists and Native Americans. There the power relationship has shifted decisively and the former are marginalized thanks to post-colonial guilt and fear of losing access. Similar fears constrain the study of Islam, but Judaism and Christianity are fair game. Forms of rational engagement with religion need to be vigorously defended and expanded worldwide, although with a tone that is not hostile or negative. If Biblical Archaeology's rationale was once defending the faith, the opposite cannot be the case now. But the Bible remains Biblical Archaeology's trump card for survival.

It seems Sisyphan, but defending the enterprise's rationale beyond the defense, illumination, or negation of the faith needs to be continually asserted. This was of course the intent behind rebranding the field as Syro-Palestinian Archaeology (Dever 1972). How much it was actually attempted, in the face of both internal and external expectations, and the general need for the discipline to market itself, is debatable. The attraction of 'Biblical' topics for researcher and the public continues to this day, and here Biblical Archaeology has nothing to be ashamed of. Perhaps by expanding the appreciation of the *method* Biblical Archaeology can go beyond simply pandering to religious or anti-religious sensibilities. The Bible is a unique way to raise general appreciation of what archaeology does, as well as of how difficult and tentative it is. Whether or not people's minds will be changed is unknown, but due diligence is in order.

Finally, there is a sense of modesty. Biblical Archaeology is called upon to defend and attack religion, and to create or bridge divides between peoples, Surely this is asking too much. Trying to work like a science, having an honest view of the potential and the limits of the discipline, are more healthy and successful means for survival.

Biblical Archaeology is not well endowed with beautiful things; the architecture, small finds, and other material culture are thin and mediocre by comparison with surrounding cultures. But it ultimately it is exceptional because it forces archaeologists to look deeply at trivial things in order to address both common archaeological questions and far larger ones, especially the origins of Great Traditions and the idea of transcendence. Having the opportunity to participate in the enterprise, to the envy of almost everyone, is something for which practitioners should be grateful.

References

Albright, W.F. (1932) *The Archaeology of Palestine and the Bible* (New York: Fleming H. Revell).

Al Rawashdeh, S., and B. Saleh (2006) Satellite Monitoring of Urban Spatial Growth in the Amman Area, Jordan. *Journal of Urban Planning and Development* 132: 211-16.

Armaly, F., with Marc-André Haldimann, J. Khoudary, J.-B. Humbert, and M. Sadeq (2007) Crossroads and Contexts: Interviews on Archaeology in Gaza. *Journal of Palestine Studies* 37/1: 43.

Banning, E.B. (2004) *Archaeological Survey* (New York: Springer).

Baram, U. (2002) The Development of Historical Archaeology in Israel: An Overview and Prospects. *Historical Archaeology* 36/4: 12-29.

—(2007) Heritage, Tourism, and Archaeology in Israel. In Kohl, Kozelsky, and Ben-Yehuda 2007: 299-325.

Baram, U., and Y. Rowan (2004) Archaeology after Nationalism: Globalization and the Consumption of the Past. In *Marketing Heritage: Archaeology and the Consumption of the Past*, edited by Yorke M. Rowan and Uzi Baram (Walnut Creek, CA: Altamira): 3-24.

Barton, G.A. (1916) *Archaeology and the Bible* (Philadelphia: American Sunday-School Union).

BASEX, Inc. (2007) *Information Overload: We Have Met the Enemy and He is Us* (New York).

Ben-Shammai, H. (1988) Jew-Hatred in the Islamic Tradition and Qur'anic Exegesis. In *Antisemitism through the Ages*, edited by S. Almog (Oxford: Pergamon): 161-69.

Biger, G. (1994) *An Empire in the Holy Land: Historical Geography of the British Administration in Palestine, 1917–1929* (Jerusalem: Magnes Press).

Braun, E. (1992) Objectivity and Salvage Excavation Policy in Mandate Palestine and the State of Israel: An Appraisal of its Effects on Understanding the Archaeological Record. In *The Limitations of Archaeological Knowledge*, edited by T. Shay and J. Clottes (Liège: Edition de Recherche Archeologique de la Université de Liège): 29-38.

Breasted, C. (1977) *Pioneer to the Past: The Story of James Henry Breasted, Archaeologist* (Chicago: University of Chicago Press).

Brink, E.C.M. van den, R. Gophna, and I. Carmi (2005) *Shoham (North): Late Chalcolithic Burial Caves in the Lod Valley, Israel* (Jerusalem: Israel Antiquities Authority).

Chatelard, G. (2005) Desert Tourism as a Substitute for Pastoralism? Tuareg in Algeria and Bedouin in Jordan. In *Nomadic Societies in the Middle East and North Africa: Entering the 21st Century*, edited by D. Chatty (Leiden: Brill): 710-36.

Cohen, S.B. (2007) Jewish Geopolitics: Nationalism and the Ties between the State and the Land. *National Identities* 9: 27-34.

Darnton, R. (2009) Google and the Future of the Book. *New York Review of Books* 56 (February 12, 2009). Online: http://www.nybooks.com/articles/22281.

Della Pergola, S., U. Rebhun, and Mark Tolts (2005) Contemporary Jewish Diaspora in Global Context: Human Development Correlates of Population Trends. *Israel Studies* 10/1: 61-95.

Dessel, J.P., and A.H. Joffe (2000) Alternative Approaches to Early Bronze Age Pottery. In *Ceramics and Change in the Early Bronze Age of the Southern Levant*, edited by G. Philip and D. Baird (Sheffield: Sheffield Academic Press): 31-58.

Dever, W.G. (1972) 'Biblical Archaeology'—or the 'Archaeology of Syria-Palestine'? *Christian News from Israel* 22: 21-22.

Dodd, L.S. (2007) Heritage Formulation in Overtly Politicized Environments: A Commentary. *Archaeologies* 3: 4-15.

El-Eini, R. (2005) *Mandated Landscape: British Imperial Rule in Palestine, 1929–1948* (London: Routledge).

Epstein, J. (2006) Are Newspapers Doomed? *Commentary* 121/1: 46-51.

Fallows, J. (1985) The Case against Credentialism. *Atlantic Monthly* (1 December 1985). http://jamesfallows.theatlantic.com/archives/1985/12/the_case_against_credentialism.php.

Feige, M. (2007) Recovering Authenticity, West-Bank Settlers and the Second Stage of National Archaeology. In Kohl, Kozelsky, and Ben-Yehuda 2007: 277-98.

Finkelstein, I., and N. Silberman (2001) *The Bible Unearthed: Archaeology's New Vision of Ancient Israel and the Origin of Its Sacred Texts* (New York: Free Press).

Finkelstein, I., and D. Ussishkin (eds.) (2006) *Megiddo IV: The 1998–2002 Seasons* (Tel Aviv: Emery and Claire Yass Publications in Archaeology, Institute of Archaeology, Tel Aviv University).

Frejka, T., and C.F. Westoff (2006) *Religion, Religiousness and Fertility in the U.S. and in Europe* (Working Paper 2006-013; Rostock, Max Planck Institute for Demographic Research).

Frisch, H. (2002) Fuzzy Nationalism: The Case of Jordan. *Nationalism and Ethnic Politics* 8/4: 86-103.

Geiger, R.L. (1993) *American Research Universities since World War II* (New York: Oxford University Press).

Glock, A.E. (1994) Archaeology as Cultural Survival: the Future of the Palestinian Past. *Journal of Palestine Studies* 23: 70-85.

Goodwin, G.M. (1998) A New Jewish Elite: Curators, Directors, and Benefactors of American Art Museums. *Modern Judaism* 18/1: 47-79, 119-52.

Guertin, C. (2004) Handholding, Remixing, and the Instant Replay: New Narratives. In *Postnarrative World: A Companion to Digital Humanities*, edited by S. Schreibman, R. Siemens, and J. Unsworth. Oxford: Blackwell, 2004. http://www.digitalhumanities.org/companion/view?docId=blackwell/9781405148641/9781405148641.xml&chunk.id=ss1-5-6&toc.depth=1&toc.id=ss1-5-6&brand=9781405148641brand

Hallote, R.S. (2009) Who Pays for Excavations? Agendas in the Funding of 'Biblical' Archaeology. *BAR* 35/2: 22, 66.

Hallote, R.S., and A.H. Joffe (2002) The Politics of Israeli Archaeology: 'Nationalism' and 'Science' in the Second Republic. *Israel Studies* 7: 84-116.

Hamilton, R.W. (1935) Excavations at Tell Abu-Hawam. *Quarterly of the Department of Antiquities of Palestine* 4: 1-69.

Holtof, C. (2006) Experiencing Archaeology in the Dream Society. In *Images, Representations and Heritage: Moving Beyond Modern Approaches to Archaeology*, edited by Ian Russell (New York: Springer): 161-76.

Israeli–Palestinian Archaeology Working Group (2007) *Israeli–Palestinian Archaeology Working Group Agreement* (Los Angeles: Cotsen Institute of Archaeology, University of Southern California).

Jenkins, P. (2007) *God's Continent: Christianity, Islam, and Europe's Religious Crisis* (New York: Oxford University Press).

—(2008) *The Next Christendom: The Coming of Global Christianity* (New York: Oxford University Press).

Joffe, A.H. (2002). The Rise of Secondary States in the Iron Age Levant. *Journal of the Economic and Social History of the Orient* 45/4: 425-67.

—(2003) Identity/Crisis. *Archaeological Dialogues* 10/1: 77-95.

—(2006a) American Jews between Best and Worst of Times. *Covenant, A Global Jewish Magazine* 1/1. Online: http://www.covenant.idc.ac.il/en/vol1/issue1/joffe.html.

—(2006b). Archaeology and the Media. *Society* 4s/6: 71-76.

—(2008) Review of Ø. LaBianca and S.A. Scham (eds.), *Connectivity in Antiquity, Globalization as Long-Term Historical Process. BASOR* 351: 99-102.

—(forthcoming a) Liberalism, Memory, and the Nation-State. In *Proceedings of the Conference 'History and Memory after the Holocaust'*, edited by E. Goodman-Thau (Berlin: Konrad Adenauer Stiftung and Hermann-Cohen-Akademie).

—(forthcoming b) The Restoration of Antiquities and the Principle of Non-Refoulment.

Kachka, B. (2008) The End. *New York Magazine* (September 14, 2008). Online: http://nymag.com/news/media/50279/.

Kensek, K.M., L. Swartz Dodd, and N. Cipolla (2004) Fantastic Reconstructions or Reconstructions of the Fantastic? Tracking and Presenting Ambiguity, Alternatives, and Documentation in Virtual Worlds. *Automation in Construction* 13: 175-86.

Kersel, M. (2008) The Trade in Palestinian Antiquities. *Jerusalem Quarterly* 33: 21-38.

Khalidi, R. (1997) *Palestinian Identity: The Construction of Modern National Consciousness* (New York: Columbia University Press).

Killebrew, A.E. (2006) Archaeologically Based Heritage Formulation in Overtly Politicised Environments. *Archaeologies* 2: 1-3.

Killebrew, A.E., S.A. Scham, H. Abu-Uqsa, W. Atrash, R. Be'eri, R. Hachlili, H. Halabi Abu Yusef, O. Nagar-Hillman, V. Raz-Romeo, and M. Weinstein-Evron (2006) From Dialogue to Polylogue: Exploring the Israeli and Palestinian Past in the Present. *Archaeologies* 2: 7-21.

Kletter, R., and A. De Groot (2001). Excavating to Excess? Implications of the Last Decade of Archaeology in Israel. *Journal of Mediterranean Archaeology* 14/1: 76-85.

Kohl, P.L., M. Kozelsky, and N. Ben-Yehuda (eds.) (2007) *Selective Remembrances: Archaeology in the Construction, Commemoration, and Consecration of National Pasts* (Chicago: University of Chicago Press).

Kohler, H.-P., Francesco C. Billari, and José A. Ortega (2006) Low Fertility in Europe: Causes, Implications and Policy Options. In *The Baby Bust: Who Will do the Work? Who Will Pay the Taxes?*, edited by F.R. Harris (Lanham, MD, Rowman & Littlefield): 48-109.

Kristof, K. (2009) The Great College Hoax. *Forbes* (2 February). Online: http://www.forbes.com/forbes/2009/0202/060.html.

Luke, H., and E. Keith-Roach (1930) *The Handbook of Palestine and Trans-Jordan* (London: Macmillan & Co.).

Maddy-Weitzman, B. (2003) *Palestinian and Israeli Intellectuals in the Shadow of Oslo and Intifadat al-Aqsa* (Tel Aviv: Tel Aviv University, The Tami Steinmetz Center for Peace Research).

Maissy-Noy, R. (2006) Palestinian Historiography in Relation to the Territory of Palestine. *Middle Eastern Studies* 42: 889-905.

McGuire, R. (2008) *Archaeology as Political Action* (Berkeley: University of California Press).

Milevski, I. (2002) A New Fertility Figurine and New Animal Motifs from the Chalcolithic in the Southern Levant: Finds from Cave K-1 at Quleh, Israel. *Paléorient* 28: 135-44.

Mishal, S., and A. Sela (2006) *The Palestinian Hamas: Vision, Violence, and Coexistence* (New York: Columbia University Press).

Moore, L.E. (2006a) CRM: Beyond its Peak. *SAA Archaeological Record* 6/1: 30-33.

—(2006b) Going Public: Customization and American Archaeology. *SAA Archaeological Record* 6/3: 16-19.

Murakami, M. (1998) Alternative Strategies in the Inter-state Regional Development of the Jordan Rift Valley. In *Central Eurasian Water Crisis: Caspian, Aral, and Dead Seas*, edited by I. Kobori and M.H. Glantz (Tokyo: United Nations University Press): 154-80.

Nigro, L., and H. Taha (eds.) (2006) *Tell es-Sultan/Jericho in the Context of the Jordan Valley, Site Management, Conservation and Sustainable Development. Proceedings of the International Workshop Held in Ariha 7th–11th February 2005 by the Palestinian Department of Antiquities and Cultural Heritage - Ministry of Tourism and Antiquities, UNESCO Office - Ramallah* (Rome: 'La Sapienza' University).

Palumbo, G., et al. (1994) *JADIS, the Jordan Antiquities Ddatabase and Information System: A Summary of the Data* (Amman, Jordan: Department of Antiquities of Jordan, American Center of Oriental Research).

Reiter, Y. (2008) *Jerusalem and its Role in Islamic Solidarity* (New York: Palgrave Macmillan).

Sasson, T., and S. Kelner (2008) From Shrine to Forum: Masada and the Politics of Jewish Extremism. *Israel Studies* 13: 146-63.

Sauders, R. (2008) Between Paralysis and Practice: Theorizing the Political Liminality of Palestinian Cultural Heritage. *Archaeologies* 4: 471-94.

Scham, S.A. (2006) Perceptions of Antiquity and the Formation of Modern Resistance Identities. In *Connectivity in Antiquity: Globalization as Long-Term Historical Process*, edited by Ø. LaBianca and S.A. Scham (London: Equinox): 132-38.

—(2008) Disinheriting Heritage: Explorations in the Contentious History of Archaeology in the Middle East. In *Archaeology and the Post-Colonial Critique*, edited by M. Liebman and U. Rizvi (Lanham, MD: Rowman & Littlefield): 165-76.

Scham, S.A., and A. Yahya (2003) Heritage and Reconciliation. *Journal of Social Archaeology* 3/3: 399-416.

Shilhav, Y. (2007) Jewish Territoriality between Land and State. *National Identities* 9: 1-25.

Snow, C.P. (1959) *The Two Cultures and the Scientific Revolution* (Cambridge: Cambridge University Press).

Suisman, D.R., S. Simon, G. Robinson, C.R. Anthony, and M. Schoenbaum (2005) *The Arc: A Formal Structure for a Palestinian State* (Santa Monica: Rand Corporation).

Tengberg, M.S., L. Naggiar-Moliner, V. Boulez, D. Faltings, M. Sadek, and P. de Miroschedji (2001) Les fouilles de Tell es-Sakan (Gaza) : nouvelles données sur les contacts égyptocananéens aux IVe–IIIe millénaires. *Paléorient* 27/2: 75-104.

Tobin, G.A. (2001) *The Transition of Communal Values and Behavior in Jewish Philanthropy* (San Francisco: Institute for Jewish & Community Research).

Tufte, E.R. (2003) *The Cognitive Style of PowerPoint* (Cheshire, CT: Graphics Press).

United States Census Bureau (2002) *The Big Payoff: Educational Attainment and Synthetic Estimates of Work-Life Earnings* (Economics and Statistics Administration).

Vajda, G. (1937) Juifs et Musulmans selon le hadit. *Journal Asiatique* 229: 57-129.

Yadin, Y. (1966) *Masada: Herod's Fortress and the Zealot's Last Stand* (New York: Random House).

—(1975) *Hazor, the Rediscovery of a Great Citadel of the Bible* (London: Weidenfeld & Nicolson).

Yannai, E., and D.T. Ariel (2006) **En Esur (*Ein Asawir) I: Excavations at a Protohistoric Site in the Coastal Plain of Israel* (Jerusalem: Israel Antiquities Authority).

Zevit, Z. (2004) The Biblical Archaeology versus Syro-Palestinian Archaeology Debate in its American Institutional and Intellectual Contexts. In *The Future of Biblical Archaeology: Reassessing Methodologies and Assumptions*, edited by J.K. Hoffmeier and A. Millard (Grand Rapids: Eerdmans): 3-19.

Zisser, E. (2003) The Mediterranean Idea in Syria and Lebanon: Between Territorial Nationalism and Pan-Arabism. *Mediterranean Historical Review* 18: 76-90.

22 Does 'Biblical Archaeology' Have a Future?

William G. Dever

Abstract

There is no simple answer to the question 'What is the future of Biblical Archaeology?' In this paper, a middle course between the radical skepticism that swept Biblical studies in the 1980s and Fundamentalism is sought to provide a way into the future. This perspective is made from one who has been deeply involved for nearly 50 years in trying to deal with the problem of relating ancient texts, especially the Hebrew Bible, to the archaeological record of the southern Levant.

Introduction

At the very moment we have come together to celebrate a remarkable event—the founding of a new, permanently endowed chair devoted to 'Biblical Archaeology'—is it appropriate to ask whether the whole enterprise has a *future*? I think that it is appropriate and indeed necessary, because, as I shall show, we stand today at a historical crossroads.

I. What is 'Biblical Archaeology?'

Let me begin with some definitions. More than 30 years ago, I began (with others) to argue for the separation of what was then popularly called 'Biblical Archaeology' from biblical studies generally, and theological studies in particular. Although novel and controversial at the time, the agenda was to establish our branch of archaeology as an independent, professional, 'secular' discipline, with its own aims and methods. The name we Young Turks (imagine!) preferred—'Syro-Palestinian' archaeology—was actually coined by Albright back in the 1920s, but it soon became a battle-cry. We won that battle (Dever 1974, 1985, 1992, 2000).

Today it is universally acknowledged that old-fashioned 'prove the Bible' archaeology is dead, and except for a few diehard Fundamentalists no one mourns its passing. I am often accused of killing Biblical Archaeology. I'm flattered; but I simply observed its death throes and was among the first to write its obituary (cf. Moorey 1991; Levy 2000; Davis 2003; Hoffmeier and Millard 2004).

Yet by the 1990s, I myself was beginning to ask whether a *new* style of 'Biblical Archaeology' might be possible, and desirable (Dever 1993). And today, both American and Israeli archaeologists (not to mention the public and the media) do use the term, albeit inconsistently and casually, mostly as a kind of 'short-hand' for what we all recognize to be the larger, parent discipline. Meanwhile, for the latter, the term 'Palestinian' has become so politicized that many of us have abandoned it for 'the archaeology of the Southern Levant', or, better, simply 'the archaeology of Israel', 'Jordan', 'the West Bank', etc. (Dever 2003a).

What I want to emphasize here is that, beyond the terminological confusion, there is a widespread consensus today that 'Biblical Archaeology' is *not* a discipline itself (certainly not a substitute for the larger discipline), but a complex, fascinating inquiry between *two* disciplines—archaeology and biblical studies—a *dialogue* at the intersection of text and artifact. It may be silly or serious; amateur or professional; but it matters, because fundamental issues of history, and faith, and self-identity are at stake. Thus 'Biblical Archaeology', properly defined, *ought* to have a future.

II. The Larger Discipline of Archaeology in Israel, Jordan, and the West Bank

In the following I want us to keep in mind that 'Biblical Archaeology' is a very small part of the larger discipline of archaeology in Israel and Jordan. At least 75 percent of fieldwork, research, and publication has nothing whatsoever to do with the Bible, although it is nonetheless important. Here I am being deliberately selective.

Call it what you will, the health of the parent discipline of archaeology is fundamental to the hoped-for dialogue. Yet it is hardly a monolithic enterprise. For purposes of analysis, let us look first at the Middle East, keeping in mind that here I am focusing almost exclusively on American work (see generally King 1983; Clark and Matthews 2003).

Israel

Israel is certainly dominant, and not just because we in the West think of it as the 'Holy Land' (i.e. ours). On the bright side, archaeology in Israel appears to have flourished in the last 30 years, as I can state as a participant and close observer. Standards in fieldwork have improved exponentially. The best digs are as good as those anywhere, and the embarrassing projects that some of us remember are no longer tolerated. There are also more projects in the field than ever, of every size, variety, and focus. There are five thriving Institutes of Archaeology, all with graduate programs, in Jerusalem, Tel Aviv, Ramat Gan, Haifa, and Beersheba. The archaeological division of the Israel Museum has its own large interdisciplinary professional staff, excellent laboratories, and modern galleries that rank it among the world's great museums. The old Department of Antiquities has morphed into a much more professional and ambitious 'Israel Antiquities Authority'. Despite the opposition of many, it has raised standards, for instance, in required conservation of sites. A new, world-class national storage and research center has been opened by the Authority at Beth-shemesh. Younger Israeli archaeologists are much more sophisticated than their venerable teachers, in their wide reading of the literature, their use of socio-anthropological theory typical of archaeology elsewhere, and their openness to cross-cultural comparisons. One simply did not see these things a generation ago. (And in the wings, unheard of as yet by most outsiders, there is a superb third generation of even younger and better Israeli archaeologists.)[1]

Israeli archaeologists, long accused of not publishing, are pouring out a flood of both analytical research papers and final report volumes. There are numerous journals and serials of the Authority and the universities, nearly all in English, which are now the leading publications. The most recent event is the publication of five lavish volumes of the excavations at Lachish by David Ussishkin and

---

1.   There is no comprehensive, up-to-date history and critique of Israeli archaeology. But see provisionally Bar-Yosef and Mazar 1982; Stern 1987; Bunimovitz 1995; Dever 1989. For the impact of Israeli archaeology on the Israeli ethos, see the perceptive essays of Elon 1997; Shavit 1997.

others, which I have hailed as a landmark (Dever 2005a). The Israelis now vastly outpace us in publication, largely because they have the institutional support that we Americans lack (below).

In all this the Israelis have grown in professionalism, so that theirs is *per capita* (Israel is a small country) arguably one of the most impressive national archaeological schools in the world, with unparalleled popular support. But there are danger signs.

First, budgets for both the Antiquities Authority and the universities have been slashed. Recently the Authority put one third of its employees on part-time non-benefit status, and let some of them go permanently. The university Institutes have suffered 10 percent cuts annually for several years. My Israeli colleagues tell me privately that without direct American subsidies to the Institutes, as well as the profits from American student volunteer programs in the Summer, Israeli archaeology could not survive. And now, with fewer and fewer American universities (and parents) willing to insure students and send them to Israel, income is dwindling further. The fact is that in today's beleaguered Israel, archaeology is simply not a high priority for the government, or all that attractive to foreign institutes.

The Israel Antiquities Authority has been compromised by rebellion within its ranks, as well as by budgets cuts. I have already mentioned the scarcity of foreign student volunteers and institutional commitment, which makes it difficult to launch new field projects. Israel continues to tolerate the black market in antiquities and to license dealers, and it does little to stop tomb robbing in the occupied territories. The latest is the scandal of fakes manufactured and traded by Israelis like Oded Golan, who still has not been convicted and sentenced. Some suggest that the 'James ossuary' and the Temple pomegranate are just the tip of the iceberg.[2]

Perhaps the most serious problem of Israeli archaeology is the inability to place younger archaeologists in secure academic positions, rather than what are perceived to be dead-end jobs in the Antiquities Authority. I can name half a dozen superb young Israeli archaeologists with Ph.D.s who have virtually disappeared in the last decade. Particularly disturbing is the fact that there are so few Israeli women who are well placed, none in prominent positions, despite some impressive talent. (Where are today's equivalents of Ruth Amiran or Trude Dothan?)

Finally, I note with some hesitation the polarization of the Israeli archaeological community. Small and somewhat ingrown, this community is becoming characterized by intense rivalries, and worse still by the 'cult of personality' swirling around Israel Finkelstein. He may have achieved celebrity status abroad, but he is not the 'centrist' he claims to be; and in the minds of many of his colleagues he has given Israeli archaeology a bad name, as though everything is about controversy.[3] (It is not.) Here there lurks the danger of politicizing archaeology in the service of radical new movements like 'Post-Zionism', although to their credit Israelis thus far have managed to avoid the alignment of archaeology and nationalism. Staying neutral has proven to be a particular challenge, since the Orthodox political parties declared open war on archaeology and archaeologists two decades ago. They have not prevailed, but neither have they given up. If they had their way, all archaeological work in Israel would be forbidden.

Jordan

I am less familiar with archaeology in Jordan, although I often visit digs there and know most of the Jordanian archaeologists personally. One thing stands out: the expanding number of field projects,

---

2.   For exposes on the Israeli Antiquities Authority, as well as the issue of forgeries (although somewhat one-sided), see Shanks 2005.

3.   Cf. the exchanges between Finkelstein and the much more mainstream Mazar in Finkelstein 1995, 1998, 2005; and Mazar 1997, 2005. In the 2005 volume (Levy and Higham 2005) note the assessment of the editors.

both Jordanian and American, some of them large and long-running (like the nearly 40-year old 'Madeba Plains Project'). Thirty years ago, Jordan was seen as the 'hinterland', largely unknown and thought to be relatively unimportant. There were few digs, especially American; publications were scant; and there was no 'national school'.[4]

All that has changed dramatically. There are now dozens of excavations, many of them Jordanian, and even more foreign excavations supported by the Department of Antiquities. The Department follows the lines of the old efficient British department, but with more modern standards. Proof of its enlightened policies under the direction of its cosmopolitan Director, Dr. Ghazi Bisheh, is that the Department issued an excavation permit to Tom Levy, a Jewish scholar with a long history of involvement in Israel—a first.[5] (I doubt that Israel would follow suit.) Despite Jordan's precarious political situation, plus the fact that several of its archaeologists are Palestinians, I see few signs that archaeology there is being politicized or perverted by nationalism—except where younger archaeologists have been subverted by European 'minimalism'.[6]

The Jordanian universities do not yet offer their own graduate degrees in archaeology; but there are more than a dozen Jordanians with Ph.D.s from abroad, including degrees from some of the world's finest universities. At one time, women were poorly represented, if at all, but today there is a growing group of women in the Department and on dig staff, some with graduate degrees. Every two years the Department of Antiquities sponsors an impressive international symposium somewhere abroad, under Crown sponsorship, with the papers published in a series of lavish volumes. Prince Hasan of the royal family is an enthusiastic patron of archaeology in Jordan, and I have met him visiting digs there. He is also a frequent visitor at our flourishing school there, founded in 1968, the 'American Center for Oriental Research'. Jordan still doesn't have a modern archaeological museum (only the old British one); but plans for one are underway. In sum, archaeology in Jordan understandably lags somewhat behind its progress in Israel, but it is making extraordinary strides. Today we know probably ten times what we knew 30 years ago about the history and archaeology of Jordan. It is no longer the neglected 'other half of the Holy Land', but a fascinating archaeological culture-area in its own right.

The West Bank

We used to speak of 'Palestinian' archaeology, but now there are *real* Palestinians in the field, native Arab archaeologists working with the 'Palestine Authority', under its own Department of Antiquities, led by Dr. Hamdan Taha. There are departments of archaeology at several Palestinian universities, like Al-Quds University in Jerusalem, where one faculty member (Dr. Nuri al-Din) holds a doctorate from the Sorbonne. At Bir Zeit University, Professor Hamed Salim teaches archaeology, having done his M.A. with me at the University of Arizona before advancing to his Ph.D., almost completed. Several young Palestinian archaeologists are collaborating with foreign excavators, as with the Italians at Jericho, or the French in the Gaza Strip.

---

4.   There is no history of Jordanian archaeology, but the essays in Stager, Green, and Coogan 2000 will give some idea of its scope more recently.

5.   See, most recently, Levy's reports in Levy *et al.* 2005, with references and more recently Levy *et al.* 2008 and Levy 2009.

6.   Larry Herr informs me that some American Christian archaeologists, despite a long and exemplary record of dispassionate work in Jordan, have now come under suspicion from a few younger Jordanian archaeologists who have bought into Whitelam's assertion that there was no 'ancient Israel' (1996), or have been influenced by Thompson's 'myth of Israel' (1999). Both scholars have facilitated Arabic translations of their heavily ideological books. And Thompson has now (2003) published papers from an international symposium he sponsored in Amman on the archaeology and history of Jerusalem—to which no Israeli or American archaeologist was invited. These are ominous signs. For a sustained critique of the biblical 'minimalists', see Dever 2001. See also n. 7 below.

Yet there are formidable obstacles. The Palestinian Authority is in such dire straits, so unstable, that archaeology is nearly at the bottom of the list of priorities. There are not even enough resources for basic conservation of sites. And, sad to say, some of the Palestinian archaeologists are not cosmopolitan enough to rise above politics and nationalist rhetoric.[7] One hope is the W.F. Albright Institute of Archaeological Research, where Director Sy Gitin has created a neutral ground where Palestinian archaeologists can not only work in the library, but can socialize with Israelis and Americans. The West Bank has marvelous antiquity sites (including many of biblical importance), and a great deal of pride in its own cultural heritage. Given half a chance, 'Palestinian archaeology' could come into its own. But everything depends upon peace, and the Messiah may come first.

III. American Archaeology

Coming closer to home now, let us look at American archaeology, first in the field abroad, and then in this country.

American Archaeology Abroad

I have already noted the numerous American projects in Israel and Jordan (none yet in the West Bank, despite the attempts of several of us). In Jordan, the number of digs has grown impressively. More of my students now work in Jordan than in Israel, partly because it is less expensive, apparently safer, and has the appeal of being 'on the frontier'. Nevertheless, at least one American archaeologist who has worked in Jordan for nearly 25 years has transferred his projects to Cyprus, because his university will no longer send students to Jordan. In Israel, on the other hand, our greatest challenge is to *launch new American field projects*. The great 20-year projects at Tell Miqne/Ekron and Ashkelon have ended their fieldwork phase, and no other large projects seem even remotely feasible. There is no university interest (on the contrary), no financial support. And there are few tenured young professors with sufficient security and resources to mount a project. To compound the difficulties, the Israel Antiquities Authority will no longer give a license to any American excavator unless he or she has an Israeli Co-Director. The problem is that we Americans provide the money and the people; but the Israeli collaborator, who has all the advantages, tends to get the credit—and the publications.

There will be a half dozen or more American projects in the field in Israel in the summer of 2006. But most are small, and to my knowledge only one is a major project of a prominent American university, under independent direction (the University of Michigan's project at Kadesh). We *desperately* need new American field projects in Israel, but at the moment the prospects are not good.

The great American 'success story' in Israel is the Albright Institute in Jerusalem already mentioned, under the brilliant guidance of Sy Gitin, now in his 25th year as Director. It is the only remaining viable foreign archaeological institute in Israel, having survived incredible difficulties both political and financial. (The French, British, and German schools are virtually defunct.)[8]

---

7. See, for example, Khaled Nashef's 2000 editorial in the first issue of the *Journal of Palestinian Archaeology*, quoting almost verbatim Whitelam's charge that 'Palestinian history has been silenced'; cf. further Dever 2001: 239-41.

8. The British School of Archaeology in Jerusalem, opened in 1919, now maintains simply a temporary director and some hostel facilities in rented quarters; it has transferred all field operations (except in Gaza) to its branch in Amman. On its history, see Davies 1988. The German school, dating back to 1890 (Weippert and Weippert 1988) has similarly moved its base of operations to Amman, continuing only field trips for clergy in Israel. The French École Biblique et Archéologique Francaise, distinguished for Biblical Archaeology since 1882 (Benoit 1988), now works only in the Gaza Strip. The secular Centre National Recherche Scientifique does, however, maintain a base in Jerusalem.

Without the unwavering support of the Albright, few if any American digs would be in the field, and a whole generation of younger American archaeologists might never have gotten their start in Israel (cf. King 1983; Clark and Matthews 2003).

American Archaeology Elsewhere in the Middle East

I am aware that I have not dealt with Syria. But there are only a couple of American excavations there; there are bleak prospects for them; and they have nothing to do directly with our assigned subject. In Cyprus, we have a thriving American institute (CAARI), and there are numerous American projects on the island. But again, the archaeology of Cyprus, while important, is beyond our purview here.

American Archaeology at Home

The foundation of American archaeology in the southern Levant as a research and teaching enterprise, not to mention as an intellectual partner in the dialogue of 'Biblical Archaeology', is here at home. How are we faring?

The good news is that the discipline has survived at *all*—survived in spite of the bitter controversy over 'Biblical Archaeology' that began 35 years ago; growing pains as the discipline 'came of age'; declining support from American academic institutions; and the worsening political situation in the Middle East. (ASOR and the Jerusalem school celebrated their centennial in Jerusalem in 2000, Dever and Gitin 2003.) And during these perilous last 30 years, we have produced at least 50 young Ph.D. graduates. As the mentor of half of them, I can attest that they are the best yet: fiercely dedicated to our discipline; willing to risk and to sacrifice beyond reasonable expectations; multi-talented; so well versed in today's archaeological theory and method that I'm glad I'm retired (I can no longer compete).

It is also a very ecumenical group. When I began nearly 45 years ago, 'Biblical Archaeology' was an exclusive old-boys club: nearly all white males, mostly Protestant clerics. The demographic makeup of the group alone demonstrates the paradigm shift. The vast majority of young people in our field today are simply not *practicing* what we used to call 'Biblical Archaeology'. And a discipline, regardless of the terminology, *is* what it *does*.

By the time younger archaeologists get their degrees, many of them have had ten years or more of field experience—and a few of them are already legendary as 'dirt archaeologists'. I'm immensely proud of them and hopeful for their future—*our* future. Perhaps the best gauge of the overall progress of our field is the annual fall meeting of ASOR. The papers read by young people, compared with those when I began 45 years ago, are light-years ahead—and not only because of Power Point. Many of the papers are more sophisticated than papers given back then by senior archaeologists. Young people are now stepping into office in ASOR. They are reading papers at national and international meetings. And their burgeoning publications are as good as anything their teachers (and mine) ever did.

On the larger scene, the American public continues to be fascinated by what we archaeologists do, as witness our bombardment by the subject in all the media, especially TV. As the success of *BAR* demonstrates, and as I can attest from huge audiences wherever I speak, 'Biblical Archaeology' in America (if not 'Syro-Palestinian') appears to be alive and well. But appearances can be deceptive.

The crucial threat to our branch of archaeology is the lack of academic opportunities for young people entering the field. We have plenty of highly qualified candidates, as we have seen, indeed a surplus. But there are very few tenure-track positions at leading universities that can provide adequate resources to support a *long-term* professional career: library; colleagues in allied fields; a graduate program; funds and commitments for field work. It is true that, miraculously, most recent

Ph.D. graduates are surviving, working at something or another. But many of them are languishing in dead-end jobs; carrying a teaching load that makes research and publication impossible; unable to continue their fieldwork; postponing personal development and family. Some of our most talented young Ph.D. graduates have simply dropped out, lost to the field. This is a tragedy, one that I personally feel deeply.

It is true that a few new jobs have been created, notably at Penn State; the University of North Carolina; Pacific School of Religion; and UCLA. After 30 years during which I headed a distinguished program at the University of Arizona, the program is closed and my budget line has gone to 'Islamic Thought'. Even Harvard let Ernest Wright's position go unfulfilled for 18 years after his death.

The fact is that with the shift of priorities from the arts and the humanities to science and technology—where the big money is—American universities have lost interest in archaeology, especially in the troubled Middle East. You would think that theological seminaries—the home of 'Biblical Archaeology' in its heyday—might take up the slack. But seminaries like Drew and McCormick, which sponsored the famous Shechem dig, no longer have any archaeological faculty or do any fieldwork. There is only one full-time professorship in archaeology in a seminary in North America, at Pittsburgh Theological Seminary (and the chair is not fully endowed).

The American public may support us; but this does not translate into what we really need: academic positions. The only hope for our field is to create endowed chairs, such as the one we are here to inaugurate today at UC San Diego, thanks to the extraordinary generosity of Norma Kershaw. To show you how extraordinary, this is only the third endowed chair in our entire field, the others being at Duke and Harvard. Now we need a few endowed positions for *junior* scholars. Without that security, our discipline will remain marginal and imperiled in American academic life.

I recently published an article in *BAR* entitled 'Death of a Discipline?' (Dever 1995). Nobody liked it; but the possibility is real. In Europe, the discipline is already dead, because the major universities have abandoned it (as they have their institutes in Jerusalem). The only place still offering a Ph.D. in our branch of archaeology (and with no emphasis on the biblical connection) is the Institute of Archaeology at the University of London; and it has no 'stars' like Kenyon on its faculty.

IV. 'Biblical Archaeology' as Dialogue

Having given a state-of-the-art assessment of Syro-Palestinian (or 'Levantine') archaeology, let me turn finally to its connection with biblical studies as a partner in dialogue, or 'Biblical Archaeology'. Over the past 35 years I have made many attempts to define 'Biblical Archaeology', its proper role, and the specific way in which it can and cannot illuminate the Bible (cf. Dever 2000 and references). Here I can only repeat a statement of the late 1980s, which is more timely than ever.

> Biblical archaeology—or, stated accurately, the archaeology of Syria-Palestine in the biblical period— may indeed survive, although not in the classic 1950s sense. But it is not a surrogate for Syro-Palestinian archaeology, or even a discipline at all in the academic sense; it is a sub-branch of biblical studies, an *interdisciplinary* pursuit that seeks to utilize the pertinent results of archaeological research to elucidate the historical and cultural setting of the Bible. In short, biblical archaeology is what it *always* was, except for its brief bid in the Albright–Wright era to dominate the field of Syro-Palestinian archaeology. The crucial issue for biblical archaeology, properly conceived as a dialogue, has always been (and is even more so now) its understanding and use of archaeology on the one hand, its understanding of the issues in biblical studies that are fitting subjects for archaeological illumination on the other—and the proper *relationship* between the two. (1985: 60, 61)

I want to look now specifically at the *American* scene, since there can be no question that 'Biblical Archaeology' is a uniquely American phenomenon, one aspect of a peculiar *religious* atmosphere that does not exist in either Europe or Israel. There is no doubt that archaeology has revolutionized our understanding of the Bible and the biblical world, as Albright had confidently predicted—but not in the way that he and most of the American public expected. I would argue that archaeology is now an indispensable tool in biblical studies, indeed a 'primary source' for writing the history of ancient Israel and early Judaism and Christianity. But the *results* have been mixed, and disappointing for those who had hoped that archaeology would 'prove the truth of the Bible'. Archaeology has provided a 'real-life context', within which the Bible now appears to many more concrete and tangible, and therefore more 'credible' in general. But the historicity of the *individual* stories of the Bible has often been thrown further into doubt, so that the question of what the supposed events 'mean' seems as elusive as ever.

I cannot go into detail here, but I have recently published three popular books that summarize the current status and results of 'Biblical Archaeology' (2001, 2003b, 2005b). Let me summarize here. (1) Relatively few lay people realize it, but archaeology today demonstrates that the Patriarchal stories, while they may have some historical basis in memory and oral tradition, are mostly legendary. (2) The story of the Exodus from Egypt has no direct archaeological support and appears to be largely fiction. (3) A pan-military Israelite 'Conquest' of Canaan never occurred, much less the annihilation of the native populace. There may have been a small 'Exodus group', but most 'early Israelites' were in fact displaced Canaanites. (4) Solomon's 'Golden Age' is a myth; he did exist (*contra* the revisionists), but he was the petty chieftain of a few highland tribes not the ruler of an empire that stretched from the Mediterranean to the Euphrates. (5) 'Mosaic monotheism' is a relatively late phenomenon, and throughout the settlement period and the Monarchy the majority of Israelites were polytheists. (6) For the New Testament era, we have to confess that, however much we can reconstruct the Palestinian world in which Jesus lived, we are as uncertain as ever in our search for 'the historical Jesus' or what he may actually have said. (7) As for early Judaism, I doubt that archaeology has contributed much that is revolutionary: even the pluralism of the Jewish community revealed by the Dead Sea scrolls was already known to good scholars.[9]

All this may appear to make us mainstream archaeologists, both American and Israeli, as much 'minimalists' as the radical European Biblicists whom we are vigorously opposing. But there is a critical difference, and there lies the *real* threat to the future of 'Biblical Archaeology'.

Biblical 'revisionism' began in the 1990s, largely in Europe around the Copenhagen and Sheffield 'schools'. The term, which I took from their own writings when I began to oppose them in the mid-1990s, may seem harmless (all good historians revise). But in fact the most radical of these skeptics are *nihilists*. When they are finished, there is no ancient Israel: the biblical stories are all 'foundation-myths', concocted late in Hellenistic Palestine by Jews desperately seeking an identity. The Hebrew Bible is a 'monstrous' (Lemche's term) literary hoax. Recently, Thomas L. Thompson has extended his deconstruction to the New Testament: there was no historical 'Jesus', it is all Christianity's self-serving lie (Thompson 2005). Elsewhere (Dever 2001) I have demonstrated that the revisionists are really closet 'postmodernists', since for them there *is* no 'truth' ('all claims to knowledge are social constructs'), no *history* ('all history-writing is fiction'). The latter are all-too-typical postmodern slogans, as typical as the method of 'deconstructing' texts, or the claim that 'all cultural values are relative' (multi-culturalism).

Now you would think that the revisionists, having discarded the Hebrew Bible as worthless historically (and, of course, theologically), would have to fall back on archaeology, the only other

---

9.   On the above, see provisionally Meyers 1994; cf. also the contribution of Jodi Magness in this volume.

possible source for history-writing. But instead, they ignore or caricature the archaeological data, and they demonize archaeologists like me. Example are too numerous to cite, but here are a few. (1) In his book *In Search of 'Ancient Israel'*, Philip R. Davies cites only one archaeological handbook, that of Mazar (1990), and that only in a single footnote discarding it because it deals with the Iron Age, and not with *Davies*'s Persian-period literary construct (Davies 1992: 24). (2) The group to which Davies belongs—the 'European Seminar on Methodology in Israel's History'—recently issued a volume on the Assyrian campaigns of Sennacherib in Judah in 701 BCE, for which we have abundant archaeological evidence, including that from 25 years of excavations at Lachish (Grabbe 2003). But there is no chapter by an archaeologist. Thomas L. Thompson recently held a symposium on the history and archaeology of Jerusalem, the papers from which have been published (Thompson 2003). Yet the symposium was held in Amman, Jordan; no American or Israeli archaeologists were invited; and the scholars included were all in the revisionist camp, a few of them so virulently anti-Israel that they sound like closet anti-Semites to me. So much for dialogue.

The fact is that the revisionists are not only totally ignorant of modern archaeology, but they are secular Fundamentalists: 'My mind is made up; don't confuse me with facts'! I have argued that in *real* intellectual circles, the revisionists' fundamental epistemology, post-modernism, is *passé*; and that, in any case, their influence outside Europe is marginal. But a few months ago, a noted biblical scholar at Yale, John Collins (2005), published a judicious, state-of-the-art analysis of American biblical scholarship in which he argues that revisionism has created a new, skeptical paradigm in biblical studies that will prevail. It irrevocably undermines our confidence in the historicity of the Bible. Henceforth, the Bible's only claims to appeal to religious beliefs or claims to moral standards will be 'philosophical'—arbitrary matters of personal need or choice. If Collins is right, there is no one out there for us *historians* to talk to. Again, it may be too late for dialogue, at least with mainstream biblical scholars, even in 'Christian America'. And they are not alone. I can tell you this much from my own widespread travels and lectures the past five years. The average liberal Protestant seminary professors are no longer much interested in the actual history of ancient Israel, only in the Bible as 'literature'. Often the biblical faculty don't bother to attend my lectures. There *is* no real dialogue with archaeology. And despite all that we've learned, no new history of ancient Israel has been written in America in the past 20 years (except for a recent evangelical work, Provan, Long, and Longman 2003).

What about other circles? The American public, which unlike the European public, still takes the Bible seriously. What about you? In some communities there probably is a future for 'Biblical Archaeology', even though it would become a purely amateur pursuit should the professional academic base collapse. It would be either ultimately unsustainable, or else wholly dependent upon the archaeological data produced by the Israelis for their own, very different purposes. That is not satisfactory. The production of data is *not* 'neutral'. How you excavate and publish influences what you find; the answers you get depend largely upon the questions you ask. Israeli-style 'Biblical Archaeology' is *different*, and not *our* future.

At the ASOR Centennial in Jerusalem in 2000, looking ahead at our prospects for the future, I expressed the opinion that 'Biblical Archaeology' as a serious intellectual dialogue (not merely the hobby of the public) might survive in America mostly in evangelical Christian circles (Dever 2003b). Why would I say that (certainly not enlightened self-interest)? Because that's where one increasingly finds the necessary *long-term institutional support*. Consider the 'Madeba Plains Project', which a consortium of Seventh Day Adventist universities has generously sponsored in Jordan for nearly 40 years (1968–), an *unparalleled* record of American archaeology. Southern Baptist seminaries also have a long and distinguished record of fieldwork. While I congratulate these Christian groups (and have trained some of their excavators), a monopoly by any one group is unhealthy.[10] And if conservative Christian groups come to dominate, suspicions about a biblical bias may arise again. Where are *mainstream* liberal Protestant seminaries?

There are still, of course, a few programs at private and state universities, among them Harvard, Toronto, Chicago, Duke, Michigan, UCLA, and happily UC San Diego. But the universities themselves do not offer much direct support; dig directors have to raise funds themselves from grants or individual donors. And the only *endowed* chairs are at Harvard and Duke, and now at UC San Diego.

One would think that Jewish institutions would have taken up the theme of 'archaeology and the Bible', especially since Jewish scholars began entering the field a generation ago. But in Judaism, *tradition* (as in the Talmud and the Mishnah) is more fundamental than biblical history. (Classic 'Biblical Archaeology' was almost exclusively a Christian, Protestant enterprise.) And in any case, most American Jews think that supporting Israeli archaeology is sufficient. The Hebrew Union College—Jewish Institute of Religion, my own first employer, still maintains an archaeological program at the Jerusalem school, but it has no faculty members in archaeology at the New York, Cincinnati, or Los Angeles campuses.

We've been speaking of inadequate funding. In the last year or so, two major endowments for our field have been established, one at Brown University (by Artemis Joukowsky), and the other in New York through a bequest of the late Leon Levy. But neither has yet clarified its aims, and I confess that I am not very sanguine about the actual benefits—particularly whether endowed chairs are envisioned.

Conclusion

Clearly the question 'What is the future of 'Biblical Archaeology'? has no simple answer. I can only suggest that we do face a crisis as serious as any that we have ever faced. I am convinced that our best hope lies in steering a cautious mid-course between radical skepticism on the one hand, which rejects the Bible altogether (and archaeology as well), and Fundamentalism, which reads the Bible in a literal, simple-minded fashion that most of us can no longer accept. The middle ground is the position that I have staked out in my recent popular books, but I get it from all sides. If the extremists prevail, as they already do in Europe and most of the Middle East, there is little hope for either our kind of 'Biblical Archaeology' or the enlightened Western cultural tradition that gave rise to the inquiry. The newly endowed chair that we are inaugurating with this volume is one *crucial* step forward. Let us celebrate it and hope that it marks a turning-point.

Bibliography

Bar-Yosef, O., and A. Mazar (1982) Israeli Archaeology. *World Archaeology* 13: 310-25.

Benoit, P. (1988) French Archaeologists. In Drinkard *et al.* 1988: 63-86.

Bunimovitz, S. (1995) How Mute Stones Speak Up: Interpreting What We Dig Up. *BAR* 21/2: 58-67, 96.

Clark, D.R., and V.H. Matthews (eds.) (2003) *100 Years of American Archaeology in the Middle East* (Boston: American Schools of Oriental Research).

Collins, J.J. (2005) *The Bible after Babel: Historical Criticism in a Postmodern Age* (Grand Rapids: Eerdmans).

Davies, G.I. (1988) British Archaeologists. In Drinkard *et al.* 1988: 37-62.

Davies, P.R. (1992) *In Search of 'Ancient Israel'* (JSOTSup 148; Sheffield: Sheffield Academic Press).

---

10. For a defense of more traditional 'Biblical Archaeology,' from a conservative/evangelical perspective, see the essays in Hoffmeier and Millard 2004.

Davis, T.W. (2003) *Shifting Sands: The Rise and Fall of Biblical Archaeology* (Oxford: Oxford University Press).

Dever, W.G. (1974) *Archaeology and Biblical Studies: Retrospects and Prospects* (Evanston, IL: Seabury-Western Theological Seminary).

—(1985) Syro-Palestinian and Biblical Archaeology. In *The Hebrew Bible and its Modern Interpreters*, edited by D.A. Knight and G.M. Tucker (Chico, CA: Scholars Press): 31-74.

—(1989) Archaeology in Israel Today: A Summation and Critique. In *Recent Excavations in Israel: Studies in Iron Age Archaeology*, edited by S. Gitin and W.G. Dever (Winona Lake, IN: American Schools of Oriental Research): 143-52.

—(1992) Archaeology, Syro-Palestinian and Biblical. In *Anchor Bible Dictionary*, edited by D.N. Freedman (New York: Doubleday): 1.354-67.

—(1993) Biblical Archaeology—Death and Rebirth? In *Biblical Archaeology Today: Proceedings of the Second International Congress on Biblical Archaeology, Jerusalem, June 1990*, edited by A. Biran and J. Aviram (Jerusalem: Israel Exploration Society): 706-22.

—(1995) The Death of a Discipline? *BAR* 21/5: 50-55, 70.

—(1999) Biblical Archaeology. In *The Oxford Encyclopedia of Archaeology in the Near East*, edited by E.M. Meyers (New York: Oxford University Press): 1.315-19.

—(2000) Biblical and Syro-Palestinian Archaeology: A State-of-the-Art Assessment at the Turn of the Millennium. *Currents in Research: Biblical Studies* 8: 91-116.

—(2001) *What Did the Biblical Writers Know and When Did They Know It? What Archaeology Can Tell Us About the Reality of Ancient Israel* (Grand Rapids: Eerdmans).

—(2003a) Why It's So Hard to Name Our Field. *BAR* 29/4: 57-61.

—(2003b) *Who Were the Early Israelites and Where Did they Come From?* (Grand Rapids: Eerdmans).

—(2005a) Review of D. Ussishkin, *The Renewed Archaeological Excavations at Lachish* (1973–1994). *BASOR* 340: 83-85.

—(2005b) *Did God Have a Wife? Archaeology and Folk Religion in Ancient Israel* (Grand Rapids: Eerdmans).

Dever, W.G., and S. Gitin (eds.) (2003) *Symbiosis, Symbolism and the Power of the Past: Canaan, Ancient Israel and their Neighbors from the Late Bronze Age through Roman Palaestina* (Winona Lake, IN: American Schools of Oriental Research).

Drinkard, J.F., G.L. Mattingly, J.M. Miller, and J.A. Callaway (eds.) (1988) *Benchmarks in Time and Culture: An Introduction to Palestinian Archaeology* (Atlanta: Scholars Press).

Elon, A. (1997) Politics and Archaeology. In Silberman and Small 1997: 34-47.

Finkelstein, I. (1995) The Archaeology of the United Monarchy: An Alternative View. *Levant* 28: 177-87.

—(1998) Bible Archaeology or Archaeology of Palestine in the Iron Age? *Levant* 30: 167-74.

—(2005) A Low Chronology Update: Archaeology, History and Bible. In Levy and Higham 2005: 31-42.

Grabbe, L.L. (ed.) (2003) *Like A Bird in a Cage: The Invasion of Sennacherib in 701 B.C.E.* (European Seminar on Historical Methodology 4; Sheffield: Sheffield Academic Press).

Hoffmeier, J.K., and A. Millard (eds.) (2004) *The Future of Biblical Archaeology: Reassessing Methodologies and Assumptions: The Proceedings of a Symposium August 12–14 at Trinity International University* (Grand Rapids: Eerdmans).

King, P.J. (1983) *American Archaeology in the Middle East: A History of the American Schools of Oriental Research* (Winona Lake, IN: American Schools of Oriental Research).

Levy, T.E. (2000) Archaeology and the Bible. In *Eerdmans Dictionary of the Bible*, edited by D.N. Freedman (Grand Rapids: Eerdmans): 88-95.

Levy, T.E. (2009) Pastoral Nomads and Iron Age Metal Production in Ancient Edom. In *Nomads, Tribes, and the State in the Ancient Near East*, edited by J. Szuchman (Chicago: University of Chicago Press): 147-76.

Levy, T.E., *et al.* (2005) Lowland Edom and the High and Low Chronologies: Edomite State Formation, the Bible and Recent Archaeological Research in Southern Jordan. In Levy and Higham 2005: 129-63.

Levy, T.E., and T. Higham (2005) Introduction: Radiocarbon Dating and the Iron Age of the Southern Levant: Problems and Potentials for the Oxford Conference. In Levy and Higham 2005: 3-14.

Levy, T.E., and T. Higham (eds.) (2005) *The Bible and Radiocarbon Dating: Archaeology, Text and Science* (London: Equinox).

Levy, T.E., T. Higham, C. Bronk Ramsey, N.G. Smith, E. Ben-Yosef, M. Robinson, S. Münger, K. Knabb, J. Schulze, P., M. Najjar, and L. Tauxe (2008) High-Precision Radiocarbon Dating and Historical Biblical Archaeology in Southern Jordan. *Proceedings of the National Academy of Sciences* 105: 16460-65.

Mazar, A. (1988) Israeli Archaeologists. In Drinkard *et al.* 1988: 109-28

—(1990)*The Archaeology of the Land of the Bible, 10,000–586 B.C.E.* (New York: Doubleday).

—(1997) Iron Age Chronology: A Reply to I. Finkelstein. *Levant* 29: 157-67.

—(2005) The Debate over the Chronology of the Iron Age in the Southern Levant. In Levy and Higham 2005: 15-30.

Meyers, E.M. (1992) Second Temple Studies in the Light of Recent Archaeology: Part I: The Persian and Hellenistic Periods. *Currents in Research: Biblical Studies* 2:25-42.

Moorey, P.R.S. (1991) *A Century of Biblical Archaeology* (London: Letterworth Press).

Provan, I., V.P. Long, and T. Longman III (2003) *A Biblical History of Israel* (Louisville: Westminster/John Knox Press).

Shanks, H. (2005) Finds or Fakes? *BAR* 31/6: 60, 61.

Shavit, Y. (1997) Archaeology, Political Culture, and Culture in Israel. In Silberman and Small 1997: 48-61.

Silberman, N.A., and D. Small (eds.) (1997) *The Archaeology of Israel: Constructing the Past, Interpreting the Present* (Sheffield: Sheffield Academic Press).

Stager, L.E., J.A. Green, and M.D. Coogan (eds.) (2000) *Archaeology of Jordan and Beyond: Essays in Honor of James A. Sauer* (Studies in the Archaeology and History of the Levant 1; Winona Lake, IN: Eisenbrauns).

Stern, E. (1987) The Bible and Israeli Archaeology. In *Archaeology and Biblical Interpretation: Essays in Memory of D. Glenn Rose*, edited by L.G. Perdue, L.E. Toombs, and G.L. Johnson (Atlanta: John Knox Press): 31-40.

Thompson, T.L. (1999) *The Mythic Past: Archaeology and the Myth of Israel* (New York: Basic Books).

—(2005) *The Messiah Myth: The Near Eastern Roots of Jesus and David* (New York: Basic Books).

Thompson, T.L. (ed.) (2003) *Jerusalem in Ancient History and Tradition* (JSOTSup 381; Sheffield: Sheffield Academic Press).

Thompson, T.L., and S.K. Jayyusi (2003) *Jerusalem in Ancient History and Tradition* (New York/London: Continuum).

Weippert, M., and H. Weippert (1988) German Archaeologists. In Drinkard *et al.* 1988: 87-108.

Whitelam, K.W. (1996) *Invention of Ancient Israel: The Silencing of Palestinian History* (Sheffield: Sheffield Academic Press).

Index of Subjects

Index of Authors

Greenberg, R. 48, 51, 108, 120, 136
Greenblatt, S. 254, 260
Greenfield, J.C. 134, 136, 138
Greenhut, Z. 111, 112, 120
Grierson, P. 205, 235
Grosby, S. 58, 67
Grove, C. 297, 302
Gsell, S. 134, 138
Guðbergsson, G. 223, 227, 235
Guertin, C. 342, 346
Guggenheimer, H.W. 289, 292
Guy, P.L.O. 129, 138

Habermas, J. 253, 260
Hägg, R. 165
Haiman, M. 107, 112, 120, 176, 177, 184
Haines, R.C. 86, 93, 94
Halbwachs, M. 214, 255, 260
Hall, J.M. 57, 58, 62, 63, 67
Hall, T.D. 222, 233
Hallo, W.W. 4, 36
Hallote, R.S. 126, 133, 138, 335, 336, 346
Hallsdóttir, M. 223, 235
Halpern, B. 11, 12, 15, 35, 36, 46, 52, 99, 120,
   151, 153, 190, 201, 207, 211, 218, 235,
   242, 249, 258-60, 264, 266, 267, 269,
   274-79, 281, 282, 306, 309
Hamilton, R.W. 333, 346
Handy, L. 297, 302
Hanks, W.F. 206, 235
Hansen, S.S. 214, 235
Har-El, M. 48, 52
Haran, M. 134, 138
Harding, G.L. 14, 41
Harrison, T.P. 86, 93, 94
Hart, S. 24, 36
Hartland, E.S. 134, 138
Hartung, U. 99, 120
Hasel, M.G. 211, 235
Haskell, T. 301, 302
Hassan, S. 101, 106, 120
Hastings, J. 138
Hastrup, K. 208, 224, 229, 235
Hauptmann, A. 12, 24, 36, 37, 107, 120, 184
Hawkins, J.D. 267, 270, 282
Hayes, J.H. 60, 68
Haywood, J. 221, 236
Heath, P. 179-81, 184
Hegel, G.W.F. 260
Helck, W. 103, 108, 120
Heltzer, M. 274, 280
Hendel, R. 251, 259, 260
Hendon, J.A. 142, 152, 153
Henrich, J. 163, 164
Herr, L.G. 14, 15, 36, 262
Herry, L.G. 282
Herschend, F. 222, 225, 236
Herscher, E. 132, 134, 138

Hertz, R. 123, 138
Herzog, Z. 43, 46, 52, 58, 145, 153, 168, 169,
   175, 176, 178, 184
Hess, R. 207, 235
Hesse, B. 63, 64, 67, 147, 153, 161, 164, 277,
   279, 282, 284
Hester, T.R. 13, 36
Hestrin, R, 274, 282
Heusler, A. 208, 235, 236
Hickman, L.A. 9, 36
Higham, T. 22-24, 36-39, 46, 47, 53, 87, 95,
   99, 121, 175, 184, 185, 201, 221, 237,
   282, 351, 359
Hirschfeld, Y. 321-23, 327
Hitchcock, A. 164
Hjálmarsson, J.R. 212, 236
Hobsbawm, E. 217, 236, 256, 260
Hodder, I. 11, 37, 48, 52, 53, 58, 62, 63, 67
Hodge, A.T. 286, 287, 292
Hodges, R. 222, 236
Hoffmeier, J. 302
Hoffmeier, J.K. 4, 37, 100, 102, 120, 299, 349
Hoffmeir, J.K. 118, 359
Hole, F. 21, 37
Holl, A.F.C. 11, 12, 38, 61, 62, 64, 67
Holladay, J.S. 49, 52, 126, 132, 134, 138, 262,
   277, 282
Holtof, C. 341, 346
Hopkins, T. 222, 236
Horne, L. 159, 163, 166
Horowitz, W. 153
Horton, M. 3, 37
Horwitz, L.K. 129, 138
Horwitz, W.J. 133, 138
Howard, M.C. 58, 67
Humbert, J.-B. 286-89, 291, 292, 321, 327
Hunt, C.O. 12, 36, 37
Huntington, R. 123, 138
Hurvitz, A. 245, 249
Hymes, D. 236

Ibrahim, M.M. 59, 67
Iggers, G.G. 252, 260
Ilan, D. 75, 79, 124, 126, 127, 131, 132, 136,
   138
Inge, C.H. 14, 41
Ingimundarson, J.H. 223, 236
Ingstad, A. 209, 236
Insoll, T. 3, 37, 124, 138
Isaac, B. 313, 317
Israel, J.I. 250, 260
Issar, A.S. 111, 116, 120

James, W. 9, 37
Jamieson-Drake, D.W. 179, 184, 275, 282
Jasmin, M. 176, 177, 184
Jayyusi, S.K. 360
Jenkins, P. 337, 346

Lowenthal, D. 254, 260, 301, 303
Luke, H. 330, 347
Lyman, R.L. 158, 165
Lynch, W.F. 170, 185

Macalister, R.A.S. 192, 201
Machinist, P. 157, 165
Maddy-Weitzman, B. 336, 347
Maeir, A. 12, 15, 21, 33, 39, 121, 156, 159, 160, 165, 299-301, 303
Magen, Y. 45, 52, 274, 281
Magness, J. 146, 154, 286-89, 292, 321, 322, 327
Maissy-Noy, R. 335, 347
Maizels, J.K. 237
Malamat, A. 48, 53, 297, 303
Mallowan, M.E.L. 266, 282
Manning, S.W. 39
Maran, J. 162, 165
Marcus, A. 303
Marcus, E.S. 99, 100, 103, 121, 124, 298
Marcus, J. 139
Margueron, J. 126, 139
Marquardt, W.H. 20, 39
Marquet-Krause, J. 14, 39
Marriner, N. 12, 39
Marshall, Y. 70, 79
Marston, C. 297, 303
Martínez, F.G. 287, 290, 292
Marx, E. 12, 39, 215
Marx, K. 237
Masalha, N. 10, 39
Maschner, H.D.G. 13, 39
Master, D. 165
Master, D.M. 85, 95, 147, 154, 159
Masters, D. 11, 12, 39
Matthews, V.H. 350, 354, 358
Mayerson, P. 169, 185
Mazar, A. 12, 15, 21, 23, 34, 39, 40, 44, 46, 47, 50, 53, 59-61, 67, 68, 100, 121, 145, 154, 157, 164, 165, 168, 178, 185, 187-90, 193, 199-201, 211, 212, 237, 242, 264, 276, 277, 282, 301, 303, 350, 351, 357-60
Mazar, B. 60, 114, 121, 312, 317
Mazar, E. 264, 276, 282, 312, 313, 315, 317
Mazow, L.B. 147, 154, 161, 165
McCown, C.C. 14, 40
McCullough, W.S. 132, 139
McEwan, C.W. 86, 95
McFarlane, A. 104, 120, 121
McGovern, T.H. 222, 223, 237, 238
McGuire, R. 347
McGuire, R.H. 58, 62, 63, 68, 340
McLaughlin, J.L. 134, 139
McNairn, B. 57, 68
McNutt, P. 169, 174, 185
McTurk, R. 237
Medcalf, P. 123, 138

Meiberg, L. 165
Meighan, C.W. 21, 40
Meitlis, Y. 297, 299, 303
Merrillees, R.S. 129, 139
Meskell, L. 216, 237
Mesoudi, A. 163, 166
Metcalf, P. 138
Meyer, M.W. 3, 37
Meyers, C. 143, 146, 154, 312, 314, 317
Meyers, E. 296, 298, 303, 356, 360
Milevski, I. 333, 347
Millar, A.R. 4, 37
Millar, F. 84, 95
Millard, A. 4, 37, 100, 118, 120, 263, 265-67, 282, 299, 302, 349, 359
Miller, J.M. 60, 68, 211, 237, 282
Miller, P.D. 134, 139
Miller, R. 116, 121
Miller, R.D. 62, 64, 68
Miller, W.I. 219, 221, 222, 227, 232
Miroschedji, P. de 103, 121
Mishal, S. 335, 347
Mommsen, H. 12, 33
Montet, P. 126, 134, 139
Moore, E.C. 9, 40
Moore, L.E. 333, 343, 347
Moore, R.I. 222, 237
Moorey, P.R.S. 4, 8, 14, 37, 40, 44, 53, 56, 68, 69, 79, 212, 237, 349, 360
Moran, W.L. 100, 121
Moreland, J. 205, 206, 217-20, 237
Morhange, C. 12, 39
Morris, C. 237
Morris, I. 126, 139
Morris, S.P. 160, 166
Moscati, S. 132, 139
Mountjoy, P. 162, 166
Moussa, A. 116, 119
Mumford, G. 103, 104, 107, 116, 121
Munger, S. 21, 40
Muniz, A. 24, 38
Murakami, M. 333, 347
Murray, O. 48, 53, 65, 68
Musil, A. 170-72, 185

Na'aman, N. 52, 59, 67, 68, 153, 175, 185, 266, 269, 270, 283
Najjar, M. 12, 23, 24, 38, 39
Nashef, K. 7, 40, 353
Naveh, J. 15, 32, 211, 232, 266, 280, 314, 317
Netzer, E. 49, 53
Neudecker, R. 286, 292
Neusner, J. 289, 290, 292
Neuwirth, A. 312, 317
Nicholas, D. 219, 232
Niditch, S. 210, 213, 218, 219, 237
Niemann, H.M. 46, 53, 243, 249
Nigro, L. 335, 347

Index of References

CPSIA information can be obtained at www.ICGtesting.com
Printed in the USA
BVOW080000130112

280396BV00002B/5/P